Banking Law and Financial Regulation in the UK and EU

Banking Law and Financial Regulation in the UK and EU seeks to blend orthodox topics covered within the banking and financial law syllabus, such as sources of banking and financial law, financial markets, financial and banking institutions, financial transactions, and banking and financial insolvency, with a careful analysis of emerging issues and more contemporary topics.

This advanced-level textbook offers a new format for the study of banking and financial law, placing it within the wider context of economic development. As such, two elements are integral to this new methodology: the rise of techno-banking and digitalisation of the financial sector, and Brexit. Departing from the approaches of more traditional textbooks in this area, the book also takes a comparative approach to UK and EU banking law, highlighting the legal consequences of the UK's exit from the EU. Aspects of human rights are integrated throughout and current debates and developments around financial crises – the advancement of technological innovations in the banking sector and contemporary topics, such as health crises, energy, and ESG and the environment – is taken into account to provide the reader with the opportunity to develop their own autonomous and broader understanding of the various concepts.

Banking Law and Financial Regulation in the UK and EU will be a valuable text for students taking advanced undergraduate and postgraduate-level courses in banking law and financial law, as well as practising lawyers, managers and accountants.

Pierre de Gioia Carabellese (PhD, PGCAP, LLM, CMgr, CMI, MA, JD) is Professorial Fellow of Advance HE (York, UK) and Professor of Banking and Financial Law (Beijing Institute of Technology, Zhuhai Campus, 2022).

Camilla Della Giustina (JD) is a PhD candidate in law at Vanvitelli University (Italy) and a visiting researcher at Plymouth University (Maritime Transport Research Group).

Banking Law and Financial Regulation in the UK and EU

Technology, Human Rights and Crises

Pierre de Gioia Carabellese
and Camilla Della Giustina

Routledge
Taylor & Francis Group
LONDON AND NEW YORK

Designed cover image: WANAN YOSSINGKUM/Getty Images ®

First published 2024
by Routledge
4 Park Square, Milton Park, Abingdon, Oxon OX14 4RN

and by Routledge
605 Third Avenue, New York, NY 10158

Routledge is an imprint of the Taylor & Francis Group, an informa business

British Library Cataloguing-in-Publication Data
A catalogue record for this book is available from the British Library

Library of Congress Cataloging-in-Publication Data
Names: De Gioia-Carabellese, Pierre, author. | Della Giustina, Camilla, author.
Title: Banking law and financial regulation in the UK and EU : technology, human rights, and crises / Pierre de Gioia Carabellese and Camilla della Giustina.
Description: Abingdon, Oxon [UK] ; New York, NY : Routledge, 2024. | Includes bibliographical references and index.
Identifiers: LCCN 2023059309 | ISBN 9781032628585 (hardback) | ISBN 9781032628578 (paperback) | ISBN 9781032628646 (ebook)
Subjects: LCSH: Banking law—Great Britain. | Banking law—European Union countries. | Financial institutions—Law and legislation—Great Britain. | Financial institutions—Law and legislation—European Union countries. | Banks and banking—Technological innovations—Great Britain. | Banks and banking—Technological innovations—European Union countries. | Human rights—Great Britain. | Human rights—European Union countries. | Bank failures—Law and legislation—Great Britain. | Bank failures—Law and legislation—European Union countries.
Classification: LCC KD1715 .D44 2024 | DDC 346.24/082—dc23/eng/20240129
LC record available at https://lccn.loc.gov/2023059309

ISBN: 978-1-032-62858-5 (hbk)
ISBN: 978-1-032-62857-8 (pbk)
ISBN: 978-1-032-62864-6 (ebk)

DOI: 10.4324/9781032628646

Typeset in Times New Roman
by Apex CoVantage, LLC

Contents

Table of Cases *ix*

1 Introduction 1

1.1 A new approach 1
1.1.1 A view to contemporary banking and financial law 2
1.1.2 The structure 3
1.1.3 Caveats 4
1.2 Regulation in the European Union 5
1.2.1 European Union statutes and their hierarchy 5
1.2.2 Financial law legislation from Brussels 8
1.3 UK regulation after Brexit 16
1.3.1 Introduction 16
1.3.2 Brexit 17
1.3.3 Financial matter 18
1.3.4 Regulation proposal 20
1.3.5 The UK regulation 21
1.3.6 Banking law in Scotland 22
1.4 The United States banking and financial regulation: a comparative analysis 31
1.4.1 Banking system 31
1.4.2 Legal sources 34
1.4.3 The approach to bank supervision 40
References 41

2 Banking law 43

2.1 Banks and their organisations 43
2.1.1 An introduction 43
2.1.2 Categories of banks 45
2.1.3 Bank and "industry" 51

2.1.4 EU banking activities 54
2.2 The supervision 56
2.2.1 European banking supervision 56
2.2.2 National supervision 58
2.2.3 Authorisation of the banking business 60
2.2.4 Prudential supervision 63
2.3 Insolvency and resolution 71
2.3.1 Introduction 71
2.3.2 The Winding-up Directive 72
2.3.3 The resolution mechanism 82
2.3.4 Creditors' protection 84
2.3.5 Moral hazard in the resolution mechanism 100
2.3.6 State aid and resolution mechanism 103
2.4 Consumer protection 108
2.4.1 Unfair terms directive 109
2.4.2 Financial and banking instruments legislation 114
2.4.3 Consumer protection in the UK 124
2.4.4 Financial training and domestic abuse 126
2.4.5 Contemporary challenges 128
2.5 Alternative dispute resolution: between banking and financial law 129
2.5.1 Restorative justice 129
2.5.2 Online dispute resolution 132
2.5.3 Financial Ombudsman 133
References 135

3 Financial law 139

3.1 The market organisation: from financial market to parallel markets 139
3.1.1 Primary market 139
3.1.2 Secondary market 158
3.1.3 Market manipulation 165
3.1.4 Disclosure of inside information; insider lists; disclosure of own account transactions by persons discharging managerial responsibilities 167
3.1.5 The other parallel markets 169
3.2 Investments and funds 176
3.2.1 Investment under MiFID regulation 177
3.2.2 The investment fund 188
3.3 Financial contracts 194
3.3.1 Loan contract 194

3.4 Security 213
3.4.1 Purposes of security 213
3.4.2 Security 213
3.4.3 Derivatives 215
3.5 Financial transactions: custody agreements 227
3.5.1 Introduction 227
3.5.2 Custody of money and securities 229
3.5.3 Security custody 232
3.5.4 Transfer of money and securities 236
3.5.5 The UK financial regulation 239
3.6 Spare banking and conduits 242
3.6.1 Introduction 242
3.6.2 Shadow banking 242
3.6.3 Securitisation 244
3.7 Islamic finance 264
3.7.1 Introduction 264
3.7.2 Principles in economic systems 265
3.7.3 Principles in the financial system 267
3.7.4 Fintech in Islamic finance 277
3.7.5 Metaverse and Islamic finance 280
3.7.6 ESG factors in Islamic finance 283
References 283

4 ESG factors, fintech and digitalisation 289

4.1 The new frontiers in banking and financial law 289
4.2 The European Union approach 290
4.2.1 The EU green finance 291
4.2.2 The EU financial policy 293
4.2.3 EU financial product 295
4.2.4 EU regulatory instruments 297
4.3 Green finance in the UK regulation 298
4.4 The role of central bank in the green transition 301
4.4.1 The concept of green bank 303
4.4.2 The role of the European Central Bank 304
4.4.3 The Bank of England approach 306
4.5 IT in financial sector: fintech 307
4.5.1 IT transaction 309
4.5.2 Digital banking 316
4.5.3 IT and financial services 335
4.6 Green and techno-digital economy 345
References 346

5 Crisis 351

5.1 Introduction 351
5.2 The 2007–2008 banking and financial crisis 353
5.2.1 The pre-existing scenario 353
5.2.2 The beginning of the crisis 355
5.2.3 Post-crisis regulation 358
5.3 Health emergency and financial instruments 363
5.3.1 The UK approach 365
5.3.2 The US management 367
5.3.3 The EU methodology 369
5.4 From credit-crunch to cost-of-living crisis 372
5.5 The 2023 financial crises: Silicon Valley Bank and Credit Suisse 374
5.5.1 The Collapse of Silicon Valley Bank 375
5.5.2 The Signature Bank case 376
5.5.3 Credit Suisse 376
5.5.4 First Republic Bank 377
5.6 From banking crisis to city council crisis: the Birmingham case 377
5.6.1 The aetiology of the insolvency of the councils 379
5.6.2 The evolution of this insolvency: from the public bail-in to the private bail-in 380
5.6.3 The consequences, also sociological, of a (global versus regional) insolvency of public entities 381
5.6.4 The US experience 382
References 386

Index *390*

Cases

Al-Nakib Investments (Jersey) Ltd v Longcroft [1990] 3 All E.R. 321.
Archibald Trotter v Messers Murdoch Cochrane, and Co. Bankers in Glasgow [1761] Mor 14607 (17 December 1761).
Ashton v Cameron County District 298 US 513 (1936). m Id at 530. 1 Id at 531.
Banco Espirito Santo SA, [2014] Gi C343/1.
BNP Paribas v Yukos Oil [2005] EWHC 1321.
British Energy Power v Credit Suisse [2008] EWCA Civ 53.
Carter v McIntosh (1862) 24 D 925–933.
Clark v West Calder Oil Co Liquidators (1882) 9 R 1017, 1024.
Colquhoun's Tr. v Diack (1901) 4 F. 358.
Criminal proceedings against Jean Verdonck, Ronald Everaert and Edith de Baedts [2001] ECR I-3399.
Deutsche Bank AG v ANZ Banking Group Lt (unreported 24 May 1999).
De Mattos v Gibson (1858) 4 De G & J 276.
Faitoute Iron & Steel Co. v Asbury Park 316 US 502 (1942).
Florida v Michel A. Espinoza, F14–2923, (11th Cir. 22 July 2016).
Grad v Finanzamt Traunstein [1970] ECR 825.
Hanover Nat'l Bank v Moyses, 186 US 181, 188 (1902).
Harbinger Capital Partner v Caldwell and Another [2013] EWCA Civ 492.
Hazell v Hammersmith & Fulham LBC [1991] 1 All E.R. 545 at 549–550.
Heritable Reversionary Co. v Millar (1892) 19 R.(H.L.) 43.
Hughes v Metropolitan Ry (1877) 2 App.Cas. 439.
In re City of Detroit, 524 B.R. 147,213 (Bankr. E.D. Mich. 2014).
Levison v Farin [1978] 2 All E.R. 1149.
Lord Advocate v Earl of Moray's Trs. (1905) 7 F.(H.L.) 116.
Marcks v Belgium, C-6833/74.
Markus Geltl v Daimler AG [2012] 3 CMLR 32.
McCulloch v Maryland (17 U.S. (4 Wheat.) 316 (1819)).
Olczak v Poland, C-30417/96.
Possfund Custodian Trustee Ltd v Diamond [1996] 2 All E.R. 774.
Pressos Compania Naviera SA v Belgium Series A 332 (1996) 21 EHRR 301.
P Commission v Italy and Others, C-425/19.
Re Lehman Brothers Holdings Inc., et al., Report of Anton R. Valukas, Examiner.

Re Lehman Brothers International (Europe) (In Administration) [2012] UKSC 6 (SC).
Re Sullivan County Regional Refuse Disposal District 165 B.R. 60, 82–83 (Bankr. DN.H. 1994).
Shepherd & Cooper Ltd v TSB Bank plc [1996] 2 All 654.
Shinhan Bank Ltd v Sea Containers Ltd [2000] Lloyd's Rep. 406.
S*katteverket v David Hedqvist*, C-264/14.
Spector Photo Group v Commissie voor het Bank – Financie & Assurantiewessen [2010] BCC 827.
Stran Greek Refineries v Greece Series A No 301-B (1995) 19 EHRR 293.
Telefonica/Caixabank/Banco Santander/JV, COMP/M. 6956 (2013).
Telefonica UK/Vodafone UK/Everything Everywhere/JV, COMP/M. 6314 (2012).
Tiffany v National Bank of Missouri, 18 Wall 409 (1874).
United States v Bekins 304 US 27 (1938).
United States v Miller 425 U.S. 435 (1976).
Universal Stock Exchange v Strachan [1896] A.C. 166 HL.
Veazia Bank v Fenno (75 U.S. 8 Wall. 533 533 (1869)).

1 Introduction

1.1 A new approach

The goals of this work are many, and very ambitious. It is a book whose primary purpose is to provide an in-depth account of the legislation and case law pertaining to that area of law called banking and financial law. However, in doing so, we decided to enlarge the scope of the legal analysis, first and foremost, from a geographical perspective.

The Brexit process reached its pinnacle on 31 January 2021, when the divorce between the United Kingdom and the European Union received its official seal. As a result of this, it is in the field of banking and financial law where the discussion constantly straddles the Channel, by identifying, for each legal concept, analogies and differences between the two legal systems: a banking common law and an EU legal system, more and more integrated as a result of the financial crisis.

Furthermore, the utilisation of the comparative analysis is also justified and corroborated by the American approach taken in the work. Thus, burning issues, such as financial crises or the insolvency of local authorities, do have their origins and/or spillovers across the ocean. Additionally, health emergency management is usually analysed from a triple approach: the EU, the British and, finally, the American one.

As far as the methodology adopted in the book is concerned, first and foremost, it is a doctrinal analysis of law, with a constant explanation, or "dissection," of the legal provisions applicable in the EU, as far as this exciting concept is concerned. The legacy of the 2007/2008 financial crises can be hardly denied in the current state-of-the-art of the EU legislation: maximum harmonisation of the legal provisions, very detailed pieces of legislation and very technical standards within EU regulation. While this process has been successful in integrating the different member states, by consequently overcoming the national legal systems, sometimes in contradiction with each other, this new integrated EU banking and financial legal system comes with a price: the lack of intelligibility of the legal provisions, given the feral technicality of the norms. This black letter of the law will be juxtaposed against the English common law and the limited legislation existing in the UK in this area. The traditional pieces of legislation existing in the UK, the FSMA 2000, will be discussed through the lens of the Brexit process.

DOI: 10.4324/9781032628646-1

Moreover, the methodology is also interdisciplinary, given the fact that banking and financial law and economics/accountancy are cognate areas. Particularly in the area of financial transactions and international contracts, a discussion of legal sources and legal provisions, if any, is not credible without keeping an eye on what happens and develops beyond the traditional legal borders. In this area attention must be paid to the soft legislation, as well as the standard practices used by operators, with non-binding documents which, *de facto*, are even more credible than laws since operators obey them without hesitation.

In a book concerned with banking and financial law, it may appear odd that a historical analysis is also encompassed. However, it is obvious, from the reading of the book, that for almost every legal concept, we must attempt to retrieve the antecedent, to ensure that both students and practitioners, and academics too, may understand the evolutionary development, up to our times, of these legal concepts.

1.1.1 A view to contemporary banking and financial law

Beyond the methodologies, the contents of the book are worthy of a brief comment and explanation. The traditional areas of banking and financial law are the subject matter of a perusal which is not self-referential. Banking law and financial law, albeit the technical legal system par excellence, so dominated by practices, constitute not only the fertile terrain of pure legal analysis but also the very busy junction and/or roundabout, where a myriad of topics converge and/or diverge.

Particularly in the aftermath of the pandemic crisis, banking and financial law has been a fertile terrain of development for ancillary themes: digitalisation, human rights and ESG (environmental, social and governance). The last one, admittedly one of the most fashionable acronyms existing in the world, holistically defines a variety of caveats, hurdles, constraints to the limits of the modus operandi of the bank. However, the ESG bank may constitute the springboard of a new typology of credit institution, projected towards a less private law model, where regulation becomes more important than what we usually call the "mask."

Human rights too represent a *fil rouge* of perusal within this work. The dogma of the bail-in and the resolution tools, experienced in coincidence with the passing of the BRRD, are going to be read though a different lens: some constitutional rights of member states cannot be derogated, despite the legal provisions to the contrary passed by Brussels. In this respect the love-hate relationship between the BRRD, the EU framework, and some norms encapsulated in some EU constitutions (the right of property as a right that cannot be derogated), appears the paradigm of this very complex scenario. The resolution tools are confirmed even more as legal instruments very easy to apply, with mechanisms which are very intuitive, but extremely complex. The BRRD, in the EU, a piece of legislation which is also applicable in the UK, albeit with a different legislative form, has been influencing both practices and *modi operandi* of credit institutions, with decisions – those of the supervisory authority – which in frequent cases have raised the eyebrows of jurists.

The question of human rights in banking and financial law is also concerned with alternative dispute resolution. Therefore, Sub-chapter 2.6. discusses the alternative approach to judicial resolution, where the recent experience of digital support has recently made its debut. Particularly, two platforms will be discussed: ProMediate and RisolviOnline.

The multiple themes which pervade the work are not limited to human rights and ESG. Under the pressure of the pandemic and its hidden forces, banking and financial law have benefitted with other areas, in the past regarded as very distant from the traditional law area: reference is made to digitalisation, digital banking and fintech. These recent phenomena provide the bank with new horizons, in the past pretty unknown.

All in all, we are very sure that this work continues in the positive streak of publications with the same authors, and not necessarily with the same publisher: both the experience in other countries (Italy), where a textbook in banking law has been written this year, and in specialised areas, such as cryoconservation, conjure up a quality and quantity of topics whose reading certainly inspires the reader, but particularly the operator and practitioner, at any level.

The strength of this research textbook is the new approach to the traditional themes relating to financial and banking law. More in depth, the traditional topics are analysis from a new and innovative approach. Hence, we can recall, at least, three examples. The first one is concerned with consumer protection: in our view it encompasses domestic abuse and the right to be forgotten in the ontological field. These two elements represent a novelty and show that financial and banking matter is pervasive also from a human rights perspective.

The second reference is to shadow banking: it will be emphasised that in the contemporary era the concept of shadow banking is anachronistic. Therefore, in light of a strong European regulation, it is more appropriate to use the concept of spare banking. Furthermore, the financial transactions have become their own soul, hence becoming even more "green" and "blue." These two colours refer, respectively, to sustainability and digitalisation: in this respect, privacy too plays a critical role in the world of securitisations. Finally, the authors stress the concept of data protection and peer-to-peer securitisations.

As far as the last example is concerned, the issue is to "other parallel markets" such as the agri-food market, the cultural heritage market and the digital market. In a nutshell, it is possible to affirm that the market is not only a purely banking area, but also it encompasses other business venues.

1.1.2 The structure

As far as the structure is concerned, this research textbook consists of five chapters. The first one is the introduction: not only does it explain the methodology, but also it gives an account of the three different legal systems crucial to a comparative approach. By contrast, the latter has its own focus on the multiple crises from 2007/2008 to 2023.

The central chapters, Chapters 2 and 3, are based on two traditional pillars: Chapter 2 is about banking law, whereas Chapter 3 discusses matters of financial law. The latter encapsulates both the traditional topics and the new ones, that is to say, the "new" shadow banking or, better, the spare banking and Islamic finance. Although it is clear that this approach is traditional, nevertheless it boasts a lot of niche arguments.

Ultimately, Chapter 4 is related to both IT and ESG factors in banking and financial law. Within this chapter, the attention is turned to environmental matters, as well as the different "philosophies" implemented by the EU and the UK. In this context, the concept of the green bank will be introduced. Finally, Chapter 4 refers to two hot topics: cryo-finance and smart finance. The first one concerns the finance relating to cryoconservation; the second one, to finance in a smart city. More specifically, the latter shall link together green and digital transitions: thanks to green financial activity, potentially, the processes of digital transition may be enhanced. For instance, via a "green" leasing a consumer may obtain a loan in order to buy a "sustainable" car.

In this context, the authors pencil the demarcation line between digital banking, on the one hand, and fintech, on the other hand.

1.1.3 Caveats

Although the authors are experts in the areas of banking and financial law, globalisation and technology developments represent a challenge for all jurists, given the fact that the traditional categories of laws constitute a "fortress under siege." Thus, the correct approach becomes even more horizontal and, at the same time, multidisciplinary and interdisciplinary.

By contrast, it is crucial not to forget the traditional lectures: only thanks to the lessons of our ancestors, is it possible to build a new temple of law. Bearing in mind the motto "*ubi societas, ibi ius*," the latter shall be shaped by the former. As a result of this, in a society based on both digitalisation and a sustainable mindset, the law would be unavoidably influenced by these two factors.

Entailed to this is also the controversial topic of the speed of IT development: the other side of this coin is the ensuing pace that the law shall take.

Finally, there are some caveats within this research textbook that need to be flagged up. First, the interdisciplinary challenge is worthy of a mention: medical law is becoming part of banking and financial law; it is also possible to make the same reasoning for environmental questions and human rights. Second, there is such a thing as the impossibility to be an expert in all fields, although this new paradigm requires us to be, at the same time, specialised practitioners and more general ones at the same time.

Beyond this, the strength of this work is its methodology because, thanks to our approach, the reader can understand the complexity and the unique elements of this area of law. To summarise, our unique selling factor in this book is to use a *fil rouge* that cuts through the different areas of banking and financial law. In doing so, both technology and sustainability come to our aid, in a fortunate coincidence.

Ultimately, IT development makes opaque the borders between human rights and economical rights, and it is, at the end of the day, the novelty of this textbook.

1.2 Regulation in the European Union

In financial law, ends commonly mark a beginning, as will be seen when charting the evolution of any legislation relating to banking and finance in general, and not only that which informs the specific focus of this textbook, *i.e.* the EU legislative framework regulating banking activity, credit institutions and financial markets. For instance, a pertinent illustration of the previous *dictum* can be observed in the wake of the Great Depression, when the US responded by devising and implementing robust legislation of the financial markets as a response to the collapse of the stock markets in 1929.

Furthermore, with the 2007/2008 financial crises still fresh in our memories, having left an indelible mark for more than a decade, and wreaked havoc on a global scale, the EU has felt compelled to implement a drive, not only relatively speedy but also bold and powerful, toward the increased integration or "harmonisation" and even (in part) unification of financial law. At a national level, in countries such as Britain, the same crisis which resulted in the collapse of major financial institutions has brought to light the inability of the supervisor to prevent this systemic failure, thereby establishing the need for the creation, within a legal framework, of a brand-new system of supervision.

In Britain, the Financial Services Act 2012[1] has put the Bank of England and its new operational arms,[2] together with its subsidiaries, in charge of prudential supervision.[3] In the meantime, pushes for more stringent legislation and harmonisation as just discussed, as well as periods of liberalisation to stimulate the financial industry can be discerned. Nonetheless, a constant factor has been the ever-closer integration of EU banking and financial law, which will be the subject of this chapter.

1.2.1 European Union statutes and their hierarchy

The focus of this book is on European banking and financial law, yet the key issues it addresses should not be considered in isolation, rather by drawing a wider perspective and glancing at the entire canvas on which this complex and wide-ranging composition has been orchestrated. In other words, an understanding of each

1 In force as from 1 April 2013.

2 More specifically, for instance, the Financial Policy Committee. For recent commentaries to the new supervisory system in Britain, see Walker and Purves (2014).

3 The Financial Conduct Authority and Prudential Regulation Authority. Similarly, almost 120 years before in late-19th-century Rome, the bankruptcy and ensuing political scandal which engulfed Banca Romana – the Italian credit institution (at the time, just one of six in that country authorised to issue currency) which, by way of an adherence to loose practices, had far exceeded the permitted threshold of banknotes to be printed and dispatched into circulation – lit the blue touch paper for the subsequent creation, in that country, of radical reform hinged upon the formation of a unified central bank, the Banca d'Italia.

specific theme (*e.g.* market abuse, prospectus, listing, consumer protection, etc.) cannot be considered in a vacuum, independent of the overarching legal structure of that complex and increasingly integrated phenomenon called the EU. Any analysis of international banking and financial law, particularly in respect to that applicable in Europe and within the EU, must therefore be preceded by a brief discussion of the legislative "sources" existing in this area of law.[4]

The treaties

Beyond the domain specific to banking and financial law, the pillar of European solidarity, *i.e.* the European Economic Community, in an early tentative step towards the current federation known as the European Union, was born and shaped from the ruins of the Old Continent, where values and institutions had been torn asunder and lay strewn across the deadly battlefields of the Second World War. It is from those battlefields that the awareness arose that a future war could and should be avoided thanks to the commitment of a commercial and financial community. This community is first and foremost a product of the European Treaties.

Of the various EU legislative sources, those which carry the most weight are the treaties. Remarkably, what are now referred to in the plural (treaties) come to life as a singular treaty – more specifically, the Treaty of the European Economic Community or the Treaty of Rome, signed in the eternal city on 25 March 1957.[5] The original treaty was concluded by the six founding states (viz. France, Germany, Italy, and the BeNeLux), although the ensuing years have witnessed a progressive rise in the number of signatories to arrive at the current formation of 28 member states.[6]

The Treaty of Rome has evolved, following a succession of subsequent treaties and an ever-increasing number of signatory countries.[7] Most significantly, the Maastricht Treaty, dated 7 February 1992, established the European Union, a denomination replacing the European Economic Community, while the Treaty

4 In law, a source is the way a precept has come into existence and, more significantly, an answer given to the following question: why is a precept binding and what the addressee of that precept is expected to comply with? (Thirlway 2014). Sources are usually divided in material or formal. The former denote the place where "the terms of the rule can be found conveniently" (*ibid.*) whereas the latter (formal sources) refer to the "legal element that gives to the rule its quality as law" (*ibid.* 5).

5 Remarkably, the signing of the Treaty of the European Economic Community was preceded, among the same six founding countries, by the European Coal and Steel Treaty, achieved in Paris on 18 April 1951, entered into force on 23 July 1952 and expired on 23 July 2002 (Kaczorowska 2011). This treaty, relating to the specific market of coal and steel rather than the more generic economic market, is generally perceived as the build-up to the signature of the Treaty of Rome. A different treaty, signed in Rome by the six founding countries, on the same day as the treaty creating the European Economic Community, is the treaty establishing a European Atomic Power Community. This treaty, relating to the niche market of the atomic power, is still in force, as a parallel treaty to the current three EU treaties.

6 The UK, for instance, together with Ireland and Denmark, joined in 1973.

7 In 2007, Romania and Bulgaria became, respectively, the 26th and 27th EU members. In 2014, Croatia has become the 28th EU member state.

of Lisbon, dated 13 December 2007, resulted into a threefold constitutional chart replacing the Treaty of Rome, specifically hinged upon the following: (1) the Treaty on the European Union;[8] (2) the Treaty on the Functioning of the European Union,[9] consisting of the basic principles of the treaty of Rome and, thus, the *de facto* successor to it; (3) the Charter of the Fundamental Rights of the European Union.[10]

As far as the TFEU is concerned, within it are still enshrined the four fundamental freedoms of the Union, to all intents and purposes mirroring (albeit not replicating word for word) those initially established under the Treaty of Rome: free movement of goods, free movement of persons, free movement of services and free movement of capital.[11] As far as the banking and financial sector is concerned, the last two principles are of particular significance, while aiding a better (methodological) understanding of the following chapters of this textbook. If a bank established in one of the (current) 28 member states wished to offer its banking services in one, some or all of the other member states, it is permitted to do so, in light of the principle of free movement of services and the body of laws which, as a result of it, have been effectuated to render this concept practically applicable.

Likewise, the free movement of capital permits individuals and legal entities of a member state freely to export their assets to another EU country, without any legal barriers. Therefore, a consumer availing themselves of a particular banking product, such as a bank account, may well conclude that the range of banking services presented in his "home country" fall short of those on offer in another member state. To take advantage of the preferable option, the consumer would only have to open the more advantageous bank account in the alternative member state and transfer his money to it. To reiterate the point specified here, as a matter of principle, this transaction should not be hampered between the relevant EU states, as this might infringe the core principles laid out by the TFEU.

While refraining from lingering on the characteristic concepts of EU law, it is nevertheless worth noting that a treaty provision is *directly applicable*, in that each individual in a member state is entitled to raise a claim before a national court requesting its application, specifically in cases where the relevant national piece of legislation contained a provision to the contrary. Simply put, the principle of the treaty takes precedence over the national norm, and once presented before the local adjudicator, the latter shall yield to the supremacy of the supranational one.[12]

Regulations and directives

As can be inferred from the analysis conducted previous, the treaties are the primary sources of EU law. Other statutes and official decisions adopted by the EU

8 Henceforth TEU.

9 Henceforth TFUE.

10 This charter was initially adopted by the Nice Council, although without any legal effect. It was the Treaty of Lisbon that made that charter a binding document (Woods and Watson 2012).

11 (Barnard 2013).

12 (Weatherill 2007).

and its multifarious bodies are considered as of "secondary nature." Such secondary legislation can be binding (a category incorporating regulations, directives and decisions) or non-binding (recommendations and Opinions).

First and foremost, binding legislation is adopted by the EU in order "to fulfil a specific function in the development of the Union law,"[13] which means, in a nutshell, that the legislation must demonstrate a legal basis and fall within the scope of the EU treaties.[14] A regulation, according to Article 288 of the TFEU, is "binding in its entirety and directly applicable in all Member States." Furthermore, a regulation is self-executing by virtue of the fact that, although domestic administrative measures of implementation are sometimes required, member states are not permitted to enact any implementing norm in order to apply it. Accordingly, the norms of each regulation are identical across the spectrum of member states, given the lack of discretion afforded to them.

Conversely, a directive is "binding, as the result to be achieved," and upon each member state to which it is addressed, "but shall leave to the national authorities the choice of the form and methods." Its implementation is mandatory within each member state and is bound by a strict time frame, although the manner in which the specific norms are worded within the relevant domestic legislation is left to the discretion of each EU country. As a general rule, directives are not directly enforceable, although, according to a well-entrenched line of case law of the European Union Court of Justice, such an eventuality could transpire should the relevant directive provisions turn out to be sufficiently detailed.[15]

1.2.2 Financial law legislation from Brussels

To chronicle the history of European banking and financial law would be to draw on an evolution of what, in essence, is the business of lending money to and raising funds from the public. In a way, this business is not dissimilar to the functioning of any other entrepreneurial activity, such as a bakery or a butcher. Nonetheless, there is a clear demarcation line between the two forms of business to the extent that they sit at polar ends of public perception, in that an awareness exists among the community at large that the manner in which a bank is managed (or mismanaged) carries far greater implications for the entire economy of a country, its financial system and sometimes also the economy outside its own national borders.

Accordingly, the bank and, more generally, other financial businesses, such as investment firms and insurance companies, enjoy a special status: the ability to

13 (Reid 2010).

14 For instance, because defence is not included in the Treaties, it would be illegal to enact a directive on it and have the purpose to legislate or to force a certain conduct of member states in this matter, notwithstanding that such directive could have been legally approved by the Council. Consistently with this, Article 296 of the TFEU requires that the legal acts must clarify the reasons they are hinged upon.

15 See, for instance, (case 9/70) *Grad v Finanzamt Traunstein* [1970] ECR 825. Among scholars, see also Dashwood et al. (2011).

commence that activity (*i.e.* to open a bank, with branches offering services to the public), even in the most "liberal countries," is not nonchalantly left to the arbitrary decision of any individual or entity. Rather, any resolution to open a bank is, as a matter of protocol, preceded by a request to the relevant incumbent authority in each respective country (traditionally, but not necessarily, the Central Bank) whereupon it will be subject to the fulfilment of a series of more or less rigorous prerequisites.

Pursuant to the more accentuated implementation, within the EU, of a single market in the 1970s and 1980s, coupled with a steady increase in the number of participating member states, a profound change of tack became evident in the *modus operandi* favoured by Brussels in regard to legislating on the banking sector. Manifested by a clear departure from the previously fragmented national rules, and in preference of the ensuing adherence to a set of pan-European norms applicable in a homogeneous way across the European Union, this revised course of direction can be regarded as a revolution, even when viewed from the perspective of the traditionally conservative jurist. This advancement in legislation, which gained a dramatic degree of impetus in the wake of the 2007/2008 financial crises, cannot be regarded as having charted a steady and progressive course, but rather as a slow and tortuous journey in arriving at its current configuration. It will be discussed in the following.

First Banking Directive

More specifically, in relation to the banking sector, an early example of the formation of common rules applicable exclusively to credit institutions is the so-called First Banking Directive, which originated in the 1970s.[16] This directive, no longer operational, specified that any banking activity ought to be preceded by communication of the relevant authorisation from the competent authority, subsequent to the fulfilment of certain prerequisites. However, this statute was rather poorly forged as, on the one hand, it failed to clarify the precise nature of these prerequisites, while, on the other, it maintained the obligation that authorisation be granted not only by the home state but also by each and every host EEC member state where the authorised bank wished to conduct its business.

Second Banking Directive and European passport

The obvious flaws of Directive 1977/78 were addressed and subsequently rectified by the ensuing Directive 89/646/EEC (the Second Banking Directive).[17] This

16 In full: First Council Directive 77/780/EEC of 12 December 1977 on the coordination of the laws, regulations and administrative provisions relating to the taking up and pursuit of the business of credit institutions.

17 In full: Second Council Directive 89/646/EEC of 15 December 1989 on the coordination of laws, regulations and administrative provisions relating to the taking up and pursuit of the business of credit institutions and amending Directive 77/780/EEC.

time around, the "reserved activities" detailed in the preceding directive were better aligned with the principle that authorisation granted to a banking business in one member state will suffice and does not therefore require that the process be repeated in another. This principle – nowadays almost sacrosanct as a European principle of banking and financial law – is commonly referred to as "passporting," which will now be discussed more extensively.

The notion of a "European passport" is inexorably linked to the parallel concept of "passported activities." Such activities are detailed in a list and termed the "activities subject to the mutual recognition." The list, in the most recent version, can be found in Annex I of Regulation no. 575/2013.[18] Although the relevant details will be comprehensively explored over the ensuing chapters of this textbook, it would not go amiss to say now that the main reserved activities are, on the one hand, the "acceptance of deposits or other repayable funds" and, on the other, the "[l]ending including, inter alia: consumer credit, mortgage credit, factoring, with or without recourse, financing of commercial transactions (including forfeiting)."[19]

Further to the explanation of "passported" activities, it might also be useful to clarify the three pillars on which the concept of the EU passport rests. First and foremost, upon authorisation by the relevant authority in its EU home member state, this green light must also be deemed to sanction all the "passported activities" that the financial institution wishes to perform in other host EU member states without this requiring the further (additional) consent of a different supervisory authority in the "host countries." Whereas no additional consent may be required, the relevant host authorities must be notified. Also, it is important to note that this universal green light applies to the activities a financial institution wishes to perform in another member state either by means of cross-border, distant services or a branch office in that other member state. As a matter of principle, the green light does not apply to the activities of a subsidiary company established in another member state, which subsidiary company – as a separate legal entity – must apply for its own authorisation(s).

The second pillar underpinning the EU passport concerns the increasing harmonisation of legislation regulating the banking industry in terms of standards and requisites applicable to the entire spectrum of EEA countries, thereby giving rise to a reduction or minimisation in disparities among the relevant legislations. We refer

18 Previously the list of the activities to mutual recognition was within Directive 2006/48, and even before, in Directive 1988/89 (Second Banking Directive).

19 Other activities subject to "mutual recognition," also referred to as "passported activities," are as follows: financial lending, money transmission services, issuing and administering means of paying (e.g. credit cards, traveller's cheques and bankers' drafts), guarantee and commitments, trading for own account or account of customers in money markets instruments (cheques, bills, certificates of deposit, etc.), foreign exchange, financial futures and options, exchange and interest-rate instruments (or transferrable securities), participation in securities issues and the provision of services related to such issues, advice to undertakings on capital structure, industrial strategy and related questions and advice as well as services relating to mergers and the purchase of undertakings, money broking, portfolio management and advice, safekeeping and administration of securities, credit reference services, and safe custody services.

to "EEA countries" here because much EU financial legislation not only applies to the EU, but also to the broader European Economic Area, which comprises the 28 EU member states plus Iceland, Norway and Lichtenstein (but not Switzerland). The process of harmonisation just mentioned has not yet accomplished an unqualified neutralisation of the prevailing "legal barriers" among the EEA for two reasons, both following from the European law principles of proportionality and subsidiarity. First, in many instances, harmonisation occurs only at a minimum level leaving member states the freedom to implement EU directives more broadly, rather than at a rigid, mandatory level (maximum harmonisation). Second, EU legislation tends to be specialist and geared towards specific products or institutions, while refraining from harmonising general areas of law. Consequently and most notably, general private or commercial law is not harmonised.

The "home country control" principle constitutes the final pillar of the EU passport. Upon the authorisation by the relevant authority in an EEA country, that consent automatically identifies the authority in charge of supervising the stability of the financial institution, irrespective of where in the EEA that enterprise wished to perform its business activities. In this scenario, the host authority will play a supervisory role where it concerns the business conducted in that host country, but, as a matter of principle, it will have no competence in the matter of the stability of the bank.

Lamfalussy Report

A discussion of the main legislative architecture of the EU concluded, attention can now be trained on the specificities of the current EU legislative process in the financial sector where it must be stressed that an initial foray into this area, as an autonomous EU tenet, came to light by way of the Maastricht Treaty, in 1992. There for the first time, principles aimed at shaping the organisation of an economic and monetary union were set out,[20] in accordance with the overarching purpose of the EU to "establish the foundations of an ever-closer union among the people of Europe."[21]

Remarkably, a significant step in the change of pace of the EU legislative process specific to the banking sector emanated from the so-called Lamfalussy Report. This report,[22] drafted by Baron Alexandre Lamfalussy and a group of like-minded "wise men" chaired by him in the late 1990s, was, upon appointment of the EU Council, entrusted with assessing the efficiency of the legislative progress in the financial sector. Ultimately, it consists of a document detailing a set of recommended guidelines conducive to a more efficient law-making process within the

20 Although this move has been hampered by the decision of two countries, the UK and Denmark, to opt out of it.

21 (Kaczorowska 2011).

22 Final Report of the Committee of the Wise Men in the Regulation of European Securities Markets, Brussels, 15 February 2001 (http://ec.europa.eu/internal_market/securities/docs/lamfalussy/wisemen/final-report-wise-men_en.pdf).

Union, in regard to the financial sector. The EU legislature has embraced the recommended process, which is now commonly referred to as the Lamfalussy process.

In brief, the Lamfalussy process discerns the following four levels of regulation:

- The adoption of directives or regulations by the EU, in accordance with the co-decision procedure (Level 1);
- The implementation of additional legislation at EU level, the purpose of which is to fill in the details (Level 2);
- A focus on cooperation among national supervisors so that "consistent implementation and enforcement" can be ensured (Level 3);
- A more effective enforcement of the EU legislation (Level 4).

The interaction between Level 1 and Level 2 of the Lamfalussy Report is fundamental, and fully deserves some more explanation. A piece of legislation appearing at the first level, usually a directive but on occasion a Regulation, allows the EU law-maker to expedite the enactment of basic principles, on the grounds of the fact that the co-decision process requires a simple majority, as opposed to complete agreement. This greases the wheels of EU law-making, as otherwise reaching a consensus on a detailed statute would be inherently more problematic and time-consuming.

Coupled with the first level is the correspondent piece of legislation represented at the second level (also, in this case, either a directive or a regulation with implementing provisions) where the detailed norms are provided. In other words, the impasse that traditionally transpired as a fly in the ointment of the EU legislative process, cleverly sidestepped by the Lamfalussy process, based on an interaction between the first-level directive or regulation and the second-level directive or regulation. Moreover, as a result of the implementation of the De Larosière Report, to be discussed further here, three European supervisory authorities have been created, consisting of the cooperating national supervisors, and are empowered to issue regulatory technical standards and implementing technical standards, which serve as detailed implementation norms of the second level. On the third level, the same European supervisory authorities may issue recommendations and guidelines.

Since the introduction of the Lamfalussy procedure, the Second Banking Directive has been superseded by an even more organic statute (viz. Directive 2006/48/EC),[23] the latter being recently amalgamated within Regulation 575/2013/EU,[24] and ancillary Directive 2013/36/EU,[25] together referred to as

23 In full: Directive 2006/48/EC of the European Parliament and of the Council of 14 June 2006 relating to the taking up and pursuit of the business of credit institutions, also referred to as Capital Requirements Directive.

24 In full: Regulation 575/2013/EU of the European Parliament and of the Council of 26 June 2013 on prudential requirements for credit institutions and investment firms and amending Regulation (EU) No 648/2012 Text with EEA relevance.

25 In full: Directive 2013/36/EU of the European Parliament and of the Council of 26 June 2013 on access to the activity of credit institutions and the prudential supervision of credit institutions

"CRD IV." This progression of the aforementioned chain of directives paints a picture of EU banking legislation which can be identified with a number of salient features.

First and foremost, the banking business is a "reserved" one on the grounds that the typical banking activities (not only to lend money and to raise funds, but also those which are ancillary)[26] are not available to anyone, but rather exclusively to those who, in satisfying the minimum legislative requirements such as having the necessary capital and adequate managerial skills, are permitted to commence such a business by means of a license or authorisation. Additionally, the business is supervised to such an extent that the sword of Damocles hangs over the head of each financial institution, thereby subjecting them to the mercy of an authority (the supervisor) who can decide, in accordance with the objective parameters, whether that business can continue to operate or, alternatively, if it should be excluded from the market by revoking its license.[27] Finally (and this is a particularly important factor at EU level and in a market which is expected to be highly integrated), banking activities are "passported." In other words, once authorisation has been granted to a bank in a given country, no further authorisation is required in other member states where it wishes to operate.

De Larosière Report

The broad picture of the legislative sources pertaining to banking and financial law is completed by the De Larosière Report. In October 2008, Jacques de Larosière de Champfeu was entrusted with a mandate, administered by the president of the European Commission (José Barroso), the purpose of which was to chair a group of experts uniquely qualified to devise practical proposals in the area of financial regulation and supervision. The report was commissioned against a challenging backdrop of economic crisis and recession. In the months pursuant to the eruption of both the eurozone crisis and the public debt crisis in 2009, the latter affecting most notably the peripheral countries of the eurozone, the EU faced a critical juncture: on the one hand, it could opt for a *chacun pour soi* solution (each country independently makes its own decisions on how to proceed) or, on the other, it could choose to strengthen cooperation within the EU countries to provide a united front against the testing economic landscape of financial recession. The latter solution found the favour of the De Larosière Report,[28] which essentially emphasised three steps to guard against any likelihood of a future collapse: (1) a new regulatory agenda, (2) a stronger coordinated supervision and (3) effective crisis management procedures.

Significantly, the De Larosière Report does not seek to alter the legislative architecture of the EU, as forged from the foundations by the treaties and, as far

---

and investment firms, amending Directive 2002/87/EC and repealing Directives 2006/48/EC and 2006/49/EC.

26 See below.

27 See the specific point about the insolvency of credit institutions.

28 (de Larosière 2009).

as the financial legislation is concerned, specified by the finishing touches of the Lamfalussy Report. In other words, the Report of 2009 does not (methodologically) amend the manner in which legislation is crafted in Brussels. However, it certainly provides the legislator with important pointers on what kind of norms and principles shall be promoted in the financial sector to address the issues and problems which crawled (or rather, leapt) out of the woodwork as the first decade of the 21st century neared its conclusion.

As emphasised by the De Larosière Report, the regulatory framework in place prior to recent crises lacked cohesiveness and therefore homogeneity. As the EU member states were afforded a significant degree of leeway over the extent to which they could implement and enforce the directives, such "options [led] to a wide diversity of national transpositions related to local traditions, legislations and practices."[29] The reason for this lack of harmonisation was the overly accentuated vagueness which characterised the first level of legislation (the directive) where the national legislator had at his disposal a multitude of options with the outcome that, at the lower level (the level 3 committees of the Lamfalussy Report), it was very difficult, if not impossible, to "impose a single solution."[30]

The De Larosière Report, and its remarks on the manner in which legislation in the financial sector should be adopted in the EU, has not gone unheard or indeed unheeded. First and most significantly, the De Larosière Report has resulted in the creation of a European System of Financial Supervision,[31] the purpose of which is to ensure the supervision of the Union's financial system. The ESFS consists of three European supervisory authorities: the European Banking Authority,[32] seated in London; the European Securities Markets Authority,[33] seated in Paris; and the European Insurance and Occupational Pensions Authority, seated in Frankfurt.[34]

As stated previously in these authorities the relevant national supervisors participate and, unlike their predecessors, are empowered to issue binding regulatory technical standards and implementing technical standards in addition to non-binding guidelines and recommendations. In addition, a European Systemic Risk Board (ESRB) forms part of the ESFS, which is "responsible for the macro-prudential

29 See "de Larosière Report," *ibid.* 27.

30 *Ibid.* 27.

31 Henceforth ESFS.

32 Henceforth EBA.

33 Henceforth ESMA.

34 Henceforth EIOPA.

See, respectively, Regulation 1093/2010/EU of the European Parliament and of the Council of 24 November 2010 establishing a European supervisory authority (European Banking Authority), amending Decision 716/2009/EC and repealing Commission Decision 2009/78/EC; Regulation 1095/2010/EU of the European Parliament and of the Council of 24 November 2010 establishing a European supervisory authority (European Securities and Markets Authority), amending Decision No 716/2009/EC and repealing Commission Decision 2009/77/EC; and Regulation 1094/2010/EU of the European Parliament and of the Council of 24 November 2010 establishing a European supervisory authority (European Insurance and Occupational Pensions Authority), amending Decision 716/2009/EC and repealing Commission Decision 2009/79/EC.

oversight of the financial system within the Union in order to contribute to the prevention or mitigation of systemic risks to financial stability in the Union that arise from developments within the financial system and taking into account macroeconomic developments, so as to avoid periods of widespread financial distress. It shall contribute to the smooth functioning of the internal market and thereby ensure a sustainable contribution of the financial sector to economic growth."[35]

Moreover, as analysed in this textbook, a great many areas of financial law underwent significant change, so as to limit the level of discretion in the hands of each member state. For instance, the deposit guarantee scheme which was previously based on a minimum harmonisation directive[36] and which thus left relative discretion to each country on the level of protection afforded to the depositor, has been replaced by a more robust maximum harmonisation directive,[37] where this discretion is significantly curtailed, if not entirely removed. In other cases, directives have been or will be replaced by regulations, so as to accomplish unification. Also, where no trace of harmonisation was to be found,[38] a legislative framework is in the pipeline and shall be presently administered accordingly.

Single Supervisory Mechanism

Despite the tumultuous evolution of the financial sector over the past 30 years, prior to the recent financial crisis, a truly European integration of supervisors had remained conspicuous by its absence. Therefore, until relatively recently, a sort of paradox prevailed within the EU where, on the one hand, a fully integrated market of credit institutions reaped the benefits of a single market which afforded them the tools to expand and operate at a greater pace across Europe, while, on the other, the fragmented subsistence of a body of supervisors as numerous as the various countries constituting the EU was evident.

In hindsight, this asymmetry, replete with myriad organisational distortions, may have been a contributory factor in the collapse of several major financial institutions in the late 2000s, too vast and pan-European to be supervised by the assemblage of authorities existing in each respective country. This flaw in the architecture of the EU banking system has recently been revisited by the creation of the Single Supervisory Mechanism.[39] This legislative structure hinges upon the European

35 Article 3 of the Regulation 1092/2010/EU of the European Parliament and of the Council of 24 November 2010 on European Union macro-prudential oversight of the financial system and establishing a European Systemic Risk Board.

36 Directive 94/19/EC of the European Parliament and of the Council of 30 May 1994 on deposit-guarantee schemes, OJ L 135.

37 Directive 2009/14/EC of the European Parliament and of the Council of 11 March 2009 amending Directive 94/19/EC on deposit-guarantee schemes as regards the average level and the pay-out delay, OJ L 68.

38 For instance, a guarantee scheme in the insurance industry.

39 By virtue of Council Regulation 1024/2013/EU of 15 October 2013 conferring specific tasks on the European Central Bank concerning policies relating to the prudential supervision of credit institutions, OJ L 287.

Central Bank,[40] which, in assuming this new additional role, is responsible, in conjunction with the national supervisors, for the prudential supervision of the credit institutions of all banks operating in the eurozone. It is hoped that this mechanism will confine to the annals of history the predicaments of the past (in other words, a largely fragmented body of supervisors, dwarfed by the giants among the credit institutions which in the interim had grown exponentially beyond the borders of a specific member state) and thus curtail the likelihood that such disarray could once again be catapulted into the public spotlight.

1.3 UK regulation after Brexit

1.3.1 Introduction

During the 1970s the United Kingdom was a major financial centre and played a central role on the international scene, becoming a leader able to influence the formation of international financial standards.[41]

More precisely, it is possible to affirm that the UK acted as an independent player; it adopted strategies to advance rules with the support of the EU and, on some occasions, with countries such as the US.[42] In other words, before the financial crisis, a series of elements made the UK one of the most relevant proponents of financial regulation in the EU and a key participant in the legislative process.[43]

This is supported by different elements:

- The quite remarkable size of the UK's economy;
- The lobbying capacity of the City of London in EU institutions;
- The UK's voting power in the EU;
- A clear strategy of technical administrative engagement of UK regulatory authorities at the EU level.

Although this picture is genuine, it is also worth mentioning that the relation between the UK and the EU changed, thanks to the transformation of the Financial Stability Forum[44] and, more precisely, when it became the Financial Stability Board.[45] Also in this circumstance, the UK remained an influential actor within the international arena, but it changed it in relation to the EU. To elaborate, before the 2007/2008 financial crises, the UK was viewed as the proponent of a distinct regulatory approach when compared to other member states;[46] the UK usually

40 The European Central Bank already existed in its capacity of Bank in charge of the monetary policy.
41 (Langevoort 2010).
42 (Moloney 2016; Conac 2015; Müller, Kudrna and Falkner 2014; Moloney, The European Union in International Financial Governance 2017).
43 (Cini and Verdun 2018).
44 Henceforth FSF.
45 Henceforth FSB.
46 (Quaglia 2012).

adopted a market-making ethos that was marked by a higher degree of openness and experimentation.

This approach contrasted with the strategy of other EU member states, *i.e.* Germany and France, characterised by a market-shaping strategy where a strict regulatory ethos was favoured.[47]

After the financial crisis, the tension between these two distinct groups deepened for multifarious reasons: (1) many of the actors involved with the financial turmoil were not subject to EU regulation; (2) a more liberal approach to regulation associated with the UK and US was viewed as being somewhat responsible for the crisis.

Therefore, with the Larosière Report in 2009, stricter and more prescriptive rules were introduced, increasing the EU's supervisory powers and creating prudential instruments at the regional level. The UK behaviour was to be a resistant force.

1.3.2 ***Brexit***

The British referendum on continuing membership of the EU in June 2016 represented a turning point in the relationship between the UK and the EU. The result led to the resignation of Prime Minister David Cameron.

During March 2017, the British government under Prime Minister Theresa May invoked Article 50 of the Treaty on the European Union: this officially epitomised the beginning of the negotiations of UK withdrawal from the EU. At the end of January 2020, the UK left the EU.

As a result of Brexit, there are multifarious implications for the relations with the UK and the EU; nevertheless, in this context the attention relies only on banking and financial matter.

Brexit means the creation of an additional influence pole between the EU and the US; moreover, the scenario results even more complex mercy the increase in market size and systemic relevance of emerging economies. China is the clearest example. The new role of emerging economies appears to be unpredictable. To explicate, on the one hand it is possible that these new economies have the capacity to boost the diversity and heterogeneity of the regulatory preferences in international fora. This could increase the legitimacy of networks and the quality of their output.

On the other hand, heterogeneity decreases the odds of achieving more granular harmonisation-based measures. Emergent economies, indeed, have different sources of risk and other structures for financial innovation. This is a circumstance that exacerbate the redistributive consequences of standards.[48]

From a UK perspective, it remains the British dilemma, born in the aftermath of financial crisis, between restoring the stability of the domestic banking system and protecting the international competitiveness of the City of London.

47 It included over-reliance, delegation of supervisory roles to financial intermediation and industry.
48 (Schilling de Carvalho 2022).

In the aftermath of the Brexit referendum, the main financial industry associations formulated a position with a view to limiting the damage for the City of London from the UK's withdrawal from the EU.

In March 2018, UK and EU negotiators reached agreement over the transition period to 31 December 2020, protecting the City's access to the EU market until at least December 2020.

Yet May's failure in her duty to support the withdrawal agreement, and her replacement as prime minister by Boris Johnson in July 2019, did little to improve relations. Therefore, it was argued that regulatory alignment was a critical element of the future UK-EU relationship, and warnings were sounded about the damage which would be done by the existing approach after a regulatory divergence.[49]

By contrast, the City engaged in pragmatic adaptation once Brexit went ahead, by partially relocating some activities to the EU, seeking to increase business with third countries and lobbying for selective deregulation of certain financial services, such as, notably, hedge funds.

Problematically, however, the EU's Chief Negotiator, Michel Barnier, continued to rule out a "special deal" for finance, as well as the prospect of mutual recognition, which was regarded as integral to the single market. Instead, he insisted that the UK ultimately had to choose between remaining in the single market (through EEA membership), or accepting more limited access, based on the EU's third-country equivalence regime for financial regulation. The government, therefore, quietly abandoned its support for the mutual recognition model: it began to signal that it now favoured a looser arrangement that would seek to build on and strengthen the EU's existing equivalence rules. It is the so-called enhanced equivalence model. Enhanced equivalence sought to import elements of a mutual recognition regime into the equivalence regime agreed with the EU. Notably, the UK proposed an independent arbitration mechanism, grandfathering clauses and a wider set of products to be covered by equivalence.

1.3.3 Financial matter

The most important priority of Bank of England was to manage financial stability implication of Brexit by ensuring that the UK financial industry was prepared for the failure of the UK and the EU to reach a deal, either on withdrawal or the future relationship.

In December 2017, the governor announced that it would allow EU banks to maintain their UK operations under current rules following Brexit, assuming that also after Brexit it was intended that a higher level of supervisory cooperation would continue with the EU.[50]

Nevertheless, branches that were considered to pose a systematic risk to London's financial centre could be forced to convert into subsidiaries. Further, banks

49 (Islam 2019).
50 (Inman and Ranking 2020).

took for granted that they reserved the right to withdraw this provision, unless it was reciprocated by Brussels.

Meanwhile, the Financial Conduct Authority[51] announced temporary waivers for over 8,000 EU financial firms to enable them to continue operating in the UK after Brexit under existing rules, even in the absence of an agreement covering financial services.

As far as the future of UK-EU relations is concerned, the governor warned explicitly against any arrangement that would leave UK regulators as "rule-takers," forced to implement EU financial regulation over which they would have no scope for influence. In this scenario, a key role was played by the Bank of England: it supported the mutual recognition model for EU-UK trade in the financial sector.

In setting out the Bank's "ideal post-EU regulatory framework" on 10 March 2020, Head of Prudential Policy, Victoria Saporta, reiterated the regulators' call for the UK to have "regulatory independence."[52]

These arguments were echoed in the UK government's negotiating mandate, which called for "regulatory cooperation arrangements" between "autonomous systems of regulation." The EU response was tilting to stress that the key instrument used to regulate interactions between the EU and the UK financial systems would be unilateral equivalence.

The preferences of UK regulators were aligned, to some extent, to theories of transnational governance. For example, clearly there was the importance of maintaining access to the EU financial markets, together with an extended transition period and/or regulatory waivers, all pointing to the importance of transgovernmental networks in shaping the Bank of England's preference for financial stability.

Even so, these economic imperatives were qualified by a bureaucratic concern to preserve (and, potentially, enhance) the role and autonomy of UK regulators post-Brexit. Crucially, this meant explicitly opposing any soft Brexit outcome, such as EEA membership, which would necessitate the full and automatic alignment of UK and EU financial rules. To reconcile these competing demands, the Bank sought to appeal to international standards as the basis of evaluating regulatory equivalence, not least because this was an arena in which UK regulators traditionally punched above their weight.[53]

It is possible to affirm that the largest UK financial firms were strongly in favour of a continued EU membership, fearing that the UK withdrawal would generate substantial political and economic adjustment costs. The political cost related to the UK's loss of influence over future EU financial regulation, while economic costs would result from diminished access to the EU single market. More precisely, UK firms risked losing lucrative "passport rights," which in the past had enabled them

51 Henceforth FCA.

52 Bank of England, The Ideal Post-EU Regulatory Framework – Speech by Victoria Saporta. 10 March, Bank of England, London, 2020.

53 (James and Quaglia 2022).

to trade across the EU without the need for further authorisation.[54] UK financial regulators were also firmly opposed to Brexit and they worked to quantify the adaptational costs of Brexit.

Therefore, senior UK financial regulators in the Bank of England became increasingly sceptical about the possibility of a soft Brexit option that, it was claimed, would leave the UK as a rule taker from Brussels.

1.3.4 Regulation proposal

It is more crystal than clear that Brexit generated an immediate adaptational pressures for domestic change by necessitating the full transposition of EU legislation into UK law and design a new financial regulatory framework.

The 2018 European Union Withdrawal Act incorporated all EU-derived domestic legislation (*i.e.* legislation implementing EU directives) and directly applicable EU law (such as regulations) onto the UK statute book, including financial services. Despite this, it was argued that it was worthwhile to recognise a tailor-made legal framework for Brexit management.

Hence, the full proposals regarding the "Future Regulatory Framework Review" were published in November 2021, and confirmed that while government and Parliament would set the broad policy framework for financial services regulation, the Prudential Regulatory Authority[55] and FCA would be responsible for issuing regulation using their existing rule-making powers and newly delegated powers.

As a result of this, the government proposed the following:

- The regulators would be given the power to set direct regulatory requirement for firms, requiring the government to gradually repeal parts of retained EU law so that the regulators would be able to replace it with regulatory requirements in their own rulebooks;
- UK regulators would be given a new secondary objective for growth and competitiveness;
- That financial regulators would be subject to greater accountability through the introduction of a new call-in power permitting the government to block or change decisions by regulators in exceptional circumstances.

In July 2022 the Financial Services and Markets Bill was published; it replaced the call-in power with a proposal in force of which the Treasury was able to force regulators to review their rules. This was unveiled without public or parliamentary disclosure.

The area with the greatest potential for UK rules to diverge and become less stringent than EU rules relates to capital markets and non-banking financial institutions. More precisely, the government has proposed to support wholesale markets

54 (James and Quaglia, Differentiated de-Europeanisation: UK policy-making in Finance after Brexit 2023).
55 Henceforth PRA.

by relaxing regulatory requirements as currently stipulated in the EU's Market in Financial Instruments Directive II.[56]

Another area concerned digital finance: in this respect, ministers have repeatedly spoken positively about the benefit to attracting fintech firms; therefore, the main idea is to expand, and implement, financial market infrastructure.

In conclusion, it is possible to affirm that Brexit shall be read as a massive opportunity to shape a new legal framework in the UK. The government had the opportunity to remove, retain or revise the body of the EU-derived law currently in force, much of which is the basis for most environmental regulation in the country.

1.3.5 The UK regulation

The Bank of England

Per the traditional approach, the role of the Bank of England is analysed in terms of banking regulation and supervision. However, it is also worth emphasising that it also exercises a significant amount of experience and influence over financial system, as a whole, via its surveillance responsibility.

The Bank of England Act 1998 had already set out the initial steps towards a single, unified regulatory body with the transfer of banking supervision to the FSA and the personnel of the Supervision and Surveillance Division.[57]

The Bank's relationship with the Treasury and the Financial Service Authority[58] was outlined in a memorandum of understanding.[59] The latter stipulates how the three organisations are expected to work together.

The main idea was that Bank played a central and crucial role, *i.e.* to monitor of stability in financial systems. This term, "financial systems," referred to both the banking sector and institutions in the wider financial marketplace that would be able to affect stability. According to the MoU, the Bank is required to monitor the infrastructure and payment system both domestically and abroad.

However, we must consider the role of the lender of last resort:[60] according to MoU, the Bank with its LORL role has the facility to ensure stability to avert systemic damage to financial markets. The power to exercise the LORL function is not prescribed in formal rules but is a discretionary power to be exercised in order to "avoid a serious disturbance in the UK economy."[61]

The LORL is utilised only in the most exceptional circumstances, after the consultation with the Treasury and FCA.

56 Henceforth MiFID II.
57 (Blair et al. 1998).
58 Henceforth FSA.
59 Henceforth MoU, see Bank of England (1997/98) Memorandum of Understanding between HM Treasury, The Bank of England and the FSA (MoU), Banking Act Report, 37–39.
60 Henceforth LOLR.
61 Bank of England (1997/98) Memorandum of Understanding between HM Treasury, The Bank of England and the FSA (MoU), Banking Act Report, 39, para 11.

From the financial services authority to the Bank of England

The FSA was incorporated in a unique way, as a private limited company by guarantee of the endogenous regulation: it is rooted within the market and detached from government interventions in terms of its day-to-day responsibilities. Even so, the FSA was accountable to Parliament and judiciary.

An independent body, such as the FSA, had grown in importance for multiple reasons; the first is the complexity of society that requires specialised bodies to take responsibility for politically sensitive areas.[62] In fact, among the reasons that the 2007/2008 crises had played havoc in the UK, one of the main ones was identified as the quintessential inability of this gigantic body, the FSA, to be independent. One of the main concerns was the dual role of the FSA, as both regulator and supervisor. Additionally, the vast area of supervision, from banking to insurance, via financial services, had made this giant partly useless. There is no doubt that the FSA was a giant, since it used to focus on multifarious objectives, that is to say:

- To maintain market confidence in the financial system;
- To cultivate public awareness and enhance the public's understanding of financial systems;
- To protect consumers, as a key rational for financial regulations;
- To reduce financial crime – that is to say, to prevent fraud.

However, not only was it a giant, but it was a giant with feet of clay. The collapse of banks in 2007/2008, with the UK credit institutions among the worst hit in the world, made the UK supervisor one of the players most contributing most to the financial crises.

Four years after the financial crisis, the Bank of England has been entrusted with this new role: not only is Threadneedle Street now in charge of the role as monetary authority, but also relied on in two areas: the Financial Conduct Authority, in charge of assessing the conduct of supervised entities vis-à-vis investors, and the Financial Regulation Authority, entrusted with the supervision of the stability of the supervised entities.

1.3.6 Banking law in Scotland

In this work, reference is made to the UK, as sovereign entity, as well as the place where banks and stock market started flourishing during the Renaissance. Although the UK is a quintessential parameter, it is well-known that, within the UK, there are different nations. One of these, Scotland, has played an important role not only in conceiving a different legal system, a common law with Roman roots, but also a different dynamic in the way credit institutions, including the central one – in Scotland, in a very peculiar way, not just Royal Bank of Scotland, but other two banks – have started operating. Additionally, the formal separation existing between

62 (Singh 2007).

Scottish legal system and English one means that some legal concepts, which are taken from granted "South of the Border," have in Scotland different contours, or different definitions, or even a completely different qualification.

To such a purpose, emphasis is placed on some notions existing in Scottish banking law. As regards securities, the person guarantee existing in English common law is replaced in Scotland by the cautionary contract, where also the cautioner is the guarantor existing "North of the Border." Additionally, the floating charge, the peculiar security that in English law, may be granted to a creditor by a debtor which is a company, did not have a Scottish counterparty until the few decades ago.

Nevertheless, although the Scottish floating charge has been introduced, scholars still continue being critic toward its impact on the Scottish legal system. Finally, as regards the undue influence – an equity concept that in English contract law has been used in the banking sector in order to invalidate a number of personal guarantees given by a spouse in order to guarantee obligations of the other spouse – the correspondent Scottish concept, in a jurisdiction whether the equity is missing, is the circumvention.

History

Before the Union, 1707, the pace of the development of the banking system was very slow in Scotland, although in Edinburgh the activities of both merchants and goldsmiths, organised as quasi business entities, were very close to a basic form of credit institutions.

Even before the Union, in 1660, bills of exchange, as a form of security bonds, were already in existence in Scotland. However, it is also true that credit instruments are reminiscent of a mercantile society. This document would be accepted only in coin and king, in order to preserve a simplistic economy and led to vulnerability if there was a shortage of coin.

While England was in war with Louis XIV of France, Scotland was enjoying a comparatively peaceful period: when England suspended the Netherlands as Europe's main money market, Scotland was indirectly affected by the shift in the power away from a traditional ally to London.

Moreover, during this period of time, the Parliament of Scotland was in a position to support enterprises which, ultimately, encouraged both manufacturing and foreign trade. Starting from this, the Scottish economy began with two major investments:

- The creation of a Scotland trading entity aimed at rivalling with the East India Company;[63]
- The establish of a public bank in Edinburgh, more specifically Royal Bank of Scotland.

63 It was sponsored by William Partrson and promoted by an act of Parliament.

John Holland, an English man, promoted the Bank of Scotland; he set out a strategy for the creation of the bank. His plan involved the drawing up of a bill to be submitted before the Scottish Parliament; in 1695 the bill was passed by the Parliament, and the Bank of Scotland was incorporated.[64] The Bank of Scotland began its business, with interests based on the African Company: the capital, having been subscribed within the appointed time, was called in, and it began issuing notes of various denomination from 100 to 5.

The strong connection with the London banking network was due to a number of factors:

- London was already the centre of international trade;
- Scottish currency lacked strength and was subjects to extreme fluctuations;
- Scots coinage should not offer the same security and certainty as the sterling.

The real progress was made when RBS began to issue its own notes: from the beginning, the bank determined that it would be prudent to use sterling units, instead of Scots pound. The notes were put into circulation by bank making payment in them to their borrowers. More precisely, "a new paper currency was to be launched in Scotland which was designed, quite deliberately, to challenge the Bank of Scotland's monopoly and extend the Bank of England's operations in Scotland."[65]

In the history of the Scottish banking system, two significant dates are worthy of recollection:

- The introduction of the system of cash-credits 12 March 1728 when marks the origin of cash-credit accounts in Scotland;
- The introduction by the Bank of Scotland of notes which an optional clause in 1730: the notes promising to pay on demand or in the handler's option, six months after demand, with, in that case, interest at 5%.
- In 1731 the establishment of branches at Glasgow, Aberdeen and Dundee.[66]

It is crucial to recall a bank war, during 1750, between a cartel of Glasgow banks, which habitually redeemed in London bills rather than species, and the banks of Edinburgh. The latter set up a private Glasgow banker, Archibald Trotter, with a supply note on Glasgow banks and Trotter demanded the banks of his city redeem them, as promised, in species. The Glasgow banks delayed and dragged their feet, until Trotter was forced to file a legal claim for damages about "vexatious delay."[67] At least, Trotter won a nominal victory but could not het the law to force Glasgow bank to pay up.

64 17 July 1695.

65 Bank of Scotland 1695–1955, 33.

66 (Fleming 1877).

67 *Archibald Trotter v Messers Murdoch Cochrane, and Co. Bankers in Glasgow* [1761] Mor 14607 (17 December 1761).

From 1716 and 1844, the Scottish banking system was characterised by free entry and unlimited note issue. Only three banks were given the privilege of limited liability, whereas all the other Scottish banks operated under an unlimited liability regime. The Peel Bank Act of 1844 prohibited new entry into the note-issuing industry in all parts of the UK. It cartelised the Scottish banking industry and prohibited new entry and competition among the existing banks.

As far as the relationship between Central Bank and Bank of Scotland is concerned, it is possible to highlight the interconnection between these two banks. Although an initial period of competition, demonstrated by the fact that Royal Bank of Scotland encourage innovation at the beginning, the two banks came to identify their best interest as lying on cartels or cartelisation.

In 1752 they set up a note exchange in which they agreed not to accept the notes of other banks, to refuse credit to specie exporters at times, of payment deficit, and to set up a permanent joint committee to promote their common interest and smooth over any differences.

A case study is represented by the growth of Ayr Bank: this bank was formed due to an excess in the credit demand, which was not met by the two public banks, one of which was heavily engaged in a credit squeeze. This credit crunch *ante litteram* was necessitated by a persistent currency exchange crisis, which two public banks attempted to relieve by borrowing from the Bank of England.[68]

The Ayr Bank failed because it attempted to subvert the implementation of necessary credit restraint policy; this continue exchange crisis, combined with the collapse of a London bank with which many Scottish banks had dealings, meant that Ayr Bank credit expansion could not be sustained. The consequences of the collapse were not so serious, thanks to the actions of the Bank of Scotland and the Royal Bank of Scotland in accepting Ayr Banks notes.[69]

As far as coins are concerned, from 1293 to 1355 coins in both England and Scotland were of the same weight and purity; however, the standard of Scotch money was sunk below that of England and by successive depreciations the value of Scotch money at the union of the crown in 1600 was only a 12th part of the value of English money of the same denomination. It remains at this point till the union of the two kingdoms in 1706 cancelled the separate coinage of Scotland; therefore, the coins now are the same. Nevertheless, the Scotch money of accounts was for some time afterwards continued and when a payment was made, it was usual to state, so many pounds, Scots, or so many pounds sterling.[70]

The origin of paper money in Scotland lies on the establishment of the Bank of Scotland in 1695, a year after its English counterpart.[71] The Bank's activities were to comprise "the Trade of Lending and Borrowing Money upon Interest, and Negotiating Bills of Exchange." In this scenario, was because of the "lending" that banknotes first began to be issued. The Continental European banks stressed that they were

68 (Checkland 1975).
69 (Dow and Smithin 1992).
70 (Lawson 1852).
71 (Malcolm 1945).

issued by way of loans, rather than against deposits, and, partly for that reason, these notes soon much exceeded any metallic money immediately available in Edinburgh.

The first banknotes were issued on 1 April 1696 and the Bank had the liabilities in notes of five times its holdings in coins. By the time that statutory monopoly originally given to the Bank of Scotland ended in 1716, paper money was firmly established within Scotland as an equivalent coin. Further, the ending of monopoly did not lead to an immediate challenge to the position of the Bank of Scotland: more precisely, in 1727 a second bank, the Royal Bank of Scotland, was established by royal charter and began to issue notes.

This was not largely accepted: for instance, Hume was hostile to the development. He referred, on one occasion, to "those institutions of banks, funds, and paper credit, with which we are in this kingdom infatuated," and he also warned against the tendency of paper money to drive out silver and gold. He also added that "we are as careful to stuff the nation with this fine commodity of bank-bills and chequer-notes, as if we were afraid of being over-burthened with the precious metals."[72] From a different perspective, it was emphasised that money let needs to circulate goods.[73]

As a result of this, it is clear that the roots of the banking business in Scotland lie back in the days before the Union of the Kingdom when Scotland was a separate country. Despite this, when the Bank of Scotland was established as the first-joint stock bank in Scotland one year after the foundation of the Bank of England, it was given a monopoly of joint-stock banking for 21 years. When this monopoly expired, the concession was not renewed and the result was that in Scotland, unlike England, there was no legal barrier to the set-up of other joint-stock companies for carrying on the trade of banking.

Moreover, under Scots law there was a generally available form of legal incorporation in the "contract of copartnery." Therefore, Scotland banking was a small-scale, local affair, as in England, two other powerful joint-stock banks were established: (1) Royal Bank of Scotland (1727) and (2) British Linen Bank (1746).[74]

Securities

A real right in security gives to a creditor, in addition to his contractual right to payment, an *ius in re* over certain specified property of the debtor to enforce payment of his debt. This right shall be distinguished from a personal right of security, such as cautionary or guarantee.

In Roman law, real securities could be in three forms:

- In fiducia;
- In dominium, ownership of the subject given in security was transferred to the creditor subject to the obligation to re-transfer it when debtor had fulfilled his undertaking;

72 (Hume 1752).
73 (Smith 1978).
74 (Gaskin 2010)

- Possession, but not ownership of the pledge was transferred in the case of pignus, or hypotheca.

The Companies (Floating Charges) (Scotland) Act 1961 recognised a statutory form of hypothec or floating charge over the assets of a registered company. Further, by the Agricultural Credits (Scotland) Act 1929 and Agricultural Marketing Act 1958 various agricultural charges may be created without delivery.[75]

The contract may take the form either of an *ex facie* conveyance of ownership to the creditor or, alternatively, the transfer to him of the subject in security. In the former case we can say that (1) his title is qualified only by a personal obligation to reconvey, (2) the creditor may sell the subject without notice to the debtor, and (3) if carried out in disregard of the debtor's rights and interests, such sale may justify the debtor in bringing a personal action for damages, a bona fide purchaser's right will be beyond challenge.

In a different hypothesis, it is settled that the trustee in bankruptcy of a security holder upon an ex facie absolute title is bound to fulfil the latter's obligation to reconvey.[76] In other words, when the creditor holds upon absolute title, his security covers not only the debt for which it was granted but also debts incurred subsequently.

- Such debts are recovered by the creditor's right of retention, unless this has been limited or excluded by the terms of the contract between the parties;
- When a subject is expressly transferred in a security, the creditor has no *ius disponendi* as proprietor and therefore can sell only by virtue of a contractual power or by order of the court;
- Such securities cover only the debt which was granted and gives no preference in respect of debts incurred after the date of the grant.[77]

Although it is arduous to give a definition of security, one of this may be the following:

> [A]ny right which a creditor may hold for ensuring the payment or satisfaction of his debt, distinct from, and in addition to, his right of action and execution against debtor under the latter's personal obligation. A creditor, in other words, who holds a right in security, has at his disposal some means of realising payment or exacting performance of the obligation due to him, distinct from, and in addition to means which are disposal of the debtors' personal credit. Whatever the special form of this right in security may be, its effect in all cases, is put the party entitled to it in a position of advantage and to render his power of realising payment of his debt more sure.[78]

75 *Lord Advocate v Earl of Moray's Trs.* (1905) 7 F.(H.L.) 116.
76 *Heritable Reversionary Co. v Millar* (1892) 19 R.(H.L.) 43.
77 *Colquhoun's Tr. v Diack* (1901) 4 F. 358.
78 (Gloag and Irvine 1897).

Securities may be qualified as follows: (1) security rights over property, (2) security over corporeal movables and (3) security over incorporeal movables.

By security rights over property, we mean hypothec and liens.

In Roman law, *hypotheca*, in contrast with *pignus*, was a real right security without possession that may took different forms. In the modern Scottish law, hypothec is a real security without the transfer of possession to the creditor. These may be either the following:

- Legal, implied by law in the circumstances;
- Conventional, *i.e.* shaped by agreement.

Although this security is recognised by Scots law, it is an obsolete tool and of a slightly different nature. These are bonds of bottomry over a ship and bond responding over a ship cargo.

As far as *pignus* is concerned, from a Roman law perspective, although *pignus* encompasses the same concept of pledge, however, the difference is that under Roman law the lender had the permitted to redeliver the goods to the borrower who held them as a balance at will of the lender and the pledge remained intact notwithstanding. Under a later development of the pignus, the borrower was never delivered possession of the good.[79]

The second one, liens, is a securities right arising by implication of law: basically, it is "a collateral or ancillary conditions implied by law in a contract whose main preoccupation will be something other than the creation of security."[80] Lies are distinguished from tacit hypotheca; hence, they demand possession by the creditor.

As far as security over corporeal movables is concerned, generally speaking, in common law, with the exception of hypotheca, there can be no securities created over corporeal movable property without delivery of possession by the debtor to the creditor. Additionally, there is no public register of interest in movable property in Scots law as "the badge of real right," although more recently a statutory pledge, on corporeal movable, has been passed. Thus, delivery possession became the overt act required at common law to vest a real right in a creditor: the general rule, in fact, is that possession presumes property, or, better, ownership. Therefore, a mere instrument of possession is not sufficient to transfer movables assigned or disponed in security. Common law requires properly a delivery of possession to create a real right in security being still considered as means of a third-party protection.

To summarise, where debtors retain possession, no security exist "a mere assignation of corporeal movables *retenta possession* is nothing but a personal obligation, and create no preference of any kind."[81]

Pledge is an express security over movable property: it is the real right of the creditor, the pledge, being constituted by both the voluntary grant of the debtor, the

79 (Pennington 1960).
80 (Sim 1991).
81 *Clark v West Calder Oil Co Liquidators* (1882) 9 R 1017, 1024.

pledgor, and the over act of delivery the property to the pledge. Pledge is a security that create a real right in the property of another, the pledgor. It is clear that two real rights coincide in the same property:

- The right pledger's right;
- The right of the holder to retain the object in security of debt for which it has been pledge.

From the fact that the pledgee's right under a contract of pledge is less than the ownership arise some consequences:

- A contract of pledge can confer no implied power to sell the property on the debtor's default but to sale by a special agreement;
- On the pledgor's insolvency, any such surplus or reversionary interest forms part of the debtor's estate and may be attached by debtor's other creditors;
- A pledge is less than an ownership; therefore, under common law, there is a presumption that the subject of a pledge cannot be retained for payment of debts for which it was expressly pledged;
- The creditor has not right to use the pledged property during his possession.

About the subject it must be capable of delivery, such as corporeal movables, goods, wares, and merchandise but not incorporeal property.[82]

The last category is security over incorporeal movables: it includes subjects so diverse as rights to debts or obligations, claims ex contractu and ex delicto, rights to shares in companies, goodwill, patents, copyright and trademarks and trade names. Personal rights may be assigned in security; however, the main forms of personal rights accepted by banks as security are life policies, stock exchange securities, interest in trust estates and debts due under contract.

In order to see an assignation it is sufficient, under Scottish law,

> any words giving authority or directions, which if fairly carried out will operate a transference . . . any words which express a present intention to transfer are sufficient as an assignation apart altogether from forms of style or the schedules of the recent statute.[83]

Floating charge

In Scottish common law, and in contrast with English common law, the floating charge was only introduced to Scotland in 1961 by the Companies (Floating Charges) (Scotland) Act 1961 and Companies (Floating Charges) (Scotland) Act

82 (Crerar 2007).
83 *Carter v McIntosh* (1862) 24 D 925–933, per Lord-Justice-Clerk Moncreiff words.

1972 introduced the officer of receiver. The latter, under a floating charge, could seek appointment of the court for control of the assets subject to the charge. Eventually, the law of floating charge may be come about in Companies Act 1958, Part XVIII, as well as in the Insolvency Act 1986, Part III, Chapter II.

Floating charge is an instrument created by an incorporated company. The Court of Session do have jurisdiction to wind up and gives the holder of the floating charge a security or charge over the assets to extent described in the charge. A floating charge may cover all or any part of the property, including uncalled capital, of the company which may from time to time be comprised in its property and undertaking. The charge "floats" over the company assets leaving the company free to intromit and deal with its assets as it wishes.

Section 410–424 Companies Act 1985 provide for the registration in Scotland if charges created by companies registered in Scotland no matter where the property is situated is made with the Registrar of Company in Edinburgh. The time limit for registration is within 21 days after the date of the creation of the charge and the date of creation is the date of the execution by the company, and in the case of a fixed security, it is the date when the right of the person entitled to the benefit of the security was constituted a real right.

Charges that require a registration are (1) charge upon land or any interest in land, (2) a security over the uncalled share capital of the company; (3) a security over incorporated movable property of any of the following categories, such as book debts of the company, calls made but not paid, goodwill, patent or licence under patent, a trademark, a copyright or a licence under a copyright, a registered design or a license in respect of such a design, a design right or a licence under a design right; (4) a security over a ship or aircraft or any share in a ship; and (5) a floating charge.[84]

Circumvention

Circumvention, in Scottish law, is recognised as a ground for reduction of contract, or of a will, and it shall be distinguished from actual fraud. In *McKellar v McKellar*[85] Lord President McNeil said that circumvention may be "legal or constructive fraud." Another circumvention definition may be seen in *Love v Marshall and Others*,[86] where Lord Kinloch stressed that this

> influence implies a course of deception . . . which is fraud in grain, but not fraud perpetuated by a single specific act. Or it implies intimidation – meaning thereby not a single act of violence, but a general course of threats and harshness, so operating on the mind as to bring the individual within entire control. Mere facility and lesion alone are insufficient. A sick man is not lightly deprived by law of his contractual capacity.

84 CA 1985, Section 410(2).
85 (1861) 24 D. 143.
86 (1870) 9 M. 291 at p. 297.

1.4 The United States banking and financial regulation: a comparative analysis

1.4.1 Banking system

In the United States,[87] there exist a variety of financial institutions: these are circumstances that do not conform to the generally accepted definition of a bank. The Uniform Commercial Code, which represents the major set of commercial laws, defines banks as "any person engaged in the business of banking, including a saving bank, savings and loan association, credit union and trust company."[88]

Another possible definition of a bank comes from an economic perspective; therefore, "a bank is an institution that offers people liquidity – the ability to convert their assets into cash on short notice – while still using their money to make long term investment."[89]

Furthermore, banks are usually divided into four main categories, such as (1) commercial banks, (2) savings banks, (3) savings and loan associations and (4) credit unions. This approach includes institutions that do not "take deposits," strictly speaking; however, it does not include institutions that both take deposits and make loans, *i.e.* the industrial bank.

The latter are also known as industrial loan companies; more precisely, the industrial bank reached its greatest prominence in the early part of the 20th century when it was identified with the Morris plan banks. It mostly offered consumer loans while financing itself primarily via consumer deposits. However, in recent years, industrial banks have largely evolved into commercial banks; a circumstance which has increasingly reinforced the controversy over their continuing exemption from the definition of "bank," originating from the Bank Holding Company Act.

Moreover, from a historical perspective, since industrial banks were not formally included in the definition of "bank," these entities, quite paradoxically, could be owned by entities which were merely commercial holding companies and not necessarily banking holding companies.

As a result of this, they proved popular with companies that wanted to offer banking services whilst not being subject to the restriction imposed by law, fettering the activities of bank-holding companies.[90]

In the modern system, virtually every bank that accepts deposits from the public, whether it is a state-chartered or a federally chartered bank, will have a federal regulator, as a consequence of carrying federal deposit insurance.

So, every state-chartered bank that takes deposits from the public will have two regulators: (1) the state chartering authority and (2) either the Federal Reserve, if it is a member, or the Federal Deposit Insurance Corporation, if it is not.

87 Henceforth US.
88 Uniform Commercial Code 1990, Official Text, Sections 1–201 (4).
89 (Krugman 2007).
90 (Felsenfeld and Glass 2011).

For instance, during the 1980s, two states, Ohio and Maryland, offered deposit insurance to their state banks through a state insurance fund. In each state, a bank failure led to fears that the state's insurance fund would be depleted, leading to a run on deposits of other state banks.

Commercial banks

Commercial banks are the wealthiest banks existing in the market; their assets of about $13 trillion in 2009 make them, generally speaking, the most significant banks in the financial system, from a quantitative perspective.

The US boasts many commercial banks,[91] hence the distaste the country traditionally has towards large banks: however, since 1996 the American attitude towards the large banks has changed. More precisely, legislative changes have enabled banks to merge and branch across State lines, resulting in large agglomeration of banking power.

Before the downturn of late 2007/2008, commercial banks were generally stable and solid and yielded record profits. Previously, in the aftermath of the cataclysmic years of the Great Depression, they had been seen as unhealthy. Again, at the beginning of 2008–2009, 25 commercial banks failed.

National banks

The 5,400 US commercial banks at year end 2009, less than 30% were national banks. These were chartered by the Office of the Comptroller of the Currency,[92] an office of the Department of Treasury.

The comptroller is appointed by the president with the advice and consent of the Senate, the same way as a full cabinet officer. The number of national banks has declined by more than 50% since 1985, but this is not much different from the drop in the number of all banks since that time. Despite the fact that national banks account for only about 30% of all commercial banks, they hold 69% of total banking assets.

The OCC, since its membership of the Treasury, is a part of the executive branch of the federal government and is also the primary regulator of national banks.

The rationale underlying the creation of national banks was to correct a peculiar structure. When national banks were established by Congress in 1863, their main function was to regularise the currency in order to assist in financing the Civil War. Most of the money was in the form of state bank obligations. Those banks were unevenly supervised and presented unpredictable, and generally uninsured, risks to their depositors. There was no satisfactory control over the money they issued. Further, in terms of pure financial risk, the paper certificates were often dirty and unsanitary to handle. All these elements discouraged investment in the government.

91 There are 6,800 commercial banks in the US, whilst European Union without England in 1986 had over 2,000 banks.

92 Henceforth OCC.

The aim of creating national banks was to correct this structure: the National Bank Act imposed a tax of 10% on the notes of state banks, while the notes of the new national bank were totally exempt from taxation.[93] This event did not happen because the state banks simply devised another way of raising funds. Rather than issuing notes, they began to take deposits directly, which is the origin of the modern checking account.

The desire to drive the state banks out of business stemmed from several factors. The first one concerned the United States Congress: they wanted to promote the new national bank system to give to government a means of financing the war effort during the Civil War. In addition, to ensure that national banks would be strong and stable and their notes would be a reliable form of currency, they generally required more capital to operate and were subject to stricter standards than their state brethren.[94]

All in all, it is possible to say that for Congress, in 1863, national banks and state banks were not equal in standing. Indeed, national banks were "superior"; they were created, first and foremost, to correct state bank inadequacies. Under the lens of the Supreme Court, "National banks have been National favorites."[95]

State banks

State banks are chartered by a state agency, with a name something like "Department of Banking." State banks are more numerous than the national banks since, as already noted, more wealth is concentrated in national banks than in state banks.[96]

The largest banks are in New York. Whether a bank charters as national, or state, is generally more a matter of taste than business necessity. The exception is represented by megabanks, such as Bank of America, JPMorgan Chase, and Citigroup, for which the national scope of their operation makes the advantages of a national charter compelling. It is well-known that Morgan was chartered by New York State and remained so after merging with Chase, which, therefore, had been a national bank. Yet in 2003 the bank converted to a national charter in order to avail itself of the clear advantage of having a single regulator for its nationwide activities. In the process, it was emphasised that the reason was economic and did not reflect any dissatisfaction with the New York State Banking Department.[97]

93 In this respect, in *McCulloch v Maryland* (17 U.S. (4 Wheat.) 316 (1819)), the Supreme Court held that a State tax on the notes of the Second Bank of the United States was unconstitutional. More precisely, the Court highlighted that the "power to tax is the power to destroy." By contrast, in *Veazia Bank v Fenno* (75 U.S. 8 Wall. 533 533 (1869)), the Court had no compunction upholding the power of federal government to destroy the state banks with taxation.

94 (Felsenfeld and Glass 2011).

95 *Tiffany v National Bank of Missouri*, 18 Wall 409 (1874).

96 More precisely, $8.2 trillion compared to $ 3.6. trillion for the state banks.

97 (Felsenfeld and Glass 2011).

Member banks

Member banks, a hybrid of the national and state bank, were members of the Federal Reserve System[98] at the end of 2009.

The Fed was created by Congress in 1913 and is in reality a central bank equivalent to the Bank of England or the European Union Central Bank.[99] It consists of a board of governors in Washington and 12 federal reserve banks around the country.

As far as its responsibilities are concerned, the first is to monitor the money supply and interest rate structures, both of which it does through setting loan rates on short term loans between banks, and buying and selling securities in the open market. Another is to regulate its member banks and, in specific areas delegated to it by Congress, the non-member banks and other financial institutions.

The Fed has the authority to modify those powers, and some generally applicable provisions in federal banking laws specifically limit the rights of member banks.[100]

Non-member state banks

Fundamentally, a federal deposit insurance corporation[101] is the primary federal regulator of the non-member state banks that have a FDIC insurance. Non-member state banks are subject to a mix of state laws, regulations and customs depending upon the state in which the bank is chartered.

Regulation by FDIC arose, given the very peculiar nature of its insurance function: as would happen for a private insurance company insuring a private household against a major risk, such as a fire, likewise the FDIC continually oversees the banks whose deposits may be affected by the actions of their managers.

The FDIC insurance function was until 2006 divided between the Bank Insurance Fund, which insured the deposits of commercial banks, and the Savings Association Insurance Fund, which concentrated on savings institutions, including savings and loans associations. National banks, member state banks and non-member state commercial banks were insured by the Bank Insurance Fund.[102]

1.4.2 Legal sources

Banking laws have the aim of governing how banks and other financial institutions deliver business.

Often, federal banking regulation takes precedence over state and local regulations. There are thousands of regulations, large and small, that banks need to understand and comply with.

98 Henceforth FED.
99 (Timberlake 1978).
100 (Felsenfeld and Glass 2011).
101 Henceforth FDIC.
102 (Felsenfeld and Glass 2011).

Bearing this in mind, the following sub-sections will discuss the legal framework in the US legal system.[103]

The National Bank Act (1863)

The National Banking Acts of 1863 and 1864 were two US federal banking acts that established a system of national banks and created the US National Banking System. The act shaped the contemporary national banking system and its support of a uniform US banking policy.

More precisely, the National Banking Acts of 1863 and 1864 gave the federal government the power to do the following:

- Charter banks;
- Require that banks hold an adequate amount of gold and silver reserves;
- Issue a national currency.

The Federal Reserve Act (1914)

The Federal Reserve Act is an Act of the Congress that created the Federal Reserve System; it also created the authority in charge of issuing federal reserve notes as legal.[104] The aim was to provide the nation with a safer, more flexible and more stable monetary and financial system. The need for a central bank, in the US, became painfully evident during the financial panic of 1907, when the stock market collapsed, banks failed and credit evaporated.

As the federal government lacked the tools to respond, it had to depend on private bankers, such as J.P. Morgan, to provide an infusion of capital to sustain the banking system. In order to correct the issue of an "inelastic currency," Congress created a National Monetary Commission. The outcome was a system that would be run by private bankers who would act as federal agents.[105]

In June 1913, the creation of a government-run Federal Reserve System was formally proposed. Today, the Federal Reserve's responsibilities fall into four general areas:

- Realise the nation's monetary policy by influencing money and credit conditions in the economy in pursuit of full employment and stable prices;
- Supervise and regulate banks and other important financial institutions both to ensure financial and banking stability, and to protect credit rights of consumers;
- Maintain the stability of the financial system and contain systemic risk that may arise in financial markets;
- Provide certain financial services to the US government, US financial institutions and foreign official institutions.

103 (Lessambo 2020).
104 The Federal Reserve was created on 23rd December 1913.
105 (Lessambo 2020).

The McFadden Act (1927)

In 1927 Congress passed the McFadden Act that was modified in 1994 by the Riegle-Neal Interstate Banking and Branching Efficiency Act. The latter allowed banks to open limited-service bank branches across state lines, by merging with other banks.

The McFadden Act allowed a national bank, to the extent to which this was permitted by state governments, to operate branches; conversely, in a state that prohibited the banking business via branch banking so that national banks could not open branches.[106] Like the Federal Reserve Act, the McFadden Act's branch banking provisions were also controversial. Those opposing the law complained that the law gave too much power to big-city bankers and hurt local communities. Financial reformers claimed that the law did not go far enough in preventing banks from adopting safe, efficient, and modern practices.

Further, the McFadden Act revised a wide range of outdated banking laws, legalised new practices requested in order to level the playing field among several banks. The McFadden Act expanded the size and types of loans that member banks could make. These expansions included the ability to invest more in real estate and to loan larger sums to single corporations. It is also said that the McFadden Act changed the structure of the commercial banks regulated by Federal Reserve. Before the act, indeed, a Fed member bank was single corporation operating out of a single building in a narrow range of activities.[107]

After the act, a Fed member could be a complex corporation with multiple legal layers operating from multiple locations.[108]

The Banking Act (1933) and the Federal Deposit Insurance Act

The Banking Act of 1933 is also known as the Glass-Steagall Act: it was passed by Congress in 1933 and prohibits commercial banks from engaging in the investment business. It was enacted as an emergency response to the failure of nearly 5,000 banks during the Great Depression.

It is well-known that the Glass-Steagall Act separated commercial banking from investment banking and created the Federal Deposit Insurance Corporation.[109]

The latter was managed, *de facto*, by the Federal Deposit Insurance Act:[110] although the FDIC was originally created by the Banking Act of 1933, which amended the Federal Reserve Act of 1913. The FDI Act set up the FDIC with the responsibility to insure bank deposits in eligible banks against loss in the event of a bank failure and to regulate certain banking activities.

106 Despite this, in a state that prohibited branch banking, national banks could not open branches.
107 (Lessambo 2020).
108 (Lessambo 2020).
109 Henceforth FDIC.
110 Named also FDI Act.

The standard deposit insurance coverage limit is $250,000 per depositor, per FDIC-insured bank, per ownership category. Deposits held in different ownership categories are separately insured, up to at least $250,000, even if held at the same bank.

FDIC insurance protects only the follows deposit products:

- Checking and savings accounts;
- Time deposits;
- Official payments issued by covered banks, including cashier's checks and money orders;
- Money market accounts.

FDIC insurance does not cover the following:[111]

- Securities, such as stock and bonds;
- Mutual funds, including money market mutual funds;
- Life insurance products, including annuities;
- The contents of safe deposit boxes.

The Bank Holding Company Act (1956)

This legal framework regulates the actions of bank-holding companies: the law was implemented both to regulate and control banks that had formed bank-holding companies to own both banking and non-banking businesses. The "1956 Act" redefined a bank-holding company as any company that held a stake in 25% or more of the shares of two more banks.

In the economy of the Banking Holding Company Act, a bank was defined as any institution that takes deposits and makes loans. Generally speaking, the law prohibited a bank-holding company from engaging in most non-banking activities or acquiring voting securities of certain companies that are not banks.

The interstate restrictions of the Bank Holding Company Act were repealed by the Riegle-Neal Interstate Banking and Branching Efficiency Act[112] of 1994. The latter allowed interstate mergers between adequately capitalised and managed banks, subject to concentration limits, state laws and Community Reinvestment Act evaluations.[113]

The International Banking Act (1978)

Only with the International Banking Act do we see the first comprehensive piece of legislation that brings foreign-owned banking operation in the US under federal regulations comparable to those faced by domestic financial institutions.

111 (Lessambo 2020).
112 Henceforth IBBEA.
113 (Lessambo 2020).

The major objectives are to promote competitive equality between foreign and domestic banks, to improve federal control over monetary policy and to provide a federal presence in the regulation and supervision of foreign bank activities in the US.[114]

Under the act, the deposits of foreign-owned bank branches operating outside of their home state are limited to the international finance related credit balances allowed by the agencies. The act allows foreign banks to obtain federal licenses for branches and agencies, a federally charted national bank under liberalised regulations. This approach ensures that in states where foreign banks are welcome, they will have a state/federal option, which is similar to that of domestic banks.

The International Banking Act of 1978 put all American branches and agencies of foreign banks under the control of US banking regulators. It allowed FDICI insurance to be provided to these branches. It also required them to conform to US banking requirements, so that all banks operating domestically are treated equally from a regulatory perspective.

The Gram-Leach-Billey Act (1999)

Under the Gram-Leach-Billey Act[115] it was required that financial institutions[116] fully explain their information sharing practices to their customers, giving the option to "opt out" if they do not want their sensitive information sharing.

The GLBA was a bi-partisan regulation, passed under President Bill Clinton, on the heels of commercial bank Citicorp's merger with the insurance firm Travelers Group. This led to the formation of the conglomerate Citigroup, which offered both commercial banking and insurance services, as well as relating to securities.

The GLBA is based on three main pillars:

- The financial privacy rules, the aim of which is to regulate the collection and disclosure of private financial information;
- The safeguard rules, which stipulate that financial institution must implement security programmes to protect such information;
- The pretexting provisions, which prohibit the practice of pretexting, such as accessing private information under false pretences.

The Dodd-Frank Act (2010)

The Dodd-Frank Act[117] was enacted in July 2010 in response to the financial crisis that hit the US during 2007–2009 years. Banks were permitted to use hidden fees and lend to unqualified consumers.

114 (Segala 1979).

115 Henceforth GLBA.

116 In this respect, a financial institution is a company that offer consumers financial products, or services like loans, financial or investment advice or insurance.

117 Also known as the Dodd-Frank Wall Street Reform and Consumer Protection Act.

The Dodd-Frank Act put regulations on the financial industry and shaped programmes to stop mortgage companies and lenders from taking advantage of consumers. It is considered the most comprehensive financial reform since the Glass-Steagall Act, which was put in place after the 1929 stock market cash.

The aim of Dodd-Frank is to place a strict regulation on lenders and banks in an effort to protect consumers and prevent another economic recession. Therefore, Dodd-Frank created several new agencies to oversee the regulatory process and implement certain changes. To summarise, the new rules including the following:[118]

- The duty for the banks to come up with plans for a quick shutdown if they approach bankruptcy or run out money;
- That every bank with more than $50 billion of assets must take an annual stress test given by the Federal Reserve, the aim of which is to help a banking institution to survive during a financial crisis;
- The prohibition for the banks to realise certain investments with their own accounts.[119]

Moreover, the Dodd-Frank Act created two new bodies: (1) the Financial Stability Oversight Council[120] and (2) the Consumer Financial Protection Bureau.[121]

The first identifies risks that affect the financial industry and keeps large banks in check. The second one, the CGPB, protects consumers from the corrupt business practices of banks. The agency works with bank regulators to stop risk lending and other practices that could hurt American consumers.

Bank Secrecy Act 2018

The Bank Secrecy Act[122] establishes a programme of recordkeeping and reporting requirements for national banks, federal savings associations, federal branches and agencies of foreign banks. Under the BSA, and related anti-money laundering, banks have some duties, such as:

- To establish effective BSA compliance programs;
- To establish effective customer due diligence systems and monitoring programs;
- To screen against Office of Foreign Assets Control[123] and other government lists;
- To establish an effective suspicious activity monitoring and reporting process;
- To develop risk-based anti-money laundering programmes.[124]

118 (Lessambo 2020).
119 For instance, banks cannot invest, own, or sponsor any proprietary trading operations or hedge funds for their own profit, with some exceptions.
120 Henceforth FSOC.
121 Henceforth CFPB.
122 Also known as BSA.
123 Also OFAC.
124 Henceforth AML.

The latter, *i.e.* AML programme, must, at minimum, include the following:

- Corporate policies, procedures and internal controls reasonably designed to assure ongoing compliance;[125]
- Designate an individual responsible for assuring day-to-day compliance with the programme and BSA requirements;
- Providing training for appropriate personnel, including training in the detection of suspicious transactions;
- Provide for independent review to monitor and maintain an adequate programme.

Furthermore, under the BSA, financial institutions are required to assist US government agencies in detecting and preventing money laundering. For example, these include (1) keeping records of cash purchases of negotiable instruments, (2) filing reports of cash transactions exceeding $10,000 and (3) report suspicious activity that might signal criminal activity.

The BSA was amended to incorporate the provisions of the US Patriot Act, in force of which every bank shall adopt a consumer identification programme as part of its BSA compliance programme. BSA reporting also allows the US to take a macro view of financial crime.

Under the BSA regime, each bank's BSA/AML compliance programme must be designed to (1) identity and verify on a risk basis the identity of each of its customers, (2) conduct appropriate risk-focused due diligence on those customers and (3) identify, monitor and report suspicious activity.

1.4.3 The approach to bank supervision

The US system regarding prudential and regulation supervision of banking is a complex structure that is not centralised in a single regulator, but the responsibility of a number of separate and independent regulators.

The dual banking system consists of two formal methods of chartering commercial banks: at state level and at the federal level. This is a consequence in many respects of the constitutional make-up of the US, which is based on a State and federal system of governance.

The dual banking system was a by-product of the legislation to introduce the national currency and put an end to states issuing their own banknotes. The dual system is not rigidly divided into two parts: a state bank could convert its charter to a national charter and vice versa. It is stressed that "the core of the dual banking system is the simultaneous existence of different regulatory options that are not alike in terms of statutory provisions, regulatory implementation and administrative policy."[126]

125 It includes the follows activities: verifying customers identification, filing reports, creating and retaining records and responding to law enforcement requests.

126 (Scott 1994).

In addition to this, the membership of FDIC and FRB have prudential responsibilities to oversee the activity of their members of the Federal Reserve and the FDIC.

However, the Glass-Steagall Act attempted to avoid concentration within the financial system by dismantling the universal banking model.[127]

References

Barnard, C. *The Substantive Law of the EU. The Four Freedoms*. Oxford University Press, 2013.

Blair, M., R. Cranston, C. Ryan, and M. Taylor. *Blackstone's Guide to the Bank of England Act 1998*. Oxford University Press, 1998.

Checkland, S.G. *Scottish Banking: A History*. Collins, 1975.

Cini, M., and A. Verdun. "The Implications of Brexit for the Future of Europe." In *Brexit and Beyond (Rethinking the Futures of Europe)*, edited by B. Martill and U. Staiger, 63–71. UCL Press, 2018.

Conac, P.H. "The European Union's Role in International Economic Fora: The International Organisation of Securities Commissions (IOSCO)." *International Organization of Securities Commissions, Paper*, no. 6 (2015), online.

Crerar, L.D. *The Law of Banking in Scotland*. Tottel Publishing, 2007.

Dashwood, A., M. Dougan, B. Rodger, E.E. Spaventa, and D. Wyatt. *Wyatt and Dashwood's European Union Law*. Hart Publishing, 2011.

de Larosière, J. "The High-Level Group on Financial Supervision in the EU." 2009. Report – Brussel, 25 February 2009, online.

Dow, S.C., and J. Smithin. "Free Banking in Scotland, 1695–1845." *Scottish Journal of Political Economy* 39, no. 4 (1992): 374–390.

Felsenfeld, C., and D.L. Glass. *Banking Regulation in the United States*. Juris Publishing, 2011.

Fleming, J.S. *Scottish Banking: A Historical Sketch*. William Blackwood, 1877.

Gaskin, M. *The Scottish Banks. A Modern Survey*. Routledge, 2010.

Gloag, W.M., and J.M. Irvine. *The Law of Rights in Security and Cautionary Obligations*. W. Green & Sons, 1897.

Hume, D. *Political Discourses*. 1752. R. Fleming, for A. Kincaid and A. Donaldson.

Inman, P., and J. Ranking. "Bank of England to Allow EU Banks to Keep UK Operations." *The Guardian*, 2020, online.

Islam, F. "Government Faces Industry Backlash on Brexit Plans." *BBC News*, 2019, online.

James, S., and L. Quaglia. "Rule Maker or Rule Taker? Brexit, Finance and UK Regulatory Autonomy." *International Political Science Review* 43, no. 3 (2022): 390–403.

James, S., and L. Quaglia. "Differentiated de-Europeanisation: UK Policy-Making in Finance After Brexit." *Journal of European Public Policy*, no. 1 (2023): 1–24.

Kaczorowska, A. *European Union Law*. Routledge, 2011.

Krugman, P. "Banks." *New York Times*, 2007, p. 19.

Langevoort, D.C. "Global Securities Regulation After the Financial Crisis." *Journal of International Economic Law* 13, no. 3 (2010): 799–815.

Lawson, W.J. *The History of Banking: With a Comprehensive Account of the Origin, Rise, and Progress of the Banks of England, Ireland, and Scotland*. Gould and Lincoln, 1852.

127 (Singh 2007).

Lessambo, F.I. *The U.S. Banking System. Laws, Regulations, and Risk Management*. Palgrave Macmillan, 2020.
Malcolm, C.A. *The Bank of Scotland 1695–1945*. R. & R. Clark Ltd, 1945.
Moloney, N. "International Financial Governance, the EU, and Brexit: The 'Agencification' of EU Financial Governance and the Implications." *European Business Organization Law Review* 17, no. 4 (2016): 451–480.
Moloney, N. "The European Union in International Financial Governance." *RSF: The Russell Sage Foundation Journal of the Social Sciences* 3, no. 1 (2017): 138–152.
Müller, P., Z. Kudrna, and G. Falkner. "EU – Global Interactions: Policy Export, Import, Promotion and Protection." *Journal of European Public Policy* 21, no. 8 (2014): 1102–1119.
Pennington, R.R. "The Genesis of the Floating Charge." *The Modern Law Review* 23, no. 6 (1960): 630–646.
Quaglia, L. "The 'Old' and 'New' Politics of Financial Services Regulation in the European Union." *New Political Economy* 17, no. 4 (2012): 515–535.
Reid, A. *European Union*. W.Green, 2010.
Schilling de Carvalho, P. "Retaining Influence in Post-Brexit International Financial Regulation: Lessons from the UK's FinTech Framework." *Journal of Financial Regulation*, no. 8 (2022): 104–131.
Scott, K.E. "The Dual Banking System: A Model of Competition in Regulation." *Stanford Law Review* 30, no. 1 (1994): 41.
Segala, P.J. "A Summary of the International Banking Act of 1978." *Economic Review*, 1979: 16–21.
Sim, A.J. "Rights in Security Over Moveables." *Stair Memorial Encyclopedia* (Lexisnexis), 1991: 67.
Singh, D. *Banking Regulation of UK and US Financial Markets*. Ashgate, 2007.
Smith, A. *Lectures on Jurisprudence*. Edited by R.L. Meek, D.D. Raphel, and P.G. Stein. Macmillan, 1978.
Thirlway, H. *The Sources of International Law*. Oxford University Press, 2014.
Timberlake, R.H. *The Origins of Central Banking in the United States*. Harvard University Press, 1978.
Walker, G., and R. Purves. *Financial Services Law*. Oxford University Press, 2014.
Weatherill, S. *Cases and Materials on EU Law*. Oxford University Press, 2007.
Woods, L., and P. Watson. *Steiner & Woods EU Law*. Oxford University Press, 2012.

2 Banking law

2.1 Banks and their organisations

2.1.1 An introduction

Banks, as we know them today, have developed from moneychangers into deposit takers. This development took place in the late Middle Ages in the Italian city-states. To be more precise, in Genoa this development may have taken place as early as around 1200, while in Venice this evolution occurred around AD 1300.[1] Back in those earliest days, deposits were credited to a current account.

It is from this early moment that banks started being frequently insolvent, for the reason that – and has been the case since – bankers held in cash only a tiny fraction of the sums received in deposit available to depositors.[2] Moreover, it is since then that they have lent on longer terms than deposits could be retrieved.[3] Consequently, from their very inception on, the banks' business model has always been inherently risky.

Also today, in essence, the banking business consists of obtaining deposits from customers, *i.e.* raising funds from the public, and lending money, *i.e.* giving credit to businesses, households and individuals. This is why a bank is, as in EU law, sometimes technically referred to as a credit institution. The bank's activity of obtaining funds and lending out the same can prove lucrative and profitable for the banker, so long as the bank is able to obtain, from the money lent to the businesses, households, and individuals (*e.g.* loans) a higher remuneration than that which is returned to the customers for the money deposited by them (*e.g.* bank accounts). The remuneration which a banker receives is referred to as "interest" and constitutes the variation of percentage on the amount of money lent from time to time. This interest is called "active" if the money is lent by the bank, while, if the money is borrowed by the bank, it is called "passive," as that money is owed to the customer.

1 (Kirshner 1974; Mueller 1997).
2 See Mueller (1997).
3 (Mueller 1997).

DOI: 10.4324/9781032628646-2

The margin between lending and borrowing is commonly referred to as the "spread." Thus, the degree of success that a banker can show depends upon his ability to obtain, from the money lent, a sufficiently high margin of interest to allow the bank not only to cover its running costs but also to secure a profit. There is another difference, already alluded to, between the money lent and the one borrowed by a bank, which may help understand why the business of banking is inherently risky: while the money deposited can, as a matter of principle, be withdrawn at any time by customers, the money borrowed is only due after a period of several years. This represents the "transformation function" of a bank.[4] Should all customers run on the bank to withdraw their money at the same time, the bank will not be able to honour its overall debts.

The banking business is generally regarded as a reserved activity. The established principle (certainly at an EU level), albeit not a universal stance,[5] is that typical banking activities (mainly, but not exclusively, the lending and borrowing functions) are regulated and such practices are therefore prohibited from use by non-authorised entities. Accordingly, an entity or individual engaged in the banking business, not duly endowed with the authorisation of the competent authority, would infringe the mandatory rules which, in some jurisdictions, constitute a criminal offence. At an EU level, this principle is encapsulated within the Capital Requirements Directive IV (CRD IV), Articles 8(1) and 9(1),[6] which stipulate that each member state, respectively, "shall require credit institutions to obtain authorisation before commencing their activities" and "shall prohibit persons or undertakings that are not credit institutions from carrying out the business of taking deposits or other repayable funds from the public."[7]

While the regulatory framework has been introduced here, the present section seeks to determine and analyse the various models of banking business whilst paying due consideration to the way financial institutions are categorised (*e.g.* commercial banks, investment banks). Additionally, emphasis is placed on the organisational structure of financial institutions, particularly in respect to the business units which emanate from them (*e.g.* branches and/or subsidiaries). Furthermore, a regulatory analysis is provided in the matter of bank ownership and, specifically, the constraints currently operating within the EU, as regards participation in banks by commercial entities and/or businesses, and vice versa, *i.e.* banks

4 (Theissen 2013).

5 The strict approach is certainly the EU one. However, still nowadays there are countries and/or jurisdictions where the pursuit of banking business is not reserved.

6 In full: Directive 2013/36/EU of the European Parliament and of the Council of 26 June 2013 on access to the activity of credit institutions and the prudential supervision of credit institutions and investment firms, amending Directive 2002/87/EC and repealing Directives 2006/48/EC and 2006/49/EC, OJ L 176. The latter directives used to be referred to as the Capital Requirements Directive (CRD) in conjunction with Directive 2006/49/EC of the European Parliament and of the Council of 14 June 2006 on the capital adequacy of investment firms and credit institutions, both published simultaneously on 14 June 2006.

7 The wording of Article 9 of Directive 2013/36/EU is identical to Article 5 of the previous Directive 2006/48.

participating in commercial and/or business entities. Finally, this section takes into account the economic climate, in assessing the legislative architecture of the bank as ultimately shaped within the EU, with a description of the various activities "subject to mutual recognition" that a financial institution is entitled to carry out.

2.1.2 Categories of banks

Banks can be categorised in a variety of ways, depending on the different perspectives from which their activities can be observed and scrutinised.

Commercial banks and investment banks

First and foremost, a point of observation of the bank comes from the operational side. A bank often is a complex organisation with myriad levels of operations. The activities that a bank can carry out are numerous and range from the most basic offer of bank accounts and investment services (retail banking) to the most sophisticated services of corporate finance (investment banking). The full spectrum of banking products that can be offered to commercial business, such as leasing and factoring (commercial banking), cannot be ignored. Banks have also sought to provide clients with tailor-made services based on the concept of wealth, the purpose of which is to optimise the assets of such clients (private wealth).

In this respect, it is common to refer to commercial banks as institutions the main purpose of which is to deal with the vast array of retail customers, predominantly via the offer of bank accounts to the general public, and the lending of money to a commercial and business clientele.

Investment banks are distinct from commercial banks in that they do not have, necessarily, a network of branches and do not liaise with retail clients. An investment bank operates with, and liaises with, corporations and/or other banks to offer them financial advice in transactions and activities of a certain level of complexity. The business we are referring to is principally advisory in nature, relating to corporate transactions such as mergers and acquisitions (usually referred to as M&A transactions) or admission of the shares of a company to the stock market (listing). These operations and transactions are typically carried out by a niche group of banks which are equipped to handle the required level of expertise. The investment bank can be a specialised autonomous bank operating as a boutique bank and not belonging to any group. However, with increasing regularity, major international banks are also availing themselves of the opportunity to widen their portfolio to operate in the investment banking business, either through specific "arms" of their business (formally within the structure of the bank), or by way of subsidiaries belonging to the parent company of that major group.

Multifunctional groups versus universal banks

An additional categorisation of banks stems from the corporate structure adopted. Irrespective of the range of activities in which a bank is engaged, a recurring dilemma arises: how a bank can better organise that plurality of businesses from a corporate structure point of view. The answers and, therefore, solutions to these questions are twofold and, to a certain extent, contradictory. On the one hand, the bank can be organised as a monolithic entity which, in practical terms, is in charge of and responsible for everything. This form of credit institution channels the broad spectrum of activities through units and sections, each being specialised in one of the specific banking businesses, such as commercial banking, investment banking, corporate finance and wealth management, but each belonging to the same corporate entity. In other words, the universal bank, as this model is commonly defined, performs the various banking activities through a unified structure, formally a single corporate entity rather than through several subsidiaries. The universal bank contrasts with the banking group model where, conversely, a parent company owns several corporate entities and, accordingly, each corporate entity operates the specific banking business concerned. Historically, it has been claimed that the universal model of bank organisation was of an Anglo-American nature, whereas the second model (the group) is traditionally associated with Germany.

First, the banking group may be a more flexible model of business. For instance, if the bank no longer wishes to perform one of the banking businesses, the obvious and relatively simple move would be to relinquish the holding in the subsidiary specialising in that business and find a purchaser who is both willing and available to step into the shoes of the current owner. Such an option is less practicable for a universal bank; in this case, the business is part of the broader structure of the bank, and therefore, any spin-off arising from the specific banking activity, no longer deemed strategically warranted, may not be executed without organisational burdens.

On the other hand, the universal bank may be a less expensive organisation; because the corporate structure does not encompass entities, rather embodying a unified corporation (with shared services), the running costs associated with the business may be, theoretically speaking, less onerous. For instance, the cost of maintaining a board of directors for each company within a group structure is a burden extraneous to the structure of a universal bank.

Perhaps even more importantly, as a response to the global financial crisis, legislatures in various parts of the world have contemplated structural reforms for their banking sector. Most of these initiatives have been prompted by the belief that retail banking is by definition less speculative and therefore less risky, as opposed to investment banking where transactions such as derivatives are concluded for the account and in the name of the bank itself, and which may be profitable in a positively trending market but dangerously give rise to huge losses in an opposite scenario. Conversely, it has been argued that the universal banks are less risky because they can better diversify their business. In the US (by means of the so-called Volcker Rule), in the UK (further to the Vicker Report), as well as on the EU level (further to the Liikanen Report), these considerations have led to legislative action.

More specifically, Section 619 of the Dodd Frank Act, known as the Volcker Rule, restricts deposit-taking banks from engaging in certain types of market-oriented activity (proprietary trading, *i.e.* trading for the account and in the name of the bank itself). The underlying intention of the rule is to safeguard the core of the banking system, i.e. commercial banks, and to prohibit it from engaging in more complex activities that are prone to conflicts of interest with the core objective of commercial banking (viz. deposits and loans).[8] Conversely, the UK independent commission on banking chaired by Vickers recommended in 2011 that large UK banks should ring-fence their retail bank operations into separate legal subsidiaries with their own prudential safeguards.

On the European level, on 2 October 2012, a high-level expert group chaired by Erkki Liikanen – governor of the Bank of Finland and a former member of the European Commission – presented its final report to the Commission. This report has now led to a draft regulation.[9] The report advises that proprietary trading and other significant trading activities should be assigned to a separate legal entity if the activities to be separated amount to a significant share of a bank's business. This would ensure that trading activities beyond the threshold are carried out on a stand-alone basis and separate from the deposit bank. As a consequence, deposits would no longer directly support risky trading activities. The report argues, however, that the long-standing universal banking model in Europe would remain untouched since the separated activities would be carried out in the same banking group. Hence, banks' ability to provide a wide range of financial services to their customers would be maintained.[10]

BRANCHES

It is customary in the banking industry to refer to branches and subsidiaries as, respectively, the units and entities through which the structure of the bank operates and functions. As alluded to earlier, the branch is the operating unit of the financial institution, usually located in close proximity to the area where that bank wishes to offer its products. Although branches – unlike subsidiaries – are not independent from a corporate point of view, they are usually organised according to a precise business model within which staff (*e.g.* cashiers) are supervised by a local, albeit "light," management structure which, in turn, reports to the "centre" (the headquarters of the financial institution). Similarly, the branch management is bestowed, in advance, with specific powers from headquarters so that, for the transactions they oversee, there is no need to receive an *ad hoc* authorisation from the central structure. This is understandable as, otherwise, the decision-making process would be embroiled in bureaucracy to the point where it could virtually grind to a halt.[11] The

8 High-level expert group on reforming the structure of the EU banking sector.

9 Proposal for a regulation of the European Parliament and of the Council on structural measures improving the resilience of EU credit institutions, /* COM/2014/043 final.

10 Liikanen Report, p. iii.

11 The limits could be of two kinds: "qualitative" and "quantitative." As to the former, banks usually adopt an internal resolution whereby exclusively some specific transactions and/or activities can be authorised by the branch management; for instance, the opening of a bank account may an ordinary activity delegated to the branch without previous authorisation of the central structure. Conversely, an advisory in the matter of M&A, quite complex, may fall within the exclusive competence of the

branch, as an established phenomenon of the banking business, is a concept duly acknowledged at legislative level. To that end, Article 4(1) of the Capital Requirements Regulation 575/2013 (CRR),[12] particularly its point 17 defines the "branch" as "a place of business which forms a legally dependent part of a credit institution and which carries out directly all or some of the transactions inherent in the business of institution."[13]

SUBSIDIARIES

Subsidiaries are corporate entities owned, either directly or indirectly, by the parent company of a banking group. Within the constraints of shareholder control as required by the applicable national corporate law, they are autonomous and independent, from a corporate point of view, from the board of directors of the holding company.[14]

Similarly, the directors of each subsidiary (in other words, those in charge of the business of that entity) reach their decisions autonomously, given that no hierarchical authorisation is required. However, this procedural blueprint does not translate into practice; *de facto*, directors are usually appointed at the shareholders' meeting, where a significant percentage of the capital – or indeed the entire capital – is owned by the parent company, and therefore, they tend to constitute a reflection of the parent company, particularly in cases where 100% of the share capital belongs to the parent company.[15] Although it would undoubtedly be too harsh to label the

central structure. As far as the "quantitative" limits are concerned, they can be connected with the value of the transaction. To further elaborate, the opening of a bank account, which is an ordinary transaction usually delegated to the branch management, may require the previous authorisation of the headquarters, if the money concerned with the transaction exceeds a certain limit. According to this line of reasoning, for instance, a personal loan, which is usually an ordinary activity "devolved" to the branch, may require the authorisation of the headquarters, if the amount of the commitment was above the threshold fixed in advance by the internal bylaws of the bank. Similarly, to authorise an overdraft of a bank account of a client, for an amount exceeding a certain amount (e.g. 10,000 euro), may be a matter well beyond the competence and power of a branch manager, and therefore, it is imaginable that an authorisation of the central function shall be required. The quantitative and qualitative limit of the transactions either devolved to the branch or reserved to the headquarters is a strategic choice of each financial institution and is adopted by a resolution of the board of directors of it. In this resolution, the powers delegated to the peripheral structures (therefore, the branches) are detailed as regards both the kinds of activities and applicable thresholds.

12 In full: Regulation 575/2013/EU of the European Parliament and of the Council of 26 June 2013 on prudential requirements for credit institutions and investment firms and amending Regulation 648/2012/EU. As elucidated by Recital (5) to Regulation 575/2013, such a regulation, alongside with Directive 2013/36/EU, "should form the legal framework governing the access to the activity, the supervisory network and the prudential rules for credit institutions and investment firms."

13 The definition corresponds to what previously used to be defined under Directive 2006/48, Article 4(3). However, it applies equally to both credit institution and investment firms.

14 Depending on the country or jurisdiction where they are located, they might have different forms.

15 It is likely that the directors of the subsidiary will be managers of the parent company or people well known to the parent company.

directors of the subsidiary of a credit institution as mere puppets,[16] nonetheless, it must be acknowledged that their decisions tend to mirror the visions of the parent company, generally adopted within the power of management and coordination of that banking group.

In this respect, the most recent bank capital requirements legislation defines "subsidiary" in Article 3 ("definitions") (15) CRD IV by referring to point (16) of Article 4(1) CRR, which, in its turn, refers to Directive 83/349/EEC, and states that subsidiary means: "(a) a subsidiary undertaking within the meaning of Articles 1 and 2 of Directive 83/349/EEC; (b) a subsidiary undertaking within the meaning of Article 1(1) of Directive 83/349/EEC and any undertaking over which a parent undertaking effectively exercises a dominant influence."[17] Thus, in essence, the control exercised by a bank over a company as a shareholder or, failing this, a dominant influence on that company would suffice as the standard which, if met, would qualify that company as a "subsidiary."

BANKING GROUPS

The organisation of a bank through subsidiaries engenders the creation of a perimeter of companies, operating akin to planets orbiting within a solar system, where the planets represent the myriad subsidiaries and the sun the parent company. From a company law perspective, the group as such does not necessarily correspond to a legal concept and its categorisation shall depend on the jurisdiction where (the parent company of) that group is incorporated.

In this respect, the paradigm in the common law system, particularly in Britain, is that tradition dictates that there is no such thing as a company group. Rather, British legislation identifies a company as a separate legal *persona*, set apart from the owners by way of the "veil of incorporation," clearly defining the legal responsibilities of the body and those of the members.[18] In other EU member states, however,

16 Usually, in any advanced jurisdiction, any director of a subsidiary may incur direct liability for any damage caused to third parties (including creditors) as a result of any decision adopted by the relevant board of directors (e.g. in Britain, see Company Act 2006).

17 The previous Directive 2006/48, at Article 4(13)(a), used to refer, directly, to Article 1 and 2 of Directive 83/349/EEC for purposes of definition of a "subsidiary." Seventh Council Directive 83/349/EEC of 13 June 1983 based on the Article 54(3)(g) of the Treaty on consolidated accounts ("Consolidated Accounts Directive"). More specifically, according to Article 1 Consolidated Accounts Directive, a company shall be subject to draw up consolidated accounts and a consolidated annual report if that undertaking (a parent undertaking) (a) "has a majority of the shareholders' or members' voting rights in another undertaking (a subsidiary undertaking)" or (b) "has the right to appoint or remove a majority of the members of the administrative, management or supervisory body of another undertaking (a subsidiary undertaking) and is at the same time a shareholder in or member of that undertaking" or (c) "has the right to exercise a dominant influence over an undertaking (a subsidiary undertaking) of which it is a shareholder or member, pursuant to a contract entered into with that undertaking or to a provision in its memorandum or articles of association, where the law governing that subsidiary undertaking permits its being subject to such contracts or provisions."

18 For the English jurisdiction, see, among others French, Mayson and Rayn (2014) and Davies and Worthington (2012).

the "group" is expressly recognised as an autonomous legal concept in addition to the concept of the company, and therefore incurring, in some cases, specific responsibilities. An example is the case of Italy, where the parent company,[19] based on a comparatively recent development of the national legislation, may be sued for damages caused to third parties, particularly the shareholders of the subsidiary, in regard to the manner in which it has managed the group.

Banking legislation promoted at an EU level and implemented in each member state does not neglect the group but rather reinforces its existence under certain conditions, particularly for purposes of supervision and accounting. In respect to the latter, Article 1 of the Consolidated Accounts Directive as evoked by the CRR, for instance, requires any undertaking to draw up consolidated accounts and a consolidated annual report if that undertaking has "a majority of the shareholders' or members' voting rights in another undertaking (a subsidiary undertaking)" (let. a) or, at least, it "has the right to appoint or remove a majority of the members of the administrative, management or supervisory body of another undertaking (a subsidiary undertaking) and is at the same time a shareholder in or member of that undertaking" (let. b).

Domestic banks and international banks

A further, albeit informal, categorisation of banks can be formed relative to the scope of their international or domestic operations. A financial institution with activities abroad is usually a major institution that, whether organised as a universal bank or as a group, is engaged in such a significant volume of activities that it may consider the market of its incorporation to be a straitjacket, restricting its plans for expansion and growth. The *extra moenia* banking business, spurred on by the phenomenon of globalisation, may encapsulate not only the retailing sector, but also investment banking. Thus, a bank may directly control branches or own subsidiaries operating in the retail/commercial sector[20] and may have operations in investment banking, manifested in sophisticated services of corporate finance offered in foreign markets.

More recently, though, such internationalisation may be a declining trend in the banking industry. The financial crisis of 2007/2008 has dealt a significant and, in some cases fatal, blow to international institutions whose financial global activities often hinged upon speculative and risky transactions, thereby jeopardising the erstwhile stability and solidity of such financial institutions and in some cases even the stability of the entire financial system. Given that bank rescues by governments have not come without a cost,[21] it has been suggested (albeit not prescribed under

19 The norm is applicable whether or not the parent company is a bank or not. See Article 2497 of the Italian Civil Code ("Management and Coordination of Companies").

20 Leasing and factoring, for instance, but also pure retail banking such as the offer of bank accounts.

21 Britain seems to be the paradigm of this: in 2008, Royal Bank of Scotland, among the other institutions, became insolvent as a result of too-risky international activities in the pure investment banking. The government had to bail out the bank, by subscribing an increase of the share capital

law) that major banks should relinquish their international business, particularly the financial one, and devote greater energy to the domestic market[22] and within the retail sector.

Financial institutions of this ilk can be more easily supervised as no strained cooperation is needed between supervisors of various countries that may have different constituencies with different interests. Moreover, the danger of contagion of a crisis in case of a default of such an institution may be thus be better controlled, possibly thereby contributing to exorbitant financial burdens on the taxpayer.

2.1.3 Bank and "industry"

The bank engages in a commercial business (it is obvious that lending money and raising funds in exchange for interest is not a charitable activity), and this, theoretically, would not prevent it from acquiring participations in commercial or industrial businesses. Similarly, under free market conditions, nothing would hinder a business from owning its own bank, because such a scenario could be perceived as a natural prerogative of any entrepreneur.

Beyond the theoretical permutations, a practical osmosis between industry and banks is traditionally perceived to be a contentious issue. A commercial company having a holding in a bank (and vice versa) conjures up a number of legitimate concerns: first and foremost, of where the risk and therefore liability for contagion lies. In view of the essential function a bank may have in the economy, the (in) solvency of a bank should not depend on the (un)insolvency of a business group entity. It would therefore be ideal to ensure and guarantee the separation between the solvent business and the insolvent one.

A second concern, which, to some extent, overlaps with issues raised by the first, is the possibility of a conflict of interest: if a bank were to be owned by a major commercial entity, a likely scenario would see it lend money preferably to its owners, as opposed to apportioning the credit risk amongst different borrowers with impartiality. It is generally believed, therefore, that a business should not buy its own bank and subsequently compel that credit institution to lend money to its group, as this would probably jeopardise a proper and impartial scrutiny of its creditworthiness. In the interests of transparency, an ideal scenario would require that a good entrepreneur should provide a convincing argument to the counterparty (the credit institution) to deserve credit based on strong balance sheets and a strong financial position rather than exploiting any competitive advantage of insiders.[23]

necessary to fill in the gigantic loss in the meantime accrued (approximately 30 billion euro). *De facto*, the British taxpayer had to pay the bail-out not for a domestic insolvency rather for the activities of the bank abroad.

22 The "rationale behind" this may also be that the competent authority may better assess the stability of the financial institution by focusing better on the domestic activities, whereas the international ones may lack intelligibility.

23 (Cranston 2002).

Thirdly, the overly invasive presence of a bank in the share capital of industrial or commercial entities, and vice versa, could contribute to the profitability of the group in booming market conditions. However, set against an uncertain economic backdrop or worse, when the house of cards comes crashing down, and businesses suffer inevitable losses or foreclosures, this may prove an unmanageable obstacle for the bank, given the degree of proximity between the commercial entities and banks, with the latter struggling to recover their money from borrowers.

If the economic risks associated with an overly strict relationship between bankers and businesses are those described, the legislation should not be, and indeed is not, averse to dictating some specific and stringent rules in this area. As a general rule of good practice for a banker a "Chinese wall" has been erected, which is also endorsed by legislation at the EU level.

Bank owning an "industry"

The reasons that a bank may wish to have a holding in a commercial entity or in industrial corporations are multifarious: aside from the hypothesis of the custodian (the bank as merely the intermediary, holding shares on behalf of its customers), the bank may purchase and sell holdings (1) to speculate on the equity of the corporation concerned[24] or, further, (2) to convert in equity loans to the company that the borrower has not been able to honour.[25]

Irrespective of the reason for the bank being or becoming an "industrialist" and regardless of specific local attitudes existing in this matter,[26] the relevant rules are quite strict and precise, at EU level. First and foremost, Article 89 CRR subjects to limits not any qualifying holding by a bank, but exclusively qualifying holdings of a credit institution outside the financial sector. In other words, the holdings that are

24 The credit institution may be totally uninterested in the specific business; however, it is confident that the value of the share may increase, and as a result of a future sale, it can attain a significant capital gain.

25 E.g. A "corporate" borrower is not in a position to pay off its debts; the bank may believe that the option of the judicial enforcement of its credit – and therefore to cause the counterparty to default – could be detrimental to the same lender. In these circumstances, the two parties may reasonably decide to renegotiate a refinancing of their previous loan, whereby the credit of the bank is written off and the owner hives down to the lender significant shares of the capital. Usually, in these circumstances, the industrial holding shall remain in the hands of the bank for a relatively short period, so long as the borrower concerned does not turn around and the relevant asset relocated in the market.

26 The model of long-term bank-industry intersection is Germany; in this country, the investment of a bank in the share capital of a commercial entity can be a long term one, accompanied also by the appointment of directors to the management body of the participated entity. This prolonged presence is viewed in a positive way by those who believe that the same commercial entity may benefit from this; a bank which is also a shareholder would be less inclined to ask for an immediate foreclosure of the participated business, in case of temporary default. In this scenario, milder option (e.g. a *moratorium* in the payment of the debts) would be the first option. On the other hand, a bank constantly acting as a "watchdog" in the board of the directors, could end up "bullying" the other shareholders, particularly the minority ones, through a dividend policy more informed by the short-term than the long-term. Ultimately, this would be detrimental to the minority shareholders and their expectation to own a solid company in the long term.

allowed under Article 89 CRR are only those of financial nature, such as (a) "a financial sector entity" and (b) "undertaking, that is not a financial sector entity, carrying on activities which the competent authority considers to be any of the following: (i) a direct extension of banking; (ii) ancillary to banking; (iii) leasing, factoring, the management of unit trusts, the management of data processing services or any other similar activity." Additionally, under Article 89(1) CRR, the limits apply exclusively to holdings "the amount of which exceeds 15% of the eligible capital of the institution." To elaborate, for holdings the amount of which is not particularly significant (again, below 15% of the capital of the bank), that holding shall not be taken into account.

Now that we have defined the perimeter of application of the norm, it is worth noting that the system of bank ownership in "industrial" entities is envisaged by CRR in a way considerably different from the past. In essence, according to Article 89(3) CRR, the global limit of industrial holdings by a credit institution must not exceed 60% of the eligible capital of that bank.[27]

Commercial businesses or industries owning a bank

The intersection between bank and industry is mitigated also in the other – and to a certain extent opposite – direction whereby a commercial entity owns a participation in the share capital of a bank. In this case, however, there is no such thing as an ad hoc rule of the kind provided by Article 89 CRR.[28] The prescription is a more general one and relates to the requirements which the EU demands any bank to comply with for the taking up and pursuit of its business. More specifically, Article 22 CRD IV[29] requires "any natural or legal person or such persons acting in concert (the "proposed acquirer") who have taken a decision either to acquire, directly or indirectly, a qualifying holding in a credit institution or to further increase, directly or indirectly, such a qualifying holding in a credit institution" to inform, first and foremost, the competent authority. Pursuant to the same provision, "qualifying holding" is regarded as the prospective acquisition or increase in the share capital of the credit institution so that the proportion of the voting rights or of the capital held "would reach or exceed 20%, 30%, or 50%[30] or so that the credit institution would become its subsidiary."

27 Under the previous regime, Directive 2006/48 required each member state to fix and impose by law (or soft legislation) a threshold of 15% of the "own funds" of a bank in respect to undertakings which were not credit institutions or financial institutions. This percentage (15%) of its "own funds" was a "single" value, relating to each non-financial undertaking of a specific bank (Article 120(1)) of Directive 2006/48). There was also a "global" limit, equivalent to 60% of the "own funds" of the bank concerned; this limit corresponded to the entire portfolio of industrial holding belonging to a specific bank. In other words, not only could each bank's total holdings in non-financial undertakings not exceed 60% of their "own funds," but the financial institution was also required not to take part in a non-financial institution for more than 15% of its own capital (Article 120(2)) of Directive 2006/48, now repealed).

28 Previously, Article 120 of CRD.

29 Under the previous Directive 2006/48, this used to be legislated under Article 19.

30 It is worth highlighting that these thresholds cannot be derogated or altered by the national legislation.

In both cases (the acquisition of a "qualifying holding" or its increase as a result of additional purchases), the competent authority is vested with the power to deny the authorisation (either to the acquisition of a "qualifying holding" or an increase by one of the percentages), within 60 days if the prospective buyer is deemed unfit considering, as a result of that perspective acquisition, "the sound and prudent management of the credit institution in which an acquisition is proposed."[31] It is crucial to note that the provision just discussed (and other than Article 89 CRR which is limited to banks holding interests in non-financials) is not limited to (the acquisition of) holdings in banks by non-financials, *i.e.* commercial entities and/or business corporations, but it applies also to acquisitions of shares or quotas of a credit institution by another bank or anyone else interested in owning a significant share of its capital.

Remarkably, the acquisition of a bank by a non-financial institution is not prohibited, nor is the holding of a significant percentage and thus, theoretically, not even in respect of the entire capital.[32] Yet each competent authority is required to assess, before the acquisition comes into effect, whether the prospective purchaser (irrespective of whether its business is financial or industrial) is in a position to ensure assessment criteria of Article 23 CRD IV, including the "sound and prudent management" of that financial institution.[33]

2.1.4 EU banking activities

Seen through the eyes of the EU legislator, the bank is an undertaking engaged in two main activities being "to take deposits or other repayable funds from the public and to grant credits for its own account."[34] The contextual exercise of accepting deposits and lending money would seem to represent the nuts and bolts of the banking business – in other words, the fundamental activities an entity must engage in for it to be defined a "credit institution."

Additionally, the ambit of CRD IV extends to "banking activities" so as to encompass the operations listed in its Annex I, where the two core activities fuse

31 See Article 23 of Directive 2013/36. The correspondent provision under the previous Directive 2006/48 was Article 19. The new Directive 2013/36 seems to leave to the authority more room in order to assess whether a credit institution can be authorised or not, given the fact that five assessment criteria are fixed by the legislator, including "the reputation of the proposed acquirer" (Article 23 of Directive 2013/36).

32 Conversely, in the opposite case of a holding in a commercial company by a bank, the limit highlighted in the previous Section 5.3.1 would be applicable.

33 This relative looseness of the discipline concerned with potential owners of a bank – whether "financial" or "industrial" – finds evidence in practice. In Britain, for instance, major retail groups, engaged in pure commercial retail sector (Tesco, Sainsbury) may be sometimes the sole owners of their own bank. This does not infringe specific rules; it is obvious, though, that the local authority in Britain authorises in advance this significant non-financial holding in a credit institution and does not raise any objection, seemingly because the sound and prudent management of the bank has not been deemed so far affected by it.

34 Article 4(1) CRR. Article 4(1) of Directive 2006/48 (now repealed) used to utilise a similar language: "to receive deposits or other repayable funds from the public and to grant credits for its own accounts."

with additional activities, the former and the latter thereby forming a "list of activities subject to mutual recognition."[35] These activities are qualified as "subject to mutual recognition" because, once the bank has been authorised by its own competent authorities, such activities can be discharged through a specific regime of communication in any other EU member state without the need for any additional authorisation.

Amongst the additional activities "subject to mutual recognition," reference can be made to "financial leasing" (no. 3 of Annex I); money transmission services, *i.e.* more technically, "payment services"[36] (no. 4); "issuing and administering means of payment (e.g. travellers' cheques and bankers' drafts), insofar as such activity is not covered by point 4" (no. 5); and "guarantees and commitments" (no. 6). Additionally, it is worth mentioning the "[p]articipation in securities issues and the provision of services related to such issues" (no. 8); the "[a]dvice to undertaking on capital structure, industrial strategy and related questions and advice as well services relating to mergers and the purchase of undertakings" (no. 9); the "[m]oney broking" (no. 10); the "[p]ortfolio management and advice" (no. 11); the "[s]afekeeping and administration of securities" (no. 12); the "[c]redit reference services" (no. 13); the "[s]afe custody services" (no. 14); and "issuing electronic money" (no. 15).

In respect to the activities catalogued here, it would appear that the range is both vast and comprehensive in its detailing of all the main businesses in which a modern bank may seek to engage: for instance, an investment bank typically offering advice in relation to M&A transactions and IPOs would fall within the activity described under number 9 of Annex 1, namely, "[a]dvice to undertakings on capital structure, industrial strategy and related questions and advice as well as services relating to mergers and the purchase of undertakings."

Amongst the activities "subject to mutual recognition" is a small selection which a credit institution shares with other supervised entities, such as investment firms.[37] In this respect, it is worth referring to number 7 of Annex 1, which particularly mentions the trading for own account or for the account of customers in "money market instruments" (let. a), "foreign exchange" (let. b), "financial futures and options" (let. c), "exchange and interest rate instruments" (let. d) and "transferrable securities" (let. e). Closely associated with this is the further activity, found under number 11, which relates to "portfolio management and advice" and which is also permitted to investment firms. In these cases of overlap (viz. activities reserved to banks but also permitted to investment firms), a bank, especially if of significant standing, may deem it opportune to organise its business within a group where the investment activities (particularly the trading on securities) are strategically

35 Directive 2006/48 used to encompass an Annex 1, with such a list. The two lists are basically identical, but for the addition of the "issuing electronic money" (no. 15), previously not a "mutual recognition activity" under Directive 2006/48, and linguistic variation in a definition of "money definition services."

36 As defined in Article 4(3) of Directive 2007/64/EC (Payment Services Directive).

37 These activities are now governed by Directive 2004/39.

delegated to a specialised entity, such as an investment firm which is totally or mainly held by a major commercial bank, the latter being the parent company. In this case, the parent company would typically not pursue the investment activities itself, but rather devolve them to the specialised company within the group, which has been specifically formed and organised for such a purpose.

2.2 The supervision

2.2.1 European banking supervision

Single Supervisory Mechanism

Since the global financial crisis started in 2007, the European legislature has been trying to create a safer and sounder financial sector for the European Union. One of the measures taken has been the creation of a European System of Financial Supervision under which three European supervisory authorities, including the European Banking Authority[38] have been established. But as the crisis evolved and turned into the eurozone debt crisis in 2010/2011, it became clear that, for those countries which shared the euro as a currency and were even more interdependent, more had to be done, in particular to break the vicious circle between banks and national finances. Consequently, in June 2012, heads of state and government agreed to create a banking union, completing the economic and monetary union, and allowing for centralised application of EU-wide rules for banks in the euro area and any non-euro member states that would want to join.

A new regulatory framework with common rules for banks in all 28 member states, set out in a "single rulebook," is the foundation of the banking union. First and foremost, common rules must help to prevent bank crises. Centre stage is taken by the most recent capital requirements legislation package, viz. the Capital Requirements Directive IV[39] and the Capital Requirements Regulation.[40] Should a bank suffer financial difficulties notwithstanding these rules of prudential supervision, a common framework has been set up to recover the bank or resolve it, *i.e.* to wind it down in an orderly way. This framework is mainly to be found in the Directive on Bank Recovery and Resolution (BRRD).[41] Common rules will also

38 Henceforth EBA.

39 Henceforth CRD IV.

40 Henceforth CRR.

In full: Directive 2013/36/EU of the European Parliament and of the Council of 26 June 2013 on access to the activity of credit institutions and the prudential supervision of credit institutions and investment firms, amending Directive 2002/87/EC and repealing Directives 2006/48/EC and 2006/49/EC, OJ L 176; and Regulation (EU) No 575/2013 of the European Parliament and of the Council of 26 June 2013 on prudential requirements for credit institutions and investment firms and amending Regulation (EU) No 648/2012, OJ L 176.

41 In full: Directive 2014/59/EU of the European Parliament and of the Council of 15 May 2014 establishing a framework for the recovery and resolution of credit institutions and investment firms and amending Council Directive 82/891/EEC, and Directives 2001/24/EC, 2002/47/EC, 2004/25/EC,

ensure that all EU retail customers are guaranteed that their deposits up to 100,000 euro per depositor (and per bank) are protected at all times and everywhere in the EU; notably, the details of these rules can be found in the Directive on Deposit Guarantee Scheme and its national implementation laws.[42]

For the member states that use the euro as their currency, the banking union will achieve uniform application of the common rules of prudential supervision by means of the so-called Single Supervisory Mechanism.[43] Within this SSM, the ECB has taken on the role as ultimate prudential supervisor of all 6,000 banks in the euro area as of November 2014. Subsequently, it directly supervises, in short, the systemically important banks of the eurozone and is responsible indirectly, *i.e.* through the national supervisory authorities, for the prudential supervision of all other banks. Thus, it is hoped a truly European supervision mechanism will be achieved, which will withstand the inclination to protect national interests, so that the link between banks and national finances will be broken.[44]

Together with the new EU-wide regulatory framework for the financial sector, the completed banking union represents a major milestone in the economic and monetary integration of the EU. It is hoped to restore financial stability and to create the right conditions for the financial sector to lend to the real economy, spurring economic recovery and job creation.

EBA

Further to the De Larosière Report,[45] the EBA was established on 1 January 2011 as part of the European System of Financial Supervision.[46] It took over all existing responsibilities and tasks of the Committee of European Banking Supervisors. The EBA is an independent EU authority which aims to ensure effective and consistent prudential regulation and supervision across the European banking sector. Its overall objectives are to maintain financial stability in the EU and to safeguard the integrity, efficiency and orderly functioning of the banking sector.

The main task of the EBA is to contribute to the creation of the European single rulebook in banking whose objective is to provide a single set of harmonised prudential rules for financial institutions throughout the EU. The EBA also plays a role

---

2005/56/EC, 2007/36/EC, 2011/35/EU, 2012/30/EU and 2013/36/EU, and Regulations 1093/2010/EU and 648/2012/EU, of the European Parliament and of the Council, OJ L 173/190–348.

42 See, more extensively, below.

43 Henceforth SSM. The SSM has been created by virtue of Council Regulation 1024/2013/EU of 15 October 2013 conferring specific tasks on the European Central Bank concerning policies relating to the prudential supervision of credit institutions, OJ L 287.

44 Please note that conduct supervision has not been unified within the eurozone, although this is harmonised within the EU under the aegis of ESMA. On ESMA, see also above.

45 See above.

46 Henceforth ESFS. By virtue of Regulation 1093/2010/EU of the European Parliament and of the Council of 24 November 2010 establishing a European supervisory authority (European Banking Authority), amending Decision 716/2009/EC and repealing Commission Decision 2009/78/EC, OJ L 331.

in promoting convergence of supervisory practices and is mandated to assess risks and vulnerabilities in the EU banking sector.

European Central Bank

The European Central Bank[47] is one of the seven institutions of the EU pursuant to the Treaty on European Union (TEU). The bank was established by the Treaty of Amsterdam in 1998, and is headquartered in Frankfurt, Germany.

The Maastricht Treaty of 1992, or TEU, mandated the creation of the European System of Central Banks,[48] of which the ECB and the 27 EU national central banks are a party to. The ESCB is governed by the decision-making bodies of the ECB. Under the aegis of the ESCB sits the Eurosystem, composed of the ECB and the 18 national central banks of those EU member states that use the euro. The ECB is the central bank for the 18-nation eurozone, and probably the 19-nation one as of 1 January 2015, on which date Lithuania is expected to adopt the euro as its currency. The ECB has a mandate to maintain price stability in countries that use the euro, by setting key interest rates and controlling the money supply.

So as to fulfil the Maastricht Treaty's goal of creating a European Economic and Monetary Union,[49] the ECB took over responsibility for monetary policy in the euro area from the member states in January 1999, two years prior to the circulation of the euro currency. Since that moment, the ECB works together with the national central banks of the eurozone countries. The aim of the single currency, albeit limited to the eurozone, is therefore to ensure price transparency, and an uncomplicated comparison of prices. This should improve competitiveness, by making it simpler to find the cheapest supplier for a product or service. It is also argued that the single currency eliminates the risk of currency fluctuations, making cross-border investments and trade within the eurozone easier. Financial markets are possibly able to operate more effectively too, as the euro facilitates their integration. So the single currency and its central bank are intended to be good for business, as well as for people who find it easier to travel, to shop or to work in other countries within the eurozone.

2.2.2 National supervision

Most of the big decisions about the shape and content of the rules governing financial market activity in Europe are now taken at the EU level and the domestic laws of member states have been relegated to an increasingly secondary role. Until the introduction of the ESFS and, especially, the SSM, this has not been matched by a simultaneous centralisation of supervisory responsibility. Instead, the tasks of day-to-day implementation and on-the-ground enforcement of this body of regulation largely fell to member states' supervisory authorities, albeit with a layer of

47 Henceforth ECB.
48 Henceforth ESCB.
49 Henceforth EMU.

EU-wide structural coordination added on top. While under the new single supervisory regime the role of the EU will increase, the national authorities will continue to be the primary supervisor for many financial institutions.

One consequence of the lack of complete centralisation with respect to supervision is that the European financial market supervisory scene may continue to resemble a cluttered landscape. Many member states divide supervisory responsibilities between several agencies, and also involve their central bank to a greater or lesser extent. The picture becomes even more crowded when the supervisory authorities from the EEA countries, the ECB and the European Commission are taken into account as well. All of these bodies participate in some way in one or more of the EU-wide coordinating structures.

Prior to the financial crisis, many countries located frontline responsibility for micro-prudential supervision of all sectors of financial market activity with a single regulatory authority that operated autonomously from the central bank. Countries in this group included Belgium, Denmark, Finland, Germany, Norway (EEA), Poland, Sweden and the United Kingdom. The Czech Republic and Slovakia also employed the integrated supervisor model, but all of the relevant functions were performed by the central bank rather than by dedicated supervisory authorities. Some other countries divided responsibilities between the central bank (for banking supervision), a securities market supervisory authority, and one or more authorities that had responsibility for oversight in respect of insurance and pensions. This system is better known as sectorial supervision – Greece, Italy, Portugal and Spain were in this group.[50] Another model has been in operation in the Netherlands, whereby prudential supervision of banking, insurance, and pensions were the responsibility of the central bank and another authority had responsibility for conduct of business regulation across all three sectors of financial market activity. The Dutch approach is sometimes dubbed a "twin peaks" model, in which there is one supervisor for prudential matters and another one in respect of conduct of business.[51]

The global financial crisis triggered a fresh look at the institutional arrangements discussed earlier, and in particular a reappraisal of the role of central banks in financial supervision. Responsibility for macro-prudential supervision (*i.e.* systemic stability oversight) is a role that seems to have been reclaimed by central banks. The crisis demonstrated both that macro-prudential supervision had not been afforded sufficient priority in the preceding years, and that it is of critical importance to ensure that macro- and micro-prudential supervision are well aligned. In 2010, France reorganised its institutional structures along, broadly speaking,

50 In Italy, for instance, the Banca d'Italia is in charge of the supervision of credit institutions, the CONSOB (Commissione Nazionale per le Societa' e la Borsa) dedicated to the supervision of listed companies, the IVASS (*Istituto per la Vigilanza sulle Assicurazioni*), previously ISVAP, deputed to review the activity of insurers, and finally the COVIP (*Commissone Vigilanza Fondi Pensione*) for pension funds.

51 For a wide-ranging meditation on the concept of "twin peaks" supervision, see Brunnermeier et al. (2009).

twin peaks lines, with a strong role for the Banque de France. The Irish legislature moved to put its central bank back at the centre of financial supervision and financial stability oversight. There have been discussions in Germany about putting the Bundesbank back at the centre of supervisory power. Belgium has also adjusted the relationship between its central bank and the financial market supervisor, and in 2010 passed a law to replace the Banking, Finance and Insurance Commission[52] by a new Financial Services and Markets Authority.[53]

The diversity that currently exists in national institutional arrangements for the oversight of financial markets indicates that there is no foundation of common transnational assumptions about what financial market supervisory architecture should look like on which to build an overarching pan-European federal structure from the bottom up. Therefore, the eurozone has chosen a top-down approach for unification of the oversight of financial markets.

As regards a non-euro country, the British government announced in June 2010 its intention to restructure the regulatory framework of the UK financial services. Central to this restructuring is the replacement of the Financial Services Authority (FSA) with a new twin peaks regulatory structure that combines oversight of the financial system as a whole with firm-specific supervision. The Bank of England (BoE) Financial Policy Committee has taken responsibility for macro-prudential regulation, focusing on the overarching stability of the financial system. Conduct of business regulation for all firms has become the responsibility of a new regulator, the Financial Conduct Authority (FCA), a BoE subsidiary. The FCA is also responsible for the prudential regulation of firms which fall outside the remit of the other new regulator, the Prudential Regulatory Authority (PRA). The PRA, also a BoE subsidiary, is responsible for micro-prudential regulation, with an objective of promoting the safety and soundness of regulated firms. Firms regulated by the PRA are therefore "dual-regulated," with the PRA responsible for their prudential regulation and the FCA responsible for conduct of business supervision.[54]

2.2.3 Authorisation of the banking business

The TFEU sets out the basics for the right of establishment and of cross-border service provision within the EU. However, the TFEU allows limitations to these freedoms for specific public health, public security and public order reasons and provides the opportunity to harmonise both the effect of the freedoms and their limitations via directives. The financial services area benefits from harmonisation. Before such harmonisation was achieved, domestic governments defined – each in different ways – what a bank was, and under which conditions it would be allowed to enter their local market (both for home-grown banks and for EU or third country banks).

52 Henceforth CBFA.
53 Henceforth FSMA.
54 (Walker 2014).

In the absence of harmonisation directives, domestic governments would be forced to set high fences around their territory and thus would invoke the right to limit the freedom of establishment and of services. The protection of the public, of the financial system and of the high standards in a member state would allow member states to act along this inclination. Conversely, the capital requirements legislation provides a commonly agreed framework on various types of cross-border market access methods within the EU. The framework intends to limit and/or eliminate such "good reasons" to limit access, in order to stimulate the single market. Combined with minimum standards on prudential supervision, it allows banks that are authorised and supervised under those minimum standards, to operate across the EU, with limited and clearly defined intervention possibilities for host member states.

Member states have to allow cross-border services to be provided and branches to be established by banks authorised and supervised by a supervisor of another member state, if the license of that bank, as granted by its own supervisor, includes the provision of those same services in its own member state. However, this obligation to permit access is linked exclusively to the specific activities.

The EU "passport"

The so-called European passport was one of the first key achievements of harmonised banking supervision in the EU.[55] The EU created a European passport to enable a legal entity with a banking license to set up branches and/or start selling services across borders in other member states. It replaced the previous need to obtain a separate banking license for each country where a bank wanted to do business, thus significantly reducing thresholds for banks to provide services in the single market. Under the European passport regime, a bank with a license in its own member state can opt to start providing services (cross-border or via a branch) in the territory of another member state (the host state).

The passport process for prudential banking supervision is very low-key indeed, in line with the freedoms of establishment and services of the treaties. Before starting its activities through the branch, the home supervisory authority must have approved this intention. Pursuant to Article 35(2) CRD IV, the application for approval must contain the following data: (1) the member state where the bank plans to set up the branch, (2) a programme of operations setting out, inter alia, the types of business envisaged and the structural organisation of the branch, (3) the address in the host member state from which documents may be obtained and (4) the names of those to be responsible for the management of the branch.

Within three months after receipt of the application and the information required, the competent authority of the home member state shall decide on the application.[56] The national supervisory authority shall approve the intention, unless

55 On the European passport, see also above.

56 This precept can be inferred from Article 35(3), first para, CRD IV.

the credit institution's operations or financial position are inadequate in view of its intention.[57] The competent authority shall also notify the host regulator.[58] Such notification contains information regarding the volume of own funds, the solvency ratio and, where applicable, information on the deposit guarantee scheme applicable to the particular branch.[59] The credit institution will be informed accordingly.[60]

The vast bulk of prudential supervision remains with the home supervisor of the legal entity, with some limited rights (more for branches, less for cross-border services) for the host supervisor of the legal entity. The process for cross-border services has been reduced to a formal process; for branches it contains minor but relatively more cumbersome material aspects. A branch is a permanent physical extension of the licensed legal entity into another member state, while cross-border services should not have such a presence in the host market (and are thus less "material" to host member state markets). The borderline between branches and services (and activities that do not require a notification at all, e.g. a visit of a bank official to another bank in the other member state) is not always clear, even though it has consequences both for the type of notification to be sent and – after the bank starts its activities – for the role of host supervisors regarding the cross-border presence of the foreign bank.

Banks from the European Economic Area (EEA) are treated as if they are banks from an EU member state for the purpose of market access. This follows from the EEA Treaty, which reciprocally allows access to and from all the EEA states, including all EU states.

This is conditional upon the non-EU EEA states taking over all prudential supervision directives. Banks from other third countries do not benefit from a European passport, unless they have a fully licensed subsidiary in one of the EU member states. Such a subsidiary is an EU entity and – once it has passed all the hurdles from the licensing process – has the same rights and obligations as any other bank with an EU authorisation to passport within the EU.

Non-compliance

If a credit institution conducting its business in another member state, either by the establishment of a branch or by way of the cross-border provision of services, has received an instruction relating to its operations or its financial situation, and the credit institution has not, or not sufficiently, complied with that instruction,[61] the home state regulator may adopt "appropriate measures,"[62] including, seemingly, the suspension of that credit institution from conducting its business through

57 *Ibid.*

58 *Ibid.*

59 Article 35(1), para 2, CRD IV.

60 This is inferable from the expression "and shall inform the credit institution accordingly" encompassed with Article 35(3), para 1, CRD IV.

61 The specific hypotheses contemplated within the CRD IV, particularly Article 41(1).

62 This is the expression utilised by the CRD IV, Article 41(1), para. 2.

either a branch or the cross-border provision of services in the other member state. The home state authority shall notify the host regulator(s) involved of this decision. From the time of this notification, the credit institution may no longer conduct its business from the branch or as a cross-border service provider in the other member state.

If a bank which conducts its business from a branch in another member state fails to comply with statutory regulations applicable in the host member state, the home state regulator, having received a notification to that effect from the host state regulator, shall, without delay, issue an instruction to the bank to adhere to the line of conduct set out in the instruction order within a reasonable term specified, in order to put an end to the violation of the statutory regulations applicable in the host member state. If the bank has not, or not sufficiently, complied with the instruction, the national regulator, having informed the host state regulator, may prevent the bank from concluding new contracts in the host member state. The host state regulator will be informed of the measures taken.[63]

In conclusion, if the banking license of a bank is withdrawn by the national supervisory authority, this authority must also inform the regulators of the member state(s) in which the bank has a branch or to which it provides services.

2.2.4 Prudential supervision

The stability of the bank

One of the main reasons to institute supervision on individual banks and banking groups is the interconnectivity of the financial system and the important role banks play in it. If a bank or banking group fails, there are risks to financial stability, as its bankruptcy could lead to the bankruptcy of its contracting parties and clients, including other banks, and so on. Moreover, a distrust of a bank may easily spill over to other banks: if one of them is no longer trusted, other banks and their services may also become suspect. Prudential supervision should therefore aim to strengthen financial stability.

Financial stability as such is not a defined concept in the CRD legislation or in any other EU legislation. Several economists have proposed definitions, but there does not appear to be any real consensus.[64] Common elements are a safe and well-functioning financial environment and the absence of shocks and "negative externalities" (*i.e.* the absence of financial instability). In this sense, anything that helps to make financial structures safer and less prone to shocks is geared towards financial stability.

When a shock to financial stability occurs, this is called a financial crisis. Financial crises are of all times and places, and can be caused by any source of instability. Financial instability may lead to damage to the general economy if shocks to it are not resolved quickly. Banks are inherently unstable, due to their short-term

63 Article 41(2), CRD IV.

64 Some commentators refer to it as a "public good" (Kaul et al. 2003).

borrowing and long-term lending business, with additional instability and contagion sources added by procyclical valuation standards, investments, cross-border business and size, as well as the use of their business to stimulate risky lending to enterprises and governments. Financial stability instruments aim to prevent or resolve this financial instability of banks (and other financial institutions).

However, the effectiveness of financial stability instruments should not be overstated, as financial stability can never be guaranteed: the business of borrowing against lending is inherently risky and that risk would render lending impossible and, therefore, limit the possibility of growth. Nonetheless, these financial stability instruments may contribute (1) to the prevention of avoidable negative shocks, (2) to dampen the negative effects or financial instability when it occurs, while attempting not to inhibit growth too much. Some negative shocks can be prevented by, for example, monitoring traders to avoid fraud and ensuring liquidity, each of which has caused crisis in the past and for which we are thus forewarned. Financial stability can be strived for by a wide range of instruments, mainly geared towards not rocking the boat or shock absorbers once the boat starts rocking in any case, and allowing economic growth and wellbeing to develop (still but also only) at a measured pace. The remainder of this chapter will pay attention to the capital adequacy requirements of the CRD legislation as a financial stability instrument, but also to CRD's provisions on liquidity risk, large exposures, corporate governance and remuneration.

Solvability and capital buffers

Thanks to the work of the Basel Committee on Banking Supervision (BCBS of the Bank for International Settlements), the basic formula of a mandatory solvency ratio has been rolled out in a reasonable harmonised fashion across the globe, including the EU. In the EU, the latest Basel Accord (the so-called Basel III Accord) has been implemented as CRD IV and CRR. Under these statutes, banks are required to have capital buffers. Capital buffers of specific quality types are required, calculated in relation to the risk the bank runs, in addition to sufficient capital for company law and licensing purposes. Subject to the availability of these capital buffers of at least the amount required for its calculated risk, the bank is allowed to attract money from companies and from consumers and subsequently to use that money for its own account by lending or investing it.

Capital buffers aim to ensure that – even if losses are made from onwards lending or investment – the money attracted from depositors and regular bondholders can be repaid. Thus, capital buffers consist of instruments on the liability side of the balance sheet that are available to absorb losses, both in a going concern, as well as in a gone concern scenario. If there is not sufficient money to pay back both creditors and shareholders, losses are borne first by the shareholders. Only if their claim has been fully written down do creditors face losses on their claims. Shareholders are therefore considered "risk investors" under company law/bankruptcy laws. This makes equity for banks rather expensive as the premium for that risk needs to be substantial (either in substantial dividends or share price rises).

The attempt to reduce those costs leads to a search for other capital buffer components that are cheaper but still provide safety – a buffer – for creditors. Subordinated loans and hybrids – *e.g.* loans that have some characteristics of shares – may be accepted as a buffer for capital adequacy purposes, such as the solvency ratio. However, the 2007–2013 subprime crisis showed that some of these components did not serve as an actual financial buffer on a going concern basis, let alone in liquidation. In sum, the intended goal of financial stability was not achieved, leading to a reassessment of several capital buffer components.

It is generally accepted that capital buffers need to have two characteristics: the buffers need to be of sufficient size, and of sufficient quality. Whereas the desirability of high-quality buffers has been the starting point, the BCBS and the CRD legislation still also accept lower quality capital buffers, such as subordinated loans. These lower-quality buffers can supplement – up to certain limits – high-quality capital buffers, such as issued and fully paid-up shares. In the latest Basel III Accord, the amount of lower-quality capital buffer types is slightly reduced, while the definition of high-quality characteristics has been slightly enhanced, with some further improvements on the overall quality of capital buffers made during the decades long transitional period. The percentages of the solvency ratio that are covered by capital buffers, which must conform to the highest set of quality requirements formulated, is gradually increased. Basel III also makes explicit that such capital buffers are useful in going concern situations, while some other financial buffers may only avail creditors in a liquidation or gone concern scenario.

The gradual enhancement, just discussed, is the result of a compromise between, on the one hand, the need to improve the safety of the banking system, and on the other, certain difficulties many banks would have encountered, should the new capital requirements have been implemented too abruptly. It has been argued that banks' lending capacity would have been significantly reduced when banks would have had to increase their capital buffers too quickly, and this argument has prevented a 'big bang' approach.

Capital can be defined in various ways. The accounting definition of capital is not identical to the definition used for regulatory capital adequacy purposes. Regulatory capital is more conservative than accounting capital. For the purposes of regulatory capital adequacy for banks, capital is not defined simply by deducting the value of an institution's liabilities (what it owes) from its assets (what it owns). Only capital that is at all times freely available to absorb losses qualifies as regulatory capital. Additional conservatism is added by adjusting this measure of capital further by *e.g.* deducting assets that may not have a stable value in stressed market circumstances (*e.g.* goodwill) and not recognising gains that have not yet been realised.

The capital adequacy requirement is the amount of capital an institution is required to hold to cover unexpected losses, relative to its total amount of assets. In the CRR, this is called the "own funds requirement" and is expressed as a percentage of risk-weighted assets. The purpose of this capital is to absorb the losses on its assets that a bank does not expect to make in the normal course of business (unexpected losses). The more capital a bank has, the more losses it can suffer before it defaults.

In order to calculate the capital an institution needs to hold against its assets, the CRR defines how to weigh an institution's assets relative to their risk. This phenomenon is known as Risk Weighted Assets or RWA. Safe assets such as cash are disregarded, other assets such as loans to other institutions are considered riskier and get a higher weight. The riskier the assets an institution holds, the more capital it has to maintain. This risk weighing of assets is done not only as regards assets on the bank's balance sheet, but banks must also maintain capital against risks related to off-balance sheet exposures such as loan and credit card commitments which are also risk weighed.

Capital comes in different forms that serve different purposes. In essence and as alluded to earlier, there are two types of capital:

- Going concern capital: this is the type of capital that has a loss-absorbing capacity so that an institution can continue its activities and prevent insolvency. This type of capital is called "Tier 1 capital." Pursuant to Article 26 CRR, the Tier 1 capital of an institution consists of the sum of the Common Equity Tier 1 capital (CET 1) and Additional Tier 1 capital (AT 1). In short, Common Equity Tier 1 can be capital instruments, and/or share premium accounts related to these capital instruments and retained earnings. CRR does not define "capital instruments," but lists its conditions in Article 28 and 29. In short, most common equity will qualify. Also, Additional Tier 1 capital is not defined in CRR, but capital instruments must comply with the list of conditions of Article 52(1) CRR in order to qualify as Additional Tier 1 capital. In short, certain subordinated loans, hybrids and convertibles, *i.e.* loans that are paid only after "senior" loans have been paid, loans which resemble common equity and loans that may be converted into shares, may qualify;
- Gone concern capital: this is the type of capital that helps ensuring that depositors and senior creditors can be repaid if the institution fails. This type of capital is called "Tier 2 capital." Also, this category of capital may include hybrid capital and subordinated debt, but the conditions to qualify as Tier 2 capital – which are to be found in Article 63 CRR – are less stringent than the conditions for AT 1.

Under the previous capital adequacy rules, banks and investment firms needed to have a total amount of capital buffer equal to at least 8% of risk weighted assets, *i.e.* a capital ratio of 8%. Under CRD IV and CRR the total capital an institution will need to hold as a capital buffer remains at 8%, but within that 8%, 4.5% (instead of 2%) has to be of the highest quality, *i.e.* Common Equity Tier 1 (CET1).

The criteria for capital instruments to qualify as either CET 1, AT 1 or Tier 2 have also become more stringent. Furthermore, the latest CRD legislation significantly increases the effective level of regulatory capital which institutions are required to have, by the introduction of five new categories of buffers – the capital conservation buffer, the counter-cyclical buffer, the systemic risk buffer, the global systemic institutions buffer and the other systemic institutions buffer; therefore, the new legislation does more than only increasing the quality of capital. In addition, on top of all these own funds requirements, supervisors may demand extra capital to cover for other risks following a supervisory review and institutions may also decide to hold an additional amount of capital on their own initiative.

Institutions can increase their capital adequacy in (at least) the following two ways:

- Increase capital: An institution can increase its capital by issuing new instruments that qualify as regulatory capital (Tier 1 or Tier 2) or not pay dividends to its shareholders, *i.e.* to retain profits, so that these new instruments and retained profits become included in its capital base. Provided the amount of risk-weighted assets[65] is not increased, such new instruments and retained profits increase the capital ratio;
- Reduce risk-weighted assets: An institution can also cut back on lending, sell loan portfolios and/or make less risky loans and investments, thereby reducing its RWAs, which has the effect of – for a given amount of capital – increasing its capital ratio.

Liquidity, large exposures and leverage

Liquidity risk is the inability of a bank to meet its obligations when they become due, because of a lack of available cash. This may be the case, notwithstanding other assets the bank may hold. In other words, a bank may be solvent but nonetheless illiquid, such as when its other assets, such as holdings in companies and/or properties, cannot be quickly sold. Liquidity risk, together with leverage (explained further here), has been a major issue in the past and, probably, a contributory factor to the global financial crisis. To avoid unwanted relapses, the recent legislation of CRD IV requires the competent authorities to ensure that "institutions have robust strategies, policies, processes and systems for the identification, measurement, management and monitoring of liquidity risk over an appropriate set of time horizons."[66] The ultimate purpose of this is to guarantee that "institutions maintain adequate levels of liquidity buffers."[67]

Furthermore, the CRD legislation contains new provisions on a bank's leverage. While, generally speaking, leverage is the ratio between total debt and equity, leverage, as defined by the CRR at Article 4(93), is the "relative size of an institution's assets, off-balance sheet obligations and contingent obligations to pay or to deliver or to provide collateral compared to that institution's own funds." What the directive aims to tackle is "excessive leverage," *i.e.* the "risk resulting from an institution's vulnerability due to leverage or contingent leverage that may require

65 Henceforth RWA.
66 Article 86(1).
67 Article 86(1).

immediate corrective measures to its business plan."[68] In this respect, CRD IV requires the competent authorities existing in each member state to ensure that "institutions have policies and processes in place for the identification, management and monitoring of the risk of excessive leverage."[69] Moreover, the same authorities shall ensure that not only the leverage risk is identified by each credit institution, but also that the institutions address, "in a precautionary manner,"[70] "the potential increases in the risk of excessive leverage."[71] More practically, the increase of risk may arise, among the several circumstances, from the reduction of the own funds of the bank due to expected or realised losses.

Finally, the large exposure regime aims to limit the maximum damage the failure of one client can do to the bank. Some banks become overly dependent on one client to the extent that if the client fails, the banks automatically fail as a result of this. For this purpose, the large exposure regime was introduced in addition to the risk weighted approach. In its most basic form, it obliges a bank to do the following:

- Add up all exposures to one client plus all exposures to other clients which are so interconnected with that one client that, should the latter fail, all these other clients can be expected to fail with it;
- Monitor all substantial ("large") exposures, meaning all exposures to a client or group of interconnected clients that exceed 10% of the bank's own funds: Article 392 CRR;
- Not allow any such large exposure to exceed a quarter of the bank's own funds: Article 395 CRR.

The underpinning concept behind the large exposure's regime is quite simple. Each affected bank shall select all exposures which are large in comparison with its own funds, and do not let an exposure become too large towards a single client (or group of clients), as that would expose the bank to failure if the client fails (or moves to another bank). Unlike the approaches to other categories of risk, the large exposures regime does not primarily rely on capital requirements to limit/manage risk. In this sense it is the odd one out of the quantitative requirements. The large exposures regime works from the premise that, even if capital requirements would cover the other risk categories, it is still not a good idea to put all the "eggs" of the bank into one basket. The large exposures regime complements the capital requirements by providing barriers to overinvestment (*e.g.* by lending) in any specific counterparty or group of connected clients, except where the risk is limited by protection measures or where it is part of normal trading policies for a limited time. In the area of the trading book, the limits may be exceeded if capital is maintained for the excess.

68 Article 4(94), CRR.
69 Article 87(1), CRD IV.
70 Article 87(2), CRD IV.
71 *Ibid.*

It is intended that the hard-wiring of absolute limits does not hamper the banks too much (as they still allow sizable loans to be made), while it attempts to limit the potential damage to a client resulting from concentration of risk. Though this basic thinking is simple, and attempts have been made to implement or make the regime so straightforward and reduce the number of national discretions, it remains riddled with exceptions, discretions and supervisory decisions, reducing its usefulness as a risk reducing factor. By way of example, exposures to a member state are exempted from the regime, which caused serious problems in the 2007–2013 subprime crisis for a wide range of banks that had excessively large exposures to their own member state or other member states.

Corporate governance and remuneration

The available systems of corporate governance of banks across the EU are multifarious, even when discounting the differences relating to each legal system. Some jurisdictions lean toward a unitary management structure,[72] others prefer a dual one,[73] in some cases even both options are possible according to the strategy of the company concerned.[74] Yet the global financial crisis and the collapse of some major financial institutions have cast serious doubts on systems of governance based on voluntary codes of conduct, rather than on binding rules.[75]

This complex scenario has shown that a loose corporate governance may drive a coach and horses through the canons of sound and prudent management of a credit institution. Accordingly, the underpinning philosophy of the EU, in the aftermath of the widespread bank failures, is based on principles and standards, to be implemented in each member state, the purpose of which is "to ensure effective oversight by the management body, promote a sound risk culture at all levels of credit institutions and investment firms and enable competent authorities to monitor the adequacy of internal governance arrangements."[76]

Against this background lie the main novelties of the rules encompassed with the CRD in the area of corporate governance.

First and foremost, all the members of the management body "shall commit sufficient time to perform their functions in the institution."[77] In this respect, it may be

72 The UK Companies Act 2006 epitomises this. Among many, see French, Mayson and Rayn (2014).

73 This is the case of Germany, see Siems and Cabrelli (2013).

74 Italy, in a creative way, has adopted a system of corporate governance that, according to the articles of association of each business entity, can be either unitary or dual.

75 Recital 53, CRD IV. At doctrinal level and with regard to the loose British system of corporate governance, see de Gioia Carabellese (2011). See also, as regards the British scandals in the area of corporate governance, (de Gioia Carabellese, "Corporate governance of British banks and duties of directors: practical implications of the Royal Bank of Scotland's demise 2014). For a broader analysis of the British system of corporate governance and its traditional voluntary approach based on "Codes" (the UK Corporate governance Code) and reports (recently, the Walker Report), see MacNeil (2012).

76 Recital 54, CRD IV.

77 Article 91 CRD IV.

inferred that the EU legislator seems to regard as non-eligible casual directors, *i.e.* bank directors dedicating a very limited time to their managerial role such as the non-executive directors.[78]

Furthermore, the piece of legislation at stake does not allow an individual to hold, as far as major banking institutions are concerned,[79] more than one of the following combinations of directorships at the same time: (1) "one executive directorship with two non-executive directorships" and (2) "four non-executive directorships,"[80] although some mechanisms of pondération are in place to ensure that specific directorships held within the same banking group are weighted as one directorship.[81] In a nutshell, the phenomenon of the jack-of-all-trades-and-master-of-none director, sitting on numerous boards of different banking groups, but in reality not seriously dedicated to any of them, should be prevented in light of rules where, *de facto*, the quality of the directorship rather the quantity is required to make sure that banks are managed properly and without unreasonable risks.

The remuneration, the second topic treated in this paragraph is a yet another area of intervention of the EU legislator. Also in this case, the financial crisis which unfolded in 2008 seems to be one of the reasons for the hitherto unknown detailed precepts promulgated in Brussels. Briefly, a remuneration of the top management too generously inclined to reward the short-term choices rather than the long-term ones, may put in danger the stability of their bank. In fact, it is now generally believed that short term high remuneration may be an opportunity for the top manager to engage in (overly) risky transactions and operations. In light of this scenario, the entire structure of remuneration, traditionally an area left to the discretion of each institution, has been the subject of decisive intervention. The new principles that, on mandatory basis, the competent authorities have to comply with, fix the remuneration for the staff and, in general terms, for any employee, as detailed under Article 92(2). Among the most important are as follows: "(a) the remuneration policy be consistent with and promotes sound and effective risk management and not encourage risk-taking that exceeds the level of tolerated risk of the institution"; "(b) the remuneration policy is in line with the business strategy, objectives, values and long-term interests of the institution, and incorporates measures to avoid conflicts of interest"; "(c) the institution's management body in its supervisory

78 Again, see de Gioia Carabellese (Non-executive Directors and Auditors in the Context of the UK Corporate Governance: Two (or Too Many?)"Pirandellian" Characters still in the Search of an Author? 2011)

It may be predicted that the recent piece of EU legislation has given the "last rite" to this controversial category, already criticised by scholars.

79 The adjective "major" is connected with "size, internal organisation and the nature, the scope and the complexity of its activities" and is defined by each member state. Article 91(3), CRD IV.

80 Article 91(3), CRD IV.

81 More specifically, pursuant to Article 91(4), some multiple directorships shall count as a single directorship: "(a) executive or non-executive directorship held within the same group"; "(b) executive or non-executive directorships held within: (i) institutions which are members of the same institutional protection scheme [*omissis*]; (ii) undertakings (including non-financial entities) in which the institution holds a qualifying holding."

function adopts and periodically reviews the general principles of the remuneration policy and is responsible for overseeing its implementation"; and "(d) the implementation of the remuneration policy is, at least annually, subject to central and independent internal review for compliance with policies and procedures for remuneration adopted by the management body in its supervisory function."

2.3 Insolvency and resolution

2.3.1 Introduction

Within the domain of banking law, the insolvency of banks has been legislated upon for more than a decade, whereas private international law – or conflict of laws – if referred to the matter of insolvency, is an area governed exclusively by the Winding-up Directive.

For insurance companies, a separate European directive, resembling the Winding-up Directive,[82] has likewise been passed. Juxtaposed with this is the question of insolvency concerning commercial business, the legislation of which, at an EU level, falls within the remit of the regulation on insolvency proceedings.[83]

Conceptually, the alignment of insolvency law is one of the most arduous legal feats a supranational law maker may face. Insolvency law is a national matter by definition, traditionally left to the discretion of each local parliament and legislature. The reason for this is that the distribution of assets amongst creditors, set in motion by a case of insolvency, is very much a reflection of national political and policy choices, which do not naturally lend themselves for a legislative cross-border alignment. Moreover, from a private international law perspective, bankruptcy law encompasses the mandatory rules of a jurisdiction, therefore applicable irrespective of any party agreement.

Despite these objective difficulties, a convergence of EU private international law regarding the insolvency of credit institutions has been achieved, through a succession of principles and law provisions, explained and discussed in this chapter. First and foremost, the principle adopted within the EU is the home country one. The UK, albeit outside the EU, still adopts this principle.

Fundamentally, the insolvency of a credit institution operating across the EU or, at least, in member state other than its own (*i.e.* the country of incorporation of the bank), is an event falling within the competence of the home "administrative or judicial authorities," irrespective of whether other branches of that bank are located outside the home country or indeed whether or not that bank provides transnational services beyond its own jurisdiction of incorporation.

82 See Wessels and Moss (2006).

83 Council Regulation 1346/2000/EC of 29 May 2000 on insolvency proceedings (henceforth also European Insolvency Regulation). Article 1(2) of the European Insolvency Regulation clearly states that the "Regulation shall not apply to insolvency proceedings concerning insurance undertakings, credit institutions, investment undertakings which provide services involving the holding of funds or securities to third parties, or to collective investment undertakings."

In referring to the "administrative or judicial authorities," the EU legislator demonstrates expert adeptness in giving a wide berth to the insidious waters of the differences existing amongst the respective national jurisdictions, and the multitude of ways in which insolvency is initiated, either overseen by a judicial authority or by an administrative one. As established by the definition provided under Article 2 of the Winding-up Directive, the administrative or judicial authorities are "such administrative or judicial authorities of the Member States as are competent for the purposes of reorganisation measures or winding-up procedures." Against the backdrop of this rather ambiguous definition, the ensuing Article 3 prescribes that the judicial or administrative authorities of the home member state "shall alone be empowered to decide on the implementation of one or more reorganisation measures in a credit institution, including branches established in other Member States." To elaborate upon this point, the provision entails that the resolution of a winding-up of a bank incorporated in a given member state belongs exclusively to the administrative authority of that country (or to the bankruptcy court located there) while that resolution of the competent authority is deemed effective across the broad spectrum of EU countries wherein that bank had opened branches.

2.3.2 The Winding-up Directive

The EU legislator has acknowledged the need to provide a definition of the insolvency procedures to which the Winding-up Directive applies.[84] In this respect, two such procedures are identified: (1) "reorganisation measures" and (2) "winding-up." The former shall be applicable to financial institutions in the case whereby the recovery of the financial institution is still within the realms of possibility. Should this be the case, the measures are intended "to preserve or restore the financial situation of a credit institution" although they could affect "third parties' pre-existing rights." Within this rather extensive category, defined under Article 2 (headed "Definition"), are to be included measures involving "the possibility of a suspension of payments, suspension of enforcement measures or reduction of claims."

The Winding-up Directive elaborates a second kind of "crisis," the winding-up, referred to as a collective proceeding "opened and monitored by the administrative or judicial authorities of a Member State with the aim of realising assets under the supervision of those authorities, including where the proceedings are terminated by a composition or other, similar measure."

Whichever procedure is adopted (either the "reorganisation measure" or the "winding-up"), the directive is resolute in specifying that any decision to initiate a procedure rests with the administrative or judicial authorities of the home member state; the relevant decision, once adopted, shall be applicable to all branches

84 For purposes of comparison, the European Insolvency Regulation, for commercial insolvencies, seems to be more explicit as it spells out the principle that the "Regulation shall apply to collective insolvency proceedings which entail the partial or total divestment of a debtor and the appointment of a liquidator."

established in other member states.[85] The other EU country (or countries) wherein the bank has opened branches shall have no grounds on which to object to the opening of the procedure, as the procedure adopted by the home authorities shall be effective across all other member states where the bank carries out activities through its branches.[86] Critically, this principle applies to "branches" but not to "subsidiaries"; it follows then that independent entities of a group will be subject to the insolvency law of that local jurisdiction, unless they themselves have branch offices.

In order to obtain the full cooperation of the authorities representing the relevant EU countries, the Winding-up Directive, at Article 9(2), requires that the administrative or judicial authority that initiates the procedure in the country of incorporation of the bank concerned communicates the decision to the authorities of any other affected countries as a matter of urgency, accompanied by a description of the practical effects which the relevant proceeding may precipitate.

It is worth noting that the cardinal principle which permeates the Winding-up Directive and, more specifically, the winding-up proceeding is, as spelled out under Article 10(1) that, save for specific exceptions, the credit institution shall be wound up "in accordance with the laws, regulations and procedures applicable in its home Member State." To elaborate, paragraph 2 of the same article stipulates that the legislation in force in the home member state shall determine "the goods subject to administration and the treatment of goods acquired by the credit institution after the opening of winding-up proceedings" (let. a) and "the claims which are to be lodged against the credit institution and the treatment of claims after the opening of winding-up proceedings" (let. f).

The claims that the creditor is entitled to lodge is certainly a hot potato when viewed from the legal perspective of the EU legislator. The EU market, but also the UK one, represents a favourable arena for consumers, wherein they can benefit from goods and/or services offered and/or provided by enterprises and banks incorporated in another EU country. It stands to reason that, in times of high competition, the free right of establishment theoretically allows the consumer to benefit from the best prices and the best conditions. However, this scenario could throw up an inextricable conundrum and an onerous predicament, were the EU bank to default on its debts, leaving its EU customers to raise claims against a foreign entity and before a foreign court and/or administrative authority. To cater for such an eventuality, Article 16(1) of the Winding-up Directive bestows upon any creditor with domicile, head office or residence in a member state different from the home member state, "the right to lodge claims or to submit written observations relating to the claims."

85 This system applicable to the banking system contrasts with that set forth under the Insolvency Regulation. In this case, the norm is that "the courts of the Member State within the territory of which the centre of a debtor's main interests is situated shall have jurisdiction to open insolvency proceedings" (Article 3(1)), whereas "the courts of another Member State shall have jurisdiction to open insolvency proceedings against that debtor only if he possesses an establishment within the territory of that other Member State" (Article 3(2)).

86 For non-banking insolvency, the rule is opposite: if the debtor has establishments in other member states, the courts of the latter shall open additional and separate proceedings. Article 3(2) of the European Insolvency Regulation.

The subsequent paragraph 2 has augmented this principle with a series of practical suggestions and prescriptions. Particularly remarkable is the stipulation that any claims "shall be treated in the same way and accorded the same ranking as claims of an equivalent nature which may be lodged by creditors of the home Member State."[87]

The directive under discussion refrains from tackling, with a properly harmonised set of rules, the issues of substantive law typically connected with cross-border insolvency. The matter is unquestionably the set-off and the possibility for a counterparty (A) of an insolvent institution (B) to compensate its debt towards B by means of its credit vis-a-vis the same entity B. In such a scenario, the Winding-up Directive recognises such a right, so long as it is permitted by the law applicable to the credit institution's claim (Article 23). Similarly, in the case of netting agreements,[88] the matter is entrusted to the law of contract governing such agreements (Article 25).[89]

To conclude, the directive on the reorganisation and winding-up of credit institutions represents a framework addressing bank failures. The degree of alignment it exhibits, however, is limited, aside from the principle of the competence of the country of incorporation of the bank for decisions relating to the commencement of the state of insolvency. Beyond the DGS Directive, the broader and more important aspects of a bank's insolvency remain reserved to the legislation of each respective member state wherein the bank operates by way of its own branches.

BRRD and SRM

The next legislative steps towards a more harmonised approach to the insolvency of credit institutions and investment firms transpired in the BRRD[90] and, for the

87 Article 16(1)(2) of the Insolvency Directive. Any information relating to measures adopted against an institution shall be disseminated using the official language/languages of the home member state (Article 17 of the Winding-up Directive). According to Article 17(2), any creditor that has established a domicile or head office in a country other than the home member state shall lodge a claim in the official language of his/its member state. However, in a slightly incongruous conclusion, the creditor "may be required to provide a translation into that language of the lodgement of the claim." There is no doubt, though, that this ideal option would have caused remarkable organisational issues for the liquidators.

88 Netting agreements are clauses whereby the parties arrange in advance that the different credit and debit transactions occurred with each other every day are not executed on an individual basis, but on a net basis, *i.e.* converted to a net sum or balance. On its turn, the balance, if positive, is given to one party by the other, if negative given by the former to the latter. There are some jurisdictions, such as Italy, where judicial courts at the beginning did not recognise the validity of the netting agreements. See also Chapter 11 below.

89 It is the Collateral Directive that brings about substantive law harmonisation on these two topics. The Collateral Directive requires each member state to ensure that any sum owed under a transaction, or any cash collateral "by sale or appropriation" of the collateral property, shall be "fit" to be set-off. In other words, provisions previously existing in a country not permitting netting or set-off are henceforth prohibited as the matter is harmonised.

90 The first draft of the BRRD was published by the European Commission on 6 June 2012. In full: Proposal for a Directive of the European Parliament and of the Council establishing a framework

eurozone member states, in the SRM. The BRRD has been in force since 1 July 2014 and was implemented into national laws by 1 January 2015.[91] The SRM Regulation becomes operational 1 January 2016. The scope of the BRRD extends to act both as a preventative measure and as a means of managing a bank failure. As a result of the BRRD, national authorities (and, in the case of the SRM: the Single Resolution Board) are empowered to intervene both by taking proactive action in respect to the credit institution, and by reacting when the actual failure occurs.[92]

The rationale behind the BRRD is to stave off any future likelihood that banks will fail in a disorderly manner, by providing a (mandatory) alternative to ordinary national insolvency rules, for such failures "not only pose risks, but could also result in a significant disruption of essential banking functions to citizens, businesses and the wider economy." Additionally, the BRRD, as a bank insolvency proceeding, is aimed to safeguard the essential services and protect certain shareholders, whereas in a normal proceeding, not addressed to banks, the main interest is to maximise creditor value. Stemming from this ontological difference of the two proceedings is the consideration that normal insolvency proceedings can be too lengthy as they involve complex negotiations with creditors, whereas, as far as the BRRD is concerned, the relevant rules are geared towards efficiency rather than fairness to creditors. Of equal importance, normal insolvency proceedings usually take place under objective judicial supervisions, according to a timescale that can be time-consuming depending on the jurisdictions, whereas the resolution measures under the BRRD are taken by the resolution authority only.

Importantly, the directive shall apply to a wide range of institutions: essentially, all credit institutions and investment firms subject to the Capital Requirements legislation (CRD IV and CRR) in addition to financial holding companies.[93] Therefore, the net of potential applicants has been cast relatively wide by the EU

---

for the recovery and resolution of credit institutions and investment firms and amending Council Directives 77/91/EEC and 82/891/EC, Directives 2001/24/EC, 2002/47/EC, 2004/25/EC, 2005/56/EC, 2007/36/EC and 2011/35/EC and Regulation (EU) No 1093/2010, 2012/0150 (COD). A first commentary to the BRRD proposal can be read in.

91 As regards the timing of the transposition of the BRRD in the laws, regulations and administrative provisions of each member state, the deadline was established, for the vast majority of its provisions, for 31 December 2014. Each member state has been permitted to apply the relevant measures starting from 1 January 2015 of Directive 2014/59 (Article 130(1) of the BRRD). The exception to this is the bail-in provisions which application can be delayed by the member states until January 2016.

92 Both the BRRD and the SRM build on global recommendations: the Financial Stability Board's "Key Attributes of Effective Resolution Regimes for Financial Institutions," published in October 2011, and the recommendations on the resolution of a cross-border bank of the Basel Committee on Banking Supervision of March 2010.

As regards the possible friction between bail-out plans and EU state aid rules, see Russo (2012).

93 Article 1(1) of the BRRD. Namely, (a) "institutions that are established in the Union"; (b) "financial institutions that are established in the Union when the financial institution is a subsidiary of a credit institution or investment firm . . . , and is covered by the supervision of the parent undertaking on a consolidated basis . . . "; (c) "financial holding companies, mixed financial holding companies and mixed-activity holding companies that are established in the Union"; (d) "parent financial holding companies in a Member State, Union parent financial holding companies, parent mixed financial holding companies and a member State, Union parent mixed financial holding companies"; (e)

legislator. Remarkably, the BRRD does not only apply to the EU member states, but to the entire European Economic Area (EEA), and the UK too. This is particularly noteworthy as its scope thus includes non-eurozone member states Sweden (and the UK, also in the post-Brexit scenario), whereas the SSM (Single Supervisory Mechanism) and the SRM (Single Resolution Mechanism) are conversely restricted to the eurozone (and countries that wish to accede to the SSM).[94]

The BRRD structure

In essence, the BRRD mainly rests on the following three pillars.

First and foremost, the initial preventive instrument provided under the BRRD is recovery planning. More specifically, in each member state, each financial institution concerned (again, not only credit institutions but also investment firms) must be obliged by law to formulate and maintain "a recovery plan."[95] This plan, to be drawn and maintained by each institution, shall set out measures that the institution may take to improve and, therefore, restore its financial situation, should this suffer a significant deterioration. Although the recovery plan is a document adopted by each financial institution independently, it shall be submitted to the competent authority for review.[96] The recovery plan shall be scrutinised by the competent authority within six months of the submission by the financial institution; the authority shall grant the authorisation to the recovery plan, so long as, mainly, two requisites are met. More specifically: thanks to the implementation of the arrangements proposed in the plan the "viability and financial position of the institution or of the group" can be maintained or restored,[97] and "the plan and specific options within the plan are reasonably likely to be implemented quickly and effectively in situations of financial stress and avoiding to the maximum extent possible any significant adverse effect on the financial system."[98]

The BRRD contains specific provisions for groups. In this respect, the BRRD[99] requires each member state to ensure that the relevant parent undertaking is in charge of drawing up and maintaining a recovery plan relating to the group, rather than the single bank. The group recovery plan shall be scrutinised and authorised by the competent authority after an assessment about its feasibility, according to

"branches of institutions that are established outside the Union in accordance with the specific conditions laid down [in the same directive]."

94 The SSM and SRM have been created in order to safeguard the financial stability in the banking union as a whole or in one or more of its member states concerned, after the so-called eurozone crisis and the risk, particularly acute in 2013, that the banking system of some EU countries could have collapsed under the public debt crisis of their respective countries.

95 Article 5 BRRD.

96 Article 6(1) BRRD.

97 Article 6(2)(a) BRRD.

98 Article 6(2)(b) BRRD.

99 Article 7 BRRD.

rules that, *mutatis mutandis*, are those applicable to the recovery plan of the single bank.[100]

Coupled with the recovery plan is the resolution planning, adopted through a process of collaboration and consultation by the "resolution authority" (all member states need to appoint a resolution authority, *i.e.* an independent public authority which performs the resolution tasks and manages the resolution process[101]).[102] The resolution plan is embraced insofar as the institution in question is, in the eyes of the resolution authority, "resolvable" in case of a crisis, *i.e.* either the financial institution may be liquidated "under normal insolvency proceedings,"[103] without the use of public money,[104] or the crisis can be resolved "by applying the different resolution tools and powers to the institution."[105]

Second, "early intervention measures" must be made available to the resolution authorities operating in each member state.[106] Any contemplation of deploying such measures implies that the financial position of the institution in question has "significantly deteriorated."[107] The specific measures made available in such a scenario are, among others,[108] to require the management body to implement one or more of the measures set out in the recovery plan and, probably the harshest one, the possible replacement, on the recommendation of the supervisor, of the management of the financial institution concerned with a "temporary administrator" appointed to such an end.

Should the aforementioned measures prove ineffective, the powers vested in the resolution authority shall extend to consider even more extreme measures, represented as a group under the third pillar of the BRRD termed "*resolution*."[109]

100 Article 8 BRRD defines "Assessment of group recovery plans."
101 Article 3 BRRD.
102 Article 10 BRRD.
103 See specifically Article 15(1), second part, BRRD.
104 This is a very important condition: the recovery plan implies that there is no "extraordinary financial support beside the use of financial arrangements," nor any "central bank emergency liquidity assistance," nor "any central bank liquidity provided under non-standard collateralisation, tenor and interest rate terms." (Article 15(1) BRRD).
105 See again Article 15(1), second part, BRRD.
106 Article 27 ff BRRD.
107 More specifically, according to Article 27(1) BRRD, when the institution infringes or deteriorates the main parameters set out under CRR.
108 According to the detailed precepts of Article 27 BRRD, measures can be as follows:

a. To require the management body to implement one or more of the measures set out in the recovery plan;
b. To require the management body of the institution "to examine the situation, identify measures to overcome any problems identifies and draw up an action programme to overcome those problems and a timetable for its implementation";
c. To require the management body to convene a meeting of the shareholders, or, alternatively, to convene the meeting ex officio, if the management body failed complying with the request of the authority;
d. To require one member of the management body or senior management to be removed if that person or those persons are found "unfit to perform their duties."

109 Articles 31 ff BRRD.

Conditions for the resolution or, better, for the adoption of one of the "resolution tools" are three: first, the relevant authority must assess "the institution [is] failing or [is] likely to fail"; second, "there is no reasonable prospect that any alternative private sector measures . . . would prevent the failure of the institution within a reasonable timeframe." and third, "a resolution action is necessary in the public interest."[110]

In this scenario, the resolution authorities shall be entitled to use the following five resolution tools:[111] (1) the appointment of a "special manager" taking over the failing institution's management; (2) the sale of the business or the shares of the institution concerned, without the prior approval of the board of directors or the shareholders, to a private sector purchaser;[112] (3) a measure whereby the assets and/or liabilities of the institution at stake are transferred to an alternate entity owned, wholly or partly, by the resolution authority (such an entity is referred to as a "bridge institution");[113] (4) a similar transfer may be effectuated with non-viable assets to a vehicle that is commonly denoted as a "bad bank" (in a process defined as "asset separation");[114] and (5) the final measure – and probably the most controversial contemplated within the BRRD – is the "bail-in tool,"[115] which can mean both the whole or partial conversion of the unsecured claims against the financial institution (*i.e.* in short, debt instruments) into shares, and the write-off, in whole or in part, of existing unsecured claims.[116]

Also, the bank may be recapitalised by write-off, in whole or in part, of the shares in order "to restore its ability to comply with the conditions for authorisation . . . and to continue to carry out the activities for which it is authorised."[117] Nonetheless, the rights of the creditors protected under the DGS Directive to be discussed further shall remain unaffected. Ultimately, the underpinning philosophy of the resolution tools is that "no financial institution shall be unconditionally protected from an orderly market exit."

Having "dissected" the main pillars of the statute under discussion, it is worth mentioning that the BRRD renders mandatory in each member state the set-up of a fund (or more than one), called "resolution financial arrangements," to be financed by way of contributions from all the banks belonging to the system of the country.[118] Fundamentally, the set-up of "resolution financial arrangements"

110 Article 32 BRRD.

111 The "resolution tools" are detailed under Article 37 ff BRRD.

112 Article 37(3)(a) BRRD. The specific modalities of this tool are detailed under Articles 38 and 39 BRRD.

113 Article 37(1)(b). Article 40 and Article 41 BRRD contain the details of this procedure. See, commenting on the draft directive rather than the final statute.

114 Article 37(1)(c) BRRD. For the details of this resolution tool, see Article 42 BRRD.

115 The terminology is reminiscent of the opposite mechanism of the bail-out, which conversely implied the use of the taxpayer money to bail out a credit institution.

116 On possible friction of the directive under discussion with the European Convention on Human Rights, particularly its Article 1, the right to peaceful enjoyment of possessions.

117 Article 43(1)(a) BRRD. Pursuant to Article 43(2)(b) BRRD, such recapitalisation can also be used for the bridge institution and asset management vehicle.

118 Article 100 and Article 103 of the BRRD. The latter law provision refers to "ex-ante contributions," as "contributions . . . raised at least annually from the institutions authorised in their

is aimed to finance the application by the resolution authority of the "resolution tools and powers."[119] On its turn, each member state shall ensure that, by a target date (31 December 2024), the "available financial means" of all the funds (or "financial arrangements," to use the jargon of the Brussels legislator) existing in that country are tantamount to at least 1% of the "covered deposits" of all institutions in that specific member state. In the intention of the EU legislator, the "financial arrangements" existing in each member state are not separate from each other rather they can borrow from each other.[120] The circumstances under which the financial arrangements are entitled to put forward a request of liquidity are exceptional, such as (Article 106(1)) (a) the inability of the amounts raised with the "ex ante contributions" to "cover the losses, costs or other expenses" of that financial arrangement; (b) if the "extraordinary ex-post contributions . . . are not immediately accessible"; and (c) "the alternative funding means . . . are not immediately accessible on reasonable terms."

For the eurozone countries, the financial arrangements just discussed will be used to form a Single Resolution Fund that is created pursuant to the Single Resolution Mechanism Regulation.[121] As stated, the same regulation creates a Single Resolution Board[122] that will act as the European resolution authority and thus be empowered to take the resolution decisions just discussed as regards all cross-border credit institutions and the institutions comprising the SSM. The national resolution authorities[123] assist the SRB by preparing and implementing the resolution decisions, as instructed by the SRB, and take the decisions about the resolution of less significant credit institutions.[124]

---

territory including Union branches." These contributions shall be proportionate to the amount of the liabilities of the institution concerned, excluding the own funds, minus the "covered deposits," "with respect to the aggregate liabilities (excluding own funds) less covered deposits of all the institutions authorised in the territory of the Member State" (Article 103(2) BRRD).

In addition to the "*ex ante* contributions," the BRRD (more specifically Article 104) refers to the "ex post contributions," which are additional contributions that the credit institutions taking part in a financial arrangement may be asked to pay, if the available financial means "are not sufficient to cover the losses, costs or other expenses incurred by the use of the financial arrangements."

Finally, Article 105 BRRD refers to "alternative funding means," as a mechanism whereby financial arrangements in each country shall be allowed to "contract borrowings or other forms of support from institutions, financial institutions or other third parties" in cases where both the *ex ante* contributions and the ex-post contributions were not adequate "to cover losses, costs or other expenses" incurred by the use of that specific financial arrangement.

119 Article 100(1) of the BRRD.

120 Article 99, in terms of principle, and Article 106, as to the specific law provision. More specifically, on the one hand, financial arrangements existing under specific jurisdictions are entitled to make a request to borrow from other financial arrangements and (Article 106(1)), on the other hand, financial arrangements shall have the power to lend to other financial arrangements (Article 106 (2)).

121 Article 67(1) SRM Regulation.

122 Henceforth SRB.

123 The role of the national resolution authority has been highlighted above.

124 Article 96 SRM Regulation.

To conclude, the legislative "bazookas," as originally conceived and implemented to cope with bank failures are aimed to preventing a bank insolvency or, if the insolvency actually materialises, to minimise the negative repercussions thereof.[125] Without these measures, mainly preventive rather than remedial, the insolvency of the bank would require the government to "step up to the plate," through an onerous deployment of public money. As a result of the BRRD and SRM, the authorities are now provided with a serious set of "weapons," allowing them to intervene "early and quickly" in relation to the unsound or failing institution.[126] It is hoped that these tools, briefly described earlier in this part, from the softer ("recovery and resolution planning") to the harshest ("resolution tools"), will achieve a continuity of the critical financial and economic functions of an afflicted institution; perhaps even more importantly, the impact of the failure of that institution on the financial system and, more in general, the economy, should be minimised.

The resolution under BRRD

In the framework of the BRRD, the resolution of the bank is part of a more complex framework of tools of varying degrees, from the more moderate to the most invasive: the latter category includes the bail-in tool, the subject of the present work. The less invasive tools include plans and measures of initial intervention which should suffice to prevent a banking crisis. However, should such measures be insufficient, the powers conferred on the resolution authority shall also include more extreme measures, which include the third pillar of the BRRD and are technically defined as "resolution."[127]

It should be noted that the term "resolution" is not specifically defined in European legislation as a whole. In a sort of circular way, at least from a linguistic point of view, Article 2 of the BRRD merely states that "resolution" means the application of a resolution tool[128] in order to achieve one or more of the resolution objectives,[129] to ensure the continuity of the core functions of the financial institution, avoid severe negative effects on the financial system as a whole, and protect public funds, depositors and investors. The banking resolution tools are, as scholars have emphasised, the sale of businesses, the creation of a bridge entity, the separation of assets, and internal banking recapitalisation, the subject of the present monograph. However, more specifically, concerning the regulation in question, a definition of resolvability is indeed provided in the BRRD.

In accordance with Article 15(1), part 1, BRRD, the resolution authority determines how resolvable an institution is when it is no longer part of a group. The

125 Recital 1 BRRD.

126 Recital 5 BRRD.

127 (de Gioia Carabellese 2019).

128 See Article 37, listed in its English version as "General principles of resolution tools," and Article 58, also listed in its English version as "Temporary public ownership tool," both related to the BRRD.

129 See Article 31(2) BRRD

legal provision then determines that an institution is resolvable if the resolution authority deems it possible or realistic to wind up the financial institution through normal insolvency proceedings or resolve it by applying the ordinary resolution tools and powers, avoiding as much as possible any significantly adverse consequences for the financial system.[130]

The regulation, seemingly transparent, actually confirms that the area between resolution tool and ordinary insolvency proceedings is extremely uncertain and perhaps even manipulated by the EU legislator. After a closer examination of the issue, it can be asserted that a financial institution should be resolvable exclusively in cases where the application of resolution tools may prevent jeopardising effects on the financial system as a whole. Therefore, it appears as though the first part of the definition is unnecessary and possibly contradictory, when comparing the resolution tools with traditional insolvency proceedings. The concrete valuation of resolvability, according to Article 16, BRRD, shall be carried out by the resolution authority at group level. This authority, together with the relevant resolution authority for the subsidiaries, after consulting the consolidating supervisor and the relevant authority of the subsidiaries, shall determine in what measure the groups may be subject to resolution.

After evaluating this, the authorities should avoid any form of assumption which may be biased and could lead to market distortions. More specifically, as can be inferred from Article 16(1), BRRD, in assessing the resolvability, the extraordinary public financial support should not influence the decisions of the resolution authority. Similarly, the central bank providing liquidity assistance should not be involved in the assessment by the regulation authority; nor, lastly, should any central bank providing liquidity assistance be involved in forms of non-standardised collateralisation, both in terms of provisions and also rates of interest.[131]

There are three resolution conditions, or rather conditions for the adoption of one of the resolution tools. Firstly, the relevant authority, namely, the resolution authority, must verify that "the institution [is] failing or [is] likely to fail."

Secondly, it must determine that "there is no reasonable prospect that any alternative private sector measures . . . would prevent the failure of the institution" and this "within a reasonable timeframe." Thirdly, the authority must reach the conclusion that "a resolution action is necessary in the public interest."[132]

Equally important is that the purpose of the resolution is, on the one hand, to prevent disruptions, and therefore damage, in provision of core banking services – essentially, deposits and payment services – and, on the other hand, to restore the economic recovery of the financial institution.[133]

With this aim, the lesson learned throughout the financial crisis still echoes in the financial markets. Bank defaults, as seen during the 2007/2008 financial crisis, can compromise the main and crucial functions of banks as payers which are reliable and

130 Article 15(1)(let. b), par. 1, BRRD.

131 Article 15(1)(let. c), par. 1, BRRD

132 Article 23, BRRD.

133 This is clearly stated in Article 34 of the BRRD, listed in English as "General principles governing resolution."

have sufficient funds: consequences which the BRRD aims at completely preventing. The resolution measures are tools to apply exclusively when faced with severe banking crises.[134] The supervisory authority should make use of them when every other "artillery" instrument (namely, every other supervisory tool) is no longer applicable.[135]

The result of such a brief description can be determined by reading in the legislative text of the directive that the only alternative to the resolution is the winding-up of the credit institution. It is self-evident that such liquidation does not prevent the crisis but rather marks the end of the bank as an entity which carries out entrepreneurial activities. Article 32, BRRD, prescribes that a resolution action shall be undertaken only when the resolution authority determines that all three conditions of Article 32 have been complied with.

In this scenario, and only when the relevant conditions have been complied with, the resolution authorities shall be entitled to exercise the five following resolution tools:[136]

- The appointment of a special manager to manage the failing bank;
- The sale of the business, *i.e.* the shares of the financial institution in question, without the prior approval of the administrative body or the board, to a private sector purchaser;[137]
- A measure by means of which the assets and/or liabilities of the financial institution in question are transferred to an alternative entity owned, in whole or in part, by the resolution authority, this institution being referred to as a bridge institution;[138]
- A similar transfer which can be carried out with regard to non-viable assets to what is commonly referred to as a bad bank; in this case, the relevant procedure shall be defined as "asset separation";[139]
- The final measure, and probably the most controversial one enshrined in the BRRD, namely, the bail-in tool, also known as the internal rescue tool.

2.3.3 The resolution mechanism

The relevant legal provision is, at a European level, Article 32 of the BRRD, together with Article 57 of the SRMR.

The credit institution is failing or likely to fail in the following circumstances:

- There are administrative irregularities or violations of legal, regulatory or statutory provisions which regulate the activity of the entity that are of such severe nature that they would revoke the license for exercising the activity;

134 Article 32 (1)(a) of the BRRD asks whether the credit institution «has failed or is likely to fail.
135 (de Gioia Carabellese 2019).
136 The resolution tools are listed in detail in Article 37 ff. of the BRRD.
137 Article 37(3)(a), BRRD.
138 Article 37(1)(b), Article 40 and Article 41, BRRD.
139 Article 37(1)(c), BRRD.

- There are very severe capital losses, so much so that they could deprive the bank of its entire capital or a significant part thereof;
- The liabilities outweigh the assets;
- The bank fails to pay back its own debts at maturity;
- Objective elements indicate that one or more of the events presented in points a), b), c) and d) will occur in the near future;
- The granting of special financial public support in their favour will be carried out.

In light of this, it is clear that the requirements which must be met for a resolution to be granted are very broad in scope, ultimately stretching from mere administrative irregularities to insolvency, including illiquidity.

Based on the legal framework of reference of the BRRD, the relevant authorities in the area of resolution, *i.e.* the Single Resolution Board for the banks under the direct supervision of the ECB[140] and the National Resolution Authority for national credit institutions, enjoy great powers in the event of a banking institution being in a situation of failing or likely filing.

These powers are so great that the themes of responsibility or accountability take on a potentially crucial role in relation to creditor protection. The greater and deeper the area of responsibility of the SRB, the greater in theory the protection for creditors; however, at the moment, the unfavourable protection resulting from the decisions of the Single Resolution Board can be explained through the level of efficiency and of detail of the existing legal appeals or decisions by the SRB itself.

It is then noted that, given the special nature of certain tasks, the parliaments of the member states can ask the Board to reply in writing to the observations or questions concerning the functions of the Board itself.[141]

As regards the set of powers, two aspects are especially remarkable. Firstly, the Resolution Authority, and in particular the Single Resolution Board, is given a set of limited powers, which is typical in the tradition of the surveillance authority in the banking sector, which are deep, limited and binding. As regards the "super binding nature" or "reinforced binding nature" of the relevant rulings, the maxim *ipse dixit* (therefore, he said and no one can raise any objection) can be employed to describe how to synthesise what the resolution authority operates. Its determinations go far beyond the traditional powers of an agency, the traditional watchdog.[142]

The new body is slowly taking the form of a two-faced Janus, who not only acts as a "watchdog" but also as the judge himself. The Board, the head of the agency and the law of the European Union, rationalises the functions of this authority through a distribution among national and supranational offices.

Not only that, but the decisions of this judge-authority, an authority which also operates as a judge, with regard to a credit to "rescue" or "kill," can even give rise to potential interference with the credit market. Admittedly, the objective of the

140 (Houben and Vandenbruwaene 2017).
141 Article 45, SRM Regulation.
142 (de Gioia Carabellese 2019).

banking resolution is, so it seems, to ensure the continuity of banking activities. However, inevitably, by doing so, the resolution authority indirectly becomes a market operator. The resolution authority, underpinning this administrative power, is the bearer of a public interest. This public interest, which in theory can take on extreme forms, at first sight collides with the interests of private subjects involved in the crisis, in particular the creditors and shareholders referred to in the analysis of the present book.

Secondly, as a consequence of the powers typical of an administrative, quasi-judging body being conferred to the resolution authority, it becomes clear why the regulation and body of laws which established such resolution bodies are so detailed. The organisation of these resolution bodies (the Single Resolution Board, at a European level, and the resolution authority at a national level) is not discussed, as this would not be relevant to the relationship between internal banking recapitalisation and the rights of creditors and shareholders. However, as a mere reference to the regulatory sources and the literature, both national and international, which has analysed the bodies mentioned here, it will suffice to outline the main traits of a figure which, albeit quite recently founded, is already consolidated in its regulation, as well as in its diverse but also contradictory aspects.

The management system for a banking crisis solution is structured at two levels, namely, the central, European level and the national level, depending on whether, after complying with the first pillar of the European Union, the bank in crisis is subject to "direct jurisdiction" by the European Central Bank or the National Central Bank. The first case scenario is founded on the Single Resolution Mechanism, while the second scenario, due to decisions of national jurisdiction, is regulated by the national law of each member state, in accordance with the principles referred to in the BRRD. The difference between the two systems can also be noted in the legal appeals.[143]

2.3.4 Creditors' protection

Undeniably, one of the main pillars of the new regulation introduced by the BRRD is the "no creditor worse off"[144] principle. In a work focusing on the relationship between the resolution tools and creditors, an analysis of the NCWO principle is crucial, in that this instrument, also defined as a "scheme," can be comprehensively assessed only in light of a specific analysis of the principle in question. It should be noted in advance that the analysis of the NCWO principle in this chapter is carried out, primarily, in accordance with Italian law and Italian regulation, but also with English and Spanish law.

Creditors are excluded from participation in the actual proceedings. The insolvency assessment, the verified lack of alternative situations, and the declaration of lack of public interest in the resolution, are all proceedings of legal situations

143 (de Gioia Carabellese 2019).
144 Henceforth NCWO.

which grant little participation to the subjects affected by the resolution measure, who would have an interest in taking part in order to protect their own positions. The bodies of the entity are themselves excluded from the procedure, although it is self-evident that they would have an interest in participating. In contrast, in ordinary winding-up procedures, stakeholders are involved simultaneously in the decision-making process, whereby their claims can only be subsequent. Even harsher judgements come from Italian scholars with regard to the unprofitable nature of the compensation mechanism of the NCWO principle.

The "no creditor worse off" principle is allegedly a form of protection within the system, aimed at providing a restoration from a capital point of view but insufficient to safeguard other needs and/or claims the creditors are entitled to. For example, it is easily noted that a shareholder who has been stripped of their own shareholding in a manner in excess of what was necessary, in accordance with the principle in question, shall be entitled to demand compensation equal to the value lost, in a scenario in which the right to veto or of option are lost.

Ultimately, the NCWO principle, clearly, does not cover rights which are not liable to economic appreciation. However, also with regard to such protection, there are certain perplexities concerning the way the instrument was designed. Shareholders and holders of debt instruments may experience further economic damage: the increase in value of the instruments following the adoption of tools aimed at healing the institution.

This can be viewed through the lens of the property law regime, where in the current framework a similar form of protection is lacking. From a more practical perspective, there are further perplexities. The NCWO principle operates on the basis of a hypothetical judgement: the advantage of the shareholder or creditor pictured in advance in a different insolvency procedure. This implies a technical assessment which is performed within the banking resolution proceedings. It should be noted that the criteria based on which the estimation of the hypothetical treatment should be carried out are rather vague. It is correctly noted that Article 88 "operates as a sort of blank cheque which does not refer, however, to another (more) precise regulation, but merely to a technical instrument, devoid of any legal connotation." The provisions on the NCWO principle, from the point of view of Italian law (just to cite one of the EU legislations), which also reflects European law, as the BRRD is reflected, may lack the assessment criteria which enable creditors and shareholders to uphold and protect their subjective rights in accordance with a specific legal framework. The regulation can therefore be described as vague and uncertain.[145]

Property right under international legislation

Another quintessential right is the property rights recognised both from the European Union and European Charter of Human Rights.

145 (de Gioia Carabellese 2019).

To elaborate, the body of law on the right to property, or rather possession, in accordance with Article 1 of Protocol 1, rules that the ECtHR shall use national laws as leverage to establish what is "a possession," as clarified in *Marckx v Belgium*.[146]

In the case at hand, the claimant had questioned the legitimacy of the provisions of the Belgian Civil Code, then in force, which prescribed that a child born outside marriage had no rights on the property of the mother, who in the case at issue had passed away. The child had the status of heir, but only as "exceptional heir," and therefore to be added in to the possession of the property they had to pursue legal action. And even in that instance, the child was entitled only to three fourths of the property, in the event of the mother having relatives still alive. The child, it was ruled, was not entitled to any of the property as long as, and unless, the mother had not passed away and had not left the property to the child, as required by Belgian law; therefore, no claim could have been brought before the State as violation of the right to property of the child. In certain cases, however, the court has applied the rule of "autonomous meaning" in the interpretation of the concept of property.[147]

In *Gasus Dosier-Und Fordertechnik GmbH v Netherlands*,[148] the claimant lamented the fact that the Dutch authorities had interfered with the right to property through the seizure of the goods the petitioner possessed. This seizure, according to the explanations of the Dutch authorities, had to continue until the purchaser of the goods, in the case at hand the unfortunate claimant, paid the taxes owed to the Dutch government. The government argued that, in accordance with Dutch law, the person to whom the goods had been sold was the true owner and the retention of the title by the claimant could be qualified as security interest.[149]

The court has reiterated in *Stran Greek Refineries v Greece*[150] that the term "possession" in accordance with Article 1 of Protocol 1 can cover monetary assets. The ruling at issue continues by saying that the owner of the property shall also have a legitimate expectation of the use of the possession. It follows that, to be qualified as a possession, a credit should be sufficiently activatable in accordance with national law.[151]

It is clear that an ordinary, non-guaranteed creditor has no right to the property of the debtor; however, it must also be acknowledged that the right of the creditor to ask the debtor for a payment constitutes a property, or better still a possession, as demanded *de minimis* by the European Convention. It can be claimed, therefore, that credits deriving from eligible liabilities in accordance with the provisions of the bail-in tool, in particular regarding obligations, constitute the property of

146 Case 17849/91 *Pressos Compania Naviera SA v Belgium Series* A 332 (1996) 21 EHRR 301, para 31.

147 (Allen 2005).

148 [1995] 20 EHRR 403.

149 (de Gioia Carabellese 2019).

150 Series A No 301-B (1995) 19 EHRR 293. In English, references to the ruling can be found in: (Fietta and Upcher 2013; Werlauff 2002).

151 Series A No 301-B (1995) 19 EHRR 293 para 63.

debtors.[152] However, in this scenario, the credit claim may indirectly comply with the parameter of the European Convention, through the regulatory procedural provisions, which guarantee to the creditor broad and persuasive forms of protection. With regard to the shareholder, the result is the same, although the reasoning seems to be even more direct and immediate.

As the shareholder is both owner and creditor, based on the general principles of company law, it can be affirmed that the potential friction between the shareholder of the bank subject to internal rescue and the rights referred to in the European Convention on Human Rights is even more direct. The first ruling worth noting is *Olczak v Poland*,[153] in which the principle whereby the shareholder owns a share of the company together with its relative rights was affirmed. Among these is the right to a share of the liquidation, together with other unconditional rights, including the right to vote and monitor corporate assets.[154]

The *Marckx* case,[155] in general, and more specifically the *Grainger* case, which concerned Northern Rock, better defined the scenario of possession, or ownership of a right. Northern Rock is the pioneering bail-in case *sui generis*, arranged by the British government in relation to the insolvency of the bank of Newcastle upon Tyne, in north-east England, in the summer of 2007.

Tragically, Northern Rock, now deceased commercially, shares with the Royal Bank of Scotland, still active in Edinburgh but *de facto* a nationalised entity, the sad record of being the first financial institution to be struck by the 2007/2008 financial crisis, at least in Europe.

In *Grainger*, the crisis of Northern Rock, which specialised in granting credit, the bank became illiquid in August 2007, with the subsequent intervention of the three British authorities then existing in the British banking supervision framework: HM Treasury, the Bank of England, and the Financial Services Authority.

It became apparent, as the months passed, that the intervention with support aid from the Bank of England, as a lender of last resort, was ineffective, given that the insolvency was worsening. Consequently, in February 2008, temporary nationalisation of the Newcastle credit institution was put into place, which then became permanent as a result of the Banking Special Provisions Act. In March 2008, the Northern Rock plc Compensation Scheme Order delegated to a technocrat the task of calculating the amount due to the shareholders, on the inescapable assumption that there would be no business continuity.

In December 2009, however, the technocrat informed the shareholders that nothing was due to them. This ruling was appealed by a group of shareholders before the European Court of Strasbourg, primarily for a violation of Article 1 of the additional Protocol. According to the claimants, the right to fair compensation had been illegally deleted, whereby upon nationalisation of the bank such shares had

152 Briefly, it may be recalled that in English common law, and also in the mixed Scottish legal system, there is no codification of general capital responsibility.

153 Case 30417/96 of 7 November 2002.

154 (de Gioia Carabellese 2019).

155 Case 6833/74, *Marcks v Belgium*, 1979, 13 June 1979.

a value of 90 pence, with a total capitalisation of 379 million pounds. The present focus is not on the ruling of the case, which is very questionable, namely, that the court ruled that the appeal was deemed inadmissible, but rather on the statement to be found in the provisions of the judges, declaring and acknowledging in a preliminary view a direct property right on the shares, ascribable to the shareholders.

The presumption of the decision, albeit unfavourable to the claimant, confirms the broad meaning of the concept of property on the part of the judges.

The Northern Rock shareholders also lost in the legal case before the English courts. In relation to the NCWO principles, the shareholders of the Newcastle credit institution brought a legal action based on the violation of Section 62(2) of the Banking Act 2009. The Court of Appeal, the second instance judge, ruled that the assessment of shares as equal to zero carried out by an independent assessor was incorrect, even if based on the NCWO principles.[156]

Provided that the right to a share is not necessarily classified as property in company law, it should be noted that the court, between the two "factions," seems to have sided with the non-technical, quite broad, concept of property, which appears to include immaterial goods too – namely, shares. The statements of the judges, in a context where the BRRD had not yet been promulgated, may have been influenced by the reassurance of the British government and by the belief that the case would be an isolated one; this was overwhelmingly refuted by the many cases of cancellation of shares recorded in Europe in less than five years following the application of the BRRD. It must be stressed that the concept of autonomous meaning adopted by the European Court also covers circumstances not attributable to the national legal systems, and therefore, it would have an autonomous scope, irrespective of the legal qualifications of a national legal system.

In light of these observations listed, both shares and credits would ensure that owners receive protection from the European Convention.

The bail-in tool may also give rise to frictions with other international sets of laws, not only the European Convention, which has already been discussed in the present chapter. Another supranational body of laws to be taken into consideration is the European legislation itself, particularly the treaties.[157]

In fact, the interaction between the BRRD and the body of laws of the EU is perhaps conceptually the first evaluation to carry out in terms of creditor protection, as the BRRD is a legislative tool which is included in a larger body of laws, based on Treaties the European Banking Scheme is by now a consolidated phenomenon as a result of the 2007/2008 financial crisis. The Charter of Nice, in Article 17, does not "sign a blank cheque" for the legislator, not even for the European legislator, to grant him private – and subversive, we can add – forms of property. As highlighted more recently in Italian literature, private property "is limited by the higher collective interest but cannot be completely altered outside of legal provisions and without the payment of the fair compensation within reasonable time."

156 *Harbinger Capital Partner v Caldwell and Another* [2013] EWCA Civ 492.

157 (de Gioia Carabellese 2019).

It is, however, true that the management of banking crises designed by the BRRD alters the relationships between fundamental rights and fundamental property rights, or at the very least leads to a new balance with fundamental rights.

The interference between the Charter of Nice and the bail-in tool was noticed by the European legislator even during the drafting of the directive. In Recital 13 of the BRRD such concern becomes manifest.

Another legal provision of the Charter of Nice is of interest, namely, Article 52, paragraph 1, which specifies that potential limitations to the enjoyment of the rights enshrined in the Charter may be applied only under one fundamental condition: these limitations of the fundamental right to property must occur: (1) in accordance with the principle of proportionality, and (2) only if necessary to achieve objectives of general interest recognised by the Union or to protect the rights and freedoms of others.

Mutatis mutandis, as regards the BRRD, after a crisis resolution of a failing institution, the investors are subject to interventions on the part of the public authority, which can be comparable to the interference of the right to property. Therefore, their analysis of legality should not be neglected by the law of the Union, indeed based on the provisions referred to in Article 345, TFEU, which sets forth the principle of neutrality as follows: the EU treaties do not decide whether a company is in private or public ownership. Consequently, as noted in the literature, member states themselves are responsible for the regulation of the right to property.[158]

However, this notion is not completely clear, in that there are two possible interpretations: on the one hand, a literal one, which highlights the legal nature of the owner; on the other, a finalistic and economic interpretation which encompasses every measure allowing the state, through intervention in the public sector, to contribute to arranging the national economic activity.

Though it is an absolute right compared to the relative right of origin, it may not be very enticing from an economic point of view which is far from a balancing situation of credits. In the two main cases of conversion of rights referred to in the BRRD, there appears to be an enhanced limitation of rights, in a framework which does not appear to fall into the legality framework envisaged by Article 45, TFEU.

The relationship between the Charter of Nice and the Convention develops on an equal level of co-existence but goes far beyond its starting point. As a result of Article 52, paragraph 3, of the Charter of Nice, if the Charter "contains rights which correspond to rights guaranteed by the Convention for the Protection of Human Rights and Fundamental Freedoms, the meaning and scope of those rights shall be the same as those laid down by the said Convention. This provision shall not prevent Union law providing more extensive protection." This disposition is defined as a disposition of equivalence, based on which the Charter shall be applied so that the level of protection ensured by the Charter to the rights also protected by the ECHR is at least equivalent to the protection guaranteed by the aforementioned tool: therefore, the European Convention constitutes a sort of "floor." By contrast,

158 (de Gioia Carabellese 2019).

the guarantee of a higher level of protection by the Charter is admissible. Consequently, there is completely legitimate cross-pollination between the European Convention and the Charter of Nice.

As a consequence of this, the jurisprudence of the European Court of Human Rights is of remarkable importance for the Charter and the judge thereof, the European Court of Justice. Therefore, when judging in the European Union Scheme the regulations in terms of property referred to in Article 345, TFEU, the decisions by the Court of Strasbourg may certainly be taken into consideration.[159]

The "no creditor worse off" principle

The BRRD takes into account the need to maintain proportionality and, therefore, prescribes that in the event of internal banking recapitalisation, no creditor, including shareholders, should be treated worse than he would have been if the bank had undergone an insolvency procedure. This principle is summed up in the English maxim, regrettably not translated into Italian, "no creditor worse off" principle or, in the more laconic acronym, the "principle" or "NCWO scheme," provided for in Article 73 of the BRRD.

The expression indicates, according to the words of the EU Commission itself, that no creditor should be treated, in the resolution, worse than he would have been if the bank had undergone liquidation in the context of the normal insolvency proceedings.[160] The principle acts in two ways: (1) the cancellation, reduction and/or conversion of debt and above all risk capital follow a *sui generis* allocation order of the losses, which is not that of normal insolvency proceedings; (2) the creditors can request compensation if they have not received a sum at least equal to the one they would have received in the context of an insolvency procedure.

Ultimately, the NCWO principle entails an imperative *de iure* replacement: the right of creditors to request payment from the bank being liquidated, according to the insolvency rules, is replaced with the right to request compensation from the resolution fund. The principle is crucial, in the issue being analysed in the present chapter, of violation of fundamental rights, given that the NCWO principle should replace the concept of *par condicio* in a normal procedure. In other words, the *par condicio* is to the judge in an insolvency procedure as the NCWO principle is to the resolution authority.

As regards strict insolvency, there is discussion concerning the legal impact deriving from the anticipation of the effects of insolvent assets. Such a circumstance would be very significant for most scholars, who highlight the fact that, upon the activation of the resolution tools, there would be an anticipation of the insolvency of creditors to the losses "upon the start of the resolution procedure."

Consequently, according to some scholars, the choice of shareholders and creditors between crisis resolution, by means of resolution tools and liquidation

159 (de Gioia Carabellese 2019).

160 Commission, EU Bank Recovery and Resolution Directive (BRRD): Frequently Asked Questions Memo (2014) 297.

proceedings, would not be the same. For others, on the other hand, the bail-in tool is neutral for creditors, as it "determines a 'not worse' situation, compared to the one the creditors would face in the event of a compulsory administrative winding-up." It is also evident, as has been noted by other scholars, that the evicted subject, if a shareholder, "shall not recover the related voting right or that of option, which shall consequently be reduced."

Furthermore, it is added that the evicted party completely and permanently loses the discussed ancillary rights. If the action of the resolution authority is particularly invasive, with the simultaneous application of cancellation, conversion or reduction, with regard to a wide series of liabilities (of debt and capital), it is clear that internal banking resolution in the end leads to an alteration of the structure of corporate governance, which may secretly entail extra-judiciary ends,[161] with consequent potential manipulations of the market.

The assessment with regard to creditors being left worse off is based on a comparison between the sums liquidated to them – as partners and creditors in accordance with the resolution procedure and as a result of an independent assessment – and the sums which such partners and creditors would have received, in theory, in the context of a normal insolvency procedure which actually is non-existent, given that the resolution is aimed at avoiding liquidation.[162]

The EBA published a technical document, in the context of assessing the difference in treatment after the resolution;[163] however, the document does not appear to offer the much-desired forms of protection which, on the other hand, a normal law governed (or at least monitored) by a judge would grant. Beyond hypothetical reassurances, the NCWO principle, however, seems to be a form of protection which is not easy to manage and not completely clear as a concept, in light of the unpredictable and unlimited burden sharing principle which governs the system.

By involving creditors in bearing the fate of the failure of the bank, there is potential confusion between the two categories of stakeholders – namely, the shareholder and the investor. Admittedly, the first category of bank investors, the holders of MREL, are holders of a type of credit which can be compared to that of a shareholder and they are exempted from the "no creditor worse off" rule. MREL is an acronym for minimum requirement for own funds and eligible liabilities, quantified case by case by the supervisory authority in relation to the bank's profile and aimed at covering the losses in the event of a bail-in tool application. In the case of banks of systemic risk, they come with the total loss-absorbing capacity.[164]

161 *Hungarian bank Magyar Kereskedelmi Bank Zrt.* See European Commission, 16 December 2015, C(2015) 9349 final.

162 (de Gioia Carabellese 2019).

163 EBA, Regulatory Technical Standards on valuation for the purposes of resolution and on valuation to determine difference in treatment following resolution under Directive 2014/59/EU on recovery and resolution of credit institutions and investment firms, EBA/RTS/2017/05 e EBA/RTS/2017/06, 23 May 2017.

164 Henceforth TLAC.

Therefore, unlike the other liabilities, which contractually cover business risk, the "MREL-able liabilities" prescribe in advance and make the relevant holder aware that they will be the first to be sacrificed. From this point of view, they seem consistent with the ECtHR principles. The act of expropriation, connected to the application of the internal banking recapitalisation, is contractually provided for with a *caveat emptor* mechanism. However, in the uncertainty of the failure requirement, referred to in the BRRD, and despite the potential differences with the company principles which are traditionally welcomed, the "MREL-able liabilities" appear to meet all the principles of the Convention, bearing in mind that they transparently inform the holder about the further causes, which he accepts, potentially leading to the extinction of the shares or of their conversion. Moreover, the MREL, together with the contingent convertible bonds (referred to as COCOs in this work), may be – and this is the thesis of the present contribution, reiterated here – the silver bullet of internal banking recapitalisation, in a new formula. Therefore, there is no arbitrary power of conversion or cancellation, but rather a simple "contractualisation" of the sacrifice of a category of creditors of the bank, aware of the bail-in tool risk entailed in their shares.[165]

Furthermore, the NCWO principle, far from clarifying the situation, will increase the controversy in light of the fact that the creditors, indeed, will deplore the negative effect on them. This is especially true in legal systems where the creditors (both senior and subordinated) usually comply with the same hierarchical order (*pari passu*), in accordance with normal insolvency procedures, and therefore share the costs.

No less importantly, as the requirement for internal banking recapitalisation is a general failure, which constitutes a very wide concept, the new system of the BRRD is sending shockwaves through the entire corporate system. As noted recently, the bondholders, or more generally the creditors of the bank, are usually holders of a right to credit, in theory also towards the holders of risk capital, and they remain as such until the liquidation if the legal entity, as a result of the insolvency rules. In the case of internal banking recapitalisation, as a result of an alleged failure, a concept which has still not been defined clearly, if not negatively, debtholders and shareholders suddenly become "venture companions," in ways and nuances which are described by the resolution authority, certainly not as a transformation of the cause of origin of the relation (of "corporate contract," in the case of the shareholder, and of "funding contract," in the case of the investor). Such characteristics, when judged against the principles of legality which must be upheld with regard to an act of deprivation of property, in accordance with the ECtHR, give rise to a number of doubts. Next, there is a dilemma concerning the funds with which to compensate the creditors: the governments of the member states will probably take over and provide financial coverage.

However, in this event, intervention seems to cloak the safety net of a normal public bail-out, although through a recourse action, rather than directly. With

165 (de Gioia Carabellese 2019).

regard to this, the BRRD requires that a minimum amount equal to 8% of the total liabilities be rescued internally, prior to intervention by the resolution authority. The decision by the Italian government in 2015[166] to offer full compensation is indicative of a need to strike a balance between public interests and individual property rights. As is well-known, the decision was justified by the public astonishment in the wake of the internal rescue of holders of subordinated bonds in four regional banks, which were not particularly large: the depositors and senior bondholders were exempted from the bail-in tool. Similarly, the Bank of Portugal offered compensation to the creditors who were affected by the re-transferring of bonds from the good bank to the bad bank.[167]

It is claimed in the literature that legislative reforms were necessary as regards the issue of banking crises, considering the serious problems of moral gambling and the costs borne by governments, and therefore by taxpayers, for the financial support offered to the banks in crisis. The BRRD would therefore be part of the concept of mandate for system reform. Indeed, this author claims and has made similar claims in the past, that there is no obligation to externally rescue banks in crisis and that their failure, without any public bail-out, would have eliminated from the market various insolvent financial institutions, thereby giving the economy a chance to recover with different and better prospects. The thesis of those who believe that, as a result of the 2007/2008 bail-out, an implicit mandate of system reform had been conferred imposes a need to carefully analyse the different issues deriving from the system implemented. This system has a cost, which has thus far been paid by the creditors of the bank, including those of capital, whose rights to property have been severely weakened.

It has been mentioned that a state, including an entity such as the EU, can waive the right to property if it can prove that its actions are legal and legitimate. With regard to this, it can be seen that there is a fundamental problem of the BRRD which does not meet the requirements of legality; it lacks consistency and sufficient generality and is applied in a prospective way, leading to disproportionate consequences, due to the fact that the creditors incur larger losses than they would have done in the context of normal insolvency proceedings. In the literature, possible solutions have been proposed regarding the legal risks which by definition are entailed in the internal banking resolution: the *ex post* solution, based on the fund, and the *ex ante* solution, based on a contractual mechanism. The former solution ensures that at the end of the bail-in tool no creditor is negatively affected thanks to ex post compensation, in the terms indicated in the following; in the latter, ad hoc financial tools are promoted whose purpose is to enable banks and creditors to decide for themselves, ex ante, how losses should be absorbed, through contractual instruments.

166 It is the decree adopted by the Italian economy and finance Secretary on 22 November 2015. Based on these, resolution plans were adopted to manage the financial distress of four major Italian banks: (1) Banca delle Marche, (2) Banca popolare dell'Etruria e del Lazio, (3) Cassa di Risparmio di Ferrara, (4) Cassa di Risparmio della Provincia di Chieti. These credit institutions were called "The 'Four Banks,'" see de Gioia Carabellese (2021).

167 (de Gioia Carabellese 2019).

The fact that there is no equivalent "no shareholder worse off" principle[168] leads us to believe that the principle cannot be applied to the shareholders of the bank subject to internal banking recapitalisation. Therefore, they are disadvantaged straightaway, with no form of protection, not even that which is in theory provided for in the BRRD thanks to the principle of the NCWO principle. And indeed, also arguing from the standpoint of corporate principles, it is without doubt that the shareholder is not a creditor, according to civil law, and therefore he does not actually enjoy the protection related to the application of the NCWO principle, simply because he is outside the boundaries of this definition.

That being said, it is difficult to trace back the reasons that, abstractly, the shareholder shall not benefit from the NCWO principle, as he is formally excluded from it. A legislator must assume that by definition the shareholder, in a situation of subsequent insolvency of the bank and, therefore, of liquidation, would receive nothing or hardly anything from that type of procedure, hence the uselessness of an equivalent NSWO principle.

Apart from believing that this circumstance is very common but is not a rule, it is not completely clear why there must be such a pre-insolvency priority order, in the event of a resolution procedure. If the value of the shares of the shareholder of the bank which underwent or is about to undergo resolution is close to zero, as a result of the current situation, he has already been negatively affected, especially in the case of quoted shares. In this scenario the "expropriation" of the shares would theoretically appear as an excessive act toward a subject and would have the sole purpose of penalising him, without any specific reason. In actual fact, beyond such theoretical discussion, it can be stated that the declared absence of a "no shareholder worse off" principle is perhaps due to the laziness of the legislator or, considering the frequent absence of technical terms in the BRRD, its inability to grasp the need for such conceptual boundaries. After reading certain recitals of the BRRD, it would be even clearer that there is a need to protect shareholders with a similar mechanism to the NCWO. This, in light of the legal cases collected in the first five years of the BRRD, should lead us to believe that an NSWO principle does indeed exist.[169]

The ex post *compensation through resolution funds*

In accordance with the BRRD and Regulation EU 806/2014, all member states, "to allow the resolution authority to apply or exercise effectively the resolution instruments and powers," shall establish "financing mechanisms" or national funds which are funded with *ex ante* annual contributions, paid by the authorised entities of their territories. Therefore, national funds have been established at a "community" level, in Italy with Legislative Decree 180/2015, Article 78, at the Bank of Italy. The funds in question constitute "national divisions" of the Single

168 Henceforth NSWO Principle.
169 (de Gioia Carabellese 2019).

Resolution Fund[170] provided for in Regulation EU 806/2014 and in force since 1 January 2016 in the context of the Single Resolution Mechanism. The national funds, after an eight-year transitional period, will gradually be merged with the transfer of the contributions collected, at a national level, to the SRF in accordance with the modalities set out in distinct intergovernmental agreements between member states adhering to the banking union. In the context of the resolution, the SRF is authorised to (1) offer a guarantee for the assets or liabilities of an institution undergoing a resolution; (2) grant the institution in question loans or purchase its assets; (3) contribute in establishing a bridge institution or a management vehicle of the assets; (4) compensate shareholders or creditors, pursuant to Article 75 of the BRRD; (5) recapitalise the credit institution under resolution, as an alternative to the bail-in tool; and (6) grant loans to other resolution funds.

With regard to the following analysis proposed, concerning the issues of legitimacy of the bail-in rules, it is emphasised that resolution funds can also be used to avoid non-proportionate results, deriving from the application of procedures provided for in the BRRD.

Essentially, and with reference to the assumption that no creditor can be compromised, the use of the resolution fund can facilitate compensation for a shareholder or creditor for their most severe losses, compared to the possible ones in a scenario of liquidation in accordance with the normal insolvency proceedings. For an effective functioning of the funds, and to ensure that they can dispose of appropriate amounts of money, it is ruled that, by 31 December 2024, the available financial resources shall reach at least 1% of the total protected deposits of all authorised institutions in the territory.[171]

Where the financing mechanisms or Funds have carried out cumulative disbursements equal to a percentage above 0.5% of the deposits protected pursuant to the BRRD of all authorised credit institutions in the respective territories, the member states are allowed to delay the initial period for a maximum of four years. In this respect, a delegated regulation of the EU Commission, the Commission Regulation on Resolution Financing Arrangements,[172] referred to as RFA, provides guidelines on the structure of resolution funds. As mentioned, the financing activity is supported by *ex ante* contributions by the banks; the contributions are collected until the objective level is reached. The contributions to the resolution fund are calculated based on the size of the institution, which is determined by the total amount of its liabilities, with the exclusion of own funds and guaranteed deposits.[173]

Larger banks are asked for larger contributions, whose total amount, however, must not exceed 30% of the total contributions collected by the fund. This basic contribution is then adjusted to the risk profile of the institution, which is calculated

170 Henceforth SRF.

171 Article 102 BRRD.

172 In English, Commission Delegated Regulation 2015/63/EU of 21 October 2014 supplementing Directive 2014/59/EU of the European Parliament and of the Council with regard to ex ante contributions to resolution financing arrangements [OJ L11/44] (RRF).

173 Article 5 RFA.

by bearing in mind the four fundamental pillars: (1) risk of exposure, (2) stability and variety of financing sources, (3) importance of the institution in relation to the stability of the financial system and (4) indicators of additional risk which can be determined by the resolution authority.

It is, however, acknowledged that the smaller credit institutions have a low risk profile and resort to resolution funds less often and, therefore, cannot be subject to the same risk adjustment systems, which is why they are asked to pay lump sums as down payments for every additional risk.[174] In the context of the European banking union, the small banks, which make up 1% of total assets, contribute 0.3% of total contributions.

Admittedly, the resolution funds can dilute the contributions in time as gradually as possible, until an objective is reached; however, such dilutions must take into due account the phases of the cycles of business and the impact that pro-cyclical contributions may have on the financial situation of the paying institutions.[175] If during a crisis the funds are insufficient, despite each institution meeting its objective, the resolution authorities may ask for ex post contributions to cover losses, costs and other expenses.[176]

However, as long as the funds are less than those referred to in the level-objective, the intervention powers of the resolution funds are reduced, and in such a scenario, it will take years for the objective in question to be reached. It had been predicted in the literature[177] that in 2018 many banks which had not fully recovered from the 2007/2008 financial crisis would still be continuing to struggle when pursuing the objective of stability. The prediction was accurate: the resolution authorities were unable to keep up with resolution requests, and therefore, governments intervened in the rescue operations with the disbursement of public money, resorting de facto to the public bail-out tool, which is what the BRRD conceptually strove to avoid. The mechanism of a resolution fund can be criticised both from a financial and a legal standpoint.

The first aspect is self-evident due to a regulation, the BRRD, whose objective, in theory, is to eliminate the risk of new public bail-outs, such as the catastrophic one which struck the Scottish bank RBS. The most daunting doubt for a legal expert actually concerns the structure of the resolution tools, fed with private financial resources, with a preventive self-financing mechanism which may indirectly give rise to a form of public intervention which the BRRD dreaded.[178]

The ex ante *negotiation of resolution tools*

The principle of non-compromised credit, designed by the BRRD, is aimed at mitigating the reasons of the creditor, in the event of a suppression (or more

174 Article 10 RFA.
175 Article 102(2) BRRD.
176 Article 104 BRRD.
177 (Maguze 2016).
178 (de Gioia Carabellese 2019).

appropriately, the cancellation or conversion) of his rights. In the decisions made thus far by the authorities, the evaluation mentioned has not been used much, in some cases becoming a mere pro forma, for objective difficulties in collecting the necessary funds to pay the compromised creditors, although, if sufficient, they would only solve the problems related to the legitimacy of the bail-in rules and, more generally, those deriving from disproportionate results.

However, the loopholes in the general rules of internal banking recapitalisation seem to constitute analogous illnesses of a human being, which require not the ordinary treatments of a compassionate local doctor, but rather the judgement of the most specialised surgeon, given the countless genetic pathologies of the BRRD, the "human body" in question, in relation to the protection of fundamental rights detailed in the body of laws of the ECHR. The criteria concerning excludable liabilities remain, sufficiently and perhaps too generic, and the BES case, described earlier, seems to confirm that the power of an administrative authority in this area is very broad, in terms of technical discretion. More generally, the administrative authority can take actions which go against the *pari passu* principle, insofar as creditors present in the same class of shares can be treated differently. The recent cases confirm that the BRRD, even if one excludes its insolvent nature, which seems agreeable, neglects the *pari passu* principle, in simple terms, technocratically and not legally.

The BRRD was created after the 2007/2008 financial crisis, and perhaps due to its emotional drive: the revenge of politicians on bankers, for having been undeservedly rescued with public money. In taking such revenge, the European legislator has perhaps gone too far, designing a mechanism which seems controversial, in that it suppresses, by administrative means and with considerable discretion, the rights of creditors of the credit institution, with uncertain judicial protections. The potential violation of fundamental rights referred to in the ECHR seems evident: the BRRD, epistemologically, marks the victory of the public sector (and therefore the suppression *sic et simpliciter* of the rights to credit) over the private creditor, who by contrast has always expected – hitherto – that such suppression could only occur with the closure of the undertaking.

In contrast to bankers being rescued in 2007/2008 and then heavily reprimanded in 2014, for a balancing of what is provided for in the BRRD, the Supervisory Authority is asked to play its role in a less invasive way so as to leave more leeway for autonomous negotiation. Although this area of the law seems completely outdated or even subject to the unrelenting attack of the public, the contractual approach offers the greatest protection to creditors who, at present, due to the resolution actions, are severely compromised. The supervisory authority is asked to adopt, regarding the bail-in tool, a contractual approach, quite the reverse of the regulatory approach, which, by definition, must comply with stricter legitimacy requirements. This regulatory approach would help to prevent violation of property rights, which constitutes the sword of Damocles hanging not only over the feasibility of the bail-in procedure but also over its very legitimacy. Currently, COCOs offer perhaps the best tool to achieve this objective. One proposal among scholars is to guarantee the implementation of the NCWO principle not in an administrative way, and therefore discretionally, but by means of negotiation, through the issuance, planned *ex ante*, of convertible bonds. COCOs constitute hybrid forms of capital which can be converted to normal capital, or be subject to cancellation, in whole or in part, of the main amount due. The banks mostly use COCOs to comply with the requirements of regulatory capital but also to absorb losses, and therefore improve their balance sheet, before becoming insolvent and undergoing resolution proceedings.

The conversion or cancellation operation is connected to the occurrence of a predeterminate event, known as a "trigger," usually related to the financial situation of the issuer. The trigger can be automatic or discretional. An automatic trigger is activated when the capital of the banking enterprise falls below a certain amount, based on the share capital book value or on its market value.

Conversely, a discretional trigger is activated by a supervisory authority which deems the banking institution insolvent or in an irreversible situation.

After the 2007/2008 financial crisis, the European governments encouraged the use of COCOs to comply with capital requirements, and consequently issued a regulation aimed at regulating the bonds in question, in compliance with the Capital Requirements Directive (CRD) and the Capital Requirements Regulation (CRR), together with the CRD IV, which sets out the minimum capital requirements for the banks. The European COCO market highlights a continual and growing trend, according to which, starting from 93 billion euros between 2013 and 2016, it is expected to reach the 226-billion-euro target by 2020, although the complexities of the current rules of the specific issue may compromise their effectiveness and destroy the financial position of banks in crisis. For the purposes of the CRR, COCOs are eligible for the treatment as Additional Tier 1 Capital (AT1) or Tier 2 Capital (T2), in relation to their characteristics. Section 1 of Chapter 3 of the CRR sets out the requirements with which the financial instruments must comply, in order to be qualified as AT1 capital.[179]

The criteria with which the financial instruments must comply to be eligible as T2 capital are less strict and are specified in Section 3 of Chapter 4 of the CRR. Again, it is interesting to note that COCOs which are eligible as T2 financial instruments: they (1) are subordinated to the credits of all non-subordinated creditors, (2) do not ensure or benefit from any of the agreements which otherwise would bring forward their level of seniority and (3) have a five-year expiration of origin.[180]

Regarding the rules listed, it is noted, first and foremost, that as the normal holders of COCOs are well aware of the risk of losing the amount of credit they have, the CRR allows banks to not carry out payment of the coupon; this is also in order to avoid violating the capital requirement. Consequently, the creditors may lose not only the capital sum, but also the interest.

179 (de Gioia Carabellese 2019).
180 Article 63 CRR.

Secondly, in AT1 COCOs, the uncertainty regarding the possibility of creditors having their capital returned is highlighted, unless the bank exercises the option, which is incidentally subject to the approval of the supervisory authority. The advocates of this financial tool do not find any absolute certainties about COCOs.

However, the tool in question seems to be a suitable mechanism for loss absorption, as it facilitates recapitalisation of insolvent institutions, while at the same time guaranteeing to the creditors their property rights. Specifically, it is noted that the conversion or cancellation of COCOs is set in advance between issuers and investors. By contrast, the bail-in tool is applied and managed by a public authority in all its aspects, also including those relevant to the conversion or cancellation, with powers whose exercise meets the limits set by the current regulations in this area, which are, incidentally, completely generic. Apart from the liabilities excluded by law, the creditors, in the case of the bail-in tool, do not know in advance whether their credit will, so to speak, be selected for the tool and therefore cannot negotiate for a coupon which reflects the risk or gives a conversion to a particular rate.[181]

In particular, COCOs offer the investor the chance to know in advance not only whether the loss will be absorbed through the conversion or cancellation but also the situation determining the conversion or cancellation (trigger) and, in the case of the conversion, the related rate.

Moreover, COCOs offer the issuers the same advantages and, more importantly, the possibility of controlling the trigger point which enables them to avoid failure, with the precocious absorption of the losses and the delimitation of the losses themselves to a determinate category of debt and the prospect of reducing the cost of further debt. In general, the market would benefit from a type of negotiation autonomy in recapitalisation, given that the role of the public authority is limited. Moreover, the resolution risk and the risk of losing the core functions of the bank are limited by the fact that recapitalisation can take place in a short time, while the bank is still a going concern.[182]

COCOs have a double function: they can be employed within the bail-in scheme and, at the same time, within the micro-system of the MREL; as a part of the capital, they reflect the possibility of absorbing losses and agree to determine the level of the MREL prescribed in accordance with the BRRD.

Therefore, when requesting to a banking institution that an amount of eligible liabilities be kept in COCOs, the surveillance authority, in a bail-in prospect, could achieve its objectives of recapitalisation, and, in the best-case scenario, of orderly resolution of the bank, without resorting to public funds or violating the property rights of creditors. One last question would be the number of COCOs a bank should issue in order to absorb the losses and ensure normal management – a crucial question to which academics have yet to find an answer.[183]

181 Article 63 CRR.

182 (Cahn and Kenadjian 2014).

183 (de Gioia Carabellese 2019).

2.3.5 Moral hazard in the resolution mechanism

Bearing in mind the legal framework of the resolution, it is possible to affirm the following:

- Bail-in tool prevents moral hazard by bankers which is inherent in the public rescue tool;
- Bail-out is a form of moral hazard.

The first sentence is justified by the fact that "any kind of recourse to extraordinary public financial support will now normally entail at least some burden-sharing (and loss absorption) by shareholders and creditors."

By contrast, bail-out undermines market discipline that is the antithesis of the concept itself. Moreover, it destabilises public finance and public debt.

Thus, it is the time to analyse the concept of moral hazard. It is well-known that moral hazard is strictly linked with financial crisis also if, in recent years, this approach has been overrated. One piece of evidence for this is the idea in force of which moral hazard has become a "fundamentalism"; hence, it is "dangerous as moral hazard itself."

As far as the expression "moral hazard" is concerned, from a non-legal perspective, this refers to a situation in which one party is responsible for the interest of another but has an incentive to put their own interest first.

The concept of moral hazard comes from the insurance industry, where it is shown that the more a policy holder insures, the higher is the risk that insured parties will incur in losses. Thus, to have multiple insurance policies tends to affect and ultimately neutralise the incentive for insured parties to take action to prevent loss.

A lot of definitions of the term still prefer to describe moral hazard by using the insurance terminology, which may lead to the false impression that this phenomenon is merely confined to insurance. By contrast, it is now accepted that moral hazard can be found in different situations where, for various reasons, economic agents do not have to bear the marginal costs of their actions.[184] Therefore, moral hazard should be defined in a much broader way.[185]

The best-known example is a worker with an incentive to shirk on the job, therefore avoiding discharging the duties of his contract of employment. From a financial perspective, by contrast, it is concerned with the fact that a subject (A) might sell to another one (B) financial products[186] knowing that it is not in the interest of B to buy it. In this scenario, not only does A pay himself excessive bonuses out of funds that he is managing on B's behalf, but also, he takes risks that B has to bear.

Although this is true, the modern financial system has increased in sophistication: this means a greater complexity and less transparency. In other words, in the modern financial business, there is a greater scope for errors, and these errors are

184 For instance, another example is the insurance medical care area.
185 (Hdjek 2009).
186 For example, mortgage.

harder to detect. Consequently, the reality is truly sophisticated and the risk management issue is overrated. By contrast, the most important reason for the failure of financial risk management lies on economic grounds.[187]

In the area of banking law, moral hazard has arisen from borrowers concealing information from banks: the latter are unable to monitor the risk to which they are exposed. Information about risk, which borrowers are presumed to know, is concealed because there is an incentive to do so. More precisely, where higher risks were identified by banks, they would charge higher interest. In a nutshell, moral hazard is a rational response to incentives to take on increased risk and to conceal information about this.[188]

Among scholars there are different schools of thought. To summarise, one position highlights that potential investors are not in a suitable position to assess the financial conditions of banks before actually committing themselves.[189] By contrast, it is also stressed that deposit insurance has undermined the incentive of depositors to monitor excessive risk taking by banks: therefore, the optimal approach shall be an unsophisticated one. In other words, in reality, depositors are not in a position to realise a strictly vigilance activity on the bank. An example of the latter was Northern Rock plc,[190] a large bank in the UK whose core business was the provision of residential mortgages, accounting for 7% of all mortgage leading in the country.[191] In September 2007, Northern Rock suffered one of the deepest crises that threatened the financial market; in order to halt the fear and prevent contagion, Parliament had to pass a law to rescue the bank and to take it to public ownership.

The main phenomenon was the inability of Northern Rock to obtain funds to run its day-to-day operations. Meanwhile, Northern Rock could no longer effectively use securitisations schemes in order to generate cash and unload risk by parcelling its home loans as bonds and selling them to willing investors.

It is also worth stressing that Norther Rock's business was a unique structure, as it was built on an investment vehicle. Originally, Northern Rock was a building society that demutualised in 1997 and became a public limited company. In order to sustain high growth in its assets, the bank changed the structure of its liabilities. In 1999, it adopted an "originate and distribute" model, thanks to which the bank originated loans – and also purchased them from specialised brokers – and, immediately after, transferred them to a special-purpose vehicle (SPV).[192]

In light of this, it is possible to affirm that Norther Rock was the archetypal case in the originate-to-distribute model: Northern Rock, for every pound in collected deposits, three were lent, so on the liability side, this bank was hugely exposed to the risk of disruption in the wholesale market. In the traditional banking approach, banks transform, extend maturity and create liquidity: a bank's liabilities are short

187 (Dowd 2009).
188 (Dow 2012).
189 (Campbell and Cartwright 2017).
190 See also Albu and Wehmeier (2014).
191 (Miranda 2010).
192 This change had a strong influence on company's strategy.

term and mainly comprised of deposits that are repayable at par on demand. Additionally, their assets are longer term and largely non-marketable.

In a physiological scenario, this last characteristic is linked with the highly private information contents of bank loans compared to market financing. This explains why bank assets are perceived as more opaque than those of most non-bank firms. In a normal situation the association does not generate problems. However, if there is a weakening of confidence in the bank's ability to meet its payment obligations, it can cause a massive withdrawal of deposits, consequently a problem[193] of liquidity with ensuing challenges in selling off assets at a normal price. The last act is the bank's insolvency.[194]

In looking at the collapse of Northern Rock through the lens of the deposit guarantee scheme,[195] there are, at least, three facts that need to be duly considered.

The first one is that, more often than not, it is argued that, where the insured are open to sustain some losses in the event of a claim, they will take more care in avoiding exposing themselves to risk.

The second is that, unless all deposits are insured to their full value, there will always be some people facing a potential loss, *i.e.* the large depositors, who may have their deposits on terms which cannot be broken in a hurry without the consent of the bank. To elaborate, the question is whether it is correct to pencil a dividing line that excludes some depositors (or parts of deposits) without inducing a run, or other financial disturbance, that the authorities find unacceptable.

The third concern is over the length of the period during which access to depositors' funds might be interrupted: standard deposit insurance protects people against loss of their deposits[196] but not against the suspension of access to deposits.

From both an empirical and data-based analysis, it is highlighted that banks with lower charter values reduce their risk taking more and more, after the introduction of explicit deposit insurance. Furthermore, it is also emphasised that large systemically important banks do not change their risk taking in response to the introduction of deposit insurance, which suggests that the introduction of explicit deposit insurance does not mitigate "too big to fail" problems.

More precisely, "moral hazard problems arise only from the additional risk taking due to higher bailout expectations, which are usually not observable. Econometrically, the identification of moral hazard therefore requires variables that well explain the likelihood of a bank bailout, but are uncorrelated with the risk taking of banks."[197]

The belief that crisis is the outcome of moral hazard is a common explanation for any excessive risk taking, including excessive risk taking by firms. More realistically, risk taking is the result of multifarious elements: for example, a

193 (Barth et al. 2021; Boccuzzi 2023).

194 (Llewellyn 2009).

195 As far as the banking supervision matter is concerned, in a nutshell, it is possible to say that traditional banking supervision does not be the better approach for this sort of financial market.

196 (Kaufman 2006).

197 (Dam and Koette 2012).

misalignment between managerial and investors' interest. However, the scenario is even more complex: the reference shall be to a potential conflict, between public and private interests. The fact is that a firm's manager engages the firm in risk taking in order to maximize profitability for the firm and its investors, principally shareholders. It is from the latter that arise the conflict and, the last result is that risk taking results which is seen as excessive from a public perspective.

In light of this, moral hazard does not cause a systematically excessive risk taking on the part of the biggest firms.

2.3.6 State aid and resolution mechanism

In the European approach to the management of banking and financial crises, it is clarified by the European Commission that financial stability remains the overarching objective, and sometimes even an obsession. The latter, indeed, ensures "that State aid and distortions of competition between banks and across Member States are kept to the minimum." The rules stipulate that state aid can only be accepted after hybrid capital and subordinated debt holders have contributed to reducing the capital shortfall "to the maximum extent."[198]

Pursuant to this communication, it is clear that states' recapitalisation measures can only be accepted under strict conditions. In other words, only exceptional circumstances, *i.e.* banking and financial crises, may justify this approach.[199] Therefore, guarantees and liquidity support can be granted before a restructuring plan is approved, but only (1) after a notification, (2) under a temporary approval, (3) to follow the conditions set in the previous communications, such as adequate remuneration and behavioural restrictions. They are restricted to banks that have no capital shortfall.[200]

This set of "recommendations" were applied in the case of Banco Espirito Santo: the state capital injection of 4.9 billion euro as capital to a bridge bank was authorised by the EU Commission.[201]

As a result of this, it is possible to affirm that aid to be granted to financial institutions is coherent with European Union approach only if it has the aim of repairing damages as a consequence of exceptional situations. Furthermore, state aid for the banking sector could be granted only in the case of the existence of a serious disturbance in the economy of a member state.[202] Additionally, they are compliant with the EU rules if the disturbance has the capability to affect the whole of the economy of the member state and not merely one of its regions, or parts of its territory.

198 European Commission, "Guidelines on State aid for rescuing and restructuring non-financial undertakings in difficulty" (2014) Gi C 249/1, 41.

199 See Lannoo (2014).

200 European Commission, "Guidelines on State aid for rescuing and restructuring non-financial undertakings in difficulty" (2014) Gi C 249/1.

201 European Commission, SA.39250 (2014/N) Banco Espirito Santo SA, decision of 03.08.2014, [2014] Gi C343/1.

202 See Article 107(3)(b).

In these cases:[203]

- The aid can be granted but it shall be proportionate to remedy the disturbance;
- The assessment of disturbance shall be done case by case;
- Only the systematically relevant bank shall be considered as a serious disturbance;
- The aid shall be temporary and precautionary in nature;
- The aid shall not be used to cover eventual future losses;
- The aid shall be confined to solvent institutions;
- The aid shall be limited to address the capital shortfall.

The Greece case

A remarkable exception was the so-called Greece case, where financial crises, with long-lasting consequences and a serious sovereign debt crisis collided with each other. The Greece bank system was affected also by a fiscal problem, a circumstance that prevented Greece from having access to international capital markets.

In Greece the measures applied would be structured in two different periods: the first period (2008–2013) and the second (2014–2016).

During the 2008–2013 years, the Greek government adopted a programme called the "recovery program" for the enhancement of liquidity in the economy, in response to the impact of the international financial crisis.[204] This support fell into the category of state subsidies under EU competition law and was authorised by the European Commission as state aid under Article 107(3)(b). Therefore, Greece notified a first package to the Commission that included the following:

- A recapitalisation scheme;
- A guarantee scheme;
- A government bond loan scheme.

After it came two "adjustment programmes." Under the first,[205] state-guarantee bonds would be issued in order to be used as collateral for obtaining funding from the European Central Bank. By contrast, no additional liquidity would be granted to the Greek banks.

The first programme stipulated the creation of the Hellenic Financial Stability Fund,[206] an administrative and financially independent legal entity, governed by private law. HFSF was competent to impose restructuring measures and monitor

203 (Miserendino 2018).
204 See Law 3723/2008.
205 The Economic Adjustment Programme for Greece, European Economy, May 2010, Occasional Papers 61, Directorate-General for Economic and Financial Affairs, available at European Commission, http://ec.europa.eu/economy_finance/publications/occasional_paper/2010/pdf/ocp61_en.pdf.
206 Henceforth HSF.

the respective procedures, while the credit institutions had to jointly set up detailed restructuring plans or amend applicable plans in line with EU state aid rules.

The second programme[207] provided for recapitalisation of the Greek banks up to 50 billion euro in the form of European Financial Stability Facility bonds and the new bank resolution scheme. Moreover, during February 2009 the HSF was transformed into the Hellenic Deposit and Investment Guarantee Fund.[208] The major development concerned the establishment of an investor compensation scheme to ensure that customers of Greek credit institutions providing investment services would be adequately covered in accordance with the provisions of Directive 97/9/EC of the European Parliament and of the Council "on investor compensation schemes." Also, in this case the EU Commission approved the measures.

During the years 2014–2015, there was a second set of general measures. In 2014 restructuring plans were put in place in order for the systematically important banks to be viable in view of the continuing economic crisis. Particularly worth noting is the case of Piraues Bank: although it received more aid than other large banks, the bank actually downsized its foreign activities.

On 14 August 2015, the Eurogroup endorsed the agreement on the memorandum of understanding – the conditions underlying the new European Stability Mechanism (ESM) programme for Greece – reached between Greece and the European institutions with input from the International Monetary Fund. On 19 August 2015, ESM's board of governors approved the memorandum of understanding. As a result, the third economic adjustment programme for Greece started on 19 August 2015 and was scheduled to run until 20 August 2018. The financial assistance of up to 86 billion euro under the programme was provided by the ESM.

On 24 November 2015, the Eurogroup issued a statement noting that the policy conditions had been met for the transfer from the ESM to the HFSF of the funds needed for bank recapitalisation purposes. The funds were transferred on a case-by-case basis, depending on the individual needs of the respective banks. In October 2015, the European Central Bank's SSM carried out a comprehensive assessment of the four systemic Greek banks to ensure they were adequately capitalised. The ESM support programme agreed for Greece included funding which was earmarked to cover the potential capital needs of the banking sector. However, under EU state aid rules, additional capital requirements should, in the first place, be covered from the market and/or other private sources. If this is not sufficient and a bank needs state aid in the form of a capital injection, such support should then be approved under EU state aid rules before it is granted, and on the basis of a restructuring plan.[209]

207 The Second Economic Adjustment Programme for Greece, available at European Commission, http://ec.europa.eu/economy_finance/publications/occasional_paper/2012/pdf/ocp123_en.pdf (visited 12 Jun. 2016). The second financial assistance programme for Greece, financed by the European Financial Stability Facility (EFSF).

208 Henceforth HDIGF. See law 3746/2009.

209 (Athanasaki 2017).

The Tercas *case*

While in the previous paragraph a discussion has been provided about the "Greece case," by contrast, in this paragraph the focus shifts towards an Italian case; the "Italian job" in discussion epitomises what, as from 2023, is a new approach by the European Commission to this matter.

The starting point is the recommendation, by the Italian Ministry of Finance to place Tercas, an Italian regional bank, under special administration under Italian law. Banca Popolare di Bari, another regional bank, agreed on a transfer deal with the administrator to inject capital into Tercas, subject to its negative equity being covered by one of the two Italian DGSs.[210]

The administrator of this Italian bank failed to find a viable solution for Tercas, this causing the latter to enter liquidation. In this scenario, Tercas would have needed to reimburse all deposits up to 100,000 euro pursuant to the DGS Directive; however, deposit reimbursement would come with a price tag significantly higher than the recovery of the bank's losses. Therefore, the FITD decided to support Tercas with an aid measure up to 280 million euro, which, unfortunately, was deemed by the Commission as a state aid, therefore illegal and incompatible with the internal market.[211]

On 2 March 2021, the Court of Justice of the European Union (CJEU) issued its decision in the *Tercas* case[212] (*Tercas* ruling) upholding the General Court's decision and rejecting the Commission's arguments by considering that the recapitalisation of *Tercas* bank by a private consortium did not constitute state aid, even though the consortium was operating as a mandatory DGS and was obliged to reimburse deposits in case of liquidation, pursuant to the DGS Directive.

In a nutshell, it is possible to affirm that in *Tercas* the only legal issue, in the arguable view of the EU Commission, was concerned with the intervention of FITD: financial sustainability originating from the FITD was ultimately money originating from the Italian Republic and, therefore, financed, directly or indirectly, through the money of Italian taxpayers.

The Commission, though, was under the duty to demonstrate that the Italian state exercised a substantial control over the entity granted the aid on the specific measure adopted.

The General Court, in its decision, rejected the Commission's arguments and stated that the "governmental nature" of an aid measure could not be grounded solely on the fact that "the absence of influence and effective control of public authorities over the private entity is unlikely," thus setting a higher burden of proof

210 It is the Fondo Interbancario di Tutela dei Depositi (FITD). The FITD constitutes a mandatory consortium established under private law that may, according to its constitution, take measures to support other members of the consortium that are under special administration.

211 See Commission Decision 2016/1208/EU of 23 December 2015 on State aid granted by Italy to the bank Tercas (Case SA.39451 (2015/C) (ex 2015/NN)) (notified under document C(2015) 9526).

212 Case C-425/19 P Commission v Italy and Others, Judgement of 2 March 2021, also named "Tercas ruling."

for the Commission to meet than what appeared to be required pursuant to the aforementioned case law.

Following the Commission's appeal, the CJEU, in its recent ruling, upheld the General Court's decision, on the basis that, in the case of private entities, such as private *consortia* that operate as DGSs, the characterisation of an aid measure as state aid requires a higher burden of proof than in the case of public entities. Therefore, according to the CJEU, the Commission had failed to adequately prove the influence and effective control of public authorities over the FITD.

From a critical point of view, one could argue that the CJEU in its *Tercas* ruling fails to acknowledge the incentive structure that the DGS Directive had imposed on the FITD. The FITD was obliged, in any event, to reimburse all covered depositors upon liquidation, in order to serve the public objective of preserving financial stability. While voluntary interventions before liquidation, such as the one under consideration, fall outside the scope of this public mandate, they are, in principle, opted for as the lowest-cost solution only because the law requires the DGS to contribute during liquidation. In other words, the fact that the "voluntary intervention" cost less than full deposit reimbursement justified the form of intervention, not the intervention itself.

While the CJEU did stress that the assessment of aid measures by DGSs will always take place on an *ad hoc* basis, the *Tercas* ruling arguably opens up the way for DGS financing to be used on a voluntary basis outside the EU crisis management framework – be it state aid or resolution rules.

Moreover, the *Tercas* ruling generates the following implications for the EU crisis management framework:

- Since the burden-sharing requirement attached to state aid may not apply in the provision of support by a DGS, early interventions prior to failure become more likely;
- Early interventions come with considerable benefits since the sooner the intervention in a banking crisis, the lower the risk for bank-runs and fire sales and thus the lower the amount of losses that need to be covered;[213]
- The risk of abusing the *Tercas* ruling cannot be neglected: supporting banks through private schemes prior to failure without bail-in or burden-sharing may ultimately doom financial stability.

To summarise, the General Court and the Court of Justice found that the Commission had not proven, per legal standards, that Italian public authorities, not even one, were involved in FITD's intervention.[214]

Finally, as final step of this saga, on 21 September 2023, the European Commission has just concluded, in accordance with the judgements of the European courts,

213 Small and mid-sized retail banks that may find bail-in unenforceable given the structure of their balance sheet.

214 (Maggiolino 2022; Boccuzzi 2022; Badia and Georgiopoulos 2023).

that support granted by the Italian mandatory deposit guarantee scheme to Banca Tercas did not constitute aid within the meaning of the EU rules.[215]

2.4 Consumer protection

Under the legal framework of the European Union, a consumer is "any natural person who, in contracts covered by this Directive, is acting for purposes which are outside his trade, business, craft or profession."[216]

More precisely, consumer protection, in the broader sense, refers to laws and regulations that ensure fair interaction between service providers and consumers. Government intervention is justified on the basis of inherent information asymmetries and power imbalances in markets, with producers or service providers having more information about the product or service than the consumers.

Generally speaking, a consumer protection framework includes the introduction of greater transparency and awareness about the goods and services, promotion of competition in the marketplace, prevention of fraud, education of customers and elimination of unfair practices.

Moreover, consumer protection includes complementary macro-areas, such as the following:

- Laws and regulation governing relations between service providers and users – the principal goal is to ensure fairness, transparency and rights of recourse;
- An effective enforcement mechanism including dispute resolution;
- The promotion of financial literacy;
- Capability by helping users of financial services to acquire the necessary knowledge and skills to manage their finances.

The evolution of "consumerist theory" in the EU is centred, at a legislative level, on a deeply ingrained piece of legislation: the Unfair Terms Directive. This statute basically stipulates that, in any contract with a consumer (as defined in the directive), disparities in the terms and conditions which are to the detriment of the weaker party shall be non-binding on the consumer. Such scenarios are elaborated upon as the present chapter unfolds, but for now, by way of an introduction, it is important to note that the directive on unfair terms in consumer contracts applies to all such contracts between a seller or supplier and a consumer. Therefore, the entire range of financial contracts, from banking contracts (including investment contracts) to insurance contracts, are subject to its authority, in as far as they involve the sale or supply of goods and services.

215 EU Commission finds that Italian support to Banca Tercas does not constitute State aid – INSIGHT EU MONITORING (ieu-monitoring.com).

216 Article 2(1) Directive 2011/83/EU of the European Parliament and of the Council of 25 October 2011 on consumer rights, amending Council Directive 93/13/EEC and Directive 1999/44/EC of the European Parliament and of the Council and repealing Council Directive 85/577/EEC and Directive 97/7/EC of the European Parliament and of the Council. (Cartwrigth and Campbell 2003). Kyei (1995) and Raymond LaBrosse et al. (2006).

The means by which protection is afforded to the benefit of the consumer shall be the topic of analysis within the present chapter.

Moreover, the commercialisation of services discharged remotely (in other words, outside the offices or premises of the supplier/seller), including those undertaken through the medium of techniques, such as the telephone, the TV, email and internet, has given birth to the passing of specific legislation relating to "distance contracts," This body of law, more specifically where it has been crafted to regulate financial contracts, is discussed within the current chapter.

Furthermore, in more recent times the level of protection afforded to a consumer acquiring services or goods in the financial sector has exceeded that provided by the framework of the Unfair Terms Directive by virtue of the development of a comprehensive body of legislation limited to the investment business. Remarkably, this body of legislation is not charged with protecting the banking/financial consumer in general, but is exclusively concerned with the consumer acquiring investment services. This legislation has been enshrined within the Markets in Financial Instruments Directive II (MiFID II) and the Markets in Financial Instruments Regulation (MiFIR). Also, this body of legislation will be the subject matter of legal analysis.

Finally, it is worthy of mention the power that, in this traditionally private law area, is increasingly bestowed upon EU authorities. An example of this is the ESMA, the European Securities and Markets Authority, and its entitlements to exercise soft-law powers in order to ensure that the financial markets for consumer products and services are consumer-friendly.

2.4.1 Unfair terms directive

As mentioned at the outset of the present section, from a contract law perspective the existence of a bargaining power imbalance between two contracting parties (*e.g.* the seller or supplier on the one hand, and the acquirer of the goods or services on the other) was traditionally perceived to be legally irrelevant, both in respect to civil law traditions and, to an even greater extent, at common law. This may have changed, but discrepancies in the way the relationship between sellers/providers of services and consumers have subsequently been regulated at each national level may hamper the EU treaty principles, according to which goods, services and capital must move freely within the Union. Therefore, the European legislator has deemed it necessary to lay down harmonising rules with regard to the responsibility each country must bear in protecting consumers against unfair terms in the contracts they conclude with sellers and providers of services. In this respect, the Unfair Terms Directive marks the emergence of a first set of European rules, and despite the differences existing in each country, aimed at harmonising "the laws, regulations and administrative provisions of the Member States relating to unfair terms in contracts concluded between a seller or supplier and a consumer." The category of consumer which the Unfair Terms Directive tackles is defined as the "natural person who . . . is acting for purposes that are outside his trade, business or profession."

A couple of observations are worth addressing in respect to the earlier definition of a consumer. First and foremost, the insertion of the adjective "natural" prior to "person" means that an entity (such as a company) is not consistent with the concept of a consumer, and therefore cannot be protected by the relevant provisions. It would appear that a consumer shall be confined to an individual. Furthermore, the "consumer," albeit a natural person, shall not benefit from any protection from the piece of legislation at stake, if he has acted for purposes connected with his professional or business activities. The reason for this seems to be that a person acquiring a good for use in the course of his business or profession (*e.g.* a lawyer buying a piece of furniture for his office) is not to be considered a weak party, acts as a professional or a businessman after all.

Before undertaking a more detailed analysis of the main terms and rules of the directive at stake, it is imperative to clarify that the provisions encompassed within Directive 93/13 apply to financial contracts, including banking/investment contracts and insurance policies. Firstly, no exclusion for these kinds of transactions is contemplated within the Unfair Terms Directive. Secondly, many financial contracts fall within the scope of "contracts concluded between a seller or supplier and a consumer"; in fact, a bank, investment firm or insurance company can be conclusively viewed as a professional supplier or seller of, respectively, banking, investment and/or insurance services and products, in many cases to consumers.

The legal protection of the consumer afforded by the Unfair Terms Directive is predominantly achieved through the provisions of its Article 3. In this respect, the main concern of the EU legislator has been that a consumer (including a bank consumer) may be unduly and detrimentally affected, in the relevant contracts, by terms that have not been individually negotiated. Put simply, these terms are not the outcome of a specific pre-contractual discussion with the seller or provider but may be a consequence of the pressure which the party with a higher bargaining power can exert on the other. Article 3(2) of the directive under discussion clarifies the specific circumstances under which a term shall be regarded as "not individually negotiated" and therefore possibly unfair: more specifically, this happens when such a term "has been drafted in advance and the consumer has therefore not been able to influence the substance of the term, particularly in the context of a pre-formulated standard contract."

A term is not binding upon the consumer, provided the term has not been individually negotiated and is "contrary to the requirement of good faith" while, in its wake, "it causes a significant imbalance in the parties' rights and obligations arising under the contract, to the detriment of the consumer."

These last two conditions, which must be met equally and therefore are cumulative rather than alternative avenues on which to dispute a contract, are worthy of a brief analysis. Firstly, the duty of good faith entails an obligation on the part of the seller or supplier (in light of this work, the bank) to the consumer to ensure that from a substantial point of view, the supplier should not take advantage of the state of necessity or lack of experience of the consumer, while from a formal point of view, terms should be written in a legible and clear way and without traps. Secondly, for the term to be unfair, the lack of good faith must cause a "significant imbalance," tipping the scales against the consumer. In this respect, the adjective "significant" is, in itself, noteworthy as it could be construed very differently from two opposing viewpoints. On the one hand, in an interpretation that is more seller and provider-friendly and, in all likelihood, more consistent with the common law tradition, the imbalance should be "serious and exceptional," otherwise it will not be material. On the other hand, taken from a civil law perspective, the imbalance shall be deemed "significant" so long as it is not trivial. Obviously, the latter interpretation is conducive to a broader scope of potential unfairness of terms and conditions within a consumer contract. The expression "to the detriment of the consumer" is also worthy of further analysis. In some EU jurisdictions, it was held that the expression does not add anything, as if it was a combination of "words of description." Some scholars, however, have voiced their contention that it holds an autonomous meaning.

Furthermore, the consumer to be considered, in order to assess the detriment, is not the specific consumer affected but rather a general consumer in that position. In other words, the criterion adopted to assess the detriment is objective as opposed to subjective in nature.

Whether or not a contractual term is unfair is ultimately a matter of interpretation. In particular, the nature of the goods and services at the time of the conclusion of the contract shall be taken into account. Furthermore, all the circumstances surrounding the conclusion of the contract, in addition to all the other terms that may have any bearing on the clause at stake, shall be duly assessed. Nonetheless, the Unfair Terms Directive, in its annex, provides a list of terms that are presumed to be "unfair" (irrespective of whether they have been individually negotiated). Among the aforementioned terms, the following are worthy of a mention: terms "excluding or limiting the legal liability of a seller or supplier in the event of the death of a consumer or personal injury to the latter resulting from an act or omission of that seller or supplier" (let. a); terms "requiring any consumer who fails to fulfil his obligation to pay a disproportionately high sum in compensation" (let. e). It would go beyond the scope of this work to delve into the full details of these terms.

Yet some other rules may deserve drawing attention to: if the terms of the contract are in writing for instance, the wording should be in a plain, intelligible language, barring such and in case of doubt, "the interpretation most favourable to the consumer shall prevail." A further important rule identified by the legislator is the legal consequence and impact of the unfair term on the contract as a whole; the term shall not bind the consumer, although the contract shall continue to exist minus the unfair term. This principle is embodied in the Latin maxim "*utile per inutile not vitiatur*," meaning that the validity of the contract as a whole cannot be affected by the invalidity of a specific clause.

Financial contract

It is trite statement that the provisions under discussion apply to the entire range of financial contracts, in as far as they involve the sale or supply of goods and services to consumers. However, while the annex to the directive determines some terms always to be unfair, this does not apply to financial contracts.

More specifically, although a term "enabling the seller or supplier to terminate a contract of indeterminate duration without reasonable notice except where there are serious grounds for doing so" is considered an unfair term by definition, a supplier of financial services reserving the "right to terminate unilaterally a contract of indeterminate duration without notice where there is a valid reason" would not leave that supplier susceptible to the same outcome. In other words, the term in the latter case would not be unfair, so long as the "supplier is required to inform the other contractual party or parties . . . immediately."

Additionally, while, on the one hand, a term "enabling the seller or supplier to alter the terms of the contract unilaterally without a valid reason that is specified in the contract" is an unfair term, on the other, this provision shall not apply in financial contracts where "a supplier of financial services reserves the right to alter the rate of interest payable by the consumer or due to the latter, or the amount of other charges for financial services without notice." This clause, if inserted in financial contracts, would therefore be binding although it will be subject to the condition that "the supplier . . . inform[s] the other contracting party or parties . . . at the earliest opportunity" and that "the latter are free to dissolve the contract immediately."

Finally, three terms listed in the annex to the directive are not determined unfair when used in certain derivative transactions or, more precisely, in transactions in transferable securities, financial instruments and other products or services where the price is linked to fluctuations in a stock exchange quotation or index or a financial market rate that the seller or supplier does not control. This derivatives exception concerns the term "enabling the seller or supplier to terminate a contract of indeterminate duration without reasonable notice except where there are serious grounds for doing so," the term "enabling the seller or supplier to alter the terms of the contract unilaterally without a valid reason that is specified in the contract," and the term "providing for the price of goods to be determined at the time of delivery or allowing a seller of goods or supplier of services to increase their price without in both cases giving the consumer the corresponding right to concept the contract if the final prices is too high in relation to the price agreed when the contract was concluded." The reason for these exclusions is that these terms represent the essence of derivatives contracts, which are, by definition, speculative transactions that may be terminated at any moment in time. Without the exceptions, these products could probably not be sold, with negative consequences for the various financial institutions and consumers who would wish to make use of such contracts.

Distance contracts

Ensuring the protection of the consumer in a contract which is negotiated at a place where the supplier or seller and consumer are physically present (*e.g.* at the branch of a bank), conjures up problematic aspects, some of which have already been identified and discussed earlier. However, the consumer may be consigned to an even more delicate position in circumstances where the negotiation with the counterparty does not occur in the physical presence of the same, but at a distance. In practical terms, this could be the result of negotiations where the various mediums of modern distance communication are utilised. The telephone is one such well-established medium which, in recent times, has been largely surpassed by the internet and, particularly, by the advent of electronic mail, so allowing the supplier or seller and the consumer to reach an agreement on the conclusion of the contract without the requirement that both parties be physically present at the time. The use of these technologies, whilst certainly beneficial to the logistical aspect of contract negotiations, may add an increased risk to the consumer. Perhaps even more importantly from the perspective of the internal market, it has been argued that without European rules, consumers would not "have access without discrimination to the widest possible range of financial services available."

With respect to primary sources concerning distance contracts, it is opportune to draw attention to two principal pieces of EU legislation: the Consumer Rights Directive, in which distance contracts are considered in a more general way, and the Distance Financial Services Directive. The latter directive is more specifically concerned with the distance marketing of consumer financial services, save for credit cards and similar products more recently subject to a different EU legislative framework. The Consumer Rights Directive excludes "financial services" so that the following will focus on the Distance Financial Services Directive. Similarly, a separate EU statute, outside the scope of this textbook, is the Directive on E-Commerce.

Distance Financial Services Directive

First and foremost, it is worth highlighting the perimeter within which the application of the Distance Financial Services Directive is confined. The task of formulating a definition for a distance contract is anything but straightforward, given the multifarious possibilities that new technology continues to serve up to parties engaged in concluding contract negotiations. Despite this, the EU legislator offers a readily understandable definition of the phenomenon at stake: the "distance contract" for financial services is

> any contract concerning financial services concluded between a supplier and a consumer under an organised distance sales or service-provision scheme run by the supplier, who, for the purpose of that contract, makes exclusive use of one or more means of distance communication up to and including the time at which the contract is concluded.

The terminology adopted refers to the "financial service," under Article 2(b), as "any service of a banking, credit, insurance, personal pension, investment or payment nature." Thus, basically, the piece of legislation at stake covers a wide range of products, in fact all the products offered at distance by "suppliers" operating in the financial industry (not only banks, but also insurers and investment firms) are accounted for. Also, the concept of "means of distance communication" is adapted relative to the nature of the products (financial in this case). In this respect, Article 2(e) refers to "any means which, without the simultaneous physical presence of the supplier and the consumer, may be used for the distance marketing of a service between those parties."

Substantively, the mechanism of consumer protection operated by the directive concerns three pillars: (1) prior information, (2) written confirmation of information and (3) right of withdrawal. First, in regard to the information which must be sent to the consumer in advance of the conclusion of the distance contract, the range of data to be provided is wide, and does not relate exclusively to the supplier and its characteristics, but includes also the financial service (main characteristics and risks) and the distance contract (particularly the right of withdrawal).

The second pillar deals with the duty of the supplier to communicate to the consumer "all the contractual terms and conditions and the information" connected with the contract and the relevant financial product, "on paper or another durable medium available and accessible to the consumer in good time before the consumer is bound by any distance contract or offer."

Finally, the right of withdrawal is enshrined within the Distance Financial Services Directive; the time by which the consumer is entitled to exercise his withdrawal right is 14 calendar days. To further elaborate on this point, Article 6 of the Distance Financial Services Directive prescribes that member states "shall ensure that the consumer shall have a period of 14 calendar days to withdraw from the contract without penalty and without giving reason." This period would appear to be a "floor" rather than a mandatory period. In other words, a member state is allowed, if it so wishes, to fix a longer period of withdrawal. Needless to say, in this case the local legislator is expected to duly consider two contrasting sides to the argument: on the one hand, the protection of the consumer (whereby a longer period – *e.g.* 30 days – would be consistent) and, on the other hand, lending support to the financial market and, particularly, to businesses operating within it. In this latter respect, to extend the cooling-off period beyond a "reasonable" number of days could ultimately discourage operators, particularly those of foreign origin, from offering products at distance in that jurisdiction.

Given the specific characteristics of the financial market, the cooling-off period does not apply to derivatives or, to use the definition of the legislator, the "financial services whose price depends on fluctuations in the financial market outside the supplier's control, which may incur during the withdrawal period." Other exclusions are those relating to "travel and baggage insurance policies or similar short-term insurance policies of less than one month's duration" and "contracts whose performance has been fully completed by both parties at the consumer's express request before the consumer exercises his right of withdrawal."

2.4.2 Financial and banking instruments legislation

As discussed earlier in this chapter, outside the financial industry and by means of the Unfair Terms Directive, the EU legislation has, for more than two decades, been fostering and promoting a legislative framework the purpose of which is to provide the consumer with a high degree of legal protection. This framework aims to ultimately ensure that, on the one hand, the consumer can be duly informed of the nature of the contract originating from (or potentially imposed by) his counterparty while, on the other hand, a specific mechanism of enforcement to the benefit of the consumer is permitted, viz. the fact that a term may not be binding on the consumer should it not meet the expected standard of fairness.

As stated, the financial industry, and particularly, the offering of banking and investment products to the public, is an area that is not exempt from the general principles of the Unfair Terms Directive. However, the general protection afforded to a consumer at EU level, in the sale and provision of goods and services, is strengthened and enhanced in the area of the "sale" and "provision" of investment products; this specific protection is the outcome of ad hoc pieces of legislation that, over the past two decades, have moulded and forged the rules specifically governing the investment business.

The rationale behind this phenomenon is understandable. The crafting of investment products is characterised by a high level of complexity which calls for specific rules. Moreover, it is a relatively recent approach by the banking sector. Historically, the bank limited its business endeavours to the offer of typical bank products (bank accounts and saving accounts, on the one hand, loans on the other), but the globalisation of world markets and the ensuing rise in competition fuelled by the presence of different players therein has radically altered the traditional landscape. It has given rise to a dual layer of products being offered by banks, viz. the typical banking products, and the investment products. Thus, the latter is offered not only by investment firms but also by banks which must be specifically authorised by their supervisory authority to do so.

From a historical point of view, the investor-oriented legislation initially hinged upon the Investment Services Directive 1993/22/EC (ISD). Upon its formulation, the ISD, although it expressly stated that investor protection must account for the differences between professional and non-professional investors, failed to administer specific rules on how the investor must be protected. Broadly speaking, generic rules of conduct were indeed laid down under Article 11 of the ISD, namely, the loyalty principle (any investment firm must act honestly and fairly in catering to the best interests of its clients); informed consent (the investment firm must adequately disclose relevant material information on risks, costs, nature of the services, etc.); and know your customer (the investment firm must seek from its clients information regarding their financial situations, the investment experience and the objectives underpinning any financial services requested). However, the widely held belief was that the ISD Directive did not succeed in creating a persuasive and convincing system of protection for the investor. The ISD has therefore been subsumed within the more comprehensive body of law consisting of the Markets in Financial Instruments Directive (MiFID) and the MiFID Implementing Directive. In 2014, these two directives have been superseded, in turn, by MiFID II and MiFIR (together: "MiFID legislation").

MiFID legislation

Following in the footsteps of the ISD, but altogether more systematic and holistic in nature, the MiFID legislation draws a better demarcation line amongst the various counterparties to investment firms and banks offering financial products. The categorisation of clients is based on a tripartite approach: the professional clients, the retail clients, and finally, the elective client who, in their turn, can be the elective professional or elective retail.

The category of professional clients assembles the "customers" who possess "the experience, knowledge and expertise to make its own investment decisions and properly assess the risks that it incurs." This category includes, among others, credit institutions, investment firms, pension funds, undertakings, central banks, but also "large undertakings" not necessarily involved with financial business. The reason being that the way the activities of these entities are carried out (businesses organised collectively) instils complete confidence in their ability to assess risk and any other relevant factors entailed to a financial product they commit to buy and/or order.

Amongst the category of professional clients are also those who should be considered as retail clients, but who have opted out of the protection granted to the category of retails clients (clients who may be treated as professions on request) or, also, elective professional clients. The waiver of this protection means that they shall be treated as professional clients, upon their own request, rather than as a result of any regulatory categorisation. Remarkably, although any retail client can opt out of the statutory protection and, therefore, be re-categorised as "professional," the onus lies with the investment firm to assess and judge the adequate expertise, experience, and knowledge of the investor beforehand. In the absence of an adequate judgement, the investor shall remain classified as a retail investor, despite having availed themselves of the opportunity to opt out. Remarkably, according to the modalities recently set out by the Annex II ("Procedure"), the waiver must be in writing, the investment firm shall give "a clear written warning of the protections and investor compensation rights they may lose," the clients "must state in writing, in a separate document from the contract, that they are aware of the consequences of losing such protections."

Retail clients represent a class of clients who, being neither professional nor eligible counterparties, are deserving of the maximum level of protection available. Although the retail client is typically an individual, it can also include an entity which has failed to meet the definition of a "professional client." This specification is remarkable, if likened to the matter of the protection of the consumer, where conversely the customer worthy of protection must be exclusively an "individual." Retail clients shall also include those classified as "elective" – therefore, those who, although considered to be professionals, have asked for the maximum protection (therefore, "elective retail" counterparties).

Finally, the MiFID II contemplates the category of "eligible counterparties." An "eligible counterparty" is a limited circle of entities, somehow connected with the financial and/or banking sector. More specifically, according to Article 30(2) of the MiFID II Directive, these are "investment firms, credit institutions, insurance companies, UCITS and their management companies, pension funds and their management companies, other financial institutions . . . , national governments and their corresponding offices including public bodies that deal with public debt at national level, central banks and supranational organisations."

In case of investment services with an "eligible counterparty," some rules of conduct under the MiFID II Directive shall not apply. Nonetheless, in dealing with "eligible counterparties," member states shall ensure that "basic" principles shall be complied with, such as honesty, fairness and professionalism in the way the investment firm liaises with the eligible counterparty. Additionally, fairness, clarity and punctuality in the information provided should be observed.

To summarise, the system of protection offered by the MiFID legislation, as far as the categories of counterparties are concerned, hinges upon two principal categories, although the opting-in and opting-out mechanism works, metaphorically speaking akin to a lift or elevator allowing each category (retail and professional) to manoeuvre itself to a minimal or maximum level of protection, respectively, if specifically requested to do so by the investment firm or financial institution. Finally, the "eligible counterparties" constitute a further category, to a certain extent partly coinciding with the "professional clients," which, given their proximity of their business to that of the investment firm, do not require the application of the detailed rules of conduct of the MiFID II, although the MiFID II nonetheless requires of them a minimum compliance with basic rules of conduct.

Not only is the MiFID legislation concerned with a nuanced categorisation of the client, it also seeks to clearly define the principles by which the investment firm is bound when offering the products to its clientele. These rules of conduct are principally those falling into step with the area of the duties of information, reporting and execution. In this respect, the first duty is to provide clear and faithful information, which is not misleading, to the client.

Irrespective of the categorisation of the client, the firm shall steadfastly act "honestly, fairly and professionally in accordance with the best interest of its clients," in accordance with Article 24(1) MiFID II. Additionally, Article 24(3) of MiFID II strikes the attention where it states as follows: "All information, including marketing communications, addressed by the investment firm to clients or potential clients shall be fair, clear and not misleading. Marketing communications shall be identifiable as such."

Furthermore, there is an additionally duty owed on the part of the investment firm, according to Article 25, headed "Assessment of suitability and appropriateness and reporting to clients." This duty is, first and foremost, the duty to act with competence and knowledge; more specifically (Article 25(1)):

> Member States shall require investment firms to ensure and demonstrate to competent authorities on request that natural persons giving investment advice or information about financial instruments, investment services or ancillary services to clients on behalf of investment firms possess the necessary knowledge and competence to fulfil their obligations.

Within the concept of suitability lies the additional duty to know the client (Article 25(2)). According to this provision, the investment firm

> shall obtain the necessary information regarding the client's or potential client's knowledge and experience in the investment field relevant to the specific type of product or service, that person's financial situation including his ability to bear losses, and his investment objectives including his risk tolerance so as to enable the investment firm to recommend to the client or potential client the investment services and financial instruments that are suitable for him and, in particular, are in accordance with his risk tolerance and ability to bear losses.

It stands to reason that any client who envisages a personal financial situation and personal investment objectives should furnish the investment firm with such information in advance, so allowing the investment firm to competently fulfil the duty owed to the client to carry out an adequate and suitable investment. The suitability of the investment for the client at hand is the parameter that the investment firm must comply with, founded on the knowledge of his/her profile. Ultimately, implied in this "brief" is the concept that the client must understand the risks, the transaction must satisfy the investment objectives of the client, and the client must be in a position to bear the financial risks implied in the transaction.

Thirdly, there is a duty to ensure the "best execution" of the client's instructions, in order that the interests of the client cannot be affected, principally in respect to costs, prices, timely execution, etc. As stated in Article 27(1) MiFID II,

> Member States shall require that investment firms take all sufficient steps to obtain, when executing orders, the best possible result for their clients taking into account price, costs, speed, likelihood of execution and settlement, size, nature or any other consideration relevant to the execution of the order. Nevertheless, where there is a specific instruction from the client the investment firm shall execute the order following the specific instruction.

Finally, a general duty that investment firms shall comply with is the identification of conflicts of interest, according to Article 23 of the MiFID II Directive. Conflicts of interest may be of various kinds and do not lend themselves for an easy categorisation. Nonetheless, the provision under the EU statute in discussion point to the potential relationship between the same investment firm (and its managers, employees and tied agents) and the clients, in so much as they "arise in the course of providing any investment and ancillary services, or combination thereof, including those caused by the receipt of inducements from their parties or by the investment firm's own remuneration and other incentive structures" (Article 23(1) Directive 2014/65). In these circumstances, the investment firm should put in place, at organisational level, measures, detailed at Article 16(3) of the same MiFID II, aimed to prevent the adverse consequences of such conflicts. Should these preventative measures not be effective, the unavoidable duty for the investment firm shall be, according to the precept of Article 23(2), the immediate disclosure to the client of such conflict of interest.

Consumer Credit Directive

As mentioned at the beginning of this chapter, credit agreements for consumers are now governed by a specific piece of legislation, which partly derogates, as far as credit contracts are concerned, from the general discipline of the Unfair Terms Directive. The body of provisions in this area is contained within Directive 2008/48 (Consumer Credit Directive), which is the latest piece of legislation applicable to this area of law. Yet an even more specific statute has been adopted recently on consumer mortgage contracts, to be discussed in the following section.

First and foremost, the area of contracts to which this legislation applies relates to credit contracts with the consumer. The definition of consumer does not differ from the general one provided under the Unfair Terms Directive. Thus, the consumer is "the natural person who, in transactions covered by this Directive, is acting for purposes which are outside his trade, business or profession."

Secondly, the transactions falling under the micro-rules of this piece of legislation under discussion, is exclusively the "credit agreement," *i.e.* "an agreement whereby a creditor grants or promises to grant to a consumer credit in the form of a deferred payment, loan or other similar financial accommodation, except for agreements for the provision on a continuing basis of services or for the supply of goods of the same kind, where the consumer pays for such services or goods for the duration of their provision by means of instalments."

Thus, bank contracts that, technically speaking, are not based on a typical creditor/debtor relationship which involves a repayment though consecutive instalments of a certain amount of money, do not fall under within the Consumer Credit Directive; similarly, credit agreements guaranteed by mortgages are outside the scope of this EU statute.

Additionally, as a result of a specific provision spelled out by the legislator, credit agreements "involving a total amount of credit less than EUR 200 or more than EUR 75,000" are outside the scope of the Consumer Credit Directive, too.

The main pillars on which the protection of the consumer in credit contracts lies are mainly (1) detailed information that the creditor shall include whilst advertising these products; (2) pre-contractual information to be provided to the consumer, before the credit contract can be concluded; (3) the adequate assessment of the creditworthiness of the client; and (4) the right of withdrawal. The latter, more specifically, shall be a period of 14 calendar days during which the consumer may withdraw from the credit agreement "without giving any reason" (Article 14(1), para. 1). According to the following paragraph of the same Article 14(1), it is stipulated, in more details, that the period of withdrawal shall begin either "from the day of the conclusion of the credit agreement" or "from the day on which the consumer receives the contractual terms and conditions and information" required under Article 10 of the same Consumer Credit Directive, "if that day is later than the date" of conclusion of the contract.

On 30 October a new piece of legislation was passed in the EU: Directive 2023/2225/EU of the European Parliament and of the Council of 18 October 2023 on credit agreements for consumers and repealing Directive 2008/48/EC. This directive revokes Directive 2008/48/EC; hence, it is designed to address challenges brought about digitalisation and technological advancements that have significantly altered the landscape of consumer credit.

The objectives of the previous directive were only partially met in a context where the regulatory landscape in the European Union was very fragmented. In other words, the pre-existed legal framework did not guarantee a higher level of consumer protection. Furthermore, both digitalisation and Covid-19 pandemic have accelerated the IT evolution in this area of law: the reference is to new market players and, consequently, to new products. The health emergency added heavy challenges to citizens and householders in dealing with their financial situation.

Recital 22 clarifies this; hence, it stipulates that from 2008,

> crowdfunding has developed as a form of finance available to consumers, typically for small expenses or investments. A provider of crowdfunding credit services operates a digital platform open to the public in order to match or facilitate the matching of prospective lenders, acting in the course of their trade, business or profession or not, with consumers that seek funding. Such funding could take the form of consumer credit. Where providers of crowdfunding credit services directly provide credit to consumers, the provisions of this Directive concerning creditors should apply to them. Where providers of crowdfunding credit services facilitate the granting of credit between creditors acting in the course of their trade, business or profession, and consumers, the obligations for creditors under this Directive should apply to those creditors. In such a situation, providers of crowdfunding credit services act as credit intermediaries, hence the obligations for credit intermediaries under this Directive should apply to them.

A new element is the so-called right to be forgotten in oncology,[217] Recital 48 stresses that

> many cancer survivors in long-term remission often experience an unfair treatment in accessing financial services. They often face prohibitively high premiums, although they have been cured for many years, even decades. For the purpose of giving consumers who survived cancer equal access to insurance related to credit agreements, Member States should require that the insurance policies are not based on personal data concerning consumers' diagnosis of oncological diseases after a relevant period of time following the end of the medical treatment of those consumers. Such period of time determined by the Member States should not exceed 15 years starting from the end of the medical treatment of the consumer.

217 (Bailo et al. 2023)

As far as the application is concerned, this Directive shall apply to credit agreements; by contrast it does not apply to the following:

- Credit agreement secured either by a mortgage or other comparable security;
- Credit agreement which purpose is to acquire or retain property rights in land or in an existing or projected building;
- Credit agreement involving a total amount of credit of more than 100,000 euro;
- Credit agreement if the credit is granted by employers to their employees as a secondary activity;
- Credit agreements that "are the outcome of a settlement reached in court or before another statutory authority";[218]
- Hiring or leasing agreement in which an obligation or an option to purchase the object is not laid down in the same agreement or in a separate one."[219]

The directive is structured according to chapters: (I) "General provisions";[220] (II) "Information to be provided prior to the conclusion of the credit agreements"; (III) "Tying and bundling practices, inferred agreement, advisory services and unsolicited granting of credit"; (IV) "Assessment of creditworthiness and database access";[221] (V) "Form and content of credit agreements";[222] (VI) "Modifications of the credit agreement and changes in the borrowing rate";[223] (VII) "Overdraft facilities and overrunning";[224] (VIII) "Withdrawal, termination and early repayment";[225] (IX) "Annual percentage rate of charge and measures to limit rates and costs"; (X) "Conduct of business obligations and requirements for staff";[226] (XI) "Financial education and support to consumers in financial difficulties";[227] (XII) "Creditors and credit intermediaries";[228] (XIII) "Assignments of rights and dispute resolution;[229] (XIV) Competent authorities";[230] (XV) "Final provisions."[231]

Chapter II,[232] "Information to be provided prior to the conclusion of the credit agreements," refers to standard information, general information and pre-contractual information. The innovative legal provision is Article 13, titled "Personalised offers on the basis of automated processing." It states, "Member States shall require that creditors and credit intermediaries inform consumers in a clear and comprehensible

218 Article 2(2)(f).
219 For the follows hypothesis see the follows letters.
220 Articles 1–6.
221 Articles 20–21.
222 Articles 18–19.
223 Articles 22–23.
224 Articles 24–25.
225 Articles 26–29.
226 Articles 32–33.
227 Articles 34–36.
228 Articles 37–38.
229 Articles 39–40.
230 Article 41.
231 Articles 42–50.
232 Articles 7–13.

manner when they are presented with a personalised offer that is based on automated processing of personal data."

Chapter III[233] discusses about a heterogenous topic and the closing legal provision is concerned the chance for member states to "prohibit any granting of credit to consumers without their prior request and explicit agreement."[234]

Chapter IX[235] is focused on financial education, which is due in order to support the consumers' education and, ultimately, to assume responsible borrowing and debt management. To achieve this goal, clear and general information shall be provided to consumer about credit granting process. The final aim is "to guide them, in particular those who take out, particularly by means of digital tools, consumer credit for the first time."[236]

The expire date for the adoption of this directive by national governments is the 20 November 2023.

Mortgage Credit Directive

A further specified category of consumer, very recently acknowledged at EU level as a category worthy of specific protection, is that of the individual who enters into a credit agreement relating to residential immovable property. In practical terms, this is the person who, for himself or on behalf of his family, lodges an application with a credit institution (the lender) for a loan to buy a property and grants the lender a security interest on the property so acquired (a mortgage).

The financial sector has proved a particularly harsh domain over much of the last decade; until 2007, against the backdrop of a booming property market, many property buyers had nonchalantly availed themselves of readily available loans on the widely held assumption that the underlying good (the property) would perpetually continue to rise in value. In reality, from 2008 the property market veered significantly in the opposite direction, with falling prices propelling property buyers inexorably towards a "negative equity." Thus, property buyers who had purchased their property at the peak of the market were forced to repay the lenders an amount that, in reality, no longer reflected the value of the property bought.

Aside from this economic consideration, a more legal concern arises in connection with the purchase of a property burdened by a mortgage. Although the borrower may have retained ownership of that property, if he proves not to be in a position to maintain the agreed repayment plan in the form of instalments which includes both the principal and, unfortunately for the borrower, also a sometimes onerous level of interest, the lender is entitled, under virtually all national systems of property law, to execute the mortgage, *i.e.* to sell the property and take recourse on the proceeds.

233 Articles 14–17.
234 Article 17.
235 Articles 34–36.
236 Article 34(1).

In the context of this complex set of circumstances, the credulous consumer jumping unwittingly onto the property ladder has become a matter of grave concern, also from the perspective of the EU legislator. To that end, a piece of legislation, Directive 2014/17 has been passed on 4 February 2014 ("Mortgage Credit Directive"), to react to and address the adverse consequences of "irresponsible lending and borrowing by market-participants including credit intermediaries and non-credit institutions." Although the transposition of this directive is not immediate, the main principles enshrined therein are undoubtedly significant.

As to the merit of the specific law provisions, the statute at stake stipulates that, although each member state is not prevented "from maintaining or introducing more stringent provisions in order to protect consumers," an enhanced support platform shall be provided to the benefit of the consumer by each jurisdiction as a means to establishing a more responsible outlook to borrowing and debt management, in particular in relation to mortgage credit agreements.

As inferable from the brief description, the area of applicability of the directive under discussion does not encompass the entire spectrum of bank contracts but rather exclusively those concerned with the mortgage market and, more accurately, the "residential" one. To elaborate, the contractual frameworks affected by the new piece of legislation are, on the one hand and according to Article 3(1)(a), "credit agreements which are secured by a mortgage or by another comparable security commonly used in a Member State on residential immovable property or secured by a right related to residential immovable property" and, on the other hand, pursuant to the following Article 3(1)(b),"credit agreements the purposes of which is to acquire o retain property rights in land or in an existing or projected building."

More stringent rules are imposed on lenders, and on the way they carry out their business in this delicate market. In this respect, three main principles are highlighted by the EU legislator. First, the Mortgage Credit Directive relates to general information administered to the public, in cases where credit agreements were offered to the market. On the one hand, the manner in which credit agreements are advertised to the public is crucial. In this respect, any advertising concerning credit agreements of this kind shall refer, on a mandatory basis, to "an interest rate or any figures relating to the cost of the credit." On the other hand, Article 13 of the Mortgage Credit Directive requires that each member state shall ensure that any communication "on paper or on other durable medium or in electronic form" is "clear and comprehensible." This obligation shall be complied with not simply by the creditors, but also by "tied credit intermediaries" and their "appointed representatives."

An additional set of rules contained within the Mortgage Credit Directive are those relating to the contracts themselves. Although the arena of contract law is traditionally deemed a national one, ergo reserved to the discretion of each member state, as it is considered part of private or commercial law, the directive does not refrain from dictating some remarkable provisions relating to the requirements for pre-contractual information. According to Article 14, the creditor, according to the specific law provisions that each member state shall set forth, is under an obligation to provide the consumer with "personalised information needed to compare the credits available on the market, assess their implication and make an informed decision on whether to conclude a credit agreement." This information is determined to be "pre-contractual" as it shall precede the conclusion of the contract or, to use the terminology of the legislator, be made available "in good time before the consumer is bound by any credit agreement or offer." Similarly, the creditor, according to Article 16 Mortgage Credit Directive, shall provide "adequate explanations" to the consumer "on the proposed credit agreements and any ancillary services." The concept of ancillary services is not clarified in terms of its boundaries, and this may encompass any product, whether of a financial nature or not and irrespective of whether or not it was issued by the same lender, as long as a causal link can be established with the subscription of the credit agreement. Regardless of the nature of the ancillary service, the general goal of the adequate explanation is to ensure that the credit agreement proposed to the client and the ancillary product is "adapted to his needs and financial situation."

The degree of creditworthiness demonstrated by the client is an additional matter of telling concern relative to the mortgage market, and is specifically dealt with under Article 18 of the directive under discussion. In this scenario, the creditworthiness of the borrower is a crucial barometer with which to assess whether the credit agreement can be entered into and, ultimately, the mortgage granted. More specifically, the assessment shall take into account "factors relevant to verifying the prospect of the consumer to meet his obligations under the credit agreement." Consistent with this approach, "the procedures and information on which the assessment is based are established, documented and maintained." Interestingly, with a provision – Article 18(3) – which constitutes a reprimand for much of the banking practices which spiralled out of control at the onset of the new millennium and where an assessment of the mortgage was superficially based on the value of the property to purchase (and the accompanying assumption that it would increase), the correct criterion to establish creditworthiness shall be based, first and foremost, on the ability of the borrower to repay the instalments from his own income. The value of the property shall be a factor, but not the prevailing one. The provisions are completed with the obligation, borne by the creditor, to ensure that once the credit agreement is concluded this contract is not altered or cancelled "on the grounds that the assessment of creditworthiness was incorrectly conducted."

2.4.3 Consumer protection in the UK

Also, before the Brexit phenomenon, a lot of studies demonstrated that in the United Kingdom, consumer protection was based on an "information" approach, to prevent market failure. On the other side, a different approach is based on pluralism and a rights-based view.

The British legal framework has its roots in the Merchandise Marks Act introduced, for the first time, in 1862 and dealing with the representation of goods, and which was repealed in 1887. Further repeals were in 1887, in 1891 and, most recently, in 1953. finally, in 1961, the Consumer Protection Act was passed.[237]

237 Committee on Consumer Protection, Interim Report, Cmnd. 1011, London 1960, p. 5.

Although under a different legal framework, British consumer legal protections have reflected a discussion as to the meaning of the consumer and his/her identity in society and politics. Furthermore, consumer protection in the UK is a *sui generis* approach: from the information-based approach it promotes a consciousness among both citizens and consumers. As a result, they should become even more responsible and informed about rapid economic and social changes.[238]

The current legal framework is the Consumer Rights Act which came into force on 1st October 2015. It introduced three main updates to existing laws:

- Consumers' rights on digital content: as a result of this, consumers have a clear right to repair or replacement of faulty digital content, such as online film, video games, music downloads and e-books.
- There were clear, well-defined new rules regarding what would happen if a service is not provided with reasonable care and skill or as agreed;
- Alternative dispute resolution became available to all businesses, to help when a dispute with a consumer cannot be settled directly.

When the UK was part of the European Union, its consumer protection regime was derived from EU legislation and was based on the following principles:

- Fairness test: consumer contractual terms, conditions and notices must not create an unfair imbalance in favour of a business;
- Transparency test: consumer contractual, terms, conditions and notices must be written in plain and intelligible language to be enforceable;
- Right to withdrawal: a consumer's legal right to cancel a contract formed at a distance within 14 days;
- Implied standards and remedies: a requirement that consumer goods, services and digital content be of satisfactory quality, fit for purpose and as described.

After Brexit, the Brexit statutory instruments[239] have either amended or repealed the "retained EU law" to reflect that the UK is no longer part of the EU. In the area of consumer protection, there are two Brexit pieces of legislation: (1) the Protection Regulation[240] and (2) the Enforcement Regulation.[241] These two achieve the aim of enforcing consumer rights both in the UK and the EU post-Brexit.

The first one, *i.e.* Protection Regulation, has the purpose to:

- Remove, or amend, references to EU laws from consumer legislation to ensure that it continues to operate effectively now, after Brexit;

238 (Hilton 2006).
239 Henceforth SIs.
240 Consumer Protection (Amendment etc.) (EU Exit) Regulations 2018/1326.
241 Consumer Protection (Enforcement) (Amendment etc.) (EU Exit) Regulations 2019/203.

- Make further amendments to clarify that, from the end of the transition period, consumer contracts concerned with imports of EEA countries will be treated in the same ways as contracts dealing with imports from non-EEA countries.

Where Enforcement Regulation is concerned, the goal is to either remove or amend references to EU legislation in relation to enforcement of various consumer protection laws. Moreover, the regulations revoke certain related reciprocal enforcement and investigatory powers across EU member States.[242]

In the banking and financial filed, the reference is to the Consumer Duty, in which it is possible to find the new rules for customers in financial and banking markets.

2.4.4 Financial training and domestic abuse

It is well-known that economic and financial security constitutes a vital and central feature for the wellbeing of both women and children, in circumstances domestic violence is in place. Both children and women are in need for economic resources in order to meet their daily needs to achieve an acceptable standard of living. Ultimately, they wish independence from an economic perspective too.

More precisely, a form of violence consists of denying access to money or providing inadequate allowances, reducing women's role in financial decision-making process, monitoring spending, restricting access to vehicles or communications or, at least, coercing women to relinquish assets.

It must be taken for granted that women who have experienced violence do have a particular economic need arising from both physical and psychological experience of violence and from an economic or financial abuse.[243] More precisely, women who have experienced violence end facing more financial challenges, associated with abuse, more inequalities and more income and wealth issues than women who have not experienced violence confront.

First and foremost, it is crucial to clarify the link between banking law and domestic abuse. Domestic violence may be defined as a physical, sexual and psychological aggression by a current or former intimate partner. Further, violence can take place both between co-habitant and non-cohabitant partner and does not require sexual intimacy.

From a banking law perspective, the reference goes to consumer protection strategies: it is quintessential to assist women in order to address debts and bills which originate from economic abuse and from the disruption of separation from domestic violence.

It is worth observing that women leaving relationships need good financial information to achieve economic security. Financial counselling and financial management services are important strategies for promoting economic security during and

242 (Conway 2021).

243 (Franzway, Zufferey and Chung 2007); (Macdonald, Catalyst paper 1: An overview of economic abuse 2012).

following violence. More in depth, financial counsellors shall be offered to help to manage immediate financial hardship and to have control on their own financial assets and to become ever more independent under an economic perspective. Therefore, a primary reason that women do not try to move on from their abusers is the lack of adequate material resources in order to do so. If a victim is financially dependent on an abuser, she may feel obliged to stay with her abuser and find it more difficult to press criminal charges or seek restraining orders.[244]

To summarise, the relationship of domestic violence and financial insecurity is circular. The abusers, indeed, control their victims' access to material resources: in turn, this engenders financial instability with an increase in the victim's further susceptibility to violence. This combination of circumstances is an obstacle for them to escape to safety.[245]

All of these actions can be summarised in financial and banking education for women. Promoting subjective financial wellbeing is important to women's financial decision-making and women's belief about their ability to provide themselves and families outside of an abusive relationship.

Furthermore, a financial support is critical in times of immediate material hardship: for instance, during a separation, as abuse may cause women to be socially isolated and reduce their options for obtaining advice and support. These supports not only do short-term but also turn into long term initiatives to assist women to build economic security throughout life course.[246]

These strategies are encapsulated into the macro-area of consumer's protection; hence, it offers a set of strategies for improving women's economy security. Consumer strategies, indeed, can help carve out pathways through which women can address the debts and bills which accumulate as consequences of economic abuse. The last goal is to build an economic independence for woman as a customer.[247]

According to this line of reasoning, it was suggested[248] that services policies and practices shall be developed to help minimise the likelihood of economic abuse. Companies could also take leadership by auditing the awareness of economic among customer service staff, by assessing the accessibility of hardship policies, ensuring opportunities to repair credit records, and ensuring their processes are efficient, so that customers don't have to retell their experiences.

By contrast, others[249] highlight the need for special financial products for domestic violence victims, such as no or low-interest loans and matched savings accounts, government funded financial counselling delivered through domestic violence services and policies in financial institutions to address financial abuse, such as loan and bill splitting for jointly generated debts.[250]

244 (Littwin 2012).
245 (Kim 2015).
246 (Macdonald, atalyst paper 4: Financial capability and economic abuse 2012).
247 (Singh 2021).
248 (Macdonald, Catalyst paper 2: Credit, debt and economic abuse 2012).
249 (Braaf and Meyering 2011).
250 (Cortis and Bullen 2015).

2.4.5 Contemporary challenges

From a global and international perspective, from the consumers' part there are, at least, three macro-areas that involve the banking sector: sustainability, the protection of assets, data and privacy and, finally, the protection of an ageing populations.

The first, sustainability, concerns issues, opportunities and challenges for financial consumers in relation to sustainable finance.

The sustainable products that may be offered to consumers are regarded sustainable, as long as they are included in a non-exhaustive list:

- Deposit products, including money deposited by the consumer provider for green, environmental and sustainable renewable lending projects, such as energy, building and waste green projects;
- Ethical, or green, credit card spending on green or sustainable projects or causes, or to offer consumers discounts when consumers make environmentally friendly product purchases using a credit card. For example, paying for second-hand clothing or purchasing plant-based meals;
- Sustainable insurance to ensure products which have social or environmental considerations.

In these circumstances, the risk that may materialise is impact washing: it is strictly linked with greenwashing, although it better refers to the risk consumers face of being misled when acquiring investment products. This situation materialises itself when this impact is not verifiable or measurable or when the said impact is overstated. The investment products marketed and sold to retail investors do not align their expectations, goals or preferences.

In other words, impact washing is the other face of impact investment, *i.e.* investments made with the intention to generate positive, measurable social and environmental impact, alongside a financial return. By contrast, impact washing can occur when the promised impact on the real economy cannot be proven, or when firms do not accurately measure their investments' impact in the way it was promised, while still claiming that an asset is having a real impact on the economy, as in making the economy more green or sustainable.[251]

As far as the second topic is concerned, it is a consequence of the Covid-19 pandemic; indeed, the latter accelerated the process of digitalisation in every sector, including banking and finance. Although the benefits for the consumers are numerous, by contrast there are also some threats. To elaborate, on the one hand, online services are lower in cost and more convenient and will become even more tailor-made. On the other hand, the risks include online fraud, data breaches, lack of privacy and manipulation of consumers' behaviour biases when operating online.

Ultimately, such an issue is linked with demographic trends: the ageing of the population is a global phenomenon. An ageing population has, at the same time, positive and negative elements. The first one concerns greater social and economic

251 (Cote 2022).

activity and value associated with longer life spans and healthier, more active older people. The second refers to physical and cognitive decline, social isolation, longer terms and unplanned financial needs and decision-making as well as lower levels of digital and financial literacy.

2.5 Alternative dispute resolution: between banking and financial law

A legacy of the 2007–2008 financial crises is the discussion around whether bankers were adequately prosecuted for their actions instrumental in the crisis. Americans believed that governments did not adequately prosecute bankers in relation to their actions and behaviour.[252] They observed that few individuals were criminally prosecuted for their role in the crisis, despite ample evidence suggesting that criminal wrongdoing was worth investigating.

Starting from this, a discussion will be made on the alternative dispute resolution[253] mechanism in the banking and financial sector. More precisely, the attention will be paid to restorative justice and financial ombudsman.

Alternative dispute resolution[254] schemes are out-of-court mechanisms that have been developed to help consumers who have been unable to reach an agreement directly with the trader, a comparatively quick solution. Traditionally, ADR schemes use a third party (arbitrator, mediator, ombudsman, complaint board) to help the consumer and the trader reach a solution. They resolve their dispute by proposing, or imposing, a solution by bringing the parties together to convince them to find a solution by common agreement.

ADR schemes are present on all developed financial markets all over the world. For instance, in the US there is a long tradition of ADR in various forms and it was developed in different ways: arbitration, mediation, conciliation, fact-finding, mini-trial, summary jury trials, court-ordered arbitration, ombudsman, med-arb, small claims courts, rent-a-judge.[255]

2.5.1 Restorative justice

Restorative justice[256] is a method whereby victims will receive restoration for the damages suffered, but it is also a means of restoring the community. The restoring activities encompass, among their objectives, property lost, personal injury and, more generally, a sense of security. Furthermore, an additional aim is to restore harmony, in light of a shared feeling that justice cannot be served while an underlying injustice still persists.[257] First and foremost, it is crucial to emphasize that RJ

252 (Erman 2013).
253 Henceforth ADR.
254 Henceforth ADR.
255 (Stone 2001).
256 Henceforth RJ.
257 (Braithwaite 2017).

should not bring to mind a romantic notion about the world and its "law and order." Rather, the purpose that RJ strives to achieve is the re-establishment of fundamental rights, proportionality, rule of law and the separation of powers.[258] A corollary of this is that RJ does not aim to abolish the key elements of the criminal judicial system of the state. However, thanks to RJ, power can be shifted – from central bodies to civil society. Consequently, the judicial system continues to be democratically administered by the community, within a pre-determined legislative framework.

The common element of RJ is the will to restore a social relationship in order to establish or re-establish social equality. More precisely, the distinctive elements of RJ are as follows:[259]

- To cover a variety of processes: from formal to informal models;
- To be based on dialogue between parties, thus conversation is central in RJ;
- To be a flexible process.

In the white-collar area, RJ makes sense because the crime is committed, typically, in an organisational context. This scenario gives regulators access to other people in the perpetrator's web of relations who can participate in conferences or be used to shame and reintegrate, among others, restorative strategies.[260]

Furthermore, banking regulations already rely on restorative justice, at least potentially: indeed, banks are investigated regularly by the supervisory authority, and the outcome of this process is an agreement between employees and bank investigators, where they agree to any necessary corrective measures. Therefore, there is a close relationship between bank investigators and banks more so than other policy areas.[261]

The first European Union legal source in this area was the "European Commission Recommendation of 30 March 1998 on the principles applicable to the bodies responsible for out-of-court settlement of consumer disputes."[262]

From this, another two documents have been passed.

The first was the "Commission Recommendation 2001/310/EC of 4 April 2001 on the principles for out-of-court bodies involved in the consensual resolution of consumer disputes,"[263] where arbitration was dropped and the focus shifted onto procedures being "consensual." The second one was "Commission Green Paper on Alternative Dispute Resolution in civil and commercial law," 19 April 2002, which broadened the scope of ADR procedures, extending the attention beyond business-to-consumer (B2C) to include also business-to-business (B2B) issues.

258 (Braithwaite, Restorative Justice 2000).

259 (Zehr 2015; Spalding 2015).

260 (Rex 2019-2020).

261 (Yackee and Yackee 2006).

262 98/257/EC, available at http://eur-lex.europa.eu/LexUriServ.do?uri=OJ:L:1998:115:0031:0035:EN:PDF (last accessed March 20th, 2012).

263 2001/310/EC, available at http://ec.europa.eu/consumers/redress/out-of- court/adr/acce_just12_en.pdf

A quintessential role is played by Directive 2014/104 on private damages actions.[264] The reference goes to its Article 18; hence, it contains an important opening towards setting up a more developed RJ-oriented institutional framework at the EU level and the member state's level.

According to the directive,

> [a]ctions for damages are only one element of an effective system of private enforcement of infringements of competition law and are complemented by alternative avenues of redress, such as consensual dispute resolution and public enforcement decisions that give parties an incentive to provide compensation.[265]

The principal objective of this directive is to give victims the right to full compensation. The latter implies a person who has suffered harm being placed in the position in which they would have been had the infringement of competition law not been committed.

Where RJ is concerned, the ambitions of the 2014 Directive remain limited to a compensatory corrective justice approach. Again, the main focus is to restore baseline equality and to compensate victims of anti-competitive behaviour by awarding them monetary damages. Meanwhile, the directive allows for consensual dispute mechanism to be set up at the member state level.

In this legal framework, dispute resolution mechanism shall be consensual.[266] Moreover, the directive proposes the establishment and setup of mixed public-private "antitrust funds."[267] It would be publicly regulated private associations set up with the specific purpose of rendering RJ processes more available and visible to victims and offenders of competition law infringements.[268]

The association, having legal personality or not, would be set up with the specific purpose of managing RJ process linked with the infringement of EU and national competition law provisions. They would be independent from government authorities, enforcement bodies and the judiciary.[269]

264 Directive 2014/104/EU of the European Parliament and of the Council of 26 November 2014 on certain rules governing actions for damages under national law for infringements of the competition law provisions of the member states and of the European Union, [2014] OJ L349/1. Henceforth, the directive.

265 Recital 5.

266 Recital 48 states that "[a]chieving a 'once-and-for-all' settlement for defendants is desirable in order to reduce uncertainty for infringers and injured parties. Therefore, infringers and injured parties should be encouraged to agree on compensating for the harm caused by a competition law infringement through consensual dispute resolution mechanisms, such as out-of court settlements (including those where a judge can declare a settlement binding), arbitration, mediation or conciliation. Such consensual dispute resolution should cover as many injured parties and infringers as legally possible."

267 It recalls the idea of the charitable trust figure under English law; see Penner (2019).

268 (de Gioia Carabellese and Della Giustina 2023).

269 (Van Cleynenbreugel 2019).

It is important to note that the presence of banking mediation institutions is becoming increasingly important and urgent: every customer's problem has the potential to cause a dispute and damage to bank's reputation. Therefore, thanks to ADR, this reputation will be maintained, increasing public trust and reducing negative publicity.

2.5.2 Online dispute resolution

Online Dispute Resolution[270] may be defined as dispute resolution processes conducted with the assistance of communication and information technology, particularly the internet. Similar expressions are e-ADR, i-ADR, cyber mediation and cyber arbitration.[271]

Usually, consumers engage in small or medium transactions which they would not usually have done in the traditional market. Further, among scholars it is emphasised that ODR would become even more popular as a result of the constant increase of e-business transactions.[272]

The concept of ODR encompasses partial or complete dispute resolutions on the internet, which have arisen both in the virtual world as well as outside it.

Entities that offer this service are, inter alia, ProMediate online mediation based in Europe and *RisolviOnline* in the UK.[273]

Within this method of managing online private disputes, some services are based on fully automated internet platforms, as well as networks which employ tools such as chat or videoconferences and, also, asynchronous forms of communications, such as emails, for example.[274]

The European legal framework states, "Consumers and traders should feel confident in carrying out transactions online so it is essential to dismantle existing barriers and to boost consumer confidence. The availability of reliable and efficient online dispute resolution (ODR) could greatly help achieve this goal."[275] Further, Recital 8 said that "ODR offers a simple, efficient, fast and low-cost out-of-court solution to disputes arising from online transactions."

Under the EU piece of legislation, ODR is a platform, a single point of entry for consumers and trades seeking the out-of-court resolution of disputes. It will be an

270 Henceforth ODR.

271 (Cyman 2017).

272 See Larson (2003).

273 ProMediate Mediation Services – What we do, ProMediate Mediation Services, www.promediate.co.uk/ (accessed 31.07.2020). 10 Online Dispute Resolution Service – Milan Chamber of Arbitration, www.risolvionline. com/index.php.

274 Directorate General for Internal Policies Policy Department A: Economic And Scientific Policy Internal Market And Consumer Protection, Cross-Border Alternative Dispute Resolution in the European Union, June 2011, www.europarl.europa.eu/meetdocs/2009_2014/documents/imco/dv/adr_study_/adr_study_en.pdf as.

275 Regulation (EU) No 524/2013 of the European Parliament and of the Council of 21 May 2013 on online dispute resolution for consumer disputes and amending Regulation (EC) No 2006/2004 and Directive 2009/22/EC (Regulation on consumer ODR), Recital 6.

interactive website which can be accessed electronically and free of charge in all the official language on the institution of the EU.[276]

ODR platform has these functions:[277]

- To provide an electronic complaint form which can be filled in by the complaining party;
- To inform the respondent party about the complaint;
- To identify the competent ADR entity or entities and transmit the complaint to the ADR entity;
- To offer an electronic case management tool free of charge via to conduct the dispute resolution procedure online;
- To provide parties and ADR entity with the translation of information which is necessary for the resolution of the dispute and exchange via platforms;
- To provide a feedback system which allows the parties to express their views on the functioning of the platform.

2.5.3 Financial Ombudsman

Financial Ombudsman[278] is an institution that operates in different countries of European Union; the Ombudsman fills different areas of competence, not only as an alternative dispute resolution entity but also and above all as independent assessors of the functioning of financial services for clients, consumers and investors.

From a European Union perspective, relevant sources are as follows:

- Directive 2013/91/EU;[279]
- Regulation (EU) 2017/2394.[280]

Moreover, in accordance with the ADR Directive, states should ensure that ADR bodies (1) are independent, impartial and not under instruction from either party or representatives; (2) are appointed for a term of office sufficient to ensure the independence of their actions and should not be relieved of their obligations without

276 (Mroczyński-Szmaj 2021).

277 See Article 5(2).

278 Named, also, Financial Ombudsman Service, therefore FOS.

279 Directive 2013/91/EU of the European Parliament and of the Council of 21 May 2013 on alternative dispute resolution for consumer disputes and amending Regulation (EC) No 2006/2004 and Directive 2009/22/EC (Directive on consumer ADR), hereinafter referred to as the "ADR Directive" [Directive 2013/91/EU of the European Parliament and of the Council of 21 May 2013 on alternative dispute resolution for consumer disputes and amending Regulation 2006/2004/EC and Directive 2009/22/EC, art. 1].

280 Regulation 2017/2394/EU of the European Parliament and of the Council of 12 December 2017 on cooperation between national authorities (AZORITI) responsible for the enforcement of consumer protection laws and repealing Regulation (EC) No 2006/2004, hereinafter referred to as CPC [Regulation (EU) 2017/2394 of the European Parliament and of the Council of 12 December 2017 on cooperation between national authorities (AZORITI) responsible for the enforcement of consumer protection laws and repealing Regulation 2006/2004,/EC art. 1].

good cause; and (3) have the necessary expertise in alternative or judicial resolution of consumer disputes.

From a general perspective, there are two main models of Financial Ombudsman: German and British.

In Germany, in 1992, on the initiative of the Association of German Public Banks, an "out of the court" procedure was established for settling disputes between banks and customers. Germany, however, had no specialised regulatory framework for regulating the activities of the Financial Ombudsman. Thus, these activities are carried out in compliance with the regulations developed by the Association of German Public Banks.

By contrast, in the United Kingdom, the concept of ombudsman provides for an independent public institution funded by public funds. Another difference consists in the fact that in the UK the institution of Financial Ombudsman was created thanks to Financial Services Act (2012).

It is crucial to read the Financial Services Act together with the Financial Services and Markets Act 2000.[281] Under the latter there are both compulsory and voluntary jurisdictions. The first includes general and life insurance, mortgage-lending, stockbroking, investment management, personal pensions and financial advice. In this case, compulsory refers to an obligation imposed on a regulated firm to submit the procedure and comply with the decision of the Ombudsman. Therefore, compliance is not obligatory. Further, there are no obligations imposed on regulated firms to submit to the voluntary jurisdiction of the FOS.

The following subjects are not eligible as customers:

- An individual, business, charity or trustee who was an intermediate customer or market counterparty in relation to the firm in question at the time of the act or omission and, in respect of the activity, which is the subject of the complaint;
- Firm whose complaint relates in any way to an activity which the firm itself has permission to carry on and which is subject to the compulsory or voluntary jurisdiction of the FOS.

Complaints brought to the FOS are determined according to what is fair and reasonable in all circumstances of the case. The Ombudsman will take into account the relevant law, regulations and regulators' rules and guidance, standards, relevant codes of practice and where appropriate what he considers to have been good industry practice at the time.

Where fair and reasonable standard is concerned, it does not require the FOS to follow the law, but only to give it consideration; it can be viewed as offering the FOS a choice as to how it formulates the fair and reasonable standard in any particular case.

281 Heceforth FSMA.

References

Albu, O.B., and S. Wehmeier. "Organizational Transparency and Sense-Making: The Case of Northern Rock." *Journal of Public Relations Research* 26, no. 2 (2014): 117–133.

Allen, T. *Property and the Human Rights Act 1998*. Hart Publishing, 2005.

Athanasaki, V. "State Aid Rules in the Financial Sector During the Economic Crisis: A Disguised But Yet Necessary Retreat or an Honest Compromise? The Case of Greece." *European Public Law* 23, no. 3 (2017): 615–639.

Badia, J.M.C., and I. Georgiopoulos. "Main Developments in State Aid Control 2021–2022." *Competition Law & Policy Debate* 7, no. 4 (2023): 178–192.

Bailo, P., F. Gibelli, A. Caraffa, and G. Ricci. "Freedom from the Stigma of Oncologic Disease: Legislative and Ethical Aspects of the Right to be Forgotten in Oncology." *Minerva Forensic Medicine* 143, no. 2 (2023): 57–63.

Barth, J.R., C. Lee, and T. Phumiwasana. "Deposit Insurance Schemes." In *Encyclopedia of Finance*, 1–17. Springer International Publishing, 2021.

Boccuzzi, G. "The Tercas Case: A Watershed." In *Banking Crises in Italy: An Application and Evaluation of the European Framework*, edited by G. Boccuzzi, 39–51. Springer International Publishing, 2022.

Boccuzzi, G. "The Revision of the Banking Crisis Management and Deposit Insurance Framework in Europe: Why Is It Important to Enhance Flexibility?" *Risk Management Magazine* 18, no. 2 (2023): 37–52.

Braaf, R., and I. Meyering. *Seeking Security: Promoting Women's Economic Wellbeing Following Domestic Violence*. Australian Domestic and Family Violence Clearinghouse, 2011.

Braithwaite, J. "On Speaking Softly and Carrying Big Sticks: Neglected Dimensions of a Republication Separation of Powers." In *The Rule of Law and the Separation of Power*, edited by R. Bellamy, 297–354. Routledge, 2017.

Braithwaite, J. "Restorative Justice." In *The Handbook of Crime and Punishment*, edited by M. Torny, 322–344. Oxford University Press, 2000.

Brunnermeier, M., A. Crockett, C. Goodhart, and A.D. Persaud. *The Fundamental Principles of Financial Regulation*. International Center for Monetary and Banking Studies, 2009.

Cahn, A., and P. Kenadjian. "Contingent Convertible Securities: from Theory to CRD IV." *Goethe-Universitat Frankfurt Am Main, Working Paper*, no. 143 (2014).

Campbell, A., and P. Cartwright. *Banks in Crisis: The Legal Response*. Routledge, 2017.

Cartwrigth, P., and A. Campbell. "Co-Insurance and Moral Hazard: Some Reflections on Deposit Protection in the UK and USA." *Journal of International Banking Regulation* 5, no. 1 (2003): 9–20.

Conway, L. "Brexit: UK Consumer Protection Law." *House of Commons Library*, no. 9126 (2021).

Cortis, N., and J. Bullen. *Building Effective Policies and Services to Promote Women's Economic Security Following Domestic Violence: State of Knowledge*. ANROWS, 2015.

Cote, C. "Impact Washing: What It Is and How to Stop It." *Harvard Business*. https://online.hbs.edu/blog/post/what-is-impact-washing, 2022.

Cranston, R. *Principles of Banking Law*. Oxford University Press, 2002.

Cyman, D. "Alternative Dispute Resolution Mechanism in the Area of Financial Services in the European Union." *Financial Law Review* 2, no. 1 (2017): 18–32.

Dam, L., and M. Koette. "Bank Bailouts and Moral Hazard: Evidence from Germany." *The Review of Financial Studies* 25, no. 8 (2012): 2343–2344.

Davies, P., and S. Worthington. *Gower & Davies Principles of Modern Company Law*. Sweet & Maxwell, 2012.

de Gioia Carabellese, P. "Non-Executive Directors and Auditors in the Context of the UK Corporate Governance: Two (or Too Many?) "Pirandellian" Characters Still in the Search of an Author?" *European Business Law Review* 22, no. 6 (2011): 759–789.

de Gioia Carabellese, P. "Corporate Governance of British Banks and Duties of Directors: Practical Implications of the Royal Bank of Scotland's Demise." *Law and Economics Yearly Review* 3, no. 1 (2014): 134–156.

de Gioia Carabellese, P. *Banking Resolution Tools, Bail-in and Fundamental Rights*. Wolters Kluwer, 2019.

de Gioia Carabellese, P. " 'Bail-in: Do Italians Do It Better (or Worse, or Not at All)?: Case Studies and a Reflection on the Italian Approach to the BRRD: the Bail-with'." *European Business Law Review* 32, no. 1 (2021): 93–116.

de Gioia Carabellese, P., and C. Della Giustina. "Restorative Justice as a New (Sustainable) Paradigm of Justice." *Amicus Curiae* 5, no. 2 (2023): 25–40.

Dow, S. "Economics and Moral Sentiments: The Case of Moral Hazard." In *Facts, Values and Objectivity*, edited by V. Neves and J.C. Caldas, 17–32. Routledge, 2012.

Dowd, K. "Moral Hazard and the Financial Crisis." *Cato Journal* 29, no. 1 (2009): 141–166.

Erman, M. "Five Years After Lehman, Americans Still Angry at Wall Street." *Reuters*. https://www.reuters.com/article/idUSBRE98E06S/, 2013.

Fietta, S., and J. Upcher. "Public International Law, Investment Treaties and Commerical Arbitration: An Emerging System of Complementarity?" *Arbitration International*, no. 29 (2013): 187–222.

Franzway, S., C. Zufferey, and D. Chung. *Domestic Violence and Women's Employment*. University of South Australia, Hawke Research Institute for Sustainable Societies, 2007.

French, D., S. Mayson, and C. Rayn. *Mayson, French & Ryan on Company Law*. Oxford University Press, 2014.

Hdjek, O. "What Is Moral Hazard and How Was It Invoked in the UK During the Northern Rock Crisis in 2007?" *Common Law Review* 11, no. 3 (2009): 27–33.

Hilton, M. "Consumer Protection in the United Kingdom." *Jahrbuch für Wirtschaftsgeschichte/Economic History Yearbook* 47, no. 1 (2006): 45–60.

Houben, R., and W. Vandenbruwaene. *The Single Resolution Board*. Intersentia, 2017.

Kaufman, G. "Using Efficient Bank Insolvency Resolution to Solve the Deposit Insurance Problem." *Journal of Banking Regulation* 8, no. 2 (2006): 40–50.

Kaul, I., P. Conceicao, K. Le Goulven, and R.U. Mendoza. *Providing Global Public Goods*. Oxford University Press, 2003.

Kim, C. "Credit Cards: Weapons for Domestic Violence." *Duke Journal of Gender Law & Policy* 22, no. 2 (2015): 281–309.

Kirshner, J. *Business, Banking, and Economic Thought in Late Medieval and Early Modern Europe*. University of Chicago Press, 1974.

Kyei, A. *Deposit Protection Arrangements: A Survey*. International Monetary Fund, 1995.

Lannoo, K. "Bank State Aid Under BRRD and SRM." *European State Aid Law Quarterly (ESTAL)* 13, no. 4 (2014): 630–635.

Larson, D.A. "Online Dispute Resolution: Do You Know Where Your Children Are?" *Negotiation Journal* 19, no. 3 (2003): 199–205.

Littwin, A. "Escaping Battered Credit: A Proposal for Repairing Credit Reports Damaged by Domestic Violence." *University of Pennsylvania Law Review* 161, no. 2 (2012): 363–430.

Llewellyn, D.T. "The Northern Rock Crisis: A Multidimensional Problem Waiting to Happen'." In *Financial Institutions and Markets. 2007–2008 the Year of Crisis*, edited by R.R. Bliss and G.G. Kaufman, 101–128. Palgrave Macmillan, 2009.

MacDonald, F. *Catalyst Paper 1: An Overview of Economic Abuse*. Good Shepherd Youth and Family Service and Kildonan Uniting Care, 2012a.

MacDonald, F. *Catalyst Paper 2: Credit, Debt and Economic Abuse*. Good Shepherd Youth and Family Service and Kildonan Uniting Care, 2012b.

MacDonald, F. *Catalyst Paper 4: Financial Capability and Economic Abuse*. Good Shepherd outh and Family Service and Kildonan Uniting Care, 2012c.

MacNeil, I.G. *An Introduction to the Law on Financial Investment*. Hart Publishing, 2012.

Maggiolino, M. "The Tercas Case, State Aid, and Antitrust: Are There Holes in the Warp?" *Italian Law Journal* 8, no. 2 (2022): 745–768.

Maguze, T.C. "EU Bank Recapitalisation and the Bail-in Option: An Analysis of the Effects of Mandatory Bail-in on Creditors' Property Rights." *UCL Journal of Law and Jurisprudence* 5, no. 2 (2016): 207–238.

Miranda, A.C. "Moral Hazard and How It Was Invoked in the Northern Rock Crisis of 2007." *King's Student Law Review*, no. 21 (2010): 27–42.

Miserendino, M.R. "State Aid for the Banking Sector: What Has Changed After the New BRRD and SRM Regulation?" *European State Aid Law Quarterly* 17, no. 2 (2018): 204–211.

Mroczyński-Szmaj, L. "Digitalisation of ADR Proceedings in Consumer Cases, with Particular Emphasis on the Institutions of the Financial Ombudsman and Coordinator for Negotiations." *Acta Iuris Stetinensis* 33, no. 1 (2021): 115–132.

Mueller, R.C. *The Venetian Money Market, Banks, Panics, and the Public Debt, 1200–1500*. Johns Hopkins University Press, 1997.

Penner, J.E. *The Law of Trusts*. Oxford University Press, 2019.

Raymond LaBrosse, J.R., and D.K. Walker. "Contingency Planning: A Practitioner's Guide Drawing from Lessons Learned from Dealing with Bank Failures." *Journal of Banking Regulation* 8, no. 1 (2006): 51–65.

Rex, J. "Restorative Justice, White-Collar Crime, and the 2008 Financial Crisis." *Appalachian Journal of Law* 19, no. 1 (2019–2020): 1–40.

Russo, C.A. "The New Course of EU State Aid rules during the 2007–09 Financial Crisis." In *Research Handbook on International Financial Regulation*, edited by K. Alexander and R. Dhumale, 171–192. Edward Elgar, 2012.

Siems, M., and D. Cabrelli. *Comparative Company Law: A Case-Based Approach*. Oxford University Press, 2013.

Singh, S. *Domestic Economic Abuse: The Violence of Money*. Routledge, 2021.

Spalding, A.B. "Restorative Justice for Multinational Corporations." *Ohio State Law Journal* 76, no. 2 (2015): 357–408.

Stone, K. "Alternative Dispute Resolution." In *Encyclopedia of Legal History, Public Law & Legal Theory Research Paper Series*. University of California, Los Angeles, 2001.

Theissen, R. *EU Banking Supervision*. Eleven Publishers, 2013.

Van Cleynenbreugel, P. "Private Damages Actions in EU Competition Law and Restorative Justice: Towards More Streamlined Institutional Framework?" *Market and Competition Law Review* 3, no. 2 (2019): 15–50.

Walker, G. "UK Financial Services Reform." In *Financial Services Law*, edited by G. Walker and R. Purves. Oxford University Press, 2014.

Werlauff, E. "Right of Possession and Interference with Such Rights." *European Business Law Review* (2002): 123–145.

Wessels, B., and G. Moss. *EU Banking and Insurance Insolvency*. Oxford University Press, 2006.
Yackee, J.W., and S.W. Yackee. "A Bias Towards Business? Assessing Interest Group Influence on the US Bureaucracy." *The Journal of Politics* 68, no. 1 (2006): 128–139.
Zehr, H. *Changing Lenses: Restorative Justice for Our Times*. Herald Press, 2015.

Table of cases

SA.39250 (2014/N) *Banco Espirito Santo SA*, [2014] Gi C343/1
Harbinger Capital Partner v Caldwell and Another [2013] EWCA Civ 492
Case 6833/74 Marcks v Belgium.
Case 30417/96 Olczak v Poland.
Pressos Compania Naviera SA v Belgium Series A 332 (1996) 21 EHRR 301.
Case C-425/19 P Commission v Italy and Others.
Stran Greek Refineries v Greece Series A No 301-B (1995) 19 EHRR 293.

3 Financial law

3.1 The market organisation: from financial market to parallel markets

3.1.1 Primary market

Historically, an ancestor of the modern stock exchange was created in the Italian Renaissance, more precisely in the 1300s, by Venetian bankers. The Republic of Venice, or *La Serenissima* – at that time an independent sovereign state with overseas territories and colonies across the Mediterranean – boasted an extensive network of trades. It was, together with Florence, the most opulent city of Europe. The active and ambitious merchants of the city-state of Venice, in order to support their increasingly booming commerce overseas and the enormous financial resources required to prop them up, needed fresh capital from outsiders. These outsiders ("investors" in contemporary finance terminology) demonstrated no knowledge of the business, but they had an interest in investing money to make a future profit. Therefore, bankers in Venice set up a system of exchange (a primordial form of the modern stock exchange), where traders were permitted to buy and sell corporate debt obligations and also government debt obligations issued by the Republic of Venice. These debt obligations represented an early form of "bonds," *i.e.* promises to pay an amount of money, issued by a merchant (in respect of corporate obligations) or the Republic of Venice (in respect of government obligations) for a nominal value to finance a specific venture; the issuer received money as a result. The remuneration for the investor would transpire, upon maturity, in the capital originally lent to the issuer, plus the interest promised, should the relevant venture reach a successful conclusion.

This system was expanded after the discoveries of Asia and the Americas and the resulting need for more extensive investments in the New World. The new ventures were decidedly hazardous, given the new inter-continental and trans-oceanic arena in which they were played out. The mechanism envisaged was therefore to separate the risk of the investment from a single venture through the release of shares. By investing in shares, the investor did not speculate in a single venture by buying the relevant bond (as was the case in the initial period), but rather he spread the risk over different ventures and/or businesses, organised by the issuer

DOI: 10.4324/9781032628646-3

of the shares, *de facto* an entity bearing some similarities to a modern joint stock company. In this new scenario, it is remarkable to note that the Dutch East India Company – a legal entity with various business operations and ventures scattered across Asia – was the first company whose shares started being traded, continuously, in the Amsterdam Stock Exchange, as early as 1611. The London Stock Exchange began operating in a coffee shop in the 18th century, as a place where shares of companies masterminding the organisation of several ventures across the ocean were initially exchanged or, to use the contemporary term, traded.

Thus, the term "stock market" traditionally conveys a venue – by definition, a trading venue – where transactions relating to financial instruments take place. From an economic point of view, the functions of a stock market are multifarious, but first and foremost it is to facilitate the exchange between demand and supply of transferrable securities or, more generally and applying the relevant technical terminology, financial instruments.[1] The conclusion of transactions within an organised stock market is rendered all the more secure as transactions therein are concluded by qualified professionals, specifically authorised as market participants to ensure such an outcome. Ultimately, these factors increase the liquidity of the market and, therefore, the prospects for firms to unearth capital in order to operate more dynamically. A salient feature of a stock market, from an organisational point of view, although this reverberates also on the way these special "venues" are regulated, is the fact that the financial instruments traded in that market are granted entry through a process of authorisation. Additionally, the dealers entitled to place orders in the regulated market are exclusively dealers authorised by their own organisation (usually from qualified investment firms and banks), and the market is an organisational structure which is overseen by a management department charged with ensuring the best functioning of it.

Stock exchange regulation

Before addressing the details of the EU law provisions governing the stock markets, it is essential to touch on the way in which the legislation existing in this area is articulated in relation to each EU member state. The legislation in question is of EU origin, the reason being that the Brussels lawmaker regards the relevant area of law, or *sedes materiae*, as adhering to the fundamental principles of the EU (particularly, the principles of free movement of capital). Accordingly, the interaction between European and national statutes in this area of law is mainly based on a dual layer, where an EU piece of legislation (usually in the form of a directive) fixes norms, and at national level these norms are subsequently implemented by each member state. This implementation tends not to materialise in a homogenous fashion across the spectrum of countries presently in possession of

1 The concept of "financial instruments" according to Directive 2014/65 (the MiFID II Directive), particularly Annex I, Section C, financial instruments are "transferrable securities," such as "shares" and "bonds," but also "money-market instruments" (for instance covered-bonds), "units in collective investment undertakings" and the important category of "derivatives."

EU membership. However, as long as the specific provisions do not infringe the relevant directive, legislative divergences do not give rise to any concern in terms of legitimacy and legality.

Each stock market is typically the product of a certain country, and its relevant legislation and regulations, where it is incorporated and operates. Nonetheless, globally, stock markets have undergone a dramatic transition over the past three decades, advancing from a scenario where they were formerly purely "public" (*i.e.* managed by an authority which was *de facto* an emanation of the government) to a more competitive system, where each market is perceived to be "private" and the entity in charge of its organisation – terminologically the "market company" or the "operator" – considered a "private" company, incorporated and functioning in accordance with the corporate law rules on private companies. Needless to say, this liberal approach does not prevent the market company from falling under the supervision of a local authority instituted at national level. The organisation and business of a stock exchange is predominantly a regulated activity, to be authorised by the national authority and thereafter subject to its supervision which is carried out, constantly and systematically, during the pursuit of the relevant business.

At EU level, the matter of the stock market has been profoundly influenced by the harmonisation process; the initial Directive 2004/39 EC of 21 April 2004 on markets in financial instruments (henceforth also the "MiFID I" or the "MiFID I Directive")[2] shall be soon phased out as a result of the passing, in 2014, of a new EU piece of legislation, Directive 2014/65 (henceforth also the "MiFID II" or the "MiFID II Directive").[3]

2 In full: European Parliament and Council Directive 2004/39 EC of 21 April 2004 on markets in financial instruments amending Council Directives 85/611/EEC and 93/6/EEC and Directive 2000/12/EC of the European Parliament and of the Council and repealing Council Directive 93/22/EEC. The MiFID needs to be read, until its full replacement by Directive 2014/65, in conjunction with two additional EU pieces of legislation, namely:

- The MiFID Implementing Directive 2006/73 ("Commission Directive 2006/73/EC of 10 August 2006 implementing Directive 2004/39/EC of the European Parliament and of the Council as regards organisational requirements and operating conditions for investment firms and defined terms for the purposes of that Directive");
- The MiFID Implementing Regulation 2006/1287 ("Commission Regulation (EC) No 1287/2006 of 10 August 2006 implementing Directive 2004/39/EC of the European Parliament and of the Council as regards record-keeping obligations for investment firms, transaction reporting, market transparency, admission of financial instruments to trading, and defined terms for the purposes of that Directive").Both these implementing statutes represent "level 2 measures" in the "Lamfalussy process" described above in this chapter.

3 In full: Directive 2014/65/EU of the European Parliament and of the Council of 15 May 2014 on markets in financial instruments and amending Directive 2002/92/EC and Directive 2011/61/EU. Directive 2014/65 has been published on the Official Gazette of the European Union on 12 June 2014 and has entered into force, according to its Article 96, on the twentieth day after its publications (ergo, on 2 July 2014). According to its Article 93, the transposition of its main rules, including those concerned with the regulated markets, dealt with in this Chapter 2, shall take place by 3 July 2016. Directive 2014/65 shall be read in conjunction with the Regulation 600/2014/EU. Together, the MiFID II and the regulation should "form the legal framework governing the requirements applicable to

More specifically, Article 44 of the MiFID II, basically corresponding to Article 36 of the previous MiFID I, details the principle that the regulated market is a reserved activity,[4] permitted exclusively to those systems complying with the provisions of Title III of the directive. The authorisation hinges decisively on the "home authority" being satisfied that both "the market company" and the systems of the regulated market (*i.e.* the organisation and structure of it) are consistent with the requirements set forth at EU level, particularly the provisions disclosed by Article 44 (and following) MiFID II.

The MiFID I required a specific dual-layer pattern as a prerequisite to a regulated market being granted authorisation: the organisation (the market itself) and the entity, distinct from the market, operating the latter, and therefore called the operator.[5] Conversely, the MiFID II seems to postulate two possible options, either a market managed and operated by an operator or a regulated market managed by itself.[6]

The operator,[7] given being ultimately responsible for the correct functioning of the regulated market, is tasked with requirements, not simply at the start of the business but also later, for the duration of its lifespan. For instance, all information relating to the programme of operations and the organisational structure of the regulated market shall be provided to the relevant competent authority by the regulated market.[8] On the other hand, the authority shall be empowered to ensure that the market itself complies with the provisions specified by the MiFID II Directive, in addition to implementing national provisions.[9] A stock market is by definition

investment firms, regulated markets, data reporting services providers and third country firms providing investment services or activities in the Union." (See Recital 7 of the MiFID II.)

4 Different from the "regulated market" is the multilateral trading facility (MTF), therefore "a multilateral system, operated by an investment firm or a market operator, which brings together multiple third-party buying and selling interests in financial instruments – in the system and in accordance with non-discretionary rules" (Article 4(1)(22) MiFID II). Although the MTFs are not officially recognised "regulated markets" and, therefore, they are not subject to the relevant rules of authorisation, the MIFID II, and previously the MiFID I too, makes sure that in each member state the investment firms and operator in charge of them establish and implement "non-discretionary rules for the execution of orders in the system" (Article 19(1) MiFID II)). A new typology of system, introduced by the MiFID II Directive, and unknown in the architecture of the previous MiFID I Directive, is the "organised trading facility"; the latter is defined (Article 4((1)(23) as "a multilateral system which is not a regulated market or an MTF and in which multiple third-party buying and selling interests in bonds, structured finance products, emission allowances or derivatives are able to interact in the system."

5 Article 36(1)(3), MiFID I.

6 This seems to be inferable from Article 44(1), para. 3, MiFID II: "In case of a regulated market that is a legal person and that is managed or operated by a market operator other than the regulated market itself."

7 Or the regulated market, in cases where the latter managed itself.

8 Article 44(1), paragraph 1, MiFID II.

However, according to the following Article 44(1), para. 3, if the regulated market was managed or operated by a market operator other than the regulated market itself, "Member States shall establish how the different obligations imposed on the market operator under this Directive are to be allocated between the regulated market and the market operator."

9 Article 44(2), MiFID II, corresponding to the previous Article 36(2)(1), second part, MiFID I.

global, as it aids both domestic and international intermediaries in gaining access to dealings on financial instruments traded in that market, but it shall be subject to the regulations of the country in which it is authorised.[10] For instance, if for public policy reasons the authority of the country where the market Is authorised suspends' transactions, that order shall take effect on the relevant regulated market of that member state.

At EU level, no time limit is specified in regard to the number of days by which the authorisation to carry out a regulated market must be granted; entailed to this is the principle – inferable indirectly–- that any national legislation will have a certain discretion as to this end. On the other hand, the MiFID II accounts for the circumstances upon occurrence of which the competent authority may withdraw the authorisation or, in some cases, suspend it.[11] In this respect, firstly, attention must be drawn to a lapse of 12 months from the time the authorisation was granted during which time the operator failed to engage in any business, an express repudiation by the market company,[12] or a lack of activity in the preceding 6-month period. Additionally, the authorisation shall be withdrawn in in cases of fraudulent activity, where the authorisation has been obtained "by making false statements or by any other irregular means."[13] Furthermore, a variation of the original conditions under which the authorisation was granted, as well as a serious and systematic infringement of the provisions adopted pursuant to the MiFID II Directive, may prompt a revocation of the authorisation.[14] Finally, Article 44(5)(e) of the MiFID II,[15] with its generic wording, would suggest that the applicable national law may contemplate additional provisions for the withdrawal of the authorisation.

Akin to any other regulated entity such as a bank, those effectively directing the business and the operations of the regulated markets (more specifically, the "management body"[16]) must be endowed with "sufficiently good repute," "sufficient knowledge" and "skills and experience to perform their duties."[17] Coupled with this provision is the obligation on each operator of the regulator market to communicate to the competent authority the identity of those in charge of the regulated

10 Article 44(2), MiFID II, previously mutatis mutandis Article 36(4), MiFID I.

11 Article 44(5), MiFID II, previously Article 36(5), MiFID I.

12 The language used by the MiFID II is slightly different: "[the regulated market] expressly renounces the authorisation."

13 Article 44(5)(b), MiFID II, previously Article 36(5)(b) MiFID I.

14 Article 44(5)(c) and (d), equipollent to Article 36(5)(c) and (d) MiFID I, respectively.

15 *Mutatis mutandis*, Article 36(5)(e).

16 The "management body" is a very neutral definition of the directive at stake, fitting both into national legal systems where exclusively a board of directors is contemplated (for instance the UK one), and jurisdictions (such as Germany) which conversely lie on a two tier body, the board of directors itself and a more enlarged supervisory board.

In the terminology of the MiFID II, the "management body" is defined as "the body or bodies of . . . a market operator], which are appointed in accordance with national law, which are empowered to set the entity's strategy, objectives and overall direction, and which oversee and monitor management decision-making and include persons who effectively direct the business of the entity."

17 Article 45(1), MiFID II, correspondent to Article 37, MiFID I.

market, and any ensuing change of personnel at that executive level.[18] The standard imposed on management of the regulated market (or its own operator, if different) is extended by the directive, albeit in terms of mere "suitability," to the "persons exercising significant influence over the management of the regulated market."[19]

Although the regulated market is typically a private organisation and the new legislative framework would appear to encourage this form of business (with the consequence that the selection of the appropriate personnel to shepherd the business is a matter of limited public concern or open to limited public interference), the competent authority shall be fully entitled to veto the appointment of management personnel in exceptional circumstances where, on the one hand, it is not satisfied that the "members of the management body of the market operator are of sufficiently good repute, possess sufficient knowledge, skills and experience and commit sufficient time to perform their functions," and on the other hand, there are "objective and demonstrable grounds for believing that [they] pose a threat to its effective, sound and prudent management and to the adequate consideration of the integrity of the market."[20]

Attention has been drawn, at the outset, to the fact that the stock market is an arena in which exclusively "admitted financial instruments" are listed. This concept of the regulated market as a "restricted club" of financial instruments is echoed in the MiFID.[21] The member states must have "clear and transparent rules regarding the admission of financial instruments to trading." These rules are engineered to ensure that "any financial instruments admitted on a regulated market are capable of being traded in a fair, orderly and efficient manner and, in the case of transferrable securities, are freely negotiable."[22] For instance, a pertinent example of shares not being "freely transferable" would be shares of an issuer, in the bylaws of which clauses are embedded so that any transfer of shares is not possible without first seeking, and being granted, authorisation from the board of directors of the issuer. An issuer which requested the listing of its shares with bylaws drafted in such a fashion should not receive the consent of the stock market to the admission of the listing; likewise, if the clause was added at a later date (*e.g.* as a result of a

18 Article 46, MiFID II.

19 More specifically, according to Article 46(1), MiFID II (in past, basically but not identically, Article 38, MiFID I), member states "shall require the persons who are in a position to exercise, directly or indirectly, significant influence over the management of the regulated market to be suitable."

According to this line of reasoning, the operator of the regulated market shall be required, on the one hand, "to provide the competent authority with, and to make public, information regarding the ownership of the regulated market and/or the market operator, and in particular, the identity and scale of interests of any parties in a position to exercise significant influence over the management" (Article 46(2)(a), MiFID II) and, on the other hand, "to inform the competent authority of and of to make public any transfer of ownership which gives rise to a change in the identity of the persons exercising significant influence over the operation of the regulated market" (Article 46(2)(b), MiFID II).

20 Article 45(7), MiFID II; in past, albeit in a looser wording, a similar provision was contained in Article 37, second part, MiFID I.

21 Article 51 (1), MiFID II, previously Article 40(1)(1), MiFID I.

22 Article 51(1), para. 2, MiFID II, previously Article 40(1), para 2, MiFID I.

resolution reached at the shareholders' meeting), in all likelihood the issuer would receive notice from the stock market to remove the relevant clause and be cautioned that an exclusion from trading could ensue, should this order not be heeded within a specific timeframe.

Because the listing renders the issued securities "public," the admission to the market of financial instruments is generally accompanied by a prospectus, *i.e.* a document disseminating and disclosing to the public not only the characteristics of the securities but also of the entity issuing the securities (the issuer). The prospectus obligations, albeit also incorporated within the MiFID II Directive,[23] are the subject matter of a specific piece of legislation – the Prospectus Directive – an analysis of which will be undertaken in the following section.

The admission of securities to a regulated market is a decidedly complex process which must negotiate several steps. Aside from the legal aspects connected with the listing, which will forthwith be discussed, it is worth acknowledging that entailed to the listing is the decision of the issuer to go "public," thereby accepting that its financial instruments will be traded publicly and, therefore, acquired by individuals and entities not necessarily known to, or welcomed by, the issuer.

It is rare that the issuer itself organises the listing; rather it relies on the cooperation of one or more financial entities (a bank, specifically an investment bank, an investment firm or a combination of them), to which a mandate is given to aid the specific securities of that issuer being admitted to the market. This financial advisor is also called the arranger. Traditionally, the mandate of the arranger involves the organisation of two activities: (1) the listing of the securities on the regulated market and (2) the drafting of the prospectus and its subsequent submission to the competent authority for approval, if indeed this is required.[24] From a financial point of view, the activities of the arranger may also include what is called underwriting. The underwriting can be of three typologies: (1) firm commitment underwriting (the underwriters purchase securities from an issuer, or one of its main shareholders, at an agreed price); (2) best efforts underwriting (an underwriter makes its best efforts to sell the securities of the offeror/issuer); and (3) standby underwriting (the offeror/issuer offers securities, with the commitment of the underwriters to purchase the remaining securities that are not purchased).[25] The issuer is typically advised by its own legal team, as are the arrangers. In some cases, the same team of legal advisors may be retained by both parties (issuer and arrangers) although, to avoid any conflict of interest, the more likely scenario is that two separate law firms are employed.

The understanding reached between the arranger(s) and the issuer is typically encompassed within a contract, with terms and conditions dictating the duties which the arranger is expected to fulfil (including any relevant indemnities and penalties), and the rights and obligations of the issuer giving the mandate. Amongst

23 And previously MiFID I too.

24 As explained later in this Chapter 2, there are cases where the issuer is exempt from the prospectus.

25 (Soderquist and Gabaldon, Securities Law 2004) "underwriting refers to the function of helping a company, or one or more of its major shareholders, see securities to the public through an offering."

such terms is obviously the right to remuneration owed to the arranger for its advice on the listing process.

The offer of securities to the public has been, for some time, the subject of a harmonisation process at EU level. A piece of legislation dating back to 1980, Directive 80/390/EEC[26] represents the earliest attempt by the E.E. Community to create a legislative framework setting forth guidelines for the drawing up, scrutiny and distribution of the relevant documentation (the listing particulars) to be published for the admission of securities to the stock markets. Directive 80/390 was later subsumed within Directive 2001/34/EC ("Listing Directive"),[27] which codifies, amongst additional features, a number of previous directives existing in this area, more specifically the following: (1) Directive 79/279EEC of 4 March 1979, coordinating the conditions for the admission of securities to official stock exchange listing (the Admission Directive); (2) the Listing Particulars Directive already cited earlier[28] of 17 March 1980, coordinating the requirements for the drawing up, scrutiny and distribution of the listing particulars to be published for the admission of securities to official stock exchange listing (the Listing Particulars Directive); (3) Directive 82/121/EEC of 5 February 1985, on information to be published on a regular basis by companies the shares of which have been admitted to official stock exchange listing (the Interim Reports Directive); (4) Directive 89/298/EEC, relating to the drawing up, scrutiny and distribution of the prospectus in its published format when transferable securities are offered to the public (the Public Offer Prospectus Directive).

A further pillar of legislation in the broad area of the public issue of securities is Directive 2003/71 EC,[29] which offers guidelines on the "prospectus to be published when securities are offered to the public or admitted to trading."

As a result of these, the legislative framework currently prevailing in this area is twofold: (1) firstly, guidelines relating to the "prospectus" and enshrined within Directive 2003/71 ("Prospectus Directive"), and (2) secondly, guidelines relating to the "listing," where the relevant rules are those incorporated within Directive 2001/34 (Listing Directive). The intention of these two pieces of legislation, alongside with the third one, the "Transparency Obligations Directive,"[30] ultimately, is

26 In full: Directive 80/390/EEC of 17 March 1980 coordinating the requirements for the drawing up, scrutiny and distribution of the listing particulars to be published for the admission of securities to official stock exchange listing ("Listing Particulars Directive").

27 In full: Directive 2001/34/EC of the European Parliament and of the Council of 28 May 2001 on the admission of securities to official stock exchange listing and on information to be published on those securities, OJ L 184.

28 Again, more specifically, Directive 80/390/EEC.

29 In full: Directive 2003/71/EC of the European Parliament and of the Council of 4 November 2003 on the prospectus to be published when securities are offered to the public or admitted to trading and amending Directive 2001/34/EC, OJ L 345.

30 In full: Directive 2004/109/EC of the European Parliament and of the Council of 15 December 2004 on the harmonisation of transparency requirements in relation to information about issuers whose securities are admitted to trading on a regulated market and amending Directive 2001/34/EC, OJ L 390. A brief commentary to the Transparency Obligations Directive can be read in (Scott, International Finance 2010).

to promote the concept of a single EU passport for issuers, so that the raising of capital can be facilitated across the EU, both as regards a listing to the regulated markets, and as regards the issue of securities.

Securities: law and regulation

LISTING DIRECTIVE

Within the EU, the admission of securities to a regulated market is governed, as already mentioned, by Directive 2001/34 (Listing Directive), which again relates to the admission of securities to the official stock exchange listing and to the information to be published on those securities.[31] From a more general perspective, its purpose is to establish a level-playing field across the Union in terms of setting minimal requirements which securities must adhere to prior to listing.

The first general rule is that "securities may not be admitted to official listing on any stock exchange situated or operating within their territory unless the conditions [of the directive itself] are satisfied."[32] To simplify, a national piece of legislation which had incorporated a decidedly loose interpretation of the guidelines, thereby not requiring any form of authorisation for securities to be listed, would undoubtedly fail to comply with the rules of the directive and, potentially, would prompt the EU Commission to initiate an infringement procedure against that country in accordance with the principles of the Treaty. In other words, the harmonisation of securities markets, manifested in standardised guidelines on authorisation, aims to ensure that an investor may safely invest in a security market with the "EU brand." Although the EU legislation, as a matter of course, does not give any guarantee on making a return on the investment, it does provide a minimal "floor" of rules which each country will be obligated to implement so that a minimal level of protection has been afforded to the investor.

A second rule, also inferable from the Listing Directive, is one which requires that all the issuers of securities to be admitted to official listing be subject "to the obligations provided for by this Directive."[33] The provisions are intended to guarantee that the issuers operating in the EU market uniformly comply with the directive at stake. All issuers, *i.e.* "companies and other legal persons and any undertaking whose securities are the subject of an application for admission to official listing on a stock exchange,"[34] operating in the community engaged in the issue of securities shall be obligated to comply with it.

The Listing Directive, when analysed further, sets forth two sets of guidelines: (1) for shares (or "equity securities"), *i.e.* securities representing the share capital of a company, and (2) for "debt securities," *i.e.* securities representing a debt of

31 Among authors, such as Grundmann (2012), the Listing Directive is sometimes also referred to as the Stock Exchange Directive.

32 Article 5 Listing Directive.

33 Article 5 Listing Directive.

34 Article 1(a) Listing Directive.

the issuer – in other words bonds, rather than the share capital. There are conditions imposed on both the issuer and the securities issues by it, although the level of information required varies relative to whether the transferrable securities are equitable securities or debt securities – the former requiring a more extensive array of information than the latter.

EQUITY SECURITIES

As regards the guidelines (for the issuer) for equity securities, an initial requirement is that the "legality" of the issuer is guaranteed. The issuer cannot be any entity, but rather must be an entity operating in conformity with "the laws and regulations to which it is subject, as regards its formation and its operation under its statutes."[35] Indirectly, given the tenor employed by the legislator, it can be inferred that an individual who wanted to issue securities to be listed would not have this venture admitted, as the sole eligible issuer is a corporation. Thus, it should be an entity having a legal personality, separate from that of its members (or owners); for instance, a partnership – in common law jurisdictions, a business organised collectively – would not fall within the ambit of "entity" as it is bereft of a separate legal personality. Additionally, the Listing Directive requires, for the admission to listing, an adequate capitalisation of the issuer, of no less than 1,000,000 euro,[36] as well as the publication of its annual accounts for the three financial years preceding the application for official listing.[37]

The second category of requirements which must be satisfied to gain successful admission of shares relates to the shares themselves, rather than to the issuer. One of the requisites stipulates that shares shall be "freely negotiable." As a means of clarifying this requisite, it is worth noting that shares, in respect of which the respective bylaws of the issuer require authorisation from other shareholders or approval by the board of directors for the transfer to be valid, would be inconsistent with the public nature of the issue. Clauses of this nature would be apt for private companies but would be decidedly unsuitable for a company which harbours the ambition of issuing shares in a regulated market. The requisite

35 See Article 42 Listing Directive.

36 Article 43 Listing Directive. This figure is a "floor," a member state or the stock exchange of that country may require a higher capitalisation. For instance, in Italy, the local stock exchange (Borsa Italiana), for the listing of shares, requires the issuer to have a minimal capital of 5,000,000 euro (see Regolamento e Istruzioni dei Mercati Organizzati e Gestiti da Borsa Italiana S.p.A.). It is also stated that the company's "capital and reserves, including profit or loss, from the last financial year, may be at least one million [euro]"; however, according to the following Article 43(2), the requisite of the minimum capitalisation can be waived by the member state, to the extent to which "the competent authorities are satisfied that there will be an adequate market of the shares concerned."

37 See Article 44 of the Listing Directive. However, according to the same law provision, such a requisite can be derogated by the competent national authority, "where such a derogation is desirable in the interests of the company or of investors and where the competent authorities are satisfied that investors have the necessary information available to be able to arrive at an informed judgement on the company and the shares for which admission to official listing is sought."

of transferability shall be required, theoretically, also for shares which "are not fully paid up as freely negotiable."[38] However, in this case, the national legislation shall be permitted to treat these shares as freely negotiable, "if arrangements have been made to ensure that the negotiability of such shares is not restricted and that dealing is made open and proper by providing the public with all appropriate information."[39]

DEBT SECURITIES

The requirements for debt securities relating to the issuer are decidedly laconic. The Listing Directive simply refers to only one – relating to the legality of the issuer: "The legal position of the undertaking must be in conformity with the laws and regulations to which it is subject, as regards both its formation and its operation under its statutes."[40] Nothing else is added in terms of requisites, markedly different from share securities, where the requirements relating to the issuer are significantly more extensive. The reason for this is an economic rather than a legal one. The investment in shares carries with it a higher level of uncertainty; they represent the capital of the company and their value fluctuates, by definition, in proportion to the performance of the issuer. As a result, information relating to the issuer is fundamental in enabling the investor to assess the level of risk involved. Conversely, the debt security is a contractual obligation on the part of the company to return the capital invested by the investors, plus interest. Other than enabling the investor to assess his counterparty's risk of default, information relating to the issuer is deemed to be less essential.

In addition to the provision according to which "[t]he debt securities must be freely negotiable,"[41] which also applies to shares, the Listing Directive requires that "debt securities" comply "with the laws and regulations in which they are subject."[42] From a theoretical perspective, this norm is intended to create a harmonisation of the type of securities admissible. However, practically speaking, this would not necessarily transpire. In fact, there seem to be as many jurisdictions represented in the EU as there are variations of legislations, some of which may take a looser approach to securities and their categorisation than others.

LISTING AND LEGAL LIABILITIES

Tort law, and, more generally, the law that governs liabilities in the context of the listing of securities, is still very much an affair of national law, as the Listing Directive has not ventured into this area. Specificities of such liability can therefore not

38 Article 45 Listing Directive. It is worth recalling that the concept of "freely transferrable" securities reverberates on Article 40 of the MiFID Directive too, as already discussed previous.

39 Article 46(2) Listing Directive.

40 Article 42 Listing Directive.

41 Article 54 Listing Directive.

42 Article 53 Listing Directive.

be covered within the context of the present book, as this would require an arduous analysis of both the contract law and law of tort existing in each jurisdiction.

Nonetheless, it is possible to indicate various legal actions possible: initiated by the issuer against the arranger (or arrangers) for responsibilities entailed to the mandate, for instance, or by the issuer against its legal advisors or financial advisors for negligence in the way the mandate has been carried out.[43] Additionally, investors too may be entitled to initiate legal proceedings against the issuer and the arranger(s) for any deceitful offer of the securities. In this respect, the range of possible scenarios which could generate such an outcome are numerous, albeit predominantly relating to the way the prospectus has been drafted, such as an incorrect description of the business of the issuer or of the securities, an incorrect reference to financial data, or an incorrect description of legal data within the prospectus. As a default response to all these potential cases, the arranger would either resist the relevant claim alone or, if contractually possible, raise an indemnity action against the accountants involved with the listing[44] or the relevant team of legal advisors.[45]

As stated, the Listing Directive does not hint at any concept of responsibility; however, an attempt of harmonisation is made under an adjacent piece of legislation.

THE OFFER OF SECURITIES

If securities are offered, a general duty arises to inform the public of the kind of financial instruments which will thereafter be offered. Such securities may take the form of shares (*i.e.* representing equity) or bonds (*i.e.* representing debt). Irrespective of the form of securities issued (either equity or debt), these instruments, if offered to the public, must comply with certain rules so as to ensure that the beneficiary of the securities (the investor) is duly informed of the specific risk entailed to that investment.[46] This objective is achieved by way of the prospectus: a document that should contain the data the investor may reasonably be expected to rely on as regards both the issuer (the entity offering the securities) and the financial instruments being offered to the market.

The following subsections will address the prospectus and the modalities whereby this document is required to be drafted, under the relevant law provisions. In addressing such provisions, emphasis shall be placed on the relevant EU directives in this matter, as it is widely acknowledged that the Brussels regulator has been particularly productive in this area of financial law.

43 The issuer may sue for professional negligence their lawyers for not correctly advising the issuer.

44 For instance, if the negligence is due to incorrect financial data provided to the arranger by the accountants involved with the listing.

45 The circumstances in this case could be several – for instance, negligence or omission in the way the legal advisors have liaised with the authority.

46 See the Prospectus Directive, particularly Recital 18: "The provision of full information concerning securities and issuers of those securities promotes, together with rules on the conduct of business, the protection of investors. Moreover, such information provides an effective means of increasing confidence in securities and thus of contributing to the proper functioning and development of securities markets. The appropriate way to make this information available is to publish a prospectus."

As alluded, the prospectus is legislated upon under the Prospectus Directive – a statute reflecting a legislative development which originated in 1980 and, ultimately, came to fruition roughly a decade ago. It still applies, although it has been amended in recent times.[47]

Historically, the concept of a prospectus does not have an EU genesis. Rather, its *ratio essendi* can be tracked back to experience across the Atlantic in the US securities markets, with its legislation enacted there since as early as the 1930s (particularly the Securities Exchange Act of 1934). The underpinning philosophy of the 1934 Securities Exchange Act, despite the highs and lows during its 80 years of lifespan, still remains basically the same, and this applies in its adaptation within the EU financial markets during the 1980s: it is based on the idea that mandatory disclosure of the issuer and its instruments is necessary and that it improves standards of corporate governance of the company.[48] It is argued in the law and economics literature that the more information is available, the closer to fairness the prices of securities are.[49]

However, the latest financial crisis engendered intriguing and, at the same time, dramatic questions as to whether such disclosure is actually effective. Nonetheless, the EU approach to the matter remains the same: mandatory instead of mere voluntary disclosure will still remain the architrave of the architecture in this area of law, although probably the real challenge in future will be the content and its effectiveness in terms of protection of the investor. Investor protection in connection with a specific financial instrument is considered one of the fundamental aims of the Prospectus Directive.[50] As indicated, the risk attached to any investment is borne by the investor and any investment in securities is intrinsically insidious. The Prospectus Directive builds on this risk and notes, at Recital 19:

> Investment in securities, like any other form of investment, involves risk. Safeguards for the protection of the interests of actual and potential investors are required in all Member States in order to enable them to make an informed assessment of such risks and thus to take investment in full knowledge of the facts.

As a result, public companies, or those which aspire to become such, are under an obligation to provide the public (and, therefore, the potential investors) with a minimal level of disclosure to ensure that the risk entailed to the investment is

47 See particularly Directive 2010/73/EU of the European Parliament and of the Council of 24 November 2010 amending Directives 2003/71/EC on the prospectus to be published when securities are offered to the public or admitted to trading and 2004/109/EC on the harmonisation of transparency requirements in relation to information about issuers whose securities are admitted to trading on a regulated market, OJ L 327.

48 The unfettered reliance on the disclosure has been questioned by authors inclined to thinking that this disclosure is far from helpful. See Benston (1969).

49 (Coffee 1984).

50 Recital 16 Prospectus Directive. The Prospectus Directive has therefore also been defined as a "product-driven" piece of legislation.

not unknown. The information should be "sufficient" (in terms of quantity of data provided) as well as "objective" (in the way both the securities and the economic circumstances of the issuer are described).[51] Coupled with this is the principle that the information must be disclosed "in an easily analysable and comprehensible form."[52]

THE PROSPECTUS DIRECTIVE

The Prospectus Directive[53] does not apply to all types of financial instruments, nor are its requirements mandatory for all issuers. As to financial instruments, the directive applies to "securities" defined as follows:

> shares in companies and other securities equivalent to shares in companies, bonds and other forms of securities debt which are negotiable on the capital market and any other securities normally dealt in giving the right to acquire any such transferrable securities by subscription or exchange or giving rise to a cash settlement excluding instruments of payment.[54]

Pursuant to the same provision, this definition of securities may be expanded and supplemented at national level.

As far as issuers to which the Prospectus Directive applies are concerned, the exemptions (for specific issuers) encompassed by the Prospectus Directive are multifarious and shall be elaborated upon here. To give at least a fleeting glimpse at the issue, however, reference could be made to some types of issuers that, given their public nature, are exempted from the Prospectus Directive, such as the European Central Bank or any central bank of EU member states.

The prospectus Is a document that, according to the intention of the EU legislator, should ensure the achievement in particular, of investor protection. Despite its central role, the "prospectus" is not defined in the legislation under discussion.[55] However, a clear description of its functions is provided under Article 5, where it is stipulated as follows:

> [T]he prospectus shall contain all information which, according to the particular nature of the issuer and of the securities offered to the public or admitted to trading on a regulated market, is necessary to enable investors to make an informed assessment of the assets and liabilities, financial position, profit and losses, and prospects of the issuer and of any guarantor, an of the rights attaching to such securities.

51 Recital 20 Prospectus Directive.

52 Recital 20 Prospectus Directive.

53 In the literature, a brief description of the main aspects of the Prospectus Directive can be read in the following: (Scott, International Finance 2010).

54 Article 2(1)(a) Prospectus Directive.

55 There is no sign of if within the "definitions" at Article 2.

Under applicable national law of contract, the prospectus may qualify as a contract.[56]

A prospectus consists of an analytical part, where emphasis is placed on both the issuer and the securities, and a summary.[57] The latter, "in a brief manner and in non-technical language, convey[s] the essential characteristics and risks associated with the issuer, any guarantor and the securities, the language in which the prospectus was originally drawn up." The summary shall also contain a series of cautions, such as an elucidation of the civil liabilities attached to those who have drafted the summary, including the translation.[58]

The responsibility lies with the EU Commission, according to Article 7 of the Prospectus Directive, to provide requirements for the "specific information" required for each type of security. In this respect, the Commission periodically publishes a list of model prospectuses which, in turn, are adopted at a national level within the prevailing legislation of each member state.[59]

Although the power exercised by the Commission in establishing model prospectuses is quite discretionary, the Prospectus Directive does not refrain from shedding some light on a few of the main rules and principles. Firstly, the principal distinction to be acknowledged is between equity securities and non-equity securities (such as debt securities).[60] In this respect, the information required is less for non-equity securities, seemingly on the assumption that the degree of risk carried by an equity investment is higher.[61]

Additionally, the various models available can be categorised in respect to retail offers and non-retail offers. The latter category, *i.e.* offers with a denomination per unit of at least 100,000 euro, typically requires less information, as they are addressed to qualified investors in a better position to assess the risk.

A further distinction can be made in relation to the issuer, according to its size and its activities.[62] For small and medium enterprises, for instance, the EU Commission is permitted to impose a less stringent level of disclosure, for purposes of simplification. Furthermore, the nature of the issuer is usually taken into consideration by the Commission so that qualified categories of issuers that are already supervised by a specific authority, are subject to less arduous models of

56 Under English law, the "prospectus constitutes a contractual document above all else" (Hudson 2013).

57 Article 5(2) Prospectus Directive.

58 Article 5(2)(letters from a) to d)) Prospectus Directive. On liabilities, see the following section below.

59 The models "created" by the EU Commission are contained in Commission Delegated Regulations issued on annual basis. See http://ec.europa.eu/internal_market/securities/prospectus/index_en.htm (accessed on 23 July 2014.

60 Article 7(2)(a) Prospectus Directive.

61 In investing in debt-securities, the simple question for the investor is to assess whether the issues is in a position (or not) to honour the relevant payment upon maturity; conversely, in an equity investment, the investor's risk assessment impinges, also, on the way the company is managed and is in a position to make a profitable activity (Panasar and Boeckman, European Securities Law 2010).

62 Article 7(2)(3) Prospectus Directive.

prospectus.[63] The rationale behind this is that these entities are already supervised by a local authority, so that a simplified model of prospectus would avoid a potential duplication in the investigation on the issuer. In the same vein, a government issuing a bond shall be permitted to publish a simplified model of prospectus, on the assumption that a government is a reliable issuer and a secure paymaster.[64]

Not every offer of transferable securities gives rise to an obligation to publish a prospectus. Conversely, two circumstances trigger such an obligation: (1) the actual promotion of an offer of transferable securities to the public and (2) the admission of transferable securities to an EEA regulated market.[65]

The first aspect of the first condition is more or less self-evident. In this respect, the Prospectus Directive stipulates, among its definitions, that a prospectus shall be qualified as "a communication to persons in any form and by any means, presenting sufficient information in the terms of the offer and securities to be offered, so as to enable an investor to decide to purchase or subscribe to these securities."[66] The definition of "offer to the public," provided by the EU legislator, is clearly wider than the notion of "contractual offer," which may have a specific meaning under the applicable national law of contract and may as such be binding on the offeror. The reason for this is that the EU legislator, so as to better safeguard the investor, has wished to further widen the ambit of the Prospectus Directive to also include mere invitations or enticements concerned with transferable securities (which under the applicable national law of contract may not be binding on the offeror).

The second condition to be met for the obligation to publish a prospectus, is the admission of the relevant transferable securities to an EEA regulated market. In other words, the publication of the prospectus is not solely dependent on the communication of an offer to the public, but also on the circumstances in which the relevant securities actually "enter" (*i.e.* are going to be listed in) a regulated market.

Some offers to the public fall within the scope of the Prospectus Directive but are exempted from the obligation that a prospectus be published. Exemptions contrast with further situations that totally fall outside the scope of the Prospectus Directive; in these cases, the Prospectus Directive shall not apply at all.[67] As to the exemptions, their rationale usually is a trade-off between the aims of the directive and the burden with which an offeror can reasonably be charged.

63 Article 7(2)(d) of the Prospectus Directive.

64 Article 7(2)(f)) Prospectus Directive.

65 It is correctly pointed out (Schammo 2011) that, although "the term 'admission to trading of securities' does not have a special or specified meaning in EU law," indeed "regulated market" is "an EU law concept" as defined by the MiFID Directive. See also Panasar and Boeckman, European Securities Law (2010).

66 Article 2(1)(d)) Prospectus Directive. Cf. also (Schammo 2011)for purposes of the definition, "the support or medium used to communicate an offer does not matter."

67 Article 1(2) of Directive 2003/71 refers to some cases of lack of applicability, such as, among the others, "units by collective investment undertakings other than the closed-end type" (let. a), the "non-equity securities issued by a Member State or by one of a Member State's regional authorities, by public international bodies of which one or more Member States are members, by the European Central Bank or by the central banks of the Member States" (let. b).

A first bunch of exemptions (*i.e.* technically defined cases where "*the obligation to publish a prospectus shall not apply*") are contemplated under Article 3 of the Prospectus Directive, and are as follows: (1) an offer of securities addressed solely to qualified investors;[68] (2) an offer of securities addressed to fewer than 100 natural or legal persons per member state, other than qualified investors;[69] (3) an offer of securities addressed to investors who acquire securities for a total consideration of at least 100,000 euro per investor, for each separate offer;[70] (4) an offer of securities whose denomination per unit amounts to at least 100,000 euro;[71] (5) an offer of securities with a total consideration of less than 100,000 euro with the threshold calculated over a 12-month period.[72]

A further area of exemptions is contemplated in detail under Article 4(1) of the Prospectus Directive. Examples are an offer to the public of shares representing, over a period of 12 months, less than 10% of the number of shares of the same class already admitted to trading on the same regulated market,[73] and shares issued in substitution for shares of the same class already admitted to trading on the same regulated market, should the issuing of such shares not involve any increase in the issued capital.[74]

68 "Qualified investors" are mainly seasoned investors whose level of expertise, experience and knowledge is such that they do not require the same level of protection as ordinary investors. In this area, the 2010 amendment of the Prospectus Directive has marked a turning point in the definition of "qualified investor." In its initial wording, the Prospectus Directive utilised is own definition and, therefore, qualified investors mainly as entities, and not individuals, with a presumable knowledge in financial products. Among these, there were banks and investment firms, but also governments and supranational institutions as well as corporations; the latter would have satisfied the definition so long as they employed 250 employees, they had a total balance sheet of over 43,000,000 euro and an annual turnover exceeding 50,000,000 euro. This first category was automatically given the status of qualified investors; in lack of the occurrence of the relevant requisites, the investor was not qualified, for purposes of the Prospectus Directive. Nowadays, the distinction in the Prospectus Directive reflects – and is connected to – the category of professional clients and retail clients, as traced in the MiFID Directive and, more recently, the MiFID II Directive. See Schammo (2011).

69 This is called a private placement; therefore, an offer addressed to a so negligible amount of investors, including individuals or "small" enterprises, that the requirement of the publication of the prospectus would be overly burdensome.

70 The required subscription, per each investor, of an number of securities for a value of no less than 100,000 euro means that, practically, exclusively major investors are concerned with the offer, rather than retail investors. Therefore, the reason for protecting the investor through the rules of the Prospectus Directive does not arise. The original threshold was 50,000 euro per investor, in 2010 increased to the latest one. See Article 7(2)(b) and 19(4) of the Prospectus Directive, as amended respectively (Schammo 2011).

71 The reason of the exclusion is similar to the previous one; a minimal amount of 100,000 euro per unit means that, *de facto*, that offer is an off-limits area for retail investors, and conversely a hunting ground exclusively for major investors.

72 In this case, the reason for the exclusion is opposite; the offer is so negligible in its value that it is presumed not to cause any possible financial harm to any investor.

73 For instance, a listed company with a share capital of 100,000,000 euro, which decided to increase its share capital by no more than 9,000,000 euro, with offer of these shares to the public, would be exempt from the publication of the prospectus.

74 In this case, the exemption is necessary to avoid what otherwise would be a duplication of administrative encumbrances, where in reality there is no need for this, as the share capital remains the same.

A further reason for an EU statute on prospectuses is that it allows for the achievement of synergies of scale in the offer of securities across the European Union. In fact, theoretically speaking, in the absence of common rules on the matter, each authority competent in every country should assume control over the approval of the prospectus in cases where the applicant decided to promote a cross-border offer of securities. To avoid any duplication of costs and legal burdens, the Prospectus Directive ensures that the prospectus is afforded an EU passport, thereby confirming that the approval of the prospectus by a competent national authority in an EU member state suffices for purposes of further approvals by other authorities of the European countries where the securities are additionally offered.[75]

The tricky issue is to identify the "competent authority." Theoretically, a supranational legislator such as the EU could have adopted a liberal approach, where the issuer decides upon an authority from those operating in EEA countries (not necessarily coinciding with the corporate office of the issuer) for purposes of the approval of the prospectus. Following this line of reasoning, once the prospectus would have been approved by this authority, the offer could proceed everywhere in the EEA without a need for any additional approval, while the offeror would benefit from a "non-home passport." However, if the system was as just described, the home-country authority of the issuer could feel to lose control over the activities and affairs of the issuer. To avoid this, the principle adopted by the Prospectus Directive is more rigorous: for transferable securities, the competent authority is the authority of the country where the issuer has its registered office.[76]

The exception to the norm arises in the case of an offer of non-equity securities with a denomination of at least 1,000 euro, or cash-settled warrants and exchangeable securities.[77] In these limited scenarios, the offeror shall be entitled to shop around before selecting, for approval of the prospectus, either the authority within the EEA of the country where the securities will be offered to the public or admitted to a regulated market, or the authority of the country of the issuer. A passported prospectus, approved in an EEA state according to the Prospectus Directive and used in a different EEA country, shall be provided with a certificate of approval of the competent authority, and a translation of the summary in the official language where it is going to be exported.

The prospectus must be approved in advance by the "competent authority" before it can be published and the subsequent offer to the public can commence. The request for approval is an administrative process whereby the prospectus is submitted to the authority which, after subjecting it to scrutiny, notifies the issuer that the publications can be released. The scrutiny undertaken by the authority does not pertain to the economic merit of the offeror; rather, it is a formal analysis of the

75 See on the EU passport also extensively above.

76 Article 2(1)(m)(i) Prospectus Directive.

77 Article 2(1)(m)(i) Prospectus Directive. As far as exchangeable securities are concerned, the additional condition is that the securities for which they can be exchanged are not those of the issuer or entity of its group.

compliance with the laws existing in the country of the authority, most notably the (implemented) Prospectus Directive.

The exact nature of the process is determined by the legislation of each respective EEA country; however, the EU legislator has codified some general guidelines, particularly in relation to the deadline for approval of the prospectus. In this respect, the time limit is 10 days from the submission of the draft prospectus by the offeror or the person requesting the admission (such as the arranger).[78] However, the time limit shall be extended to 20 days, "if the public offer involves securities issued by an issuer which does not have any securities admitted to trading on a regulated market and who has not previously offered securities to the public."[79] This time proviso, although ostensibly strict, is in reality mitigated by a provision, enforced by authorities to the point where it has become standard practice, allowing the authority to suspend, "on reasonable grounds," the time permitted if "the documents submitted . . . are incomplete" or "supplementary information is needed."[80] Finally, it is worth elucidating that should either deadline (10 or 20 days, respectively) lapse without the authority having granted the approval, this shall not be taken by the applicant as silent consent (Article 13(2)). Should such a scenario arise (*i.e.* lack of action on the part of the authority), the applicant, in accordance with the applicable national law, may have the option to sue the authority for damages. A likelier solution, however, would see the offeror (or arranger, on its behalf) set up amicable conversations so that the impasse may be clarified.

Tort law generally, and professional liability law in particular, continues to remain largely a matter of national discretion,[81] although some recent attempts at harmonisation have been made within the body of EU legislation.[82] Yet the Prospectus Directive, in this area, does not aim to achieve a proper harmonisation of the civil liability regimes.[83]

78 Article 13(2) Prospectus Directive.

79 Article 13(3) Prospectus Directive.

80 Article 13(4) Prospectus Directive.

81 As far as English law is concerned, any "negligent misstatement" of a party to another usually falls within the sphere of the tortious liability. So long as the defendant realises that the claimant may rely on the false representation, a common law liability will arise (*Shinhan Bank Ltd v Sea Containers Ltd* [2000] Lloyd's Rep. 406). However, the real issue remains as to whether a person, particularly an investor or categories of investor, is able to rely on that statement (see *Possfund Custodian Trustee Ltd v Diamond* [1996] 2 All E.R. 774; *Al-Nakib Investments (Jersey) Ltd v Longcroft* [1990] 3 All E.R. 321). Among scholars, see Hudson (2013). Under the same English law, the offer of securities via a prospectus would give rise to a contract between the offeror and the subscriber; therefore, theoretically, an incorrect statement in a prospectus should be regarded as a breach of contract. However, the courts in Britain have been so far quite reluctant to hold such a liability, on the basis that the statement is not simply a term of a contract (Panasar and Boeckman, European Securities Law 2010).

82 Article 35a(1) of the Regulation 1060/2009/EC of the European Parliament and of the Council of 16 September 2009 on credit rating agencies Credit Rating Agency Regulation (as amended by Regulation 462/2013/EC) contains, for the first time, a direct ground for a liability claim against credit rating agency.

83 The German proposal to introduce an effective common field of civil and tort liability in this area was abandoned in the final draft of the Prospectus Directive (Schammo 2011).

More specifically, under Article 6(2) Prospectus Directive, each member state is required to ensure that, in each jurisdiction, "laws, regulation and administrative provisions on civil liability apply to those persons responsible for the information given in a prospectus."[84] This provision seems vague enough to avoid any conflict with national laws, as it will probably suffice for each member state, to have its civil liability regime apply to the prospectus.[85] However, it is theoretically possible to infer that a member state will be held to be in breach of the EU legislation, if it proved to have inadequate internal rules to tackle for the issue of misleading information in the prospectus. Those who should be held responsible are at least the "issuer" (and its management), the "offeror"[86] and "the person asking for the admission to trading on a regulated market" or "the guarantor," as the case may be.[87] The role each of those persons plays in connection to the listing should be identified in the prospectus, so as to avoid any issues of transparency at a later point.[88]

3.1.2 Secondary market

From an economic point of observation, the secondary market differs markedly from the primary market. The latter deals with the issuance of securities and possible admittance of those securities to the market for the first time, whereas the former is concerned with the trade of securities which have already been issued and may be traded in a regulated market. This distinction in definition is echoed in the legal framework. More specifically, the legislation addressed to the primary market deals with the way financial instruments must be introduced to the market for the first time (therefore, listing and/or prospectus topics discussed previously in

84 An example of implementation of this rule is the British legislation. Sect. 90 of the Financial Services and Markets Act 2000 cuts out the requirement, existing in the law of tort of that country, to prove breach of a duty of care, as the causation will suffice for purposes of a tortious liability. In this respect, the British statute transposes into the legislation the common law rule encapsulated in *Possfund Custodian Trustee Ltd v Diamond* [1996] 2 All E.R. 774.

Additionally, pursuant to Section 84(1)(d) of the same Financial Services and Markets Act 2000, paragraph 5.5.3R of the Prospectus Rules identifies some categories of professionals responsible for the prospectus: (1) the issuer; (2) directors and any other individual and/or professional giving the authorisation to be named as responsible for the prospectus; (3) any other individual and/or professional who has authorised the prospectus or part of it.

85 (Panasar and Boeckman, European Securities Law 2010). In this contribution, it is correctly emphasised that the mosaic of differing liability regimes, still inevitable in this phase of the EU integration, may still represent an impediment to the development of a pan-European market (ibid. 40).

86 Remarkably, according to the definitions of Directive 2003/71 (Article 2)(1), the "issuer" is "a legal entity which issues or proposes to issue securities" (let. h); the "offeror" (or "person making an offer") means, conversely, a "legal entity or individual which offers securities to the public" (let. i).

87 Article 6(1) Prospectus Directive.

88 Again, Article 6(1), part 2.: "The persons responsible shall be clearly identified in the prospectus by their names and functions or, in the case of legal persons, their names and registered offices, as well as declarations by them that, to the best of their knowledge, the information contained in the prospectus is in accordance with the facts and that the prospectus makes no omission likely to affect its import."

Chapter 2). Conversely, legislation relating to the secondary market concerns the modalities whereby securities may be transferred, whilst also accounting for the legislator's interest in protection of the investor and the credibility of the market against any lack of transparency or general confusion which may befall it. Accordingly, the legislation at EU level in this area tackles two possible issues: firstly, the abusive nature by which securities once issued are dealt with from time to time and, secondly, the protection which investors must be afforded in cases where significant holdings in listed securities are transferred.

Regulation on market abuse

A regulated market of transferable securities must be based on principles of transparency, as the investor invests his money in a publicly traded company (either in its shares or bonds or in other securities) on the assumption that he can be informed of all relevant information relating to the securities (and the issuer). In contrast to a transparent market is an opaque market, where crucial information is withheld or even misleading.

If speculated upon from an ultra-liberal perspective, the market would ideally rule itself and would therefore not require any form of government regulation aimed at ensuring transparency. Following this line of reasoning, the stock market should be self-governing. The prevailing approach nowadays is that the investor – and his legitimate expectations to be furnished with transparent information – cannot rely on the benevolent cooperation of the issuer and its management. Therefore, it is generally believed that strict rules must be imposed on the issuer and, to a certain extent, on the market in which it operates. At EU level, this imposition is conveyed by way of legislation which, for more than a decade, has been adopted in order to protect the investor: principally embodied in European Parliament and Council Directive 2003/6/EC of 28 January 2003 on insider dealing and market manipulation (henceforth also the "*Market Abuse Directive*" or "*MA Directive*"), and entered into force in April 2003 through Implementing Directive 2003/124.[89]

89 In full: Commission Directive 2003/124/EC of 22 December 2003 Implementing Directive 2003/6/EC of the European Parliament and of the Council as regards the definition and public disclosure of inside information and the definition of market manipulation, OJ C 161. The MA Regulation was published on 7 June 2014 and entered into force on the 20th day following this application, *i.e.* on 28 June 2014. It shall replace the current MA Directive no earlier than 3 July 2016 for its main body of provisions: Article 39 MA Regulation. However, for some specific law provisions contemplated in the same Article 39, the applicability has already started on 2 July 2014.

The "expiry date" for the MA Directive to be implemented in each member state was 12 October 2004. Among the ancillary EU pieces of legislation following up on the MA Directive and Implementing Directive, it is worth highlighting the following ones: Commission Directive 2003/125/EC implementing Council Directive 2003/6/EC as regards the fair presentation of investment recommendations and the disclosure of conflicts of interest; Commission Directive 2004/72 implementing Directive 2003/6/EC as regards accepted market practices, the definition of inside information in relation to derivatives on commodities, the drawing up of lists of insiders, the notification of managers' transactions and the notification of suspicious transactions. See Wood, Regulation of International Finance (2007b).

More recently, the MA Directive and its ancillary legislation has been surpassed and overtaken by a new EU legislative structure mainly based on the following:

1. Regulation (EU) No 596/2014 (henceforth also the "Market Abuse Regulation" or the "MA Regulation");[90]
2. Directive 2014/57/EU of the European Parliament and of the Council of 16 April 2014 (henceforth also the "New Market Abuse Directive" or the "New MA Directive").[91]

The underpinning philosophy of both the MA Directive and the MA Regulation still remains identical in its substance. Recital 12 of the MA Directive stipulates as follows:

> The objective of legislation against insider dealing is the same as that of legislation against manipulation to ensure the integrity of Community financial markets and to enhance investor confidence in those markets. It is therefore advisable to adopt combined rules to combat both insider dealing and market manipulation. A single Directive will ensure throughout the Community the same framework for allocation of responsibilities, enforcement and cooperation.

The ultimate MA Regulation seems to adhere to the same line of reasoning, more specifically at Recital 2, which emphasises as follows:

> An integrated, efficient and transparent financial market requires market integrity. The smooth functioning of securities markets and public confidence in markets are prerequisites for economic growth and wealth. Market abuse harms the integrity of financial markets and public confidence in securities and derivatives.

Nonetheless, the MA Regulation marks a significant step forward for the EU financial legislation; it reflects how significantly different the financial markets now are from those which, more than a decade ago, inspired the creation of Directive 2003/6. It is worth mentioning, among multifarious phenomena: (1) the emergence of new markets, platforms and over-the-counter markets trading in financial instruments; (2) inefficiencies in the way the previous legislation had regulated commodities and commodity derivatives; and (3) the lack of effective enforcement of the MA Directive by the authorities.

90 Regulation 596/2014/EU of the European Parliament and of the Council of 16 April 2014 "on market abuse (Market Abuse Regulation) and repealing Directive 2003/6/EC of the European Parliament and of the Council and Commission Directives 2003/124/EC, 2003/125/EC and 2004/72/EC."

91 Directive 2014/57/EU of the European Parliament and of the Council of 16 April 2014 "on criminal sanctions for market abuse."

Against the backdrop of this ever-changing and dynamic background, the EU legislator has developed an ambitious programme. It does not only focus, as already purported by the MA Directive, "on financial instruments admitted to trading on a regulated market or for which a request for admission to trading on such a market has been made,"[92] but also on "any financial instruments traded on a regulated market, an MTF or an OTF, and any other conduct for action which can have an effect on such a financial instrument irrespective of whether it takes place on a trading venue."[93]

In this new scenario, the principal activities subjected to the spotlight of the MA Regulation are, fundamentally, still those sanctioned by the previous statute, namely, "insider dealing," "unlawful disclosure of inside information" and "market manipulation."[94] Accordingly, detailed explanation shall be provided later in this chapter, in respect to each. But first, it is worth clarifying the magnitude of the pertinent piece of legislation in this area, in terms of securities and markets involved, particularly in light of the MA Regulation recently passed in Brussels.

Directive on market abuse

In regard to securities, the MA Directive adopted an already broad outlook, as inferable from the definition provided under its Article 1(3). Actually, when juxtaposed with other examples of EU legislation, including the Prospectus Directive which exclusively deals with "transferable securities,"[95] the scope was even greater, given the fact that the wording of the MA Directive referred to "financial instruments" and therefore also covered: units in collective investment undertakings; money market instruments; financial-futures contracts; forward interest-rate agreements; interest-rate, currency and equity swaps; options to acquire or dispose of any instrument falling into these categories, including equivalent cash-settled instruments, derivatives on commodities; and any other instrument admitted to trading on a regulated market in a member state or for which a request for admission to trading on such a market has been made.

The MA Regulation even enlarges and expands the magnitude of the previous legislation. Pursuant to Article 3(2) of the MA Regulation, this Regulation mainly relies on a dual layer: on the one hand, it covers "securities" (let. a),[96] roughly corresponding to what previously defined by the MA Directive; on the other hand, it also covers "associated instruments" (let. b), including those which "are not admitted to trading or traded on a trading venue, or for which a request for admission to

92 Recital 8 of the MA Regulation.

93 Again, Recital 8 of the MA Regulation.

94 Recital 7 of the MA Regulation. In broader terms, market abuse is "a concept that encompasses unlawful behaviour in the financial markets."

95 See above.

96 More specifically, according to Article 3(2)(a) of the MA Regulation, "securities" are (1) "shares and other securities equivalent to shares," (2) "bonds and other forms of securities debt" or (3) "securitised debt convertible or exchangeable into shares or into other securities equivalent to shares."

trading on a trading venue has not been made."[97] Remarkably, the MA Directive used to connect the "financial instruments" to the "regulated markets," and in this respect, it is thought the MA Regulation will improve the effectiveness of the past legislation. In other words, not every category of financial instruments used to fall within the previous legislation, rather exclusively those which, in every EEA country, resulted in being admitted to officially recognised markets and included in the list that the EU Commission, in cooperation with each national authority, used to keep updated.[98] For financial instruments not admitted to trading on a regulated market in a member state, but whose values depended on financial instruments indeed admitted to trading in an EU, or better, in an EEA financial market, the main provisions of the MA Directive used to apply (Article 2, 3 and 4) but not the entire piece of legislation.

Pursuant to Article 2 of the new MA Regulation, it shall apply not only to "financial instruments admitted to trading on a regulated market" (as already prescribed under the MA Directive) but also to those "for which a request for admission to regulated market has been made." Additionally, and in a way significantly different from the past, the MA Regulation shall apply also to "financial instruments traded on an MTF, admitted to trading on an MTF or for which a request for admission to trading to an MTD has been made,"[99] "financial instruments traded on an OTF"[100] and "financial instruments [different from the previous ones, MH, PdG], the price or values of which depends on or has an effect on the price of a financial instrument referred to in those points, including, but not limited to, credit default swaps and contracts for difference."[101] By way of interpretation of the new rules and their enlarged scope, well beyond the perimeter of the regulated markets, it can be affirmed that the EU legislator wants to ensure, in light of the exponential dimension of the market of OTC derivatives which many believe has contributed to the last financial crisis, that the rigorous provisions on market abuse existing in the regulated markets be not circumvented through practices left unlegislated in the adjacent non-regulated markets. The outcome of this is that obligations and duties applicable to the operators in both markets are made symmetric.

INSIDER DEALING

The first category of behaviour which falls within the scope of the MA Regulation is "insider dealing." Those in possession of inside information are prevented from

97 The list of letter b is multifarious: among the different "associated instruments" mention can be made to (1) "contracts or rights to subscribe for, acquire or dispose of securities" or (2) "financial derivatives of securities." The MA Directive did not apply to this typology of financial instruments.

98 In other words, the provisions encompassed with the *corpus iuris* of the previous MA Directive were triggered by an important condition: that is to say, the financial instruments concerned be admitted to trading on a regulated market in at least one member state, or at least a request of admission to trading in one of the EU regulated market has been lodged. See Article 9(1) of the MA Directive.

99 Article 2(1)(b) of the MA Regulation.

100 Article 2(1)(c) of the MA Regulation.

101 Article 2(1)(d) of the MA Regulation.

using such knowledge to acquire or dispose of, or try to acquire or dispose of, for their own account or on behalf of others, either directly or indirectly, financial instruments to which that information relates.[102] In light of this brief description, insider dealing, as described by the MA Regulation,[103] is centred on the concept of both "insider" and "inside information." The insider, for purposes of the EU piece of legislation under discussion, is the person possessing this information because he is, somehow, connected with the issuer and/or financial instruments. To elaborate, according to the terminology of the MA Regulation,[104] the insider shall be

> any person who possesses that information as a result of (a) being a member of the administrative, management or supervisory bodies of the issuer . . . ; (b) having a holding in the capital of the issuer . . . ;[105] (c) having access to the information through the exercise of an employment, profession or duties; or (d) being involved in criminal activities.[106]

In other words, insiders are those engaged in a strategic endeavour within the confines of the issuer's business[107] or in connection with it[108] or, in any case, those who obtain the information by virtue of their criminal pursuits.

Inside information constitutes any information, "of a precise nature,"[109] "which has not been made public" and that relates, "directly or indirectly, to one or more issuers or to one or more financial instruments."[110] Information, as articulated in

102 Article 8(1) of the MA Regulation. To fulfil the intellectual curiosity of the reader, it may be recalled that the predecessor of such a norm was Article 2(1), subparagraph 1, of the MA Directive. Under the previous legislation, in a preliminary ruling the ECJ ((case 45/08) *Spector Photo Group v Commissie voor het Bank – Financie & Assurantiewessen* [2010] BCC 827) held that, where a person is in possession of inside information, there is a rebuttable presumption that the information has been used.

103 So was, basically, the previous MA Directive too on this specific point.

104 Article 8(4) of the MA Regulation, previously Article 2(1), subparagraph 2 MA Directive.

105 The provisions under let. a and b are extended to the "emission allowance market participant." The latter, according to the "definitions" of the MA Regulation (Article 3(1)(20)), is defined "any person who enters into transactions, including the placing of orders to trade, in emission allowances, auctioned products based thereon, or derivatives thereof."

106 It is remarkable to note that any "person" referred under Article 8(4), subparagraph 2, MA Regulation, must be extended, if a legal person, to the "natural persons" taking part in the decision "to carry out the acquisition, disposal, cancellation or amendment of an order for the account of the legal person concerned" (Article 8(5) of the MA Regulation, *mutatis mutandis* Article 2(2) of the MA Directive).

107 For instance, the management, the shareholders or those discharging professional duties within the issuer (any employee who had to come across with the inside information).

108 For instance, legal advisors, auditors or accountants.

109 Accordingly, information of generic nature should be outwith the scope of the definition.

110 This is the tenor of Article 7(1) of the MA Regulation. Previously, the basic rules were, fundamentally, the same, albeit enshrined within Article 1(1) of the MA Directive.

In a preliminary ruling of the EUCJ (case 19/11) *Markus Geltl v Daimler AG* [2012] 3 CMLR 32), the chairman of the multinational company Daimler informed the supervisory board that he was thinking of resigning, but actually he did not do so for another two months. At that time, the stock exchanges were notified and the share prices rose. Shareholders who had previously sold

this definition, if made public, should, in all likelihood, impart a telling blow (positive or negative) or, in the terminology of the MA Regulation, have "a significant effect," "on the prices of those financial instruments or on the price of related derivative financial instruments."[111]

Finally, the MA Directive required each member state to implement at national level administrative sanctions for the violations of the principles, while it was left to the discretion of the local legislator which nature those sanctions would have (either criminal or civil).[112] In a significant move from the past, the new EU body of law by way of the Directive 2014/57[113] establishes "minimum rules for criminal sanction for insider dealing," but also for the other two categories of conduct of unlawful disclosure and market manipulation, "to ensure the integrity of financial markets in the Union and to enhance investor protection and confidence in those markets."[114]

UNLAWFUL DISCLOSURE OF INSIDE INFORMATION

The underpinning philosophy of the MA Regulation is to prohibit the persons concerned (the "insider," as defined in the same statute) from disclosing inside information to any other person ("except where the disclosure is made in the normal

---

their shares sued for compensation. It was held that intermediate steps in a protracted process might have been tantamount to *"precise information."*

111 Article 7(1)(a) of the MA Regulation, previous, *mutatis mutandis*, Article 1(1) of the Market Abuse Directive.

Remarkably, as a result of the MA Regulation, the concept of "inside information," if relating to "commodity derivatives," shall "bask" in a larger perimeter of application. More specifically, as a result of the Article 7(1)(b) of the MA Regulation, the "inside information" relating to commodity derivatives is independent of the fact that the contract shall be listed in a market.

As far as persons in charge of the execution of orders concerning financial instruments, "inside information" shall mean, additionally (Article 7(1)(d) of the MA Regulation, previously Article 1(1) of the MA Directive), "information conveyed by a client and related to the client's pending orders, which is of a precise nature, relating, directly or indirectly to one or more issuers or to one or more financial instruments, and which, if it were made public, would be likely to have significant effect on the prices of those financial instruments, the price of related spot commodity contracts, or on the price of related derivatives financial instruments."

Finally (and this provision does not have any bearing with the previous text of Directive 2003/6), it is stated (Article 7(1)(c) of the Market Abuse Regulation) that, as far as emission allowances (or auctioned products based on them) are concerned, "inside information" is the "information of a precise nature, which has not been made public, relating, directly or indirectly, to one or more such instruments, and which, if it were made public, would be likely to have a significant effect on the prices of such instruments or on the prices of related derivative financial instruments."

112 This seems to be also the interpretation of scholars such as (MacNeil 2012).

113 It is remarkable that in the new "nomenclature" of the EU legislator, the directive at stake is called Market Abuse Directive. To avoid confusion with what, historically, has been the Market Abuse Directive for more than a decade (the Directive 2003/6), in this Chapter 2 the recent Directive 2014/57 shall be referred exclusively by its number.

114 Article 1(1) of the Directive 2014/57. The purpose of the legislation is also to introduce and harmonise across the EU a criminal regime in this area, in light of the fact that some jurisdictions, in the past, did not cater for criminal sanctions.

exercise of an employment, a profession or duties"[115]), or to recommend or induce "another person, on the basis of inside information, to acquire or dispose of financial instruments to which that information relates."[116]

Interestingly, the EU law provisions relating to insider dealing, when the MA Directive was still in force, used to set out "minimum standards," from which each national legislator could derogate. Thus, an EU member state which had decided to make more stringent the prohibitions of use of inside information would not infringe the MA Directive, so long as the concept of "inside information" remains correspondent to that forged in Brussels.[117]

Within the "unlawful disclosure of inside information," the MA Regulation makes reference, for the first time, to a special conduct, the "market sounding." This is basically, according to Article 11(1) of the MA Regulation, "the communication of information, prior to the announcement of a transaction, in order to gauge the interest of potential investors in a possible transaction and the conditions relating to it such as its potential size or pricing, to one or more potential investors by . . . the issuer."[118] Although conducting market soundings is a valuable tool to gauge the opinion of potential investors and therefore are quite beneficial to the financial markets (particularly when the latter either lack confidence or do not rely on a relevant benchmark or, anyway, are volatile[119]), they may require disclosure of inside information to potential investors. Market sounding, therefore, is not prohibited in principle. However, it shall require a cautious approach by the disclosing market participant; the latter, according to Article 11(3) of the MA Regulation, "shall specifically consider whether the market sounding will involve the disclosure of inside information" before the start of a market sounding. If this is the case, it shall make a written record of its conclusion and the reasons for it, with obligation to provide the authority of these records, upon request of the latter.[120]

3.1.3 Market manipulation

A further category of behaviour prohibited under the MA Regulation is that of market manipulation.[121] According to Article 1(2) of the MA Directive, the general activity of market manipulation used to branch out into three subcategories:

115 Article 0(1) of the MA Regulation, basically but not *verbatim* correspondent to Article 3(a) of the previous MA Directive.

116 Article 10(1), second part, MA Regulation, previously Article 3(b), MA Directive.

117 Under the previous MA Directive, so was the *decisum* of the ECJ (Case C-28/99 *Criminal proceedings against Jean Verdonck, Ronald Everaert and Edith de Baedts* [2001] ECR I-3399). On this assumption, see, among scholars, MacNeil (2012).

118 In addition to the "issuer," the communication can originate, according to the same Article 11(1) also by a secondary offeror of a financial instrument, an emission allowance market participant or a third party acting on behalf of them.

119 See Recital 32 of the MA Regulation.

120 See, again, Article 11(3) of the MA Regulation.

121 In a very explicit way, Article 5 of the MA Directive used to state that "Member State shall prohibit any person from engaging in market manipulation."

to mislead in terms of supply, demand or price of financial instruments; fictitious devices and deception; and dissemination of false information. Article 12 of the MA Regulation revamps the categories previously legislated, by adopting a quadripartite definition. In essence, a fourth conduct of market abuse makes its debut in the recently enacted EU statute under discussion, namely, the dissemination of false information relating to benchmarks.[122] This further *genus* may address problems of speculation as emerged during the financial debt crisis, when it may have been incorrect information relating to the sovereign debt of some eurozone countries and their capacity to repay their debt, that played havoc across the financial markets.[123]

As to the first category of market manipulation, Article 12(1)(a) of the MA Regulation refers to a defined perimeter of activities; more specifically, transactions or orders to trade or any other behaviour which does the following:

- "[G]ives, or is likely to give, false or misleading signals as to the supply of, demand for, or price of, a financial instrument, a related spot commodity contract or an auctioned product based on emission allowances" or
- "[S]ecures, or is likely to secure, the price of one or several financial instruments, a related spot commodity contract or an auctioned product based on emission allowances at an abnormal or artificial level."

According to the same article of the MA Regulation, the person entering these orders or transactions or, more in general, engaging in such behaviour shall be exempt from sanctions, if it was established that his reason for so doing is "legitimate" and that these transactions or orders to trade conform to "accepted market practice."[124]

The second area of market manipulation is concerned with a "transaction, a placing of an order to trade, or any other activity or behaviour, which employ a fictitious device or any other form of deception or contrivance."[125]

The third conduct is defined, according to Article 12(1l) of the MA Regulation, as the dissemination of information,

> through the media, including the internet, or by any other means, which gives, or is likely to give, false or misleading signals as to the supply of, demand for, or price of, a financial instrument, a related spot commodity contract or an auctioned product based on emission allowances or secures, or is likely to

122 Article 12(1)(d).

123 The dissemination of false information relating to benchmarks is not an absolute novelty; in some EU countries such as Britain, the prohibition had already been introduced before the recently enacted MA Regulation, more specifically by the *Financial Services Act 2012*.

124 The "accepted market practice" is better defined, in the MA Regulation, under Article 13. These "accepted market practices" may be established also by the competent authority on the basis of criteria defined under Article 13(2).

125 Article 12(1)(b) of the MA Regulation, previously, *mutatis mutandis*, Article 1(2)(b) MA Directive.

secure, the price of one or several financial instruments, a related spot commodity contract or an auctioned product based on emission allowances at an abnormal or artificial level, including the dissemination or rumours.

Finally and as already anticipated, the last category of conduct, introduced by the MA Regulation and not contemplated in the previous piece of legislation, is the transmission of "false or misleading information" or the provision "of false or misleading inputs in relation to a benchmark where the person who made the transmission or provided the input knew or ought to have known that it was false or misleading, or any other behaviour which manipulates the calculation of a benchmark."[126]

In all of these four circumstances, the essential condition is that "the person who made the dissemination knew, or ought to have known, that the information was false or misleading."[127, 128]

3.1.4 Disclosure of inside information; insider lists; disclosure of own account transactions by persons discharging managerial responsibilities

As when the MA Directive was still in force, the MA Regulation continues to enjoin issuers to disclose to the public inside information directly concerning them as soon as possible.[129] Nonetheless, as far as the matter of the disclosure in concerned, new notions previously missing, have been codified by the MA Regulation, namely, the "insider lists" and "the disclosure of own account transactions by persons discharging managerial responsibilities." A brief account of all shall be provided in this chapter.

As to the first category (disclosure of inside information), the relevant rules are detailed in Article 17 of the regulation under discussion.[130] The main purpose of these provisions is to ensure that one of the main values of the MA Regulation, viz. market integrity, is not affected, nor prejudiced, also in connection with an issuer.

126 Article 12(1)(d) of the MA Regulation.

127 Article 12(1)(c) of the MA Regulation.

128 Article 4 of the Implementing Directive 2003/124 used to provide details of such categories of conduct. As regards these misleading signals, mention used to be made to "the extent to which orders to trade given or transactions undertaken represent a significant proportion of the daily volume of transactions in the relevant financial instrument on the regulated market concerned, in particular when these activities lead to a significant change in the price of financial instrument." As regards all the other signals provided under Article 4 of the Implementing Directive 2003/124, now repealed, see, among scholars, (Swan and Virgo 2010). A more detailed elucidation of the concept of market manipulation was provided by an implementing document of the EU commission published on 22 December 2003, the Implementing Directive 2003/124/EC where a non-exhaustive list of "signals, which should not necessarily be deemed in themselves to constitute market manipulation," was provided.

129 See Linklaters, EU "gets tough" on Market Abuse, 20 October 2011, 4, www.linklaters.com/pdfs/mkt/london/Market_Abuse_briefing.pdf, accessed on 15 July 2014.

130 Previously, Article 6 of the MA Directive.

The MA Regulation requires the issuer to inform the public "as soon as possible" of "inside information which directly concerns that said issuer."[131] As a result, the issuer shall guarantee that "inside information is made public in a manner which enables fast access and complete, correct and timely assessment of the information by the public."[132]

Therefore, the principle of transparency adopted would require the issuer to proceed immediately to the disclosure of the inside information relating to or concerned with the same issuer. Remarkably, Article 17(4) of the MA Regulation, in the same fashion as the previous MA Directive, allows a significant exception to the norm; the dissemination of the inside information may be delayed by the same issuer in three – alternative – circumstances: (1) the immediate disclosure is likely to prejudice the legitimate interests of the issuer,[133] (2) the delay of disclosure is not likely to mislead the public or (3) the issuer[134] is in a position to keep the information confidential.[135]

As far as the "insider lists" are concerned, this is a significant and remarkable novelty of the MA Regulation. It is legislated in its Article 18 that the issuer[136] is required to draw up a list of the persons who, on the one hand, "have access to inside information" and, on the other hand, "are working for them under a contract of employment" or "performing tasks through which they have access to inside information, such as advisers, accountants or credit rating agencies."[137] Such a list, the "insider list," shall be updated "promptly" by the issuer, according to the specific modalities of Article 18(4) of the MA Regulation.[138] The provision is made even more persuasive and stringent, due to Article 18(1)(c) requiring the issuer to provide the "competent authority" with such a list.

Finally, as far as the transactions of people discharging managerial responsibilities is concerned, the MA Regulation, more specifically Article 19,[139] requires them to notify the issuer[140] and the competent authority of "every transaction conducted on their own account relating to the shares or debt instruments of that issuer or to derivatives or other financial instruments linked thereto."

131 Article 17(1), first subparagraph, MA Regulation.
132 Article 17(1), second subparagraph, MA Regulation.
133 Or the "emission allowance market participant."
134 Or the "emission allowance market participant."
135 Article 17(4) of the MA Regulation.
136 The obligation applies also to the "emission allowance market participant."
137 Article 18(1)(a) of the MA Regulation.
138 Article 18(1)(b) of the MA Regulation.
139 More specifically, Article 19(1).
140 Or, alternatively, any "emission allowance market participant." Additionally, the concept of issuer shall be that provided by the same MA Regulations, Article 3(1)(21), namely: "a legal entity governed by private or public law, which issues or proposes to issue financial instruments, the issuer being, in case of depository receipts representing financial instruments, the issuer of the financial instruments represented." Therefore, if the manager of the issuer decided to buy and sell securities issued by an entity different from the issuer, the law provisions under discussion shall not apply.

The notification at stake shall be made "promptly" and, anyway, "no later than three business days after the date of the transaction,"[141] and the content of the notification shall comply with the requirements set out under Article 19(6).[142]

Two aspects, relating to the new concept of "managers' transactions" are worthy of a clarification. Firstly, in terms of persons subject to the obligation at stake, the norm under comment is extended to "persons closely associated" with the managers of the issuer. The relevant definition of "persons closely associated" is given under Article 3(1)(26) of the MA Regulation, where, basically, reference is made to the "spouse," "a dependent child," "a relative" and "a legal person, trust or partnership the managerial responsibilities of which are discharged" by the same manager or by a person closely associated with the latter. Secondly, as far as the transaction to be communicate, not every transaction falls within the duty, but exclusively a transaction or a series of transactions exceeding a minimal threshold of 5,000 euro "within a calendar year"[143] or the higher threshold fixed by the national authority, although in this latter case, despite the discretionary power, the threshold cannot be higher than 20,000 euro.[144]

3.1.5 The other parallel markets

The IT impact and development imposes to rethinking the "market" definition. Not only does, the latter, only financial, or economics, but also shall encompasses others strategic sectors, such as agri-food, the cultural heritage or, the digital ones.

The milestone idea is that, in the contemporary era, it materialises an increasing of businesses related to others sectors. Thus, also these three examples shall be discussed further. Under particular attention will be the technological market due its pervasive and intrusive approach.

The agri-food market

Markets can be defined as "collective devices that allow compromises to be reached, not only on the nature of goods to produce and distribute but also on the value to be given to them."[145] Therefore, the main function of markets is the exchange the value based on specific context-specific rules shaped by public regulation, cultural customs, civic norms and, or, private contracts. Agri-food market encompasses the totality of the complex production, *i.e.* transformation and distribution activities making. It is also should be noted that agri-food markets are under pressure of

141 Article 19(1) of the MA Regulation.

142 Namely, the notification shall comprise of "(a) the name of the person; (b) the reason for the notification; (c) the name of the relevant issuer or emission allowance market participant; (d) a description and the identifier of the financial instrument; (e) the nature of the transaction(s) . . . ; (f) the date and the place of the transaction(s); and (g) the price and volume of the transaction(s)."

143 Article 19(8) of the MA Regulation.

144 Article 19(9) of the MA Regulation. If the national authority decided to exercise this power, the ESMA, the European Securities and Markets Authority, shall be informed of this.

145 (Callon and Muniesa 2005).

different elements: global climate change, social and economic problem, population growth, food insecurity and malnutrition, resource scarcity, ecosystem degradation and biodiversity.[146]

After the 2007–2008 financial crisis, capital has increasingly targeted food and farmland as an investment opportunity. At the beginning, scholars sought to make sense of the broad trends, others were critical and focused their attention on higher and volatile food prices. For this second approach, the main problem concerned price speculation and its impact on poor, who spend a significant portion of their income on food.[147]

The "financialisation" of both food and agriculture is expanding into areas beyond the dominant agriculture export states, such as Canada, the United States and the European Union.

The agri-food market is a complex market, given its dynamics: financial investors are attracted, due to the promise that this market gives them. In other words, the expectation rise of food prices, in a strict connection with the fundamental elements of this peculiar market (population growth, changing diets in the emerging economies, climate change, limited land resources and increased production of biofuels feedstock), attract investors.[148]

Therefore, a financial speculation issue arose: from a critical perspective, it was stressed that financial investment in specific areas (Africa, Asia, Latin America and post-Soviet Eurasia) may be qualify as speculative.[149]

The link between agriculture and finance may be explained as follows. From an historical perspective, the modern state in rich countries has played an important role in creating institutions to support industrialised models of agriculture.[150] At the same time, agrarian movements have pushed the state to develop unique forms of financial regulation and legislation in the US and Canada.[151]

Furthermore, since 1990s agricultural economist have highlighted the unique requirement of capitalising agriculture. In other words, farms are risky financial investments in comparison with other economic sectors, such as manufacturing or services. Thus, private capital has been reluctant to invest without assurances from the state. The reference, more precisely, is to a contract enforcement, bankruptcy law and state-backed collateral.

The States' responses consist in provide financial support for farmers in the form of credit institutions starting in the 19th century. Moreover, states provide agriculture with price and income supports, export trade financing and other subsidies. For example, it would enhance policies for agricultural credit to encourage commercial

146 (Borsellino, Schimmenti and Bilati 2020)

147 (Clapp, Food Price Volatility and Vulnerability in the Global South: Considering the Global Economic 2009; Gosh 2010).

148 (Visser, Clapp and Isakson, Introduction to a Symposium on Global Finance and the Agri-food Sector: Risk and Regulation 2015).

149 (Cotula 2012; Borras and Franco 2011; Borras et al. 2012; Visser, Mamonova and Spoor, Oligarchs, Megafarms and Land Reserves: Understanding Land Grabbing in Russia 2012).

150 (Chang 2009).

151 (Carney 2011; Prasad 2012).

agriculture: the US supported industrial agriculture via farm mortgages whose aim is to provide capital for the purchase of input and equipment.[152] In this respect, the US government established the Federal Farm Loan Act of 1916 and created federal land banks: the latter turned farm ownership into collateral for mortgages.

In Europe, cooperative and credit unions were established by agrarian interests, to both fund and support farmers.

Another relevant topic is agricultural commodity trade as a good under-market regulation. Canada and Australia were the first countries that established marketing boards to manage a commodity trade in grains. The objectives were dual: on the one hand to restrict the manipulation of grain markets and to provide stable prices and orderly marking for exports. On the other hand, to offer credit to importing countries.[153] Farmers and the commodity trading interests of exporting countries benefitted from these supports, however, farmers in importing countries had to compete with "dumped" commodities. Traditionally, the latter was given in the form of food aid.[154]

Also, this link, *i.e.* between financial investors and trade in agricultural commodities, has a long history. During the 18th and 19th century, commodity exchanges created fungible agricultural commodities via a combination of technology innovation and both state and market regulation.[155] In London, for instance, additionally, agriculture exchanges were established. These markets, together with the US agricultural market, provided a means by which buyers and sellers of contracts could purchase and sell agricultural commodities for delivery at a date in the future. Furthermore, these parties had the opportunity to hedge their risks against the uncertainty of agricultural production and long-distance trading.

Likewise in the agricultural market there is a private speculative activity: private speculative capital has long been active in agricultural commodity marketing and trade, even before to the commodities exchange formalisation. Speculation refers to the prediction of price movements with the uncertain possibility of a reward.

Nevertheless, farmers and farmer organisations have been always criticised over the commodity exchanges, due to their distrustful aims. More precisely, under the commodity exchanges there are non-agricultural interests, used to manipulate prices and markets. Due to this, some of the United States had banned futures trading. By contrast to some curbs of financial speculation in commodities markets, the futures trade grew and eclipsed the physical trade of commodities in centres free from restrictions, such as Chicago.[156]

These exchange centres have been criticised, and the response, such as in the US, was to pass legislation aimed at reducing the opportunities for private market manipulation. In this respect, it is worthy to recall the US Grain Futures Act of 1922 and the 1936 Commodity Exchange Act. The keys were to rein in financial speculators in agricultural markets.

152 (Fitzgerald 2003).
153 (Turner 1949).
154 (Clapp, Hunger in the Balance: The New Politics of International Food Aid 2012).
155 (Cronon 1992).
156 (Cowing 1957)

The first one required that all futures transactions were to take place on approved exchanges, thus outlawing manipulation of the market.

The second, *i.e.* the Commodity Exchange Act, limited the number of futures contracts that speculators were legally allowed to own at any one time.

More recently, the Commodity Futures Modernization Act of 2000 prohibited in an express way the Commodity Futures Trading Commission, the US regulatory body that oversees commodity exchange markets, from regulating OTC derivatives. This change made an alignment between US and EU regulation.[157] The consequence of this new legal framework was a commodities' grown into global corporations with a significant reach into markets of emerging economies.

The combination between relaxed position limits and exemption of OTC derivatives from reporting fuelled the creation of new financial products lead to a massive growth of agriculture-based derivatives.[158]

An excessive speculation in this niche sector can result in increased volatility in agricultural and land prices, and, in the latter case, can result in hardships both for consumers and for farmers. Additionally, the latter does not benefit when prices rise; hence, the volatility introduces greater uncertain and complicates planning.[159]

Another side of this coin concerns the relationship between farmland acquisition in developed countries and land rights losses for small-scale producers. Another impact of this approach was also ecological. Despite this, large agricultural trading interests have benefited from these changes because they have had the opportunity to increase joined financial institutions in offering agricultural commodity derivative products to investors.[160]

In order to prevent externalisations, the government may prevent dispossessions in different ways:[161]

- To develop a national regulation to realise a borders zone security;
- To protect land, ecosystem and local social groups;
- To ensure food sovereignty.

It is important to highlight that the main investors in these agricultural commodity derivatives are large-scale investment funds that are seeking to gain exposure to commodity markets. In such investments, governments have also taken a role, thanks to pension funds and foundation endowments.

The government regulations is quintessential because a lack of regulation encourages private speculative investments.[162]

157 (Tett 2009).

158 For example, financial speculation increased from US$65 billion in 2006 to some US$126 billion by early 2011; see Worthy (2011). Further, as far as coffee market is concerned, it is estimated that 1 kilogram of coffee is traded 8,000 times over in speculative trade (Breger Bush 2012).

159 (FAO 2011).

160 (Murphy, Burch and Clapp 2012; Hudson 2013; McMichael 2010).

161 (Fairbairin 2015).

162 (Martin and Clapp 2015).

In this scenario, it is possible to refer to index-based agricultural insurance:[163] a novel type of derivative that plays a crucial role in initiatives to "climate-proof" agriculture. UBAI was born in derivatives markets developed by US energy traders, well-known as Enron. There, derivatives were seen as a means for enterprises to hedge against the potentially damaging effects of climate variables on their business practices. Thanks to the support of the World Bank, the model was extended to agricultural production in the early 21st century, giving rise to IBAI.

In a different way from a normal situation, index insurance links indemnity pay-outs not to the actual losses that farmers suffer in their fields. More precisely, it serves as a proxy for loss, from such as rainfall, temperature, wind speed or the level of water in a river. To elaborate, farmers who hold IBAI policies receive pay-outs only when environmental measures meet or exceed specified thresholds; actual agricultural performance is irrelevant. This is possible because indexed products are weather derivatives for farmers, not insurances that guarantee recompense for losses.[164] Again, this presumes that astute farmers can and should manage environmental risk through offsetting bets on financial products.

The benefits ascribed to index insurance are (1) the reduction in the transaction costs of verifying losses, (2) resolving the problem of moral hazard, and (3) alleviation of adverse selection problems. Furthermore, it is possible to say that index insurance is championed as a pro-poor initiative, that expands opportunities to smallholders who are often excluded from insurance markets.

Although in more recent times, it is possible to speak about the democratisation of financial capital markets,[165] this is not applicable to the financial agricultural sector. Supporters of financial inclusions argue that this problem is a direct consequence of "market failure." Therefore, if the financial inclusion is to be successful, it seems to be necessarily focused on one element: the expansion of both the scale and variety of products offered.

In this scenario, IBAI has, as the same time, positive and negative effects. The first one is related to its aim: to offer means for mitigating the risk of agricultural modernisation in an era of increasing climate volatility.[166] Nevertheless, in doing so it is not possible to say that it epitomises a win-win-win financial approach. The reasons for this are multifarious:

- Its relation with basis risk: potentially, an individual farmer's experience could differ from that estimated by the index upon which indemnity payments are based;

163 Henceforth IBAI

164 (Johnson 2013).

165 By this expression we refer to the fact that the poor populations who were previously excluded from formal finance are now actively included in a number of financial markets. More precisely, the latter includes microloans, subprime mortgages and credit cards. A more critical approach suggests that these financial instruments maintain a "poverty finance" to mask the causes of economic marginalisation. See Rankin (2013); Roy (2010); Taylor (2015); Soederberg (2014).

166 (Isakson 2015).

- IBAI does not reduce the probability of crop failure resulting from environmental events and, perhaps, it may exacerbate it;[167]
- The agricultural modernisation motivated by IBAI increases farmers' exposure to economic risk; hence, IBAI does not protect farmers from rising input costs or increasingly volatile outputs prices;
- The market mediation relations promoted by index insurance will not cultivate mutuality and compassion.[168]

The cultural heritage market

It is well known that in a market economy, every organisation, regardless of its funding statute, enters into various relationship with other entities in horizontal or vertical systems and structures. Where the horizontal asset is concerned, it includes market relations and reflects the totality of the relationship with suppliers of goods and services. This applies to both commercial and non-profit organisations.

The latter also applies in the civil sector, which includes both non-profit organisations and quasi-non-profit-organisations. These not only achieve social goals but also pursue parallel, or secondary, objectives by entering into numerous and varied market relationships, characteristically for purchase and sales transactions. These quasi-profit-organisations also manage, for instance, cultural heritage sites, which include historic buildings, historic property or historic building complexes.[169]

From this, it is possible to speak about cultural heritage[170] market which consists into historic sites, historic buildings and cultural heritage as a result of their qualities, value and importance for future generations. Furthermore, cultural heritage also has a market potential, that is its potential economic utility. This is the market potential of the site, *i.e.* the ability to generate the expected market flows.[171]

From the discussion on the subject of cultural heritage sites as a modern market of entities, arises a question relating to the marketisation of the function of this niche market and the functions played by the quasi-non-profit organisations.[172]

In this context, the use of databases containing economic information about transactions in the real asset market may represent a great advantage. For instance, in Netherlands, "landmark status" is a proxy that offers the opportunity to measure cultural heritage.

167 More precisely, adoption of the new technologies promoted by most IBAI initiatives exposes farmers to a high probability of crop failure. In other words, the reduction of risk of credit failure is not equivalent to the increased probability of having smallholders stuck with food, compared with traditional agricultural practices, which are relatively more resilient than their modern counterparts.

168 (Bowles 1998).

169 (Starr 2013).

170 It should be noted that heritage is a comprehensive word that includes both brands of breakfast cereals to luxury tableware. Further, it refers also to objects, monuments and landscape. See Grey and Kuokkanen (2019).

171 (Parsons 2008).

172 (Szromnik 2019).

The cultural heritage market is also called a grey market, when alluding to the illicit antiquities trade. More precisely, the grey market refers to antiquities for which provenience or findspot documentation has been lost. These goods were acquired and exported before the country of origin had patrimony laws in place to prohibit their removal. Hence, these objects have been in circulation so long that they now are considered licit simply through the passage of time.[173]

Digital market

The rapid progress in technology and the widespread use of the internet have brought in a new era in digital economy. Digital platforms have become essential in our life and daily routine. As a consequence of this, a small number of powerful platforms have gained unprecedent market power. Thus, there is a need for regulated digital markets to balance innovation, protecting consumer and promoting competition.

The key of digital market regulation concerns to safeguard consumers from potential harm and unfair practices in the online world. It aims to ensure that consumers can trust the information they receive and assert their rights using digital platforms.[174]

As far as regulation is concerned, the European Union passed the Digital Service Act[175] one of the most comprehensive pieces of internet regulation. It will apply to Facebook, Instagram and a number of other tech platforms and services.[176] DSA is designed to keep users safe online and stop the spread of harmful content that is either illegal or violates a platform's terms of services. It protects also Europeans' fundamental rights like privacy and free speech.

There are five key issues:

- The platforms' duty to combat the sale of illegal products and services;
- The duty to fight against illegal content, such as Russian propaganda, interference with elections, hate crime and online harms, including harassment and child abuse;
- Protection of children and the prohibition of targeting children with advertising based on their personal data or cookies and to ensure a high level of privacy, security and safety for minors;
- To prohibit the use of sensitive personal data, including race, gender and religion;
- Ban dark partners.

173 (Browman 2008).

174 (Rakhmatovna 2023).

175 Henceforth DSA. Regulation 2022/2065/EU of the European Parliament and of the Council of 19 October 2022 on a Single Market for Digital Services and amending Directive 2000/31/EC (Digital Services Act).

176 More precisely: TikTok, X (formerly known as Twitter), YouTube, Instagram, LinkedIn, Pinterest, Snapchat, Amazon, Booking.com, China's Alibaba and AliExpress as well as Germany's Zalando, Google Play and Apple's App Store are subject, as are Google's Search, Microsoft's Bing, Google Maps and Wikipedia. This list does not definitive.

In the UK, Parliament passed its final Parliamentary British[177] equivalent of the DSA: the Online Safety Bill. Its aim is to manage the risk of digital markets by establishing a more flexible, collaborative and forward-looking approach. The proposal is in two main parts: (1) new powers to tackle harms in all markets and (2) to give the CMA's[178] Digital Markets Unit[179] powers to oversee a new regulatory regime for the most powerful firms – those which have significant and entrenched market power, giving them Strategic Market Status.[180]

The second part consists of three main pillars:

- Legally enforceable conduct to manage the effects of market power;
- Pro-competitive interventions, to address issues such as personal data mobility, interoperability and data access;
- A leading approach to competition concerning UK business and consumers given particular consumer harm arising from these transactions.

As a result of this new piece of legislation, digital platforms will be expected to do the following:

- Remove illegal content or prevent it from appearing in the first place, including content promoting self-harm;
- Prevent children from accessing harmful and age-inappropriate content;
- Enforce age limits and age-checking measures;
- Ensure the risks and dangers posed to children on social media platforms; thus, the latter shall become more transparent, including by publishing risk assessments;
- Provide with clear and accessible ways to report problems online when they do arise.

In a nutshell, the bill assumes that technology is consistent with the new duties, but there is no specific obligation to use "proactive technologies."

3.2 Investments and funds

Alongside banks, insurance companies and pension funds, the investment firm is traditionally considered one of the key players in the financial industry. By definition, investment firms are the operators of investment services and investment activities relating to financial instruments. Thus, the investment firm is to the capital markets what the bank is to the banking sector and, finally, what the insurance company is to the insurance market. For instance, the execution of an order to sell or buy securities listed on a stock market is a typical example of activity reserved to

177 Among scholars, see Coe (2022); Dittel (2022).
178 Competition and Market Authority.
179 Henceforth DMU.
180 Henceforth SMS.

investment firms. However, whilst three of the aforementioned four sectors (banking, insurance and pension funds) have maintained a well-established constitution and adhere to clearly defined boundaries, the same cannot be said of the investment business.

Capital markets have been swept up in a three-decade-long wave of intensification triggered by the globalisation of economies and the burgeoning role played by stock markets, the shift from small, "boutique" brokerage firms to modern investment firms, and the direct involvement of banks in investment activities. As a result of this last development, the once prominent demarcation line between investment firms and banks has steadily been whittled away, with investment banks (that is, banks operating principally in the capital markets) fulfilling an increasingly important role on the stage dominated by investment businesses and traditional investment firms (or brokerage houses). Thus, investment firms have been progressively integrated within major banking groups in accordance with the composition of a universal bank. Where in this chapter we refer to "investment firms," we therefore mean both investment firms *per se*, *i.e.* traditional boutique firms, and banks acting in a capacity as investment firms, *i.e.* banks performing investment services and activities.

The investment business, in its own right, has grown enormously, quantitatively speaking, which is due in part to the emergence of new channels of marketing and selling of the relevant products – namely, door-to-door and online activities.

Furthermore, the evolution of the markets and incorporation of new technologies has equipped investment businesses with an array of new financial products and innovative forms of organisation. Besides investment firms, the investment business is dominated by investment funds. Where investment firms, in essence, facilitate the sale and purchase of financial instruments, investment funds form financial instruments themselves. This is certainly the case when it comes to the undertakings in collective investment, and the specific securities – the units – representing the participation of the investor in the common fund. So as to leave no stone unturned, this form of investment business, as well as the alternative investment funds, shall also be discussed later.

3.2.1 Investment under MiFID regulation

The investment firm

The investment firm, as an entity operating in the financial sector, is legislated upon by the EU; the relevant pieces of legislation in this case are Regulation 600/2014 on markets in financial instruments (MiFIR)[181] and Directive 2014/65 on markets in financial instruments (MiFID II).[182] According to Article 4 of the latter statute,

181 In full: Regulation on markets in financial instruments and amending Regulation Emir on OTC derivatives, central counterparties and trade repositories. OJ L 173.

182 In full: Directive 2014/65/EU of the European Parliament and of the Council of 15 May 2014 on markets in financial instruments and amending directive 2002/92/EC and Directive 2011/61/EU,

the investment firm is defined as, "any legal person whose regular occupation or business is the provision of one or more investment services to third parties and/or the performance of one or more investment activities on a professional basis." This definition encapsulates the economic reality of modern capital markets, where boutique investment firms together with banks are the main operators in the stock markets to accommodate the pursuit of investment activities.

In turn, "investment services and investment activities"[183] – in other words, the investment contracts that the investment firm (and the bank) enters into with its customers[184] – are elaborated upon under Annex I of the MiFID II, section A of which specifies nine "undertakings":[185] the "[r]eception and transmission of orders in relation to one or more financial instruments," the "[e]xecution of orders on behalf of clients," "[d]ealing on own account," "[p]ortfolio management," "[i]nvestment advice," "[u]nderwriting of financial instruments and/or placing of financial instruments on a firm commitment basis," "[p]lacing of financial instruments without a firm commitment basis,"[186] "[o]peration of an MTF [multilateral trading facility, MH, PdG]" and[187] "[o]peration of an OTF [organised trading

OJ L 173. The MiFID II has been published in the *Official Journal of the European Union* on 12 June 2014 and, according to its Article 93, its transposition in each member state shall take place for the nearly totality of its provisions, by 3 July 2016. The previous Directive governing this area, Directive 2004/39 or MiFID I, shall be phased out by 3 January 2017, according to Article 94 of the MiFID II.

183 From a legal point of view, investment services and investment activities are different: "investment services" are services carried out by the investment firm in the interests of the client, even though under its own name, whilst investment activities are carried out by the investment firm in its own interest. A typical example of the latter is the activity of organisation of Multilateral Trading Facilities (MTF).

184 The definition "investment contract" is commonly adopted in the US, where the legislation misses a concept of investment services and investment activities. See, among others, Soderquist and Gabaldon, Securities Law (2004). From a comparative analysis between the EU and the US, it is also worth noting that the comprehensive category of "investment activity" carried out by an investment firm would correspond, basically, to the following categories of professionals: (1) the "broker" as "the person engaged in the business of effecting transactions in securities for the account of others"; (2) the "dealer" as "the person engaged in the business of buying and selling securities for his own account"; (3) the "investment adviser" as "the person who, for compensation, engages in the business of advising others . . . as to the advisability of investing in, purchasing or selling securities." See Hazen (2009).

185 In the MiFID I the investment activities and investment services used to be eight; this is because the OTF, recently introduced by the MiFID II (see later), was not part of the definition.

186 An EU definition of underwriting and placement is not provided, although an interpretation of them can be inferred. More specifically, underwriting and/or placing, if relating to financial instruments, are agreements between the issuer (or the offeror) and the investment firm in charge of the placement. In force of the relevant terms and conditions, the latter undertakes to offer to the public the financial instruments issued, at a specific price and, in some cases, in previously defined slots of time. The placement "on a firm commitment basis" entails a full responsibility of the investment firm to buy the residual financial instruments that were not offered; it is quite obvious that this placement, differently form the other one ("without a firm commitment basis") shall be more onerous for the offeror/issuer as the specific commitment of the investment firm is usually "priced."

187 A multilateral trading facility is "a multilateral system, operated by an investment firm or a market operator, which brings together multiple third-party buying and selling interests in financial

facility, MH, PdG].”[188] Of these nine investment services and investment activities, portfolio management might be worthy of a brief clarification. Individual portfolio management refers to the contractual relationship existing between a customer and a professional (the investment firm), where the latter uses its expertise as an investment adviser for the investment of securities and money of an individual customer. It is different from collective portfolio management, where the investment firm is an adviser to a fund, the units of which belong to a plurality of investors, rather than a single investor.[189]

Pursuant to Annex 1 of the MiFID II, Section C,[190] the investment services and investment activities just referred to must relate to “financial instruments,” which are, in essence, distinguished between “transferrable securities,” such as shares, bonds and derivatives.[191] In respect to the latter, Article 4 of Section C of Annex 1 contemplates “[o]ptions, futures, swaps, forward rate agreements and any other derivative contracts relating to securities, currencies, interest rates or yields, emission allowances or other derivatives instruments, financial indices or financial measures which may be settled physically or in cash.” Additionally, financial instruments are also, inter alia, “money-market instruments” (such as covered bonds) and “units in collective investment undertakings.”

Finally, MiFID II also addresses the category of “ancillary services,” which cannot be defined as reserved services; theoretically, they could be discharged by non-investment firms also. However, the EU legislator does not allow an investment firm to carry out exclusively one or more ancillary services, if at least one “main” investment service or investment activity has not been authorised. The definition of these ancillary services is furnished under Annex 1 of the MiFID, particularly within section B.[192] Amongst these activities, reference can be made to (1) “Safekeeping and administration of financial instruments for the account of clients, including custodianship and related services such as cash/collateral management and excluding maintaining securities accounts at the top tier level”; (2) “Granting credits or loans to an investor to allow him to carry out a transaction in one or more financial instruments, where the firm granting the credit or loan is involved in the transaction”; (3) “Advice to undertakings on capital structure, industrial strategy

instruments – in the system and in accordance with non-discretionary rules – in a way that results in an [investment contract].” Article 4(1)(22), MiFID II.

188 An organised trading facility is “a multilateral system which is not a regulated market or an MTF and in which multiple third-party buying and selling interests in bonds, structured finance products, emission allowances or derivatives are able to interact in the system in a way that results in an [investment contract].” Article 4(1)(23) MiFID II. This specific investment activity did not use to be included in the previous Directive 2004/39, MiFID I, and therefore, it is a novelty of the MiFID II.

189 See Busch and De Mott (2012).

190 Also in the MiFID I, the “financial instruments” used to be defined under Annex I, Section C.

191 “Security,” rather than “financial instrument,” is the terminology adopted in the US. See sect. 2(a) of the Securities Act (Soderquist and Gabaldon, Securities Law 2004).

192 It is worth noting that the “ancillary activities” contemplated under Annex I, Section B, of the MiFID II are basically similar to those previously mentioned in the MiFID I, and contained in the same Annex I, Section B.

and related matters and advice and services relating to mergers and the purchase of undertakings"; (4) "Foreign exchange services where these are connected to the provision of investment services"; (5) "Investment research and financial analysis or other forms of general recommendation relating to transactions in financial instruments"; 6. "Services related to underwriting."

Initial capital and authorisation process

Similarly, to what is required for credit institutions, an investment firm must be endowed with a minimal capital so as to ensure that the business has a financial buffer to accommodate losses, and is carried out seriously and with certain degree of commitment. In this respect, the EU legislator established floors for the member states, also connected with the kinds of services provided. The relevant provisions, initially secluded in a piece of legislation (viz. Directive 2006/49, specifically concerned with the capital adequacy of investment firms and credit institutions), have now been transposed into the recent CRD IV legislation which concerns, among others, "prudential supervision of credit institutions and investment firms." Apart from the cosmetic variation of the pertinent legislative instrument, the substance of the provisions has remained basically the same: (1) the initial capital of an investment firm shall be of at least 730,000 euro;[193] however, (2) such minimal capital may be reduced to 125,000 euro for investment firms having a more limited activity;[194] and finally, (3) the floor may, at the discretion of the relevant member state, be further reduced to 50,000 euro[195] for an investment firm that "is not authorised to hold client money or securities, to deal for its own account, to underwrite issues on a firm commitment basis."

As a result of the definitions provided by Annex I of the MiFID, any undertaking of investment services and investment activities on financial instruments is a reserved activity, permissible solely to those individuals or entities securing prior authorisation from the competent authority, as established in each member state. In this respect, Article 5 MiFID II[196] stipulates that: "Each Member State shall require that the provision of investment services and/or the performance of investment activities as a regular occupation or business on a professional basis be subject to prior authorisation in accordance with this Chapter."[197] Such authorisation shall be granted by the home member state competent authority designated in accordance with Article 67. The competent authority grants the authorisation, to the benefit of

193 Article 28(1) of CRD IV.

194 More specifically, according to Article 29(1) of CRD IV, an investment firm not dealing "in any financial instruments for its own account or [not underwriting] issues of financial instruments on a firm commitment basis, but which holds client money or securities and which offers one or more of the following services . . . : (a) the reception and transmission of investors' orders for financial instruments; (b) the execution of investors' orders for financial instruments; (c) the management of individual portfolios of investment in financial instruments."

195 Article 29(3) of CRD IV.

196 This provision basically mirrors Article 5 of MiFID I.

197 Chapter I, Title II.

the investment firm, for one or more investment services and/or investment activities[198] required by the applicant. As already stated, the reserved investment services and investment activities can be exercised by an authorised EU bank also. In this case, however, no specific authorisation under the MiFID II is prescribed, which means that, *de facto*, the authority overseeing a bank (*e.g.* the Bundesbank in Germany, the Banca d'Italia in Italy) shall rubber-stamp the pursuit and undertaking of investment services by EU banks.[199]

It can be inferred from Article 6 of the MiFID II[200] that a request lodged with the home country authority may relate to the full spectrum of investment services and activities, but also just one investment service may be requested and allowed. Any initial authorisation(s) granted for one or more of the activities does not prohibit the investment firm concerned from making a further request, at a later stage, for an extension of the authorisation, so that additional activities can be included.

The principle of an EU passport, firmly entrenched in the operations undertaken by banks, is *mutatis mutandis* adopted by the MiFID II in order to define the kinds of cross-border activities that the authorised entity can perform, either through the establishment of branches or in the cross-border provision of services.[201]

198 Remarkably, the authorisation may cover also one or more of the ancillary services, although the principle is spelled out (Article 6(1)) that authorisation "shall in no case be granted solely for the provision of ancillary services."

199 See Recital 38 of MiFID II, basically mirroring Recital 18 of Directive 2004/39.

"Credit institutions . . . should not need another authorisation under this Directive in order to provide investment services or perform investment activities. When a credit institution decides to provide investment services or perform investment activities the competent authorities, before granting an authorisation under Directive 2013/36/EU, should verify that it complies with the relevant provisions of this Directive."

200 "The home Member State shall ensure that the authorisation specifies the investment services or activities which the investment firm is authorised to provide. The authorisation may cover one or more of the ancillary services set out in Section B of Annex 1. Authorisation shall in no case be granted solely for the provision of ancillary services."

201 Article 6(3) MiFID II. The details of this cross-border activity and the relevant modalities are contained in the same MiFID II, Article 34, as far as the freedom to provide cross-border invest services and activities is concerned and, Article 35, as regards the freedom to establish a branch. Basically, without entering into the minutiae of the specific provisions, the rules are, mutatis mutandis, those provided for credit institutions and, therefore:

a. The competent authority of the home Member State, within one month of receiving the information of the investment firm to provide services in a further EU country, will "forward it to the competent authority of the host Member State" and the "investment firm may then start to provide the investment services and activities concerned in the host Member State" (Article 34, MiFID II);
b. As regards the freedom to establish branches, communication by the investment firm to its home country authority of its intention to open branches in a different Member State (Article 35(2), MiFID II Directive); as such, "unless the competent authority of the home Member State has reason to doubt the adequacy of the administrative structure or the financial situation of an investment firm, taking into account the activities envisaged," the home authority shall provide, within three months, this communication to both the authority of the designated host country and the investment firm concerned (Article 35(3), MiFID II Directive). Eventually, according to Article 35(6), MiFID II Directive, the branch shall be established and shall be

From a practical point of view, the request, and subsequent wait, for authorisation from the home country authority may be a time-consuming process. This is indicative of the legal complexity inhibiting the administrative procedure, where the supervisor shall be thorough to the point that he "is fully satisfied that the applicant complies with all requirements under the provisions adopted pursuant to this Directive."[202] However, the time allocated to the relevant authority is not without restriction. Article 7(3) MiFID II suggests an allotted time period for each member state of six months in which the process must be completed and the approval or rejection of the application disclosed. It is a prerequisite of any application that the information provided be extensive and must include "a programme of operations setting out *inter alia* the types of business envisaged and the organisational structure."[203]

Fitness of the directors, notification of qualifying shareholders

The investment firm business, and the delicate area in which it operates, is acknowledged by the EU legislator. Article 9(3) of the MiFID II prescribes that each member state shall be required to ensure that

> the management body of an investment firm defines, oversees and is accountable for the implementation of the governance arrangements that ensure effective and prudent management of the investment firm including the segregation of duties in the investment firm and the prevention of conflicts of interest, and in a manner that promotes the integrity of the market and the interest of clients.[204]

Coupled with this is the provision, comparable with that applicable to banks under the corresponding legislation, stipulating that the national legislations ensure the management of the investment firms be undertaken by at least two persons meeting the requirements laid down earlier.

The identity of persons having, directly or indirectly, a qualifying holding in an investment firm must be communicated to the relevant supervisory authority,

---

able to commence its business, one it has received such a communication from the competent authority of the host Member State or, if this was not communicated, "at the latest after two months from the date of transmission of the communication by the competent authority pf the home Member State." It is worth noting that, according to Article 35(5), where "the competent authority of the home Member State refuses to communicate the information to the competent authority of the host Member State, it shall give reasons for its refusal to the investment firm concerned within three months of receiving all the information."

202 Article 7(1) of the MiFID II.

203 Article 7(2) of the MiFID II.

204 The previous correspondent provision of MiFID I, at Article 9, used to be less rigorous: the EU used to require each respective member state to ensure that the person who effectively directs the business of an investment firm is "of sufficiently good repute and sufficiently experienced"; these requisites, to be detailed at national level, should be conducive to effecting "the sound and prudent management of the investment firm."

typically as an essential part of the application.[205] As for investment firms (and similar to banks), the EU approach turns out to be more rigorous than for a company carrying out its business in a non-reserved sector. More specifically, the relevant supervisory authority assesses the identities of persons wishing to obtain, directly or indirectly, a qualifying holding in an investment firm, whereupon each member state, according to the prescriptions set out in Article 10(1), paragraph 2, of the MiFID II Directive,[206] shall refuse authorisation if the identities of the shareholders are deemed likely to jeopardise "the sound and prudent management of the investment firm."[207]

The communication, to the supervisory authority, of the identity of the persons having a qualifying holding in the investment firm at the time of the application underlines the urgency with which each EU member state must request notification of any variation of the ownership structure of the firm, also for sale and purchases of qualifying holdings.[208] Such communication must precede the conclusion of the relevant sale and purchase agreement, although it would seem allowed if a contract has been concluded but is made subject to the conveyance of further communication to the competent authority and its subsequent approval.[209]

The same rationale behind the sale and purchase of qualifying holding in the investment firm applies to the increase of holding by the same person; any rise or fall above and below certain thresholds (namely, 20%, 33% and 50% or the acquisition or cessation of control of the firm) shall be conveyed to the competent authority and encounter the possibility of objection, should the supervisor deem the variation prejudicial to the "*sound and prudent management*" of the investment firm.[210]

The financial salesman

In the contemporary format of investment business, the conclusion of the investment contract is increasingly conducted beyond the physical confines of a traditional

205 This is not clearly prescribed, although it is indirectly inferable from the tenor of Article 10 of MiFID II:

"The competent authorities shall not authorise the provision of investment services or performance of investment activities by an investment firm until they have been informed of the identities of the shareholders or members, whether direct or indirect, natural or legal persons, that have qualifying holdings and the amounts of those holdings."

206 Basically correspondent to Article 10 of the MiFID I.

207 Likewise, according to Article 10(3) of the MiFID II, in cases where the influence exercised by qualifying shareholders is "likely to be prejudicial to the sound and prudent management of an investment firm, the competent authority take appropriate measures to put an end to that situation."

208 Therefore, the notification of the relevant ownership structure is not simply in coincidence with the authorisation but also later in connection with future variations of it.

209 Article 10(3), subparagraph 2 MiFID II; more specifically: "the competent authority shall have up to three months from the date of the notification of a proposed acquisition [omissis] to oppose such a plan if, in view of the need to ensure sound and prudent management of the investment firm, it is not satisfied as to the suitability of the persons [having a qualifying holding] [omissis]."

210 Article 11 of the MiFID II, corresponding to Article 10(3)(2) of the MiFID I.

branch of the investment firm, or bank offering the same contract. The relatively recent phenomenon of online banking, for instance, can no longer be deemed a new phenomenon given the degree to which it has become fully entrenched in banking operations.

A further avenue along which investment services relating to financial instruments can be offered is through the medium of door-to-door sales discharged by individuals who are not necessarily employed by the investment firm. Door-to-door sales basically constitute a promotion and sale of investment services beyond the premises of the principal, *i.e.* the headquarters or branches of the investment firm or bank. This activity is discharged by people who are not necessarily employees of the principal but rather agents, *i.e.* a self-employed category earning their living by charging a percentage based on the volume of deals they conclude on behalf of the investment firm. In both cases (either employees or agents connected with the principal), the local legislation usually requires that these categories of professionals be enrolled on a special register,[211] whilst the enrolment is subject to the prior successful completion of a training course organised by the local authority or of a relevant exam.

It is worth stressing that not all legislations acknowledge the category of the agent engaged in promoting and selling the investment services of the investment firm (or bank). Nonetheless, the EU legislator requires that for those member states adopting the "financial agent," adequate rules are in place in order to safeguard the investors. The relevant provisions worthy of a closer look are those of Article 29 MiFID II.[212] More specifically, Article 29(1) of the same directive stipulates that it is the discretion of the member state "to allow an investment firm to appoint tied agents for the purposes of promoting the services of the investment firm." The mandate of such a tied agent usually includes "soliciting business or receiving orders from clients or potential clients and transmitting them, placing financial instruments and providing advice in respect of such financial instruments and services offered by that investment firm."

It can then be deduced that, in other words, the tied agent is not a mandatory figure, given that a member state may decide not to contemplate them. However, if the local legislation did decide to opt in, the principles to comply with are those to be found under Article 29 of MiFID II. In this respect, the first discernible principle is clarified, where Article 29(2) concerns the concept of vicarious liability of the tied agents. If the tied agent has been appointed by an investment firm, the principal shall remain "fully and unconditionally responsible for any action or omission on the part of the tied agent when acting on behalf of the investment firm." Linked to this is the relevant provision (again, Article 29(2)), requiring any state permitting this category of persons, to ensure they disclose "the capacity in which [there are] acting and the firm which [they are, *omissis*] representing when contracting or before dealing with any client or potential client."

211 (Wood, International Loans, Bonds, Guarantees, Legal Opinions. Vol 3, The Law and Practice of International Finance Series 2007a).

212 Correspondent, with some differences, to Article 23 of the MiFID I Directive.

Not only is the investment firm vicariously liable for acts and omissions of the tied agent, but it is further required, under the auspices of each applicable local legislation, to monitor the activities of their agents in order to ensure full compliance with the EU statute.[213]

The tied agent is not an ordinary agent working for a principal but rather is a qualified professional discharging a delicate activity with the potential to influence investors. As a result of this special statute, an EU member state choosing to recognise tied agents must ensure that a public register (as defined in MiFID II) is formulated.[214] Enrolment is subject to, on the one hand, the "*good repute*" of the prospective tied agent and, on the other, an "*appropriate general, commercial and professional knowledge*" of the activity he will discharge.[215]

The tied agent, if contemplated for use by an EU member state, is a reserved category of professionals whose license to operate is conditional on enrolment with the public register. The firm shall take full responsibility, when appointing these tied agents, in ensuring that exclusively those enrolled are appointed. This onus on the investment firms can be inferred, indirectly, from Article 29(5) MiFID II.

The monitoring process undertaken by the investment firm operates not simply at the outset of the activity (when the mandate is delivered to the tied agent by the investment firm), but stretches throughout the tenure of the mandate. In this respect, the provisions existing in each national country must ensure that "investment firms appointing tied agents take adequate measures in order to avoid any negative impact that the activities of the tied agent . . . could have on the activities carried out by the tied agent on behalf of the investment firm."[216]

All in all, the tied agent is an optional category engaged in the promotion and sale of investment services beyond the premises of the investment firm, through the medium of door-do-door sales. Insofar as an EU member state has chosen to create a register of tied agents, the rules to be complied with shall be those of Article 29 of MiFID II. Of these, the most significant probably is the principle of vicarious liability on the part of the principal for any act and/or omission the tied agent should incur in discharging the activity.

The new regulation of investor protection: EU and UK

On 24 May 2023, the European Commission published its Retail Investment Package in the line of the Capital Markets Union Action Plan, recently published (2020). In the latter the European Commission announced its intention to put forward a strategy for retail investments in Europe.

The aim of this package is to address perceived shortcomings in the current EU regulatory framework for retail investment, *i.e.* the retail investors struggle to access relevant, comparable and easily understandable information to take

213 Article 29(2), para. 3 MiFID II.
214 Article 29(3), para. 1 MiFID II.
215 Article 29(3), para. 2 MiFID II.
216 Article 29(4), para. 1 MiFID II.

informed investment choice. The underlying idea is that some investment products do not offer value for money. It is worthy to be noted that the same reasoning was made by the final rule set out by FCA on 27 July 2022.

Also under the European lenses, the aim is to empower retail investors, such as the "consumer" investor) to make investment decisions that are aligned with their needs and preferences, ensuring that they are treated fairly and duly protected. In other words, these measures shall enhance a retail investor's trust and confidence to safely invest in their future and take full advantage of the EU's Capital Markets Union.

In more detail, the package includes the following measures:

- Improve the way information is provided to retail investors about investment products and services, in ways that are more meaningful and standardised;
- Increase transparency and comparability of costs by requiring the use of a standard presentation and terminology on costs;
- Ensure that all retail clients receive at least annually a clear view of the investment performance of their portfolio;
- Address potential conflicts of interest in the distribution of investment products by banning inducements of "execution-only" sales while ensuring that the financial advice is aligned with the retail investor's best interest;
- Protect retail investors from misleading marketing by ensuring that financial intermediaries, advisors, are fully responsible for the use, and misuse, of their marketing communication (this provision includes, also, marketing via social media);
- Preserve high standards of professional qualifications for financial advisors;
- Empower consumers to make better financial decision, in order to encourage member states to implement national measures than can support citizens' financial literacy;
- Reduce administrative burdens and improve accessibility of products and services for sophisticated retail investors, by defining eligibility criteria for becoming a professional investor;
- Enhance supervisory cooperation to make it easier for national competent authorities and European supervisory authorities to ensure that rules are properly and effectively applied in a coherent manner across the EU.

By contrast, in the UK legal system, the terminology used by FCA is Consumer Duty. The reference goes to the final rules set in a new Consumer Duty Feedback to CP21/36 and final rules.[217] It consists in three elements: (1) a consumer principle, (2) cross-cutting rules and (3) four consumer outcomes. The complete rules come into force on 31 July 2024; before this deadline, firms will be expected to share implementation plans, board papers and other relevant material with supervisions and ought to expect challenge from the regulator on their approach.

217 FCA, A new Consumer Duty Feedback to CP21/36 and final rules, Policy Statement, PS22/9, July 2022.

The consumer principles require that firms act to deliver good outcomes for retail customers.[218] The second one, *i.e.* the "cross-cutting rules," requires that firms do the following:

- Act in good faith;
- Avoid causing foreseeable harm;
- Enable and support retail customers to pursue their financial objectives.

The latter area, the outcomes, focuses on the following:

- Products and services;
- Price and value;
- Consumer understanding;
- Consumer support.

Consumer Duty[219] achieves, at least, two main objectives. The first one is consumer protection. In this respect, the Duty sets higher, clear and standard rules by requiring firms to ensure their products and services are fit for purpose and offer fair value to help consumers to make effective choices or act in their interest.

The second one is aimed at creating a fairer and more consumer-focused playing field on which firms can compete and innovate in pursuit of good consumer outcomes. The main idea is that competition can more effectively act in the interest of consumers where firms design products and services to meet consumer needs. Thus, consumers are put in a position to make informed decisions and act in their own interests.[220]

Furthermore, this regulation discusses also "consumers in vulnerable circumstances" – circumstances that may be either temporary or permanent. If a customer's circumstances change, it could mean that limited channel(s) of support no longer meet their needs.

In a nutshell, "The Duty will set a higher standard of care that firms must provide to customers. Firms will need to focus on delivering good outcomes for customers, this will enable them to identify problems earlier, and prevent problems escalating or becoming widespread."[221]

The Duty will apply to firms engaging in regulated activities in the UK across the retail distribution chain. More precisely, both the UK distributors of non-UK products/services will be within scope. UK manufacturers of products sold through non-UK distributors will also be in scope.

218 FCA, A new Consumer Duty Feedback to CP21/36 and final rules, Policy Statement, PS22/9, July 2022, para 1.15.
219 Henceforth "the Duty."
220 FCA, A new Consumer Duty Feedback to CP21/36 and final rules, Policy Statement, PS22/9, July 2022, para 1.14.
221 FCA, A new Consumer Duty Feedback to CP21/36 and final rules, Policy Statement, PS22/9, July 2022, para 14.1.

3.2.2 The investment fund

This paragraph is dedicated to the discussion and analysis of one of the most sophisticated and controversial of financial instruments: the units in collective investment undertakings.

By way of an introduction, it is worth emphasising that the units at stake are "financial instruments," for MiFID II Directive explicitly includes the units in collective investment undertakings within Section C of Annex 1. Although the units in collective investment undertakings fall within the category of financial instruments, a specific *ad hoc* legislation has been in place for a number of years at EU level, due to complexity of these financial products. In fact, the units do not, in themselves, represent securities, but rather quotas or shares in an investment fund.[222] The fund is fed by the (cash) contributions of a number of investors, undertaking one or more quotas or shares. Subsequently, the fund invests this cash in securities (but possibly not exclusively securities), in accordance with the investment strategy tailored to each fund and laid down in its investment programme. From a legislative perspective, funds may be distinguished between the funds that qualify as undertakings for collective investment in transferable securities (UCITS) and are covered as such by Directive 2009/65/EC (UCITS Directive),[223] and collective investment undertakings that are not covered by the same Directive. These latter investment undertakings, *i.e.* alternative funds, are covered by Directive 2011/61/EU on Alternative Investment Fund Managers (AIFMD) and the Alternative Investment Fund Managers Regulations (AIFMD and the latter regulations together: "AIFMD legislation").[224] As a gross generalisation, it could be stated that these alternative investment funds use investment strategies more innovative than a traditional fund and may have a limited number of investors providing significant amounts of money. These alternative funds include hedge funds and private equity funds. A legal analysis specifically addressed to the alternative investment funds and the comparatively recent piece of EU legislation is provided further here.

222 In some countries, the fund is called an "investment fund"; in others, a "mutual fund." Entailed to the adjective "mutual" is the fact that the relevant units can be underwritten by any investor.

223 Directive 2009/65/EC of the European Parliament and of the Council of 13 July 2009 on the coordination of laws, regulations and administrative provisions relating to undertakings for collective investment in transferable securities (UCITS) (recast). Most recently, this directive has been recast by Directive 2014/91/EU of the European Parliament and of the Council of 23 July 2014 amending Directive 2009/65/EC on the coordination of laws, regulations and administrative provisions relating to undertakings for collective investment in transferable securities (UCITS) as regards depositary functions, remuneration policies and sanctions, OJ L 257.

224 Directive 2011/61/EU of the European Parliament and of the Council of 8 June 2011 on Alternative Investment Fund Managers and amending Directives 2003/41/EC and 2009/65/EC and Regulations 1060/2009/EC and 1095/2010/EU; Commission Delegated Regulation 694/2014/EU of 17 December 2013 supplementing Directive 2011/61/EU of the European Parliament and of the Council with regard to regulatory technical standards determining types of alternative investment fund managers, OJ L 183; Commission Implementing Regulation 447/2013/EU; and Commission Implementing Regulation 448/2013/EU.

UCITS V

The specific nature of the units in collective investment undertakings (or "mutual funds," to use the American terminology) is the justification underlying the need for a detailed EU legislation in this matter, originally administered by Directive 85/611/EEC.[225] This directive has been recast by several subsequent amendments and replaced by the mentioned UCITC Directive. In its turn, this directive has been amended most recently by Directive 2014/91/EU (UCITS V Directive; UCITS Directive and UCITS V Directive together: UCITS V). The rationale behind these pieces of legislation is to harmonise, as far as is possible, the prevailing rules in each respective member state on this matter so as to ensure a better circulation of the units can be realised, together with a strong protection of the unit-holder.[226] Additionally, the harmonisation process provides the UCITS with an EU passport; once the UCITS is initially authorised in one member state, that shall suffice for purposes of authorisation in any other member state where the units are to be marketed.

UCITS V clarifies, from the outset, the concept of undertakings for collective investment in transferable securities. Pursuant to Article 1(2) of UCITS V, "UCITS" are "undertakings" "with the sole object of collective investment in transferable securities or in other liquid financial assets referred to in Article 50(1) of capital raised from the public and which operate on the principle of risk-spreading" and "with units which are, at the request of holders, repurchased or redeemed, directly or indirectly, out of those undertakings' assets. Action taken by a UCITS to ensure that the stock exchange value of its units does not significantly vary from their net asset value shall be regarded as equivalent to such repurchase or redemption." Thus, the UCITS covered by UCITS V are exclusively of an open-ended nature, meaning that their units can be redeemed or repurchased by the fund at the request of the investor. Closed-end UCITS are outwith the scope of UCITS V,[227] likewise are, for instance, UCITS which raise capital without promoting the sale of these units to the public within the EU.[228]

Looked at from a practical point of view, investing in a UCITS can be of considerable advantage to an investor: when subscribing one or more units (*i.e.* when paying for one or more participation rights in a UCITS), the investor relies on the ability

225 In full: Council Directive 85/611/EEC of 20 December 1985 on the coordination of laws, regulations and administrative provisions relating to undertakings for collective investments in transferrable securities, OJ L 375/3.

For literature concerned with Directive 85/611, see Wood, International Loans, Bonds, Guarantees, Legal Opinions. Vol 3, The Law and Practice of International Finance Series (2007a).

226 (Scott and Gelpern, International Finance. Transaction, Policy, and Regulation 2012).

227 Closed-end funds are collective investment funds the units of which cannot be disinvested upon request of the investor but during a specific period of time. Conversely, in the open-end fund, the investor is always entitled to ask for – and obtain – the redemption of his units by the same fund, according to the modalities indicated by the fund itself.

228 Article 3(a) and (b) UCITS V, respectively. Conversely, closed-end funds may fall under the scope of the AIFMD regulation; see Article 1 Commission Delegated Regulation 694/2014/EU of 17 December 2013.

of the management company to optimise his capital through an investment policy bound by the principles of risk-spreading. The more the management company invests money of the fund in profitable securities, the greater the likelihood that the unit-holder will see the value of his units rise. Any profits realised by the unit-holder are therefore dependent upon a future increase in the values of the units, together with the distribution of "dividends" at the discretion of the management company.

From the earlier discussion, it follows that a UCITS is inexorably linked with a management company (a concept defined in UCITS V) tasked with overseeing and managing the investment of the fund. Metaphorically speaking, the management company constitutes the head of operations while its apparatus (directors and managers) is in charge of professionally investing the funds raised from the public. The fund then is the body or the object, the volume of money that, once raised from the public, must be invested in securities with a favourable outcome dependent on the ability of the management company to exercise the correct choice of investment. The activity at stake is speculative: the investor will have to put faith in an increase in the future value of the unit so that, as a result of the sale or redemption of the unit, he can realise a profit.[229] Conversely, he cannot be offered any guarantee on the profitability of this activity. The investment in the fund may turn out to be unprofitable; in this case, the investor forgoes any right to claim back the sum of money given at the time of the subscription. The difference between the higher value of the units at the time of the subscription and the lower value, when the unit is sold or redeemed, constitutes the loss reported by the investor.

The limited possibilities of reclaiming any money invested, as just discussed, do not include potential proceedings, under the applicable national private or commercial law, against the management company for a mismanagement of funds if it could be demonstrated that the maladministration had been instrumental in furthering the loss beyond what might be expected of a professional entity operating in that sector. From a private law point of view, although in various EU jurisdictions there is no such thing as a legal concept of asset manager, scholars tend to characterise the relationship between investor and management company as agency, where the investor, as principal, has given a mandate to the management company as agent to invest.[230]

Because of the delicate nature of the activity tasked to the management company, it must be authorised in advance in the country where it is established, so long as the home authority has ascertained that the specific requisites are in place, more specifically (1) an initial capital of, in principle, 125,000 euro; (2) the names of the directors, who shall manifest the necessary good repute and experience; (3) a programme of activity; and (4) information on the close ties which may exist between the directors and natural or legal persons owning the entity. In this respect,

229 A partial way out for the investor – but this applies exclusively to open-end funds – is to ask for the redemption of the unit; however, in the closed-end funds, the investor relinquishes any right to claim back that sum of money.

230 In a pure common law jurisdiction, the paradigm of this is England and Wales. See Van Setten and Plews (2012). From the perspective of a mixed legal system, see Cabrelli (2012).

it is important to ensure that these ties do not prevent the effective exercise of supervisory functions by the competent authorities.[231]

In the execution of its business activities, the management company is supported by a depositary responsible for the safekeeping of the assets of the mutual fund. The depositary (usually an authorised bank) is an entity which establishes a close working relationship with the management company but which remains independent of it. Actually, Article 25(1) UCITS V expressly prescribes that "[n]o single company shall act as both investment company and depositary." The reason for this is that, in discharging its safekeeping role, the depositary acts "solely in the interests of the unit-holders."[232] It is important to note that the mutual fund is one thing, but the capital and own funds of the management company itself are quite another. Therefore, the borderline etched to separate the assets of the two entities is rigorously marshalled.

Investment funds and rules of transparency

At the outset of this paragraph, it was alluded to that UCITS may invest in securities in accordance with the programme of each specific fund. This programme must be made public to the prospective investors from the start. In this respect, two aspects should be emphasised.

First and foremost, any opportunity for the management company to invest the fund in securities and cash is constrained by specific mandatory rules set forth under the UCITS Directive. In the context of this book, it is not feasible to enter into the details of these regulations given their exhaustive nature. The fundamental underlying principle is that UCITS shall spread the risk rather than concentrating it within a single pursuit. In adhering to this line of reasoning, a UCITS "may invest no more than 5% of its assets in transferrable securities issued by the same body."[233] To allow for a higher percentage would overexpose the fund to the same issuer. Similarly, some UCITS V rules reflect the underpinning philosophy of an investment fund, viz. an investment fund is not so much concerned with the management of the company it invests in as it is not an entrepreneur but rather an investor holding a financial interest in the profitability of the shares in which it has invested its money. In this vein, UCITS V clearly prohibits that the management company acquire, to the benefit of the fund, "shares carrying voting rights which would enable it to exercise significant influence over the management of the issuing body."[234]

That said, in the adjacent area of the rules of transparency, the UCITS Directive prescribes that essential documents connected to the fund be published – namely, the prospectus, an annual report for each financial year, and a half-yearly report covering the first six months of the financial year.[235] Of these documents, the greatest significance can be attached to the prospectus. In a similar vein to the general

231 Article 7(1)(a), (b), (c), and Article 7(2) UCITS V, respectively.

232 Article 25(2) UCITS V.

233 Article 52(1) UCITS V.

234 Article 56 UCITS V.

235 Article 68 UCITS V.

prospectus,[236] it contains the "information necessary for investors to be able to make an informed judgement of the investment proposed to them."[237] The prospectus relating to UCITS shall comply with the standards provided in Schedule A of Annex I of the Directive under discussion. This standard represents a "floor" of information which the management company cannot fall short of while it is, of course, fully entitled to exceed the minimal level of data required under the statute.

Alternative investment funds

As has previously been alluded to in this chapter,[238] alternative investment funds are funds which are less traditional than UCITS. They are more speculative, in the sense that their investment strategy can be more innovative and the single investor may invest a larger amount of money. Yet legislation, at least at EU level, was absent prior to the introduction of the AIFMD legislation in 2011. The purpose of this comparatively recent piece of legislation was, fundamentally, to "provide for an internal market for AIFMs and a harmonised and stringent regulatory and supervisory framework for the activities within the Union of all AIFMs."[239] The rationale behind the legislation at stake is practical in nature and its pertinence to the recent financial crises is clear: a number of AIFM strategies are "vulnerable to some or several important risks in relation to investors, other market participants and markets."[240] As a result of this, the legislator has envisaged the need to establish "a framework capable of addressing those risks taking into account the diverse range of investment strategies and techniques employed by AIFMs."[241]

Interestingly, the AIFM Directive, which prescribes specific rules relating to the manager of the fund (the AIFM), does not make reference to the fund itself. Accordingly, the fund shall be subject to the legislation existing in each country. It is beyond the scope of the current chapter to elaborate at length upon the details of the piece of legislation under discussion. Nevertheless, it might be helpful to discuss the main provisions applicable to these funds.

First and foremost, the AIFM, *i.e.* the manager directly responsible for an alternative investment fund (AIF), shall have secured prior authorisation from the relevant home country authority. It should be noted that, subsequent to being granted such authority, the AIFM shall be permitted to carry out only limited activities, specifically those detailed under Annex I of the directive under discussion, including portfolio management and risk management. Accordingly, the full spectrum of investment activities and investment services pertaining to financial instruments, usually granted to investment firms, are precluded from the ambit of authority exercised by AIF managers.

236 See also above, Chapter 2.
237 Article 69 UCITS V.
238 Section 8.3.1.
239 Recital 4 to the Directive 2011/61/EU.
240 Recital 3, Directive 2011/61.
241 *Ibid.*

The conditions to be satisfied prior to granting the authorisation just mentioned are those detailed under Article 8, where one of the most important requirements is an initial capital of 300,000 euro.[242] Also, in cases where the value of the portfolios managed by the AIFM exceeds 250 million euro, the AIF's own funds must constitute 0.02% of the amount by which the value of the portfolios of the AIFM exceeds 250 million euro.[243] The authorisation shall be regarded as withdrawn by the competent authority, should one of the circumstances detailed under Article 11 transpire, the most important of which are, seemingly, the obtainment of the authorisation "by making false statements or by any other irregular means" or in cases where the AIM "no longer meets the conditions under which authorisation was granted."

Once the AIFM has acquired authorisation in its own (*i.e.* home) member state, by way of the EU passport the authorisation shall be immediately valid in each member state,[244] and the AIFM shall have the capacity to both manage and commercialise funds to professional investors within the Union, without the need for any further authorisation by the authority of the other member state where the funds are either managed or commercialised.[245] But if the units of AIF were offered to the public, then the decision will rest with the authority of the other member states as to whether or not the commercialisation of the AIF is granted authorisation.[246]

In light of the speculative nature of the AIF, clear guidelines have been installed to ensure that their managers, *i.e.* the AIFMs use "at all times, adequate and appropriate human and technical resources that are necessary for the proper management of AIFs."[247] In this scenario, according to the precepts of the EU legislator, the competent authorities of the home member state of the AIFM shall require that "the AIFM has sound administrative and accounting procedures, control and safeguard arrangements for electronic data processing and adequate internal control mechanism."[248] In perusing the details of the organisational requirements, it is worth acknowledging that the legislation under discussion expressly requires that the AIFM put in place "appropriate and consistent procedures" to ensure that "a proper and independent valuation of the assets of the AIF can be performed."[249]

The delegation of the functions of a fund manager opens the door to a number of possible risks: the investor typically relies on the credibility and reliability of the delegated manager, the entity formally in charge of the management of the fund. Conversely, a delegation of functions to third parties may in turn jeopardise the principles of transparency and affect the same credibility of the management functions. This concern, already relevant across the spectrum of mutual funds, is magnified when dealing with a fund (alternative investment fund) which is more

242 However, the minimum capital shall be reduced to 125,000 euro if the AIM was appointed exclusively as "external manager."
243 Article 9(3) AIFMD.
244 Article 8 AIFMD.
245 Articles 31-33 AIMFD.
246 Article 43 AIFMD.
247 Article 18(1) AIFMD.
248 *Ibid.*
249 Article 19(1) AIFMD.

speculative in nature. In light of this, the EU legislator ensures that the delegation of functions, albeit permitted, is subject to a control of the authority of the competent member state. Thus, when delegating to third parties, the entity aimed to carry out the management of an AIF be notified to the authority.[250] Also, the effectiveness of the agreement must comply with several conditions, amongst which a special mention can be made to the following: the alternative investment fund manager "must be able to justify its entire delegation structure on objective reasons";[251] "the delegate must dispose of sufficient resources to perform the respective tasks and the persons who effectively conduct the business of the delegate must be of sufficiently good repute and sufficiently experienced";[252] "where the delegation concerns portfolio management or risk management, it must be conferred only on undertakings which are authorised or registered for the purposes of asset management and subject to supervision";[253] the alternative investment fund manager delegating these functions "must be able to demonstrate that the delegate is qualified and capable of undertaking the functions in question, that is was selected with all due care and that the AIFM is in a position to monitor effectively at any time the delegated activity, to give at any time further instructions to the delegate and to withdraw the delegation with immediate effect when this is in the interest of the investors."[254] In other words, the delegation is not – and cannot be – an opportunity for the authorised intermediary (the AIFM), on the one hand, to eschew its responsibilities and, on the other, to expose the investor to a risk that is more considerable that originally envisaged.

Finally, the AIF shall engage the services of an authorised institution to act as a depositary, by definition a bank,[255] and the appointment of this depositary, which is mandatory, shall be documented by virtue of a written contract.[256]

3.3 Financial contracts

3.3.1 Loan contract

A loan contract constitutes one of the simplest forms of commercial contracts: in essence, a lender advances money to a borrower who is then obligated to pay it back, usually with the addition of interest. Within the context of loan finance, loans may be distinguished in various ways. Firstly, a demarcation line can be

250 Article 20(1) AIFMD.
251 Article 20(1)(a) AIFMD.
252 Article 20(1)(b) AIFMD.
253 Article 20(1)(c) AIFMD.
254 Article 20(1)(f) AIFMD.
255 Article 21(1) AIFMD.
256 Although the terms and conditions of this contract are left to the discretion of the contracting parties, the legislation in discussion takes pain to highlight (Article 21(2) AIFMD) the main aspects of the agreement that shall be necessarily indicated in the contract: particularly, "the flow of information deemed necessary to allow the depositary to perform its functions for the AIF for which it has been appointed as depositary, as set out [in the AIFMD, MH, PdG] and in other relevant laws, regulations or administrative provisions."

drawn between term loans and overdrafts. Term loans are loans which are extended for a fixed term, cancellable only if certain conditions are satisfied and repayable prematurely only in the event of default or the occurrence of certain other predefined events. This form of finance is very predictable and starkly contrasts with overdrafts. Overdrafts are loans that can be extended but also cancelled and repaid at any time. Loans may also be distinguished by the parties involved. For example, a bilateral loan may be entered into between a borrower and a single bank, whilst a syndicated loan may occur by way of the involvement of multiple banks or other financial institutions. The group of lenders may be relatively small in number, sometimes referred to as a "club loan," or conversely, may be more heavily populated, and in exceptional cases, the number may run into hundreds of lenders. In regard to the borrower, a distinction can be made in accordance with the size of the company or group. Bank loans can be granted to corporate and governmental borrowers but also can be extended to small or medium-sized private companies and, as a matter of course, to private individuals. This chapter will deal primarily with loans advanced by several banks (typically referred to as "syndicated loans") to large enterprises and governmental bodies.

Loan finance has not been subject to much statutory European private law harmonisation. Loans, therefore, largely remain governed by the applicable national law of contract, which may vary considerably from one country to another. However, when it comes to large bank loans the standard documentation of the Loan Market Association[257] is habitually used. In accordance with the LMA documentation, parties typically opt for English law but other applicable laws may also be selected and relevant versions of the LMA documentation are available for each respective option provided. Nonetheless, the LMA documentation has brought about a significant degree of harmonisation and this chapter will therefore pay considerable attention to it.

In a typical loan document, the financial terms form the core element of the agreement between the parties. Yet, of at least equivalent importance are the non-financial (*i.e.* legal) terms, such as the covenants and events of default. In establishing these conditions, to be discussed further here, the bank wishes to generate as much certainty as possible that the loan will eventually be repaid by the borrower. The borrower, for his part, has a vested interest in securing as much flexibility on the repayment of the loan as possible.

Purposes

Companies typically use a mix of sources of funding, *i.e.* capital, to finance their growth and business development. In essence, sources of capital can be distinguished between equity capital and debt capital. Equity capital is self-funded from retained cash and equity share capital. Debt capital may include long and short-term bank loans, syndicated loans by a syndicate of banks and perhaps institutional

257 Henceforth LMA.

investors, transaction specific finance, and short-term (less than one year) capital market debt.

With every finance transaction the company has to determine which type of finance is most suitable. Sometimes, especially in larger finance transactions, more than one source will be used. Both equity capital and debt capital have their own characteristics which influence the choice to use either one of them or both for the financing of the company. In contrast with equity capital, debt capital can be characterised as follows: (1) debt capital providers, *i.e.* lenders, bear less risk than equity capital providers in that they rank *pari passu* with other creditors while equity providers are subordinated to debt providers (which is particularly relevant in the company's insolvency); (2) in Europe, debt capital is most commonly provided as a loan; (3) debt capital creates a repayment right, *i.e.* claim, for the lender/creditor; (4) the return on the loan is provided as interest (which may be tax-deductible for the company) and does not depend of the company's profit or reserves; and (5) the relation between lenders and the company is to a large extent laid down in the credit documentation and applicable contract law.

Syndication of bank loans

The essence of syndication is that two or more banks agree to make loans to a borrower on common terms governed by a single agreement between all parties.[258] The syndication is generally initiated by the grant of a mandate by the borrower to an arranging bank or group of arranging banks setting out the financial terms of the proposed loan, and authorising the arranging bank(s), or "arrangers," to arrange syndication, *i.e.* find other banks to participate in the loan. The actual terms of the mandate naturally depend upon the type of borrower and its credit standing. Nevertheless, there is a core market practice. Investment grade borrowers (rated BBB− or above) can typically obtain better terms than borrowers rated speculative. The financial terms are set out in a "term sheet" which states the amount, term, repayment schedule, interest margin, fees, any special terms and a general statement that the loan will contain representations and warranties, covenants, events of default and other usual clauses.

The arranging bank (1) assists the borrower in preparing an information memorandum about the borrower and setting out the terms of the loan for despatch to potential bank participants, (2) solicits expressions of interest from these potential participants and (3) negotiates the loan documentation. Once the loan documentation is agreed, then all of the banks sign up to the syndicated loan agreement with the borrower and, in the agreement, appoint one of their number, usually the lead arranging bank, as their agent to administer the loan. It is for convenience of administration that one of the banks is appointed agent of the syndicate through whom payment and communications are channelled.[259]

258 See Proctor (2010); Ellinger, Lomnicka and Hare (2011).
259 (Hudson 2013).

In the syndicated market it is common that each bank will make loans up to its specified commitment and that each bank's obligations are not meant to be joint and several, as syndications are not intended to be a partnership. Therefore, banks do not underwrite each other or guarantee to the borrower that other banks in the syndicate will remain solvent. At the same time, the participating banks do have to cooperate because certain decisions have to be made as a group during the term of the loan. The banks may agree between themselves to delegate certain decisions to majority control, *e.g.* certain waivers of non-payment obligations and the right to accelerate the loan on an event of default. But most commonly, the more important decisions are subject to all lenders consent.

Under the usual method of syndication, all banks sign the loan agreement. But at a later stage, a bank may wish to transfer its claim under the loan for multiple reasons. For example, the original bank might transfer its claim to make a profit out of this trading, to remove the claim from its balance sheet, as it would cause an undesired capital adequacy requirement, or to securitise the claim. For all these reasons, the marketability of the claims arising from a loan is essential. The main methods of transferring the claims, or, more specifically, the participations in a syndicated loan are (1) by assignment, in which the original bank assigns (a portion of) the loan to the new bank; (2) by sub-participation, in which the original bank agrees to pay to the new bank amounts equal to the new bank's share of payments received by the original bank from the borrower; or (3) by novation, in which the original bank, the new bank and the borrower all agree to novate (a portion of) the loan agreement to the new bank.

Loan Market Association

The Loan Market Association[260] is an association of international banks active in the London market.[261] One of its key objectives is to harmonise certain provisions of the documentation for syndicated credits, *i.e.* claims arising from loans that are made available by a group or syndication of banks. The harmonisation is primarily with a view to enhancing the tradability of these credits and reducing the time and cost of negotiations, and therefore improving liquidity, efficiency and transparency in the syndicated loan markets in Europe, the Middle East and Africa. The LMA does not seek to standardise deal-specific terms, which depend upon the circumstances of the credit, but the commercially less important areas of the documents, so as to allow lenders and borrowers to focus on the more important commercial aspects of individual transactions.

260 Henceforth LMA.

261 Since the establishment of the LMA in 1996, its memberships have grown steadily and now in 2014 stands at 512 organisations covering 52 nationalities, comprising commercial and investment banks, institutional investors, law firms, service providers and rating agencies.

Documentation structure and facilities

In current standard LMA documentation, broadly speaking, the agreement can be divided into three sections. The first section consists of the core provisions of the loan, such as the facilities to be provided (to be discussed further here), the principal amounts, the repayment instalments and repayment dates, the interest rates and periods, the fees and the specifics of payment such as the currency, time and place. Also, a provision is included regarding a tax and other unforeseeable additional costs.

The second section contains the conditions precedent. Only if these conditions are satisfied, is the bank obliged to lend the agreed amount under the loan agreement. First, there are conditions precedent to all loans. These are to ensure that all legal matters, including the required security, are in order. The conditions precedent in this second section provide in outline that the bank is not obliged to make any loans until the bank has received such items as constitutional documents of the borrower and its authorisations, *e.g.* board resolutions, process agency appointment under a forum section clause, and legal opinions as to the validity of the documentation and other matters. Secondly, there are conditions precedent to each loan separately. These clauses provide in outline that the bank is not obliged to make a loan unless, at the time of the request for the loan and the borrowing of the loan, and immediately after the loan is made, the representations and warranties are true and up-to-date, no event of default has occurred (or will occur in the near future) and there has been no material adverse change in the borrower's financial conditions. In addition to the conditions precedent, the second section also consists of the covenants, the representations and warranties, as well as the events of default. The events of default are events which give the banks express permission to accelerate outstanding loans, suspend further loans and cancel its obligations. Finally, this section determines which security has to be granted to the lenders.

The third section deals with various (operational) issues regarding the syndicated nature of the loan, such as the role of the agent and the transfer of loan participations. This section also contains the boilerplate clauses, such as the choice of law and forum clause.

Most commonly, the lenders offer different kinds of facilities in the loan agreement. Regardless the type of facility, the agreement always concerns a lender providing a loan to a borrower who has to repay the principal amount and an additional amount as interest. When the bank provides a loan facility it will commit itself to provide the borrower a fixed amount of money which can be drawn in a lump sum or in parts. Loan facilities can be categorised in different ways, of which the most important ones will be discussed further here. However, one has to keep in mind that the classifications are merely meant as an illustration of existing possibilities. New types can be developed and existing types might become obsolete. The classifications under discussion are as follows:

Term loan, that is a loan which is made available to the borrower on the basis that it will be repaid in specified instalments over a set period of time or at

> once (which is then called a "bullet loan"). Generally, the drawdown of a term loan by the borrower is only possible within a short time after closing *i.e.*, conclusion of the agreement. This is called the availability period or commitment period. Once repaid, a term loan cannot be redrawn. If parties agree on a fixed interest rate, the term loan is called a fixed rate term loan, but in most cases the rate is floating instead of fixed, in which case the loan is called a floating rate term loan. From an economic point of view the floating rate term loan is very similar to the roll over term loan. A roll over term loan is a loan which has to be repaid at the end of an interest period, but will then again be redrawn for a new period. This makes it possible to agree on a long-term loan with a short term interest rate. Term loans are generally used for a specific financing requirement such as an asset purchase. It is a long-term debt on the borrower's balance sheet.

A revolving loan is a term loan which can be drawn at any moment during the term of the loan and can be redrawn after a (partial) repayment. Such a facility is most commonly used for credit needs that increase in a specific season.

A demand loan is a facility which the lenders make available but which the lenders are able to cancel or require repayment of at any time (or "on demand"), although sometimes a notice period has to be taken into account. Therefore, the facility might also be called an "uncommitted facility." Facilities of this type do not require lengthy documentation as there is no need for undertakings or events of default, the lender being free to terminate the facility at will. The lack of a commitment by the lender is a significant disadvantage to a borrower. On the other hand, the capital adequacy treatment of such facilities may result in them being cheaper for a borrower than committed facilities of a longer duration.

A stand-by loan materialises when a borrower desires to have more flexibility. In this scenario the banks commit themselves to provide a loan at the request of the borrower. Because the banks enter into this commitment, they have to reserve the amount during the term of the loan. For this commitment a commitment fee will be charged to the borrower, calculated on the non-drawn part of the stand-by facility.

Another possibility is that the borrower has fluctuating financing requirements, *e.g.* for working capital. For this situation the overdraft facility was invented. An overdraft facility is a facility that the borrower may draw down, repay and then draw again. This is different from a term loan which, once the borrower has repaid, cannot be reborrowed. By having the ability to repay and reborrow, the borrower is able to ensure that levels of borrowing at any time do not exceed his financial requirements at that time. An overdraft facility may be committed or uncommitted. In a committed facility, the lenders would commit to lend up to a specified sum for a given period, such as 12 months. The borrower could draw up to the limit at any time, repay as and when desired, and have the comfort of being able to draw again, up to the limit, at any time within the committed period. However, the borrower will need to pay a commitment fee to the lenders for any part of the facility which the borrower is not using at any time, and which the lenders remain committed to lend. If the facility is uncommitted or if the period of the commitment is short then the facility will usually be a current liability on the borrower's balance sheet. Sometimes an overdraft facility contains a clause to make sure the facility is used only for predefined temporarily increased credit needs. Thus, the overdraft facility slightly differs from a revolving credit, as a revolving credit is used for specific foreseeable credit needs while the overdraft facility commonly is used as a working capital facility, meaning it might be used for temporarily increased credit needs.

Another – albeit unconventional – type of facility is the contingent liability facility. Under this facility the bank takes on the obligation to pay a certain amount of money to a creditor of the borrower, instead of to the borrower itself. Thus, this facility makes it possible for a borrower to guarantee the payment of a debt since the bank has to fulfil the borrower's payment obligations. Important examples of such a facility are the bank guarantee or a letter of credit, which are both quite similar.

In the present context, a corporate finance transaction is one in which there is neither a specific asset nor a specific stream of income on which the lenders' credit decision is based, but rather they are relying on the general financial position of the borrower. This is also known as "balance sheet lending."

An asset finance transaction is one in which the future value of a certain asset is a key factor in the lenders' credit risk assessment. This, of course, has major implications for the security required and the documentation.

A project finance transaction is one in which the income generated by the project is a key factor in the lenders' credit decision. In the context of asset and project financing, it should be noted that the lenders are often taking a mixture of asset risk, project risk, and corporate risk. For example, lenders providing ship finance (which is regarded as asset finance) will not only assess the future value of the ship. They will often also look at the operator's balance sheet and financial ratios and at the likely income which the ship will generate. In other words, the lenders will take asset, project, and corporate risk into account when they consider making available a facility which is traditionally regarded as an asset finance transaction. Some transactions (most commonly project finance) are put together on a "limited recourse" basis. This means that the lenders accept that they will only be repaid out of prespecified assets. This may be done by having a contractual limitation on recourse. Alternatively, it may be done structurally, by establishing a special-purpose entity which will own only the assets (*e.g.* project assets and income) to which the lenders are intended to have recourse, with the lender lending to that entity.

Purpose of the loan

Based on the goals to be achieved by loans, we can have different typologies:

- Acquisition finance: finance used to acquire something, usually a company;
- Bridge finance: finance made available to bridge a funding gap. For example, when a company requires financing for a corporate acquisition, it may intend to raise the bulk of that finance through issuing bonds on the capital markets, but it may need interim finance to cover the period during which the bonds have not

yet been issued and paid up, etc. A bridge loan is also often used in acquisition finance when there is not enough time to negotiate complete finance documentation including the security, before the take-over has to take place. Therefore, banks have created the possibility of a simpler bridge loan with only minimal security (most commonly a pledge over shares of the target company) for a short period of time, with the objective to negotiate the actual finance documentation prior to the maturity date of the temporary bridge loan. To speed up the negotiations for the take-out loan, *i.e.* the full-fledged loan, the bridge loan quite often consists a step-up clause which determines that the interest rate will increase after a certain lapse of time. A bridge finance loan is usually a high-interest, short-term debt provided by the house bank of the borrower;
- Mezzanine finance or venture capital: finance used where traditional finance is not available in sufficient amounts to meet the borrower's needs. Generally, companies meet their financing requirements by a mixture of debt and equity. Where the level of debt is high compared to the amount of equity, the company is described as "highly leveraged" or "highly geared." When equity plus the amounts available from traditional lenders is insufficient to meet the needs, borrowers may approach mezzanine financiers to make up the difference. The claims that arise from the finance they provide will be subordinate to the claims that arise from a traditional loan. Thus, it will carry more risk and therefore the interest will be higher. Usually, the mezzanine financier will also require some form of "equity kicker" – that is, in addition to the margin they will require a share in any profits from the transaction;
- Refinancing: finance made available to repay existing debt. This may be done to achieve less onerous covenants or more favourable margins, to reflect new corporate structures, to increase leverage, as part of a restructuring following a default, or for other reasons;
- Mismatch facilities: these are facilities which seek to match the difference between what is available to a borrower from a given source and what the borrower needs. For example, in a securitisation a borrower may require a mismatch facility to bridge the gap between the dates when the payments on receivables come in, and the dates on which the issued bonds have to be paid.

Documentation clauses

In the following, we will discuss some of the most common and important clauses in finance documentation, with a specific focus on LMA documentation.

Under the purpose clause, the borrower undertakes to use the loan for a specified purpose. This does not, in itself, provide a great deal of protection for the lenders, for three reasons. Firstly, the borrower may disregard the clause, using money for other, unauthorised purposes (and thus putting the lenders in the position of, at best, having assumed a different credit risk from the one intended). Additionally, the loan may be used for the intended purpose, but its availability may result in other moneys being able to be diverted to a purpose which the lenders would not have funded. Third, the purpose stated is often quite vague, for example, "general corporate purposes," leaving a lot room for interpretation.

Nevertheless, the purpose clause is of some value. It may assist in good faith arguments by the lenders (*e.g.* to demonstrate their lack of awareness of any illegal use or use in contravention of a regulation). It will, in most cases, be likely to trigger discussions about intended use of the facility, which may then become more specifically detailed. It can, in the worst cases, assist in establishing a claim in fraud if the borrower uses the funds for any unauthorised purpose.

One of the most essential elements of the credit agreement, at least from the lender's perspective, is the repayment of the loan, including the accrued interest. The repayment clause therefore is an important clause in the contract. Repayment may be made in instalments or in a single amount ("bullet"). Instalments must often be made in equal semi-annual amounts, commencing after a "grace period." The jargon for a larger final instalment is a "balloon."

Prepayments, *i.e.* payments made prior to the agreed moment(s), are generally discouraged. If the borrower would like to repay the loan any earlier than agreed upon, so-called "break costs" will be calculated. The reason behind these additional costs in case of an early prepayment is that the bank is assumed to fund the loan by matching deposits in the (interbank) market, which it on-lends to the borrower. In case of an early prepayment the bank wants to be compensated for the costs it has made in the interbank market for the availability of sufficient funds, since these costs now will no longer be compensated by the interest payments of the borrower.

Also, the way a repayment or prepayment has been made is determined by the payments clause. This clause provides in outline that the borrower and the bank will make all payments in the specified currency, in immediately available funds, to the specified bank account in the country of currency, without set-off or counterclaim. Both bank and borrower are invariably required to make payments in the financial centre of the country of the currency (*e.g.* US dollars in New York City, sterling in London, yen in Tokyo and euros in the principal financial centre of a member state or London). Although technically payments could be made by other means, large payments are always made through a clearing system of the country of the currency.

In syndicated loans, the borrower makes payments to the agent bank who distributes them to the bank pro rata of their participation in the loan. Under English law, the borrower is discharged after paying the agent even if the agent of the banks fails to pay the banks. This is because the agent is the agent of the banks, and payment to an agent is deemed to represent payment to the principal.

The prohibition of set-off would prevent, for example, a set-off by the borrower of its debt following from the loan against its claim following from a deposit with the lender. The lenders' arguments for the prohibition on set-off and counterclaims by the borrower are commonly (1) the maxim "pay now, litigate later,"[262] (2) the

262 Or *solve et repete* clause, to put it in a Latin terminology.

cash flow principle (the bank uses payments to repay the underlying interbank loan) and (3) the clause improves the transferability of loans, as the transferee bank thus will not have to fair the risk that the borrower might invoke a set-off right it had against the transferor bank.

Interest, margin, costs and fees

The interest calculated by the bank usually consists of three elements: (1) a compensation for the costs the bank makes; (2) a risk element which depends on the creditworthiness of the borrower; (3) a profit mark-up for the bank. All of these elements are generally expressed as "basis points." One basis point is one-hundredth of 1%, so that 50 basis points is 0.5%, or half a per cent. The borrower commonly pays interest at a percentage that is calculated as a "margin" or "spread" in basis points, *e.g.* 100 basis points, above EURIBOR or LIBOR. This is the rate at which the bank is offered deposits matching as to currency and maturity, respectively in the European or London, interbank market, as shown on a market provider's screen service – usually at 11:00 a.m. local time in the funding market, two business days before the interest period concerned.

In floating rate loans, the interest rate changes periodically. The borrower may choose interest periods of (generally) one, three or six months (and sometimes even nine or twelve months) during which the interest rate is fixed. A longer interest period gives more security but at the same time will be relatively more expensive. Interest is calculated on a 360- or 365-day-a-year basis and interest is payable at the end of an interest period or at least six-monthly. In case of a default the borrower will have to pay default interest at about 100 to 200 basis points higher than the regular interest rate.

Several clauses have been designed to protect the margin or spread payable to the bank. First, under the tax-grossing up clause, if the borrower must deduct taxes, it has to pay extra so that the bank receives the full amount. Second, under the increased costs clause, if any law or official directive increases the bank's underlying costs, the borrower must compensate those costs. Central bank reserve requirements, special taxes, capital adequacy rules and liquidity requirements may impose costs on the bank which are attributable to the loan but which are not reflected in the costs of funding deposits. The weakness of this clause is the practical difficulty of allocating certain costs to particular loans and also the commercial acceptability of passing on some costs. Probably because of this an increased cost claim is highly unusual in international loans. Additionally, the borrower is usually obliged to bear all costs in connection with the negotiation, drafting and amending of the credit documentation.

Besides the different cost provisions just discussed, there are also some arrangements with regard to the fees. First, the borrower has to pay an "arrangement fee" to the lead manager of the arranging banks, which is commonly stipulated in a confidential fee letter. In the case of a stand-by loan facility, a commitment fee will also be payable by the borrower. As a common practice, this commitment fee is a percentage of the stand-by amount.

Guarantees, representations and undertakings

Next to the condition precedent, it is the guarantees, representations, undertakings and events of defaults that form the second part of the loan agreement. This part regulates the working relationship between the lenders and the borrower, and hence is often the most heavily negotiated part of the document.

A bank will consider security for repayment of the loan of the utmost importance. Therefore, it is commonly agreed that the borrower has to grant different types of security. Not only property law or real security interests, such as pledges and mortgages are granted, but also personal security rights. A prime example of such a personal security right can be found in the guarantee clause. Under the so-called "all moneys" guarantee, for instance, a third-party guarantor guarantees whatever monies the borrower owes the lenders from time to time. In the context of major financings, "all moneys" guarantees are unusual. In typical major financings loan documentation such as LMA documentation, the guarantee clause constitutes a primary obligation on a guarantor to pay sums under the loan agreement if these sums remain unpaid by the borrower. The intention is to ensure that any difficulties with the underlying debt do not affect the guarantor's liability. Therefore, the LMA documentation also contains an indemnity for losses resulting from unpaid sums because of invalidity, illegality, or unenforceability. Furthermore, the guarantee is a continuing guarantee. This means that the guarantee relates not only to the original loan (which may well have been repaid) but also to the readvanced loans from time to time. This is especially important in a revolving credit.

Representations and warranties are typical English-law-inspired statements inserted into the contract that list the basic assumptions that inspired each side to agree to the deal.[263] The idea is for one side to put the other side on notice that it is relying on certain facts, both past and present, and that it expects those facts to survive into the future. Technically speaking, representations and warranties are distinct legal concepts. Each gives rise to a different legal remedy if a deal goes sour and ends up in court. Representations are past and present facts that spell out why each side was brought into the deal. A misrepresentation claim, if proved, gives rise to damages and a remedy called rescission, which is the unwinding or undoing of the deal. Warranties are inserted to protect a party if losses arise because the future does not unfold in the way that was represented by those facts. A breach of warranty gives rise to damages. However, for most practical purposes, if any of the statements (whether a representation or a warranty) transpires to be untrue, the lenders will rely on their contractual rights (not to lend and/or to accelerate) which arise as a result. These rights are the same for a misrepresentation as for a breach of warranty.

Credit agreements contain an elaborate series of mainly standardised representations by the borrower. Banking practice distinguishes between legal representations and commercial representations. The former basically deal with the legal

263 (Wood, International Loans, Bonds, Guarantees, Legal Opinions. Vol 3, The Law and Practice of International Finance Series 2007a).

validity of the agreement,[264] while the latter deal with the borrower's financial condition and credit standing. In practice, the representations are investigatory and therefore, (hopefully) flush out problems in advance because they trigger disclosure of information, which is especially useful under English law because there is no general duty to negotiate in good faith in that jurisdiction.[265]

A frequently used representation is the representation regarding the *pari passu* ranking of the debt.[266] Together with the negative pledge and cross-default clauses, this clause is especially important for unsecured lenders to ensure that they are and remain on equal footing with other lenders with regard to the borrower.[267] The intention is to ensure that the syndicate of lenders for this loan is at least equal with all other unsecured creditors or, if not, that they know which creditors have priority. The *pari passu* clause requires the loan to be of at least equal ranking with other unsecured debts. In other words, it requires that the borrower confirm that on the borrower's insolvency, the lenders will share the borrower's assets that are available to unsecured creditors *pro rata* with other unsecured creditors. However, the clause does not prevent the borrower from paying other debts before making payment on the loan, giving security for other debts[268] and agreeing to different, more favourable terms in any loan agreements with other creditors.

The purposes of the undertakings are to ensure the lenders have the information they need, to ensure good housekeeping by the borrower, to give the lenders' leverage and to protect the borrower's assets. Usually the undertakings cover (1) provisions of information, (2) financial covenants and (3) positive and negative covenants relating to protection of assets.

Within provision of information is concerned, the most important information undertakings relate to the financials of the borrowing company or group. Therefore, generally, the parent company has to supply to the lenders, via the agent, its audited financial statements. Both consolidated statements, and statements of each member of the group who is a party to the finance documents separately, are commonly required. A consolidated statement concerns the highest level in the group to which the lenders have recourse, which thus gives financial information for the whole of the group below that company. Together with the audited annual

264 Legal representations include such matters as legal status of the borrower (*e.g.* duly incorporated company, powers and authorisations of borrower and the legal validity and enforceability of the borrower's obligations). Commercial representations include such matters as no litigation, actual or known to be threatened (material on group basis); borrower's last (group) accounts are materially correct; the information memorandum is materially correct and not misleading, projections reasonably based, no material omissions (to best knowledge and belief of the borrower); no material adverse change in (group) financial condition since date of last accounts; and no (material) default on contracts or other debt.

265 Actually, in English law there is no such thing as a good faith principle as a whole. See McKendrick (2012).

266 Sometimes, the *pari passu* clause is also a warranty and even sometimes a covenant as well.

267 (Cranston, Principles of Banking Law 2002).

268 This is something the negative pledge clause tries to avoid.

statements the lenders might require an auditor's certificate confirming compliance with the financial ratios.

Furthermore, the company commonly must provide to the lenders all documents dispatched by the company to its shareholders or its creditors. This is intended to ensure that those events that are significant enough to be notified to shareholders and/or creditors are, at the same time, notified to the lenders. However, in the case of private companies, it may be appropriate to limit this requirement since the shareholders of private companies are often immediately involved in the day-to-day management and may receive more information than would be appropriate for a lender.

In the same vein, the borrower may have to supply to the lenders all details of a litigation, arbitration or administrative procedure, as soon as the company becomes aware of it (and if it might, if adversely determined, have a material adverse effect).

The financial covenants relate to the financial ratios that are agreed upon in connection with the monitoring of the borrower. More specifically, these covenants determine which aspects of the borrower's financial condition will be monitored and tested by the lenders, at which level of the group the tests are run; in respect of what periods the tests are run; and what the consequences of breach of a ratio are.

The general positive covenants are minimal; the most important positive covenant is to comply with laws affecting the loan. The negative covenants usually consist of the negative pledge clause, a no disposal clause and a clause prohibiting mergers or change of business.

The negative pledge is especially important from a legal point of view. The clause prohibits the borrower from giving security to a third party[269] unless that security falls within one of the exceptions to the clause.[270] There are many different reasons for inclusion of a negative pledge and its significance varies from transaction to transaction, but first of all, its role is to preserve equality among the lenders and it protects the borrower's pool of assets from being dissipated. In a secured transaction, lenders may also want to have the negative pledge installed so as to facilitate the lenders' control of the company, enable the lenders to easily sell the company as a going concern should an event of default occur, and reduce the likelihood of other creditors taking action against the company.

The consequence of a breach of the negative pledge is not entirely clear from a legal point of view and somehow problematic from a practical point of observation. The clause aims to ensure that if the lenders need to enforce their rights against the borrower, all of the borrower's assets will be shared equally. If the borrower breaches the clause, the lenders may be contractually allowed to accelerate (*i.e.* to demand immediate repayment of the loan in advance of its normal due date). Yet if they do so, they will then be in the situation which the clause was

269 (Cranston, Principles of Banking Law 2002).

270 Generally, only few exceptions as to the negative pledge undertaking are permitted. Exceptions might concern (among others): existing security, netting or set off in the course of ordinary banking arrangements, operation of law, after acquired property/companies and security entered into pursuant to the finance documents themselves.

intended to avoid – that is, of having to enforce but not having equal access to the borrowers' assets. In other words, the clause does not in fact protect the lenders against a borrower which breaches the clause. The position may be different if the person taking security knew, or should have known, that that security was given in breach of the negative pledge.[271]

Events of defaults

An event of default is a predefined event which allows the lender to demand immediate repayment of the loan in advance of its normal due date ("acceleration").[272] Especially in revolving credit facilities, the occurrence of an event of default normally also allows the lender to cancel any obligations to make further loan advances. The events of default are not concerned with fault, but only of risk, as they set out the circumstances on which parties have agreed that the level of risk has changed. Calling a default is a last resort and will usually lead to the immediate demise of the borrower. Thus, the ability to call a default is primarily to provide a sanction and to strengthen the hand of the bank in restructuring negotiations unless the case is hopeless. The existence of these rights gives the lenders leverage to negotiate adjustments to the transaction (such as a change in security or interest) if any of the specified events occurs.

An (actual) default such as a breach of an undertaking is something which may or may not mature into an "event of default" as defined in the agreement. Both a default and an event of default automatically result in the release of the lenders from their obligation to lend new money unless the majority of the lenders waive the default. Nevertheless, some defaults are also automatically considered events of default. An example is a breach of financial ratio, which is automatically an event of default in most loan agreements. Many defaults become events of default only after a period of time (grace period) and/or the giving of notice. Once a default occurs, the borrower is obliged to notify the lenders. Failure to do so results in a separate (usually automatic) event of default. Once an event of default has occurred, the lenders have the right to accelerate the loan. Acceleration does not happen automatically. The lenders can elect whether or not to exercise that right and the loan will only become repayable early if the lenders make a demand for such payment. The lenders' right to accelerate the loan or not to lend additional moneys will cease to be exercisable in certain circumstances, if the loan document states that those rights are only exercisable while the event of default is "continuing."

Roughly, there are two types of events of default: actual events of default (such as the failure to pay principal or interest when it falls due for payment) and

271 Under English common law, in these exceptional circumstances, the beneficiary of the promise would be entitled to sue the third party and successfully ask for the invalidation of the security granted in breach of the negative pledge. This is referred to as the "rule of De Mattos," named after the *decisum De Mattos v Gibson* (1858) 4 De G & J 276. Among scholars, see Cranston, Principles of Banking Law (2002).

272 (Cranston, Principles of Banking Law 2002).

prospective events of default (such as when payment is not yet due, but it is clear that it will not be capable of being paid when it does fall due). Events of default commonly have four main effects by the express terms of the loan contract. First, an event of default expressly permits the bank to accelerate outstanding loans. Second, an event of default permits the bank to cancel its obligations to extend further loans. Third, it enables the bank to suspend further loans under the "conditions precedent" clause. Last, an event may constitute a default under other (credit) agreements of the borrower under a cross-default clause (see further the immediately following paragraph).

Three commonly used events of defaults in loan documentation are discussed in more detail. It concerns the cross-default clause, the material adverse change clause and the change of control clause.[273] All three are important from a legal point of view because of their use or effect.

CROSS-DEFAULT

Cross-default means that the borrower fails to pay another financial debt outside of the loan agreement when due, or other financial debt is accelerated, or a commitment to lend other financial debt is cancelled, an event of default or pending event of default occurs in relation to any other financial debt, or collateral security for financial debt becomes enforceable or is enforced.[274] This clause is of critical importance because a default under any other financial indebtedness of any group member constitutes an event of default under the facilities agreement itself. This clause constitutes a phase in the negotiations on which borrowers usually spend some time in striking an acceptable deal with lenders.

The aim of the cross-default clause from the lenders' point of view is to ensure that they are on an equal footing with all the other creditors of the group. If another lender is not paid and accelerates, demanding repayment at once, or if another lender has the right to accelerate, the lenders also wish to be able to accelerate repayment of the facilities themselves (even if the borrower has not otherwise defaulted under the facilities agreement).[275] The borrower will wish to restrict the circumstances in which the lenders can demand repayment under the facilities agreement on the basis of defaults under other financing arrangements. Express limitations on the clause may include the scope of "debt" that is relevant for the

273 To be more complete: the main events of default are non-payment; non-compliance with other terms, such as covenants, breach of representation and warranty, cross-default, actual or declared insolvency, creditor executions, change of control, and material adverse change. Materiality tests and grace periods may be agreed, especially if the borrower has a strong bargaining position.

274 (Wood, International Loans, Bonds, Guarantees, Legal Opinions. Vol 3, The Law and Practice of International Finance Series 2007a).

275 As the bank thus has the sanction of acceleration to bring the house down, it gives the bank the ability to be present at the table in debt restructuring negotiations. In practice however, the cross-default has an "inertia effect." If everybody can accelerate, then nobody can, since this inevitably leads to bankruptcy, which might not be to the lenders' benefit (Wood, International Loans, Bonds, Guarantees, Legal Opinions. Vol 3, The Law and Practice of International Finance Series 2007a).

cross-default clause. For instance, debt may be limited to borrowing and guarantees of borrowing and exclude operational debt, such as trade debt, because otherwise many borrowers would often be in default. Another way of limiting the scope can be reached by agreeing on a threshold amount. Thresholds may be different for principal and interest. Sometimes the default is limited to actual acceleration of other loans, rather than the potential occurrence of either a pending default or an event whereby the debt is capable of being accelerated. This is often called cross-acceleration, as opposed to cross-default.

MATERIAL ADVERSE CHANGE

Under the material adverse change clause,[276] an event of default shall be deemed to have occurred if any circumstances arise which, in the (reasonable) opinion of the majority banks, might be/is likely to/will have a material adverse effect on the financial conditions of the borrower or on the ability of the borrower to comply with its obligations under this agreement.[277]

Generally, an adverse change in financial conditions would be "material" if the circumstance, if known at the time of the conclusion of the contract, would have caused the bank not to lend at all or to lend on significantly more onerous terms, *e.g.* as to interest, maturity or security. Consideration could be given also to the criteria used by recognised rating agencies in posting significant credit downgrades. Often there is a double test: any "material adverse change" must also affect the ability of the borrower to perform.[278] From a lender's point of view, the clause should apply only to significant deteriorations, whereas a precise financial test would confer greater predictability for both sides.

The material adverse change clause is important in practice for the lender, as it allows the bank to exercise a suasion and pressure on the counterparty. Although the bargaining power balance between lender and borrower varies significantly depending on the practical circumstances, the inclusion of this clause is fairly standard. Nevertheless, sometimes borrowers can successfully argue that lenders are adequately protected by all the other representations, covenants and events of default and do not need, in addition to the latter, to embed in the contract the ability to accelerate or stop a drawing on the grounds that there has been a material adverse change.

276 Henceforth MAC.

277 See, under English common law, *BNP Paribas v Yukos Oil* [2005] EWHC 1321. In this case the controversy was centred on whether two events subsequent to the conclusion of the facility (namely, the imprisonment of the directors of the borrower and an unexpected US $3 billion tax bill charged on the borrower itself) could constitute a "material adverse change." It is reminded by Hudson (2013) that, in a scenario where the borrower reported a fall of 20% in its net assets, it was held (*Levison v Farin* [1978] 2 All E.R. 1149) that this was tantamount to a "material adverse change."

278 (Wood, International Loans, Bonds, Guarantees, Legal Opinions. Vol 3, The Law and Practice of International Finance Series 2007a).

CHANGE OF CONTROL

Change of control means that it constitutes an event of default if a single person (or persons acting in concert) acquires control of the borrower and/or existing controllers of the borrower lose control. Especially where the borrower is a public company and becomes controlled by a single shareholder, for instance, as a result of a takeover, it is easier for the new shareholder to manipulate the assets than if the borrower remained a public company.[279]

Boilerplate

The provisions in the third and last part of a typical loan agreement are commonly referred to as boilerplate. The boilerplate contains clauses relating to issues such as loan transfers, the agency role, notices, and jurisdiction. Usually also various schedules are attached to the loan agreement. These are used to attach additional documents and lists, such as the drawdown notice, confidentiality letter and list of conditions precedent.

CHANGES TO PARTIES

One of the most important boilerplate clauses concerns changes to the parties of the agreement. Usually, the loan agreement foresees a possibility for the lenders to transfer their part of the loan to another financial institution. There are multiple methods by which a new lender can acquire an interest in the loan. For the agreement itself the most important possibilities under English law are a transfer of rights and obligations (classically, by novation) or an assignment of rights.[280] Other options (such as sub-participation or credit derivatives) do not involve the borrower and therefore do not have to be stipulated in the agreement.

Transferring secured loans gives rise to specific problems. Therefore, syndicated credits generally contain largely standardised and detailed provisions whereby a lender may novate its rights and obligations to another bank or financial institution. The novation may amount to a complete substitution of the new lender or rather as an assignment of the rights of the old lender and the assumption by the new lender of obligations under the loan agreement plus the release of the old lender.[281] The difference between the two is that a novation cancels old loans completely (which might have adverse effects on any security for the loan unless held by a trustee or

279 (Wood, International Loans, Bonds, Guarantees, Legal Opinions. Vol 3, The Law and Practice of International Finance Series 2007a).

280 Under English common law, "assignment" is not technically possible, although rights can be assigned under to the equity theory and, as regards properties, under sect. 136(1) of the *Law of Property Act 1925*. See McKendrick (2012). In the neighbouring jurisdiction of the British Isles (Scotland), the English assignment is referred to as "assignation": a different term defining a similar phenomenon. See MacQueen and Thomson (2020); Black (2014).

281 The assignment could be prohibited under the terms of the loan, particularly in cases where the borrower prefers to control who the lender is. A lender with a too aggressive policy on acceleration clauses, for instance, would not be a comfortable counterparty for the lender (Hudson 2013).

agent for the lenders), whereas an assignment and assumption preserves the old loan and its security.

Not only the lenders, but also borrowers or guarantors might change during the term of the loan. As a general rule, the loan agreement prohibits the borrowers and guarantors from transferring their rights or obligations under the agreement. However, most commonly it is allowed that new additional group members become entitled to make drawings under the facility. However, this will only be allowed if the new party is approved by the lenders, signs an accession letter and delivers certain conditions precedent.[282]

THE AGENT

The boilerplate clauses on the agent reflect the intention of a syndicated loan that the agent should have an administrative role only and should not be obliged to look after the interests of syndicate members nor to exercise any discretions on their behalf.[283] Instead, it is intended that the agent should merely act as a conduit for receipt of money and information. The extent to which (other) lenders are relying on the agent, therefore, is limited as far as possible. The loan agreement does, in certain cases, allow the agent to take decisions on behalf of the syndicate (as opposed to requiring it to do so). In exercising these rights, and in the relationship with the borrower(s) generally, the agent should be aware that, if in practice it takes decisions on behalf of the syndicate (such as the decision to approve conditions precedent, or to approve a legal opinion for the purpose of accepting a new obligor), it may expose itself to liability to the syndicate.[284]

WAIVERS

In the loan agreement the issue of waivers and (especially under English law) estoppel have to be addressed.[285] The main concern in relation to a loan is that, following a default, the lenders may lead the borrower to believe that they do not

282 Conversely, it is possible that a borrower or guarantor resigns from the credit agreement. This party will then have to request such resignation by delivering a resignation letter to the agent. The agent will only accept such letter and notify the other parties, if the borrower or guarantor has repaid its loans and other moneys due from it under the agreement, provided there is no default at that time.

283 The agent should be distinguished from the arranger. The latter's role comes to an end with the signing of the facility agreement, whereas the former's one continues, with the main purposes of the agent being the administering of the agreed facility. See Proctor (2010).

284 For example, as regards the rights of the syndicate agent to enforce the obligations of the loan vis-à-vis the borrower, it was held in *British Energy Power v Credit Suisse* [2008] EWCA Civ 53, that the agent would act as "principal" if this was inferable from the terms of the loan.

285 In English law, the doctrine of estoppel is based on an entrenched court decision, *Hughes v Metropolitan Ry* (1877) 2 App.Cas. 439 (Peel 2010). Among the different estoppels (promissory, proprietary, by convention, contractual), the estoppel by representation would be, *mutatis mutandis*, applicable to the parties to a loan contract: it will occur when "a person who makes a representation of existing fact which induces the other party to act to his detriment in reliance on the representation will not be permitted subsequently to act inconsistently with that representation." See McKendrick (2012).

intend to exercise their rights, and ultimately, they may be held to have waived the rights or be estopped from exercising them. As a matter of course, the lenders wish to make sure this will not happen. Furthermore, if the borrower defaults and the lenders do not plan to exercise their rights immediately, the lenders might write to the borrower advising that they are reserving their rights to be exercised as they see fit in the future.

GOVERNING LAW

Lenders commonly require loan agreements for large sums of money to be governed by English or New York law. The reasons for this are, first and foremost, historical: Britain (until the First World War) and America (until now) have been the largest economies in the world. Additionally, banks prefer their "own home" law by definition, and because so many major financial institutions are still located either in London or New York, they tend to feel safe with a choice for either of those two laws.[286] Irrespective of the rationale behind this trend, the convergence worldwide towards two main legal systems (either the English or the New York one) generally makes syndication of very large sums of money easier. Lenders also commonly argue that these laws respect freedom of contract to a large extent and are reluctant to interfere in negotiated agreements, making for a fair degree of certainty in relation to the effect of the agreement.[287]

CONDITION PRECEDENT

The borrowers usually require mainly corporate documents and legal documents as conditions precedent to be submitted. For the lenders it is normal to require copies of the constitutional documents and of board resolutions of the borrowers, as lenders do not want to be involved in unauthorised transactions. The resolutions will, of course, need to have been made in accordance with the company's constitution, including such matters as quorum, notice of meeting and declaration of directors' interests. Sometimes also a shareholder's resolution will be required.

Quite often also legal opinions are required as a condition precedent. Those opinions have to be obtained from lawyers from the governing law jurisdiction of the agreement and from lawyers from the countries in which the borrowers are incorporated. Because under the conflict of laws rules of many jurisdictions, the law where these are incorporated will govern issues such as how the documents are authorised and, assuming that the place of incorporation is also the main place of business of the companies, will also govern issues relating to winding up and

286 (Wood, International Loans, Bonds, Guarantees, Legal Opinions. Vol 3, The Law and Practice of International Finance Series, 2007a).

287 Ibid. 13. A further aspect is the predictability and the attitude of English courts to "enforce the bargain of the parties strictly" and not to acknowledge civil law principles, such as the good faith one. In other words, less discretion is given to the court in English law. See, for instance, *Shepherd & Cooper Ltd v TSB Bank plc* [1996] 2 All 654.

enforcement of judgement against the borrower. Yet lenders need to consider all countries which may have an impact on the enforceability of the borrower's obligations to repay the loan and of any security given, to decide whether to obtain legal opinions in those countries.

3.4 Security

3.4.1 Purposes of security

From the lenders' perspective, the primary purpose of security is to reduce the credit risk, *i.e.* the risk that the loan is not repaid, and to obtain priority over other creditors in the event of the debtor's bankruptcy or liquidation. A security interest gives a creditor a property right over an asset (in this context also called "collateral") which enables the creditor to realise the collateral in case the debtor defaults on his repayment obligation(s). In other words, it enables the creditor to sell the collateral and satisfy his claims on the debtor. Importantly, a security interest is a protection against the insolvency of the debtor, as the secured creditor takes free of any claims of the debtor's unsecured creditors.

A secondary but important consideration may be that security gives the creditor a certain measure of influence or control. This is particularly true if a creditor holds a general security interest such as a floating charge, which covers substantially the entirety of a debtor company's assets.[288] The priority enjoyed by the security taker is likely to deter unsecured creditors from enforcement actions and thus may contribute to the orderly reorganisation of the company, the sale of it as a going concern, or the effective realisation of its assets.

There may also be other reasons for taking security.[289] The holding of a security may allow the beneficiary (the bank) to weight its counterparty risk originating from the corresponding claims; ultimately, this risk weighting results in being extremely useful for purposes of capital adequacy of the credit institution itself.

From the viewpoint of the borrower, the ability to furnish security may reduce the lenders' credit risk assessment so that they may be willing to advance funds which might not otherwise be available, or so that they may offer them on less onerous terms.

3.4.2 Security

Where security is to be given to more than one secured creditor, *e.g.* a syndicate of banks, it is useful for a trustee to hold the security for the common benefit of the

288 The floating charge is a security historically tied with Britain and the jurisdictions existing in the British Isles. In the latest Companies Act 2006, the relevant legal provisions are in Part 25, Sect. 859A-894. Among scholars, see Boyle (2014); Davies and Worthington (2012); Dignam and Lowry (2012).

289 For a general overview on guarantees and securities in the banking and financial sector, from an British perspective, see Proctor (2010).

creditors. In the case of syndicated bank loans, the trustee usually is the agent bank. In essence, a trust is an arrangement whereby the trustee holds title to an asset (in the present context: the secured claims plus the security interest) for beneficiaries (in the present context: the syndicate participants) so that the asset is immune from the personal creditors of the trustee (the agent bank).

One of the main advantages of a security trustee is that it would be impracticable to grant security interests to each individual creditor when numerous creditors are involved. Also, the use of a trustee makes easier and more practical both the common monitoring of covenants and the control over the collateral. Moreover, because the trustee holds the security interest(s) and hence can be authorised to deal with the collateral without involving the (sometimes numerous) syndicate participants, the trustee can facilitate and control the distribution of the realisation proceeds and other payments amongst the creditors. Another advantage of the trustee materialises in the context of a large syndicated loan; in particular, because of the use of a trustee, creditors can transfer their claims by novation so that their part of the loan is transferred, while new creditors can be added without the need to grant new security in their favour. As the trustee is the holder of the security, the trustee essentially only needs to determine the creditors' identities when the time comes to distribute the trust property. Under common law, the trustee itself may be changed without re-creating the security in favour of the new trustee – a simple vesting declaration would suffice.

However, a trust cannot be created under all legal systems. First, a trust is a typical common law concept[290] and is not possible under many civil law jurisdictions, although some European countries have ratified the Hague Trust Convention so that a common law trust may be recognised there. Furthermore, some civil law jurisdictions require that the holders of a security interest should also be the creditors of the secured claim(s). In a syndicated loan, this is usually not the case, as the (non-lending) trustee or agent holds security for all lenders.

In transactions governed by Dutch law this has often been solved by the creation of a so-called parallel debt. As it has been developed in the Netherlands, in a parallel debt structure, the borrower acknowledges an additional debt to the agent, which debt equals the aggregate of the borrower's obligations to the lenders under the syndicated loan. Also, it is contractually agreed that a payment to the agent of an amount under the parallel debt discharges the borrower from the corresponding obligations to the lenders. Thus, the parallel debt never exceeds the borrower's combined obligations towards the lenders and a parallel, but independent, separate debt has been created between the borrower and the agent. The borrower then secures its obligations to the agent under the parallel debt. As a result of the parallel debt, the security taker can remain the same entity, viz. the agent, also if the

290 From an English perspective, see Moffat (2005); Gardner (2011). The latter scholar provides the following definition of trust: "A trust is a situation in which property is vested in someone (a trustee), who is under legally recognised obligations, at least some of which are of a proprietary kind, to handle it in a certain way, and to the exclusion of any personal interest. The obligations may arise either by conscious creation by the previous owner of the property (the settlor), or because some other legally significant circumstances are present."

composition of the lenders changes. Also, it removes the concern that a security right cannot be validly created in favour of a party who is not the creditor of the secured claim, as is generally assumed under Dutch law.

3.4.3 Derivatives

Derivatives are agreements whereby one party contracts with another to receive a financial benefit from the variation of a specific, underlying asset or to seek protection against the same variation. The parties to a derivative agreement are usually a bank with another bank, but also a bank and a non-financial counterparty, and even also non-financial parties between themselves conclude derivative agreements. The asset that underlies a derivative is the yardstick for (the value of) the derivatives on which the derivative's value is calculated. Thus, the value of derivatives is not fixed in advance by the parties; rather it is derived from the underlying asset that the parties have decided to indicate in the contract.[291]

Historically, derivatives have a lineage which can be traced back to a bygone era; in ancient Greece, the price of olive oil was fixed at the time of the conclusion of the contract of sale – in seasonal terms, this could have occurred in springtime – although the product itself would not reach the customer until the following autumn, as harvest-time brought it to fruition. Thus, the producer as much as the customer was protected against any fluctuation of the olive oil price that might have occurred between the sale and harvest-time. Although this contract can hardly be equalled with a "future" on olive oil in the present-day financial sense of the word, some aspects of the transaction unquestionably bear the hallmarks of the contemporary "financial future on a commodity," to be discussed more extensively here. Similar derivative transactions were prevalent in the Dutch Renaissance of the 17th century, when the most venerable of its local products, the tulip, succeeded the olive oil of ancient Greece as the preeminent underlying product to represent this specific commodity derivative.[292]

Derivatives may be concluded over-the-counter, *i.e.* they may be concluded between parties outside the securities exchange.[293] Thus, the contracting parties will fix their contractual relationship by way of a one-to-one negotiation over the relevant terms and conditions, and may or may not elect to use a standardised contract (see also the following). But derivatives may also be traded on an organised exchange. In that case, the agreements are necessarily standardised.

Legal structure

As indicated earlier, the reason for entering into a derivative may be, from an economic point of view, (1) hedging or (2) speculative.[294] In the first case, a party seeks

291 (de Gioia-Carabellese 2010; Masera and Mazzoni 2013).
292 (Hudson 2013).
293 (Hudson 2013).
294 Considerations on the construction of financial contracts can also be read in Bamford (2011).

to obtain protection against a possible variation in value of a pre-existing asset or a loss. A classic risk against which parties may seek protection is the credit risk a lender runs on his borrower, *i.e.* the risk that the borrower/debtor might default and thus causes the lender/creditor to incur a loss. The lender may enter into a financial derivative for the purpose of hedging so that the lender pays a fixed amount to his counterparty (commonly a financial institution), and this counterparty undertakes to supply the lender a cash flow at short notice, should the borrower actually default. Thus, the lender has swapped his credit default risk for a payment obligation of a fixed amount and has created the potential to counter-balance the loss originating from the loan.[295],[296] Contrary to hedging, the speculative purpose occurs when the party (or both parties) to a derivative "speculate on the performance of some identified, underlying marketplace," although in reality "the investor does not necessarily need to invest directly in that marketplace because derivatives replicate the performance of a real market in a virtual form."[297] More specifically and by way of example, parties may enter into the very same credit default swap (CDS) as just discussed, while that CDS does not protect against an actual credit risk one of the parties runs under a loan to a borrower. Thus, the derivative has become a gamble between two parties on the default occurring in a contract between two other parties.

From a legal perspective, the dichotomy between hedging and speculative purposes entailed to the investment in derivatives was underlined by numerous court decisions in Britain, dating back to the early '90s. In a controversy concerning a number of banks selling derivatives to local authorities,[298] it was held that the sole reason for such authorities acquiring derivatives was of a speculative, rather than a hedging nature, given the fact that they were exclusively seeking a profit from the fluctuation of interest rates.[299] In these circumstances, such a speculative purpose endangered the enforceability of the derivative, thereby rendering the bank ineligible to claim money arising from any transactions concluded in the interim.[300] Thus, the actual purpose entailed to the purchase of a derivative may be a concern for the bank selling the product in cases where the counterparty is prohibited, under the applicable law or by its articles of association,[301] from concluding derivatives for speculative purposes.

295 (Hudson 2013).

296 (Hudson 2013).

297 (Hudson 2013).

298 In the specific case, boroughs belonging to Great London Council.

299 See particularly Lord Templeman's statements in *Hazell v Hammersmith & Fulham LBC* [1991] 1 All E.R. 545 at 549-550: "The swap market enables a borrower to raise funds in the market to which the borrower has best access but to make interest and principal payments in its preferred form of currency. . . . Swaps may involve speculation or may eliminate speculation."

300 In some jurisdictions, such as the Italian one, the widespread sale of derivatives to public local authorities (such as *communi* or *regioni*) has also sparked off, doctrinally, serious issues as regards their consistency with the constitution of that country (*i.e.* Article 81 and Article 97) and, particularly, the obligation to ensure balanced budgets and public debt sustainability. See Passalacqua (2013).

301 Alternatively, as far as public authorities are concerned (such as municipalities/councils and, more in general local authorities), reference shall be made to the regulations applicable to them.

In the same vein, the validity of financial derivatives becomes doubtful when speculative derivatives may potentially be qualified as "gaming or wagering" contracts. Historically, this category of contracts is regarded as "null and void" under English legislation,[302] mainly as a matter of public policy, coupled with the moral concern that accruing (and surrendering) money in this fashion is unethical. Under English law, which is statistically speaking the jurisdiction governing the vast majority of derivative transactions in the European market, the precedent upon which financial institutions and market operators confidently (or conveniently) opt to rely is *Morgan Grenfell v Welwyn Garden and Hartfield DC*,[303] where the possibility of assimilation (*i.e.* derivatives being tantamount to gaming or wagering, and thereby invalid) was unceremoniously quashed. Thus, and despite *decisa* to the contrary in the past,[304] scholars[305] have acknowledged that financial derivatives are unlikely to be regarded, nowadays, as gaming or wagering, at least under English law, as they are typically entered into at arm's length and in good faith.

Main categories of derivatives

In contemporary financial practice, derivatives can, in essence, be distinguished between the option, the forward and the swap. These main types of derivatives will be subsequently discussed further here. Additionally, specific attention will be paid to credit derivatives. All these types share the characteristic that they typically have the capacity to be sold or transferred to third parties, although their value, despite these events, will continue to be dependent on the market value of the underlying asset.

OPTIONS

An option affords a beneficiary the right to buy or to sell an underlying asset (*e.g.* a commodity such as oil, wheat or gold, or a security such as shares or government bonds) specified in the contract at the time of its conclusion. More specifically, the right to sell an underlying product at some point in the future (a put option) is a contract deriving its value from that of the underlying asset at the future juncture. The party entitled to sell the share at this prospective juncture (the "holder" or "beneficiary" of the option) will exercise the option, seemingly, if the value of the underlying asset at the given time specified in the contract (the settlement date)

302 An example, among others, is English law, where, as early as the *Gaming Act 1845*, particularly sect. 18, it is stated as follows:

> "All contracts or agreements, whether by parole or in writing, by way of gaming or wagering, shall be null and void . . . no sum shall be brought or maintained in any court of law and equity for recovering any sum of money or valuable thing alleged to be won upon a wager."

303 [1995] 1 All E.R. 1.

304 *Universal Stock Exchange v Strachan* [1896] A.C. 166 HL. The case, concerned with a pure contract for differences, where parties were speculating on an underlying price and its performance, was regarded void simply because a gaming.

305 (Hudson 2013).

is lower than the value at the time of the conclusion of the contract. Conversely, an option to buy an underlying asset at some point in the future (call option) will allow the beneficiary to exercise the option (and, therefore, purchase the underlying asset) if the value of the asset at the future time agreed between the parties (the settlement date) is higher than the value agreed at the conclusion of the contract.

For example, if a party wants to negotiate a call option relating to shares for an overall amount of 100 euro, it is likely that the premium paid to the other party shall be a percentage of the nominal amount of the transaction, for instance, 5%, therefore 5 euro. It can be presumed that the holder will exercise the option, at the settlement date, if the value of the shares concerned with the negotiation has risen to more than 105 euro. In this case, the transaction shall be defined, from the holder's economic point of view, "in-the-money." Conversely, if the overall value of the shares has decreased to, for instance, 50 euro, it is likely that the holder will not exercise the call option; it does not make sense to him to buy share the current value of which is 50 for a price as much as twice that initially stipulated in the contract. From the holder's economic point of view, the transaction shall be "out-of-money." In this second case, the holder will probably not exercise the option and will lose the premium.

It is worth noting that in both cases (call option and put option), the decision to exercise the option is not an obligation, but rather a right for the holder/beneficiary. However, this right bestowed on the beneficiary to exercise the option is not gratuitous, rather it is the outcome of a price paid to the other party – a price which is commonly referred to as a premium. Thus, if the value of the underlying asset has not played out as the holder of the option hoped, he will elect not to exercise his option and his loss is confined to the premium. The counterparty or "writer" of the option, on the other hand, is always under the obligation (both in call options and put options) to deliver or accept the asset, respectively, should the beneficiary elect to exercise the option. Thus, the financial risk is far greater for the writer of an option than for the holder/beneficiary.

As far as the settlement is concerned, the typologies of options fall into two categories: the European one, in which the right can be exercised by the holder at a specific date agreed at the outset in the contract, and the American option in which the right can be exercised by the holder within a specified window of opportunity, rather than on a fixed date.

FORWARDS

The legal feature characterising this form of financial derivatives is the promise to supply an underlying asset at a specified price and on a prearranged date. Differently from the option, though, the forward does not permit the holder (*i.e.* the party paying the price) to choose whether or not to fulfil his obligation in connection with the conditions of the market; in dealing with a forward, irrespective of the conditions of the market and, therefore, irrespective of whether the transaction is in-the-money or out-of-money, the two main contractual obligations (to pay money, on the one hand, and to consign the underlying asset, on the other) shall be mandatory.

SWAPS

The third main category of financial derivatives are swaps. We have already discussed one previous example, the CDS. As another classic example, parties may wish to protect themselves against the risk associated with the payment obligation arising from a floating interest rate on a loan. In such an instance, the floating interest rate may increase to the point that the debtor, *i.e.* the borrower to the loan, may incur a loss. In order to secure protection against that risk, the borrower may enter into a financial derivative with a counterparty for the purpose of hedging, so that the borrower pays the counterparty a fixed rate, and receives the floating rate in return which the borrower may then forward to his creditor, *i.e.* the lender. Thus, the borrower has swapped his payment obligation of a floating interest rate for a payment obligation of a fixed interest rate, and has created the potential to counterbalance the loss originating from the floating rate.[306]

CREDIT DERIVATIVES

Credit derivatives may be regarded as a specific category of financial derivatives. Under these contracts, the parties do not hedge or speculate on a variation in value of an underlying asset (as typically happens with other derivatives), but rather on the creditworthiness of an entity, or a "reference entity," as is the technical term applied in the contractual frameworks. The reference entity may be connected with the holder of the derivative, such as if the holder of the derivative holds a bond issued by the reference entity. Pursuant to the credit derivative, the holder will receive an amount calculated on the credit performance of this reference entity. For instance, if the reference entity has issued a bond and the interest on the bond turns out to be less than agreed upon, the derivative counterparty (usually a bank or another financial institution) shall pay the deficit to the holder of the credit derivative. A recent spate of transactions has shown how credit derivatives can also be entered into not to avail of a specific protection, but rather with a speculative purpose, relating to the prospective and/or expected default of a reference entity.

The terms of a credit derivative commonly refer to a "calculation agent," *i.e.* a party (either an external entity or one of the two parties to the contract) charged with the task of assessing whether the "credit event," *i.e.* the event giving rise to an amount to be paid under the derivative relating to the credit performance of the reference entity, has materialised. Credit events will usually transpire under actual and defined circumstances, such as the non-payment of an underlying asset. However, in more complex credit derivatives, credit events may refer to publicly available information. In such instance, the degree of discretion placed in the hands of the

306 (Hudson 2013). In *Hazell v Hammersmith & Fulham LBC* [1990] 2 Q.B. 697, the swap has been defined as follows: "[A]n agreement between two parties by which each agrees to pay the other on a specified date or dates an amount calculated by reference to the interest which would have accrued over a given period on the same notional principal sum assuming different rates of interest are payable in each case."

calculation agent in consideration of whether a credit event has actually occurred may cause a certain level of legal contention.[307]

Contractual frameworks

ISDA MASTER AGREEMENT

Parties entering into financial derivatives are unlikely to draft new contracts from scratch each and every time they engage in a derivative transaction. Rather, it is common practice that parties agree on over-arching or umbrella documentation to regulate the various derivative transactions which they will thereafter engage in. Such umbrella documentation is widely referred to as a master agreement for the reason that, in anticipation of the series of derivative transactions that the contracting parties will effect in the future, they contain the general terms and conditions applicable to each of them. The rationale behind the adoption of a master agreement between two parties is predominantly practical in nature; two parties committed to undertaking several financial derivatives in the future may prefer to rationalise the contracts in a unified document. Proponents of master agreements also argue that they allow for the parties concerned with the transactions to benefit from minimised risks under standardised and uniform terms and conditions.[308]

Amongst the various frameworks available in the market for derivatives, market participants tend to adhere mainly to the ones drafted by the International Swaps and Derivatives Association (ISDA).[309] This chapter will therefore focus on the derivatives documentation made available by ISDA, of which the latest version dates of 2002 but is updated regularly.[310] In essence, the ISDA derivatives documentation consists of (1) a master agreement (MA) encompassing the main clauses applicable to the contractual relationship between the two parties concerned; (2) a schedule, in which the intention of the parties to conclude the MA is formalised, and which schedule contains derogations and/or amendments to the main clauses of the MA;[311] and (3) the confirmation, a document specifying the specific transaction that, from time to time and during the efficacy of the MA, the parties may elect to conclude.

307 *Deutsche Bank AG v ANZ Banking Group Lt* (unreported 24 May 1999) as recalled by (Hudson 2013).

308 This is called "legal safety." As emphasised by scholars, the "terms have been considered in depth and so are more likely to be legally safe and sophisticated. Hence, market confidence" (Wood, International Loans, Bonds, Guarantees, Legal Opinions. Vol 3, The Law and Practice of International Finance Series 2007a).

309 (Wood, International Loans, Bonds, Guarantees, Legal Opinions. Vol 3, The Law and Practice of International Finance Series 2007a).

310 The latest version of the ISDA Master Agreement (2002) is available at www.isda.org. For a brief commentary to the ISDA MA, see Wood, International Loans, Bonds, Guarantees, Legal Opinions. Vol 3, The Law and Practice of International Finance Series 2007a, Proctor (2010) and Harding (2010).

311 Fundamentally, the schedule will override the MA for provisions of the latter that the schedule refers to as expressly deleted or redrafted therein (Hudson 2013).

Section 14 of the ISDA MA 2002 defines the various typologies of transactions to which the MA will apply. The MA defines these transactions as specified transactions which include, for instance, swaps, options and futures. In principle, the schedule does not derogate from this wording, meaning that the MA will apply to all transactions falling within the ambit of the standard definition of specified transactions. Nevertheless, contracting parties may opt to either (1) expand the list of transactions falling within the scope of the MA or, conversely, (2) restrict the scope of the definition by means of an express exclusion of one or more of the transactions specified under Section 14. In any case, should the parties enter into a transaction which corresponds with one of the categories specified under both the MA and the relevant schedule, the same transaction shall automatically fall within the contractual ambit of the MA and the accompanying terms and conditions (as derogated by the schedule, as the case may be) will apply automatically. Consequently, no new separate contract needs to be signed and the existing MA and Schedule will suffice for the purposes of the relevant transaction.[312]

PRINCIPAL TERMS AND CONDITIONS

The ISDA MA comes replete with clauses and terms which give rise to subtle interpretations and, sometimes, contentious wrangling. In the following, we will briefly analyse those which crop up most frequently.

Sect. 2(a)(iii) of the MA prescribes that the obligation on each party is subject to two preceding conditions: (1) that no instance of default with respect to the other party has occurred or is having an enduring impact and (2) that no early termination in respect to that transaction has transpired. The two preceding conditions afford a right to the party with control over the payment, *i.e.* the right to play that card and terminate the MA if, at a future juncture, it emerged that either of the aforementioned conditions had not been satisfied at the time the payment is due.[313]

A default on the part of either one of the two parties to a contract is sometimes not regulated under the contract but is left to the rules of the applicable general contract and insolvency law, including those rules which determine how the contractual relationships relevant to the insolvent or defaulted party shall be treated. Given the heterogeneity of rules of contract and insolvency law prevailing across various jurisdictions, the MA ensures that the remedies are stipulated uniformly. Under sect. 5(a), for instance, a series of events is listed which are regarded to be "events of default" in respect to the implicated party. Consequently, the non-defaulting party may be entitled not only to terminate the MA, but to claim termination, acceleration and set-off of all transactions based on it.

312 Even if the MA is terminated, Section 2(a)(i) of the ISDA MA prescribes that the payment made by each party (or the delivery under the confirmation) is subject to the remaining provisions of the MA. The proviso suddenly becomes crucial and essential, if regarded in connection with the termination of the entire framework. In brief, such a termination will transpire, triggered by the non-defaulting party, in cases where such an obligation to pay was not fulfilled.

313 (Hudson 2013).

Of these events of default, specific reference can be drawn to the "failure to pay or deliver" (sect. 5(a)(i)). Under normal rules of applicable contract law, a failure to fulfil an obligation arising from a contract may entitle the non-defaulting party, depending on the jurisdiction, to either claim damages, terminate the contract or even seek both remedies. As the MA is used by parties operating in different jurisdictions, sect. 5(a)(i) serves to regulate uniformly the consequence of any failure to pay or deliver, viz. the termination of all transactions in place between the parties based on the MA.

Similarly, the bankruptcy or insolvency of a party to a MA is uniformly regulated under the terms of the MA at sect. 5(a)(vii). As rules of insolvency law are multifarious in various jurisdictions, the MA strives to align and uniformly define insolvency events as "events of default" so that, irrespective of the applicable insolvency law, they shall be categorised for purposes of the MA as tantamount to insolvency and allow the other party to terminate. It could be argued that it is necessary to format these events into a contract, if only to bring some uniform order to a set of events or circumstances, which otherwise would not be considered in a harmonised manner across the different jurisdictions. A pertinent example would be the appointment of an administrator, provisional liquidator or trustee. These appointments may be treated as insolvency events by a particular jurisdiction but not necessarily so by another. In light of this, the MA, under sect. 5(a)(vii)(6), defines them as events of default, thereby leaving little room for doubt that any such appointment entitles the other party to terminate the contract.

Moreover, the insertion within the MA of insolvency events serves to further enlarge the perimeter of termination. For example, the general assignment of goods under many jurisdictions would not qualify as insolvency. The MA, conversely, adopts a practical approach on the assumption – irrefutable from a practical point of view – that a number of activities such as the general assignment of goods may be an indication of its insolvency (although technically speaking they are not). Under the MA, their occurrence would not permit the party to raise any objection, and they will allow the other party to terminate.[314]

A dilemma which parties usually face when negotiating the MA arises over which events should lead to the automatic termination of the contract, *i.e.* which events take effect immediately, and of which events, conversely, notice should be given by the non-defaulting party. The ISDA MA in its 2002 version specifies that, as a general rule, termination is to be initiated by way of a notice served by the non-defaulting party, informing the counterparty that a termination event has occurred.

314 Interestingly, the "events of default" apply not solely to each party but also to any relevant credit support provider or specified entity. The credit support provider is an entity acting as guarantor to one of the parties. If so indicated in the schedule, the other party shall be entitled to terminate the contract if one of the events of default occurs in connection with this third party. In a similar vein, with respect to the specified entity, also other parties may be referred to, such as a corporation belonging to its company group. If this has been drafted in the schedule, the occurrence of one of the events of default in respect to that party will allow the other party to claim the termination of the MA.

Pursuant to sect. 6(a) of the MA, the exception to the rule is the bankruptcy event discussed earlier, which leads to an automatic early termination. However, parties may also decide either to apply automatic early termination to all termination events rather than exclusively to bankruptcy[315] or, conversely, have the bankruptcy event exempt from automatic early termination so that termination of the MA shall require the notice of the non-defaulting party also in the instance of any bankruptcy event as defined under the MA.

From a non-legal perspective, it is no mean feat to establish whether automatic early termination or termination by notice would be appropriate for which events. Automatic early termination might be advisable where parties are poorly acquainted with one another, for instance, when they are geographically disconnected, and the non-defaulting party would be oblivious to whether or not a termination event has occurred.[316] Yet automatic early termination is not without complications; a situation may develop where the defaulting party continues to honour its obligations under the contract regardless of the occurrence of a termination event. Should this transpire, the non-defaulting party would prefer to benefit from the payment which occurred subsequent to the termination event rather than be required to relinquish these monies as would be the case if the termination event would have qualified as an automatic termination event.[317]

NETTING ARRANGEMENT

One of the most important features of the ISDA MA constitutes its netting arrangement. Netting under the umbrella of an MA allows each party to add outstanding obligations and set off the aggregate value of those obligations against the aggregate of the counterparty's obligations. Thus, netting is a concept inexorably linked with set-off.[318] The following forms of netting will subsequently be discussed: settlement netting, close-out netting and insolvency netting.

Settlement netting allows the parties to an MA to determine a net balance, *i.e.* set off their reciprocal obligations which follow from the derivative transactions that are due on the same date.[319] For instance, upon completion of a specific working day, the various amounts resulting from the transactions concluded over the course of that day may be converted into a single balance, which is due to be paid by one party to the other or, indeed, due to be received by that party from the other, depending on whether the sum is negative or positive. In the underpinning

315 (Hudson 2013).

316 (Hudson 2013).

317 (Hudson 2013).

318 (Wood, International Loans, Bonds, Guarantees, Legal Opinions. Vol 3, The Law and Practice of International Finance Series 2007a). The set-off is usually regarded as a form of payment: "A debtor sets off the cross-claim owed to him against the main claim which he owes his creditor. Instead of paying money, he uses the claim owed to him to pay the claim he owes."

319 (Wood, International Loans, Bonds, Guarantees, Legal Opinions. Vol 3, The Law and Practice of International Finance Series 2007a).

philosophy of the ISDA MA, the netting applies to transactions of the same nature[320] and conducted in the same currency. In contrast to some national laws of contract, however, the ISDA MA would also allow the parties to apply netting to different (outstanding) transactions, so long as a uniform currency is adopted. Settlement netting is typically contractual in nature, given that it is created by contract.

Perhaps even more importantly, close-out netting entails, subsequently, (1) the cancellation of the outstanding contracts of two parties to an MA, such as by virtue of the default of one of the two parties; (2) the valuation of all outstanding obligations under the cancelled contracts, and the valuation is usually done by the non-defaulting party; and (3) the determination of a net balance. Thus, close-out netting hinges upon the cancellation of the non-performed contracts within the MA which, via valuation of obligations, result in a set-off of "*gains and losses of each contract so as to produce a single net balance owing one way or the other.*"[321]

Thirdly, insolvency netting occurs in cases where one of the parties to an MA becomes insolvent. Insolvency netting is virtually identical to close-out netting, save for the reason for termination, viz. the event that one of the parties becomes insolvent: (1) first, the outstanding contracts between the two parties are cancelled, (2) then all outstanding obligations under the cancelled contracts are valued and (3) a net balance is determined which the non-insolvent shall receive from or have to pay to the insolvent.[322] The insolvency netting clause is catered for by common law jurisdictions, whereas in some civil law jurisdictions (particularly in the French legal tradition) its legal validity could be called into question by the court upon request of the non-insolvent party.[323]

320 As a result, it is possible to set off different transactions of swaps between the same parties, but not also a swap with an option.

321 (Wood, International Loans, Bonds, Guarantees, Legal Opinions. Vol 3, The Law and Practice of International Finance Series 2007a).

322 (Wood, International Loans, Bonds, Guarantees, Legal Opinions. Vol 3, The Law and Practice of International Finance Series 2007a). Without the insolvency set-off, the non-insolvent party (A) would incur in a potential risk of uncertainty. To elaborate, as regards two reciprocal obligations on a future maturity, A would be under an obligation to discharge immediately to the insolvent party (B) his obligation, whereas, as far as his reciprocal credit is concerned, A should prove it to the liquidator of B, and once this condition is met, A would have to compete with the other (unsecured) creditors in B's insolvency and thus receive, seemingly, only a part of his credit.

323 An example is the Italian legislation. The bankruptcy legislation of that country, hinged upon an entrenched statute still in force (Royal Decree no 267 of 17 March 1942, also referred as the Italian Bankruptcy Law), does not clearly cater for a specific termination of derivative contracts in case of insolvency of one of the parties. This is due to the fact that Article 76 of the Italian Bankruptcy Law applies exclusively to "forward stock exchange contracts," i.e. not over-the-counter derivatives (contra: Court of Appeal of Milan, 17 October 1986, where it was held, controversially, that Article 76 applies also to contracts for the exchange of currency concluded outwith the stock exchange). However, after the passing of Legislative Decree no 58 of 24 February 1998 (the Italian Consolidated Finance Act), particularly Article 203 encompassed therein, the mandatory rescission of derivatives in case of insolvency of one of the parties, whether or not the contract is out-of-the-counter or not, is eventually unquestionable in that jurisdiction too. (Wood, International Loans, Bonds, Guarantees, Legal Opinions. Vol 3, The Law and Practice of International Finance Series 2007a); (de Gioia-Carabellese 2010).

Legislative framework

Derivatives have, for many years, not been the subject of specific legislation and regulation. The financial crisis of 2008, which some claim has been caused to some extent by an absence of legislation in the matter of over-the-counter speculative transactions, has prompted a general rethink of this area and a call for stricter regulation. Warren Buffett, for instance, famously wrote in 2002: "In my view, derivatives are financial weapons of mass destruction, carrying dangers that, while now latent, are potentially lethal."[324] On the global level, the G20 in Pittsburgh on 26 September 2009 called for mandatory centralised clearing for derivatives.[325] On 4 July 2012, the EU legislature followed up and adopted the European market infrastructure regulation (EMIR).[326] Under EMIR, in short, mandatory centralised clearing and reporting requirements are introduced. ESMA (the European Securities and Markets Authority) is made responsible for supervising the application of the regulation and implementing secondary legislation in this area.[327] By virtue of this innovative body of rules, it is hoped that the market of OTC derivatives, which has been described by EU commissioner Barnier as a "Wild West territory" prior to the 2008 crisis,[328] can now be regarded as more transparent, clearly defined and less pernicious.

EMIR

The first salient feature of EMIR is that it imposes on two counterparties dealing with derivatives the use of an intermediary to facilitate the clearing of the transaction. The intermediary may be a central counterparty (CCP). Pursuant to Article 2 EMIR, a CCP means "an entity that legally interposes itself between the counterparties to the contracts traded within one or more financial markets, becoming the buyer to every seller and the seller to every buyer and which is responsible for the operation of a clearing system."[329] Also, parties to a derivative may use institutions ("clearing members"), one for each party, that participate in the clearing system

324 Berkshire Hathaway annual report for 2002. Cf. also Hudson (2013): "[OTC derivatives have] contributed to the spreading of the crisis beyond its point of origin . . . and to magnifying it into a full-blown global financial crisis than almost brought the financial system, and with it the global economy, to its knees."

325 On the concept of clearing, clearinghouse and CCP.

326 In full: Regulation 648/2012/EU of the European Parliament and of the Council of 4 July 2012 on OTC derivatives, central counterparties and trade repositories, OJ L 201/1. See also the EU Commission, *Driving Economic Recovery*, published on 4 March 2009, preceded by the "de Larosière Report" published in February 2009 (The High-Level Group of Financial Supervision in the EU, *Report*, Brussels, 25 February 2009, http://ec.europa.eu/internal_market/finances/docs/de_larosiere_report_en.pdf> accessed 3 August 2014).

327 Theoretically, the supervision on derivatives could have been granted to the European Central Bank. However, the Larosière Report dismissed this option, on the assumption that this different architecture would hamper the main role of the central bank, aimed to guarantee the monetary stability (Hudson 2013).

328 *Driving Economic Recovery*, published on 4 March 2009.

329 Again, on the concept of clearing, clearinghouse and CCP.

operated by a CCP. The purpose is to ensure that operational and systemic risks that originate from the entering into derivatives is reduced given the safety net of the entity or entities that step into the shoes of the counterparty, thus also taking over any default risk of that counterparty.

More specifically, in accordance with Article 4(1) EMIR, any over-the-counter derivative entered into between financial counterparties is subject to the centralised clearing requirement.[330] As far as derivatives concluded between a financial counterparty and a non-financial one are concerned or, alternatively, between two non-financial counterparties, the clearing will be mandatory if the magnitude of the derivative transaction of this non-financial counterparty exceeds a specified threshold, fixed under Article 10(1)(b) of the regulation at stake.

The EMIR also imposes on the parties to a derivative transaction the obligation to provide a "trade repository" with detailed reports of the derivatives which they have entered into, modified or terminated. The requirement that channels of communication are maintained, which applies to both parties equally, must be fulfilled within one working day. The trade repository to which the information must be communicated is defined in the EMIR as an entity that collects and maintains the records of OTC derivatives, holding them for a period of five years. The trade repository can be also be defined as an information agency that operates under supervision of ESMA for the sole purpose of accumulating data relating to financial derivatives to which the legislation at stake is applicable.

Finally and importantly, the EMIR requires that a CCP must be in position to transfer or, to use the appropriate technical term, "port" the positions in derivatives held by any clearing member to another clearing member should the former clearing member default.[331]

MIFIR

The regulation stage in the matter of derivatives has become populated by additional characters: a significant development has been the recent enactment of the EU Regulation on Markets in Financial Instruments Regulation (MiFIR).[332] MiFIR, enacted on 15 May 2014, is geared towards ensuring that all trading is conducted on either exchanges, *i.e.* multi-lateral trading platforms (MTF), or through organised trading facilities (OTF).[333] Coupled with this provision is the norm under Article 25 MiFIR, granting the operator of a regulated market the responsibility of ensuring that every class of derivatives is subject to clearing by a CCP as prescribed by EMIR.

330 More specifically, financial counterparties include any investment firm authorised under MiFID (on MiFID), any authorised bank, any authorised insurance company, an occupational pension fund, or any hedge fund properly licenced.

331 Article 48 EMIR.

332 In full: Regulation 600/2014/EU of the European Parliament and of the Council of 15 May 2014 on markets in financial instruments and amending Regulation 648/2012/EU, OJ L 173.

333 Article 24 of the MiFIR.

3.5 Financial transactions: custody agreements

3.5.1 Introduction

Banks, as we know them today, have developed from their original role as simple moneychangers to include, within their contemporary scope of activities, the business of deposit taking, *i.e.* the accepting of monies from the public for purposes of custody.

Historically, in the Italian city-states of the 13th century, people brought their coins to a banker primarily for the safe keeping of these monies, but also so that the banker could facilitate, upon a transfer order by his client(s), cross-border[334] transfers of this cash. Even at this pioneering stage of the banking business, deposits were already credited to accounts and the banker could effectuate a cross-border transfer order simply by orchestrating the relevant credit and debit entries in the accounts he maintained in his books or, to use a more technical terminology, by making the relevant book-entries in his ledgers.[335]

It is not difficult to envisage how this system of book-entry transfers was instrumental in minimising the multitude of risks that would stem from a physical cross-border transfer of monies. This system has thus been conceived and put in practice for dealings with money and has subsequently been refined over the ensuing centuries. It was only over the course of the last century that the invention of accounts and book-entry transfers has also been generally applied to the custody of securities.

As a result of the technological advancements which have materialised at a seemingly perpetual rate of knots over the latter half of the last century, the accounts maintained on (physical) books just referred to, in relation to both money and securities, have been replaced by electronic accounts. Thus, the bulk of monies and securities, in contemporary banking, are held and transferred through the medium of electronic book-entries in electronic accounts.

As a matter of principle, from the 13th century onwards, virtually the full spectrum of jurisdictions embarked on the adoption of a system whereby claims of money depositors rank *pari passu*, *i.e. pro rata parte*, with claims of the bank's other creditors. Back in those formative years, deposits for safekeeping were classified as *depositum regulare* ("regular deposit"), while deposits into a current account were distinguished as *depositum irregulare* ("irregular deposit"). Under the Roman law concept of *depositum (regulare)*, a depositor has a property right in individual deposited assets.[336] In practice, this obligated the custodian bank to register the individual assets held for each individual depositor. This concept applied both to monies and, later, also to securities. However, as the practice of

334 In the medieval context the term "cross-border" should be contextualised as referring to transaction aimed to be executed between two different city-states sometimes not far from each other, yet formally under a different sovereignty.

335 (De Roover 1974; Mueller 1997).

336 (Du Plessis 2010).

individual custody involved increasingly burdensome administrative costs, assets became merged in the custodian's coffers and administered on a collective basis. Moreover, as its assets were essentially fungible and, therefore, interchangeable, the banker could only return equivalent properties, *i.e.* not the very same assets that the client had deposited, but synonymous with the original assets in terms of both quality and quantity.[337] Consequently, in most legal systems, such a commingling implies the loss of ownership, which leaves the investor with a *pari passu* claim against his custodian and provides little or no protection in the case of the custodian's insolvency. This form of custody, under which the depositor essentially loses ownership and the custodian is obligated to return equivalent assets, has been coined *depositum irregulare*.

This chapter deals with the custody and transfer of money, *i.e.* cash, and securities. From a private or commercial law perspective,[338] the custody of money and securities has not been the subject of much European harmonisation. However, in the immediate aftermath of the recent global financial crisis, the issue of the custody of money and securities, and specifically segregation, *i.e.* the segregation of client assets from the bank's own assets and from the assets between clients, has caught the eye of many advisory groups and legislators across the globe. In the following, the rules of segregation that follow from the MiFID II legislation[339] and the recent CSD Regulation[340] will be discussed while attention shall be drawn to the various solutions which, in the private law field, the relevant jurisdictions have developed for securities custody, in order to deal with and, ultimately, minimise the issue of loss of ownership under the *depositum irregulare* concept.

Subsequently, consideration will be given to the transfer of money and securities by way of book-entries (or giro-transfer, as it is more commonly referred to in many continental European jurisdictions). It should be noted that this area, which forms such a critical aspect of daily life, has not been the subject of much European private law harmonisation. Nevertheless, the transfer of money is currently governed by an ambitious European project, viz. the Single European Payments Area,[341] which consists of the EEA in addition to Switzerland and the principality of Monaco. Under the SEPA Regulation,[342] banks, or, more broadly and

337 (Haentjens 2007).

338 As the following chapters, this takes a transactional perspective and is therefore more concerned with private or commercial law aspects than regulatory elements.

339 Most importantly: Directive 2014/65/EU of the European Parliament and of the Council of 15 May 2014 on markets in financial instruments and amending Directive 2002/92/EC and Directive 2011/61/EU, OJ L 173 (MiFID II); and Regulation 600/2014/EU of the European Parliament and of the Council of 15 May 2014 on markets in financial instruments and amending Regulation (EU) No 648/2012, OJ L 173 (MiFIR).

340 In full: Regulation 909/2014/EU of the European Parliament and of the Council of 23 July 2014 on improving securities settlement in the European Union and on central securities depositories and amending Directives 98/26/EC and 2014/65/EU and Regulation 236/2012/EU, OJ L 257/1.

341 Henceforth SEPA.

342 In full: Regulation 260/2012/EU of the European Parliament and of the Council of 14 March 2012 establishing technical and business requirements for credit transfers and direct debits in euro and amending Regulation 924/2009/EC, OJ L 94.

accurately, payment services providers, must implement certain technical requirements for credit and debit transactions in euros within the EU. Furthermore, a crucial aspect of SEPA is the Payment Services Directive,[343] which aims to harmonise the regulatory framework regarding payment services providers, *i.e.* credit institutions, and, in short, the range of institutions which manage payment transactions in euros.[344]

Thus, it introduces an authorisation requirement for the pursuit of the payment services business. These technical and regulatory guidelines put in place via SEPA and the Payment Services Directive[345] will not be subject to an extensive discussion in the present chapter. Rather, as this chapter takes a private or commercial law perspective, greater attention will be attributed to the Settlement Finality Directive, which deals with transfer (orders) of both money and securities and which aims to reduce the systemic risk associated with participation in payment and securities settlement systems, and, more specifically, the risk that materialises when a participant in such a system becomes insolvent.[346]

3.5.2 Custody of money and securities

As stated earlier, nowadays depositors hold the greatest part of their money and securities in electronic accounts with their bank; this custody can commonly be qualified as *depositum irregulare*.

This practice is made complicated by two factors. First and foremost, in today's financial system, cash and securities are virtually always centrally stored: cash with a central bank and securities with a central securities depository (CSD). Practically, clients, particularly retail clients, never hold their assets (cash and securities) with these central depository institutions, as these are held on an account with a financial institution. On its turn, the latter, which is often a bank, may hold these assets on an account with the central depositories. On the account with the central depository, duly registered in the financial institution's name, is credited the aggregate of all client assets of this institution. This account is therefore commonly denoted as an "omnibus" account. Thus, this omnibus account does not distinguish (either legally or operationally) between the underlying retail clients, and may or may not include the financial institutions' own assets.

Moreover, between the retail client and the central depository, multiple financial institutions may be interposed; in this scenario, several omnibus accounts will exist

343 In full: Directive 2007/64/EC of the European Parliament and of the Council of 13 November 2007 on payment services in the internal market amending Directives 97/7/EC, 2002/65/EC, 2005/60/EC and 2006/48/EC and repealing Directive 97/5/EC, OJ L 319.

344 Scholars (Proctor 2010) point out the main objectives of Directive 2007/64: first and foremost, "to allow wider range of participants (including non-banks) in the market of for payment services"; additionally, to strengthen the consumer protection, "with rules requiring clarity and transparency of charging structures."

345 In full: Directive 98/26/EC of the European Parliament and of the Council of 19 May 1998 on settlement finality in payment and securities settlement systems, OJ L 166.

346 For a brief commentary to the Settlement Finality Directive, see Proctor (2010).

between the retail client and the central depository, as the financial institution, in our example, may hold an omnibus account with a second institution and so on.

Second, today's multiple-tiered system is only rarely purely domestic. Financial institutions holding (*omnibus*) accounts with each other may be located in different jurisdictions, and it is seldom that a client's securities portfolio consist of securities issued by issuers located in only one jurisdiction. These different jurisdictions may treat the holding and protection of client assets differently, which "may give rise to legal disputes as to ownership and entitlement to the assets, and complicate transfers or the rapid return of the assets to clients."[347]

Furthermore, under the conflict of laws rules which have been introduced into European Union law by the Settlement Finality Directive and the Collateral Directive,[348] the law of the place applies where the "relevant" securities account is located, *i.e.* the account on which the securities in question are credited. This means that in a securities custody chain, where multiple financial intermediaries are interposed between client and central securities depository, multiple laws may apply which may have different (substantive) rules on the holding and protection of the same client assets.

Cash is the most fungible thing, by definition. As stated earlier, from the 13th century onwards, depositors of cash money rank *pari passu* with other depositors and, more generally, with other creditors of the bank. In most continental European legal systems, client money forms part of a bank's property and segregation (again, the separation of client assets from the bank's own assets and from the assets between clients) is therefore usually accomplished by operational rules only, rather than via law.

Under English law, however, client money does not form part of the property of a bank that has accepted client funds. Upon receipt, those funds form part of a statutory trust and thus exist free of the bank's own creditors' claims. In the insolvency of Lehman Brothers International (Europe), the UK Supreme Court decided, in short, that even where funds have not been operationally segregated from the firm's own accounts, these funds apply free of the firm's own creditors. This also means that, if losses occur within the trust formed by client funds, these losses must be shared amongst the clients, whether or not they have been operationally segregated.[349]

347 Basel Committee on Banking Supervision, Report and recommendations for the resolution of cross-border financial institutions (2010) ("BCBS Report"), p. 40.

348 Article 9(2) Settlement Finality Directive – to be discussed below; and Article 9 Directive 2002/47/EC of the European Parliament and of the Council of 6 June 2002 on financial collateral arrangements, OJ L 168/43. On this directive, see more extensively below Chapter 12. The same rule can be discerned in § 8-110 (1994) of the US Uniform Commercial Code enacted in all US states, and in the (not yet enacted) Convention on the law applicable to certain rights in respect of securities held with an intermediary, although these latter two instruments give primacy to party autonomy. These rules show that there is not even a global uniform conflict of laws rule to determine, which (substantive) rules apply to the holding and protection of client assets.

349 *Re Lehman Brothers International (Europe) (In Administration)* [2012] UKSC 6 (SC). See, amongst many, Gruyaert and van Loock (2014).

In the Lehman Brothers case, the Court also considered the Markets in Financial Instruments Directive I.[350] MiFID gave the principal and most general European rule regarding segregation both for cash (*i.e.* "funds" in MiFID terminology) and for securities: "An investment firm shall, when holding funds belonging to clients, make adequate arrangements to safeguard the clients' rights."[351] Just as was the case for securities, this rule was further substantiated for cash in the MiFID Implementing Directive.[352]

This general rule for cash will be retained under MiFID II and MiFIR, albeit under a different article number. MiFID II now stipulates in its Article 16(9): "An investment firm shall, when holding funds belonging to clients, make adequate arrangements to safeguard the rights of clients and, except in the case of credit institutions, prevent the use of client funds for its own account." What applies to cash applies to securities also: pursuant to Implementing Directive Article 16, the member states shall require that, for the purpose of safeguarding clients' rights in relation to funds belonging to them, investment firms comply with the requirement that they must keep such records and accounts as necessary to enable them at any time and without delay to distinguish assets held for one client from assets held for any other client, and from their own assets. If, for reasons of the applicable law, including in particular the law relating to property or insolvency, the arrangement made by investment firms in compliance with the requirement are not sufficient to satisfy the requirement of Article 13(8) MiFID, member states shall prescribe the measures that investment firms must take in order to comply with those obligations.

The MiFID apply to investment firms, but they have a far wider scope as they also apply to banks,[353] as well as to "market operators, data reporting services providers, and third-country firms providing investment services or performing investment activities through the establishment of a branch in the Union."[354] They may apply not only to legal persons but also to natural persons.[355] Remarkably, in most European jurisdictions, investment firms will not be allowed to hold cash on behalf of clients other than cash in connection with the providing of investment services, because it is not allowed to act as a bank without being licensed as such.[356] Payment

350 In full: European Parliament and Council Directive 2004/39/EC of 21 April 2004 on markets in financial instruments amending Council Directives 85/611/EEC and 93/6/EEC and Directive 2000/12/EC of the European Parliament and of the Council and repealing Council Directive 93/22/EEC, OJ L 145 (henceforth MiFID I).

351 Article 13(8) MiFID I.

352 Article 16 of Commission Directive 2006/73/EC of 10 August 2006 implementing Directive 2004/39/EC of the European Parliament and of the Council as regards organisational requirements and operating conditions for investment firms and defined terms for the purposes of that Directive, OJ L 241.

353 In cases where these entities also provided investment services. Article 1(3) and (4) MiFID II.

354 Article 1(1) MiFID II.

355 Article 4 caput and (1) MiFID, now Article 2(1)(1) MiFIR.

356 Pursuant to Article 4(1) under (1) of the Capital Requirements Regulation (CRR), a bank is an undertaking, the business of which is to take deposits or other repayable funds from the public and to grant credits for its own account. Similarly, it may be prohibited to attract repayable funds from the public without an exemption or a dispensation from a prudential regulatory authority.

institutions are under a separate obligation to safeguard their clients' funds. Interestingly, under the Payment Services Directive, member states are offered the choice to accomplish this either through property law segregation or insurance.[357] As a matter of principle, property law regulation is left to the discretion of the member states.[358]

3.5.3 Security custody

If a bank or investment firm does not record the individual numbers of the securities it holds for each client separately, or, more generally, if these securities are not in any way identifiable as a specific client's property, most civil law jurisdictions will deem these securities to form part of that bank's or investment firm's (own) property.

As stated, this phenomenon is commonly denoted as *depositum irregulare* and involves the "commingling" of the assets of various depositors held collectively by one financial institution. This does have dramatic consequences: without specific legislation having been enacted or special measures having been taken, the commingling of securities to which multiple clients are entitled, would mean that these securities are deemed to be part of the bankruptcy estate in the event of the bank or the investment firm that holds those securities falling bankrupt. Civil law jurisdictions therefore need both legal and operational rules to accomplish asset segregation and client protection.

In common law jurisdictions, as a general rule, client securities do not form part of the property of a bank or an investment firm, at least in as far as the bank's or the investment firm's administration holds the securities for the benefit of clients. Such securities form part of a statutory trust and thus take free of the bank's or the investment firm's own creditors' claims. Common law jurisdictions, therefore, need operational rules to achieve asset segregation and client protection.

MiFID

What has been stated in the context of custody of cash also applies to securities custody: MiFID I gave the principal and most general European rule in this regard: "An investment firm shall, when holding financial instruments belonging to clients, make adequate arrangements so as to safeguard clients' ownership rights, especially in the event of the investment firm's insolvency."[359] This rule was further specified and substantiated in Article 16 MiFID Implementing Directive. Recently, MiFID II and MiFIR, *i.e.* the recast of MiFID, have been enacted. In these instruments, the mentioned rule will be retained albeit under different article numbers.[360] MiFID II now states in its Article 16(8):

> An investment firm shall, when holding financial instruments belonging to clients, make adequate arrangements so as to safeguard the ownership rights

357 Article 9(1)(a-c), Payment Services Directive.
358 Article 16(2), MiFID Implementing Directive.
359 Article 13(7), MiFID I.
360 Articles 16(8), 16(9), MiFID II and 2 caput and (1) of MiFIR, respectively.

> of clients, especially in the event of the investment firm's insolvency, and to prevent the use of a client's financial instruments on own account except with the client's express consent.

These cited provisions pertain to financial instruments (*i.e.* securities – not defined in this directive). They provide for two rules: a general requirement for investment firms to "make adequate arrangements so as to safeguard the ownership rights of clients" and, additionally, a prohibition for investment firms to use a client's financial instruments "on own account." This second rule means that an investment firm is not allowed to use the financial instruments it holds for its clients for its own purposes if and when the client has not expressly consented.[361] The first rule has been further explained in Implementing Directive Article 16(1), which is still in force and reads as follows:

> 1. Member States shall require that, for the purposes of safeguarding clients' rights in relation to financial instruments belonging to them, investment firms comply with the following requirements: (a) they must keep such records and accounts as are necessary to enable them at any time and without delay to distinguish assets held for one client from assets held for any other client, and from their own assets.

Article 16(1) thus is mainly an operational rule. However, the European legislator realised that operational segregation may not be sufficient to accomplish client protection. Article 16(2) MiFID Implementing Directive therefore reads:

> 2. If, for reasons of the applicable law, including in particular the law relating to property or insolvency, the arrangements made by investment firms in compliance with paragraph 1 to safeguard clients' rights are not sufficient to satisfy the requirements of Article 13(7) and (8) of Directive 2004/39/EC, Member States shall prescribe the measures that investment firms must take in order to comply with those obligations.

Indirectly, the MiFID rules also apply to investment funds. More specifically, the recent Alternative Investment Fund Managers Directive (AIFMD) as well as the amended Undertakings for Collective Investment in Transferable Securities Directive require that fund assets are held with a depositary, and that such depositary must segregate these fund assets from its own assets under the MiFID rules just referred to. More specifically, Article 21(8)(a) AIFMD reads:

> The assets of the AIF or the AIFM acting on behalf of the AIF shall be entrusted to the depositary for safe-keeping, as follows: (a) for financial

361 The investment firm might wish, for instance, to enter into securities lending transactions and thus make a profit on the portfolios held.

> instruments that can be held in custody; (i) the depositary shall hold in custody all financial instruments that can be registered in a financial instruments account opened in the depositary's books and all financial instruments that can be physically delivered to the depositary; (ii) for that purpose, the depositary shall ensure that all those financial instruments that can be registered in a financial instruments account opened in the depositary's books are registered in the depositary's books within segregated accounts in accordance with the principles set out in Article 16 of Directive 2006/73/EC, opened in the name of the AIF or the AIFM acting on behalf of the AIF, so that they can be clearly identified as belonging to the AIF in accordance with the applicable law at all times.[362]

Private and commercial law

It has just been discussed how MiFID and the MiFID Implementing Directive have introduced, on the European level, statutory operational standards for the custody of securities. However, international harmonisation (let alone unification) of private or commercial law rules for securities custody seems to be a mere utopia, as different jurisdictions have developed different legal regimes of securities custody. Nevertheless, there have been attempts and initiatives of harmonisation, which we will discuss further here.

The principal distinction between the current regimes of securities custody is between jurisdictions that confer clients some kind of co-property interest in their securities and jurisdictions that have developed other views. Co-property interests are known in civil law jurisdictions such as Germany, Spain and the Netherlands, where it is based on the *Depotgesetz*, the *Ley del Mercado de Valores* and the *Wet giraal effectenverkeer*, respectively. Fungible custody in Belgium and Luxembourg is based on *Koninklijk Besluit* (Royal Decree) *no. 62* and several *règlements grand-ducal* (grand-ducal decrees) respectively, which establish co-ownership in notional pools of securities.[363]

To give an example of a system that confers clients some kind of co-property interest in their securities in order to eliminate the consequences of commingling, the *Wet giraal effectenverkeer* – the Dutch act for securities custody and transfer – makes securities that are subject to this specific statute and which are deposited on behalf of a client with an "intermediary" form part of a collective deposit (or "pool") of securities of the same kind, *i.e.* securities that are mutually interchangeable, deposited with that institution on behalf of clients. By virtue of the Dutch

362 Article 22(5)(a), UCITS V. is identical, *mutatis mutandis*. See also Article 22a(3), added by the European Parliament, on specific requirements when the depositary delegates its tasks to a third party.

363 Of 17 February 1971, of 8 June 1994, of 7 June 1996, of 16 August 2000 and a statute of 3 September 1996. See also the EU Clearing and Settlement Legal Certainty Group Questionnaire (2007), 130 (EU Questionnaire).

piece of legislation under comment, clients who have deposited their securities with an intermediary, give up their individual ownership of the securities deposited and become joint owners of the relevant collective deposit, pro rata to the quantity of securities deposited. Since a collective deposit does not form part of the assets of the intermediary, the securities are not available to the intermediary's liquidator if the intermediary becomes insolvent, and are therefore protected. Each joint owner of a collective deposit has a claim *in rem* against the intermediary. On the same basis as the collective deposits are established with intermediaries, so-called "giro deposits" are established with the CSD. Just as a collective deposit is a pool consisting of securities of a particular kind deposited with an intermediary by its clients and administered by the intermediary, a giro deposit is a pool consisting of securities of a particular kind deposited by intermediaries with the CSD and administered by the CSD.

The "other views" just referred to can be distinguished in the Anglo-American models and so-called transparent models. Under UK and US law, investors enjoy a bundle of rights *in rem* as well as *in personam* against their intermediary. In the UK, account holders' contractual rights follow from their contract with the custodian, while their property law rights classify as co-ownership rights, which may follow from the concept of trust.[364] In the US, the Uniform Commercial Code (UCC) Article 8 provides investors with proprietary and contractual rights in respect of the securities to which they are entitled.

Brazilian and Chinese law represent examples of jurisdictions where client accounts are segregated on all levels of the custody chain. Thus, these systems qualify financial intermediaries as mere account operators and (fictionally) regard securities custody as *depositum*, *i.e.* the administration of individual assets per individual client.

It requires little imagination to realise that the differences in legal regimes "may give rise to legal disputes as to ownership and entitlement to the assets, and complicate transfers or the rapid return of the assets to clients" as the Basel Committee on Banking Supervision warned.[365] Consequently, securities custody has been the subject of various international harmonisation initiatives, many of which have not yet been enacted. On the European level, the European Commission has been working on harmonisation of securities custody law since the so-called Giovannini Reports of 2003, but at the moment of writing, no draft proposal has yet been published.

Recently adopted is the Central Securities Depository Regulation.[366] This regulation is primarily directed at financial market infrastructures, of which Central Securities Depositories are of relevance in the present context. It mirrors the MiFID

364 See EU Questionnaire (2007), 143–144.

365 Basel Committee on Banking Supervision, Report and recommendations for the resolution of cross-border financial institutions (2010) ("BCBS Report").

366 In full: Regulation 909/2014/EU of the European Parliament and of the Council of 23 July 2014 on improving securities settlement in the European Union and on central securities depositories and amending Directives 98/26/EC and 2014/65/EU and Regulation 236/2012/EU, OJ L 257/1 (Henceforth CSD Regulation).

Implementing Directive and provides that a CSD shall segregate the accounts held by financial intermediaries with the CSD (in this regulation: "participants") from those of other participants and its own assets. It also provides that a CSD must enable its participants to segregate the securities of that participant's clients from those of the participant's own. Also, CSDs and participants must give participants and their clients, respectively, the choice to either register omnibus accounts or accounts per individual client.[367]

3.5.4 Transfer of money and securities

Settlement and clearing

Before, we have discussed the multiple tiered model in which cash and securities are held through financial institutions, with an emphasis on the legal position of the client/account holder in that model. In this context, we will focus less on the static situation in which cash and securities are held on accounts with a financial institution, but rather on the dynamic scenario in which the same assets are transferred, or, as commonly referred to, "settled."

So as to introduce the topic, let us consider the following two, simplified examples of a securities transfer or "settlement." First, assume transferor A and transferee B are clients of the same bank X, which bank X maintains omnibus accounts with the local central securities depository. Upon A's order, this bank debits A's securities account and credits B's account with the same amount. The bank's omnibus account with the CSD remains unchanged, as the transfer can be perfected solely on the books of the bank.

Now assume transferor A and transferee C are not clients of the same bank. A remains a client of bank X, while C is a client of bank Y. Also in this instance, A orders his bank X to debit his securities account. Bank X then debits A's account and the local CSD consequently debits X's omnibus account. Assuming C's bank Y is located in the same jurisdiction and therefore also maintains omnibus accounts with the CSD, the CSD then credits bank Y's account. Finally, bank Y credits C's securities account, by which the transfer is completed.

A transfer of money largely follows the same pattern as the two examples of a securities transfer just given. For a money transfer, one only needs to substitute "payor" for transferor and "payee" for transferee, and "central bank" for CSD.

It is important to note that the relationships between A and his bank, as well as between B/C and their bank, must be considered separately, as these relationships are legally to be distinguished from the relationship between A and B/C – this relationship may nonetheless have given the cause for the securities transfer. In the case of securities transfers that have been concluded on a stock exchange, transferor and transferee are normally even unaware of each other's identity and merely order their respective financial institutions to buy or sell securities of a certain type.

367 Article 38, CSD Regulation.

Also, important to note is that, for most cash and securities transfers, the financial institutions that effectuate these transfers for their clients and themselves make use of a "clearinghouse" or a "central counterparty" (the latter is also referred to as CCP). Such clearinghouse or CCP have in common that they calculate the aggregate of the obligations of all transactions that the participants, *i.e.* the financial institutions that participate in the system managed by the clearinghouse or CCP, conclude between themselves on a given day. Whilst the actual delivery or transfer of assets is called "settlement," this calculation process is called "clearing."

Whereas trade-for-trade settlement systems, *i.e.* systems wherein payment and transfer of every single transaction is calculated individually and no netting or set-off takes place, might provide a high level of transparency, they are costly and technically difficult to realise. Moreover, netting or set-off of securities and payment transfers reduces the risks associated with individual transfers and thus results in a cost reduction. In most systems, both delivery and payment obligations are therefore netted, which is performed by a CCP, or a clearinghouse.

In a clearinghouse system, the clearinghouse calculates the net positions of all its participants' obligations or all their transfer orders. At the end of the trading cycle, the clearinghouse typically submits the netted orders to the CSD and central bank, and the CSD and central bank credit and debit the participants' accounts accordingly. Where the clearinghouse does not become a (central) counterparty to its participants, a central counterparty or CCP is interposed between the participants' transactions and in that capacity takes over their obligations by novation. Thus, for all transactions, the financial institution of the transferor (in the case of a securities transfer) or payor (in the case of a cash transfer) has to deliver to the CCP instead of to the financial institution of the transferee/payee. The CCP consequently also takes over all the risks attached to non-performance by a defaulting party, and the use of a CCP therefore results in a considerable reduction of settlement risk.

Although similar, the netting by a CCP and a clearinghouse must be distinguished, as in a CCP system, the net balance has to be paid/delivered to or by the CCP, whereas in a clearinghouse system, the net balance is paid/delivered between the participants themselves through accounts with the CSD and the central bank. For that purpose, the CCP's participants maintain so-called clearing member accounts with the CCP, and consequently hold both a clearing member account with the CCP and a securities and cash account with the CSD and central bank.

Settlement Finality Directive

Other than for reasons of (operational) mistakes by the financial institutions that maintain cash and securities accounts, the reversal of entries in cash and securities accounts is mainly prompted by the insolvency of one of the parties involved. The European legislature has addressed the reversal of transfers relatively early. Based on this legislative framework, it is acknowledged that legal uncertainty should be minimised, particularly in the context of such a vital element of modern economies, and recognised that in payment and securities settlement systems, an enormous number of transactions between numerous participants is multilaterally effectuated on a daily basis, while the reversal of settlements in that context is cumbersome and often impossible.

Consequently, the Settlement Finality Directive was adopted on 19 May 1998.[368] Its main purpose has been to reduce the systemic risk associated with participation in payment and securities settlement systems, and, more specifically, the risk that materialises when a participant in such a system becomes insolvent.[369] Therefore, the Settlement Finality Directive, first and foremost, determines that transfer orders and payment netting be final and non-revocable in nature, it determines which insolvency rules are applicable to claims and obligations in a payment/securities settlement system, and it insulates (the enforcement of) collateral, *i.e.* the assets that are used to secure an obligation, from insolvency proceedings. Moreover, the Settlement Finality Directive provides for a conflict of laws rule regarding some proprietary issues of securities custody and transfer law. As a general matter, the Settlement Finality Directive constitutes a departure from traditional European financial law legislation where the focus lies on mutual recognition of home-country supervision, whereas the Settlement Finality Directive gives primacy to the law and the rules of the settlement and payment systems.

Article 3 is the Settlement Finality Directive's pivotal provision of substantive law. It requires national laws to ensure that transfer orders and netting are enforceable once entered into a payment or securities settlement system. Enforceability is to be ensured regardless of the commencement of insolvency proceedings against a participant of the system after that entry, while Article 3 further states that the moment of entry should be defined by the rules of the system itself. The moment from when a transfer order can no longer be revoked is also to be defined by the rules of the system; Article 5 Settlement Finality Directive.

Article 7 determines that the insolvency of a participant in a payment or securities settlement system has no retroactive effects with regard to this and other participants' rights and obligations towards the system. This provision is complemented by Article 9(1), requiring the EU member states to implement legislation that insulates (the enforcement of) collateral from the effects of insolvency proceedings commenced against a participant in a system.

Conflict of laws rules are found in Articles 8 and 9. The rationale behind both provisions is that neither the operator of a payment or securities settlement system, nor its participants should have to take into account the national law of the participants, particularly those of pertaining to insolvency, for the purposes of determining their rights and obligations against the system. Article 8 provides that the effects of the insolvency of one of the participants be determined by the law designated by the operator of the settlement system, thus deviating from the general rule under which the law of the jurisdiction where insolvency proceedings commenced

368 In the UK, Directive 98/26 was transposed by means of the Financial Markets and Insolvency (Settlement Finality) Regulations 1999. See Proctor (2010).

369 See Recitals 2, 4 and 9, Settlement Finality Directive.

will apply (*lex concursus*).[370] Where a participant has obtained collateral in the form of securities, Article 9(2) refers to the law of the EU jurisdiction where this participant's/collateral taker's rights are registered to determine their nature.[371] The Settlement Finality Directive has been implemented in all member states with no significant deviations.[372]

3.5.5 The UK financial regulation

As a result of Brexit, in 2023 the Financial Services and Markets Act 2023 was passed, the aim of which is to make important updates to the regulatory framework for financial services. More precisely, this act implements the outcome of the Future Regulatory Framework (FRF) Review and, at the same time, revokes retained EU law relating to financial services and enables HM Treasury and financial services regulators to replace it with legislation designed specifically for UK markets.

As far as the revocation of retained EU law is concerned, the act revokes the following types of retained EU law, such as the following:

- All direct principal EU legislation, such as regulations;
- Secondary legislation made under primary legislation, such as instruments made to implement EU obligation under the European Communities Act 1972 and instruments made under the European Union Withdrawal Act 2018 which addressed deficiencies in EU law;
- All EU tertiary legislation, such as delegated regulations, commission decisions and implementing acts;
- Some part of the primary legislation.

Furthermore, there is also the "Associated Powers": a provision to allow retained EU law to be replaced in a way that creates a comprehensive FSMA model of regulation. Under the FSMA, the UK Parliament, through legislations, sets the overall approach to financial services regulation including the regulators' objectives. Moreover, it is the power of Parliament to establish the parameters which HM Treasury sets for the "regulatory perimeter" through secondary legislation. In this, it will specify which financial activities should be regulated.

In order to establish a comprehensive FSMA model, the regulators need to have the appropriate powers to make rules when retained EU law is revoked. In other instances, the regulators have not sufficient regulatory rule-making powers to replace the rules that are currently in retained EU law. The restatement power will allow HM Treasury to address this by enabling (1) the restatement into domestic

370 See Ooi (2003). EU Insolvency Regulation Article 9 (Council Regulation 1346/2000/EC of 29 May 2000 on insolvency proceedings (OJ L 160/1)).

371 In a different wording, the Winding-up Directive, Article 25.

372 *Report from the Commission, Evaluation report on the Settlement Finality Directive 98/26/EC (EU 25),* COM(2005), 657 final/2, 9.

legislation of any existing regulator rule-making powers there are set out in retained EU law, (2) the modification of the existing regulator rule-making powers and (3) the creation of new rule-making powers in areas covered by retained EU law.

The "Associated Powers" encompasses, also, the power of modifying the retained EU law: although this process may involve so many passes, it is contemplated that there will be finite a transitional period, during which the regulator may be restricted in how he is able to pursuant its statutory objectives.

In addition, we can find amendments to the Markets in Financial Instruments Regulation (MiFIR) and the European Market Infrastructure Regulation (EMIR). The starting point is that the UK played a significant role in designing the MiFID II framework and the government believes that the resilience and effectiveness of the UK's capital markets has been significant strengthened by the post-crisis reforms that it implemented. Nevertheless, the main points where it is crucial to make changes are as follows:

- To share trading obligation (STO) that is under modification;
- To replace the pre-trade transparency waiver regime and remove the double-volume cap;
- To change the definition of a systematic internaliser regime as it moves to a systemic internalised regime and gives to FCA the power to specify how the new definition should be interpreted (this may ensure a more flexible regime, all the better for account evolution; ultimately, this may increase the transparency requirement and price formation);
- The FCA has specific and permanent power to modify or suspend the derivatives trading obligation (DTO) in order, also, to simply the transparency regime for fixed income and derivatives;
- Amendments to EU Securitisation Regulation.

Ultimately, another topic is the new regulatory powers, of which the main areas are (1) the designated activities regime, (2) the financial market infrastructure, (3) sustainability, (4) digital settlements assets,[373] (5) the definition of the new objectives and (6) the Bank of England's regulatory powers.

The first one, the designated activities regime, is created to allow activities related to financial markets to be regulated within a framework which is compatible with a comprehensive FSMA model.

The financial market infrastructure encompasses the various process that need to be performed to complete each transaction. These process, more precisely, are performed by several different entities, many of which are collectively referred to as a financial market infrastructure (FMI). Every type of FMI performs a vital function in supporting financial markets: this activity ranges from collecting data on financial transactions, to performing unique services aimed at enabling firms, active in financial markets, to meet their regulatory obligations. To shape a

373 Sustainability and digitalisation further.

comprehensive FSMA model, the regulators need the appropriate powers to make rules when retained EU law is revoked. That includes the ability to make rules for FMI and the appropriate powers to supervise and oversee them. Due to this, the act introduces general rule-making powers for the Bank of England in relation to two types of FMI, CCPs and central securities depositories (CSDs). In this respect, the act does the following:

- Introduces a general rule making power for the Bank over CCPs and CSDs;
- Establishes the concept of a systemic third-country CCP.

Ultimately, there are also the recognised investment exchanges:[374] a multilateral system which brings together multiple third-party buying and selling interests in financial instruments, in accordance with non-discretionary rules.

The second point, financial market infrastructure, is focused on the regulatory powers of the Financial Conduct Authority. In this scenario, a central role is played by the data reporting service providers[375] as a type of FMI. More precisely, there are at least three types of DRSPs:

- Approved publication arrangements,[376] which publish trade reports on behalf of investment firms which are required to publish information, such as price, and the size of the executed trades they perform;
- Approved reporting mechanisms,[377] which report details about transaction to FCA on behalf investment firms, for market surveillance purposes;
- Consolidated tape providers,[378] which collocate trading data for financial instruments for a variety of sources.

Another FCA duty is to be responsible for the regulation of financial service and, the latter comprehends also the Financial Ombudsman Service. This is an alternative dispute resolution service for financial service complainants, for such as consumers and smaller business which have a complaint about a financial services firm or claims management company.

As far as the new objectives are concerned, the government has recognised that the financial services sector is an "engine" whose purpose lies on an objective: to help the wider economy grow. Therefore, there are secondary objectives for the FCA and the PRA to provide greater focus on international competitiveness and medium to long-term growth. The last goal is the increasing UK role, on an international level: more precisely, the UK may become a global leader in promoting high international standards.

374 Henceforth RIE.
375 Henceforth DRSPs.
376 Henceforth APAs.
377 Henceforth ARMs.
378 Henceforth CTPs.

The last point refers to the regulatory powers of Bank of England: in addition to its traditional objectives, the Bank of England has also the duty to facilitate innovation in the clearing and settlement services provided by CCPs and CSDs. In order words, the additional elements concern the improving of quality, efficiency and economy of the services they provide.

3.6 Spare banking and conduits

3.6.1 Introduction

Traditionally, the 2007–2008 financial crises are automatically linked with structure finance, and, more precisely, securitisations. The latter have been considered, for a long time, a threat to the stability of financial markets.

Another topic strictly connected with securitisation is shadow banking. At the beginning, shadow banking implied special-purpose vehicles or special-purpose entities (SPEs) used in securitisation and structure finance transaction.

Bearing this in mind, in this chapter, the main issue is not the 2007–2008 financial crisis,[379] rather shadow banking, securitisations and, more in general, the financial and banking regulation in the area of structured finance arising out of the 2007–2008 crises, particularly in the area of structured finance.

Yet this approach is innovative because it describes, from a historical perspective, the evolution of both shadow banking and securitisations. Therefore, it will be clear, as a result of this analysis, that shadow banking was a phenomenon relating to securitisation: in the aftermath of the financial turmoil, the regulation has been even more strict, in that the traditional structure finance transactions have been totally changed.

Furthermore, shadow banking has changed its own skin, at the mercy of digital and technological transactions, particularly when those have become "greener" or "more techno."

Additionally, here other issues will be discussed, albeit linked with shadow banking, such as deposit guarantee schemes, moral hazards, depositor protection and financial stability as a quintessence of the whole legal system.

3.6.2 Shadow banking

The term "shadow banking" refers to a variety of forms from country to country: for example, in China, shadow banking institutions consist of trust loans, wealth management products, undiscounted banker acceptance, and peer-to-peer lending. In Indonesia, shadow banking, known as non-bank financial institutions, includes trust companies, securities companies, bank wealth management arms, entrusted private entities and financial technology companies (fintech) such as peer-to-peer lending and crowdfunding. All of these institutions represent a shadow banking system where, and if, they carry out credit intermediation activities.

379 See below.

Per the Financial Stability Board definition, shadow banking concerns credit intermediation that, at the same time, involves entities and activities outside of the regular, or traditional, banking system.

Other alternative definitions stress different elements, such as the following:

- Shadow banking as the result of financial crisis;[380]
- Shadow banking as a consequence of financial innovation during financial crisis;[381]
- The activities of both slightly regulated and unregulated entities.[382]

As a result of this, shadow banking has a more negative connotation due to its reference to credit intermediation outside the regular banking sector. By contrast, a school of thought stresses that shadow banking may be a positive element too: it supports the real economy and provides competition for the banking sector.[383]

To summarise all of these definitions, it is possible to say that shadow banking is the activity carried out by specific institutions, the conduits, whose task is to carry out functions of transformation of both the credit and the relevant expiry. This transformation materialises through the issuance of securities, albeit without granting the traditional depositors' protection. Again, this transaction does not provide the investor with a guarantee of repayment in relation to their own investment, which is typically afforded to depositors.[384]

A problem connected with shadow banking is its connection with traditional bank activity. The controversy concerns the link between the practice of taking out short-term deposits and providing long-term financing. This activity, potentially, can become risky in circumstances where banks failed to manage their risk in a practical and effective way.[385] By contrast, within the realm of shadow banking, this mismatching is neutralised or, at least, its risk minimised, since the assets transferred to the SPV and the bonds issued by the latter, tend to coincide with each other, as far as their maturity is concerned.

The demarcation line between shadow banking and traditional banking is that the latter receives direct support from the public sector, while the first, does not appear to be subject to the copious prudential rules to which public banks are subject.[386] Should a credit institution fail, depositors, or at least a large representation of them, will be protected via a specific depositors' protection scheme, which is mandatory in major jurisdictions. By contrast, shadow-banking activities turn out to be only indirectly or implicitly supported. As regards securitisation activities, the credit institutions from which they originate are allocated off their relevant balance sheet.

380 (Bengtsson 2013).
381 (Pozsar et al. 2010).
382 (Elliott, Kroeber and Qiao 2015).
383 (Rogge 2021).
384 (de Gioia Carabellese and Della Giustina 2023).
385 (Alexander 2019).
386 (Moloney, Ferran and Payne 2016).

It is crucial to emphasises another aspect: after the EU regulation, to find a lack of legislation is a "mission impossible." Within a harmonised regulatory environment in which supervised entities – *i.e.* those in charge of these transactions – are subject to heavy burdens, limiting the entitlement to purchase structured products, it is arduous and even speculative to conceive the shadow nature of these financial transactions. The same inference can be made for SPV, vehicles which, now disguised as SPPE, in the new EU Securitisation Regulation, are likewise in the mirror of the EU supervisor and supervisors.

Thus, the conclusion is that it is possible to conclude that shadow banking encompasses activities carried out in areas where regulation, albeit existing, is unconventional.[387] These financial activities, which intermediaries are authorised to carry out since they are not prohibited, are indeed influenced by rules, although the latter may seem vague or even non-existent.

These stances are corroborated by the new legislature recently passed.

The unique aspect of the ultimate piece of legislation in the financial area is mainly concerned with a new, increased sensibility to the environment[388] and technological development.[389] Thus, the banking regulation, that may now fill the "green banking" box too, is considered essential for the ecological transition.

Also in connection with this postulation, most scholars underline that shadow banking may augment the quality of sustainability, in addition to being an opportunity for "actors" (such as banks and, more in general, businesses) to play an active role of in the transitional, ecological process: the final stage of this "grand tour" is an economic system where the major themes of the sustainable development may be dealt with.

Traditionally, the *modus operandi* of the banking business has led to an increase in polluting emissions.[390] Also in view of this, the speculative financial transactions have been hardly considered so far environmentally conscious. By contrast, the new underpinning idea of future financial markets is that there is a strong relationship between banking systems and ecosystems; as a result of this, the regulation, broadly considered, is expected to act as a thread connecting those different issues.

The body of law existing in the financial sector is now adamant that its aims and objectives include those relating to both the environment and environmental risk. Hence, the banking legislation turned, linguistically, on the expressions "sustainable finance" or "green finance."

3.6.3 Securitisation

Although securitisations were under the spotlight during 2007–2008 years, they do not constitute a new phenomenon.

387 (de Gioia Carabellese and Della Giustina 2023)
388 (Chiu, Lin and Rouch 2022).
389 See below.
390 (Pettifor 2019).

Historic perspective

Some primordial, albeit raw, forms of structured financial agreements can be traced back to the Genoese Republic, one of the four Italian maritime republics. In the 12th century, the sale of tax credits, carried out at that time by that sovereign state, would have been somehow reminiscent of contemporary securitisation.

Furthermore, the ancestor of the current concept of the modern mortgage securitisation would be the sale of loans linked with the plantation and the relevant crops.

Similarly, it can be held that financial innovation shall be interpreted as a process of evolution, growth and improvement. The outcome of this coincides with the establishment of the same market. From a historical point of observation, it can be recalled that the first derivatives were exchanged at the time of the Mesopotamian civilisation, as a support for the exchange of agricultural goods and to insure against the risks of disasters that would starve the population. Added to this is the circumstance that the first futures on wheat were the subject of exchange at the temple. The members of the clergy acted as guarantors, for purposes of the good end of the operation to be concluded.[391]

To elaborate, in 1695, a structured, negotiated and secured credit instrument was conceived on the West Indies assets and was pegged to the plantation revenues, these plantations consisting of either coffee or sugar. However, this market was not sustainable, because all the risks that were borne were reflected on the return on the investment itself.

To find the first successful securitised market of loans it is necessary to move to Germany and France, a few decades later. The German mortgage-backed bond market was a response to the financial crisis following the Seven Years' War. Known as *Pfandbriefe*, or guarantee bonds, these instruments became a pillar of the European market of those years. However, in the United States, three attempts were made, all of which were unsuccessful, to convert loans into negotiable securities, which took place in the 1870s, 1880s and 1920s.[392]

The first US securitisation market was, at least initially, a privately funded one. However, probably because it was unregulated, it ended in an unceremonious way since it caused serious defaults and provides an incorrect and misleading reconstruction of the European experience.

Within the modern securitisation literature, three phases of the development of these transactions are usually outlined. At the end of the 1960s, mortgage securitisations were seen and perceived as an effective response to the risk of both early repayment and the variation of interest rates. Some further scholars[393] refer to securitisations as a delayed response to "monetarism." This phenomenon started precisely from savings and lending institutions. Since many financial institutions sought additional revenues by turning their attention to fees and commissions, this made the practice increasingly popular and widespread.

391 (Riley 1980; Rouwenhorst 2005).

392 (Snowden 1995).

393 (Minsky and Wray 2008).

In the late 1980s, because of the savings and loans crisis, the Resolution Trust Corporation (RTC) used securitisation operations in order to operate this procedure as much as possible, from commercial mortgages to automotive loans. In 1992, the SEC recognised that securitisation was becoming one of the most dominant means of funding in the US.

Between 2002 and 2004, the market switched to non-regulated securitisations, otherwise known as PLS, typically managed by investment banks. In light of the securitisation system, all global institutions benefited from this. The time was no longer favourable to a business model where banks carried out their activities merely to the benefit of the local securities markets. By contrast, with these transactions, banks started relying on the possibility of passing on credit risks to both international investors and hedge funds; therefore, a coverage was no longer limited to the local context.

The legal central role of securitisations is not played by the paper, the *papel*, which is issued by the vehicle, and in which the metamorphosis of the receivable (from credit to debt) materialises, as a consequence of the assignment. Rather, it is the definitive transfer of credit risk and the segmentation of securities (protected or backed by the transferred assets) in different risk classes: these two combined features, in the end, allow the placement of the securities in the market at different rates, whereas, without this metamorphosis, the placement would not have occurred.

Indeed, securitisation alluded to the risk transfer from the banking sector to outside investors. In order to realise this transaction, banks were induced to reduce regulatory capital, a practice that eventually contributed to the largest banking crisis since the Great Depression.[394]

The transfer, or broadly speaking the sale, from which the securitisation stems, describes only a part of the phenomenon, the initial one, in which the originator, as a result of the true sale, is protected from the risk of insolvency of the debtors of the assigned claims or the insolvency of the SPV.

The remaining, albeit preponderant, part of the securitisation lies on both the issuance of securities and the fragmentation of investors' risk according to classes, which shall be at least two. Credit segmentation, therefore, seems to be the term that describes securitisations better, since their distinctive and quintessential connotation is the creation of classes of securities. By contrast, the mere sale of the assets, which in itself defines a financing transaction, is not tantamount to an investment transaction.

In the development of the financial markets of the United States and the United Kingdom, securitisation operations[395] pursue different objectives. They prop up public policy objectives, such as supporting the development of financial markets with particular regard to capital and loan markets. Second, they help comply with regulatory requirements for financial institutions, in particular as regards capital

394 (Acharya, Schnabl and Suarez 2013).

395 (Engel and Mccoy 2010; Bonsall 1990).

adequacy and lending limits applicable to banks. Finally, they carry out risk transfer transactions in the context of impaired assets and portfolio diversification.

The usefulness and practical help provided by these financial transactions has led both operators and relevant legal systems around the world to seek to develop similar practices and contractual/legislative frameworks in their own financial markets. The most successful examples have taken place within the European Union, whose regulation, alongside that in the UK, constitutes the main focus of this work.

This trend, however, shall be contextualised within a broader reflection: asset securitisation is a structured finance transaction which takes place in a complex capital market.

It follows from this that the traditional asset securitisation structures cannot be transferred, nonchalantly, to different financial markets, especially to emerging countries whose economies may be too different and too peculiar. Additionally, the transplant of securitisations may result in being problematic in financial markets whose legal system is based on civil law. In these cases, the financial transactions at stake must cater for the functions for which they were designed in the financial markets and legal systems of origin, the US and the UK, whereas the different legal systems and heterogenous principles of law of the target market may be quite different.

Structure

The principal elements around which a securitisation is constructed are the transaction, the structure and the parties.

The central part of a securitisation transaction is the sale of assets: it refers, traditionally, to receivables, from the originating party, the originator, to a special-purpose vehicle.[396]

The receivables used in a securitisation transaction come in great variety and numbers, for example, home mortgage loans, *i.e.* loans that have been extended to finance a house and which have been secured with a mortgage, and other consumer receivables, such as credit card receivables, lease obligations and even monthly charges for telephones. Receivables also encompass loans to professional parties, such as commercial real estate mortgages, which could be securitised.

Differently from other forms of banking contracts, such as factoring, the vehicle pays receivables not with its own money,[397] but with what it collects because of the placement in the relevant capital market of the securities issued alongside the purchase of the assets.

The parties to a securitisation transaction are special-purpose vehicle, originator, debtors, servicer, investors, swap counterparty and rating agencies.

The SPV, also referred to as the issuer, is the vehicle that is essential to the securitisation transaction. It buys the receivables from the originator with capital raised

396 Henceforth SPV.
397 In fact, the vehicle is a thinly capitalised company, without assets.

by issuing different types of bonds (further discussed here). The SPV is usually a limited liability company, and the shares of the SPV are owned by a foundation or a trust office. Thus, the SPV's shares are not held by the originator, as it is important that the SPV is not consolidated on the originator's balance sheet.

Even more importantly, the SPV must be "bankruptcy remote." Bankruptcy remoteness is achieved by several means: (1) the objects of the articles of association are limited in such a manner that the SPV is not allowed to conduct any business that does not regard the securitisation transaction; (2) all possibilities for counterparties to initiate liquidation proceedings against the SPV are excluded by incorporating a covenant in all its contracts that prohibits the contracting party from initiating liquidation proceedings against the SPV; (3) the SPV does not hire employees and restrains the number of creditors to a minimum. Fourth, independent directors are appointed, *e.g.* by contracting a corporate service provider.

The SPV has a crucial role; hence, it does the following:

- Receives the purchase amount it has to pay for the receivables to the originator by issuing bonds, which are typically rated by a rating agency, to investors;
- Pays principal and interest on these bonds with the proceeds on the receivables (*i.e.* principal and interest) that have been transferred to the SPV.

The parties buying bonds from an SPV are often other banks, institutional investors and hedge funds. They are named as investors. With a securitisation, investors with different risk appetites may be satisfied, as the bonds are commonly issued in (at least) two classes: senior and junior bonds, while the junior bonds are subordinated to the senior ones. Distinguishing senior and junior (and other classes of bonds, such as in the previous illustration) is called tranching.

Investors may have a big advantage of buying bonds issued by an SPV in a securitisation transaction: properly, the possibility to invest in assets with a relative low credit risk and therefore high ratings, and high returns. Also, a securitisation enables them to invest (indirectly) in assets such as mortgage loans and credit card loans, that would otherwise not have been available for them to invest in directly.

An originator is the entity that initially has the receivables, *i.e.* that holds the claims on clients, that are to be securitised. An originating party typically is a bank, but it can also be another financial institution such as a credit card company, or any other company that has many receivables.

Originators enter into a securitisation transaction for different reasons. First, the originator may want an off-balance treatment of receivables and a "leverage ratio." This is a goal that can be pursued by the originators because they no longer hold the credit risk of the receivables, duly transferred to a different party, for which they receive immediate cash. The latter is the consideration that the SPV pays for receivables. The advantage of this structure is obvious: the originator receives the payment straightaway, without having to wait for the expiry of the credits. In doing so, and thanks to the cash payment, the originator is in a position relieve the outstanding liability in order to obtain, because of this, a better "leverage ratio." In this way, therefore, a better balance between equity and debt is achieved.[398]

An additional reason (the second one) why the originator may decide to securitise its assets is that a securitisation may represent a cheap funding, in comparison with the funding which the originator might obtain in a traditional fashion – namely, the issuance of bonds. The cost of funding of a securitisation – the money that the originator receives from the SPV – turns out to be relatively low (particularly if compared with the funding of a bond). The reason for this is that the rating of the bonds issued by the SPV is, usually, higher than the one at which the underlying assets would have been valued in the absence of a securitisation transaction.[399] In light of this, securitisations may represent a less expensive alternative than other funding methods, such as, for example, a syndicated loan, or the issuance of corporate bonds.

A third motive underpinning the arrangement of a securitisation is that these transactions allow the originator to offer its assets to a wider audience than the ordinary issuance of bonds. In essence, securities issued by an SPV are easier to trade than the underlying assets.

A fourth motivation for opting for a structured finance transaction relates to the regulatory capital relief that can be achieved through the transfer of the receivables from the originator to the SPV. The credit risk that the originator bears on his claims impacts on the regulatory capital of a bank. At a time when the credit risk is not borne by the books, the originator releases regulatory capital which, in the opposite case, would be required to keep.[400]

Finally (the fifth reason), a bank may opt for securitising its portfolio since the European Central Bank accepts some bonds issued by the SPV as collateral. In this case, credit is provided to the banks: otherwise, the ECB would not accept a security interest on the receivable underlying assets. Needless to say, the last two circumstances just mentioned are applicable exclusively to a scenario where the originator is a bank.

The debtors of the receivables securitised can be consumers as well as companies. Consumer debts, eligible for securitisation, comprise, among others, credit card debts and mortgage loans. Company debts include long-, medium- and short-term obligations. In the vast majority of cases payment of the debt is secured, *e.g.* by a bank mortgage.

The collector of the receivables is referred to as "the servicer" and receives a fee for its work. It is very well possible that, after the transfer of the receivables to the SPV, the originator continues to collect the proceeds on the receivables and thus acts as the servicer, but this role can also be performed by a third party.

398 In synthetic securitisations, off-balance sheet treatment is not possible, by definition, since assets are not transferred to the SPV.

399 This more generous rating may be also due to the fact that, as already emphasised, the SPV, differently from a multiple purposes company, does not incur in the risks of carrying out an unfettered range of businesses, with the ensuing problem of unleashing a huge variety of creditors.

400 (Alexander 2019).

Another party that is commonly involved in a traditional securitisation transaction is the rating agency. Its role is to rate the bonds issued by the SPV. These bonds are usually tranched as rating agencies focus primarily on the credit risk of the receivables: the bonds connected with the receivables with the lowest default risk obtain the highest rating, the bonds connected with the highest default risk obtain the lowest. The rating can vary from AAA to D (also depending on the rating method used). Thus, a triple-A rating ensures investors that the SPV is highly probable to pay the returns and interest on the bonds.

Finally, we can say that the security trustee is the party that links together SPV, debtors and investment. The security trustee is mandated by a contract to enforce the security rights against the SPV, and debtors on behalf of investors.[401] More precisely, a liquidity facility can be concluded between the SPV and a liquidity provider, which is usually another bank, which allows the SPV to have cash to pay the bond holders. In the same way as in a syndicated loan context, a securitisation transaction requires a trustee that acts for the full range of bond holders in a similar way as the trustee does for the Lender in a syndicated loan. Security rights protecting claims must be transferred to the security trustee in order to allow the security trustee to execute these security rights. As a result of the transfer, investors will be able to claim security rights in the event of non-payment of the SPV.

FLOWS

From the SPV's party may originate some flows, such as (1) receivables, (2) bonds, and (3) swap counterparty.

The receivables that may be used in a securitisation transaction come in great variety and numbers. One could think of home mortgage loans, *i.e.* loans that have been extended to finance a house and which loans have been secured with a mortgage, and other consumer receivables, such as credit card receivables, lease obligations and even monthly charges for telephones. But also loans to professional parties such as commercial real estate mortgages could be securitised.

One of the main objectives in a securitisation transaction is to reduce the credit risk on the receivables. Credit risk is the risk of inability to pay principal and interest. Mitigating this risk could be achieved in multiple ways. First, the credit risk on the receivables, *i.e.* the risk of non-payment of principal and interest on the claims, is reduced by a careful selection of which receivables are to be transferred to the SPV. In order to receive a high rating of the bonds issued by the SPV, only receivables with a low default risk, *i.e.* claims that are highly probable to be paid, should ideally be transferred to the SPV. Second, credit risk on the receivables may be reduced by a guarantee from the originator or one given by a third party to the SPV. Such a guarantee would secure payment on the receivables, but should not be overly extensive because of a possible recharacterisation risk. A third possibility to reduce the credit risk on the receivables is by pool insurance. This means

401 (Haentjens and de Gioia Carabellese 2020).

that payment of principal and interest on certain pools of claims are insured by a professional party.

As far as bonds are concerned, the risk of the SPV's inability to pay principal and interest on the bonds qualifies as a credit risk for the investors. This risk could be mitigated in several ways.

First, the credit risk on the SPV is mitigated by tranching. Because junior notes are subordinated to the senior ones and thus bear the first losses, the credit risk on notes with more seniority is mitigated. Second, over-collateralisation is a way to mitigate credit risk on the SPV: the originator transfers more receivables to the SPV than are needed to pay the investors. Also, the interest the SPV receives on the receivables from the debtors is usually higher than the interest the SPV has to pay to the investors. The surplus that follows can be credited to a so-called reserve account. Third, and importantly, the structure is set up so that the investors may benefit from, *i.e.* eventually exercise the security interest(s) that the debtors have granted to the originator, to secure the receivables.

In the most classic example of a securitisation, these security interests would be the residential mortgages the borrowers vested in the property financed by the loans from which the receivables follow. Fourth, the credit risk on the SPV is mitigated by a subordinated loan from the originator to the SPV: a loan that is only to be paid back to the originator if, should the SPV fall insolvent, all "senior" claims, viz. the investors' claims (including junior bonds), have first been satisfied. This loan is therefore also called the equity piece. Fifth, a liquidity facility is entered into between the SPV and a liquidity provider (see also the following), under which facility cash must be provided to the SPV, enabling it always to pay its bond holders.

As mentioned earlier, the SPV is able to purchase the originator's receivables by issuing bonds to investors. The SPV can pay principal and interest on these bonds from the proceeds, *i.e.* principal and interest, on the receivables that the originator has transferred to the SPV. The interest rate (the SPV has to pay to bond holders) on the bonds is usually floating. The interest rate (the SPV receives from the debtors) on the receivables, on the other hand, is usually fixed. To mitigate this mismatch/interest rate risk, the SPV commonly enters into a swap contract with a swap counterparty. Under this financial derivate contract, the counterparty accepts variable interest flows and provides fixed flows in return. The SPV thus always receives a fixed interest rate payable to the bondholders.

Ultimately, it is worthwhile to recall the GIC and liquidity providers. As just mentioned, it may possible that a mismatch occurs for some reasons: on the one hand, a surplus can arise, such as when debtors prematurely repay their loans. On the other hand, a deficit may occur when debtors default. For the situation of a surplus, the SPV and an account provider may enter into a guarantee investment contract (GIC), which enables the SPV, in case of an incidental surplus on the receivables, to invest this surplus temporarily. Usually, the return on that temporary investment is a few basis points below LIBOR. In case of a temporary deficit on the receivables, a liquidity facility entered into between the SPV, and a liquidity provider may provide cash, thus enabling the SPV always to pay its bond holders.

LEGAL ISSUES

The study of a securitisation transaction requires the consideration of multiple legal issues. These mainly represent regulatory and property law rules, as these rules are commonly of a mandatory nature and cannot be contracted away. In this chapter some of the main legal concerns will be discussed, of which the true sale requirement features most prominently.

More precisely, the reference is to true sale, security rights, assignability and set-off.

The first one, true sale, is the transfer of receivables from the originator to the SPV. This qualification is justified by the fact that under the laws of various jurisdictions, including the US, the amount payable by the SPV to the originator may otherwise be recharacterised as a loan secured by the receivables. Also, under some jurisdictions, a fiduciary transfer that is not the result of a true sale but has only security purposes is forbidden. If such recharacterisation occurs, the results for the parties involved are often dramatic.[402] Off-balance treatment of the receivables will then be cancelled and the originator has thus remained liable for the credit risk on the receivables. Also, property laws are applied to the recharacterised securitisation transaction so that all regular requirements for security interests in receivables are applied – and will probably not have been complied with.

This generates a host of difficulties, including unsatisfied publication or registration requirements. Moreover, under most property law regimes, any surplus on the collateral needs to be returned to the creditor after realisation of the security interest, while in a securitisation transaction (at least part of) the surplus is destined for the bondholders (see also the following). Finally, enforcement of a regular security interest is commonly subject to restrictive rules which are absent in the case of a full title transfer as is intended in a securitisation.

As a matter of course, the mechanics of recharacterisation depend on the applicable (property) law. Generally, however, in order to prevent recharacterisation, it is of the essence that the transaction does not contain the main characteristics of a regular security interest for a loan. First, the originator must have no remaining liability for the assets that are transferred to the SPV. This means that the originator cannot guarantee the returns and interest on the receivables and has no obligation to repurchase in case of losses on the receivables. Second, it is paramount that the SPV obtains exclusive control over the assets and is allowed to take all sorts of actions that a regular owner would be allowed to do. In other words, the SPV should obtain full power of disposal for purposes of, *e.g.*, selling, pledging or managing the assets. Third, the assets must be isolated from the originator in case of its bankruptcy.

Depending on the applicable law, a court might also take other circumstances into account when determining whether a securitisation transaction qualifies as a secured loan. For instance, and as already alluded to earlier, under common property law, a security taker is allowed to benefit only from the proceeds of the

402 (Wood, Law and Practice of International Finance 2008).

realisation of his security interest to the extent that the proceeds do not exceed the initial secured debt. Thus, they must transfer any surplus on the proceeds back to the debtor.

Also in a classic securitisation, the SPV transfers back some surplus to the originator for profit extraction purposes, while other surplus is for the benefit of investors. It depends on the particular transaction whether the profit extraction is considered as material. If it is, recharacterisation might follow. Second, an originator sometimes holds a right to repurchase any surplus receivables. Whether this is considered as material also depends on the particular conditions of a transaction. In any case, the repurchase of the receivables cannot be without consideration, *i.e.* gratis, due to the recharacterisation risk. Third, if the originator continues to service and collect the receivables after their transfer to the SPV (see previous discussion), this could be an indication for recharacterisation since in a true sale, the selling party is usually not committed to collect. Fourth, the originator could to some extent continue to be liable for the underlying receivables, as it usually would have made a subordinated loan to the SPV that bears losses on the receivables prior to the SPV's bondholders. This depends on the specific transaction, and again, it depends on the applicable (property) law whether this is a decisive factor for recharacterisation.

This is quintessential, to ensure that the sale is genuine and, by no means, the originator shall return the price received. A consequent aspect is that, according to some legal systems, a transfer for fiduciary purposes which takes place only for the purpose of security is prohibited.[403] From this perspective, the true sale is also instrumental in ensuring that the amount paid by the SPV to the originator may not qualify as a loan, secured by the claims.

Should this recharacterisation[404] take place, the results for the parties involved would be catastrophic.[405] Specifically, the off-balance sheet treatment of receivables will be affected and the originator will have a remaining responsibility for the receivable credit risk. In addition, all the requirements for the provision of credit-related securities will be applied and, as a result of recharacterisation, they will no longer have to be met. Investors, who have not subscribed the securitised financial instruments in relying on the creditworthiness of the company, will see their money in jeopardy.

This combination of unexpected events leads to a number of difficulties, such as the reversal of publication or registration requirements linked with the ostensive sale. Also, depending on the different property rights regimes, any surplus on collateral will have to be returned to the creditors, following activation and enforcement of the collateral, whereas, conversely, the surplus in a securitisation transaction is reserved to bondholders. Finally, the enforcement of the security is subject to restrictive rules that are absent in the hypothesis of full transfer in the case of a securitisation.

403 Article 3:84(3) del *Dutch Civil Code* (Haentjens and de Gioia Carabellese 2020).

404 That is, if the trust transfer is not the result of a true salt but has taken place solely and solely for the purpose of guarantee.

405 (Wood, Law and Practice of International Finance 2008).

In order to prevent recharacterisation, it is necessary that the transaction in question does not possess the main characteristics of a credit-related security interest. This goal could be achieved via different strategies. First, it must be excluded that the originator has residual liability for the assets that are transferred to the SPV. The originator, in other words, cannot guarantee the repayment of the principal and the interest of the receivables and, therefore, is not encumbered by any obligation to repurchase the securities in the event of losses on the receivables. Second, it is essential for the SPV to obtain exclusive control over the assets and for the vehicle to be allowed to take any action that a normal owner is authorised to take. From an accounting point of view, thirdly, the assets must be solidly included within the perimeter of the SPV and, therefore, isolated from the originator in the event of its insolvency. Finally, depending on the applicable law, a court might consider other circumstances to assess whether a securitisation can be qualified as a secured loan.

Fourthly, the originator could continue to be liable for the underlying claims even if indirectly. This would be the case with a subordinated loan to the vehicle, the SPV, if the originator's creditor bears credit losses before the bondholders are forced to do so.[406] The described would integrate a delicate circumstance which could be appreciated differently depending on the legal regime applicable in a specific legal order. In other words, one element will be regarded as decisive on the basis of the sensitivity of a legal order.

Another topic concerns the transfer of the security rights that secure the receivables, to the security trustee. As a general rule of property law, security rights are accessory, *i.e.* they follow the claim which they secure. Thus, security rights securing the receivables would generally transfer, with the securities themselves, from the originator to the SPV. But it is quite common that the security rights securing the receivables are so-called bank mortgages. These mortgages have been vested in immovable property to secure the loan to finance that property, but under the applicable contract, secure also any other claim the bank might have on the debtor, following, *e.g.* from overdrafts on a current account. Where a house loan is securitised and transferred to an SPV, it becomes questionable to what extent the bank mortgage securing the house loan also transfers to the SPV. Depending on the applicable law, the answer could be that the mortgage splits *pro rata*, which means that the percentage of the mortgage that regards the loan is transferred to the SPV while the originator retains the remainder.

Where the security interests on the receivables (such as mortgages and pledges) have been transferred to the SPV, they subsequently need to be transferred to the security trustee. Depending on the applicable law, this could be achieved in various ways. Under Dutch law, for instance, the mostly commonly used way is a parallel debt construction, which means that the SPV obliges itself to pay the same amount to the security trustee as it has to pay to the bondholders so that the debts are parallel. The SPV subsequently vests a pledge on the receivables in favour of

406 This operation is defined as equity price.

the security trustee to secure payment on this newly created debt. By virtue of the accessory principle discussed earlier, the security interests that secure the receivables (*e.g.* mortgages) become available, with the pledge, to the security trustee. Consequently, the security trustee has become empowered, in case of the SPV's inability to pay principal and interest on the bonds, to enforce those security interests and recoup losses for the investors.

Under the property laws of some jurisdictions, most notably of jurisdictions with a civil code tradition, the assignment of receivables without notice to or consent of the debtor cannot be asserted against third parties, including the debtor itself. Since in a classic securitisation transaction several thousands of receivables on debtors are involved, noticing or asking for consent is impractical, may jeopardise the effectiveness of the transaction and is therefore expensive. This issue can be solved by the creation of an undisclosed pledge (instead of undisclosed assignment) under some property law regimes or by a synthetic securitisation to be discussed further here.

Also, under property law regimes that allow for undisclosed assignments enforceable against third parties in securitisation transactions, debtors commonly remain empowered to discharge their obligations by paying to their original creditor (*i.e.* the originator) until notice of assignment (to the SPV) is given. In common law jurisdictions, such payments of debtors to the originator prior to notice of the assignment may be held in a separate trust that is unavailable for the other creditors of the originator, *e.g.* in its insolvency. In civil law jurisdictions that do not recognise the creation of such a trust, this may be problematic as, in the originator's insolvency, payment of the debtors to the originator becomes part of the originator's insolvency estate and thus available for distribution amongst all ordinary creditors of the originator.

From these, it follows that it is of paramount importance to be able to unequivocally establish which property law regime applies to the transfer of the receivables from originator to SPV. However, this is not an undisputed issue and the Rome I Regulation does not provide a definite answer, although its Article 14(2) does clarify that the law governing the assigned claim determines its assignability, the relationship between the assignee and the debtor, the conditions under which the assignment can be invoked against the debtor and whether the debtor's obligations have been discharged. Consequently, under the conflict of laws regimes of some member states, the (proper) law of the receivables themselves (in the words of Article 14(2) Rome I: "the law governing the assigned claim") also determines the property law requirements for their transfer, while under other member states' laws, the property law requirements for the transfer are determined by the law of the transfer agreement. The benefits of the last option are obvious in the context of securitisations: in such instances, the parties to the securitisation arrangement need to investigate the substantive law of the transfer agreement and comply with the property law requirements of only that law, rather than having to investigate which laws apply or have been made to apply to any and all of the receivables to be transferred, and possibly comply with different property law requirements of those laws.

Finally, linked with the assignment of the receivables is whether the debtors are allowed to set off their debts against the originator against any claim they may have against the same, also after those debts have been transferred to the SPV. Again, it depends on the particular property law applicable, but under many jurisdictions, debtors are allowed to set off, at least until notice has been given of the assignment.

European Union regulation

The global financial crisis, with its widespread "wrecks," has resulted, quite unceremoniously, in being the milestone for the start of a new regulation in the financial and banking sector: after this crisis, in fact, the European legislature has attempted to create a safe harbour, in the financial and banking sector, in the European Union and elsewhere.

The academic debate has been focused for a long time on the possible development on prudential regulation, with the aim of preventing banking crises. Thus, a more stringent framework has been urged, in order to reduce the intensity of such crises.

In order to "resuscitate the securitisation market,"[407] the EU legislature, at that time still encompassing the UK, took a legal approach to this market, previously informed by a total laissez-faire approach. The ultimate aim is to promote securitisations transaction, albeit with a more rigorous regulation, informed to market discipline. This will avoid the negative consequences of shadow banking.

Bearing this in mind, the EU Securitisation Regulation[408] has engendered, essentially, three changes. At the first level, financial markets have to comply with stringent measures; at the second, a more pervasive supervision is carried out by the authority; and, finally, a harmonisation and, to a certain extent, a full unification of national rules has been achieved.[409] The last two elements are closely related with each other.

In light of the scenario just depicted, it is possible to infer that the central principle of the overall regulation lies on the quintessential importance of the "health" of credit institutions. A "healthy" banking system is strategic for both economic development and social stability.[410]

In force of a literal interpretation of the EU Securitisation Regulation, particularly as regards the STS Securitisations, this piece of legislation is to make the securitisations' market a more secure one.[411] It is obvious that the STS securitisations aim at minimising the risks, these "dangers" being immanent to all financial

407 (Bavoso 2018).

408 Regulation 2017/2402/EU of the European Parliament and of the Council of 12 December 2017 laying down a general framework for securitisation and creating a specific framework for simple, transparent and standardised securitisation, and amending Directives 2009/65/EC, 2009/138/EC and 2011/61/EU and Regulations 1060/2009/EC and 648/2012/EU.

409 (Haentjens and de Gioia Carabellese 2020).

410 (Cranston, Avgouleas, et al. 2017).

411 By the word of EU Commission, the approach is a more risk sensitive regulatory (EU Commission Proposal, 2015, 7).

systems. As a result, the asset-backed securities, linked with STS securitisations, should bear a lower level of risk and, in exceptional negative circumstances, of losses for financial institutions which had to hold them. Ultimately, these are the "terrain" on which the STS Regulation pillars firmly lie.

In essence, the EU Securitisation Regulation deals with a set of rules, whose final objective is the establishment of a European register of "quality" securitisations, known by the acronym "STS."[412]

The STS brand recognised for securitisation transactions reflects the need to create a sustainable securitisation market[413] in which the benefits of securitisation transactions can be realised at the same time. Thus, the criteria are follows:

- Simple: Article 20 requires that (1) all the originator, sponsor and SPV be established in the EU; (2) true sale, assignment or transfer with the same legal effect of the underlying assets to the issuer SPV; (3) the proof that any underlying asset is clear, predetermined and unambiguous; (4) originators or lender have the necessary expertise;
- Transparent: Article 22 stresses that (1) originator and sponsor have a duty of providing environmental performance of assets financed in a residential mortgage or auto loan; (2) it is necessary that originator and sponsor be compliant with transparency requirements; (3) there applies an external verification of underlying exposure data by an appropriate, independent party;
- Standard: Article 21 imposes the duty: (1) to satisfy risk retention requirement; (2) to document conflicts between classes of investors, bondholder voting provisions and trustee responsibilities; (3) to report historical loan-level static and dynamic performance data provided at pricing.

THE GREEN SECURITISATION

As will be discussed, there is a new approach to economy and, therefore, also to securitisations. More precisely, Regulation 2019/2088/EU:[414] the latter requires banks and businesses to apply a duty of transparency in connection with the ESG nature of financial products. The purposes of the sustainability shall be clear, concrete, transparent and measurable. Hence, the banking legislation turned, linguistically, on the expressions "sustainable finance" or "green finance."

As the regard of the ESG securitisation matter, some scholars[415] may be sceptical for how securitisations may qualify as ESG-tainted. In particular, the gist is,

412 (Cullen 2018).

413 Entailed to this is the need to build a quality market for securitisation transactions; those which contributed to this programme are the European Central Bank and the Bank of England.

414 In full: "Regulation 2019/2088/EU of the European Parliament and of the Council of 27 November 2019 on sustainability-related disclosures in the financial services sector" (OJEU, 22 June 2020 L 198/13).

415 There is a dearth of official scholarly work on this, yet. However, the relevant question seems to be reasonable.

particularly for investors but for issuers too, to grasp the real nature of a marketable product and to determine if a product can be considered suitable for the final users (the investors, by definition). Another point is the difficulty of qualifying as a green a securitisation: in other words, it is not clear what are the sustainability criteria for a securitisation which aspires to be qualified as green.

Despite this, the ESG securitisation concept was crystallised in the legislative securitisation framework, long before the adoption of the "European Green Deal" and the "Action Plan on Financing Sustainable Growth," already mentioned previously. On such a ground, references are made to Regulation 2017/2402/EU (the EU Securitisation Regulation).

In force of Regulation 2021/557/EU,[416] it is prescribed that, in order to integrate sustainability-related transparency requirements in Regulation 2017/2402/EU, EBA, in conjunction with the other EU financial authorities,

> should be mandated to publish a report on developing a specific sustainable securitisation framework. That report should duly assess, in particular, the introduction of sustainability factors, the implementation of proportionate disclosure and due diligence requirements, the content, methodologies and presentation of information in relation to environmental, social and governance-related adverse impacts, and any potential effects on financial stability and on the scaling up of the Union securitisation market and of bank lending capacity. Based on that report, the Commission should submit a report to the European Parliament and to the Council on the creation of a specific sustainable securitisation framework, together with a legislative proposal, if appropriate.

Article 1(1), par. 30, of Regulation 2021/557/EU, refers to Article 2(24) Regulation 2019/2088/EU[417] for a definition of "sustainability factors," *i.e.* "environmental, social and employee matters, respect for human rights, anti-corruption and anti-bribery matters." In this way, the European Regulation 2021/557 highlights that, in order to complement the transparency requirements relating to sustainability, the ESBA in agreement with the EMA should be responsible for publishing a report on the development of a specific framework for sustainable securitisations.

> [The report] should duly assess, in particular, the introduction of sustainability factors, the implementation of proportionate disclosure and due diligence requirements, the content, methodologies and presentation of information in

416 In full: "Regulation 2021/557/EU of the European Parliament and of the Council of 31 March 2021 amending Regulation 2017/2402/EU laying down a general framework for securitisation and creating a specific framework for simple, transparent and standardised securitisation to help the recovery from the COVID-19 crisis" (OJEU, 6 April 2021, L 116/1).

417 "Regulation 2019/2088/EU of the European Parliament and of the Council of 27 November 2019 on sustainability-related disclosures in the financial services sector" (OJEU, 22nd June 2020 L 198/13).

> relation to environmental, social and governance-related adverse impacts, and any potential effects on financial stability and on the scaling up of the Union securitisation market and of bank lending capacity. Based on that report, the Commission should submit a report to the European Parliament and to the Council on the creation of a specific sustainable securitisation framework, together with a legislative proposal, if appropriate.[418]

The crucial aspect is the consideration that the disclosures to investors of both the integration of sustainability risks and the consideration of adverse sustainability impacts on investment decision-making "are insufficiently developed because such disclosures are not yet subject to harmonised requirements."[419]

COVID-19 SECURITISATIONS

One of the purposes of Regulations 557/2021 and 558/2021[420] is to provide support to both credit institutions and financial intermediaries to remove non-performing exposures from their balance sheets in order to be able to continue to provide credit to enterprises necessary for managing the economic crisis determined by Covid-19.

The idea behind this new approach is that the credit institution can continue to lend to the real economy: from this perspective, securitisations can play a key role in transforming loans into actionable securities. The European Commission is currently preparing a proposal for a Council Directive on the approximation of the laws of the member states relating to the approximation of the laws of the member states relating to the approximation of the laws of the member states.

Precisely, the Regulation 2021/557 contains legal provisions aimed at amending the EU Regulation 2017/2402 by establishing specific rules regarding simple securitisations, transparent and standardised as necessary to support the recovery following the crisis from Covid-19. This Regulation introduced, for the first time, the category of securitisations of non-performing exposures. This "genre" is the securitisation

> hedged by an aggregate of non-performing exposures whose nominal value represents not less than 90% of the entire nominal value of the portfolio at the time of creation and at any subsequent point in time when assets are added to the portfolio underlying or withdrawn from it because of a reconstitution, restructuring or any other relevant reason.

In other words, they refer to transactions with exposures that qualify as "defaulting" in accordance with industry regulations and to an extent of not less than 90%.

418 Recital 28.
419 Recital 29.
420 This new European securitisation regime entered into force in January 2019 and will only be subject to a comprehensive review by January 2022. See the EBA Report, *Developing a Framework for Sustainable Securitisation*, EBA/REP/2022/06, online.

Another new element, compared to the discipline contained in the Securitisation Regulation, relates to the legal provision that the obligation to maintain the relevant economic interest at 5% should be calculated on the net value of the underlying exposure, rather than on the gross value. Thirdly, in the logic of the new European intervention, it did not seem appropriate that net economic interest could be held exclusively by the originator, promoter or original lender, in relation to transactions in which the originator and original lender are often extraneous.

The most recent development in the EU legislation on securitisations is Regulation No. 2021/558, concentrated on Regulation No. 2013/575. The latter relates to the adaptation of the securitisation framework to support the post-Covid-19 economic recovery. This regulation contains a treatment, defined as prudential, as far as affected exposure securitisations are concerned. The ultimate purposes, in this specific scenario, is to ensure that the legislation cannot turn out to be an obstacle to market developments for this particular type of transaction.

The innovative aspect relates to the approach of the 2021 EU regulation. The new regulatory approach, given the consideration that the market for non-performing exposures following the crisis is likely to grow from Covid-19, adapted the risk weight for the securitisation positions of non-performing exposures.[421]

UK regulation

In the UK legal system, after the Brexit transition period has meant that a parallel regime for securitisation in the UK has been implemented. These amendments are contained in an *ad hoc* piece of UK legislation.

Some changes are "cosmetic" and are due to the fact that the UK is no longer a member state of the EU. The same term "member states" or "the Union" is now replaced with, fundamentally, "the United Kingdom." Likewise, the reference to ESMA, EBA and EIOPA (the EU financial supervisory authorities) has been replaced with the FCA and/or the PRA, the UK supervisory authorities.

Other changes concern the concept of a sponsor, the management portfolio by the sponsor, due diligence, and so.

In order to facilitate the transition from the EU Securitisation Regulation regime to that under the UK Securitisation Regulation, the UK regulators have put in place various transitional norms under temporary transitional powers granted to them by the UK Treasury for a limited period until 31 March 2022 (the so-called TTP period). This means that in many cases, UK regulated entities can continue to comply with the previous requirements under the EU Securitisation Regulation instead of the UK Securitisation Regulation, while they prepare to comply with the new UK regime. In particular, UK originators, sponsors and SSPEs may use the EU disclosure templates rather than the UK disclosure templates during the TTP period.

There are a number of points to consider in terms of the practical impact of the separate EU and UK securitisation regimes. Firstly, in each transaction it is

421 (de Gioia Carabellese and Della Giustina 2023).

important to consider to what extent there will need to be compliance with each regime by entities which are directly subject to it.[422]

Transaction parties will also need to consider whether the transactions will be targeted at, or be funded (initially or in the future) that is, by, EU and/or UK investors. The related wording in prospectuses and other offering documents, transaction documents and documents such as risk retention memos will need to be drafted accordingly, and we are currently seeing a range of different approaches in the market, depending on the degree of compliance required under the directly applicable requirements of the Securitisation Regulations, or contractually agreed to by non-EU or non-UK entities.

Moreover, on July 2023 it was published the Securitisation Regulation 2023, Policy Note,[423] it states that securitisations activity in the UK is primarily regulated under the European Securitisation Regulation.

However, with this new piece of legislation new provisions shall be introduced or modified within the legislation. In this respect, there are five main points.

First, the power of the FCA: the FCA will not be permitted to make rules under the Designated Activities Regime,[424] regarding rulemaking powers in certain areas for PRA-authorised firms. The FCA does have a new power, addressed to both authorised and unauthorised firms subject to its rules under the DAR.

Second, regarding due diligence, it introduces obligations to make due diligence rules for institutional investors when investing in a securitisation and sets the definition of "institutional investor" for these purposes. The main goal is to ensure clarity in legislation regarding the scope of firms which should be subject to due diligence requirements.

Another area is still concerned with due diligence, albeit on occupational pension schemes: in this case, the duty to control information, management decisions and to give more information, turns out to be boosted.

Further, the official document highlights that this piece of legislation "is unique to many other pieces of retained EU law on financial services"[425] because FCA, PRA and TPR are responsible for supervising compliance with this new legal framework.

Finally, HM is authorised to designate other jurisdictions if a jurisdiction's law and practice has equivalent effect to applicable UK law. The latter requirement refers also to requirements for STS securitisations currently in retained EU law, which will be repealed and replaced by regulator rules.

422 Where, for example, one of the parties is located in the EU and another party is located in the UK, there will need to be compliance with the relevant aspects of the two regimes, and this will need to be considered carefully.

423 Securitisation_Regulations_2023_-_Policy_Note__1.pdf (publishing.service.gov.uk).

424 Also DAR, introduced by FSMA 2023, is designed to enable the FCA to make rules in respect of activities, products, or conduct which may not be regulated activities under FSMA 2000 and which apply to a broader range of entities than authorised persons.

425 Securitisation_Regulations_2023_-_Policy_Note__1.pdf (publishing.service.gov.uk), para. 4.16.

To summarise, it is possible to say the following:

- The EU regulatory regime will be maintained for securitisation repositories (SRs) and third-party verifiers (TPVs);
- In the UK TPV authorisation is named registration;
- Key definitions, provisions and certain requirements, such as the requirement for originators and/or sponsors of STS securitisations, will be restated.

Privacy aspects in securitisations

In a traditional securitisation, where a copious number of claims are involved, as are many debtor counterparties, the notice cannot be considered a viable solution. Indeed, the mechanism described could undermine the effectiveness of the operation and, if it were to be carried out in practice, it would become extremely expensive. The solution could be the use of a pledge or the creation of a synthetic securitisation.

If reference is made to the different systems of transfer of ownership that allows undisclosed assignment to become effective against third parties via public forms of publicity, debtors remain entitled to fulfil their obligations, via a payment to be made to the original owner, therefore the originator. This would be possible until notification of the sale to the SPV would take place.

In common law systems, debtors' payments to the originator, prior to the notification of the assignment, may be made to a trust. The relative amount of money flowing into the trust, cannot be "attacked" by other creditors of the originator in case of insolvency.

Within a securitisation transaction, an important number of parties could have access to pieces of information about the assets, which are the subject matter of the principal transaction (the sale of receivables). In this way, by example, rating agency, SPV and trustees are only potential parties that could have access to information belonging to the originator.

This aspect may be assessed within the GDPR legislative framework:[426] the aim of the GDPR Regulation is to have a global disposition, in the European Union area regarding personal data protection.

In turning the focus on securitisations, the privacy aspect and its underpinning legal "universe," at least the EU version, entails that the correct information to interested parties shall be verified. Every securitisation transaction implies the processing of personal data pertaining to the debtor and, more in general, the successors thereto. These elements are basic information or personal data, earnings, capital (or assets). They are usually included in paper and electronic documents which are passed by the transferor to the transferee.

426 Regulation 2016/679/EU of the European Parliament and of the Council of 27 April 2016 on the protection of natural persons with regard to the processing of personal data and on the free movement of such data, and repealing Directive 95/46/EC (General Data Protection Regulation).

Bearing this in mind, there is a crucial problem: it is extremely complex to provide the privacy policy to a very important number of people. In other words, the performance of the servicer is very excessive in relation to the protected right.

The way out, in this scenario, thanks to the business practice that has unfolded, is to obtain a statement from the debtor in which the last one certifies the authorisation for the processing of personal data by the guarantee. The duty of the bank, in application of the principal of due diligence, shall lie on the assessment as to whether this has been fulfilled.[427]

Personal data and peer-to-peer securitisations

A new scenario could unfold dependent on the role played by owners of platforms: not only does this engender a potential labour law problem, but also privacy issues entailed to the users of these services may be sparked off.

More in detail, should we admit that personal data can become the subject matter of securitisations, the funding of the platform economy could originate from personal data securitisations.

Tentatively, in personal data securitisation, a new transaction is concerned: the economic transaction may be identified in the QR code. This system is hinged upon the management, in a synthetic way, of personal data which are transferred to ensure that a smart city – in fact, a smart society – can be implemented.

In this "mosaic," the piece of personal data becomes a loan to be assigned to a third party, the SPV. However, the way the personal data will be transferred, in a more heterodox model of securitisation, is via the "QR" code. It is not too speculative to affirm that in the future the QR code will be to the securitisation, as the smart card was initially to the payment of commercial transactions.

The "green caveat" of this techno-oriented securitisation is given by the "green nature" of the underlying purpose of the loan, that it to say the fact that the loan caters for an environmental finality. Admittedly, this ultra-synthetic securitisation seems to be partly reminiscent of a peer-to-peer mechanism of lending. In fact, although this kind of transaction is still more potential than actual, their characterisation as mixed transactions is the likely outcome of their legal perusal, as things are at present.

To sketch out the contours of this heterodox securitisation, a few points are worthy of further analysis.

In the last ten years, the peer-to-peer business has interfered with the banking activity, particularly the one of lending money. This has unleashed a de facto competition of individuals, and entities too, both outside the supervisory perimeter of the regulator, against traditional banks. The strength of these centrifugal forces has been so much as to shake the foundations of the traditional banking sector.

Likewise, the heterodox securitisation, as an unconventional form of structured finance transaction, in cases where it related to personal data to be assigned with a

427 (de Gioia Carabellese and Della Giustina 2023).

high degree of velocity via a QR Code, could be regarded as a new financial phenomenon – namely, a peer-to-peer securitisation.[428]

THE NEW SEASON FOR SHADOW BANKING

Bearing in mind the burning question is, if we can discuss it again in 2023, about shadow banking.

The existence of a strong regulation in the aftermath of financial crisis requires the rethinking of this concept. In this respect, shadow banking is classified between two other typologies: shadow banking 1.0. and shadow banking 2.0.

The first one, shadow banking 1.0., shall refer to the 2007–2008 years. The second one, shadow banking 2.0., refers to decentralised finance:[429] this, as a result of its own complexity, creates a kind of opacity that obfuscates risks. Therefore, shadow banking may refer to this unregulated financial area.[430]

Consequently, there are, at least, three chances. The first one shall use shadow banking in order to identify the new financial activities based on platforms. The second one may lead to the adoption of a new terminology: for instance, the emerging financial activities shall be qualified as parallel or spare banking.

The latter, potentially, may encompass the concept of speculative finance. For instance, if we admit personal data securitisation, based on a platform system, de facto we refer to an unregulated activity. Moreover, in this new scenario, the potential bubble does not have a financial aim, but properly a human one. To elaborate, an individual may have access to the financial markets' borrowing, via a sale of personal data. The securitisation of personal data may inadvertently induce individuals to engage in practices of a dubious ethical compliance. In other words, the possibility to get money easily, via a techno-synthetic system of creation of money, may engender practices where the real nature of the individuals results in being overwhelmed by a synthetic one.[431]

Thus, this can shape shadow banking 5.0.

3.7 Islamic finance

3.7.1 Introduction

Before starting the financial and banking analysis, it is essential to focus attention on the principal concepts of Islamic finance. It is well-known that Islam propounds guiding principles and prescribes a set of rules for all aspects of human life.

Islam postulates a unique nexus of contracts between the Creator, man and society on the basis of divine law that affects, in a direct manner, the working activity of the various social, political, economic and financial systems.

428 (de Gioia Carabellese and Della Giustina 2023).
429 See below.
430 (Allen 2023).
431 (de Gioia Carabellese and Della Giustina 2023).

Thus, the principal pillars of Islamic ideology are the belief in (1) the unity and oneness of the Creator (*tawhid*), (2) prophethood (*nubuwwa*) and (3) the ultimate return of everything to the Creator for the final accountability and judgement (*ma'aad*). These axioms are comprehensive and govern all of man's actions and decisions: they constitute an integrated and whole society.

The strength of ideology realises the strength of compliance and the strength of Institution that determine the performance and efficiency of an economic system.

Shari'ah is the network of rules that embodies the divine will in terms of specific code of behaviour, by virtue of acceptance of which, through the exercise of his free choice, a person becomes a Muslim, and according to which an individual lives both his private and social life. The *shari'ah* rules are derived from the *Qur'an* and its operationalisation by the Prophet (*pbuh*) through a rigorous process of investigation and thinking across time and geographical regions.

The life of a Muslim, as individual and part of society, is managed by a different set of rules. To beginning, *aqidah* (faith) concerns the core relationship between people and the Creator and deals with all matters related to a Muslim's faith and beliefs. Subsequently, there is the *shari'ah*, and finally there is *akhlaq* that covers the behaviour, attitude and work ethics according to which a Muslim lives in a society. *Shari'ah* is comprehensive, also, of two elements: *ibadat* and *muamalat*.

The first one is rituals or, better, rites and ritual via which each individual comes to an inner understanding of their relationship with Allah. The second one, *muamalat*, defines the rules governing social, political and economic life. Properly in *muamalat* are laid down the rules for commercial, financial and banking systems.[432]

3.7.2 Principles in economic systems

The economic and banking system proposed by Islam has some peculiarities where it is seen from an Occidental point of view. The behaviour rules and norms of an Islamic system shape also the economic field.

In this respect, crucial is the unconditional prohibition of *riba* – that is, the prohibition of pure debt security and of leverage through debt. Also, debts based on a predetermined rate tied to the principal are prohibited. This prohibition is based on an argument of social justice, equality and property rights. More precisely, this is based on two main ideas:

- Profits, determined ex post, symbolise successful entrepreneurship and creation of additional wealth;
- Interest, determined ex ante, is a cost that is accrued irrespective of the outcome of business operations, and may not create wealth if business incur losses.

As a result of this, money is "potential" capital; its value is recognised only as a capital, not as a potential capital.

432 (Iqbal and Mirakhor 2011).

In a nutshell, the Islamic banking, and also financial system, is based on discouragement of hoarding and the prohibition of transactions featuring extreme uncertainty, gambling and risk.

Property rights in light of social justice are of extreme importance; hence, such rights are designed to give effect to the interdependence of the members of the community, with a view to recognising explicitly that they cannot live in isolation. Thus, the word "property" is defined as a bundle of rights, duties, powers and liabilities with respect to an asset. The main principle is that the Supreme Creator is the ultimate owner of all properties and assets, but in order that humans become materially able to perform duties and obligations prescribed by the Law Giver, they have been granted a conditional right of possession of property.

Another principle is risk sharing, based on the basis of taking responsibility, possibly even becoming responsible for the loss and its consequences. Islam has its own definition of mutual exchange, or *al-bay*: one bundle of property rights is exchanged for another, therefore allowing both parties to share the risk of transaction. One verse in the *Qur'an* (2:275) states as follows: "they say that indeed an exchange transaction (*bay'*) is like a *riba* (interest-based) transaction. But Allah has permitted exchange transactions and forbidden interest-based transactions." It is clear that, in these circumstances, there are two elements:

- *Al-Bay* is a contract of exchange of one commodity for another whether the property rights over one commodity are exchanged for those over the other;
- *Riba* in which the lender retains rights over the sum lent but property rights over the additional sum to be paid as interest is transferred from the borrower to the lender at the time of contract.

Although there is the prohibition of *riba*, in 1989 a legal opinion (*fatwa*) issued by Egypt's highest legal scholar, Sheikh al-Azhar Muhammad Sayyid al-Tantawi, gave rise to considerable controversy. His opinion was that banks may fix the rate to be paid to depositors: this legal opinion may have been valid for a specific situation, while it was never intended to lead to a general acceptance of the practice of paying or receiving bank interest.

It is essential that parties are able to exchange under a principle of freedom, as well as a concept of clear definition of the pertinent property rights: therefore, freedom to produce what caters for well-protected property rights, in order to permit the production to proceed. Some corollaries are entailed to this conceptual premise:

- To exchange freely and conveniently, the parties need markets;
- To operate in a successful way, markets need rules of behaviour and enforcement mechanisms to reduce uncertainty in transactions and ensure the free flow of information:
- Trust is crucial in both markets and parties.

Therefore, it is clear that rules governing market conduct relate to appropriate behaviour on the part of all participants to the market. The rule is that market transactions be based on mutual consent, and the latter shall be based on freedom of choice and freedom of contract.

A market supervision is critical to ensure compliance with the rules of conduct in the market place which are internalised by participants before their entrance into the market. This compliance has the role of ensuring that prices are fair and just.

The structure has, at least, five main pillars:

- Property rights;
- The free flow of information;
- Trust;
- Contract;
- The right not be harmed by others.

All of these elements together serve to reduce uncertainty and transactions costs and enable cooperation and collective action to proceed unhindered.

The concept of cooperation and competition is vital in structuring the ideal society via harmonisation and reconciliation between these opposites. The greatest distinguished characteristic of Islam is its forceful emphasis on the integration of human society as a necessary consequence of the unity of Allah (*swt*).

The components of economic justice are as follows:

- Equality of liberty and opportunity for all members of society with respect to the utilisation of natural resources;
- Justice in exchanging;
- Distributive justice.

The result of these factors leads to the fair price: pursuant of justice in exchange, the *shari'ah* required an ethical and moral behaviour of all participants in the market. A market that operates on the basis of these rules, which are intended to remove all factors inimical to justice in exchange, yields prices for factors and products that are considered "fair" and "just." The Islamic concept refers to the price prevailing as a result of the interaction of economic forces operating in a market in which all rules of behaviour specified by the *shari'ah* are observed and adhered to by all participants.

Ultimately, it is important to emphasise that the law is the direct rule of God: the market's rules are based on the general principles of *shari'ah*. It is the result of the fact that economy is part of a healthy and moral society, *i.e.* the central objective of Islam.[433]

3.7.3 Principles in the financial system

The primary role of a financial system is to create incentives for an efficient allocation of financial and real resources to complete aims and objectives. A well-functioning financial system promotes investment by identifying and funding good

433 (Iqbal and Mirakhor 2011).

business opportunities, by mobilising savings, by monitoring the performance of managers, by enabling the trading, by hedging and diversifying risks, and, ultimately, by facilitating the exchange of goods and services. The ultimate aim is an efficient allocation of resources.

It is expected that an efficient financial system performs several functions:

- To facilitate efficient financial intermediation, to reduce information and allocation costs;
- To be based on a stable payment system;
- To offer efficient and liquid money markets and capital markets;
- To have a well-developed market for risk trading.

The financial model

The structure of the financial system is based on three models: (1) two-tier *mudarabah*, (2) the "two windows" model and (3) the *wikala*-based model.

The first one, two-tier *mudarabah*, is characterised by the fact that the contract is utilised on each side of the bank's balance sheet and integrates the assets and liabilities. It envisages depositors entering into a contract with a bank to share the profits accruing to the bank's business. The fundamental concept is that both the mobilisation and utilisation of funds are conducted on the basis of profit shared among investors, depositors, the bank itself and the entrepreneur or the users of the funds. In this scenario:

- The first tier of the contract is between the investor, who is a "character" that is tantamount to a depositor, and the bank, which acts as the *mudarib* on their behalf; banks can accept and demand deposits that yield returns and are repayable on demand at par;
- The second tier represents the *mudarabah* contract between the bank, as the supplier of funds, and the entrepreneurs, who are seeking funds and agree to share profits with the bank according to a certain percentage stipulated in the contract.

As far as the two-windows model is concerned, it divides the liabilities side of the bank's balance sheet into two windows: one for demand deposits and transactions balances, and the other for investment balances. The choice of the window is left to the depositors. It requires a 100% reserve for the demand deposits, although it stipulates no reserve requirements for the second window. This structure is based on the assumption that the money deposited as demand deposits is placed as an *amanah* and must be backed by a 100% reserve. The motivation is that these balances belonging to the depositors do not carry with them the intrinsic and automatic right for the bank to use them as the basis for money creation through fractional reserves.

On the other hand, money deposited in investments accounts is placed with the depositors' full knowledge that their deposits will be invested in risk-bearing projects.

The *wikala*-based model is based on a *wikala* contract where an Islamic bank acts purely as a *wakil* (agent) of the investors, and manages funds on their behalf on the basis of a fixed fee. The mutual agreement between bank and investors determines the terms and conditions of the contract.

Banking system

The structure of a hypothetical Islamic bank or financial intermediary of any kind combines the activities of commercial and investment banking.

One of the distinctive elements is the *shari'ah* board: it comprises religious scholars, and this board of experts is very influential on the operation of the bank. An Islamic bank cannot introduce a new product without the prior permission and approval of their *shari'ah* board and, depending on the affiliation of the religious scholars on the board to any particular school of jurisprudence, this can determine the success, or failure, of a product with its target clients. The existence of *shari'ah* board provides satisfaction to depositors that the board is monitoring the institution's compliance with *shari'ah* principles.

There are also Islamic private banks: they are a group that are becoming some of the largest private-sector financial institutions, with growing networks through branches and/or subsidiaries within the Islamic world. There is no standard way of grouping Islamic financial institution, but they can be divided into the following categories: Islamic windows, Islamic investment banks and funds, Islamic mortgage companies and *mudarabah* companies.

The structure and the current practices In Islamic banks differ in several aspects between the theoretical models and the reality.[434]

The first element concerns the deviation of the structure of the assets from that which the theory prescribes. On the asset side of the balance sheet, as expected, a clear preference for asset-backed securities, based on trade finance, is evident, as opposed to partnership-based instruments, requiring the sharing of profit and losses. This preference is justified by the fact that sales-related securities are considered low risk and resemble familiar conventional fixed-income securities in their risk-return profile.

However, Islamic banks have not utilised partnership-based instruments, such as *mudarabah* and *musharakah*, on their assets side, due to the high monitoring costs associated with these instruments resulting from asymmetrical information and moral hazard. The reasons for that are as follows:

- Banks are not willing to allocate their limited resources for monitoring purposes;
- The market for partnership-based financing requires a well-functioning infrastructure where information about potential entrepreneurs and their projects is readily available;
- The majority of Islamic banks are operating correctly, while lacking such sophisticated infrastructure.

434 (El-Gamal 2011).

A reliance on trade financing is often referred to by critics, as a "*mudarabah* syndrome," and is not considered as a positive feature. Furthermore, Islamic banks prefer leasing because it is considered to have less uncertain returns than the partnership-based *musharakah* or *mudarabah*.

A further divergence is the choice, and application, of accounting policies that affect the allocation of income between shareholders and account holders or between different classes of account holders. From a theoretical perspective, Islamic finance has clear barriers in the deployment of assets between those funded by demand deposits, general investment accounts, special investments accounts and equity.

Current practice shows that these barriers are non-existent; in its function, an Islamic bank is a hybrid of both commercial and investment bank.

Scholars stress also the critical issues with the current practice, such as illiquidity, limited scope, limited maturity structure fragmentation and concentrated banking.

In the first case, illiquidity, the predominant transactions on the assets side of Islamic banks consist of customised or tailor-made transactions between the banks and their clients. There is no organised market to securitise the bank's assets and to trade the securities in the market. Thus, Islamic banks have limited the liquidity of the financial institutions. The consequence is that Islamic banks have limited themselves to a small set of classes which constrain their opportunities for portfolio diversification and its benefits. It is true that this practice is conservative, but it has associated costs from the additional exposure to credit and operational risk.

In absence of debt markets and with the lack of derivatives markets, the role of the financial intermediary, providing Islamic financial services becomes critical. The financial intermediary not only becomes the main source of capital and risk mitigation, but is also expected to undertake other activities with a wider scope.

The development of global finance expects Islamic banks to go beyond their traditional core commercial banking role and develop other areas dealing with securities, risk management, and insurance businesses.[435]

As far as limited maturity structure is concerned, Islamic banks shy away from instruments requiring a medium, and long-term commitment; additionally, Islamic banks are unable to offer opportunities to investors who are interested in long-term investments.

Furthermore, although the number of financial institutions has grown, the average size of their assets is still small by comparison with their counterparts in the conventional system. Consequently, given their small size, Islamic banks are unable to reap the benefits of the economics of scale and scope, and attendant efficiency gains.

Finally, Islamic banks tend to be concentrated in their deposit base or asset base, often concentrating on a few select sectors and avoiding direct competition. For instance, some Islamic financial institutions may specialise in financing the

435 (Aldohni 2013).

agriculture sector, but they do not diversify into other sectors. It is clear that this behaviour exposes banks and financial institutions to cyclical shocks in their specific sector.[436]

Capital markets

The development of a secondary market is important and essential to the development of the primary market. All savers have a liquidity preference, and this can also exist in an Islamic system. To the extent that savers can sell securities quickly and at low costs, they will be more willing to devote a higher portion of their savings to long-term instruments than they would otherwise. The probability is higher that primary securities in the Islamic system would be tied to the projects and management of particular enterprises, and there are various risks that must enter into the portfolio decisions of savers.

There is also another class of risk that is closely tied to the secondary market for a given security: if two securities are identical in all respects except that one has a well-organised secondary market while the other has a poor one, investors in the latter run the risk of liquidating their securities holdings at depressed prices, compared to the prices offered for the former. Furthermore, the degree of this marketability risk is directly related to factors such as the extent of the knowledge of the participants as well as the numbers of traders in the market, which determine the depth and the resilience of the secondary market.

In an Islamic system, more than in other economic systems, the role of both government and central banks are quintessential in the different levels – that is, development, promotion, supervision and control. The purpose is to ensure their compliance with *shari'ah*.

As far as the money market is concerned, one of the main purposes is to make arrangements by which the surplus funds of the financial institutions are channelled into profit-sharing projects of others. It is conceivable that excess funds may be available with some banks but no assets, or assets attract their risk-return characteristics on which they take a position. By contrast, there may be banks with insufficient financial resources to fund all available opportunities, or with investment opportunities requiring commitments of what the banks may consider excessive funds for them to take a position, and for which they may prefer risk sharing with a surplus bank. In such cases, the development of an interbank funds market is a distinct possibility. It may also be possible for some banks to refinance a certain position that they have taken, by agreeing to share their prospective profits in these positions with other banks in the inter-bank funds market. At least, it is also possible that a subset of their assets-portfolios comprising an equity share can be offered in the money market exchange for liquidity.

Both for secondary market and money market, the change is to ensure compliance with the *shari'ah*.

436 (Vogel and Hayes 1998).

In this respect, the concept of a market to trade equities is fully compatible with the *shari'ah*, but the operations and trading rules and practice should also be compliant. As far as Islamic funds are concerned, they emerged in the late 1980s operating on the basis of a principal-agent model. Clients invest capital in the fund, which in turn channels capital only to select companies which satisfy *shari'ah* requirements.

Funds may be restricted to a specific asset class, such as real estate, leasing, commodities or equities, or could be general purpose and diversified across asset classes, such as a hybrid of equities and commodities. Islamic investment funds operate on the basis of a variety of *shari'ah* compliant contracts.

In order to achieve the dual functions of credit intermediations and the effective allocation of excess liquidity, Islamic investment funds have earned a reputation as a fundamental pillar of the Islamic financial industry.

In the Islamic equity funds the stock of companies involved in business considered unlawful under the *shari'ah* are screened out before a filtration process is applied by each fund manager regarding certain financial ratios, such as the existence of debt or income from debt securities.

The first part, construction, is simple, by contrast the second part is not as straightforward because it relies on the judgement of individual fund managers and different jurisdictions have different practices with regard to other filtering criteria. Some general guidelines used to screen and filter the stock of a company are as follows:

- The business compliance with *shari'ah*;
- Stocks of companies that depend heavily on debt financing as determined by their debt ratio are eliminated; different funds set different levels of tolerance depending on how strictly they want to adhere to the *shari'ah*;
- Interest income, because fund managers also try to avoid those stocks where companies have substantial amounts of income derived from interest on securities;
- The shares of the company are negotiable only if the company owns some illiquid assets;
- Ordinary shares are permitted.

Also, commodity funds are popular among Islamic investors whose contributions are used in purchasing commodities for resale. The profits generated by the sales represent the income of the fund which is distributed pro rata among the subscribers. Commodity funds are subjects to certain conditions, such as (1) short sales are not allowed, (2) forward sales are allowed only in the case of *salam* and *istisna* and (3) dealing in certain commodities, such as pork or alcohol is prohibited.

The intermediation and disintermediation activities

The prohibition against interest generates an important opportunity for the integration of financial markets; the latter does not operate on the basis of interest resources, which shall be allocated on the basis of profit sharing, and it would be free from their relative ability and efficiency in exploiting market imperfections: it would determine the size of financial activities to be carried out by the unorganised market.

In order words, an unorganised market exists, based on the productivity of small-scale investment, the extent of the familiarity with agent-entrepreneurs and their availability to closely monitor projects. However, it is expected that the spread between the rates of return in an organised and an unorganised market would not be as wide as that which exists in the two markets in an interest-based developing economy where the organised financial sector is regulated and interest rates are kept artificially low.

An efficient financial intermediation requires more-efficient resource allocation in an Islamic finance system: it can be expected that the monitoring costs would be higher. Additionally, the need for specialisation and expert portfolio diversification and management far greater in the initial phase of operation-based system.[437]

With financial intermediation in Islam, the intermediary simply passes through the performance and its assets to the investors/depositors on its liability side. There is an element of risk sharing in the contractual agreement between the financial intermediary and depositors/investors. The assets, on the side of the balancer sheet, could be in the form of over-the-counter assets financed by the Islamic bank or direct investment in marketable securities of *shari'ah*-compliant assets.

The Islamic banks have more fiduciary responsibilities which have a direct impact on the governance of the financial institution. The focus of an Islamic bank is on the return on the physical investment, because its own profitability is directly linked to the real rate of return.

Islamic financial contracting encourages banks to focus on the long term in their relationship in profit-/loss-sharing arrangements. This means that there might be higher cost in some areas, particularly with regard to the need for monitoring the performance of the entrepreneur. There is a tendency in Islamic banks to rely on financial instruments that are acceptable under Islamic principles but may not have the best risk-sharing properties, because in some respects they are closer to debt than to equity.

ISLAMIC SECURITISATION

In order to ensure the compliance with *shari'ah*, a securitisation transaction shall be shaped in a two-stage process.

First, the pool of assets that will potentially support the bond offering are scrutinised to determine whether they offend Islamic prohibition, by involving assets that are connected with what Islam considers as sinful activities.[438] An issuer with excessive debt, or one who directly or indirectly provides conventional financial

437 (Iqbal and Mirakhor 2011).

438 These are gambling, alcohol, lewd entertainment and sale the pork products, among others.

services and charges interest would technically be barred from issuing interest bearing *sukuk*[439] because of the prohibition. In a similar way, the prohibition on uncertainty would prevent issuing bonds in connection with the projects that are considered under *shari'ah* to be overly speculative or risky, which technically would potentially bar issuers in certain types of hedges, forward contracts and contracts for differences.

Since *shari'ah* forbids engaging in activities involving excessive risk, the offering document provided to investors must clearly set out material terms of the lease, so that the investor can make an informed decision as to the creditworthiness of the bonds.

Once a pool of assets has been isolated and approved as *halal*,[440] the second stage involves ensuring the *sukuk* offering itself is *halal*, including the underwriting, standard, issues placement and the procurements of ratings. Moreover, *sukuk* offerings marketed at non-Islamic investors or non-Islamic jurisdictions also need to comply with local laws of the relevant jurisdiction. Local laws dealing with bankruptcy, trust, corporations, prospectuses, securities, secured transactions, perfection of security and tax will have also an impact on the *sukuk* offering.

In Islamic securitisations transactions, investors share an exposure to the business risk associated with the asset pool, and each investor is compensated for such exposure with a share of the profits commensurate to the amount of exposure in lieu of a pre-determined interest payment.

Contemporarily, an Islamic *sukuk* shows similar characteristics to conventional asset backed securities, issued by a SPV under securitisation transactions. The *sukuk* represents an ownership interest in the underlying assets or its usufructs. More specifically, they are

> certificates of equal value representing undivided Investment *Sukuk* are certificates of equal value representing undivided shares in ownership of tangible assets, usufruct and services or (in the shares in ownership of tangible assets, usufruct and services or (in the ownership of) the assets of particular projects or special investment ownership of) the assets of particular projects or special investment activity, however, this is true after receipt of the value of the *Sukuk*, the activity, however, this is true after receipt of the value of the *Sukuk*, the closing of subscription, and the employment of funds received for the closing of subscription, and the employment of funds received for the purpose for which the *Sukuk* were issued.[441]

Generally, they are characterised as either asset-backed *sukuk* or asset-based bonds. The first one offers predictable returns to their holders based on the

439 It is a negotiable financial instrument, the Islamic bond.

440 It is investing in anything that is not made haram by *shari'ah* law.

441 Shari'ah Standard 17(2) published by Accounting and Auditing Organisation for Islamic Financial Institution (AAOFI) in November 2002.

underlying assets. The second offers less predictable returns due to the profit and loss sharing in the underlying investment.

Islamic *sukuk* are structured in many ways depending on how parties' relationship with each other is structured and the nature and intended ownership of the underlying assets.[442]

ISLAMIC BONDS MARKETS

Illiquidity remains a key problem with Islamic *sukuk*, as there is no effective second-hand market. This is because *sukuk* represents a debt of the holder which cannot be traded under *shari'ah*, for a debt cannot normally be traded for amount other than its face value. Therefore, the holder is often effectively obliged to hold the *sukuk* until maturity or sell them *at par*, which is not always practical.

This follows properly from *shari'ah* that permits only that holding of *sukuk* reflects a direct interest in an underlying asset, as well as the fact that a debt can normally only be sold on at its full value.

Sukuk can normally only be traded on a secondary market at par value: it is clear that at this price in normal market conditions there would be no economic incentive for anyone to buy. Nevertheless, there is an exception where the *sukuk* issue is financed by physical assets. As such assets can be sold at a discount, so can any *sukuk* that represent them.

Sukuk must satisfy two elements:[443]

- The bond holder cannot be paid interest but must instead be sharing in the risk of the business issuing the bonds; any return must be calculated by reference to that firm's performance;
- The activities carried out by the bond issuing must not be un-Islamic so that the bond holder is not financing something to which their religion is opposed.

Equity markets

The Islamic economic system is also based upon vibrant markets for equity-based securities. In this respect, the most important question is as to the best contractual agreement representing a share in a joint stock company with limited liability. The latter is an issue about how to deal with a legal entity such as a corporation, which has a legal "personality" and needs to be treated as "juridical person."

Moreover, there are two categories of *musharakah* contracts:

- *Musharakah mulk* which gives the partner ownership rights to the value of assets without any specific linkage to any real asset;
- *Musharakah aqd* in which grants the partner ownership rights to the value of assets without specific linkage to any real asset.

442 (Haynes 2018).
443 (Haynes 2018).

The third burning question refers to negotiability, transferability and tradability of stocks in primary and secondary markets. Islamic law encourages trading and markets in all tangible goods and properties, although it restrains – and even prohibits – the trading of financial interest under the suspicion of trading leading through a back door to the prohibited element of *riba*.

The law blocks trading in monetary obligations[444] (such as *dayn* – debt) and even contingent or future rights generally. The *shari'ah* ruling is that the stocks of a company are negotiable only if the company owns some non-liquid assets. If all the assets of a company are in liquid form (that is, money), the stock cannot be purchased or sold other than at par value. With the changing economic structure where there is a large number of economic entities engaging in providing services and holding illiquid assets, this poses serious problems. Consequently, a financial intermediary cannot exist in the form of a public company.

The accepted practice of maintaining a margin account to purchase stocks can be questioned for the follow reason. Margin accounts allow a buyer to purchase stocks using leverage and borrowed funds at the prevailing interest rate: this situation cannot exist, nor would it work, in the Islamic economy. The usage of leverage in stock trading will eliminate a large number of buyers from the market, which in turn will directly hamper the liquidity in the market and result in higher transaction cost and operational inefficiency.

Further, it is said that trading in the stock market opens the door to speculation and leads to practices amounting to gambling. It is another element prohibited by Islam. Within trading practices, this raises the question of speculation. Recently, distinction has been made between speculation and calculated risk taking, based on information available in the market. Several measures have been suggested to reduce unwanted speculation and to eliminate the element of gambling. Among these, we can find (1) a tax structure that is linked to the holding period of investment, (2) introduction of greater transparency, (3) regulation of institutional investors who influence the market and (4) imposition of restrictions on price changes.

It is important to recall the concept of *ghabun*: the difference between the price at which a transaction is executed and the fair price. This makes for unethical transactions. The consensus seems to be that marginal over-pricing is permissible but gross over-pricing should be curbed. It should also be noted that the principle of fair price is tricky; hence, it is a pricing based on the information available in the market and the expectations of investors regarding the market and security.

Ultimately, the practice of short selling a stock is not compatible with the principles of Islam. Under Islamic law, an exchange contract is void unless the intention of the buyer is to buy and of the seller to sell, and that no one sells what he does not have. From this the question arises of trading a borrowed financial claim which does not appear to be compatible with *shari'ah*. By eliminating the short-selling

444 The references are to currency, or equivalents of currency), obligations demarcated in generic goods (for example, so many bushels of a particular grade of wheat).

facility, markets will discourage speculative behaviour, but will also eliminate arbitrage opportunities, which may hamper price discovery.

Equity contracts and markets for equity-based capital are so vital in the Islamic financial system, that the absence of such markets will hinder achievement of the full potential of the system.[445]

3.7.4 Fintech in Islamic finance

As mentioned, from the *shari'ah* perspective, finance has an impact on people's lives and overall economics cannot be left entirely in the hands of individuals. Fintech[446] applications cover the whole spectrum from the negotiation phase- up to post-execution matters, such as dispute resolution.

There is a significant increase in the adoption of technology and innovative solutions in leading jurisdictions offering Islamic financial services. For instance, in Malaysia, the Investment Account Platform (IAP) was introduced as a cross-border multi-currency platform for facilitating regional and global financing opportunities for emerging business ventures. The IAP is based on a consortium of several Islamic banks who help as financial intermediaries to channel the funds to deserving business ventures. Another example is Dubai Multi Commodities Centre (DMCC)'s Commodity Murabahah Trading Platform (CMTP) that became fully functional in 2013.

Besides this fintech application in the Islamic capital market, there is an increasing use of crowdfunding platforms for financing *shari'ah* complaint projects and, particularly for small-to-medium-sized enterprises (SMEs), housing and agricultural financing.

Within the concept of *taktech* or *takāful* technology we refer to *shari'ah*-compliant variants of the conventional insurtech. *Tartech* is a subset of fintech in Islamic finance that combines the world *takāful* and technology, seeking to revolutionise the *takaful* sector by complementing existing initiatives to extend *takāful* to the underinsured segments of the population. *Taktech* refers to the application of technology in different aspects of *shari'ah*-compliant insurance schemes or *takāful* to complement existing practices, enhance financial inclusion, serve the underinsured and promote best practices in service delivery to policy holders or participants.[447]

As a result of this, it is clear that the complexity of *shari'ah*-compliant finance does not exempt Islamic banks from technological disruption. Islamic account holders also make fewer visits to branches, relying on smartphone and tablet apps and web-based online services for everyday transactions. As a consequence of this, Islamic banks need to employ more IT staff and fewer administration.

Properly the technology disruption resulting from IT innovation requires to monitoring in a continuous way these "new" financial products with the

445 (Iqbal and Mirakhor 2011).
446 This topic will be discussed below.
447 (Oseni and Ali 2019).

shari'ah boards in order to ensure that they do not deviate from the approved templates.[448]

These monitoring activities can be undertaken by internal *shari'ah* audit staff by random sampling of the contracts, to verify compliance. Every contract must be under a strict control; hence, any irregularities should be reported by the auditing staff to the *shari'ah* board for discussion and action. In order words, every product introduced by Islamic financial institutions or substantial revision to existing products, should be subject to *shari'ah*-board approval, before they are offered to customers.

An important aspect of technological advancement in financial services is the empowerment of customers who have greater knowledge of finance than ever before. This also applies to users for Islamic financial products who are highly motivated to learn more about the subject, both from personal interest and religious conviction. There is a wealth of information on the web concerning Islamic finance, which is available to everyone. Thus, the wealth of information readily available from online resources can facilitate risk-sharing as a fundamental principal in Islamic finance.[449]

Investor decision-making and subsequent actions have been greatly empowered by technological advancement. This has increased the efficiency of securities markets by providing comprehensive information and more secure brokerage systems. With settlements being made instantaneously, there is no delay between purchasing and selling orders for securities being issued and the execution of transactions. Indeed, today, all brokerage is conducted online, with the client making purchasing or sale orders from a computer, tablet or smartphone. They are given a few seconds to confirm the order, otherwise it will be cancelled.

Often, there is the possibility for the clients to follow the prices of securities on a different screen, and in making their decision whether to confirm they have to decide themselves if their offer is best. If they do not confirm, the clients may lose the opportunity to deal at a favourable price point, so they have to assess whether price trends are in their favour or not. Consequently, the responsibility for getting the best price has shifted from the broker to the client.

From an Islamic perspective, these online and speculative activities, called day trading, appear highly speculative and contrary to the principle of participatory finance and risk sharing.[450]

Under the *shari'ah* lenses, there are, at least, two main areas: payment exchanges and capital holders and capital seekers.

The first one, payment exchange, refers to blockchain technologies; furthermore, blockchain will affect traditional uses of money in three different ways: medium of exchange, the store value and, finally, the unit of account. The behaviour is both to elaborate and develop guidelines for these three uses of money rather than react to any new product.

448 (Billah 2020).
449 (Mansour and Bujosa Vadell 2023).
450 (Wilson 2019).

As far as capital holders and capital seekers are concerned, it is crucial to distinguish between online crowdfunding platforms, on the one hand, and peer-to-peer lending, on the other. In the first one, investors can receive in return either the following:

- The capital invested (in form of *qard hasan*, or benevolent loan);
- The capital with a markup (*murābahah*), received in exchange a product (as a way to advance sales, which is equivalent to *salam* or *istisna*');
- Non-cash-related compensation (e.g. a small role in a movie, tickets to the performance of the movie produced, a book signed by the author, along the lines of a gift or *hibah* given in a safe-custody contractual arrangement or *wadiah*).

Within peer-to-peer lending, payments can be made on a *murābahah* basis: theoretically, it would be acceptable from a *shari'ah* perspective.[451] There are few studies that have scrutinised the relationship between Islamic finance and *shari'ah*.

The main idea is that tangible and intangible properties (*māl*) are defined among scholars as anything that is legally possessed and that is valuable which can be exchanged and compensated for a damage.[452] The conclusion is that *māl* whether physical, usufruct or service, can be developed through proper earnings and spending; it is critical that the means and outcome of developing *māl* must conform to *shari'ah*. In this respect, it is possible to affirm that the fundamental values are as follows:[453]

- Transparency;
- The existence a socio-economic perspective, *i.e.* a socio-economic welfare of the entire ecosystem;
- Trust;
- Honesty;
- Accountability;
- Generosity.

To summarise all, fintech is welcomed so long as it brings real benefits to human beings and removes hardship in financial transactions. Furthermore, fintech in Islamic finance must follow *sharī'ah* and it means that (1) Islam encourages innovation in financial services to facilitate mankind's activities in transactions; (2) fintech application should observe the prohibition such as interest (*rib*a), gambling (*maysir*), uncertainty (*gharar*), harm (*darar*) and cheating (*tadlis*); (3) fintech applications should observe the rules in contract, which is the pillar and the conditions; (4) fintech applications should observe Islamic ethics in transactions; (5) fintech applications should aim at realising benefits and avoiding harms in society.[454]

451 (de Anca 2019).
452 (Al-Shatibi 1997; Al-Suyuti 1997).
453 (Mohammed and El Amri 2019).
454 (Laldin and Furqani 2016)

3.7.5 Metaverse and Islamic finance

Another challenge that Islam faces, and needs to handle, is the metaverse[455] and, in the economy of this work, the finance in the metaverse, therefore the digital assets. The main question is if these digital assets incorporate risk, *gharar*:[456] in this latter scenario investment is not permitted.

After the metaverse started erupting, several forms of Islamic financing options were adapted to fit in with the needs of the metaverse. In this respect, an empirical example shall be meta-*murabaha*. *Murabaha* financing is a form of financing, where the financier will purchase the asset and sell it to an entity for an amount consisting of the asset price, in addition to a profit margin.

This financing form in the metaverse has become meta-*murabaha*:[457] the first main parties are the metafinancier and the metaentity. The latter may be an avatar or digital company that engages in a transaction with the metafinancier. The metafinancier may be a digital financial provider, such as individuals or a lending company or a digital bank within the metaverse. The digital asset may take various forms, such as digital clothes, equipment, avatars and others.

The asset is purchased by the metafinancier to a third party and, then, the metaentity either pays the metafinancier with a single payment or a series of a phased payments. All of these transactions are conducted with the metaverse's cryptocurrencies, and are based on a smart contract.

Meta-*murabaha* has a lot metaverse services, such as commodities, parallel banking activities, the equity market, leasing and the *sukuk* market.

Beginning with virtual commodities, they may be in the form of various shapes, but non-fungible tokens[458] have been amongst the most valuable commodities in the metaverse. The metafinancier purchases the virtual commodities, such as NFT or virtual, which then forms the basis of the master meta-*murabaha* agreement.[459]

This provides long-term meta-financing without the necessity to acquire the virtual asset and the risk associated with it. The metaentity will serve an e-notice to the metafinancier in the agreement that the metafinancier will sell a virtual commodity to the metaentity. The metafinancier will purchase the commodity on the spot from a third party within the metaverse. Then, the virtual commodities are immediately sold to the metaentity on the *murabaha* contract, and the metaentity acquires the title of it. Despite this, the crypto-consideration is deferred for a certain period of time, generally, three months.

455 A more detailed analysis will be realised among this work.

456 In Islamic finance, the concept of *gharar* provides a measure of legitimacy of a risk investment. *Gharar* is, of course, subject to interpretation (Brown 2017; Alam, Gupta L. and Zameni 2019).

457 After the Facebook transformation into Meta, financial data and transaction management will become key parts of the metaverse enabling individuals and corporations to transact and operate within these universes (Katterbauer, Syed and Cleenewerck, Financial cybercrime in the Islamic Finance Metaverse 2022).

458 Herein NFT.

459 Henceforth, also, MMAA.

Crypto-consideration includes the cost of commodities and the profit amount agreed in the e-agreement. The metaentity will immediately sell it to a third party in a metaverse based on the market value: the resulting crypto-funds can be utilised by the metaentity for other purposes, such as the acquisition of an asset. By the end of the meta-*murabaha* period, a new agreement is set up to purchase the virtual commodities and sold on the spot. It is clear that metafinancier engaged in the meta-*murabaha* agreement has some security.

As far as parallel commodity meta-*murabaha* is concerned, the structure of this financial transaction combines the crypto interest-bearing facility agreement with a SPV structure. To elaborate, the metaentity provides an e-notice to the SPV within the master meta-*murabaha* agreement to sell the virtual commodity to the metaentity. The digital SPV takes out the loan within the facility agreement and, then, the SPV purchase the commodities from a third party. Thus, the SPV sells the digital commodity on the basis of the meta-*murabaha* agreement. The metaentity then sells the virtual commodity in order to perform another purchase with the received funds. In conclusion, the metaentity will repay the cost in addition to a profit margin to the SPV that will cover the repayment of the crypto-loan.

Equity meta-*murabaha* represents another financing format that overcomes the concerns with respect to the security of the asset. More precisely, equity meta-*murabaha* has two parallel structures:

- One is based on a crypto-interest bearing facility;
- One is based on *shari'ah* compliance.

Although these two structures are adjacent to each other, the main difference to the parallel meta-*murabaha* agreement is that the income is utilised to service the interest within the crypto-facility agreement.

In the metaverse there are also lease options, that is meta-*ijara* and meta-*istisna/ijara*.

The first, meta-*ijara* lease agreement, is one of the Islamic finance forms available to parties. In this, the metafinancier and the metaentity engage in agreement where the right to use an asset is granted for a specific period of time. The rental crypto payments are predetermined: for instance, this may work well for digital asset financing to rent virtual land within the metaverse. The lease process is initiated by the metaentity that specifies the asset it wants to acquire and the metafinancier purchases the digital asset. The metaentity enters into a meta-*ijara* lease agreement with the metafinancier, where the metaentity leases the digital asset from the metafinancier. The periodic crypto-rental payments represent the cost of the asset in addition to a mark-up payment. At the end, the metaentity is responsible for the maintenance and insurance of the digital asset.

Meta-*istisna/ijara* is a contract that specifies an item to be manufactured or constructed where the contractor is required to deliver the item upon completion. This specific contractual scheme provides an Islamic principle-compliant project financing framework within the metaverse. The metafinancier and the metaentity enter into a meta-*istisna* agreement where the metaentity will deliver a project to the metafinancier within a specific timeframe. The metafinancier makes scheduled crypto payments to the metaentity that may mirror conventional payment advances in projects. After the beginning of the meta-*ijara* lease the metafinancier assumes the title of the digital project upon completion. The metaentity will lease back and operate the project from the metafinancier. Moreover, the metaentity has the opportunity to purchase the digital project for the meta-*istisna/ijara* agreement outlined crypto-amount.

Ultimately, there is the meta-*sukuk*, although this is at an embryonic stage. The first step concerns the establishment of a meta-SPV issuer that will issue the e-*sukuk* in the metaverse. The meta-SPV issuer will issue an e-*sukuk* in the form of trust certificates that either represent an undivided ownership interest in certain digital assets or a usufruct of assets. The e-*sukuk* holders do the following:

- Obtain the right to the income that is generated by the meta-SPV from the assets;
- Subscribe to the meta-*sukuk* and pay the proceeds to the meta-SPV issuers.

As a result of this, the meta-SPV issuer than declares its trust in the proceeds and the digital assets from the metaentity or a third party, with the proceeds of the *sukuk* issuance. Afterwards, the meta-SPV issuer then leases the digital assets to the metaentity under the *meta-ijara* lease. The metaentity is required to pay periodical rental payments to the meta-SPV issuer which may be done at a fixed or variable rate. The meta-SPV issuer receives the period payments and will make periodic distribution payments to the e-*sukuk* holders. There will be guarantees such that at maturity or in the case of default, the meta-SPV issuer will sell, and the metaentity will buy the digital asset at the prescribed price. The amount will be equal to what is owed by the metaentity to the meta-SPV issuer. The funds are then distributed to the e-*sukuk* holders. If there is maintenance and insurance required, the metaentity will engage in an agreement with the meta-SPV issuer to service the digital asset.

A peculiar meta-*sukuk* is meta-*sukuk al murabaha*: the metaentity will establish a meta-SPV issuer in order to issue the *Sukuk*. The meta-SPV issuer purchases the meta-commodity on the spot basis and the metaentity purchases the meta-commodity and makes a deferred crypto-payment. Immediately, the metaentity sells the metacommodity and may utilise it for the purchase of other digital assets. After a specific period of time, the metaentity will conduct a deferred crypto-payment and a new meta-*murabaha* contract will be created. The metaentity pays the meta-SPV issuer the profit margin which will be distributed to the e-*sukuk* holders.[460]

Also, for the metaverse space, it is crucial this complies with *shari'ah* principles and Islamic values. Properly in this scenario, *shari'ah*-compliant laws and regulations must shape a new ethical approach to ensure that these new technologies are used in a way that is beneficial both to society and which does not contravene Islamic values.[461]

460 (Katterbauer, Syed, et al., Islamic finance in the metaverse–a meta-finance framework for supporting the growth of *shari'ah*-compliant finance options in the metaspace 2022).
461 (Mohamed 2023).

3.7.6 ESG factors in Islamic finance

In financial sector is growing a new sector: the responsible investment with a focus on environmental, social and governance (ESG) elements.[462] It should be noted that Islamic finance has the same basic principles as sustainable finance: financial stability, economic growth, poverty alleviation and distribution of wealth, financial and social inclusion and environmental preservation.[463]

More precisely, the aim of Islamic finance industry is to advance companies that are included in sectors or industries that provide added value to the real economy. Investments in fixed-income financial instruments, such as preferred stocks, bonds and some derivatives are unacceptable as they promise a fixed rate of return and do not provide voting rights.

Furthermore, Islamic investors are not allowed to buy shares of companies whose main business activities are alcohol, gambling, conventional financial services, entertainment, products related to pork, tobacco and weapons.

Prima facie, it appears clear that the ESG concept and Islamic finance have the same values: however, *shari'ah* investment is carried out based on *shari'ah* principles to protect Islamic values. Moreover, it is also possible to affirm that Islamic banks shall qualify as green banking; hence, the majority of Islamic bank financing portfolios must be green or socially beneficial. Due to Islamic finance principles, banks may not invest in unethical industries but banks have the duty to encourage investment in projects that benefit the natural environment and society.[464]

By contrast, a school of thought stresses that Islamic investment criteria are more focused on excluding some religious non-compliance elements rather than including ESG factors. However, it is also true that Islamic finance has an untapped potential for Islamic social finance the aim of which is to promote and finance agriculture-based programmes.[465]

References

Acharya, V.V., P. Schnabl, and G. Suarez. "Securitizations without Risk Transfer." *Journal of Financial Economics*, no. 107 (2013): 515–516.

Agustin, F., R. Muhtadi, and S. Sahal. "The Importance of Implementing Environment, Social and Government. (ESG) and Maqasid Sharia-Based Islamic Finance in Islamic Bank." *Journal of Islamic Economic Laws* VI, no. 2 (2023): 133–158.

Alam, N., L. Gupta, and A. Zameni. *Fintech and Islamic Finance: Digitalization, Development and Disruption*. Palgrave Macmillan, 2019.

Al Ansari, R., and F. Alanzarouti. "ESG and Islamic Finance: An Ethical Bridge Built on Shared Values." *Journal of Islamic Financial Studies* 6, no. 1 (2020): 5–11.

Aldohni, A.K. *The Legal and Regulatory Aspects of Islamic Banking: A Comparative Look at the United Kingdom and Malaysia*. Routledge, 2013.

462 This concept will discuss further.

463 (Al Ansari and Alanzarouti 2020)

464 (Agustin, Muhtadi and Sahal 2023).

465 (Ma'ruf, Mahomed and Mohamad 2021).

Alexander, K. *Principles of Banking Regulation*. Cambridge University Press, 2019.
Allen, H.J. "DeFi: Shadow Banking 2.0?" *William & Mary Law Review* 64, no. 4 (2023): 919–968.
Al-Shatibi, A.I. *Almuwafaqat*. Dar Ibn Affan Press, 1997.
Al-Suyuti, J. *Al-Ashbah wa al-Naza'er*. Maktabt Nizar Mustafa al-Baz, 1997.
Bamford, C. *Principles of International Financial Law*. Oxford University Press, 2011.
Bavoso, V. "Market-Based Finance, Debt and Systemic Risk: A Critique of the EU Capital Markets Union." *A Convivium* 11, no. 3 (2018).
Bengtsson, E. "Shadow Banking and Financial Stability: European Money Market Funds in the Global Financial Crisis." *Journal of International Money and Finance* 32, no. 1 (2013): 579–594.
Benston, G. "The Value of the SEC's Accounting Disclosure Requirement." *Accounting Review* 44, no. 3 (1969): 515–532.
Billah, M.M.S. *Islamic Fintech. Insights and Solutions*. Palgrave Macmillan, 2020.
Black, G. *Woolman on Contract*. W. Green, 2014.
Bonsall, D.C. *Securitization*. Butterworths, 1990.
Borras, S.M. Jr, and J. Franco. *Political Dynamics of Land-Grabbing in Southeast Asia: Understanding Europe's Role*. Transnational Institute, 2011.
Borras, S.M. Jr., C. Kay, S. Gomez, and J. Wilkinson. "Land Grabbing and Global Capitalist Accumulation: Key Features in Latin America." *Canadian Journal of Development Studies* 33, no. 4 (2012): 402–416.
Borsellino, V., E. Schimmenti, and H.E. Bilati. "Agri-Food Markeets Towards Sustainable Patterns." *Sustainability*, no. 12 (2020): 2193–2228.
Bowles, S. "Endogenous Preferences: The Cultural Consequences of Markets and Other Economic Institutions." *Journal of Economic Literature* 36, no. 1 (1998): 75–111.
Boyle, A.J. *Boyle & Birds Company Law*. Jordan, 2014.
Breger Bush, S. *Derivatives and Development a Political Economy of Global Finance, Farming, and Poverty*. Palgrave Macmillan, 2012.
Browman, B.A. "Transnational Crimes Against Culture: Looting at Archaeological Sites and the "Grey" Market in Antiquities." *Journal of Contemporary Criminal Justice* 24, no. 3 (2008): 225–242.
Brown, J. *Hadith: Muhammad's Legacy in the Medieval and Modern World*. Simon and Schuster, 2017.
Busch, D., and D.A. De Mott. *Liability of Asset Managers*. Oxford University Press, 2012.
Cabrelli, D. "Scotland." In *Liability of Asset Managers*, edited by D. Busch and D.A. De Mott, 507–533. Oxford University Press, 2012.
Callon, M., and F. Muniesa. "F. Peripheral Vision Economic Markets as Calculative Collective Devices." *Organic Studies*, no. 26 (2005): 1229.
Carney, R. "The Domestic Political Origins of Global Financial Standards: The Agrarian Roots of American Securities Regulation." *Business and Politics* 13, no. 3 (2011): 1–39.
Chang, H.-J. "Rethinking Public Policy in Agriculture: Lessons from History, Distant and Recent." *The Journal of Peasant Studies* 36, no. 3 (2009): 477–515.
Chiu, I.Y.-Y., L. Lin, and D. Rouch. "Law and Sustainable Finance." *European Business Organisation Law Review* 23, no. 1 (2022): 1–7.
Clapp, J. "Food Price Volatility and Vulnerability in the Global South: Considering the Global Economic." *Third World Quarterly* 30, no. 6 (2009): 1183–1196.
Clapp, J. *Hunger in the Balance: The New Politics of International Food Aid*. Cornell University Press, 2012.

Coe, P. "The Draft Online Safety Bill and the Regulation of Hate Speech: Have We Opened Pandora's Box?" *Journal of Media Law* 14, no. 1 (2022): 50–75.
Coffee, J. "Market Failure and the Economic Case for a Mandatory Disclosure System." *Virginia Law Review* 70, no. 4 (1984): 717–753.
Cotula, L. "The International Political Economy of the Global Land Rush: A Critical Appraisal of Trends." *Journal of Peasant Studies* 39, no. 3–4 (2012): 649–680.
Cowing, C.B. "Market Speculation in the Muckraker Era: The Popular Reaction." *The Business History Review* 31, no. 4 (1957): 403–413.
Cranston, R. *Principles of Banking Law*. Oxford University Press, 2002.
Cranston, R., E. Avgouleas, K.V. Zwieten, C. Hare, and T.V. Sante. *Principles of Banking Law*. Oxford University Press, 2017.
Cronon, W. *Nature's Metropolis: Chicago and the Great West*. W.W. Norton, 1992.
Cullen, J. "Securitisation, Ring-Fencing, and Housing Bubbles: Financial Stability Implications of UK and EU Bank Reforms Get Access Arrow." *Journal of Financial Regulation* 4, no. 1 (2018): 73–118.
Davies, P., and S. Worthington. *Gower & Davies Principles of Modern Company Law*. Sweet & Maxwell, 2012.
de Anca, C. "Fintech in Islamic Finance." In *Fintech in Islamic Finance*, edited by U.A. Oseni and S.N. Ali, 47–63. Routledge, 2019.
de Gioia-Carabellese, P. "'Derivatives' in the Light of the Recent Financial Crises (Lehman Brothers) and Through Glimpses of Comparative Analysis." *Rivista Trimestrale di Diritto dell'Economia* (2010): 234–257.
de Gioia Carabellese, P., and C. Della Giustina. *The Law of Securitisations. From Crises to Techno-Sustainability*. Routledge, 2023.
De Roover, R. "New Interpretations of the History of Banking." In *Business, Banking, and Economic Thought in Late Medieval and Early Modern Europe,* edited by J. Kirshner, 38–77. University of Chicago Press, 1974.
Dignam, A., and J. Lowry. *Company Law*. Oxford University Press, 2012.
Dittel, A. "The UK's Online Safety Bill: The Day We Took a Stand Against Serious Online Harms or the Day We Lost Our Freedoms to Platforms and the State?" *Journal of Data Protection & Privacy* 5, no. 2 (2022): 183–194.
Du Plessis, P. *Borkowski's Textbook on Roman Law*. Oxford University Press, 2010.
El-Gamal, M.A. *Islamic Finance: Law, Ecnomics, and Practice*. Cambridge University Press, 2011.
Ellinger, E.P., E. Lomnicka, and C.V.M. Hare. *Ellinger's Modern Banking Law*. Oxford University Press, 2011.
Elliott, D., A. Kroeber, and Y. Qiao. "Shadow Banking in China: A Primer." *Economic Studies at Brookings*, no. 3 (2015): 1–7.
Engel, K., and P. Mccoy. *The Subprime Virus*. Oxford University Press, 2010.
Fairbairin, M. "Foreignization, Financialization and Land Grab Regulation." *Journal of Agrarian Change* 15, no. 4 (2015): 581–591.
FAO. "The State of Food Insecurity in the World." 2011.
Fitzgerald, D.K. *Every Farm a Factory: The Industrial Ideal in American Agriculture*. Yale University Press, 2003.
Gardner, S. *An Introduction to the Law of Trusts*. Oxford University Press, 2011.
Gosh, J. "The Unnatural Coupling: Food and Global Finance." *Journal of Agrarian Change* 10, no. 1 (2010): 72–86.

Grey, S., and R. Kuokkanen. "Indigenous Governance of Cultural Heritage: Searching for Alternatives to Co-Management." *International Journal of Heritage Studies* 26, no. 10 (2019): 919–941.

Grundmann, S. *European Company Law Ius Communitatis*. Intersentia, 2012.

Gruyaert, D., and S. van Loock. "UK Supreme Court Decision on Lehman Brothers Client Money: Equity or Lottery." *European Review of Private Law*, no. 2 (2014): 217–250.

Haentjens, M. *Harmonisation of Securities Law*. Kluwer Law International, 2007.

Haentjens, M., and P. de Gioia Carabellese. *European Banking and Financial Law*. Routledge, 2020.

Harding, P. *Mastering the ISDA Master Agreements: A Practical Guide for Negotiation*. FT Press, 2010.

Haynes, A. *The Law Relating to International Banking*. Bloomsburry, 2018.

Hazen, T.L. *Securities Regulation in a Nutshell*. West Publishing/Thomson Reuters, 2009.

Hudson, A. *Hudson: The Law of Finance*. Sweet & Maxwell, 2013.

Iqbal, Z., and A. Mirakhor. *An Introduction to Islamic Finance*. John Wiley & Sons, 2011.

Isakson, S.R. "Derivatives for Development? Small-Farmer Vulnerability and the Financialization of Climate Risk Management." *Journal of Agrarian Change* 15, no. 4 (2015): 569–580.

Johnson, L. "'Index Insurance and the Articulation of Risk-Bearing Subjects'." *Environment and Planning* 45, no. 11 (2013): 2663–2681.

Katterbauer, K., H. Syed, and L. Cleenewerck. "Financial Cybercrime in the Islamic Finance Metaverse." *Journal of Metaverse* 2, no. 2 (2022): 56–61.

Katterbauer, K., H. Syed, L. Cleenewerck, and S.Y. Genc. "Islamic Finance in the Metaverse – A Meta-Finance Framework for Supporting the Growth of Shariah-Compliant Finance Options in the Metaspace." *Researchgate – Preprint Version*, 2022.

Laldin, M.A., and H. Furqani. "Innovation Versus Replication: Some Notes on the Approaches in Defining Shariah Compliance in Islamic Finance." *Al-Jāmi'ah: Journal of Islamic Studies* 54, no. 2 (2016): 249–272.

Ma'ruf, A., Z. Mahomed, and S. Mohamad. "Sustainable Finance and a Shari' Analysis of Environmental, Social and Governance (ESG) Criteria." In *Islamic Finance and Sustainable Development. A Sustainable Economic Framework to Muslim and Non-Muslim Countries*, edited by M.K. Hassan, M. Sarac and A. Khan, 193–217. Palgrave MacMillan, 2021.

MacNeil, I.G. *An Introduction to the Law on Financial Investment*. Hart Publishing, 2012.

MacQueen, H.L., and J. Thomson. *Contract Law in Scotland*. Bloomsbury Professional, 2020.

Mansour, N., and L.M. Bujosa Vadell. *Islamic Sustainable Finance, Law and Innovation. Opportunities and Challenges*. Springer, 2023.

Martin, S.J., and J. Clapp. "Finance for Agricolture or Agricolture for Finance?" *Journal of Agrarian Change* 15, no. 4 (2015): 549–559.

Masera, R., and G. Mazzoni. "'Derivatives' Pricing and Model Risk." *Law and Economics Yearly Review* (2013): 296–311.

McKendrick, E. *Contract Law. Text, Cases, and Materials*. Oxford University Press, 2012.

McMichael, P. "Agrofuels in the Food Regime." *The Journal of Peasant Studies* 37, no. 4 (2010): 609–629.

Minsky, H.P., and L.R. Wray. *Securitization*. Economics Policy Note Archive, Levy Economics Institute, 2008.

Moffat, G. *Trusts Law Texts and Materials*. Cambridge University Press, 2005.

Mohamed, H. "Shariah Concerns in the Metaverse." 2023. Muzakarah.

Mohammed, M.O., and M.C. El Amri. "Fintech in the Light of Maqāsid al-Sharī'ah." In *Fintech in Islamic Finance. Theory and Practice*, edited by U.A. Oseni and S.N. Ali, 93–112. Routledge, 2019.

Moloney, N., E. Ferran, and J. Payne. *The Oxford Handbook of Financial Regulation*. Oxford University Press, 2016.

Murphy, S., D. Burch, and J. Clapp. *Cereal Secrets: The World's Largest Grain Traders and Global Agriculture*. Oxfam International, 2012.

Ooi, M. *Shares and Other Securities in the Conflict of Laws*. Oxford University Press, 2003.

Oseni, U.A., and S.N. Ali. "Fintech in Islamic Finance." In *Fintech in Islamic Finance*, edited by U.A. Oseni and S.N. Ali, 3–15. Routledge, 2019.

Panasar, R., and P. Boeckman. *European Securities Law*. Oxford University Press, 2010.

Parsons, E. *Non-Profit Marketing*. SAGE Publications Ltd, 2008.

Passalacqua, M. "Derivative Financial Instruments and Balanced Budgets: The Case of the Italian Public Administration." *Law and Economics Yearly Review* (2013): 447–479.

Peel, E. *Treitel on the Law of Contract*. Sweet & Maxwell, 2010.

Pettifor, A. *The Case for the Green New Deal*. Verso Publisher, 2019.

Pozsar, A., T. Adrian, A. Ashcraft, and H. Boesky. "Shadow Banking. Federal Reserve." *Bank of New York Staff Report*, no. 458 (2010): 3–9.

Prasad, M. *The Land of Too Much: American Abundance and the Paradox of Poverty*. Harvard University Press, 2012.

Proctor, C. *The Law and Practice of International Banking*. Oxford University Press, 2010.

Rakhmatovna, D.D. "Digital Market Regulation." *Science and Innovation. International Scientific Journal* 2, no. 7 (2023): 72–75.

Rankin, K. "A Critical Geography of Poverty Finance." *Third World Quarterly* 34, no. 4 (2013): 547–568.

Riley, J. *International Government Finance and the Amsterdam Capital Market 1740–1815*. Cambridge University Press, 1980.

Rogge, E. "Economic Regulation: Regulating Multinational Banks." In *Multinational Enterprise and the Law*, edited by P.T. Muchlinski, 385–469. Oxford University Press, 2021.

Rouwenhorst, K.G. "The Origins of Mutual Funds." In *The Origins of Value. The Financial Innovations That Created Modern Capital Markets*, edited by W.N. Goetzmann and K.G. Rouwenhorst, 249–270. Oxford University Press, 2005.

Roy, A. *Poverty Capital: Microfinance and the Making of Development*. Routledge, 2010.

Schammo, P. *EU Prospectus Law*. Cambridge University Press, 2011.

Scott, H.S. *International Finance*. Foundation Press, 2010.

Scott, H.S., and A. Gelpern. *International Finance. Transaction, Policy, and Regulation*. Foundation Press and Thomson Reuters, 2012.

Snowden, K.A. "Mortgage Securitization in the US; Twentieth Century Developments in Historical Perspective." In *Anglo-American Financial Systems: Institutions and Markets in the Twentieth Century*, edited by M.D. Bordo and R. Sylla, 261–295. Irwin, 1995.

Soderquist, L.D., and T.A. Gabaldon. *Securities Law*. Foundation Press and Thomson West, 2004.

Soederberg, S. *Debtfare States and the Poverty Industry: Money, Discipline, and the Surplus Population*. Routledge, 2014.

Starr, F. *Corporate Responsibility for Cultural Heritage: Conservation Sustainable Development and Corporate Reputation*. Routledge, 2013.

Swan, E., and J. Virgo. *Market Abuse Regulation*. Oxford University Press, 2010.

Szromnik, A. "Market and Marketing within the Concept of Functioning and Development of Cultural Heritage Sites." *International Entrepreneurship Review* 5, no. 3 (2019): 79–94.

Taylor, M. *The Political Ecology of Climate Change Adaptation: Livelihoods, Agrarian Change, and the Conflicts of Development*. Routledge, 2015.

Tett, G. *Fool's Gold: How the Bold Dream of a Small Tribe at J.P. Morgan Was Corrupted by Wall Street Greed and Unleashed a Catastrophe*. The Free Press, 2009.

Turner, A.H. "Federal Marketing and Price Support Legislation in Canada." *Journal of Farm Economics* 31, no. 4 (1949): 594–609.

Van Setten, L., and T. Plews. "England and Wales." In *Liability of Asset Managers*, edited by D. Busch and D.A. De Mott, 331–368. Oxford University Press, 2012.

Visser, O., J. Clapp, and S.R. Isakson. "Introduction to a Symposium on Global Finance and the Agri-Food Sector: Risk and Regulation." *Journal of Agrarian Change* 15, no. 4 (2015): 541–548.

Visser, O., N. Mamonova, and M. Spoor. "Oligarchs, Megafarms and Land Reserves: Understanding Land Grabbing in Russia." *The Journal of Peasant Studies* 39, no. 3–4 (2012): 899–931.

Vogel, F.E., and S.L. Hayes. *Islamic Law and Finance: Religion, Risk and Return*. Kluwer Law International, 1998.

Wilson, R. "Implications of Technological Advance for Financial Intermediation in Islamic Finance." In *Fiintech in Islamic Finance. Theory and Practice*, edited by U.A. Oseni and S.N. Ali, 33–46. Routledge, 2019.

Wood, P.R. *International Loans, Bonds, Guarantees, Legal Opinions. Vol 3, The Law and Practice of International Finance Series*. 2007: Thomson/Sweet & Maxwell, 2007a.

Wood, P.R. *Regulation of International Finance*. Thomson/Sweet & Maxwell, 2007b.

Wood, P.R. Law and Practice of International Finance. Sweet & Maxwell, 2008.

Worthy, M. "Broken Markets: How Financial Market Regulation Can Help Prevent Another Global Food Crisis." *World Development Movement*. https://www.globaljustice.org.uk/wp-content/uploads/2014/12/broken-markets.pdf, 2011.

4 ESG factors, fintech and digitalisation

4.1 The new frontiers in banking and financial law

Digitalisation has developed rapidly in the financial field: scholars, too, stress that this change engenders many benefits. They refer to the improvement of some quintessential factors: corporate financial performance, corporate resilience, mitigation of corporate bankruptcy and promotion of risk taking.

Although this statement is true, from another perspective it should be emphasised that this approach may not be totally consistent with the concept of sustainability.

To elaborate, with the increasingly urgent threat coming from global climate change, people are asked to pay more attention to corporate, social and environment performance. Therefore, ESG factors have become a business model.

Beyond this short introduction, in this chapter the topics under scrutiny are, mainly, technological developments in the banking and financial area and, at the same time, the sustainability goals that credit institutions are required to achieve, particularly under the pressure of global regulation. The new factor is concerned with the balance point that may be found between these two different aspects.

In other words, it is not totally clear if IT applications in the financial area shall be qualified as part of the more comprehensive sustainability concept.

Therefore, this chapter highlights the European agenda, including that of the UK, regarding both sustainability and digitalisation. A further step is constituted by the discussion about the two different pillars, that, from a metaphorical perspective, we can identify with two colours: blue and green.

The financial sector plays a crucial role in supporting growth by providing an efficient intermediary function between suppliers and demanders of capital. The reason for this lies on the fact that, usually, banks use significantly more resources than non-financial firms: therefore, they are under greater pressure to provide social benefits. For this reason, too, bankers' managers are going to expect to allocate economic resources in better ways.[1]

1 (Azmi et al. 2021).

DOI: 10.4324/9781032628646-4

4.2 The European Union approach

Early in 2019, under President Charles Michel, the European Council[2] would discuss, for the first time, climate change and the relevant actions in order to achieve climate neutrality by 2050.

The European leaders endorsed the objective of making the EU climate-neutral by 2050 in line with the Paris Agreement. The underlying idea is that the transition to climate neutrality will bring significant opportunities for economic growth, markets, jobs and technological developments. Thus, the European leaders recognised the need to put in place an enabling framework to ensure a cost-effective as well as a socially balanced and fair transition to climate neutrality.

It is worth noting that the Paris climate conference is an important milestone to support environmental welfare across the world. A prestigious outcome is the promotion of investment that supports sustainable business models; more precisely, this investment is pivotal in achieving the goals of the conference.[3]

The first document is the "European Grean Deal,"[4] in which, among other objectives, there is also the pursuance of a green finance which, as a final goal, aims to ensure this transition via green investments.

In this respect, there are at least three strategies. The first one is to shape, and boost, the foundations for sustainable investments: a crucial role would be played by the Parliament to adopt a taxonomy for classifying environmentally sustainable activities. As far as the second one is concerned, reference shall be made to the opportunity, for both companies and investments, to identify such peculiar investment. The final case is concerned with introducing climate and environmental risk management into the financial system.

One of the main roles of the financial sector is to help businesses acquire the financial resources they need and to give them opportunities for investors. The sustainability aim plays a crucial role; hence, the traditional financing options are likely to affect the environment in a negative way.[5] Furthermore, investors are becoming more aware of the value of green energy for environmental welfare, and this has led to an upswing in green finance. The latter is also to refers to a lowers credit risks because sustainable business models have less volatility in earnings: borrowers with less credit risk means lender can benefit from lower loan loss provisions and capital requirements. This is a way to helping environmental goals.[6]

The adjective sustainable, in the financial matter, refers to the process whereby environmental, social and governance (ESG) factors are taken into account when making investment decisions in the financial sector. Environmental considerations

2 European Council 12-13 December 2019.

3 (Ji et al. 2021).

4 Communication from the Commission to the European Parliament, the European Council, the Council, the European Economic and Social Committee and the Committee of the Regions, *The European Green Deal*, Brussels, 11.12.2019 COM(2019) 640 final.

5 (Kim, Wu and Lin 2020).

6 (Afzal, Rasoulinezhad and Malik 2022).

might include climate change mitigation and adaptation as well as the preservation of biodiversity, pollution prevention and circular economy.[7]

In this respect, a system of classification is needed in order to define, in a precise manner, the criteria that have be fulfilled by sustainable or green investment products. Such taxonomy should support investor decisions, avoid greenwashing and help channel capital flows into sustainable investment. The reference is to the Establishment of a Framework to Facilitate Sustainable Investments.[8]

The final aim for the European Union is to become a global leader of climate change, as environmental degradation requires a global response, which can be aided by "Green Deal diplomacy" activity across the world.

Strictly connected with the Green Deal is the new approach adopted by the European Commission for a sustainable blue economy in the EU: "On a new approach for a sustainable blue economy in the EU Transforming the EU's Blue Economy for a Sustainable Future."[9] The objectives of the latter are to safeguard biodiversity, food, mobility, security, data and more. Therefore, the blue economy contributes to climate change mitigation by developing offshore renewable energy, decarbonising maritime transport and greening ports. More precisely, the blue economy, a sustainable economy, offers a lot of solutions to achieve the European Green Deal's objectives due to reduce the carbon footprint and to contribute to carbon neutrality.

In this respect, the European document speaks about BlueInvest as a way to support sustainable and innovative technologies and solutions for a blue economy. It provides investment and market readiness assistance to innovative SMEs and start-ups, promotes to its growing investor community and helps them to raise finance.

4.2.1 The EU green finance

To define in an exact manner if an investment product is sustainable (either green or not), it is essential to have a classification system. As already mentioned, such taxonomy should support investor decisions, avoid greenwashing and help to channel capital flows into sustainable investment. In this respect it takes into force EU Regulation on the Establishment of a Framework to Facilitate Sustainable Investments, better known as Taxonomy Regulation.

It is worth distinguishing six environmental objectives by which economic activities can be classified as sustainable. In order to explain such taxonomy, we

7 (Berrou, Dessertine and Migliorelli 2019).

8 Regulation EU 2020/852 Taxonomy Regulation came into force on 12 July 2020. However, many details are established through Delegated Acts.

9 Communication from the Commission to the European Parliament, the Council, the European Economic and Social Committee and the Committee of the Regions, *On a new approach for a sustainable blue economy in the EU Transforming the EU's Blue Economy for a Sustainable Future*, Brussels 17.5.2021, COM(2021) 240 final.

can divide the area into three main pillars. The first one is about climate change and it is concerned with the following factors:

- Climate change adaptation: it covers activities that contribute to a reduction of greenhouse gas emission coherently with the goals of the Paris agreement; for instance, we can consider renewable energies;
- Climate change mitigation: the reference, in this case, is to activities that may reduce the adverse impacts of current and expected future climate change on people or nature, such as reforestation.

A second group is about the protection of natural resources, such as water, marine resources and protection of biodiversity and ecosystem. Strictly connected with this is both the control and reduction of pollution.

As far as the third area is concerned, there is the concept of transition to a circular economy.

According to this scheme, the activities that shall be classified as sustainable are as follows:

- Activities that directly contribute to the defined sustainability goals;
- Enabling activities that facilitate the achievement of such goals by providing enabling technologies or services;
- Transitional activities that support the transition to a CO2 neutral economy as long as technological alternatives remain unavailable.

This piece of regulation has applied since 1 January 2022 for the objectives of "climate change mitigation" and "climate change adaptation" and for other environmental objectives from 1 January 2023.

This legal framework is corroborated by the delegated acts, named Implementation of Taxonomy. These acts are the follows:

- Climate Delegated Act:[10] this establishes the technical screening criteria for activities that substantially contribute to climate change mitigation or climate change adaptation. It has been in force since 1 January 2022 and will cover sectors that are responsible for almost 80% of direct greenhouse gas emissions in Europe. More specifically, it includes sectors such as energy, forestry, manufacturing, transports and buildings;
- Disclosure Delegated Act: this refers to the disclosure requirements of financial institutions and corporates that enable investors to make informed investment decisions and to provide other stakeholders with sustainability-related information;
- Environmental Delegated Act: this was published on 27 June 2023, and it includes a new set of EU taxonomy criteria for economic activities making a

10 Brussels, 4.6.2021 C(2021) 2800 final, the Climate Delegated Act.

substantial contribution to one or more of the non-climate environmental objectives, such as sustainable use and protection of water and marine resources; transition to a circular economy; pollution prevention and control; protection and restoration of biodiversity and ecosystems.

4.2.2 The EU financial policy

The EU attention on the green matter is justified also by the fact that among scholars, there is a new underpinning idea involving the environment and banking systems: the traditional banking business model led to an increase in polluting emissions.[11]

Therefore, a new concept of sustainable banking, ontologically coupled with sustainable finance and, more precisely, the first one, *i.e.* sustainable banking, encapsulates both sustainable products, sustainable investments and sustainable projects.

Thus, the Sustainable Finance Disclosure Regulation[12] was developed to improve transparency, reduce greenwashing and direct capital towards more sustainable investment products and business. Following the launch of Level 1 requirements going into effect in March 2021, Level 2 requirements also came into effect on 1 January 2023.

The regulation applies to both all financial market participants[13] and financial advisors.[14] The first one, more specifically, includes the following:

- An insurance company that makes available an insurance-based investment products;
- Investment firms that provide portfolio management;
- An institution for occupational retirement provisions;
- A manufacturer of pension products;
- An alternative investment fund manager;
- A pan-European personal pension product provider;
- A manager of a qualifying venture capital fund;
- A manager of a qualifying social entrepreneurship fund;
- A management company for UCITS (undertakings for the collective investments in transferable securities);
- A credit institution that provides portfolio management.

The products that it encompasses include, but not exhaustively, investments and mutual funds, insurance-based investments products, and private and occupational pensions and insurance and investment advice.

11 (Pettifor 2019; de Gioia Carabellese and Della Giustina 2023).

12 Regulation 2019/2088/EU of the European Parliament and of the Council of 27 November 2019 on sustainability-related disclosures in the financial services sector. Henceforth SFDR.

13 Henceforth also FMPs.

14 Henceforth FAs.

The SFDR has two levels of disclosure: entity level and product level. As far as the first is concerned, the disclosure places obligations for the entities themselves, concerning their policies on decision-making on sustainability risks. The second level is at product level about the reporting obligations concerning the financial products and their sustainability risks.

From the firm's perspectives, there are, at least, three main obligations. Within the first one, the firms are obliged to disclose the potentially negative consequences an investment decision on sustainability factors and how they are mitigating the impacts. These sustainability factors include environmental aspects, such as energy performance and water usage, as well as social one.

The second one is concerned with ESG risk factors in investment processes, and requires a disclosure where an ESG event could negatively impact material investment, so as to align remuneration policies with sustainability management. As far as the latter is concerned, there is a need for additional disclosures about two peculiar products: (1) products that involve environmental and/or social factors amongst their characteristics, and the companies in which the investments are made have good governance practices; (2) products that have sustainable investment as their core objective.[15]

Also in this scenario, it is crucial to recall the Non-Financial Reporting Directive[16] enshrined a set of rules for the disclosure of non-financial information for certain large companies. The goal is to enhance the transparency on sustainability related issues. To elaborate, capital market-oriented companies, banks, insurance companies and other larger non-listed firms with more than 500 employees are under an obligation to report on matters regarding the environment, employees, respect for human rights and anticorruption issues.

There is some criticism surrounding this matter: the main concern originates from the observation that only a small proportion of firms need to comply with the requirement of the NFRD and that the disclosed information is often not relevant or detailed enough for investors to integrate sustainability information into their investment process. Consequently, on 21 April 2021, the Commission adopted a proposal for Corporate Sustainability Reporting Directive[17] which will extend the scope of sustainability reporting to all larger companies. This new directive entered into force on 5 January 2023.

In this latest scenario, the term "ESG" is used to allude to environmental, social (including human rights) and governance factors. A further novelty is about the "double materiality" standards that are both inside-out and outside-in: the impact of the company, firstly, and the financial impact on the company, secondly.

15 See SFDR Articles 8 and 9.

16 Directive 2014/95/EU of the European Parliament and of the Council of 22 October 2014 amending Directive 2013/34/EU as regards disclosure of non-financial and diversity information by certain large undertakings and groups, henceforth NFRD.

17 Directive 2022/2464/EU of the European Parliament and of the Council of 14 December 2022 amending Regulation 537/2014/EU, Directive 2004/109/EC, Directive 2006/43/EC and Directive 2013/34/EU, as regards corporate sustainability reporting, henceforth CSRD.

In more detail, the impact materiality refers to company's actual, or potential, influences, both in a positive and negative manner, on the environment and people, over various time spans. This includes the impact that emanates from the company's operations, value chain, products, services and business relationships.

The second, *i.e.* financial materiality, concerns the risks or offered opportunities capable of affecting a company's financial status, its performance and even its ability to secure financing.

These two elements, the financial and impact materiality, are deeply connected because a sustainability impact could be financially material or become so over time. Thus, this incorporation attracted the attention of investors and stakeholders since they are keen to understand that not only does a company have an influence on both people and environment, but also vice versa.

Based on CSRD, companies have a duty to publish annual sustainability reports that mandate reporting on the following:

- Company business model and strategy;
- Sustainability targets and their progress regarding pollution, biodiversity, climate change, and circular economy;
- The role of administration/management of the company regarding sustainability;
- How the company's business model and strategy integrate the interest of stakeholders;
- Sustainability-related practices, including the necessary due diligence process to identify actual/potential adverse impacts connected with the value chain and actions to prevent/mitigate actual or potential adverse impacts;
- Risks related to sustainability matters and how the business is managing those risks (the ESG factors);
- Information on intangible resources, including intellectual, human and social capital.

Non-compliance may expose EU-established group companies and, potentially, their individual directors and officers to regulatory scrutiny and potential sanctions. In addition to any regulatory penalties, established by law, it is expected that disclosure will be also closely monitored by members of the public, including advisory groups, shareholders, customers, activists, peers and other stakeholders.

4.2.3 EU financial product

This piece of regulation is expected to significantly improve the practice of sustainability disclosure. Furthermore, at the same time, it bridges the gap between the real economy and products/services in the financial sector. According to this line of reasoning, the development of standards for green financial products can support the further development of ESG-oriented market segments by helping investors identify products that comply with low-carbon criteria.

The most important example is European Green Bond Standard, which is the first stepping stone towards shaping a legal framework of green financial products.

From a historical point of view, during October 2021, the European Commission issued its first green bond raising a total of 12 billion euros, to be used exclusively to finance green and sustainable investments across the EU.[18] Further, the European Commission could issue up to 250 billion euros in green bonds as part of the post-Covid-19 recovery fund to help member states conduct their environmentally friendly initiatives.[19] In a similar way, via European Green Deal, the European Commission announced the establishment of a comprehensive framework for the transition to sustainability, targeting climate investment.[20] Also, the European Commission declared that it would establish the EU Green Bond Standards as an element of European Green Deal.[21] Finally, in 2021 the European Commission published the Proposal for a Regulation on European Green Bonds.[22] Thus, it introduced the EU green bonds standard as well as establish a comprehensive framework for the issuance of green bonds within the EU.

Despite the European Commission's aim to introduce regulation, the details of the proposal raised some eyebrows. Despite this, green bonds are still unregulated by the European Union, since the main actors are, merely, private governance bodies including the International Capital Market Association (ICMA) and the Climate Bonds Initiative (CBI).

This lack of legislation is not be perceived as a negative element rather than a sign of fragmentation or a dispersive approach of the legal order. To elaborate, among scholars it is highlighted that "the greenness of a green bond is determined by a multi-modal validation framework governed by private third-party organizations that safeguard the market from the risk of greenwashing."[23]

Therefore, the Proposal for a Regulation on European green bonds serves both environmental and financial market purposes: in this scenario, therefore, the financial market dimension does not remain a remote topic; hence, the proposal constitutes part of the main green European agenda on sustainable finance.

Nevertheless, the European Green Bonds Regulation is a novelty for three main reasons. Initially, European green bonds should be allocated, mostly, to taxonomy-aligned projects, better known as environmentally sustainable assets and economic activities, in line with the Taxonomy Regulation. Furthermore, issuers

18 (Parks 2018).

19 (Sivaramakrishnan, Basu and Dereskeviciute 2021).

20 European Commission, Communication from the Commission to the European Parliament, the Council, the European and Economic and Social Committee and the Committee of the Regions, Sustainable Europe Investment Plan, European Green Deal Investment Plan, 14 January 2020, COM(2020) 21 final.

21 European Commission, Communication from the Commission to the European Parliament, the Council, the European and Economic and Social Committee and the Committee of the Regions, Sustainable Europe Investment Plan, European Green Deal Investment Plan, 14 January 2020, COM(2020) 21 final.

22 European Commission (2021b) Communication from the Commission to the European Parliament, the Council, the European Economic and Social Committee and the Committee of the Regions. Strategy for Financing the Transition to a Sustainable Economy, 6 July 2021, COM(2021) 390 final.

23 (Parks 2018, p. 35).

will be subject to enhanced disclosure requirements based on proceeds and the environmental impact. Ultimately, external reviewers, which should confirm that all disclosures comply with the requirements of European green bonds, have to be registered with and supervised by European Securities and Markets Authority.[24]

In this scenario, the European Green Bonds Regulation recognised green taxonomy as a benchmark to define whether an economic activity and the related assets are green and whether full compliance with minimum safeguards is ensured.

Nevertheless, the proposal covered only green bonds and not all GSS bonds, that is "green, social and sustainable bonds."[25] An amendment to the Proposal that was put forward in the Report of the Committee on Economic and Monetary Affairs of the European Parliament of May 2022 better reflects the specific nature of the GSS bond.[26]

As a result of the green bond's growth, it increases also phenomena such as, primarily, greenwashing. Therefore, it becomes crucial to ensure that these bonds will be allocated according to the Taxonomy Regulation. In addition, these green criteria achieve the aim to foster market integrity by avoiding greenwashing and, at the same time, enhancing investor confidence and issuer transparency.

Greenwashing may be defined as "the difference between what the company says it does in terms of commitment to sustainability, and what the company actually does as evaluated by external parties."[27]

4.2.4 EU regulatory instruments

In order to ensure the transparency of the market, there is also a legislative framework. First at all, benchmark regulation plays a critical role in financial markets under different points of view, such as to fix the reference point for pricing financial instruments and transactions. For instance, this parameter refers to equity and debt capital markets and derivatives markets in various asset classes. Furthermore, a benchmark is a measure for performance of financial instruments and to determine financial obligations arise from financial contracts.

A further reference shall be made to EU the Benchmarks Regulation.[28] In its original version, this regulation is concerned with indices, used as benchmarks in financial instrument and financial contracts, or to measure the performance of investment funds.

24 ESMA.

25 (Pyka 2023).

26 European Parliament Committee on Economic and Monetary Affairs (2022) Report on the proposal for a regulation of the European Parliament and of the Council on European green bonds (COM(2021)0391 – C9-0311/2021–2021/0191(COD)), 20 May 2022.

27 (Ruiz-Blanco, Romero and Fernandez-Feijoo 2022).

28 Commission Implementing Regulation 2021/1848/EU of 21 October 2021 on the designation of a replacement for the benchmark euro overnight index average and Regulation 2016/1011/EU of the European Parliament and of the Council of 8 June 2016 on indices used as benchmarks in financial instruments and financial contracts or to measure the performance of investment funds and amending Directives 2008/48/EC and 2014/17/EU and Regulation (EU) No 596/2014

The legal architecture of this piece of regulation is based on three levels. The first one is the current consolidated version entered in force on 13 February 2021; the second one is concerned the implementation of the measures. The latter encompasses the implementing of delegated acts, including technical standard. As far as the latter, *i.e.* the third level, is concerned, it is based on ESMA questions and answers about Benchmark Regulation.

Some amendments refer to climate and green transition, such as the following:

- EU Climate Transition Benchmarks (EU CTB);
- EU Paris-aligned Benchmarks (EU PAB) and sustainability related disclosures for benchmarks (Regulation (EU) 2019/2089);
- Delegated Regulations ((EU) 2020/1816 and Delegated Regulations ((EU) 2020/1816.

In the EU Climate Transition Benchmark, the underlying assets are selected in order to be coherent with the decarbonisation portfolio; the EU Paris-aligned Benchmark denotes a benchmark portfolio whose carbon emissions are aligned with the objectives of the Paris Agreement. A decarbonisation objective, or better, decarbonisation trajectory, means a measurable science-based and time-bound trajectory towards alignment with the objectives of the Paris agreement. This decarbonisation encompasses three different areas:

- Emissions directly generated from the respective entity;
- Emissions from the consumption of purchased electricity, steam or other sources of energy;
- All indirect emissions that occur along the value chain of the reporting company.

Where the administrators' duty is concerned, they have the following duties:

- To disclose the calculation method of the respective benchmark as well as the methodology for selecting, weighting and excluding the underlying assets;
- To disclose how carbon emissions of the underlying assets were measured, their respective values, the total carbon footprint and the type/source of the data used;
- To provide in their benchmark statements detailed information about whether and how ESG factors are reflected in each benchmark.
- To use a specific disclosure template to ensure standardised formats and facilitate comparability for investors.

4.3 Green finance in the UK regulation

In the UK legal system, the government has published a document entitled Green Finance Strategy to deliver the transition to net zero. This approach has been developed by HM Treasury,[29] and it refreshed the original strategy set out in 2019.

29 It is a new Department for Energy Security and Net Zero and the Department for Environment, Food and Rural Affairs.

In the latest version of this official documents, “Mobilising Green Investment – 2023 Green Finance Strategy,”[30] the UK government sets down these objectives:

- To promote growth in financial sectors and competitiveness in order to support the transitional global economy;
- To enhance the private investment in the green economy field to achieve net zero, to build climate resilience and supporting nature’s recovery;
- To ensure financial stability also thanks to an effective green finance framework;
- To incorporate into the financial matter nature and climate adaptation;
- To realise an alignment between two different sectors, *i.e.* financial regulation and both climate and nature.

The Mobilising Green Investment document had three main pillars: (1) the objectives pursuant by the UK government both at national and international level; (2) the will to realise an alignment with climate and environmental goals; (3) the creation of opportunities for green investment.

In the first of these, we can find a definition of green finance: “any structured financial activity – a product or service – that has been created to ensure a better environmental outcome. It includes an array of loans, debt mechanisms and investments that are used to encourage the development of green projects or manage the impact of climate change on investments.”[31]

The connection between financial sectors and industry is also pursuant by the three different nations – Scotland, Wales and Northern Ireland. As far as Scotland is concerned, it is worthy to emphasise that Edinburgh is the second largest financial centre in the UK and plays a key role in the UK’s net zero targets.

A particular example comes from Northern Ireland; hence, the Irish government proposed a range of key packages regarding green finance, such as (1) Green Innovation Challenge Fund, (2) the Green Growth Support Package and (3) Energy and Resource Efficiency.

In this respect, we can recall the “British Airways Case”:[32] in 2021, BA was the first airline to receive a sustainability-linked loan tied to one of its sustainability targets. More precisely, BA entered into a sustainability-linked assets-finance structure with a total of $785 million to finance seven new-generation fuel-efficient aircraft. The mechanisms used were enhanced equipment trust certificates, commonly referred as EETCs.

In order to support the financial purposes, in the Chapter 2, the UK government has the duty to build a framework to achieve the ambitious global sustainable financial standards. In this respect, quintessential is transparency, in order to inform both investors and consumers through the disclosure of information by corporates and in the financial sector. Further, it is essential that investors and consumers are able to access the sustainability information, therefore, the access to sustainability information is central to pursuant this. Another objective is to identify investment

30 Mobilising Green Investment – 2023 Green Finance Strategy (publishing.service.gov.uk).

31 Mobilising Green Investment – 2023 Green Finance Strategy (publishing.service.gov.uk), 18.

32 British Airways will be also defined as BA.

opportunities, to ensuring sustainability claims and protect consumers against greenwashing.

Another milestone of this second chapter is the transition plan. Should we define this expression, transition plan refers to: "a) high-level targets organisations are using to mitigate climate risk, including greenhouse gas reduction targets, b) interim milestones, and c) actionable steps the organisation plans to take to hit those targets."[33]

It is stressed that the transition plans have the potential to mobilise green and transition finance at a transformation scale globally, creating new economic opportunities. Thus, the UK government wishes to encourage companies to plan for their transition but does not wish to place undue burdens onto companies whose size or scale makes mandatory disclosure unreasonable. Moreover, the UK government will work with the Financial Conduct Authority to ensure transition plan requirements are delivered across the financial services sectors alongside requirement across listed private companies.

Ultimately, Chapter 3 is focused on mobilising and creating opportunities for green investment: the goal is to become the most competitive, attractive and innovative in the world.

The investments priorities across the green objectives are the following:

- Net zero and energy security;
- Nature: the finance made up principally of investment nature-based solutions for carbon sequestration, food risk management and water quality;
- Climate adaptation and resilience.

In this respect, the document recalls a case study of offshore wind; this example shows the effectiveness of UK policy framework in attracting private investment. In 2014, the UK government supported the offshore wind sector via a support scheme named "Renewables Obligation and Final Investment Decision Enabling for Renewables." At the moment, the UK has the highest deployment of offshore wind capacity in Europe and it is also the site of the first, second, third and fourth largest operational offshore wind farm projects in the world.

The actions set out to support business and investors are as follows:

- Research and innovation support in new and emerging technology;
- Commercialisation to support the new technologies;
- Help actions coming from government to grow green sectors;
- Support transition to greener practices in the established sectors;
- Enable and stimulate investment into climate resilience and supporting the adaptations across the economy.

As far as the support transition to greener practices, a case study is the well-known Clean Growth Fund.[34] In the 2019 Green Finance Strategy committed £20 million

33 Mobilising Green Investment – 2023 Green Finance Strategy (publishing.service.gov.uk), 40.
34 Henceforth also CGF.

to a new clean growth venture capital fund with a view to catalysing the Clean Growth equity financial market. This fund is a venture capital fund backed by both public and private investors.

CGF is an independent venture capital fund managed by Clean Growth Investment Management LLP, and it is based on speeding up the commercialisation of innovative UK-based clean technologies. The aim of the latter shall be to reduce GHG emissions. CGF makes direct investments in companies seeking to commercialise promising technologies. Investments, more precisely, are made across the technology spectrum, including hardware, software, process systems, materials, deep tech and business model innovations.

About the investment in nature markets, the UK government is investing £30 million Big Nature Impact Fund (BNIF), a fund managed by Federated Hermes and Finance Earth.[35] BNIF will accelerate, across the England, high-integrity nature projects that generate revenue from ecosystem services such as carbon sequestration, biodiversity and water quality by creating biodiversity woodlands and other priority habitats and restoring peatlands.

In order to support the transition to net zero, resilient and nature positive economy, the lines on which the government works are as follows:

- Circular economy;
- Decarbonising oil and gas production in the North Sea through electrification of infrastructure and cessation of routine flaring;
- Supporting energy security;
- Enhancing investment in landscape for renewable energies in order to decarbonise the energy sector;
- Supporting local areas via monetisation of insurance benefits from flood resilience to climate risk and innovation in financing mechanisms to support residents in properties impacted by sea level rise.

4.4 The role of central bank in the green transition

Climate change is perceived as one of the most pressing social and economic issues of the day. One of the consequences of this pressure is the presumption that central banks play a significant role play in addressing environmental challenges.[36] As a result of this, both the Bank of England and the European Central Bank have argued that central banks have a new role.[37] The latter shall be interpretated in order to encompass, climate and environmental risks.

35 UK Government (2022), Press notice: Update on the The Big Nature Impact Fund, www.gov.uk/government/news/update-on-the-big-nature-impact-fund.

36 (Cullen 2023).

37 European Parliament, "New ECB boss quizzed for the first time by Economic Affairs Committee" (Press Release 2 December 2019) (www.europarl.europa.eu/news/en/press-room /20191202IPR 67811/new-ecb-boss-quizzed-for-the-first-time-by-economic-affairs-committee).

Another example comes from the US: the president of the Federal Reserve Bank of San Francisco has indicated that studying climate risk is "essential" to its mission of economic and financial stability.[38]

These central bankers are now taking action collectively at the global level: a group of eight central banks, including the Bank of England and Banque de France, formed the Network for Greening the Financial System[39] as organised, in a voluntary way, an examination to what central banks can do to address climate change.[40]

The climate change has become a better example of operational risk because heavy damage to bank property, diminished operating capacity and associated reputational risk could impact on the value of a shareholder's investment in a bank. To elaborate, emergency or catastrophic events, such as severe or abnormal whether conditions, become more chronic and have disruptive effects on the business activities.[41]

This point is central for the Central Bank; hence, it provides critical services for the economy, such as payments and credit transactions, which require their physical system to remain functioning smoothly.[42] Mainly, regulators address operational risk by requiring banks to hold an additional capital charge reflecting an estimated loss from an operational event which requires banks to use historical data and information about the bank's business environment and control systems, to assess themselves a capital surcharge.[43]

To elaborate, not only do central banks have an interest to assess the impacts of climate change in the economy, but also, in some cases, they are under an obligation to do so for some reason. These are the follows:

- Climate change and policies to counter it affect the structure and dynamics of the economy and the financial system, posing risks to both price and financial stability;
- Climate change could increase the riskiness of the assets held on central banks sheets potentially leading to financial losses;
- Climate change could also be translated into higher credit risk by affecting the ability of counterparties, issuers and debtors to service their obligations;
- The mandate of various central banks obliged them to support general economic policies of their respective governments in some cases subjects to the requirements that such actions do not prejudice the price stability mandate.

38 Mary C. Daly, President & CEO, Fed. Rsrv. Bank of S.F., Speech at the Economics of Climate Change Conference: Why Climate Change Matters to Us 4 (8 Nov. 2019), www.frbsf.org/our-district/press/presidents-speeches/mary-c-daly/2019/november/whyclimate-change-matters-to-us/.

39 Henceforth NGFS.

40 Origin and Purpose, Network for Greening the Fin. SYS., www.ngfs.net/en/about-us/governance/origin-and-purpose (last visited 14 Sept. 2021) [https://perma.cc/8NZ3-AQJG].

41 See JPMorgan Chase & Co., Annual Report (Form 10-K), at 20 (25 Feb. 2020).

42 (Skinner 2021).

43 Basel Comm. on Banking Supervision, Operational Risk-Supervisory Guidelines for the Advanced Measurement Approaches (2011), www.bis.org/publ/bebs196.pdf [https://perma.cc/Q697-BXDS].

In this scenario, central banks are, on the one hand, in a position to promote green finance through fair pricing of climate risks by financial intermediaries. On the other hand, central banks' implicit or explicit responsibility for financial and macro-economic stability urgers monetary authorities to address climate-related and other environmental risks on a systemic level. It is clear that the role and the potential of central banks and financial and regulation authorities in green finance is crucial.[44]

Among scholars, it is emphasised that climate disasters may engender a systemic risk: if the company cannot insure themselves against catastrophe risk, unless they charge customers on the relevant price, their ability to withstand losses occurring due climate-related events will be unbearable. Furthermore, if they are the counterparties to the bank, any distress they have may be part of a banking system.[45]

Central banks respond to climate change via two different methodologies. The first category of measures includes protecting the bank's sheets and preserving their ability to deliver on price stability mandate against materialisation of climate risk. The protective action is regarding as supporting the central bank's price stability mandate. For example, these activities include the effect of climate change on the economy and financial policy, and consequently monetary policy, to develop a monetary policy strategy that is resilient to climate change and to incorporate climate change into the analytical toolkit.

By contrast, proactive measures are to enhance greening non-monetary portfolios, such as pension funds; to support greening foreign reserves management; and to promote greening the collateral framework for monetary policy operation.

The second category is concerned with central bank actions aimed at raising awareness of climate risk. These actions help to promote green finance and sustainable growth without an active use of central bank's sheet. The reference is to a range of policy about communication to the public and financial community about climate risk, to informing financial markets and the public via disclosure about the carbon footprint of a central bank's own balance sheet.

This approach will not come without a price and a risk: a green monetary policy could realise a distortion of financial markets, especially when green bonds become a scarcity. The transmission of monetary policy could be hampered if certain financial institutions are excluded from accessing central bank facilities. Furthermore, given the absence of a clear taxonomy and accepted market standards (what it is green and what is polluting investment), central banks lack an objective definition and a legal ground for their green policies.[46]

4.4.1 The concept of green bank

Based on this, among scholars it is possible to find the concept of "green bank," which is a bank whose operations and achievements are to encourage environmental

44 (D'Orazio and Popoyan 2019).

45 (Cullen, After "HLEG": EU Banks, Climate Change Abatement and the Precautionary Principle 2018).

46 (Boneva, Ferrucci and Mongelli 2022).

activities and reduce carbon emissions, within and outside the banking system. Moreover, a bank may be considered "green" when providing services associated with ecological commitments to green and clean production. Additionally, a green bank provides financial assistance for loans and purchase of green cars, energy-efficient mortgages, eco-savings and green credit cards to help make environment sustainable.

Another aspect involves the fight against climate change: gradually, green banks promote green banking operations and direct credit flows to sponsor environmentally friendly projects and promote green productions service and consumption industries, clean energy and renewable energy.[47]

Furthermore, the concept of green banking is part of the macro-notion of sustainable banking. The latter has the aim of supporting sustainable development goals: banking is sustainable where it may be considered as a global initiative to transform the traditional banking concept and develop new sustainable business models.

In this respect, sustainable banking involves green banking practices to incorporate environmental considerations, community practices and ethical values. Green banking, thus, has various types of practices: it provides, for instance, low interest rate loans for greener investment in the early period of green banking development; it supports the development of certain industries with environmental concerns, such as renewable energies, energy efficiency and green building.[48]

4.4.2 The role of the European Central Bank

Although climate change is a global issue, in the European Union the discussion between central banking and environment is particularly crucial for three different reasons:

- The mandate of the European Central Bank[49] is framed in the treaties that make up, *de facto*, the EU's constitutional charter;
- There are important court decisions coming from the European Court of Justice[50] about ECB's mandate;
- There is also a dialogue between national and supranational level regarding environmental matters. It is worthy of emphasis that ECB has 20 counterparties.

As far as case law is concerned, the reference is to *Weiss and Others*[51] and the position on this by the German Constitutional Court.[52] The latter held that the ECJ exceeds its judicial mandate as determined by the functions conferred upon it.[53]

47 (Thin Hang 2022).
48 (Gunawan, Permatasari and Sharma 2022).
49 Henceforth ECB.
50 Henceforth ECJ.
51 C-493/17.
52 BVerfG, Judgment of the Second Senate of 5 May 2020–2 BvR 859/15 -, paras. 1-237.
53 See Article 19(1) Treaty on European Union.

Weiss is a case stemming from an action against German institutions in the context of the ECB's Public Sector Purchase Programme (PSPP) an asset purchase programme launched in 2015 and still in force. The German Federal Constitutional Court referred the case to the Court of Justice, questioning the validity of the ECB's decisions: the first one had doubts over the compatibility of the PSPP's decision with the prohibition, established by the treaty, on monetary finance and the principle of conferred powers. Despite this, the ECJ confirmed the legality of the ECB's decision.

Unlike other central banks, the ECB has as primary objects to maintain price stability; therefore, if its first objective is in a situation of conflict with others, the first takes precedence.

As far as the environment is concerned, the latter has little to do with maintaining price stability: Article 127(1) TFEU first sentence states, "The primary objective of the European System of Central Banks [hereinafter referred to as 'ESCB'] shall be to maintain price stability." Therefore, at first sight, the environment has little relevance. Therefore, the second sentence of Article 127 (1) TFUE says, "Without prejudice to the objective of price stability, the ESCB shall support the general economic policies in the Union with a view to contributing to the achievement of the objectives of the Union."

This second principle shall be read under the lenses of the EU constitutional law and, more precisely, the principle of institutional balance[54] in force of which the ECB shall exercise its power with due regard for the powers of other institutions.

Article 127(1) second sentence says also that another goal of EU is to work to realise a "sustainable development of Europe based on balanced economic growth and price stability, a highly competitive social market economy, aimed at full employment and social progress, and a high level of protection and improvement of the quality of the environment."[55]

Ultimately, the reference to "general economic polices" is encapsulated into Article 127(1), which includes not only the economic matter but also the policies. In the latter there is also the sustainability principle; indeed, Article 3 TEU states that one of the goals of the internal market is "the sustainable development of Europe based on balanced economic growth and price stability . . . and a high level of protection and improvement of the quality of the environment."

Consequently, if we read together these two legal provisions, it becomes clear that one of the duties of the EU is to take into account broader objectives, when setting its broad economic guidelines aiming at sustainable development.[56]

Ultimately, although ECB is an independent technical institution with a specific competence, *i.e.* to maintain price stability, it has also other two duties: (1) to incorporate environmental consideration in pursuing this objective and (2) to support general economic policies in the Union to achieve the objectives of the EU. As a

54 See Article 13(2) TEU.

55 More precisely the reference is to Article 3(3) TUE recalled by Article 127(1).

56 Recommendation for a Council Recommendation on the economic policy of the euro area, COM(2020)746 final.

result of this, under certain conditions, treaties require the ECB to take into account climate change considerations.[57]

4.4.3 The Bank of England approach

It is well known that in early 2015, the Bank of England[58] emerged as one of the first movers on climate change among high-income economy central banks. However, it is also noted that BoE should be enabled to respond about climate change as a result of a piece of policy actions.

The government legislation was crucial to both catalysing the BoE's approach to climate change and providing the certainty of a transition pathway. The BoE's initial report about climate change was prompted by a request from the Department for Environment, Food & Rural Affairs (Defra) for the PRA to complete a Climate Change Adaptation Report.

This report was established as a part of the 2008 Climate Change Act landmark legislation that set up legally binding carbon targets for the purpose of informing the government's climate strategy.

Moreover, the government has utilised the BoE's annual remit letters from the chancellor of the exchequer to provide political legitimacy for the BoE to support this transition in the face of criticism.

Bearing this in mind, the BoE's market-shaping attention to climate change is a significant development in realising a link between climate change actions and prices and financial stability. A second market was also utilised in doing so. The result of this is a proactive approach to addressing climate change when setting low-carbon transition.[59]

As far as the second market is concerned, we can recall two alternative markets: the voluntary carbon markets and nature markets.

The first one enables carbon credits to purchase, usually via organisations, for use against voluntary climate commitments, as opposed to legally binding emissions reductions obligations.

The second one, nature markets, enable farmers and natural resources managers to sell carbon and other ecosystem services through sustainable management and nature restoration projects. Empirical cases are the Peatland Code and the UK Saltmarsh Code: these are voluntary certification standards for UK peatland restoration projects. These certifications show that a consistent approach to projects wishing to attract carbon finance is viable.

Despite this, the BoE does not work alone, because it is surrounded by others, such as the Green Finance Institute.[60] It was launched in 2019 with seed funding by the UK government and aims to support the mainstreaming of green finance both in the UK and overseas. Its strategy has been to identify the barriers to investment

57 (Zilioli and Ioannindis 2022).
58 Henceforth also BoE.
59 (DiLeo 2023).
60 Henceforth GFI.

in real economy decarbonisation by sector and committing to develop the solutions to overcome them.

Moreover, the UK has been a pioneer in the use of market mechanisms to mobilise finance for climate and nature since 2002 when it was established European's first Emissions Trading Schemes.

Thanks to this, the capital market has also changed and, in the contemporaneous era, has truly become a venue in which nature and finance work together. An empirical case is the Farmer and Finance project; this is a working group on financing a farming transition that identifies barriers and corresponding enablers under the themes of data, priority environmental outcomes, environmental markets principles and aggregation models. The UK government will progress work in each of these areas including through actions set out in this strategy and help farmers to identify and have access to private sector investment to pay for nature outcomes.

As a result of this, a new market arises, which is the voluntary carbon and nature market, to contribute to net zero and wider environmental improvement.

Prima facie these organisations appear not to be encompassed into the activity of the Bank of England; however, it should be noted that these policies come from studies conducted in 2017.[61]

In conclusion, it seems that UK's Central Bank is still playing a key role as a global actor in order to facilitate the transition to net zero.[62] The other face of this coin is the need to give a new interpretation of this mandate to define the governance and finance. In a nutshell we can say the following:

- This approach is hybrid;
- The Bank of England shows a greater institutional sensitivity to environmental impact;
- The future of the role of the Bank of England remains uncertain;
- The Bank of England is playing a crucial and central role in the global economy in the Anthropocene era.[63]

4.5 IT in financial sector: fintech

As demonstrated earlier, one of the achievements of the green transition is to realise also the digital transition. The milestone idea is that an innovative development can become a lever of competitive advantage in international markets and, at the same time, the level of innovation is currently becoming quite specialised. More precisely, the impact on the economic has also an influence on financial sector. New technologies have been emerging and have appreciably changed the existing financial services. The references are to new marketing approach (e-banking, mobile banking), new typologies of financial services

61 (Skinner 2021).
62 (Jackson and Bailey 2023).
63 (Dikau, Robins and Volz 2021; Siderius 2022).

(online financing thorough crowdfunding and peer-to-peer platforms) and a new coin, the cryptocurrencies.[64]

All of these topics are encapsulated into a big word: fintech. This involves all kinds of channels that connect technological companies and their innovation with finance. Fintech, thus, includes both small start-up players and big-tech companies that offer any kind of financial product or service. There is also a more specific approach which restricts the fintech sector to start-up companies that offer financial solutions and to banks born as pure digital institutions, also called neobanks, to use a neologism. It is clear that big tech does not belong to the realm of the financial sector. Nevertheless, fin tech does include also big-tech companies since the latter have been showing increasing interest in financial services.

Within fintech we refer to a financial technology field that represents "entities using new technologies to offer products that are either complementary or competitive to related products offered by regulated financial institutions."[65]

The interaction between financial systems and big tech was described as an "elephant in the banking room."[66]

Another phenomenon is the metaverse: it is a link between two dissimilar words, "meta" and "universe," *i.e.* "among" or "with" and "universe." In technical jargon, a metaverse is used to identify a post-reality universe that merges physical reality with a virtual digital world. The metaverse is generating several business opportunities for industries; hence, thanks to this metaverse, companies are altering their ways of functioning and ability to offer their services and products.

In this respect, one of the potential uses of the metaverse is also a creation of branches of banks. In light of the key role played by banks in the financial industry, a virtual bank in the metaverse is a digital financial institution that functions within a simulated world or virtual atmosphere. These new "meta-banks" provide services and products which are similar to those of a conventional bank, such as accepting deposits and providing long and short-term loans and various types of investment opportunities, yet in a digital format.[67]

Moreover, the metaverse is also to refer to virtual products to the financial industry, such as virtual banking, virtual stock exchanges, virtual insurance companies, virtual trading floors and virtual financial education centres.[68] For instance, KB Bank of South Korea introduced a VR version of its branch in the metaverse where employees are represented by avatars.[69] Customers can have access to banking services without the constraints of working hours or queues, and banks can potentially provide these services at a reduced cost through location-independent virtual customer representatives.

64 (Pakhnenko et al. 2021).
65 (Kuszewski 2018).
66 (Valverde and Fernandez 2020).
67 (Sarkar 2023).
68 (Narin 2021).
69 (McConville 2023).

There is not a consensus on the definition of the metaverse; thus, the most successful approach is to describe what this world is and how it works. From a literal perspective, the "father" of the metaverse is Neal Stevenson with his science fiction novel *Snow Crash*, published in 1992. It describes a parallel virtual reality universe created from computer graphics, which users from around the world can access and connect to through goggles and earphones.[70]

From a technical perspective, the metaverse, a properly parallel world,[71] is populated by avatars, virtual beings used by users, and it may be defined as a users' virtual self-representation.[72]

4.5.1 IT transaction

It is properly cryptocurrencies, and therefore blockchain technology, which fill the gap between fintech, on the one hand, and currencies, on the other.

Many transactions are carried out thanks to cryptocurrencies. Moreover, blockchain uses P2P transactions and decentralised protocols to "eliminate" third parties from banking operation.

As a result of this, both fintech and blockchain have an impact on both the banking and financial systems.

Blockchain

Blockchain technology is suitable for many applications in Industry 4.0, and it has become one of the main pillars of the whole organisation.

Blockchain technology, a distributed ledger technology, is a network software protocol that enables the secure transfer of money, assets and information via the internet without a third-party organisation, such as a bank, or an intermediary. Thanks to this platform, safely stored transactions, cryptocurrencies or data information about debt and digital assets can be safely carried out.

The piece of information, once stored, cannot easily be forgotten, or tampered with, due to the approval mechanism based on distributed nodes.

According to the European Central Bank, a blockchain is "the ledger (book of records) of all transactions, grouped in blocks, formulated with a (decentralized) virtual currency scheme."[73] A different definition comes from a law in the US, specifically in one US state, Arizona. Here, a blockchain is a "distributed ledger technology that uses a distributed, decentralized, shared and replicated ledger, which may be public or private, permissioned or permissionless, or driven by tokenized crypto economics or tokenless. The data on the ledger is protected with cryptography, is immutable and auditable and provides an uncensored truth."[74]

70 (Mystakidis 2022).
71 (Cheong 2022).
72 (Franks 2011).
73 ECB, Virtual currency schemes – a further analysis (ECB 2015), p 33.
74 Arizona House Bill 2417, www.azleg.gov/legtext/53leg/1r/bills/hb2417p.pdf (accessed 18 November 2018).

From a UK definition, blockchain is a database typology that takes a number of records and puts them into a block: every block is chained into the next block via a cryptographic signature. Therefore, blockchains can be used like a ledger which can be shared and corroborated by anyone with the appropriate permission.[75]

The blockchain structure has four major elements:

- Hash, using one-way mathematical functions to assign unique indexes;
- Digital signatures, implemented as public cryptographic keys;
- Peer-to-peer (P2P) network, which serves as a routing structure for nodes to use distributed hash;
- Consensus mechanism, which is a set of a digital procedures designed to ensure the accuracy and consistency of the stored information across the participating nodes.

The blockchain technology platform is gradually shaping up into three components: (1) underlying infrastructure which includes facilities for mining and manufacturing of specialised computer hardware to perform blockchain-related tasks; (2) middle layer between the blockchain platform and client application services, including smart contracts, blockchain platform and financial services; (3) hotspot distributed applications in various industries, including finance.

As far as the economic perspective is concerned, blockchain promotes the convergence of computer and communications technologies to digitise all assets and then register and transfer notarised digital assets on the blockchain. Cryptocurrencies should not be issued by the central bank of a government but should be completely decentralised and owned by non-state entities. All kinds of digital currencies can be exchanged freely in the blockchain economy. It was argued that blockchain can achieve the optimal allocation of resources through the form of digital rewards for mining to establish decentralised credit for universal participation.

Within the major finance and economic applications, these may summarise as follow:[76]

- Cryptocurrency and its platform;[77]
- Cross-border payment;
- Digital asset register and management, such as transferring and verifying asset ownership, home, auto, stocks, bonds, mortgages and insurance and, on the other hand, preserving the integrity and authenticity of sensitive documents, *e.g.* passports and visas.

75 Distributed Ledger Technology: beyond blockchain, a report by the UK Government Chief Scientific Adviser, 2016, https://assets.publishing.service.gov.uk/government/uploads/system/uploads/attachment_data/file/492972/gs-16-1-distributed-ledger-technology.pdf (accessed 18 November 2018), p 17.

76 (Zhang et al. 2020).

77 See below.

From an EU perspective,[78] the main goal, the "gold standard," is to become a leader in blockchain technology and an innovator in blockchain. The gold standard for blockchain includes the following:

- Environmental sustainability; hence, blockchain should be sustainable and energy-efficient;
- Data protection;
- Digital identity;
- Cybersecurity;
- Interoperability.

A token, generally speaking, is an object that represents something else, such as another object, either physical or virtual, or an abstract concept. Tokenisation is the act of converting rights over a physical or intangible assets into tokens, which are recorded on a blockchain. Again, a token is a sequence of characters that serves as an identifier for a specific asse or asset type. In a nutshell, in a blockchain system any digital asset digitally transferable between two or more people, is called a token.

Cryptocurrencies

One of the main blockchain applications is to develop and support cryptocurrencies. The latter are a digital peer-to-peer currency created by a cryptography. More precisely, cryptocurrency may also qualify as "a system of currency that uses cryptography to allow secure transfer and exchange of digital tokens in a distributed and decentralised manner."[79]

The most famous cryptocurrency is bitcoin: created by a person or a group who identify bitcoin as a "purely peer-to-peer version of electronic cash that allows online payments to be sent directly from one party to another without going through a financial institution."[80] The underlying idea is that a fund transfer may be conducted without an intermediary; in addition, bitcoin can only be stored on a computer or smartphone.

In this scenario, a key role is played by mining: it creates cryptocurrencies, by solving in an automatic way mathematical puzzles towards processing transactions of users. Thus, "mining is the competitive process of collecting transactions and adding them to the blockchain in the form of blocks."[81] It appears the relation between blockchain and cryptocurrency; hence, the first one, blockchain, "is a sequence of blocks, which holds the complete record of transactions (a public ledger) indicating the order in which the transactions occurred."[82]

78 Blockchain Strategy | Shaping Europe's digital future (europa.eu).
79 (Dourado and Brito 2014).
80 (Nakamoto 2015).
81 (Barski and Wilmer 2015).
82 (Kuo Chuen 2015).

From a historical perspective, the creation of bitcoin coincided with the 2008 global financial crisis: it is commonly accepted that bitcoin was the result of the financial turmoil, although there is no evidence of this.

The main characteristics of cryptocurrencies are as follows:

- Lower cost transactions because it does not involve third-party intermediaries that charge fees. This was true at the beginning but not yet;
- Thrustless, because "no one actor is trusted, and no one needs to be trusted." There is not a central authority, or trusted third party, in a distributed consensus network.[83] However, it is also clear that parties shall trust in the platform or digital system;
- Decentralised, because blockchain is available to anyone who is able to engage in mining by dedicating their computational skill. Being decentralised, more precisely, lays on the fact that transactions are based on nodes, in computer networks;
- Pseudonymous: transactions are publicly visible, but users are represented by a public key, which is a unique set of numbers and letters serving as a pseudonym.[84]

Cryptocurrency was a novelty in the law scenario; therefore, it is important to create a definition. To elaborate, the importance of determining this legal category transcends anti-money-laundering law. At the time, there are licensed cryptocurrency exchange platforms that perform exchange between the traditional and "new" currencies. However, a new intermediary for cryptocurrency providers, the custodial wallet, which offers custodial services to users, like banks providing bank accounts (deposit service) to customers, has emerged. A lack of regulation could lead to a different treatment of different financial institutions.[85]

Thus, in Europe cryptocurrencies are a commodity,[86] and the attribution of tangibility to commodities removes cryptocurrencies out-right from the definition of commodity. A decision of the Florida Court did not qualify bitcoin as money.[87]

Under the implementation of the Single Euro Area Payment (SEPA) Regulation,[88] cryptocurrencies do not qualify as debit transactions but cryptocurrency exchanges should comply with SEPA Regulation. This finds a proof in a report on cryptocurrencies adopted in 2015 by the European Central Bank in which it was stressed that under EU law, "virtual currency is not currently regulated and cannot be regarded as being subject to the (current) PSD or the EMD. As the phenomenon is still

83 (Antonopoulos 2014).

84 (Franco 2015).

85 (Gikay 2018).

86 (Fuller 2014).

87 *Florida v Michel A. Espinoza*, F14-2923, (11th Cir. 22 July 2016).

88 Regulation (Eu) No 260/2012 of the European Parliament and of the Council Of 14 March 2012 Establishing Technical and Business Requirements for Credit Transfers and Direct Debits in Euro and Amending Regulation (Ec) No 924/2009, Ojeu, L 94/22.

relatively new and also moving into different areas, it would be too early to try making new, tailor-made legislation."[89]

Also under the EU legal order, as a result of a European Court of Justice decisions, bitcoin did classify as a money but as a means of payment accepted by the parties since "the 'bitcoin' virtual currency has no other purpose than to be a means of payment."[90]

In 2023 both UK and EU have passed a new regulation on cryptocurrencies.

The HM Treasury in February 2023 published the final document about cryptocurrencies, titled "Future financial services regulatory regime for crypto-assets. Consultation and call for evidence."[91]

Although there is not a universal definition of "crypto-asset" or related terms, virtual assets or digital asset, there is an increasing consensus around the definition of crypto-asset as "any cryptographically secured digital representation of value or contractual rights that – (a) can be transferred, stored or traded electronically, and (b) that uses technology supporting the recording or storage of data (which may include distributed ledger technology)."

The government's will includes to included the financial services regulation of crypto-assets within the legal framework established by the UK's Financial Services and Markets Act 2000 (FSMA). Crypto-assets are a means of doing a lot of activities:

- Issuance of coins;
- Payment;
- Exchange of money;
- Investment and risk management.

The proposal is to adopt a similar approach to that used for securities and apply a regulation when an asset is admitted to trading on a regulated crypto-asset trading venue and, therefore, becomes exchangeable for fiat currency or subject to a public offer. As a result of the difference between bitcoin and securities, the proposal is to establish an issuance and disclosure regime for crypto-assets grounded in the intended reform, tailored to the specific attribute of crypto-assets to refer to public offer and admission to the trading regime.

In addition, the proposal distinguishes between different financial activities: intermediation, trading venue and custody.

From an EU perspective, the reference is to Markets in Crypto-assets (MiCA) Regulation,[92] which will enter in force between mid-2024 and early 2025. Crypto-assets, in this respect, "are digital representations of value or of rights that have the

89 European Central Bank, *Virtual Currency Schemes- A Further Analysis*, 24 (2015).

90 *Skatteverket v David Hedqvist* Case C-264/14, 6 (July 2015), 52.

91 HM Treasury, *Future financial services regulatory regime for cryptoassets. Consultation and call for evidence*, 2023, online.

92 Regulation 2023/1114/EU of the European Parliament and of the Council of 31 May 2023 on markets in crypto-assets, and amending Regulations 1093/2010/EU and 1095/2010/EU and Directives 2013/36/EU and 2019/193/EU.

potential to bring significant benefits to market participants, including retail holders of cryptoassets."

Crypto-assets do not encompass the following:

- Financial instruments such as transferable securities, money-market instruments, options, futures, swaps, etc., relating to securities, currencies, commodities because they are regulated under MiFID II;
- Electronic money under the Directive 2009/110/EC;
- Deposits under the directive 2014/49/EU on deposit guarantee schemes;
- Structured deposits pursuant to the MiFID II directive;
- Any kind of securitisations.

Further, MiCA draws a demarcation line between utility tokens and e-money tokens. The first one represents crypto-assets whose main purpose is not based on keeping their value but on ensuring access to certain asset or service available on DLT. The e-money tokens are crypto-assets whose purpose is to be used as means of exchange. The value remains relatively stable by their reference to the value of fiat currency that is a legal tender.[93]

MiCA Regulation proposes two new categories of subject: issuers of crypto-assets and crypto-asset service providers.[94]

The first one is limited to legal person/entities that offer any of crypto-assets to public or are putting efforts to have the crypto-assets admitted to trading platform for crypto-assets.[95] Despite this, there is an analogical institute for the users of securities: for the latter, it's the prospectus, while for crypto-asset issuers, it's the white-paper. The latter contains specific requirements, such as information obligations and transparency of the structure and proper distribution of roles and responsibilities.

Services of crypto-asset service providers[96] means the following activities or services linked with crypto-assets: "(a) the custody and administration of crypto-assets on behalf of third parties; (b) the operation of a trading platform for crypto-assets; (c) the exchange of crypto-assets for a fiat currency that is legal tender; (d) the exchange of crypto-assets for other crypto-assets; (e) the execution of orders for crypto-assets on behalf of third parties; (f) placing of crypto-assets; (g) the reception and transmission of orders for crypto-assets on behalf of third parties; (h) providing advice on crypto-assets."[97]

An important section concerns potential outsourcing activities:[98] if crypto-asset service providers "outsource services or activities to third parties for the performance

93 See Title III.

94 Among scholars, see Bočánek (2021).

95 "A legal person or other undertaking whose occupation or business is the provision of one or more crypto-asset services to clients on a professional basis, and that is allowed to provide crypto-asset services" Article 6(1)(15).

96 Henceforth CASP.

97 Article 3(1)(15).

98 See Article 73.

of operational functions shall take all reasonable steps to avoid additional operational risk." They remain fully responsible for discharging all of their obligations and ensuring that outsourcing does not do the following:

- Result in the delegation of the responsibility of the crypto-asset service providers;
- Alter the relationship between the crypto-asset service providers and their clients nor the obligations of the crypto-asset service providers towards their clients;
- Alter the conditions for the authorisation of the crypto-asset service providers.

There is also a duty to cooperate with the competent authority of the crypto-asset service providers' home member state by the third parties involved in the outsourcing.

Furthermore, the duties of crypto-asset service providers are to (1) ensure that third parties involved in the outsourcing meet the data protection standard of the EU, (2) exercise the direct access to the relevant information of the outsourced services, and (3) adopt the expertise and resources necessary for evaluating "the quality of the services provided, for supervising the outsourced services effectively and for managing the risks associated with the outsourcing on an ongoing basis."[99]

Decentralised autonomous organisation and decentralised finance

Another application of blockchain is the decentralised autonomous organisation (DAO): in 2013, for the first time, it was used in the term "decentralised autonomous corporation."

Only in 2016 it was the term DAO used to refer to an automated investment fund set up on the Ethereum blockchain. People transferred the cryptocurrency ether to the DAO and in return they received DAO tokens. In turn, a proposal would be submitted to the DAO and token holders vote on whether to fund those projects; the projects that were approved would be funded, and profits were remitted to the DAO and distributed to the DAO token holders. The human involvement was limited to only a group of curators, checking the identity of people submitting proposals, and DAO token holders would vote on which proposal to fund. No managers or board of directors were necessary: the token holders would vote on which project to fund.[100]

This experiment failed as a result of hackers exploiting the experiment: the DAO's code was accessed and a considerable number of DAO tokens were transferred to a wallet the hacker controlled.[101]

However, DAOs refer to different typologies that may achieve different purposes within the blockchain ecosystem. For instance, many DAO protocols are

99 Article 73(1)(e).
100 (Winkler and Mattheis n.d.).
101 (Sims 2021).

oriented towards decentralised finance (DeFi) purposes, such as lending, borrowing and mortgages. DeFi DAOs provide financial services eliminating the need for traditional intermediaries, like banks. The goal is to create a more inclusive and efficient financial ecosystem by leveraging blockchain technology and smart contracts.[102]

"Decentralised finance" is an umbrella term used to describe a number of services in the crypto world that seek to mimic functions of the traditional financial system without financial intermediaries. The latter, indeed, are taken over by computer or, better, by smart contracts based on blockchain technology. DeFi lays on the continuation of a trend on the digitisation of financial markets, started 50 years ago.

In other words, DeFi may be defined as the transformation of traditional financial products into products that operate without an intermediary via smart contracts or blockchain. It is clear that DeFi (1) is an ecosystem of financial applications (2) based on smart contracts (3) that achieved the properties as integrity and securities and that (4) these properties are achieved via blockchain.

From another perspective, the majority of such financial services consists of translating monetary banking systems, providing peer-to-peer lending and borrowing platforms, and enabling advanced financial instruments such as decentralised exchanges (DEX), tokenisation platforms, derivatives and predictions markets.

4.5.2 Digital banking

Digital banking services has become a trading topic in the financial industry. By digital banking we refer to the use of internet, mobile phones and any other electronic mediums as delivery channels for banking services, which includes all the traditional services, such as balance enquiry, statement printing, transfer of funds to other accounts, bills payment and new banking services, such as electronic bill presentment and payment, without necessarily visiting a bank.

It is also possible to distinguish between online and digital banking: the first one alludes to the use of telecommunications networks and internet to provide an extensive array of financial services and products to clients through a website or a system operated by financial institutions. The second one, *i.e.* digital banking, is the digitalisation, or moving online, of all the traditional banking activities and programs that historically were only available to customers when physically inside a bank branch. It includes money deposits, loan management, bill payments, opening a digital bank account and so on.[103]

Mobile payment

Mobile banking is a growth technology, strictly linked with the development of the commercialisation of 3G phones, which also fosters the advancement of mobile

102 (Lee and Li 2023).
103 (Wadesango and Magaya 2020).

financial services. At the first stage, IT development offered the opportunity for the growth of mobile commerce; hence, customers were keen on adopting the mobile services if three requirements are met: simplicity, cheapness and rapidity.

The mobile banking development was also facilitated by a suitable legal framework: there was a general agreement between banks and bank supervisors that mobile banking activities should be approached similarly to traditional banking practices. Mobile banking includes the whole range of services with which a banking activity is involved.

Mobile payment too belongs to the realm of mobile banking, that is to say, the range of mobile commerce services involving payment transactions initiated or confirmed using a mobile phone.[104] In this respect, mobile payment (M-payment) is the future alternative to cash and, at the same time, represents a suitable technology for consumers. Although there is no such thing as a formal definition and a specific regulation, mobile payment shall be adopted to describe mobile commerce and the way in which mobile commerce involves a transaction that is carried out between a merchant and a customer. The latter is entitled to purchase goods and/or services through wireless handheld services.[105]

An informal, and not binding, definition may be found in a whitepaper issued by the European Payments Council in 2014; it prescribed that "[the mobile payment is a] payment service made available by software/hardware through a mobile device. [Then, the whitepaper analyses the definition of a mobile device, according to which a mobile device is a] personal device with mobile communication capabilities such as telecom network connection, Wi-Fi, Bluetooth . . . which offers connections to the internet. Examples of mobile devices include phones, smart phones, tablet."[106]

Further, the Committee on Payment and Settlement Systems has qualified a mobile payment as "payments transmitted by access devices that are connected to the mobile communication network using voice technology, text messaging (via either SMS or USSD technology) or NFC."[107]

At least, in a competition case decided by European Commission in 2012,[108] Three UK, a British telecommunications and internet service provider, recognised the importance of digital mobile wallets. More precisely, it said,

> Three UK submits that the availability of a mobile wallet will become a key parameter of competition when consumers decide on a tariff plan with an operator, as handsets will become increasingly multifunctional and the

104 (Weber and Darbellay 2010).
105 (D'Alvia 2021).
106 European Payments Council, "Mobile Wallet Payments," EPC White Paper EPC163-13 (2014), p. 9.
107 Committee on Payment and Settlement Systems, "Innovations in Retail Payments" Report of the Working Group on Innovations in Retail Payments of the Bank for International Settlements' (2012), pp. 1–96.
108 COMP/M. 6314 (2012) *Telefonica UK/Vodafone UK/Everything Everywhere/JV*.

> mobile wallet is going to be the next step of an already existing natural evolution, becoming a "hygiene factor" in the sense that it will be an integral part of the mobile phone, like for example the camera, or access to the internet.[109]

In this respect, the European Commission qualified digital mobile wallet as a product, rather than a service; hence, in most cases, the mobile wallet is based on remote money transfer function. Therefore, mobile wallet is not a payment instrument, but an access channel to orders forms of payment instrument, such as debit or credit cards, checks.[110]

Smart-banking contract

Smart contracts are general purpose programmes that allow secure transactions without the help of third parties and reduce costs associations with the bargaining practices. Smart contracts can be defined as a self-executing and self-verifying computer-aided programme that takes place between two parties based on the terms of contract. The transaction of the contract is controlled by the blockchain network.

From an EU perspective, the legal framework to which reference is made is the proposal for a regulation on the Data Act.[111] In this legal framework, smart contracts are the main pillars in the data governance architecture because the goal is data sharing. Therefore, for the Commission, smart contracts are a suitable solution to make data transfer easier: the proposal lays down a regulatory framework for smart contracts and a new vision for how they should operate in the context of data transfer.[112]

The party that offers smart contracts has some duties, such as[113] (1) to ensure a higher degree of robustness and an ad hoc control on the contract's mechanism, (2) to ensure the existence of a mechanism that is able to "reset or instruct the contract to stop or interrupt the operation to avoid future (accidental) executions"[114] and (3) to guarantee the confidentiality of trade secrets.

From the UK perspective, we recall a report of Law Commission where it was concluded that the existing law of England and Wales can apply; hence, "anything further is required in law to confirm this and . . . we do not think that any

109 COMP/M. 6314 (2012) *Telefonica UK/Vodafone UK/Everything Everywhere/JV*, para 521.

110 COMP/M. 6956 (2013) *Telefonica/Caixabank/Banco Santander/JV*, para. 5: "the digital wallet does not constitute a payment method, but it is only the place where digitalized means of payment are stored and can be accessed in order to make a payment. The retail wallet will not have field communication (NFC) functionality for payments without the use of the internet (mobile or static)."

111 Proposal for a Regulation of the European Parliament and of the Council on harmonised rules on fair access to and use of data (Data Act) 2022/0047 (COD).

112 (Casolari et al. 2023).

113 See Article 11.

114 Article 11 b).

confirmatory legislative statement to such effect would be helpful."[115] Also in the same direction, it is highlighted that

> smart legal contracts can satisfy the requirements for a contract, a legislative statement that smart contracts are capable of being legally enforced (or to confirm that a contract is not unenforceable merely because it is a smart legal contract) seems unnecessary. In the absence of a real need for legislation, we do not think it would be justified.[116]

In the area of banking and financial law, the process can be simplified, to ensure a strict adherence to regulation guidelines. Moreover, thanks to financial contracts it is possible to (1) reduce transaction costs, (2) supply automated insurance claim process to the finance industry, (3) eliminate infiltration and enhance blockchain storage transparency and (4) optimise operations.

Payment system under IT control

European policy introduced changes on data portability and payment systems with the objective of allowing their consumers and citizens a much better control of their personal data. Furthermore, this piece of legislation achieved the objective of changing the industrial and dynamic in banking and in financial services. Also in this scenario, another goal is to realise more transparency and lower costs for consumers.

Bearing this in mind, harmonised payment markets in the European Union is a precondition for a single European market. Thanks to the Payment Services Directive, or PSD1,[117] the European Union established some common payments rules to remove entry barriers and to provide fair conditions that would increase competition in the payment market. This directive is the first comprehensive payment legislation aimed to facilitate access to new market players. It provided a great transparency and reduced consumer information.

As a result of the change in financial services industry and the payment sector, there was the needs to shape a new regulation for payment and banking services across the EU. Therefore, the European Authorities have adopted a revised Payment Services Directive (PSD2),[118] whose aim is to extend the framework to all foreign currencies across the EU/EEA as well as the payment transactions in all currencies in which only one participant is within the EU/EEA territory.

115 Law Commission Law, *Smart Legal Contracts, Advice to Government*, no. 401/2021, para 3.142.

116 Law Commission, *Smart Legal Contracts, Advice to Government*, no. 401/2021, para 3.146.

117 Directive 2007/64/EC of the European Parliament and of the Council of 13 November 2007 on payment services in the internal market amending Directives 97/7/EC, 2002/65/EC, 2005/60/EC and 2006/48/EC and repealing Directive 97/5/EC.

118 Directive 2015/2366/EU of the European Parliament and of the Council of 25 November 2015 on payment services in the internal market, amending Directives 2002/65/EC, 2009/110/EC and 2013/36/EU and Regulation 1093/2010/EU, and repealing Directive 2007/64/EC.

PSD2 entered into force on 13 January 2016 with a duty for all EU member states and European Economic Area (EEA) countries to implement their national laws by 12 January 2018. The real change is concerned with how the region will overcome an overly fragmented centralised hierarchically inherited framework to allow for the necessary changes to respond to digital market initiative.

The revised PSD2 is a key directive for borderless banking and payment services that has set the stage for a pan-European open banking. Furthermore, another significant regulatory trend is the implementation of General Data Protection[119] to control customers over their financial and personal data through consent mechanisms.

Prima facie, it seems that these two legal frameworks are in contrast to one another, with the former endorsing the stimulus for expansive data sharing: GDPR seems to protect and restrict the freedom to share them. In the lack of derogations, the signature GDPR should read the processing of big data in financial services, including account data in Open Banking.[120]

The harmonisation between GDPR and PSD2 shall be the users' consent as regards authorisation of a payment transaction. Article 64 of PSD2 states that "a payment transaction is considered to be authorized only if the payer has given consent to execute the payment transaction." Also, the following Articles, that is Articles 65 and 66, do not refer to consent, but to "explicit consent." In this scenario, consent, or explicit consent, refers not to processing data but to the authorisation to a Payment Initiation Services[121] or Account Information Services.[122]

By contrast, under GDPR, consent is the element that permits the personal data processing by data controllers that would otherwise be forbidden. If a subject gives valid consent, data controllers are released from the restrictions provided by law. Thus, the processing becomes lawful from the moment consent is unambiguously expressed. GDPR states that consent shall be "freely given, specific, informed and unambiguous."[123] The explicit consensus refers to sensitive personal data.

A coordination came from the European Data Protection Board:[124] it considered "explicit consent," under Article 94(2) PSD2 as contractual consent that does not interfere with contractual necessity. More precisely, EDPB highlighted that

> Article 94(2) of PSD2 should be interpreted in the sense that when entering a contract with a payment service provider under PSD2, data subjects must be made fully aware of the purposes for which their personal data will be processed and have to explicitly agree to these clauses. Such clauses should be clearly distinguishable from the other matters dealt with in the contract,

119 Henceforth GDPR.
120 See recital 90 PSD2.
121 Also, PIS.
122 Also, AIS.
123 Article 4(11) GDPR.
124 Also, EDPB: the European Authority in charge of supervision and consistent application of the GDPR.

> and would need to be explicitly accepted by the data subject. The concept of explicit consent under Article 94(2) of PSD2 is therefore an additional requirement of a contractual nature and is therefore not the same as (explicit) consent under the GDPR.[125]

Another problem is concerned with the "silent parties" *status*, *i.e.* third-party individuals whose data are in a payment account for being the payee, the beneficiary of a payment, or a joint account holder. Due to this, the reservation whether the processing of silent-party data is legitimate when "explicit consent" for the processing of such data has been given by another data subject, the payment service user, or other grounds for processing are accepted.

The problem is the following one: the third-party providers of digital services[126] have access, granted by banks, to silent-party data; this is a data protection operation under Article 4(2) GDPR. Further, TPP does not rely on the consent of the silent data subject. In this respect, European members of Parliament highlighted, "A lawful basis for the processing of these silent party data by PIP and AIS – in the context of payment and account services under PSD2 – could be the legitimate interest of a controller or a third-party ex Article 6(1)(f) to perform the contract with the service user."[127]

In order words, as a result of the increasing power of the biggest competitors in the financial market, fintech, and as a result of PSD2 implementation, new major players have emerged in the market:

- ASPSPs (account servicing payment service providers);
- TPPs (third-party payment service providers).

The latter, TTPs, are payment institutions that cannot rely on payment accounts, in addition to having a limited scope of activities. For instance, they can be (1) PISP, or a provider of payment initiation service on behalf of the client or (2) AISP, or a client account information service provider.

The first case, PISP, plays a mediation role between buyer and merchant, offering them a new payment initiation service (PIS), which is an alternative to making online payments without using a payment card. When making online purchases, the purchase details are transferred to the PISP, which will, alternatively, do the following:

- Redirect the consumer to the bank for authentication and checking with the bank whether the purchase transaction can be carried out, where after the banks' verification the customer will be redirected to the online store to complete payment and order the goods;
- Conduct login information to and from the bank so that payment can be made without interruption of service.

125 European Data Protection Board, Letter to Sophie in 't Veld.

126 Henceforth TPP.

127 European Data Protection Board, Letter to Sophie in 't Veld.

The second, *i.e.* AISP, helps consumers to gain an overview of their financial situation. As a result of the consumer's consent, AISP can share data with other companies such as price comparison websites which offer additional services from which the customer may benefit.

It is crystal clear that, as far as banks are concerned, this system cannot be totally suitable for the traditional banking sector. Thus, banks are subject to an obligation to maintain, and provide, a system that facilitates access to customer information. Also, credit institutions need to comply with a duty to repay an unauthorised or faulty payment transaction, even if the transaction is initiated thorough a payment-initiated service provider.

Furthermore, banks have a new competitor which is causing them to have a lower direct interaction between them and their customers, which weakens their ability to sell other products or services. At the same time, this mechanism reduces their institutional position in the everyday life of customers. To elaborate, as a result of this legal framework, the expected legal barriers to entry for non-bank, payment, and service providers is likely to add to the competitive pressure for incumbents. Credit institutions must comply with higher regulation requirements than non-bank providers, forcing the former to be more optimised for regulatory compliance security. It is clear that non-bank providers can offer more attractive services.

Moreover, it is not totally correct to emphasise the higher level of security ensured by the third-party provider. Indeed, the banking industry, while adhering to PSD2 guidelines, will need to find a way to ensure secure access to data and permit management, while preventing application manipulation. This is corroborated by the fact that in PSD2 it is quite clear that banks will be responsible for the ownership and security for the customer and confidentiality data.[128]

To elaborate, PSD2 is not just a further regulation that requires a mere operational and compliance approach from banks, but an evolving IT development in the banking sector and payment model. The reference is to Payment Initiation Services and Account Information Services (XS2A). As far as Payment Initiation Services are concerned, it means services to initiate a payment order at the request of the payment service user with respect to a payment account held at another payment service provider. Account Information Service is an online service to provide consolidated information on one or more payment accounts held by the payment service user with respect to a payment account held at another payment service provider.

The difference between PSD1 and PSD2 is that the first one realised a disintermediation on banks by payment institutions in the merchant acquiring business. On the other side, PSD2 is expected to add disintermediation on the consumer side. Moreover, not only did PSD1 function in pre-euro currencies but also enabled the operability of new end-to-end providers. The latter are new firms, in the form of closed platforms that interact digitally with the payer and the payee arranging for the payment transaction within their closed system.

128 (Petrović 2020).

Via PSD2, European Union fundamentally, but also substantially, shifts its policy approach to digitalisation. Therefore, thanks to this legislative framework, in Brussels they baptise the novel concept of open banking. This new banking model fluctuates from the money business to the data business, and vice versa. As a result, pieces of account data are shared with new market players of the fintech industry capable of capturing or creating value around an existing asset that is underexploited.[129] Furthermore, in an open banking environment, financial services are market segments and they achieve a disintermediation of the banking industry.[130]

It Is worth stressing that the most debated part of PSD2 is concerned with the provision of XS2A regarding the strong customer authentication.[131] These procedures shall include, at least, two of the following three factors: (1) something that only the user knows, such as a password or PIN; (2) something that only the user possesses, such as a mobile phone or token; and (3) something belonging to the user, such as a fingerprint.[132]

On 28 June 2023, the European Commission has published its proposed revision of EU payment services legislation as a review of the PSD2. More precisely, under this proposal, PSD2 would be split into two different instruments:

- A third Payment Services Directive (PSD3) that would deal, in particular, with the authorisation process for payment institutions (Pls) and the prudential regime;
- A separate Payment Services Regulation (PSR) that would deal with rules, and related penalties, for the PSPs and users.

In addition to these two new proposals, the European Commission proposed to merge the EU E-Money Directive (EMD2) with the proposed PSD3 and PSR text in order to have a coherent regime for both payment services and e-money services.

It is crucial to stress the differences between PSD3 and PSR. The first one, PSD3, remains an EU directive and provides rules for the authorisation of payment institution. PSR is an EU regulation that provides rules in relation to (1) transparency of conditions and information requirement for payment services and (2) rights and obligations in relation to the provision and use of payment services including provisions for open banking.

The PSD3 proposal defines that payment services "unless specified otherwise, any reference to payment services shall be understood in this Directive as meaning payment and electronic money services."[133] Thus, a payment account "means an account held by a payment service provider in the name of one or more payment service users which is used for the execution of one or more payment transactions and allows for sending and receiving funds to and from third parties."[134]

129 (Chesbrough 2010).
130 (Ferretti 2022).
131 (Cortet, Rijks and Nijland 2016).
132 In this respect, the facial recognition authentication system will be discussed further.
133 Article 1(3) Proposal.
134 Article 2(13) Proposal.

Furthermore, revising the payment service directive, that will change from PSD2 to PSD3, in addition to PSR, shall be a legal package of measures, which does the following:

- Combat and mitigate payment fraud;
- Improve consumers' rights;
- Level the playing field between banks and non-banks;
- Improve the functioning of open banking;
- Improve the availability of cash in shops and via ATMs;
- Strengthen harmonisation and enforcement.

All of these shall be read jointly with legislative proposal for a Framework for Financial Data Access. This will establish clear rights and obligations to manage customer data sharing in the financial sector. More precisely, the goals are as follows:

- The possibility, but not obligation, for customers to share their user data;
- Obligation for customers' data holders to make this data available to data users;
- Full control by customers over who accesses their data and for what purpose;
- Standardisation of customer data and required technical interfaces as part of financial data sharing;
- Clear liability regimes for data breaches and dispute resolution mechanisms.

Personal data as a money: Directive 2019/770/EU and 2019/771/EU

In the scenario of digital single market strategy for Europe,[135] a critical role is played by two European Directives: Directive 2019/770/EU[136] and Directive 2019/771/EU.[137]

The first one, Directive 2019/770 introduces the express qualification of personal data as a consideration in the contract for the supply digital content or services and as an obligation similar in all to the payment of the price. Nevertheless, the directive does not omit to highlight that the "protection of personal data is a fundamental right and that therefore personal data cannot be considered as a commodity." In order to achieve this result, "this Directive should ensure that consumers are, in the context of such business models, entitled to contractual remedies."[138] Therefore, the recognition of damages is a quintessential part of the directive.

135 Communication from the Commission to the European Parliament, the Council, the European Economic and Social Committee and the Committee of the Regions of 6 May 2015. A Digital Single Market Strategy for Europe; COM(2015) 192 final, in https://eur-lex.europa.eu/legal-content/EN/TXT/?qid=1447773803386&uri=CELEX:52015DC0192.

136 Directive (EU) 2019/770 of the European Parliament and of the Council of 20 May 2019 on certain aspects concerning contracts for the supply of digital content and digital services.

137 Directive (EU) 2019/771 of the European Parliament and of the Council of 20 May 2019 on certain aspects concerning contracts for the sale of goods, amending Regulation 2017/2394/EU and Directive 2009/22/EC, and repealing Directive 1999/44/EC.

138 Recital 24.

More in general, the purpose of this directive is to contribute to the proper functioning of the internal market and to promote a higher level of consumer protection in the area of digital contents or digital services.[139]

In this scenario, personal data shall be defined as a money because, Article 3(1), second part, states that Directive 2019/770

> shall also apply where the trader supplies or undertakes to supply digital content or a digital service to the consumer, and the consumer provides or undertakes to provide personal data to the trader, except where the personal data provided by the consumer are exclusively processed by the trader for the purpose of supplying the digital content or digital service in accordance with this Directive or for allowing the trader to comply with legal requirements to which the trader is subject, and the trader does not process those data for any other purpose.

More precisely, the consideration is not to be in money but personal data. This directive does not apply when personal data provided by consumers are exclusively processed by the trader to supply the digital content or digital service in accordance with the directive or to allow the trader to comply with legal requirements to which the trader is subject. Further, the trader does not process those data for any purpose.[140]

The second one, 2019/771, applies to sales contracts and to contracts "for the supply of goods to be manufactured or produced";[141] that includes in its scope "digital content or digital services which are incorporated in or inter-connected with goods [. . .] and are provided with the goods under the sales contract, irrespective of whether such digital content or digital service is supplied by the seller or by a third party."[142]

This directive applies if a consumer buys a sweatshirt and if the consumer buys a car with a GPS application installed. This is a good endowed with digital elements.[143] It is also a good with digital elements if the seller commits to updating the application for a period of time.[144]

Digital euro

As a result of an increasingly digitalised global economy, on 1 November 2023, and after two years in a "preparation phase," a digital euro has been launched. From this very date, fraught with symbolism, an experimental phase shall begin, in order to test this new currency.

139 See Article 1.
140 Article 3(3).
141 Article 3(1) and (2).
142 Article 3(3).
143 Article 2(5)(b).
144 (Carvalho 2019)

Digital euro is the virtual version of the currency, issued by the European Central Bank, that could be used free of charge in the eurozone, alongside cash. To elaborate, digital euro is an electronic system of payments and transactions that the ECB is on the verge of introducing.

It may represent an opportunity for the ECB to provide people with a public digital alternative to private bank deposits. Positive Money Europe advocates for a digital euro that is universally accessible, free of costs and privacy-compliant. It is crucial to emphasise that it should not replace cash; rather, the option of using banknotes and coins will be protected.

An implication of digital euro is that it represents a payment system that would provide a universally accessible and safe electronic form of public money, offering people a real alternative to private bank money. In other words, digital euro would ensure that the eurozone continues to provide money as a public utility service instead of letting private companies run our money system.

In a nutshell, digital euro is "a liability from the European Central Bank"; the aim of this virtual currency is "to be a digitalized form of cash." Moreover, from a broader perspective, by its own nature, digital euro may be "classified as a financial, intangible, centralized issuance and elastic supply asset."[145]

From a regulatory perspective, it is mandatory to recall the ECB's summary report on digital euro.[146] At the same time it is essential to refer to the proposal for a regulation of the European Parliament and of the Council to establish a digital euro.[147]

In this scenario, digital euro[148] is seen as a consequence of the digital era;[149] therefore, there are some advantages to this new digital currency:

- Widely accepted and easy to use;
- Free for basic use;
- Usable for any digital payments in the euro area;
- Not requiring an online connection; hence, it is possible to use both online and offline;

145 (McGreevy 2023).

146 European Central Bank – Eurosystem – A stocktake on the digital euro. Summary report on the investigation phase and outlook on the next phase, see ecb.dedocs231018.en.pdf (europa.eu).

147 Proposal for a Regulation of the European Parliament and of the Council on the establishment of the digital euro {SEC(2023) 257 final} – {SWD(2023) 233 final} – {SWD(2023) 234 final} Brussels, 28.6.2023 COM(2023) 369 final 2023/0212 (COD).

148 For a definition see article no. 2 and ff of the European Parliament and Council proposal.

149 Recital no. 4 of the European Parliament proposal states that "the digital euro should support a variety of use cases of retail payments. Those use case include person to person, person to business, person to government, business to person, business to business, business to government, government to person, government to business, and government to government payments. In addition, the digital euro should also be able to fulfil future payments needs, and in particular machine to machine payment in the context of Industry 4.0 and payments in the decentralised internet (web3). The digital euro should not cater for payments between financial intermediaries, payment service providers and other market participants (that is to say, wholesale payments), for which settlement systems in central bank money exist and where the use of different technologies is being further investigated by the Eurosystem."

- A higher protection of privacy;
- Inclusive and leaving no one behind;
- Settling payments instantly;
- Secure;
- Risk-free as money issued by the ECB;
- Usable for payments at the point of sale and person-to-person.

Digital euro thus represents a different means of payment; hence, it offers additional freedom of choice to end users. Moreover, thanks to digital euro, people would have more choices in how to pay and a secure solution that fully respects their privacy. The central bank has no interest in monitoring people's payment patterns and no commercial aspirations. Digital euro has the aim to achieve a cash-like level of privacy for offline payments, as it would require no third-party validation and would simply rely on the direct transfer from the payer to the payee.

Via digital euro, the European Union will not be dependent on foreign service providers; therefore, digital euro can strengthen Europe's resilience in three ways:

- It ensures that, in addition to private solution payments, there would be a payment solution for the euro area under European governance;
- It would be able to rely on its own underlying infrastructure, and it enhances Europe resilience on electronic payment systems in the event of cyberattacks and technical disruptions:
- It provides a pan-European platform on which European PSPs[150] could build services with a pan-European reach for their customers.

Properly, PSP methodology plays a vital role in the distribution and management of digital euro and providing digital euro-related services in all euro area countries. In addition, digital euro would be a standardised means of payment services, thanks to which there will also be the opportunity to develop financial products and services.

In the same fashion as fintech, non-bank PSPs could offer the same integration of digital euro payments into their platform and services attracting a larger euro area-wide user base and benefiting from economies of scale.

Moreover, this can implement competition between banks and non-bank PSPs, creating new business partnership and driving innovation in the payment industry.

From a monetary policy, digital euro is designed to have no material impact on financial stability or the transmission of monetary policy.

A digital euro can be used both online and offline. In the first case, the references go (1) to ensure coverage of all use cases in most payment situations (2) for payment made remotely (3) so people would not have to rely only on a bearer instrument to be able to hold central bank money.

The offline mode is designed to maximise certain cash-like characteristics, such as a bearer payments instrument that is not dependent on an online connection but

150 This acronym means person-to-person transactions.

is limited to proximity payments and would need to be prefunded, and which is to offer a cash-like level of privacy for offline payments.

These two ways accomplish different goals. Where online payments are concerned, the users could pay on a remote basis or they could use budgeting applications to analyse their spending. Validation by a PSP as a third party would be required to complete online transactions and comply with payment regulations.

The offline solution would allow a peer-to-peer validation model, where people would be able to make and receive payments in physical proximity without the need to involve a PSP in the transaction. The payment would be settled locally, between two devices, with no connection to any third party for validation or recording. The monetary value relating to the payment would be exchanged between the secure elements of the two users' devices in accordance with the rules laid down in the legislative framework and the technical implementation by the Eurosystem.

The offline functionality would require prefunding, for which an online connection would be required. Therefore, provided users have prefunded their offline wallet beforehand, the offline digital euro could offer a fallback option when no internet connection is available. Nevertheless, the device used for offline digital euro transactions would still need to go online for verification of security features at regular intervals.

The digital euro could be used to make any digital payment throughout the euro area instantly and at any time. the digital euro can also be qualified as a public good, for people to use in all their daily digital payments.

The digital euro requires a collaboration between public and private sector to maximise their respective advantages. People who would open and manage digital euro accounts with PSPs are responsible for their relationship with end users. Thus, PSPs meet the requirements established by the Payment Services Directive[151] for the provision of payment account services and that provide retail payment services would be expected to offer digital euro services. It is crucial to stress that these PSPs would have a contractual account management relationship with end users.

The account-based system or the server could provide the digital euro's transfer method: a third party will keep track of deposits made from the payer's bank account to the payee's bank account, providing evidence of successful transactions. It is clear that the digital euro works as a current money transaction.

The European report emphasises also the social soul of digital euro. More precisely, the digital euro is designed to be inclusive and accessible for people with low digital and financial skills and resources, as well as those with disabilities or functional limitations. In this line of reasoning, the digital euro payment card is designed for those are vulnerable to digital financial exclusion and prefer a physical card to an app. Further, an offline functionality would also support digital euro payments in areas with poor network coverage.

151 See in this Chapter.

The last topic concerns privacy[152] and data protection as fundamental rights. The starting point is the idea that users of any digital payment services need to identify themselves to their PSP before they can start making use of such service. Under the draft proposal, digital euro shall be treated in a similar way to other digital payments services. Also in this case, it becomes critical to distinguish between online and offline privacy models.

In the second case, i.e. offline payments, a higher level of privacy may refer to (1) offline proximity transactions or (2) the prohibition of sharing transaction data with PSPs, the Eurosystem or any potential providers of supporting services. The only exception would be steps required to avoid the forgery of digital euros.

As far as online payment is concerned, the amount of data related to online digital euro payments available to the respective PSPs would be limited to what is necessary to perform basic digital euro services, and consistent with what is required by regulation in compliance with GDPR. Moreover, data available to the Eurosystem would be limited to what is necessary to perform critical digital euro-related tasks within the regulatory framework and would also be pseudonymised.

Digital euro users would have full control over how their own personal data are used. This includes an opt-in rather an opt-out for allowing PSPs to process a users' personal data for commercial purposes or to provide additional services. Without express consent from digital euro users, their personal data cannot be used for any purposes beyond what is legally required for the purposes of onboarding and the processing of digital euro services.

PSPs would be able to see the data shared by their respective end users to the extent necessary to provide basic digital euro services within the regulatory framework. Any user data obtained by a PSP during the onboarding process and, in their role as digital euro distributors, initiators of transactions and providers of additional services would remain with the respective PSP unless it is necessary to perform digital euro-related tasks within the regulatory framework.

The Eurosystem, as operator of the settlement component, would not be able to identify any natural person making or receiving digital euro payments. Pseudonymisation is the correct way to achieve this goal. Moreover, data available to the Eurosystem would be limited to what is necessary to perform its tasks within the regulatory framework and would also be pseudonymised.

The objective of the legislative European proposal, *i.e.* to establish a digital euro, is to ensure that central bank money with the status of legal tender remains available to the general public while offering a state-of-the-art and cost-efficient means of payment. At the same time it is also mandatory to ensure a high level of privacy in digital payments, maintain financial stability and promote accessibility and financial inclusion.

A crucial point concerns the legal tender status of the digital euro: Article 7 of the European Parliament and Council proposal states that this legal tender status "shall entail its mandatory acceptance, at full face value, with the power to

152 See Articles no. 34-35 of the European Parliament and Council Proposal.

discharge from a payment obligation."[153] As a result of this, the payee shall not refuse digital euros tendered in payment, to comply with that obligation. Another consequence is that the value of digital euros in payment of a debt shall be equal to the value of the monetary debt. This status is confined to the euro zone.[154]

Therefore, "Cross-currency payments between the digital euro and other currencies shall be subject to prior agreements between, on the one hand, the European Central Bank and, on the other hand, the national central banks of the Member States whose currency is not the euro and the third countries."[155] Thus, the ECB has a duty to cooperate with the national central banks of member states whose currency is not the euro, to enable interoperable payments between the digital euro and other currencies.

Article 9 sets forth some exceptions to the rule encompassed within Article 7. More precisely, Article 9 stipulates that a payee shall be entitled to refuse digital euro in the following cases:

- "Where the payee is an enterprise which employs fewer than 10 persons or whose annual turnover or annual balance sheet total does not exceed EUR 2 million, or is a non-profit legal entity";
- If the "refusal is made in good faith and where such refusal is based on legitimate and temporary grounds in line with the principle of proportionality in view of concrete circumstances beyond the control of the payee." In this scenario, the payee has on its side the burden of proof to establish that legitimate and temporary grounds have existed in a particular case and that the consequent refusal was proportionate;
- In the case in which "the payee is a natural person acting in the course of a purely personal or household activity";
- If, prior to the payment "the payee has agreed with the payer on a different means of payment."

The last topic that the EU proposal discusses is action to prevent money laundering: in this respect, Article 37 refers to the pre-existing European Regulation on anti-money laundering. More precisely, particular attention is on offline payment methodology. Additionally, it is also crucial "to prevent money laundering and terrorist financing while not unduly restricting the use of the offline digital euro as a means of payment."[156] In this respect, a duty of the European Commission is to take into account the following elements "(a) an assessment of the money laundering and terrorist financing threats, vulnerabilities and risks of the digital euro when funding and defunding their payment instrument; (b) relevant recommendations and reports drawn up by international organisations and standard setters with

153 Article 7(2).

154 Article 8(2) states, "The digital euro shall have legal tender status for online payments of a monetary debt denominated in euro to a payee residing or established in the euro area."

155 See Article 21(1).

156 Article 37(6).

competence in the field of preventing money laundering and combating terrorist financing; (c) the objective of ensuring the usability and acceptance of the digital euro as a legal tender instrument."[157]

Although it is a regulation perspective, the other side of the coin is the sustainability issue. To elaborate, as a single bitcoin transaction uses 200 kWh[158] the same problem applies to digital euro transactions. For the second digital currency, i.e. the euro, the ECB estimates that its user amount will be 400 million consumers and the total transactions would be hundreds of million per day. As a result of this, the result energy usage would be 27,700 GW. It is clear that this type of energy consumption can endanger the climate targets: in other words, the digital euro alone could take up 8% of the 40 GW of ocean energy and 300 GW offshore wind energy.[159]

In this scenario, the sustainable solutions may be the following: the use of a decentralised system based on the proof-of-stake.[160] A PoS system is based not on mining but on validators to approve the transaction. The validators have a stake in the transaction. Initially, they pay the system to become validators; if they approve a fraudulent transaction, their stake is decreased. If the transaction is approved correctly, they receive a commission.[161] From an energy perspective, the energy consumption is therefore estimated at 10^3 joule per transaction rather than the 10^9 joule required through a PoW system.[162]

From the EU perspective, however, digital euro can result in a reduction in both cost and carbon footprint of the current payment ecosystem, because, via digitalisation, physical transportation and manipulation will be reduced.[163]

A final consequence of the digital euro is the impact on banking and financial institutions; indeed, central banks are preparing to introduce digital central bank money, the central bank digital currency.[164]

The latter may play a crucial role[165] on the international scene; hence, CBDCs can do the following:[166]

- Help to protect a country's monetary autonomy by preventing private stablecoins;
- Realise a banking international network;

157 Article 37(6).
158 (Brosens 2017).
159 See Commission Proposal for a Directive of the European Parliament and of the Council Amending Directive 2018/2001/EU of the European Parliament and of the Council, Regulation (EU) 2018/1999 of the European Parliament and of the Council and Directive 98/70/EC of the European Parliament and of the Council as Regards the Promotion of Energy from Renewable Sources, and Repealing Council Directive 2015/652/EU, 8, COM (2021) 557 final (July, 14 2021).
160 Henceforth PoS.
161 (Mooij 2022).
162 It is a system based upon proof-of-work verification.
163 (Wagner, Bruggink and Benevelli 2021).
164 Henceforth CBDC.
165 By contrast, see also Ozili (2023).
166 (Boonstra 2022).

- Balance held at central bank by certain financial institutions, such as mutual funds, pensions funds, and insurers and larger industrial companies.

CBDCs aim to enlarge access to central bank reserves from the small realm of commercial banks to the public at large, in order to represent a reserve for all. Thus, cash would no longer be the only form of central bank money thorough which the public could transact and save. One could do the same with reserves deposited at the central bank or with a tokenised CBDC.[167]

Privacy

As shown earlier, it is clear that data has become a critical resource for many business models as a result of digitalisation and globalisation. It is also clear the link between GDPR and finance: fintech development processes a large amount of sensitive data. For instance, payment data can retain information about ethnic origin, political opinions, religious beliefs and so on. In a nutshell, fintech business models always rely on artificial intelligence, big data, cloud computing and so on. Therefore, it materialises a challenge for consumer privacy and financial personal data.

As a result of the steady growth of the financial sector, there are significant implications for consumer privacy derive:

- Personal data collection by a growing number of non-bank service providers and other third parties, *i.e.* big tech companies, and third-party intermediaries;
- The collection and analysis of personal financial data is of an increasing economic importance to entities operating in the financial sector; hence, the access to data provides an informational advantage over competitors;
- Personal data represents a lucrative source of revenue;
- Many companies collect personal financial data to sell personal data to data brokers, commercial enterprises or debt collectors.

The EU and UK approach, at the moment, is based on PSD2.[168] In this respect, PSD2 requires TPPs to obtain the "explicit consent" of consumer before accessing their personal data. It also requires them to comply with the consumer privacy criteria of the GDPR. Additionally, PSD2 prohibits TPPs from accessing, storing or using any customer data that is not relevant to the services that the customer requests.[169]

In this specific area, the demarcation line of regulation between the EU and the UK regulation is quite obvious. The UK has gone farther afield, by implementing additional rights for its customers in terms of the unlimited guarantee provided to every UK bank customer through the UK direct arrangements.[170] Furthermore, the

167 (Minesso, Mehl and Stracca 2022).
168 See above.
169 Article 66(3).
170 (Courtneidge 2012).

UK requires all open banking participants to adhere to specific technical requirements, intended to create a single data sharing ecosystem that operates through a uniform set of standards.

In 2016–2017 the UK Financial Conduct Authority and Competition & Markets Authority[171] issued a series of orders that required the country's nine largest banks to share certain types of financial data through APIs, using a common set of technical rules know as Open Banking Standard.[172] This is based on the recommendations of the Open Banking Working Group, which is an entity established by the UK government.

In this scenario there is also the Open Banking Implementation Entity:[173] it is a quasi-governmental organisation responsible for developing the technical standards that apply to all companies that participate in open banking in the UK. Those standards ensure, among other things, that banks and TPPs use a common API format for data sharing and a common user interface. That user interface allows consumers to select which TPPs they wish to share their data with, to determine how long the TPP will have access to their data and to choose the precise purpose for which their data may be used.

In other words, the main objective is to shape a "larger ecosystem" for IT companies in banking sector and developers to work within as a single application could then connect with, and be used by, customers from any bank.[174]

By contrast, the US adopted a more hands-off approach:[175] under the Trump administration the US Department of the Treasury recommended an industry-led approach to open banking and advised against imposing substantial regulatory requirements governing financial data sharing. However, the Biden administration has advocated for new regulation that given consumers rights to share their banking data with third parties.[176]

In the US there is the Right to Financial Privacy Act of 1978 that protects the confidentiality of personal financial records by creating a statutory Fourth Amendment protection for bank records. This act was a reaction to *Miller*,[177] where the US Supreme Court found that bank customers had no legal right to privacy.

Finally, in the relation between the US and EU, as a result of EU-US Data Privacy Framework,[178] in the matter of financial privacy, it was recognised that in

171 Henceforth CMA.

172 298569302-The-Open-Banking-Standard-1.pdf (theodi.org)

173 Also, OBIE: it is defined as "the custodian of the Open Banking Standards for APIs and owns and maintains the Directory of Open Banking Participants (also referred to as the Directory)." Report (openbanking.org.uk), p. 4.

174 U.K. Competition & Markets Auth., Retail Banking Market Investigation: Provisional Decision On Remedies 40 (2016)

175 In *United States v Miller* 425 U.S. 435 (1976) the United States Supreme Court did not recognised to a bank investor a constitutional right about privacy interest in bank records.

176 (Wilson 2022).

177 See also *California Bankers Association v Schultz* 416 U.S. 21.

178 Commission Implementing Decision of 10.7.2023 pursuant to Regulation (EU) 2016/679 of the European Parliament and of the Council on the adequate level of protection of personal data under the EU-US Data Privacy Framework, Brussels, 10.7.2023 C(2023) 4745 final.

the US the Right to Financial Privacy Act provides a government authority with the power to obtain financial records held by financial institutions pursuant to an administrative subpoena only under specific circumstances. In other words, in the US there is a stricter requirement, following on from individual statues, for specific matters, such as financial privacy. At the moment, under the EU regulation, cross-border access to data, including the financial, will be regulated by the Framework for Financial Data Access (FFDA).

Facial recognition technology

As a consequence of IT development, which has become impressive during and since the global pandemic, the banking sector uses, as a security mechanism, biometric recognition in order to guarantee security in banking transactions. The most well-known mechanism is facial recognition that uses biometric methods.

Facial recognition[179] is easy to conceive and can be efficiently utilised for "bulk scanning," which, otherwise, would appear difficult to other biometrics technologies, such as fingerprint and iris recognition.

To elaborate, in order to enhance mobile banking facilities and to ensure that banking transactions will be more secure, transactions will also become more efficient. The traditional mechanisms, such as PIN, can easily be hacked. In this scenario, FRT shall be used in online transactions, which is more reliable and builds trust between the users of online banking systems.

FRT involves a system based on a comparison between the actual user and her/his counterpart stored in a bank; this comparison is made with the help of neural networks. The latter increase in accuracy, while comparison and ensuing approval are used for the execution of the transaction.

In the banking system, the algorithm used for facial recognition is FaceNet, an algorithm which involves proxy detection: the system does not accept an image of the user as an input, and also when there is a group of persons visible during image recognition, the system takes the face that has the majority percentage in the input image.[180]

The advantages of FRT payments are as follows:

- Rapidity, because the entire validation process takes only several seconds;
- A contactless methodology, because all that is necessary is a device, such as a mobile phone, with a camera able to scan a human face;
- Convenience, because it is useful when users forget to carry credit cards or mobile phones with them or when their hands are full with other purchased goods and they cannot enter a PIN or scan their fingerprint while making another purchase.
- Security, because it is safer than some traditional payment methods, such as using a password to authorise credit card or mobile payments.

179 Also, facial recognition technology, or FRT.
180 (Venkatesan et al. 2021).

By contrast, FRT is surrounded in uncertainty and risks for users, especially privacy and security concerns because:

- FRT systems can be hacked: hackers can obtain targets' photographs or videos from non-FRP sources (e.g. social network sites) and present these images to an FRP system;
- FRT providers can use or share collected facial information with the government or other surveillance companies and these data can be used to identify people outside of FRP, such as in street cameras or workplace surveillance. Rules and regulations are needed to govern the collection, storage, and use of facial information and to protect users' privacy.[181]

4.5.3 IT and financial services

In this sub-chapter, we refer, more precisely, to fintech. This term does have a general meaning that encompasses both banking and financial sector, albeit a specific one.

In other words, "digital banking" refers to the IT usage, such as websites and mobile applications to provide banking services from banks. By contrast, fintech banking is the enablement of financial services and transactions methods for a variety of financial and non-financial business.

It is also true that the neo-banks, such as the IT bank, constitute the broader part of the fintech world. More precisely, fintech refers to, in this specific sub-chapter, financial intermediation activity based on IT and digital solutions. Thus, fintech means specialisation in the financial and IT sectors: it offers financial products via a financial circuit, such as digital platforms, and other technological support. Further, fintech, often, is perceived as an entity able to offer traditional banking and financial services but without a bank.[182]

Ultimately, from Fintech is derived insurtech: the insurance industry was not immune from the fintech approach. Insurtech concerns the applications of a variety of technologies in the field of insurance, to cut costs and enhance processes.[183] More precisely, insurtech involves the use of blockchain, AI, the internet of things (IoT), social networks and other technologies.[184]

Roboadvice

The term roboadvice is a portmanteau consisting of two words: "robo," an abbreviation of "robot," which is "a machine controlled by a computer that is used to perform jobs automatically," and "advice," an opinion offered about what to do or how to act in a particular situation.[185]

181 (Li and Li 2023).
182 (Tanda and Schena 2019).
183 (Lin and Chen 2020).
184 (Lauria 2018).
185 Cambridge Dictionary 2021.

Based on this, roboadvice can be outlined as an automated system that advises on finance, especially wealth meanings: the entire financial advisory becomes managed via a digital and automatic system.

As with a human financial advisor, the roboadvisor analyses the financial situation of a customer thanks to an algorithmic system. The latter achieves an association between customers' information to a suitable portfolio allocation and implementation of its recommendation.

This mechanism may be described as a process divided into three phases:

- Initiation and profiling: via an online module, customers make a self-assessment about of their risk-affinity and investment characteristics and provide investment goals;
- Matching and customisation: the risk profile is transferred automatically into the recommendation of a portfolio allocation. At the end of this phase, it is marked an offer and the implementation of the portfolio for the customer;
- Monitoring and rebalancing: the customers have permanent online access to their portfolio, and get reports about the performance as well as financial news and occasionally education content.

Roboadvice shall be informed by level of trust, transparency, ease of use, usefulness and roboadvice expertise.

In order to achieve a higher level of trust, some scholars found that giving a name and a human form to an avatar means increasing factors of trust, especially when the task complexity is perceived as low. In order words, a higher degree of humanisation increases the perceived social presence and trust.[186]

As far as transparency is concerned, potential users should be in a position to totally understand the process and bring familiarity with this new technology. Ultimately, regarding the perceived expertise, it is crucial that it is manifest in the decision-making process.[187]

From a historical perspective, roboadvice became widespread in the aftermath of the financial crises, 2007–2008, in small start-ups.[188]

From a risk perspective, roboadvice technology can be tied both to consumer and systemic risk: the first is microfinancial and the second one is macrofinancial risk. The most prevalent consumer risk seems to be the unsuitability of the individual advice: the output does not always fit the actual situation and risk preferences of the respective individual. In other words, roboadvice does not realise an assessment of the individual's situation including all particular events exhaustively. Further, the unsuitable recommendation is likely to affect a large number of customers and therefore cause damage on a much bigger scale than incorrect human advice. Finally, roboadvice may be vulnerable to third-party manipulation or hacking.

186 (Morana et al. 2020).
187 (Torno, Metzler and Torno 2021).
188 (Chiu and Deipenbrock 2021).

From an opposing view, there is also systemic risk in financial stability and cyber risk. These are likely to appear when roboadvisors grow in scale and become a major force in the financial market. The systemic risks are related to two phenomena: herding risk and flash crash.

Herding risk is when roboadvice has the potential to exhibit greater herding behaviour than traditional portfolio advisors, leading to concentration risks. Since market participants can act in ways that exacerbate the degree and impact of fluctuation on economic growth and market prices, herding can increase the amplitude of swings in asset prices and lead to an increased incidence of unidirectional portfolio shifts. It is clear that can lead to, at least, a financial problem.

Flash crash: the most prominent took place in 2010 when American stock indices collapsed and dropped by about 9% for approximately half an hour.

As far as the regulation is concerned, within the European Union there is no specific regulation on the matter of roboadvisors. The main legal frameworks are as follows:

- The Digital Operational Resilience Act (DORA) – Regulation (EU) 2022/2554[189] as a part of the digital finance package to support the potential of digital finance in terms of innovation and competition.
- Markets in Financial Instruments Directive[190] and more precisely Article 17: it states that if an "investment firm that engages in algorithmic trading shall have in place effective systems and risk controls suitable to the business it operates to ensure that its trading systems are resilient and have sufficient capacity, are subject to appropriate trading thresholds and limits and prevent the sending of erroneous orders or the systems otherwise functioning in a way that may create or contribute to a disorderly market";[191]
- European Securities and Markets Authority's guidelines,[192] in which it is classified how firms can assess suitability when providing roboadvice. The firms shall inform their client about the suitable assessment and its purpose in a clear and simply way; establish, implement and maintain adequate policies and procedures; and collect all necessary information about the client's knowledge and experience before providing investment advice or portfolio management services.

189 Regulation of the European Parliament and of the Council on digital operational resilience for the financial sector and amending Regulations 1060/2009/EC, 648/2012/EU, 600/2014/EU and 909/2014/EU Brussels, 24.9.2020 COM(2020) 595 final 2020/0266 (COD).

190 MiFID II – Directive 2014/65/EU of the European Parliament and of the Council Directive 2014/65/Eu of the European Parliament and of the Council of 15 May 2014 on markets in financial instruments and amending Directive 2002/92/EC and Directive 2011/61/EU.

191 Article 17(1).

192 ESMA, final guidelines on certain aspects of the Mifid 2 appropriateness and execution-only requirements.

Sandbox regulation

From an etymological perspective, sandbox alludes to a safe playground in which an experiment's collective experiences can take place without having to face the strict rules of the "real world." In more recent years, this concept has been applied in several, also non-financial, areas. A sandbox for programmers was established, where potentially unsafe codes could be run and studied, without risk of infecting the entire system. Furthermore, sandbox is also used in medicine, where it refers to clinical trials for new methods of treatment: a drug is being tested on a limited and specified group of patients to evaluate its effect before becoming authorised for the market.

All of these have in common the circumstance that, before an innovative product is being put on the market, it is tested in a safe environment where potential harm is strongly limited and cannot break out of the box, causing widespread damage.

In the financial sector, sandbox refers to a controlled space in which business can test and validate innovative products, services and business models and delivery mechanism with the support of an authority for limited period of time.

The idea of a regulatory sandbox for financial services was pioneered by the British Financial Conduct Authority[193] in 2016, and after, also the Financial Stability Board adopted its own "sandbox."[194] From an EU perspective, on 14 February 2023 the European Commission launched a regulatory sandbox for innovative use cases involving Distributed Ledger Technologies (DLT).

The EU sandbox establishes a pan-European framework for regulatory dialogues to increase legal certainty for innovative blockchain technology solutions. Its aim is to provide a framework for regulators, supervising authorities and blockchain innovators to engage in regulatory dialogue, identify obstacles from a legal regulatory perspective in a safe and confidential environment, and increase legal certainty for innovative decentralised technology solutions, including blockchain.

Each regulator defines certain requirements to determine which firms should be granted access to the sandbox. In other words, every organisation publishes a list with the eligibility criteria for the upcoming cohort.

Numerous approaches are taken to protect customers who participate in the sandbox testing, FCA, for instance, ensures consumers protection on a case-by-case basis with the follows standard:

- Retail customers: if a firm fails, they have always a right to complain to the firm, then to Financial Ombudsman Service, and have access to the Financial Services Compensation Scheme (FSCS);
- Sophisticated customers: depending on the specific trial and where it is legally possible, it shall be considered a test that only engages with sophisticated customers who have consented to limiting their claim for compensation;

193 FCA, Regulatory Sandbox.
194 FCA, Regulatory Sandbox.

- Additional safeguards connected with the size, scale and risks from the trial; additional safeguards may be necessary.

In the case of roboadvice additional safeguards were established: most cases require the firm to include qualified financial advisers checking the automated device outputs generated by the underlying algorithms, in order to avoid unsuitable advice.

In most cases sandbox participants must provide an exit strategy as part of their application. The objective is to minimise the potential detriment to participating consumers and it can, therefore, be partly understood as an investor protection advice.

Also, FCA in 2023 launched the Digital Sandbox to test the environment. This means that firms can be supported at a very early stage of product development by "enabling experimentation." Participants in a digital sandbox will have permanent access to datasets and application program interfaces (APIs), including public, synthetic or anonymised data sets to testing and validation the T system.

It will also have data security protection to allow experimentation while safeguarding the data assets on the platform and will be a collaborative platform to allow diversity of thought, share experiences, and foster an ecosystem between teams, observers and mentors.

Generally speaking, a sandbox for the IT financial sector does have some advantages. First, the dialogue between regulator and the regulated make it straightforward for fintech to seek clarification when encountering IT problems. Further, sandboxes would reduce the time-to-market cycle by smoothing the authorisation process. Strong support by the competent authority makes identifying and complying with respective rules much faster and much more cost-efficient. Sandbox, indeed, results also, in a smooth entrance in financial markets for small firms. Finally, thanks to sandbox regulation, an early close supervision ensures safety for consumers because they are able to identify and address risk for consumers and the system as a whole. In other words, supervision, together with transparency and enhanced communication with all market participants, are further able to create trust and mitigate scepticism towards some digital-based financial services.

Sandbox is also a means of supporting financial stability, because this piece of legislation creates trust in financial products and makes new firms more attractive to potential investors.[195]

From a different perspective, FCA sandbox regulation may also encounter some risks, at least two. The first one is called risk-washing fintech. A sandbox engages in risk-washing, to the extent that it provides a stamp of marketability for fintech without being able to control for systemic risk. To elaborate, a lack of transparency of its operation creates an opportunity for framing fintech's riskiness. Furthermore, its involvement in the creation of an adequate risk-profile makes it incapable of independently evaluating that same risk-profile.

195 (Ringe and Christopher 2020).

The second risk is named risk-taming: this means attempting to produce the characteristics of an economy market, client or asset class that decreases the risk of engaging with it at an acceptable level in terms of profits. Risk-taming aims to increase firms' profit seeking capacity generally, but in particular, their capacity to provide bankable assets which function as a place to park wealth, and as collateral in the shadow banking system.

Risk-washing is also different from de-risking: the latter occurs when financial companies withdraw their services from clients and even entire markets, because the profits to be made are outweighed by the risk involved. De-risking can take several forms, such as disengaging from an economy market, client or asset class because their characteristics impose more risk that can be justified by possible profits.[196]

It is crucial to note that risk-washing resembles greenwashing, but from the sandbox perspective, at least three risks can arise:

- Information generated by sandbox tends to obscure the systemic economic and social dangers of individual fintech efforts. If the specific assessment criteria for fintech products in the sandbox are not adequate a problematic effect may arise for consumer interest and financial stability;[197]
- Sandbox design contains a level of opacity or lack of transparency: although it promotes a dialogue between regulator and regulated and it promotes transparency between these two parties, it remains opaque for the others, *i.e.* firms and consumers;[198]
- Sandbox involved the development of fintech firms and products; as a fintech firm goes through the testing period, the firm's risk profile is jointly shaped by the fintech developer and the correspondent sandbox officials. Therefore, at the end of the testing period, the sandbox team is not independent, and it is not in a position to adopt an independent evaluation.

Crowdfunding

Crowdfunding is a digital economy in which funds provided by large numbers of individuals, the crowd, are aggregated and distributed through online platforms to a range of actors and institutions.

The digital economy of crowdfunding emerged in the US and the UK around a decade ago; it is closely related to the wider trends of crowdsourcing, coproduction, and the sharing economy where ideas, knowledge and other assets are made available and accessed by geographically distributed online communities.

Crowdfunding circuits transfer funds that are provided by large numbers of individuals who are collectively referred to as the crowd. Funds are aggregate and distributed through online platforms to a range of actors and institutions.[199]

196 (Brown and Piroska 2022).
197 (Omarova 2020).
198 (Allen 2019).
199 (Langley 2016).

Financial-return crowdfunding[200] is a manifestation of marketplace investing, representing a significant part of the fintech industry. From an overview, crowdfunding includes either lending transactions, whereby the investors/lenders expect to receive the principal and interest and the end of the lending periods or equity transaction. The last refers to securities, offered by a privately held company, to the general public through the medium of an online platform. Therefore, it is possible to draw a distinction between the following:

- Loan-based (LB) crowdfunding, basically refers to P2P lending;
- Equity crowdfunding or investment-based (IB) crowdfunding.

As far as regulation is concerned, national approaches among member states shall be either traditional or innovative. The first one extends prior banking or financial regulation to crowdfunding, and the second consists of the adoption of ad hoc rules or a fully fledged regime.

In the European Union legal system, platforms do not lend money directly but only facilitate loans among their clients. In some business models, either the platform takes a participation in the loans made through it or a bank extends the loans on behalf of crow-lenders.

F-R crowdfunding seems to represent an important alternative form of finance, especially for small- and medium-sized enterprises[201] bridging existing funding gaps and expanding financial inclusion. At the same time, it is also an interesting investment opportunity in terms of diversification in the financial market and financial/non-financial/ethical returns.

As a result of European crowdfunding service providers for business,[202] crowdfunding services will be offered in the EU only by legal persons that are established in the EU territory and authorised under the same regulation.[203] It is required that crowdfunding service providers shall act honestly, fairly and professionally in accordance with the best interest of their clients. Further, the EU regulation does not consent that "service providers shall not pay or accept any remuneration, discount or non-monetary benefit for routing investors' orders to a particular crowdfunding offer made on their crowdfunding platform or to a particular crowdfunding offer made on a third-party crowdfunding platform."[204]

As far as the borders are concerned, this regulation does not cover donation-based and reward-based crowdfunding due to the lack of any financial return and investment perspective. Further, offering of tokens (initial coin offerings – ICOs) does not cover by the EU regulation.

200 Also, F-R crowdfunding.

201 SMEs.

202 Regulation 2020/1503/EU of the European Parliament and of the Council of 7 October 2020 on European crowdfunding service providers for business, and amending Regulation 2017/1129/EU and Directive 2019/1937/EU.

203 See Article 3(1).

204 Article 3(3).

A problematic topic is concerned with the Brexit situation: in this respect British crowdfunding providers should be treated as third countries' providers and, therefore, denied access to the European crowdfunding service providers[205] regime, unless establishing a separate stable and effective organisation in one of the member states. In this, the same UK government confirmed that the regulation will not be transposed in the UK law, after Brexit.[206]

In the UK legal system, crowdfunding must be authorised by the FCA: all firms authorised by the FCA are required to comply with FCA rules set out in the FCA Handbook of Rules and Guidance. The UK regulation is not confined to participation by an individual either as a lender or borrower, and it covers investment beyond the mere granting of loans.

Lending technologies

Peer-to-peer lending, or P2P, has emerged an appealing new channel of financing. Online P2P lending platforms allow individual lenders to aggregate their funds to finance loan request from an individuals and businesses. Essentially, it may define as a debt form of crowdfunding.

P2P lending platforms constitute, essentially, an online market that matches the supply and demand of funds. The fact that the internet facilitates disintermediation by allowing parties to communicate directly with one another is a fundamental reason. However, the potential for the growth is also because of a number of competitive advantages of P2P lending platforms over the banks.

More precisely, the P2P financial market helps investor and borrowers to invest or obtain loans without a traditional financial intermediary: it is a fast-growing technology trend that can displace traditional retail banking.

An efficient regulation of the financial services market combined with technological innovation make P2P platforms more competitive compared to commercial banks.

P2P lending is the most popular form of alternative finance by amount of capital raised: it is part of the broader lending-based crowdfunding market. Among scholars, it is defined as an umbrella term. It refers to digital business models that connect those who can lend or invest money directly with those who need financing.[207]

As a new model of organisation alternative to the traditional banking, in P2P lending, a legal person, in the form of a digital platform, collects and pools separate amounts of funds from individuals or businesses in a crowd, to finance collectively a larger loan to other needful individuals, in their capacity of consumers or small entrepreneurs.

Relating to the different model, this is lending and borrowing between private parties through the intermediation of a for profit online platform that matches

205 ECSP.

206 (Macchiavello 2021).

207 Crowdfunding, European Commission, https://ec.europa.eu/info/business-economy-euro/growth-and-investment/financing-investment/crowdfunding_en (last visited Dec. 2, 2020).

lenders with borrowers. Properly IT development permits this technological innovation in the financial services sector.

The dealings among the three parties of a P2P lending transaction define the private law relationship: fundamentally, it is a basic unsecured form. The borrower makes an inquiry or application to the platform indicating the amount and maturity of the sought loan. Further, the platform makes an assessment of the credit risk involved and sets the related interest rate to be published to potential lenders subject to the borrower's arrangement of the platform's terms and conditions. The latter includes the obligation to repay the capital with interest in the agreed timeline and penalties for delays. The lenders, creditors or investors, undertake a contract with the platform: this includes a contract for the benefit of a third party and places their offers. At least, the loan is originated and the platform channels the funds from the lenders to the borrowers.[208]

The crucial element is the lack of contract between lenders and borrowers: moreover, these two parties remain anonymous to each other. There are different platform models that shape the information changed between the parties:

- The platform matches the lenders with the borrowers;
- Lenders may choose the borrowers in a pool by their characteristics or profile supplied by the platform – that is, loan size, maturity, a basic risk scoring or rating, interest rate and return on investment.

In the P2P model, the relations between the parties may be described as a triadic relationship consisting of providers, intermediaries and consumers, where the value creation control is decentralised.

Different from this is B2C model: a relationship between provider and consumer, which is referred to as a dyadic relationship. This model has a governance structure characterised by centralisation where the primary focus is to possess unique and hard-to-imitate resources.

Finally, there is the B2B model, where the value is created by the synergies between the parties. The B2B economy realises a value for its stakeholders and, simultaneously, created value and opportunities.[209]

Cryo-finance

Cryo-finance refers to a way to find funding in order to payment the cryonics services offer by different Russian and American cryo-organisations.

Human cryonics, the preservation of the body, or even only the head of a human being in liquid nitrogen, is the technology at the moment. If at the beginning of its "story" this medical treatment saw its utilisation as applying to at the earliest moments of life, in recent times it is now possible that a grown human being could

208 (Lenz 2016).
209 (Breunig, Johansen and Kristiansen 2022).

be surrounded by liquid nitrogen at a temperature of −196°C. The ultimate goal is to give another chance of life to a cryo-patient.

Not only has cryonics a strong link with medical law but also with the financial and economic fields. In this respect, one of the cryo-organisations, Alcor Life Extension Foundation, in order to ensure that the cryonic suspension does not come to halt due to the insufficiency of funds, adopts a care trust fund. More precisely, there is a dual financial system of separate trusts.

At the beginning, the Patient Care Trust (PCT) was established and, only in the following years, came the introduction of the Alcor Care Trust Supporting Organization (ACT).

The first one of these[210] was a legal entity of which the title of beneficiary is Alcor: a dead person, indeed, holds no rights as beneficiary. The mechanism is a conservation fund used to deposit a sizable share of the cryo-patients' funding. In other words, before being accepted into Alcor's programme, the member shall provide proof that the minimum funding is payable to Alcor. The proof defined as acceptable is different if there is an insurance policy or a prepayment.

With the insurance policy, the member shall transfer ownership of the policy to Alcor; Alcor provides a buy-back agreement guaranteeing no changes will be made to the policy without the member's written consent. Additionally, Alcor must be identify as the beneficiary of the policy. If the individuals choose the prepayment, he shall provide Alcor with the minimum cryopreservation amount though such payment method. These funds will be placed into either a bank account or Alcor's pre-approved trust agreement.

It is also important to highlight that there are also standby charges, and their costs change in relation to the different types of documentation and/or contractual commitments.

The second species of fund is the ACT and was established in 2016. ACT is instrumental in guaranteeing, for an indefinite period of time, the arrangement and costs for storage and preservation. The ACT works in conjunction with the PCT. The ACT shall be for the exclusive not-for-profit research and educational purpose of providing care for individuals[211] who have been placed into cryopreservation or other forms of biostasis. It is worth mentioning that this pattern, concerned exclusively with long-term research donors, is particularly used by Alcor. The expiry is the future time which is the moment when it will be possible to repair and revive them and, more precisely, when it will be possible to regard them legally "alive," functional and independent.

ACT is also strategic to support the scientific research directly related to contribute to development of resuscitation technologies. To achieve this further goals, ACT trustees may create a separate reserve account for research with the ACT. The latter reserve account will be a bookkeeping account within the ACT trust estate and will be invested in the same manner as all ACT funds.

210 Alcor Life Extension Foundation.

211 They, in the Alcor terminology, are called patients.

Alcor establishes the terms and conditions of the ACT trustees. First at all, there shall be five ACT trustees, and all of these must be cryopreservation members of Alcor. In this respect, only three individual trustees shall be members of Alcor's board of directors. A goal is to have as many trustees as reasonably feasible who are related to or have had a significant personal involvement with an Alcor biostasis patient.

Additionally, no individual trustee may be an employee of Alcor or receive compensation from the ACT, the PCT or Alcor. An exception is for those benefits available to any Alcor member or as otherwise expressly provided herein or in the ACT trust agreement.[212]

In light of this, it is obvious that not only is cryonics a bioethical matter, but also it impinges on a financial field. As it is corroborated in this work, before signing a cryo-conservation agreement, an individual shall rely on both financial sources to pay his suspension and to live in the future. Potentially, the solution shall be the revival trust.[213]

Thanks to the revival trust, assets are set aside. The deposit is in the interest of any cryonically frozen individual, should they ever be given a second life. A person, who wishes to be cryonically frozen, merely creates a trust holding various assets and names themselves as beneficiary.[214]

As far as the trust in the cryonics world is concerned, this refers to the personal revival trust (PRT),[215] a peculiar type of trust that is set up to hold assets for a person in a cryonic preservation until they are revived.[216] It should be noted that in the vast majority of countries, PRTs are not legal because they are inconsistent with perpetuities (RAP).[217] By contrast, the RAP poses no obstacles in states that have either repealed or significantly modified perpetuities. To summarise, in such post-RAP states, practitioners such as lawyers are able to incorporate dynasty trusts which can last for centuries or be even perpetual. This depends on the laws existing in that country.

4.6 Green and techno-digital economy

The green growth, discussed at the beginning of this chapter, shall be support by finance, which is green and smart finance. The green development level reflected in green finance indices have an important effort. It can create a new business model in which it may be encompassed energy, environmental, business, financial and banking services.

In this context, "smart city" refers to a whole city organisation from infrastructure, to transport and environment. For instance, it is possible to realise a link

212 Alcor Care Trust Supporting Organization Operating Agreement – Alcor.
213 (Taylor 2021).
214 (Dedon 2018).
215 (Regaldo 2006).
216 (Engelhardt 2006).
217 More precisely: "a contingent future interest must vest, if it all, within twenty-one years after the expiration of some life in being when the interest was created" (Dukeminier and Krier 2003).

between financial and a business activity, *i.e.* the farming sector. Thanks to green support it becomes possible to achieve multiple goals: support a critical sector, enhance the use of IT systems in farming, and reduce carbon emissions thanks to a green approach both to banking and finance.

Moreover, via sustainable finance, a lot of sustainable projects, both from an EU and UK perspectives, may be funded. For example, it could support the increased use of "drones" as a part of an EU agenda or autonomous vehicles on the UK side.

Furthermore, thanks to sustainable investment and a cooperation between IT development and fintech, a support is also given to the green port strategy, the latter being an investment and encouragement to an environment-friendly approach to maritime business activities and ship industries. The reference, in this case, is to the UK Maritime 2050 – Navigating the Future.

In summary, green and blue, sustainability and technology, finance and ecosystem, potentially, may all be heading to the same outcomes.

References

Afzal, A., E. Rasoulinezhad, and Z. Malik. "Green Finance and Sustainable Development in Europe." *Economic Research* 35, no. 1 (2022): 5150–5163.

Allen, H. "Regulatory Sandboxes." *The George Washington Law Review* 87, no. 3 (2019): 579–645.

Antonopoulos, A. "Bitcoin Security Model: Trust by Computation a Shift from Trusting Math." *Radar*. http://radar.oreilly.com/2014/02/bitcoin-security-model-trust-by-computation.html, 2014.

Azmi, W., M.K. Hassan, R. Houston, and M.S. Karim. "ESG Activities and Banking Performance: International Evidence." *Journal of International Financial Markets, Institutions & Money*, no. 70 (2021): 1–18.

Barski, C., and C. Wilmer. *Bitcoin for the Befuddled*. No Scratch Press, 2015.

Berrou, R., P. Dessertine, and M. Migliorelli. "An Overview of Green Finance." In *The Rise of Green Finance in Europe*, edited by M. Migliorelli and P. Dessertiine. Cham: Palgrave Macmillan, 2019.

Bočánek, M. "First Draft of Crypto-Asset Regulation (MICA) with the European Union and Potential Implementation." *Financial Law Review* 22, no. 2 (2021): 37–53.

Boneva, L., G. Ferrucci, and F.P. Mongelli. "Climate Change and Central Banks: What Role for Monetary Policy?" *Climate Policy* 22, no. 6 (2022): 770–787.

Boonstra, W. "CBDC and the International Position of the Euro." *SUERF The European and Finance Forum*, no. 269 (2022): 1–11.

Breunig, K.J., H. Johansen, and J.R. Kristiansen. "Digital Entrepreneurship Across P2P, B2C and B2B Contexts: A Bibliometric Analysis Deconstructing Extant Research on Sharing Economy Business Models." In *Digital Entrepreneurship and the Sharing Economy*, edited by E. Vinogradov, B. Leick, and D. Assadi, 52–72. Routledge, 2022.

Brosens, T. *Why Bitcoin Transactions Are More Expensive than You Think*, 2017. Economic and Financial Analysis, Global Economics.

Brown, E., and D. Piroska. "Governing Fintech and Fintech as Governance: The Regulatory Sandbox, Riskwashing, and Disruptive Social Classification." *New Political Economy* 27, no. 1 (2022): 19–32.

Carvalho, J.M. "Sale of Goods and Supply of a Digital Content and Digital Services – Overview of Directive 2019/770 and 2019/771." *EuCML – Journal of European Consumer and Market Law* 8, no. 5 (2019): 194–201.

Casolari, F., M. Taddeo, A. Turillazzi, and L. Floridi. "How to Improve Smart Contracts in the European Union Data Act." *Digital Society* 2, no. 1 (2023): 9–15.
Cheong, B.C. "Avatars in the Metaverse: Potential Legal Issues and Remedies." *International Cybersecurity Law Review* 3, no. 2 (2022): 467–494.
Chesbrough, H. "Business Model Innovation: Opportunities and Barriers." *Long Range Planning* 43, no. 2–3 (2010): 354–363.
Chiu, I.H.-Y., and G. Deipenbrock. *Routledge Handbook of Financial Technology and Law*. Routledge, 2021.
Cortet, M., T. Rijks, and S. Nijland. "PSD2: The Digital Transformation Accelerator for Banks." *Journal of Payments Strategy & Systems* 10, no. 1 (2016): 13–27.
Courtneidge, R. "The Implications of the Payment Services Directive and the Second E-Money Directive." *Journal of Payments Strategy & Systems* 6, no. 3 (2012): 219–224.
Cullen, J. "After 'HLEG': EU Banks, Climate Change Abatement and the Precautionary Principle." *Cambridge Yearbook of European Legal Studies*, no. 20 (2018): 61–87.
Cullen, J. "Central Banks and Climate Change: Mission Impossible?"*Journal of Financial Regulation* 9, no. 2 (2023): 174–209.
D'Alvia, D. "Legal Costants and the 'Costant' Outside the Law: Mobile Payments in Comparative Perspective Under European Union Law." *Maastricht Journal of European and Comparative Law* 28, no. 3 (2021): 332–355.
Dedon, J. "Preserving Assets in Trusts for Clients Considering Cryonics." *Estate Planning Magazine*. https://www.dedononestateplanning.com/wp-content/uploads/2018/07/ETPL-August-2018-Dedon.pdf, 2018.
de Gioia Carabellese, P., and C. Della Giustina. *The Law of Securitisations. From Crises to Techno-Sustainability*. Routledge, 2023.
D'Orazio, P., and L. Popoyan. "Taking Up the Climate Change." *LEM Working Paper Series*, no. 19 (2019): 1–35.
Dikau, S., R. Robins, and U. Volz. *Ulimate-Neutral Central Banking: How the European System of Central Banks Can Support the Transition to Net-Zero*. Grantham Research Institute on Climate Change and London School of Economics and Political Science, 2021.
DiLeo, M. "Climate Policy at the Bank of England: The Possibilities and Limits of Green Central Banking." *Climate Policy* 23, no. 6 (2023): 671–688.
Dourado, E., and J. Brito. "Cryptocurrency." *The New Palgrave Dictionary of Economics*. https://www.mercatus.org/research/journal-articles/cryptocurrency, 2014.
Dukeminier, J., and J.E. Krier. "The Rise of the Perpetual Trust." *UCLA Law Review* 50, no. 6 (2003): 1303–1344.
Engelhardt, E. "Issues Facing Trustees of Personal Revival Trusts." *Journal of Person Cyberconciousness* 12, no. 1 (2006).
Ferretti, F. "Open Banking: Gordian Legal Knots in the Uncomfortable Cohabitation between the PSD2 and GDPR." *European Review of Private Law* 30, no. 1 (2022): 73–102.
Franco, P. *Understanding Bitcoin: Cryptocurrency, Engineering and Economics*. Wiley, 2015.
Franks, M.A. "Unwilling Avatars: Idealism and Discrimination in Cyberspace." *Columbia Journal of Gender and Law* 20, no. 2 (2011): 224–232.
Fuller, C. "Bitcoin vs. Bank of Finland: Cryptocurrencies Ruled as Commodities after." *International Business Times*, 2014, online.
Gikay, A.A. "Regulating Decentralized Cryptocurrencies under Payment Services Law: Lessons from European Union Law." *Case Western Reserve Journal of Law* 9 (2018): 1–35.
Gunawan, J., P. Permatasari, and U. Sharma. "Exploring Sustainability and Green Banking Disclosures: A Study of Banking Sector." *Environment, Development and Sustaibability* 24 (2022): 11153–11194.

Jackson, J., and D. Bailey. "Facilitating the Transition to Net Zero' and Institutional Change in the Bank of England: Perceptions of the Environmental Mandate ant Its Policy Implication within the British State." *The British Journal of Politics and International Relations*, 2023.

Ji, X., Y. Mirza, M. Umar, and S.K.A. Rizvi. "The Impact of Carbon Neutrality on the Investment Performance: Evidence from the Equity Mutual Funds in BRICS." *Journal of Environmental Management* 297 (2021): 113–228.

Kim, D.H., Y.C. Wu, and S.C. Lin. "Carbon Dioxide Emissions and the Finance Course." *Energy Economics*, no. 297 (2020): 104–788.

Kuo Chuen, D.L. *Handbook of Digital Currency: Bitcoin, Innovation, Financial Instruments, and Big Data*. Elsevier, 2015.

Kuszewski, P. "Impact of the PSD2 Directive and Strategic Use of Costly Innovation." *Warsaw School of Economics, Banking Institute*, 2018, online.

Langley, P. "Crowdfunding in the United Kingdom: A Cultural Economy." *Economic Geography* 92, no. 3 (2016): 301–321.

Lauria, V. "Free from Legacy Baggage, Asian Insurtech Firms Are Reimagining the Insurance." *Forbs*. https://www. forbes. com/sites/vinnielauria/2018/06/20/free-from-legacy-baggage-asian-insurtech-firms-are-reimagining-the-insurance-industry, 2018.

Lee, J., and R. Li. "Law and Regulation for Decentralised Autonomous Organisations (DAOs)." *SSRN Online*. https://papers.ssrn.com/sol3/papers.cfm?abstract_id=4455052, 2023.

Lenz, R. "Peer-to-Peer Lending: Opportunities and Risks." *European Journal of Risk Regulation* 7, no. 4 (2016): 688–700.

Li, C., and H. Li. "Disentangling Facial Recognition Payment Service Usage Behavior: A Trust Perspective." *Telematics and Informatics*, no. 77 (2023).

Lin, L., and C. Chen. "The Promise and Perils of Insurtech." *Singapore Journal of Legal Studies*, no. 1 (2020): 115–142.

Macchiavello, E. "The European Crowdfunding Service Providers Regulation: The Future of Marketplace Lending and Investing in Europe and the 'Crowdfunding Nature' Dilemma." *European Business Law Review* 32, no. 3 (2021): 557–604.

McConville, P. "The Metaverse: What Does It Mean for Banks?" *Retail Banker International*. https://www.retailbankerinternational.com/comment/peter-mcconville-synechron-expert-comment-banking-in-the-metaverse/, 2023.

McGreevy, J. "Digital Euro: Design and Reasons for Its Creation." Thesis Project, 2023.

Minesso, M., Mehl A., and Stracca, L. "Central banking digital currency in an open economy." *Journal of Monetary Economics* 127, no. 2 (2022): 54–68.

Mooij A. "The Digital Euro and Energy Considerations: can the ECB Introduce the Digital Euro Considering the Potential Energy Requirements?" *German Law Journal* 23, no. 9 (2022): 1246–1265.

Morana, S., U. Gnewuc, D. Jung, and C. Granig. "The Effect of Anthropomorphism on Investment Decision-Making with Robo-Advisor Chatbots." 2020.

Mystakidis, S. "Metaverse." *Encyclopedia* 2, no. 1 (2022): 486–497.

Nakamoto, S. "Bitcoin: A Peer-to-Peer Electronic Cash System." *Bitcoin.org*, 2015.

Narin, N.G. "A Content Analysis of the Metaverse." *Journal of Metaverse* 1, no. 1 (2021): 17–24.

Omarova, S.T. "Technology v. Technocracy: Fintech as a Regulatory Challenge." *Journal of Financial Regulation* 6, no. 1 (2020): 75–124.

Pakhnenko, O., P. Rubanov, D. Hacar, V. Yatsenko, and I. Vida. "Digitalization of Financial Services in European Countries: Evaluation and Comparative Analysis." *Journal of International Studies*, no. 2 (2021): 267–282.

Parks, S.K. "Investors as Regulators: Green Bonds and the Governance Challenges of the Sustainable Finance Revolution." *Standford Journal of International Law*, no. 541 (2018): 1–48.

Petrović, M. "PSD2 Influence on Digital Banking Transformation – Banks' Perspective." *(JPMNT) Journal of Process Management – New Technologies, International* 8, no. 4 (2020): 1–14.

Pettifor, A. *The Cas for the Green New Deal*. Verso Publisher, 2019.

Pyka, M. "The EU Green Bond Standard: A Plausible Response." *European Business Organization Law Review*, no. 1 (2023): 1–21.

Regaldo, A. "A Cold Calculus Leads Cryonauts to Put Assets on Ice With Bodies Frozen, They Hope to Return Richer." *Wall Street Journal*, 2006.

Ringe, W.G., and U.O.F. Christopher. "Regulating Fintech in the EU: the Case for a Guided Sandbox." *European Journal of Risk Regulation* 11, no. 3 (2020): 604–629.

Ruiz-Blanco, S., S. Romero, and B. Fernandez-Feijoo. "Green, Blue or Black, But Washing – What Company Characteristics Determine Greenwashing?" *Environment, Development and Sustainability*, no. 24 (2022): 4025.

Sarkar, S. "Banking in Metaverse Opportunities and Challenges." *The Management Accountant Journal* 58, no. 1 (2023): 63–67.

Siderius, J. "An Unexpected Climate Activist: Central Banks and the Politics of the Climate-Neutral Economy." *Journal of European Public Policy*, no. 30 (2022): 873–897.

Sims, A. "Decentralised Autonomous Organisations: The State of Play." *New Zealand Law Journal*, no. 4 (2021): 337–340.

Sivaramakrishnan, S., R. Basu, and R. Dereskeviciute. "European Commission Issues Its First – and the World's Largest – Green Bond." *National Law Review* IX, no. 313 (2021).

Skinner, M.P. "Central Banks and Climate Change." *Vanderbilt* 74, no. 5 (2021): 1301–1364.

Tanda, A., and C.M. Schena. *FinTech, BigTech and Banks: Digitalisation and Its Impact on Banking Business Models*. Springer, 2019.

Taylor, G. "Dead on Arrival: A Call for Legislative Action with Respect to State and Federal Laws Surrounding Cryonics." *SMU Science and Technology Law Review* 24, no. 2 (2021): 383–412.

Thin Hang, N.P. "Policy Implications for the Green Bank Development in the Context of Global Climate Change." *Emerging Science Journal* 6, no. 4 (2022): 817–833.

Torno, A., D.R. Metzler, and V. Torno. "Robo-What?, Robo-Why?, Robo-How?-A Systematic Literature Review of Robo-Advice." Twenty-fifth Pacific Asia Conference on Information Systems, Dubai, 2021.

Valverde, S.C., and F.R. Fernandez. "Financial Digitalization: Banks, Fintech, Bigtech, and Consumers." *Journal of Financial Management, Markets and Institutions* 8, no. 1 (2020): 2040003.

Venkatesan, R., B. Anni Princy, V.D. Ambeth Kumar, M. Raghuraman, M.K. Gupta, A. Kumar, A. Kumar, and A.K. Khan. "Secure Online Payment Through Facial Recognition and Proxy Detection with the Help of TripleDES Encryption." *Journal of Discrete Mathematical Sciences and Cryptography* 24, no. 8 (2021): 2195–2205.

Wadesango, N., and B. Magaya. "The Impact of Digital Banking Services on Performance of Commercial Banks." *Journal of Management Information and Decision Sciences* 23, no. Special Issue (2020): 343–353.

Wagner, E., D. Bruggink, and D. Benevelli. Preparing Euro Payments for the Future: A Blueprint for a Digital Euro. *Journal of Payment Strategy & Systems* 15, no. 2 (2021): 165–187.

Weber, R.H., and A. Darbellay. "Legal Issues in Mobile Banking." *Journal of Banking Regulation* 11, no. 1 (2010): 129–145.

Wilson, C.M. II. "Data Sharing Is Caring: Consumer Privacy and International Approach to Open Banking." *George Washington International Law Review* 53, no. 3 (2022): 601–644.

Winkler, N., and B. Mattheis. "FinTech and Blockchain – Keep Bubbling? Or Better Get Real?" In *Digital Marketplaces Unleashed*, edited by C. Linnhoff-Popien, R. Schneider, and M. Zaddach, 382. Springer, n.d.

Zhang, L., Y. Xie, Y. Zheng, W. Xue, X. Zheng, and X. Xu. "The Challenges and Countermeasures of Blockchain in Finance and Economics." *Systems Research and Behavioral Science* 37, no. 4 (2020): 691–698.

Zilioli, C., and M. Ioannindis. "Climate Change and the Mandate of the ECB: Potential and Limits of Monetary Contribution to European Green Policies." *Common Market Law Review* 59, no. 2 (2022): 366–394.

5 Crisis

5.1 Introduction

Some scholars have claimed that banks are not susceptible to failure, as such institutions are deemed the paymasters par excellence in financial and international transactions. However, in truth, and as dramatically brought to light by the global financial crises of 2007/2008, banks may be illiquid or, even worse, become fully insolvent.[1] This should not have come as a surprise – although in reality it did – for the business of a bank is inherently risky. In fact, bank failures have occurred since banks have existed in the form as we know them today, *i.e.* since the 13th century. Moreover, the word "bankrupt," which can be found in practically all languages of the world to mean insolvency, even derives from the failure of a bank. *Bankruptcy* (English), *bankroet* (Dutch), *Bankrott* (German), *bancarota* (Portuguese) and *банкротство* (Russian) all find their origin in the Italian *banca rotta*. The ritual act of breaking a banker's table or *banco*,[2] behind which he conducted his business, used to signify this banker's insolvency.

An important issue that may arise when dealing with the insolvency of banks is the cross-border magnitude of the results of such insolvency; the globalisation of markets and the transnational activity of banks mean that international groups may operate across a wide spectrum of jurisdictions, with subsidiaries and/or branches established in each respective country.[3] In this scenario, the declaration of insolvency of the entire group, or of specific subsidiaries in a specific country,

1 Although the definition of insolvency and illiquidity varies per jurisdiction, from an accounting perspective, "insolvency" occurs when a company (or a financial institution) does not have adequate liquid assets (cash or assets easily converted into cash) to pay its debts when they fall due. The entity may be otherwise profitable and have a healthy balance sheet but may fall into insolvency if too many of its assets are difficult to convert quickly into cash (*i.e.* they are illiquid assets). Companies can, therefore, often recover from insolvency if they can persuade their creditors to give them long enough to convert fewer liquid assets into cash.

2 In Italian, the masculine *banco*, rather than *banca*, corresponds to the English "desk." Therefore, the original term *banco* (the masculine form) has more recently been usurped by the feminine *banca*, which is also the name defining a bank in contemporary Italian. Interestingly, the medieval term *banco* (again, literally "desk") is a synonym of the more recent *banca* (bank), albeit an archaic one, nowadays basically in desuetude.

3 See also above.

DOI: 10.4324/9781032628646-5

may give rise to delicate legal issues regarding the way in which the assets of the group, scattered across a diverse range of jurisdictions, must be treated. The seminal case epitomising the "mayhem" caused by a cross-border bank insolvency is that of BCCI, a financial institution with headquarters in London, Luxemburg and the Cayman Islands. In 1992, upon the onset of its crisis, insolvency procedures were initiated in the three aforementioned countries. As a matter of course, the three competent local courts within each of the three respective jurisdictions ruled that the assets relating or pertaining to the operations of BCCI should be distributed. However, these rulings appeared to be influenced by the different approach taken by some courts in further countries (that is to say, countries other than those where the headquarters were located), where BCCI had branches. Notably, a US court held that the assets of the BCCI branch located in New York should be ring-fenced and distributed preferentially to US creditors. These rulings, though, were inconsistent with the reality of BCCI's operations in New York; in fact, the branch located there did not have these assets on its own account but rather exclusively on behalf of the three headquarters for purposes of payment obligations in US dollars. An alternative course of action would have seen the relevant money deemed by the US courts as assets belonging to the three headquarters, rather than pertaining solely to the US branch.

The BCCI case is an example of the inherent difficulties which the organisation of insolvency proceedings may present for the operational activities of a bank at an international level. These proceedings, in more recent times, have been the subject matter of intervention in the form of a host of EU legislation. First, the Winding-up Directive[4] sets out harmonised private international law rules about the insolvency of credit institutions throughout the EU. This directive takes on board the legal dilemmas which came to prominence in the BCCI case and the inextricable difficulties originating from that; essentially, this piece of legislation dictates a general rule – the details of which are explained as the present section unfolds – according to which insolvency proceedings initiated against a bank in their home country must be recognised across the EU, while separate proceedings against branches located in further EU countries are precluded.[5]

Since the 2007/2008 financial crises, it is possible to infer that the history has been seen a never-ending chain of heterogenous turmoil. Although all of these are not related to financial and banking matter, in direct or indirect manner, they made an impact on economic ground. Therefore, the attention will start with Lehman

4 In full: Directive 2001/24/EC of the European Parliament and of the Council of 4 April 2001 on the reorganisation and winding up of credit institutions.

5 Ultimately, these rules aim to prevent any attempt, in a jurisdiction where the bank has got branches, to ring-fence the assets located there, to the benefit of the local creditors; all the assets of the bank, wherever located in the EU, must be deemed part of the global assets of the bank incorporated in its home country and, therefore, to be apprehended to be distributed among the creditors of the bank. Corollary of this rule is that the jurisdiction of the incorporation of the bank must treat all the creditors according to their rights.

Brothers' collapse, and discuss also the latest financial crises, such as Silicon Valley Bank and Credit Suisse.

5.2 The 2007–2008 banking and financial crisis

In order to discuss financial crises, it is essential to provide an overview of this phenomenon. In this respect, not only is a discussion about the single event but also a proper analysis focused on the banking turmoil which may result.

5.2.1 The pre-existing scenario

In order to regulate the entire financial market from an international perspective, consider the Basel Accord signed by Basel Committee on the banking supervision and established in 1974. The second one, *i.e.* Basel II, passed in 2006, was based on three pillars:

- Minimum capital requirement;
- Supervisory review;
- Market discipline.

This legal framework used to be affected by a number of flaws:

- It was not implemented in the USA during the boom in subprime mortgages and did not apply to non-bank lenders, nor to investment banks, nor once again to credit rating agencies;
- It tried to standardise capital requirements, although this contributed to the house market bubble;
- It legitimated the separation of the balance sheet of a bank and its operations;
- It encouraged banks to hold securities backed by residential mortgages, including subprime mortgages.

Moreover, Basel II placed emphasis on self-regulation, disclosure and transparency, and it overrated the principle of "home country rules." Consequently, banks from lax areas of supervision were free to operate according to their domestic norms, first and foremost in the European markets, but in America too.[6]

The years preceding the crisis were defined by scholars[7] as the period of Great Moderation in order to encompass the decline in macroeconomic volatility over the preceding 25 years, after the 1979 and 1980 crises.

The features of this period were (1) low inflation, (2) economic growth and (3) mild recession. The basic foundations of the Great Moderation were reduced inflation and the establishment of basic price stability. However, there was a decline of prices globally and, particularly, the prices of commodities, energy and

6 (Kolb 2010).

7 (Sher and Iyanatul 2010).

manufactured goods all fell together. Due to financial innovation and deregulation, banks started exploring and, then, decisively entering real estate lending.

Another important factor that contributed to the global financial crisis was the global imbalance and, more precisely, (1) the excessive saving by surplus countries, especially China, and (2) the excessive consumption by deficit countries led by the USA.[8]

In the Asian countries, such as South Korea, Indonesia and Thailand, governments were faced with serious economic difficulties. In order to provide them with financial assistance the IMF imposed harsh policies on Asian countries and asked them to raise their interest rates whilst cutting government spending at the same time.

As a result of this, Asian countries realised that they did not need to become economically independent in order not to ask again for financial support in future crises. To achieve this goal, they accumulated trillions of dollars of assets.[9] This led to the capital flows from emerging economies to advanced economies, and these had a preference for the US dollar. The preference for dollar reserves came from Asia, the net capital inflows from Asia to the US grew rapidly, and this phenomenon, which is related to the asset price inflation in the USA, is known as a savings glut.[10]

China, as well as Asian countries, invested in debt instruments and bought a lot of treasuries, Fannie and Freddie mortgage-backed securities, and other debt instruments: the large supply of debt helped drive down lending standards: obviously, there was enough demand for debt from house buyers and other borrowers.[11]

It is clear that capital inflows from Asia caused an indirect influence on US mortgage market; before the crisis, the USA have experienced the absorption of foreign capital, which drove down the cost of credit, by making loans cheap. Hence, the accessibility to credit in the US led to a housing construction boom and enabled debt-financed consumer spending.[12]

Another element that corroborated the financial crisis was the technology stock bubble, or the dot-com bust: coupled with this is the central banks' attitude to adopt the policy of low interest rates, hence the house bubble, and the ensuing mortgage market bubble. To elaborate, investors wanted to hold these relatively safe assets instead of government securities: for example, pension funds, hedge funds and insurance companies all held MBS instead of government securities.

However, bundling and insuring mortgages can be profitable when the house price is rising: due to the risk premium effect, they were no more profitable to hold than prime mortgages because there was a reduction of risk through insurance diversification.

The logic consequence was a change of mortgage system: banks holding the mortgages as it was in a traditional "originate-to-hold model": the bank would

8 (Verick and Islam 2010).
9 (Franklin and Carletti 2010).
10 (Ramskogler 2015).
11 (Franklin and Carletti 2010).
12 (Taylor 2009).

originate them and start selling them to be securitised. This new process was called "originate-to-distribute model": the originators were paid on the number of mortgages they approved, so they were encouraged to approve as many mortgages as possible. It is clear that this system deteriorated the quality of mortgages, and the following occurred:

- Banks were not motivated to use their screening and monitoring methods;
- Thanks to this model, banks received benefits from origination fees without bearing the credit risk of borrowers;
- If the secondary market was functioning well, they were able to pass those loans to a third party.[13]

Other elements that made a contribution to the financial crisis were (1) the rise of subprime mortgages, (2) securitisations, (3) the role of rating agencies and[14] (4) the failure of risk management.

More precisely, rating agencies played a crucial role because their aim was to rate these securities by whether they met the payment and performance obligations. One of the main reasons that led to a failure of this activity was that the issuer was paying for the rating. It was a situation characterised by a conflict of interest between obtaining issue business and objective rating. Further, there was also a difficulty in gaining access to the necessary loan information in order to calculate the rating. Managers were under pressure for a credit estimate but without being given any loan documentation.[15]

5.2.2 The beginning of the crisis

The crisis began in early 2007 with the deflation of the US housing boom: the housing price started to fall for the first time in more than a decade, and this was the first significant decline. As a consequence of this, private consumption was influenced, and there was both an increased unemployment and mortgage defaults. The asset value of houses was less than the value of the mortgages, the delinquency rate (namely, the default on the instalment of the mortgage) grew. Other pathological elements started materialising:

- Mortgages had insufficient reserves, so risk of default of insurers rose;
- The value of credit-backed security fell, as the potential buyers were asking for the higher risk premiums;
- The stock prices of insurers fell as their losses accumulated and they could not raise new money by selling stock or borrowing support on the value of the equity capital.[16]

13 (Purnanandam 2011).
14 As far as securitisations and subprime mortgages is concerned, we have just discussed before.
15 (Hosp 2010).
16 (Congleton 2010).

During 2007 summer it was clear that it was a financial fallout, and it was marked by different events. The first one was that announced, by BNP Paribas, concerning the intention of freezing three of their funds; the explanation was "the complete evaporation of liquidity in certain market segments of the US securitisation market had made it impossible to value certain assets fairly regardless of their quality or credit rating."[17] In other words, the assets could not be used as collateral and, without a collateral, there is no funding.

In September of that year Britain's largest mortgage lenders, Northern Rock, failed. Northern Rock was a building society, that is a mutually owned savings and mortgage bank, until its decision to go public and float its shares on the stock market in 1997. As with other building societies in the UK, Northern Rock traced its origin to the cooperative movement of the 19th century. Despite its modest origins, Northern Rock grew rapidly and it became the fifth-largest bank in the UK in terms of mortgage assets.

When it expanded its mortgage assets, the size of its balance sheets far outstripped its traditional funding base of branch-based retail deposits; however, the bulk of retail deposits at the time of its run were non-branch-based deposits such as postal and telephone accounts. These two have a similar element, which is the fact that customers send in their withdrawal or deposit request by post or via telephone, and customers are rewarded for their inconvenience with a slightly higher deposit interest rate. These non-branch retail deposits enabled Northern Rock to expand their retail deposits beyond their narrow regional base (the traditionally poor North-East of England), but these deposits proved most vulnerable to withdrawal in the aftermath of the run on the bank.

The gap in funding between the amount lent out and the amount depositors put in was made by securitised notes and other forms of nonretail funding, such as interbank deposits and covered bonds.

As far as securitisations are concerned, there is a difference between US and the UK. In the first one, the securitisation process used special-purpose entities that were considered separate from the bank and makes the loans.[18] By contrast, in the UK and, more precisely, in the Northern Rock case study, the special-purpose entities operated under the assumption that the special-purpose entities were consolidated within the Northern Rock's main balance sheet. Thus, the rapid growth of Northern Rock's balance sheet reflected the accounting regime along with the flow of new loans originated.

This is not the only difference one can see in comparing Northern Rock and its "motherland" (the UK) with US and EU banks. US and EU banks sponsored off-balance sheet entities, such as conduits and structured investment vehicles. These short-term liabilities needed to be rolled over several times each year, which made banks highly vulnerable, in cases where credit markets had started becoming unwilling to fund new issues. By contrast, the notes issued by the British counterparts had

17 BNP Paribas Suspends Funds because of Subprime Problems," New York Times, 9 August 2007.

18 They represent an off-balance sheet vehicle.

relatively longer maturities: for example, Northern Rock had 31.1 billion pounds of securitised notes outstanding at the end of 2005. The total redemptions during 2006 of these notes were 7.12 billion pounds, therefore just a fraction.

The reason for the deposit run affecting Northern Rock was fundamentally due to small fluctuations in the market. If the borrower was highly leveraged, which was the Northern Rock scenario in 2006/2007, small fluctuations in its implied haircut could have, and in fact did, cause large shifts in available funding. Again, Northern Rock could initially borrow with a haircut of just 2%; however, the Newcastle-upon-Tyne credit institution found itself, shortly after, needing to borrow at a much higher haircut. In other words, the required reduction in leverage for Northern Rock would have been extreme. Ultimately, the Northern Rock demise was just a matter of time, inevitable when the following pullback in funding conditions arrived. The tide eventually turned, meaning institutions such as Northern Rock, with extreme leverage and balance sheet mismatches, were literally left "on the beach."

From Northern Rock a harsh lesson came for banking and financial regulation: it demonstrated that, if a financial institution relied on access to a continuous stream of short-term liquidity to roll over expiring short-term debts, when the latter, the short-term debts, did not materialise, the market started alienating these institutions.[19]

However, Northern soon proved not to be an isolated case. One year later, in 2008, came the Lehman Brothers' collapse,[20] with scholars providing a number of possible interpretations for this turmoil. These explanations can be summarised as follows:[21]

- The fact that it was required to compete with commercial banks, which had highly leveraged positions: Lehman merged and acquired many commercial and investment banks. This merging of activities exposed them to several risks, leading to their bankruptcy;[22]
- Unethical management practices contrasting with prudent corporate governance practices: the reference is to financial frauds, a violation of most Sarbanes – Oxley Act provisions, and so on;[23]

19 (Song Shin 2009).

20 Lehman Brothers was born in Alabama in 1844 when Henry Lehman and his two brothers (Emmanuel and Mayer) established a small shop to sell to local cotton farmers, groceries, utensils and other commodities. After the growth of the cotton industry, Lehman Brothers envisaged the need to enhance their liquidity. Initially, the company was run as a family business for many decades until they formed a partnership with retail giants, such as Goldman Sachs, in the 1990s. The main purpose was to build a strong team to fund the emerging retail business in the first years of the 1990s. Afterwards, with the company growing fast, they were designated by the Alabama government to sell state bonds. Their entry to the financial market came when the US decided to transform the economy from an agrarian to an industrialised basis and develop the railway system. Lehmann Brothers subsequently raised the fund for firms engaged in the railway industry.

21 (Pichardo and Bacon 2009).

22 (Boot and Marinč 2008).

23 (Mensah 2012).

- Central was their inability to meet short term obligation despite a high asset base;[24]
- The crisis of collateralised debt obligation and derivatives crisis. More precisely, Lehman Brothers not only lacked a robust product control process to account for residential whole loans coupled with misstatement but also capitalised on speculative opportunities. The latter was aimed by reducing its exposure to credit risk in the financial market;[25]
- A high-leveraged structure and ratio increased year on year: as a consequence of the financial crisis, coupled with increased interest rates, Lehman's position was adversely impacted, leading to their bankruptcy;[26]
- A complex capital structure;
- Unsuccessful bail out and takeover attempts.[27]

5.2.3 Post-crisis regulation

In aftermath of the financial crises, the regulation started pursuing three goals: (1) to reduce the probability of any larger financial institution going a similar way, (2) to limit the harmful spillovers to the broader economy and (3) to reduce the risk that taxpayers would absorb loses in a potential future crisis.

It started to be argued that to have enough cushion of equity capital was crucial for the banks for the following reasons. First, with a cushion, banks will be the first ones which would absorb the losses in a crisis, rather than taxpayers. Furthermore, it could help reduce distortions connected with the "too big to fail" problems. Finally, with the heightened capital requirements, banks would be able to survive with large losses without failing, on the assumption that a large failing of banks can bring broader economies into crisis.[28]

Although this is the common ground, the approach to the problem was different between legal systems. Thus, we will next discuss the US, the EU and the UK legal frameworks.

The US approach: Dodd-Frank Act

The response to the crisis in the US was the adoption of the Dodd-Frank Wall Street Reform and Consumer Protection Act.[29] In more detail, Title 1 of this piece of legislation shaped the Financial Stability Oversight Council (FSOC), which was granted the authority to designate systematically important non-bank financial companies and is aimed toward an enhanced prudential regulatory regime for certain large bank-holding companies and the non-financial companies.

24 (Murphy 2008).
25 (D'Arcy 2009).
26 (Vlukas 2010).
27 (Anderson 2008).
28 (Greenwood et al. 2017).
29 Henceforth, also, Dodd-Frank Act and DFA.

Title 2 created from scratch the Orderly Liquidation Authority (OLA) for resolution regime available outside the Bankruptcy Code for the systematically important financial institutions.[30]

Furthermore, the Federal Reserve's annual Comprehensive Capital Analysis and Review[31] achieved the aim of assessing whether the largest banks in the USA would have enough capital to continue lending to households and companies in the situation of an economic downturn. Moreover, it assessed if banks had robust forward-looking plans for rebuilding capital were there significant losses. This periodical stress test, to be carried out on an annual basis, was one of the most useful regulatory reforms after the crisis: it helped, and still helps, the risk-based capital framework to be more dynamic and progressive.[32]

Under the Dodd-Frank Act, the FSOC is responsible to monitoring systematic risk and migration across jurisdictions.

Again, as far as banking industries are concerned, traditionally federal regulation has been rather favourable to "big banks" since the broad principles of financial regulation are the same for all banks. In this scenario, the Dodd-Frank Act shifted this traditional one-size-fits-all principle by establishing specific asset-size thresholds tailored to benefit small banks in terms of regulatory reform.

In a nutshell, the Dodd-Frank Act is a massive piece of federal regulation from the US, whose aim is to "promote the financial stability of the United States by improving accountability and transparency in the financial system, to end 'too big to fail,' to protect the American taxpayer by ending bail-outs, to protect consumers from abusive financial services practices, and for other purposes." Also, according to this line of reasoning, it is possible to infer that the Dodd-Frank Act, together with the Consumer Protection Act, signed in 2010, resulted in a new approach to financial regulation in response to the 2008 financial crisis.[33]

As a result of this legal framework, the financial stability is achieved via three different types of regulation on financial institutions:

- Higher requirement of loss cushions, which is capital requirement;
- Enhanced supervision and disclosure requirement on a bank's activities;
- Consumer protection requirements.

Despite these positive elements, DFA had a negative impact on small banks: the impact to the latter concerned entry barriers, dramatic rises in compliance costs and higher capital requirements. The "discrimination" lies in the fact that the large banks are able to economise over these additional regulatory burdens by expanding their balance sheets. By contrast, small banks, such as community banks, show a lack of capacity to quickly expand their size, and therefore, these costs appear disproportionate.[34]

30 (Sykes 2018).
31 Henceforth CCAR.
32 (Greenwood et al. 2017).
33 (Leledarkis and Pyrgiotakis 2022).
34 (Liu 2023).

The EU regulation

Before the financial crisis, the regulation was built by the Basel II agreement based on three pillars:

- Minimum capital requirement: this refers to specific rules for the estimation of credit risk for banking books based on the use of credit ratings and the introduction of a minimum capital requirement for operational risks. In force of this, banks are provided with two options in order to measure their credit risk, the choice between the standard method or the internal rating-based approach;
- Supervisory review: this introduces the prudential control process whereby banks can determine their capital needs and cover the risk undertaken by planning any necessary action to maintain a level of adequate capitalisation.
- Market discipline: focused on information sharing and, more precisely, a set of disclosure requirements to enable market participants to be properly informed about the risks to which a bank is exposed and the capital adequacy that can claim against those risks.

The lesson from the 2007–2008 crisis was that the existence of the gap in standards caused key issues for two main reasons.[35] First, the quantity and quality of capital requirements proved to be insufficient. To elaborate, during the crisis, it became clear that some liabilities, including the regulatory definition of capital, were able to absorb the losses only in the event of a full-blown disaster and could give rise to contagion phenomena. The second was the imbalance between the prudential treatment of credit and financial risks.[36]

Bearing this in mind, the Committee published the first draft of Basel III (published in 2010), whose essential elements are as follows:

- More capital with the provision of additional buffers which are themselves diversified in relation to the systemic relevance of the bank;
- Better quality capital or, more precisely, financial instruments capable of effectively absorbing unexpected losses in the absence of default;
- New requirements for previously overlooked risks, such as credit evaluation adjustment;
- Liquidity requirements;
- Limits on leverage.

It is also worth recalling the De Larosière Report tailored in 2009. Its aim was to challenge the backdrop of crisis and recession with three essential steps against any future collapse: a new regulatory agenda, stronger coordinated supervision and effective crisis management procedures. Therefore, a European System of

35 (Alexander 2009).
36 (de Gioia Carabellese and Della Giustina 2023).

Financial Supervision[37] was created, with a purpose to ensure the supervision of the Union's financial system, and it consisted in three European supervision authorities: the European Banking Authority, the European Securities and Market Authority and the European Insurance and Occupational Pensions Authority.[38]

This legal framework was also complemented by two directives:

- Capital Requirements Directive;[39]
- Capital Requirements Regulation.[40]

In 2017 the Basel Committee introduced several revisions to Basel IV: the new revisions became effective in January 2022. The crucial points of this quintessential piece of legislation can be summarised as follows.

The key element is the revised standardised approach to credit risk whose aim is to enhance robustness and sensitivity to this approach. Further, it constrains the use of the internal model approach. Moreover, it removed the possibility for the banks to use internal models for estimating CVA. Finally, operational risk shall be based on measures relating to both a bank's income and its losses.

The UK approach

Before discussing the approach in the aftermath of the crisis, it is vital to emphasise the particular nuance of the UK background. In a system such as the UK, it was noted that there were real systemic dangers in giving supervisors discretionary powers to set regulatory capital for individual institution since they are unlikely to exercise their power in an independent way.[41] Additionally, in the UK system, the regulator had enough freedom in selecting and balancing the regulatory techniques through which the objectives of regulation were to be pursued and in determining the intensity of regulation via the pertinent enforcement rules. Therefore, the legal structure of regulation could be of much less significance than the manner in which regulation was practised.

The main cause of crisis seemed to be both a lack of regulation and a failed model of supervision. To elaborate, the Turner Review[42] and the FSA Regulatory Response[43] highlighted that FSA, as a banking supervision, failed to use its power to require higher levels of capital and liquidity, as credit expanded in individual institutions and across the system. Moreover, the Treasury Select Committee failed in the case of Northern Rock.[44]

37 Henceforth ESFS.
38 As far as these authorities is concerned, see before in this work.
39 Henceforth CRD IV.
40 Henceforth CRR.
41 (Brunnermeier et al. 2009).
42 FSA, The Turner Review, A Regulatory Response to the Global Banking Crisis (March 2009).
43 FSA Discussion Paper 09/2, A Regulatory Response to the Global Banking Crisis (hereafter FSA Regulatory Response) (March 2009).
44 House of Commons Treasury Committee, The Run on the Rock HC 56-1 (Fifth Report of Session 2007-08).

The style of regulation was an adaptation of international and EU measures to fit the local legal order. However, this implementation was realised via practices and not via adjustment of rules.[45] As far as the regulatory structure is concerned, the UK had its own peculiarity that will be exposed further.

After the crisis, there was a review of the institutional structure of regulation in the UK and, more precisely, in 2010 the "twin peaks" model[46] was adopted, in which prudential regulation would be separate from the conduct of business regulation to be undertaken by a new Consumer Protection and Markets Authority. It introduced the Council for Financial Stability, whose objective was, and still is, to regulate and guarantee macroeconomic regulation and financial stability. Nevertheless, some characteristics of the UK system will remain distinctive:

- Regulation will operate on an integrated basis across the banking, securities and insurance sectors;
- Prudential regulation will be located within the central bank.

Also, as a result of the "twin peaks" model, the Financial Policy Committee,[47] a subsidiary of the Bank of England, would be, and still is, responsible for macro-prudential regulation. By contrast, the micro-prudential regulation will be the responsibility of the new PRA: it is responsible for prudential and financial regulation but will also be a subsidiary of the Bank of England.[48]

Finally, corporate governance measures have also been constituting a central component of the prudential regulation framework in the post-2008 scenario. As a result of the examination of professional standards and culture in the banking sector in the UK,[49] the Banking Reform Act of 2013 was passed.

The latter introduced a new "senior persons" regime and new powers for the PRA and FCA to impose regulatory sanctions on individual senior managers when a bank violates a regulatory requirement.[50] It established a new regulatory crime of "misconduct," as well as a criminal regime for senior managers.

More precisely, Section 36 of the Financial Services (Banking Reform) Act, 2013, shaped a new "offence relating to a decision causing a financial institution to fail," which may be committed when a senior manager of a financial institution (1) "takes, or agrees to the taking of, a decision by or on behalf of the financial institution as to the way in which the business of a group institution is to be carried

45 (MacNeil 2010).

46 The precedent model saw the collaboration, albeit problematic, between Bank of England and FSA. In this scenario, (1) the Treasury was responsible for general policy and the overall structure of regulation, (2) the Bank of England for financial stability, and (3) FSA for prudential supervision. It is important to noted that this model was adopted in Australia in 1998 and in Australia had not any bank failed (Cooper 2006).

47 Henceforth FPC.

48 (Lui 2012).

49 House of Lords and House of Commons, *Changing Banking for Good: Report of the Parliamentary Commission on Banking Standards. First Report of Session 2013-2014* HL Paper 27-I, 2013.

50 (Cranston et al. 2017).

on" or (2) "fails to take steps that the senior manager could take to prevent such a decision being taken."[51]

Finally, the Executives' Remuneration Reports Regulations 2013 make certain revisions to the existing remuneration regulations. The main goal is to promote transparency in the remuneration of directors, boost shareholder accountability, and offer a more effective performance linkage.[52]

5.3 Health emergency and financial instruments

The Covid-19 health emergency represented one of the biggest crises of modern times: if the 2007–2008 financial crisis kick-started in New York, by contrast this coronavirus came from China. These two crises have both common and different elements. The first one is in reference to international and financial connections. As far as these differences are concerned, it is possible to summarise in the following ways:[53]

- The Covid-19 crisis is endogenous;
- The financial uncertainty in Covid-19 was the duration of the economic turndown, whilst in the financial crisis, it was the extent of losses to be incurred on home mortgage loans;[54]
- Covid-19 is truly global with direct consequence on every country of the world.

Nevertheless, not only did Covid-19 have an impact on the health sector but also on the economic one.[55] In this work, an overview of this from a banking/financial perspective is given. In a similar way to the discussion about the 2007–2008 financial crises, the methodology relating to the financial consequences of Covid-19 is based on a comparative analysis between three different legal systems: (1) US, (2) UK and (3) EU.

First and foremost, it is critical to say that, in financial markets, the pandemic triggered a flight to liquidity or a "dash for cash" with sales of risky assets.[56] A section of research papers show that, with the growing number of infections and death in continental Europe, and particularly Italy, stock markets started sliding, with investors moving money away from stocks and putting them into safer assets like bonds. In March 2020, both the US and UK governments were downplaying the threat of the pandemic. Similarly, foreign exchange markets, based on London and New York, remained unmoved.

51 Financial Services (Banking Reform) Act 2013 Section 36.
52 (Rizk 2022).
53 (Wojcik and Ioannou 2020).
54 (Jackson and Schwarz 2021)
55 It was emphasised that potentially "a widespread wave of small business failures-even if they are not individually systemic actors-may ripple across other parts of the economy and eventually trigger contagion and collapse" (Hafiz et al. 2020).
56 (Gros 2020).

When it became clear and obvious that the Italian government would introduce a lockdown, the OPEC countries did reduce production, although this was more than compensated by the hugely decreasing demands for oil, hence the decrease in the price of oil.

This event accelerated the stock market decline, and on 12 March, President Christine Lagarde announced low-cost funding for assets purchased from banks. Yet she did not decide to cut interest rates, and stated that there was no ECB intention to start buying newly issued government bonds of eurozone member states.

Another approach was in the US: on 15 March 2020, the central bank cut interest to zero and offered to buy USD 700 billion of asset from banks. The following day, it opened liquidity swap lines, used in 2008, offering the UK GBP, CHF, EUR, and JPY for USD in unlimited amounts. ISS, European and Japan central banks to exchange. On 18 March, the Bank of England announced the purchase of GBP 200 billion government bonds; similarly, the European Central Bank announced buying EUR 750 billion of government and corporate bonds.

This mechanism recalls the crucial role of the state and the nature of global finance because the dominant position of the US state in the global financial system was confirmed.

From a financial perspective, it is possible to highlight the following:

- Banks entered into the pandemic better capitalised than in the run-up to the global financial crisis of 2008;
- Governments and central banks prevented the immediate financial panic from spiralling out of control: this prevented an immediate recession triggering in turn a financial crisis;
- The pandemic accelerated the digitalisation of banks;
- Consumer behaviour was changed by the pandemic.

Furthermore, the financial system failed to incorporate, or discounted, pandemic risk into loan pricing and risk models because a pandemic is, similarly to the 2008 financial events, a "black swan" event.[57] Thus, Covid-19 parallels the last financial crisis or other financial panics in its force as a precipitator of event which saw the emergence of new information which disrupted prior expectations. To elaborate, the 2008 failure had its roots in prior market expectations about the future and sustainability of housing price increases and the capacity of individual borrowers to sustain home mortgage payments.[58]

The link between Covid-19 and banking/financial matters is that the pandemic may be a systemic risk for a financial system: therefore, financial regulators could play a productive role in helping public health officials estimate the aggregate costs of failure to contain pandemic risks. Consequently, financial regulators could play a productive role in helping public health: if financial regulators play a crucial role

57 (Jackson and Schwarz, Protecting Financial Stability: Lessons from the COVID-19 Pandemic 2021).

58 CORELOGic, *Evaluating the Housing Market Since the Great Recession*, 2018.

in order to contain pandemic risk, public health authorities too could benefit from input from financial regulators to complete a comprehensive cost-benefit analysis for pandemic risks.[59]

From this becomes clear that the financial sector has a crucial role for the economy and its resilience: the Covid-19 crisis would be worst, under financial and economic view, where banking sector has been a shock-transmitter. The keys are financial resilience and a strong, but at the same time flexible, prudential regulatory regime.[60]

To summarise all, the main risk was that a health crisis caused an economic crisis or, at least, a financial crisis.[61]

5.3.1 The UK approach

In order to fight the shock occurred by Covid-19, the UK government guaranteed the Coronavirus Business Interruption Loans Scheme (CBILS) and Bounce-Back Loans Scheme (BBLS) and had collectively provided around £30 billion of new credit to more than half a million businesses across the UK. Further, the Government's Coronavirus Corporate Financing Facility (CCFF) provided a further £20 billion in funding addressed to larger companies. Net bank lending to UK non-financial corporates increased by over £30 billion in March alone, from an average of £1 billion per month over the previous three years.[62]

From the Bank of England's perspective, the action was to pump billions of dollars into financial markets in exchange for governmental debt, leaving investors flush with cash and looking for somewhere to invest it.[63]

From a further perspective, the spread of the virus made investors, the public and policymakers aware that a serious economic damage was on the verge of unfolding due to external uncertainties and the consequences would be on an unknown scale. There was also an aggregate impact of the pandemic over the stock market in the UK and the spending behaviour of households changed. Indeed, they are more defensive and resistant to investing.

To elaborate, the role of the latter is crucial in determining the performance of financial markets. In this respect, there are three elements to be considered in investment behaviour: (1) risk perception, (2) satisfaction and (3) rate of profitability.[64]

Bearing this in mind, during Covid-19, the UK policy concerns the effect of credit arrangements on households and corporations which are in debt and/or need additional financing by debt. More precisely, borrowers, both households and corporations, need temporary relief from the pressures of debt. Moreover, access to finance and credit to businesses should continue in order to avoid key social losses,

59 (Jackson and Rothesian, The Analysis of Benefits in Consumer Protection Regulations 2019).
60 (Giese and Haldane 2020).
61 (Jackson and Schwarz, Protecting Financial Stability: Lessons from the COVID-19 Pandemic 2021).
62 Bank of England Discussion Paper, December. – (2020), Interim Financial Stability Report, May. (2020).
63 (Blakeley 2021).
64 (Nguyen et al. 2020).

such as protecting jobs and business supplier from negative effects. All of these measures were explicit in the UK.[65]

Explicit loan forbearance was introduced in the UK in March 2020 suspending the operation of contractual obligations for FCA-regulated lenders in consumer credit and household mortgages.[66] Regulators required mortgages lenders to grant payment holiday to any customers who indicates they will potentially experience difficulties. Other consumer credit customers had a similar relief in the payment holidays, including personal loans and credit cards. Furthermore, in order to support loan forbearance, Financial Policy Committee of the Bank of England,[67] relaxed the micro-prudential regulatory measures known as a countercyclical buffer.

The main idea in the UK following from PRA is that banks should use all elements to support the economy:[68] UK business with turnover of less than £45 million could benefit from the Coronavirus Business Interruption Loan Scheme.[69] In force of this, a credit lender could provide loans and overdraft facilities of up to £5 million, guaranteed at 80% by the government, to be repaid over up to six years; smaller UK businesses could borrow £5 million, guaranteed at 80% by the government, to be repaid over up to six years.

This scenario was corroborated by a relax of micro-prudential regulation, more specifically concerned about some fundamental factors:

- An encouragement to banks to allow businesses, with credit lines and undrawn credit, to draw upon such lines even if this means the bank's liquidity ratios may fall below the mandatory 100% they are supposed to maintain;
- The liquidity coverage ratio was intended to be maintained at all times at 100% so that banks can meet their cash outflows for a period of 30 days, to prevent a liquidity-driven crisis.

This approach was complemented by the suspension of externally administrated stress testing[70] that, for 2020, was postponed in order to reduce pressure on banks and focus them on the relief and rescue agenda.

65 Corporate Insolvency and Governance Act 2020, c. 12 (UK).

66 This act was passed by Parliament: FCA Mortgages and Coronavirus: Updated Guidance for Firms. (17 Nov. 2020), www.fca.org.uk/publications/finalised-guidance/mortgages-and-coronavirusupdated-guidance-firms,

67 Henceforth FPC, which has oversight of the systemic health of the financial system, and it is able to exercise flexible power to adjust a prudential regulatory measures known as the countercyclical buffer (CCyb).

68 Prudential Regulation Authority, Q&A on the Usability of Liquidity and Capital Buffers BANK OF ENG. (6 July 2020), www.bankofengland.co.uk/prudential-regulation/publication/2020/buffer-usability-qanda (last visited 29 Aug. 2020).

69 Apply for the Coronavirus Business Interruption Loan Scheme, U.K. DEP'T FOR BUS., ENERGY & INDUS. STRATEGY (May 1, 2020), www.gov.uk/guidance/apply-for-the-coronavirus-business-interruption-loan-scheme [https://perma.cc/R776-ZQTK].

70 Every year the Bank of England carries out annual cyclical and biennial exploratory stress test so that supervisors can understand the bank's capital resilience and potential for continuity in stressful scenarios.

The "legal elastic" was the critical approach based on the "relief and rescue" philosophy, while adverse consequences arose from this, such as (1) a higher supervision activity from the authorities, (2) the possibility to suspend regulatory requirements and (3) a strike balance between economic welfare/justice and bank resilience.[71]

5.3.2 The US management

The Covid-19 economy shock brought an aggressive response from the Federal Reserve due to a quick deployment of US Financial Crisis monetary policy tools and programmes. More precisely, the Federal Open Market voted twice to lower the target range for the federal funds rate by a total of a 1–1.5% bringing the range to 0–25% for the first time since the financial crisis.

At the same time, the Federal Reserve expanded also its purchase agreement operations, by purchasing massive amounts of Treasury securities. More precisely, the Federal Reserve, at the beginning, committed to purchase $500 billion in Treasury securities and $200 billion in agency mortgage-backed securities (MBS). However, one week later these purchases became open ended, with the promise to purchase "in the amounts needed to support smooth market functioning and effective transmission of monetary policy."[72] Thus, the Federal Reserve re-instated dollar swap lines for foreign central banks, which were designated to ease overseas liquidity in the dollar.

All of these financial provisions were encapsulated into the Coronavirus Aid, Relief, and Economic Security Act,[73] whose goal was to provide fast and direct economic assistance to American workers, families, small businesses and industries. It was passed by Congress on 25 March 2020.

After cutting interest rates, the Federal Reserve invoked its emergency authority under Section 13(3)(a) of the Federal Reserve Act; this legal provision stated that, where there are "unusual and exigent circumstances, the Board of Governors of the Federal Reserve System . . . may authorize any Federal reserve bank." It encapsulates a singular power of the Federal Reserve to permit Federal Reserve banks to provide liquidity directly to non-bank and commercial entities.

As far as this power is concerned, it was surrounded by limitations. First, it was only available in times of crisis and when it was approved by a vote of five governors that ascertain the presence of "exigent and unusual circumstances."

Once it is invoked, the Federal Reserve had broad authority to create a facility or programme based on the eligibility to discount for "any participant" pledging certain eligible collaterals.

In this respect, the limits on such facilities programme were as follows:

- Any participant shall demonstrate that is unable to obtain adequate credit accommodations from other baking institutions;

71 (Chiu, Kokkinis and Miglionico 2021).

72 Press Release, Bd. of Governors of the Fed. Res. Sys., Federal Reserve Announces Extensive New Measures to Support the Economy (Mar. 23, 2020, 8:00 AM).

73 Also known as CARES ACT.

- The secretary of the Treasury must approve of the facility and its terms;
- It is crucial to ensure that such facilities security for emergency loans is sufficient to protect taxpayers from losses;
- The Federal Reserve may not provide credit to an insolvent borrower.

In the Covid-19 scenario, the Federal Reserve initiated the use of its emergency lending authority by reviving four lending facilities that were used during the financial crisis to provide liquidity to nonbank financial entities and corporations. These are as follows:

- Primary Dealer Credit Facility,[74] which was aimed to keep credit markets functioning by lending to primary dealers with investment grade debt securities as collateral;
- Money Market Mutual Fund Liquidity Facility,[75] which experienced high rates of investor redemptions during times of financial turbulence;
- Commercial Paper Funding Facility,[76] which allowed the Federal Reserve to purchase commercial paper, providing support to eligible issuers, including financial and commercial companies;
- Term Asset-Backed Securities Loan Facility,[77] which lends to holders of asset-backed securities collaterised by loans including student loans, auto loans and credit card loans.

One of the novelties unleashed by the pandemic was the Federal Reserve's decision to support lending to large corporations and medium-sized businesses: this approach goes by the name of Main Street businesses. The Federal Reserve announced two facilities aimed at supporting large corporate employers, the Primary Market Corporate Credit Facility (PMCCF) and the Secondary Market Corporate Credit Facility (SMCCF).[78] At the beginning, these two programmes were limited to investment grade debt but later expanded to those companies who had been newly downgraded. The SMCCF allows for the purchase of US-listed exchange-traded funds (ETFs), including bond funds which allows for broader investment rather buying individual corporate bonds.

In a nutshell, the Federal Reserve's Main Street lending program is a highly innovative but complex effort to support mid-market lending, and since it is so recently operational, it is yet to be proven. In order to apply the mechanism, the Federal Reserved partnered with the following:

- Treasury, whereby it is the provider of first-loss credit protection;
- Private-sector commercial banks as underwriters and allocators of credit.

74 Henceforth PDCF.
75 Henceforth MMLF.
76 Henceforth CPFF.
77 Henceforth TALF.
78 Press Release, Bd. of Governors of the Fed. Res. Sys., Federal Reserve Announces Extensive New Measures to Support the Economy (Mar. 23, 2020, 8:00 AM).

To qualify an eligible borrower, a company must have either less than $2 billion in its 2019 annual revenues or fewer than 15,000 employees. In general, the company's leverage cannot exceed six times its 2019 EBITDA.[79]

Another measure shaped by Federal Reserve was the Municipal Liquidity Facility (MLF) aimed at offering loans directly to states, countries and cities. The Federal Reserve will purchase bonds issued by states, cities and countries that meet certain requirements as to their credit ratings and population size. Funds can only be used to manage the cash flow impact of the pandemic, such as the deferral of tax revenue due to the extension of tax filing deadlines.

This was corroborated by a supervisor activity known as a stress test on a bank-by-bank basis, in order to reflect distinct periods of systemic distress. This can provide critical "just in time information" to policymakers and others. With the stress test results, the Federal Reserve also announced that it is requiring large banks to suspend repurchases, cap dividends based on past income, and resubmit their capital plans later this year. In other words, the interaction between stopping dividends and share price is of major concern to the banking sector, but regulators will need to decide whether in the public interest they should require conservation and raising of equity given to the potential for future losses from the global pandemic.[80]

5.3.3 The EU methodology

Bearing in mind the worst experience of bailout austerity as a policy solution to managing crises, the EU approach was to realise a lifting of fiscal restrictions on public spending by the European Commission during the pandemic. All EU countries had the same fiscal room to increase public debit as a response to pandemic. The austerity policy that had sadly marked the aftermath of the 2007/2008 financial crises would be counterproductive in reviving growth and reducing unemployment which were urgently needed in aftermath of a health emergency.

More precisely, as far as the health emergency is concerned, the EU approach was to limit the negative impact of the Covid-19 pandemic, at the same time maintaining the EU legitimacy and role.[81]

Without EU support, fiscally weaker members would lack the capability to recover from recession. The outcome of this, politically, would be to reinforce populist demand for leaving EU in these countries.

In order to help EU economies, the EU adopted a joint recovery fund which would authorise the Commission, on behalf of the EU, to borrow up to €750 billion from capital markets in form of bond issuance. The loans would be repaid through EU budgets and possible new resources between 2027 and 2058. From this point, €390 billion would be distributed in the form of grants to countries and sectors most affected, with the remaining €360 billion in loans. Combined with

79 This refers to earnings before interest, taxes, depreciation and amortisation. It is commonly used as a measure of a company's net income.

80 (Barr, Jackson and Tahyar 2020).

81 (Di Mascio, Natalini and Profeti S. 2022).

the Multiannual Financial Framework 2021–2027 (MFF) – the joint package of recovery funds and MFF is designed to launch EU investments into three main areas: (1) green and digital transitions, (2) key value chains of strategic sectors and (3) health security.[82]

The EU recovery fund was revolutionary for a number of reasons:

- It was investment-driven;
- It had the form of collective actions at the EU level;
- It was seen as a return to the Keynesian economics.

In this respect, the corona bond had the function of facilitating repayments by members' contribution to the EU budgets, and possible new taxes were the realisation of debt mutualisation in all but name. This showed that the allocation of recovery funds would be based on member's needs and not on their budgetary contribution; additionally, the fund comprised grants, not loans.

The underpinning philosophy of the corona bond is the joint debt instrument, issued at a eurozone level, with a collective guarantee from all involved member states. The last goal was to ensure that there would be an easy access to funding throughout the eurozone, particularly for the countries that were in a weaker financial position. Corona bonds, in other words, were and still are specific forms of eurobonds because they are limited in time, scope and type of expenditure.

The corona bonds' issuance would allow countries, such as Italy and Spain, to borrow money at a lower interest rate than by issuing their own government bonds. South European countries were to use these bonds only to proceed from such issuance to finance national measures designed to mitigate the damage caused by the pandemic, such as financial support to business.[83]

The implications of EU's recovery fund for European integration were multidimensional:[84]

- From the eurozone perspective, it epitomises the first step towards a fiscal union and creates the potential to realise a full fiscal union;[85]
- It marked the moment of the New Deal, able to reshape industrial development;
- It represents the second Marshall Plan, the first and proper one being the post–Second World War Marshall Plan.

More precisely, the European Council agreed on an exceptional temporary recovery instrument called Next Generation EU,[86] which establishes a joint funding

82 European Council (2020) Special European Council, 17–21 2020: main results. Brussels: European Council; European Commission (2020) Europe's moment: repair and prepare for the next generation. Press Release, issued on 27 May 2020, Brussels: European Commission.

83 (Bush 2022).

84 (Luo 2021).

85 (Leino 2020).

86 Henceforth NGEU.

model to support governmental spending and reform in those member states most severely affected by the pandemic. The core of the NGEU[87] is constituted by the Recovery and Resilience Facility:[88] its purpose is to support investment and reform in member states to pave the way for a sustainable recovery.

As far as the RRF is concerned, the novelty is the fact that it envisages a share of grants almost equal to that of loans, which represents a significant change from the management of the sovereign debt crisis. To have access the RFF funds, member states had to draft national recovery and resilience plans,[89] setting out their reform and investment agendas for the years 2021–2023. In order to manage and supervise the implementation of the NRRPs, a new task force, named the Recovery and Resilience Task Force,[90] was established. Its main duty is to work jointly with the Directorate-General for Economic and the Financial Affairs European Commission's Secretariat General.[91]

From a European perspective, and taking into account general principles, recovery and resilience plans[92] could provide a comprehensive, long-term investment and reform strategy for successful twin transition while ensuring social and territorial cohesion. The keyword here is "twin," *i.e.* sustainable and digital transition as a mandatory element in order to avoid the drastic effects of climate change and its impact on the economy. This approach is quintessential also because it demonstrates the link between the Covid-19 virus, on the one hand, and pollution, environment and climate change, on the other.[93]

In order to have access to RRPs, member states must submit a national RRP which outlines the investment and reform they plan to finance, under that RRP, to be submitted to the European Commission before 30 April 2021. The Commission[94] would then have two months to assess and, eventually, endorse or reject it before the Council can provide the final approval.

Within RRPs, investment is defined as "capital formation in areas such as fixed capital, human capital, and natural capital. This would also cover, for instance, intangible assets such as R&D, data, intellectual property and skills."[95]

The RRF adopts a bottom-up approach that has the potential to ensure domestic ownership of NRRPs who achieved the following goals:[96]

- To address challenges identified in the relevant Country Specific Recommendations[97] issued in the European Semester;

87 (Schramm, Krotz and De Witte 2022).
88 Henceforth RRF.
89 Henceforth NRRPs.
90 Henceforth RECOVER.
91 Henceforth DG ECFIN.
92 Also named RRPs.
93 (Weaver et al. 2023).
94 As far as the role of the European Commission is concerned, see Bokhorst and Corti (2023).
95 European Commission (2021), "Guidance to Member States Recovery and Resilience Plans – Part 1," Commission Staff Working Document, Brussels.
96 (Di Mascio, Natalini and Profeti S. 2022).
97 Henceforth CRSs.

- To report on the progress made in the achievement of investment and reform commitments which take place in the context of the Semester.

The RRF's general purpose is to promote the EU's economic, social and territorial cohesion by improving resilience and sustainable growth potential contributing to the implementation of European Pillar of Social Rights, encouraging green and digital transition. It is based on five pillars:[98]

- Green transition;
- Digital transformation;
- Social and territorial cohesion;
- Smart, sustainable and inclusive growth, including economic cohesion, jobs, productivity, competitiveness, research, development and innovation, and a strong, well-functioning internal market;
- Policies for the next generation.

5.4 From credit-crunch to cost-of-living crisis

Credit crunch is a concept that has a long history, dating back to the Great Depression of the 1930s. The decline in the supply of credit marked the 1990–1991 recession. It also affected the previous recession going back to the 1960s.

From a financial perspective, the credit crunch includes the consequences of the storage of financial capital and declining quality of borrowers' financial health, caused by the banks cutting the loans supply in the 1990s.

It was said that credit crunch is strictly linked with the shortage of bank capital: a large reduction in bank capital lowers push to capital-to-asset ratio below that required by capital regulation, and therefore, banks need to increase their capital-to-asset ratio. Banks with low or no earnings have only two options: (1) raise new capital or (2) reduce assets and liabilities. Thus, capital crunch describes the problem of a capital decline that causes a bank to shrink. By contrast, credit crunch is a situation in which loan supply has fallen faster than loan demand: this is a possible, but not necessary, outcome of a capital crunch.[99]

Moreover, the phrase "credit crunch" is also used to explain curtailment of the credit supply in response to both (1) decline in the value of bank capital or (2) conditions imposed by regulators, bank supervisors or banks themselves that require banks to hold more capital than they previously would have held.

A milder version of this concept is "credit squeeze," and it was used in the years 2007 and 2008: in this case, credit crunch has a global implication because international investors were involved. Moreover, the 2007–2008 credit crunch was more complex than earlier crunches; hence, financial innovation has allowed new ways

98 (Pilati 2021).
99 (Peek and Rosengren 1995).

of packaging and reselling assets. With regard to this financial crisis, the peculiarities were as follows:

- This crisis arose from of the mispricing of the risk of these products;
- New assets were developed based on the subprime mortgage market in the US;
- New assets were developed based on subprime and other mortgages which were then sold to investors in the form of repackaged debt securities of increasing sophistication.[100]

More recently, the concept has changed its own denomination, with the cost-of-living crisis as a consequence of both the Covid-19 pandemic and the Russia-Ukraine conflict. Both of these events have recently sparked off a global energy crisis and, from this new turmoil, global energy prices surge.

Indeed, Russia is a major exporter of oil and natural gas: European countries reliant on oil and natural gas used to import from Russia, already at high risk, since gas storage were nearly and probably deliberately emptied before the war. This faced unprecedent fuel supply shortages, only slightly tempered by slowing economic growth and a mild winter in 2022–2023. At the same time, emerging economies suffer from high fuel-import costs and fuel deprivation.

Furthermore, the potential opportunity to redirect investment after Covid-19 crisis with huge amounts of money to be used to kick-start the economy has been missed. In reality, the progress towards an energy transition is still lower, and this is reflected in and has been amplified by the dependency on fossil fuel imports.

All of these factors have recently caused cost-of-living crises. This new crisis has pushed a number of economies into recession, caused higher inflation and put painful cost-of-living pressures on households around the world. Households suffered, and are still suffering, the higher energy prices as a result of two factors:

- Fuel prices increases directly increase household fuel bills, such as for heating, cooling, cooking and mobbing (mobility);
- Energy and fossil feedstock inputs, needed for the production of goods and services for final household consumption, lead to higher prices of household-expenditure items.

Another critical element is the unequal distribution of income reflected in different household consumption patterns: this means that surging energy prices could affect households in different ways.[101]

It is possible to argue that finance may play a quintessential role in this scenario via the financialisaton of the renewable energies and energy community. This may realise via the secondary market within the SPV being refinanced or on-sold just before, or after, project construction.[102]

100 (Milzen 2008).
101 (Guan et al. 2023).
102 (Baker 2023).

5.5 The 2023 financial crises: Silicon Valley Bank and Credit Suisse

In early 2023 central banks around the world began raising interest rates: the hike interest rate to led to banking crisis in the US, which led to the failure some regional banks in the US and, finally, the collapse of a systemic bank in Europe. This happened in a different manner from the 2007–2008 financial collapse due to the fact that in 2023 banking sector was more capitalised and it is tightly regulated.

The collapse of Silicon Valley Bank,[103] Signature Bank, Credit Suisse and First Republic Bank fuelled a financial instability. The first reaction of regulators was to issue unconventional deposit guarantees, such as granting full deposit insurance to all depositors.

The 2023 financial crisis have its roots in the Russia-Ukraine war and Covid-19 pandemic. The contribution of the first one brought in the low interest rate and the significant fiscal stimuli which were introduced to stimulate aggregate demand in order to exit the Covid-19-induced recession in 2020 and 2021 and an increase of interest rates to tame the rising inflation in the US.

The war caused supply chain disruption and led to fuel, energy and food shortages, which led to inflation.[104]

In order to curb rising inflation, central banks had to make a choice between stimulating economic development after Covid-19 or increasing interest rates to slow economic growth and inflation. Central banks began to raise interest rates to control rising inflation, consequently borrowing costs also increased for many kinds of loans. As a result of this approach, the banks' ability to service their debts, which could otherwise plunge banks into financial difficulties, was reduced.

The consequences of the 2023 financial crisis are as follows:

- A widespread reduction in lending, as a result of an increase in interest rates in the US, tightened financial conditions;
- Loss of investor confidence and a bank run;
- An increase in the cost of borrowing;
- More inflation;
- An increase in unemployment;
- A consumer spending reduction.

It is important to highlight that SVB sparked off the collapse of other banks. SVB, in fact, was not a traditional bank due to the nature of its clients. SVB provided banking services and credit to thousands of start-up companies, and venture debt had been a core part of their lending practice for decades.

103 Henceforth SVB.

104 (Ozili, Global economic consequence of Russian invasion of Ukraine 2022).

5.5.1 The Collapse of Silicon Valley Bank

SVB was a regional bank that served US venture capitalist and technology start-ups with large, uninsured deposits. The collapse of SVB had, at least, two main factors: (1) SVB's poor investment strategy during the tech boom 2020–2021 and (2) the US Federal Reserve's decision to raise the interest rate.

As we said earlier, SVB was not a traditional bank for many reasons.

First and foremost, SVB business was focused on the venture capital ecosystem with a high concentration of customers in the tech start-up space. In the recent years, the boom in speculative investment in small technologies firms resulted in more than 200% growth in both the bank's assets and deposits. This was possible thanks to a channel of financing, which facilitated and benefitted SVB.

Furthermore, SVB managed its balance sheet in a peculiar way: more precisely, this bank invested in long-term and fixed-rate government bonds. As interest rates have risen over the last two years, the value of these assets declined at the same time as inflow into tech start-ups and other ventures capital funding slowed. This mechanism exacerbated the slowdown in growth of its deposits, while its funding costs rose as well.[105]

Within the first element, during 2020–2021, SVB took money it received from deposits and invested the latter into long-term treasury bonds when interest rates were low during the tech boom. This strategy would have been profitable, had interest rates remained low. However, it would become problematic in cases where interest rates began rising. Subsequently, since the US Federal Reserve began to raise interest rates to control inflation, the Treasury bonds held by SVB lost their value until below cost price. Thus, SVB was forced to sell its bonds at a big loss and indeed made a loss on nearly all of its securities that were available for sale. A consistent part of these were US Treasury securities.

Depositors who received early information about SVB's distress had made deposit withdrawal requests and had quickly withdrawn enough funds from the bank; due to this, the bank was in a severe cash shortage and a liquidity crisis. The price shock affected the bank's ability to raise additional equity capital. On 10 March 2023 SVB collapsed.[106]

From a theoretical perspective, SVB was a bank that mixed illiquid assets (business or mortgage loans) and liquid liabilities (deposits which may be withdrawn at any time). This model acted as an intermediation between savers and borrowers: the former prefer to deposit in liquid accounts; the latter prefer to take long-maturity loans. In normal circumstances, banks act as intermediaries between these two parties:[107]

- Hence, each bank provides a valuable service by channelling funds from many individual deposits into loans for borrowers;

105 (Khoo 2023).
106 (Ozili 2023).
107 (German 2023).

- Also, thanks to the aggregation funds from many different depositors, banks help depositors save the high transaction cost they would have to pay in order to lend directly to business.

SVB's collapse is crucial also from another perspective: it is well known that SVB was a crypto-friendly bank and, therefore, provided a view of the behaviour of this new coin during a turmoil. Among scholars, it has been argued that bitcoin, in this specific case, played a role as a safe-haven for assets. More precisely, these cryptocurrencies absorbed influences from the US banking market across timeframes: bitcoin outperformed gold in terms of return and volatility stability, showcasing its crisis-resistant volatility.[108]

Although this is true, the digitalisation was not helpful in SVB's case because of the following factors:[109]

- Online banking facilitated a huge bank run;
- The digitalisation transformed the information society into an information warfare, via social media;
- Data-driven disinformation was a "force multiplier" for "information war agents."

5.5.2 The Signature Bank case

SVB collapse made its first casualties in Signature Bank or, better, Signature Bank was a case of forced-death-by-association. Indeed, Signature Bank had large exposure to the crypto sector – an abnormally large share of uninsured deposit reaching US$79.5 billion as of December 2022. Yet it was not due to bad investment strategy as in the case of SVB.

As a result of the panic which arose around SVB, depositors had already withdrawn more than $10 billion in deposits from Signature Bank; thus, the Federal Deposit Insurance Corporation immediately seized and shut down Signature Bank. This decision was based on the fact that this first contagion could trigger a system-wide bank run and the contagion would reach systemic proportions. In other words, the aim was to contain the panic in the banking system.[110]

5.5.3 Credit Suisse

The Financial Stability Board defined Credit Suisse as a "global systemically important bank" but also named it a "problematic child" as a result of ongoing scandals, litigations, fines and financial losses connected with the 2007–2008 subprime mortgage crisis and other events. Clearly, Credit Suisse could represent a problem for the global banking system.

108 (Changlun and Xiujuan 2023).
109 (Ciuriak 2023).
110 (Ozili 2023).

As far as the 2023 collapse is concerned, Credit Suisse is also a victim of SVB; after the SVB collapse, Credit Suisse needed capital injection from its largest shareholder, Saudi National Bank, who refused to do this. The main reason was the regulatory rules that prevented banks from holding more than 10% ownership of other banks.

Consequently, Credit Suisse was not able to raise additional equity capital quickly; this element, combined with investor apathy towards new investment, put Credit Suisse in significant distress. This scenario was also boosted by the depositors' withdrawal of an amount of US$35 billion.

The last element was the sale of Credit Suisse to Union Bank of Switzerland[111] as a result of the Swiss Central Bank order.[112] Due to do this, shareholder approval was bypassed, bringing about a swift resolution of uncertainty; thus, shareholders did not have to put public money at risk by setting up a complex special-purpose vehicle to de-risk the Credit Suisse balance sheet.[113]

5.5.4 First Republic Bank

First Republic Bank was affected by the Federal Reserve's interest hike in early 2023. It was a regional bank that focused on high-net-worth clients. Its trouble began in March, after the collapse of the other two banks.

After these events, First Republic Bank witnessed a deposit injection of $30 billion by the biggest US banks: it was a moral suasion deal brokered by US bank regulators and aimed at strengthening the bank and improving the resilience of the US system.[114]

The first report showed a massive deposit withdrawn.

5.6 From banking crisis to city council crisis: the Birmingham case

From a theoretical perspective, municipals are, for some elements, like commercial enterprises: cities have a formal similarity to hotels with paying residents, services, transportation and public/private spaces.

Fifteen years ago, in September 2008, the financial crisis reached its more obvious pinnacle too. Footage from the Lehman Brothers headquarters in London hit the headlines: scared employees were told overnight that they needed to vacate their offices. Obedient bank managers, secretaries and workers of all kinds were seen, sometimes shedding tears, leaving the premises with their huge file boxes containing papers and notes of an entire career with their home institution.

One of the ancient banks continuously operating for more than two centuries would enter a winding-up procedure, an actual insolvency process. The board of directors would be replaced by administrators, in charge of dealing with the

111 Also, UBS.
112 (Ozili 2023)
113 (Bolton, Jiang and Kartasheva 2023).
114 (Ozili 2023)

liquidation of assets. A glorious bank would shut for good, with scared employees battening down the hatches, and beleaguered counterparties at best dealing with a default problem, at worst facing the consequences of a contagion.

Financial crises were mainly private and concerned with private organisations. These institutions were left to their destiny; therefore, they were liquidated, such as Lehman Brothers, or they were rescued by the government of each country of incorporation: the British government was, among the different Western countries, the one more "sadly" active in this activity. A few weeks after the collapse of Royal Bank of Scotland, in October, the chancellor of the exchequer signed one of the most expensive cheques ever seen, for the roughly 30 billion pounds, necessary to bail out (therefore, to rescue with public money) the Edinburgh bank.

Fifteen years on, still from the UK, we have now a different insolvency. It does not relate to banks but rather to councils, or public bodies. For those who are not from the UK, it is worth mentioning the role of these institutions. Councils constitute the legacy of the Local Government Act 1974, a piece of legislation which reformed the structure of local entities in the UK. Councils, in a legislative framework which is still alive and, perhaps quite too, kicking after nearly 50 years, constitute fundamentally the most granular form of public entity in the UK. In fact, for centuries, before the enactment of devolution, to Scotland first, in 1998, and later to Wales and Northern Ireland, councils have been the main local entity. With dimensions that can vary – from the city council, which corresponds to the city (*e.g.* Edinburgh, Leeds), to the council that, for historical reason, coincides with a broader territory (*e.g.* Highlands and Islands, West Yorkshire, Northumberland), the council is the most granular form of local government. They are financially augmented by the contributions of the residents (mainly those who live in it, whether or not they are owners of property there): these contributions are tantamount to what is called council tax.

It is worth noting that this system has worked very well, and it has been quite functional: pay-as-you-use. You live in a council, you pay for all services provided, albeit indirectly. The council tax charged and collected does not go to the government; it stays within the council, according to a principle of autonomy and independence. However, it is also flagged up that the council does not have a huge power to raise funds, given the fact that these resources would be quite limited anyway, in comparison with what would be needed and expected.

However, more recently, we can see a new dawn rising across the Channel: the insolvency of councils. The most obvious case, so far, is Birmingham. The city, the "second city of the Empire" during the 19th century, with a council, therefore a local authority, which is the second most populated one in Europe (continental and non-continental), has declared its own insolvency. By serving the Section 114 notice, the council has notified that it is not able to balance its financial resources.[115]

In technical-legal jargon, the council has activated this Section 114, pursuant to which a council which is either illiquid or insolvent, although not technically

115 See, among the first comments, (Marique and Vaccari 2023).

declared insolvent, or both, is exempt from honouring all of its obligations but the essential ones. It is quite arduous to ascertain what is essential and what is not. The demarcation line is thin. However, it is not too speculative to figure out that essential services will be scrapped, and these relate to major activities, such as the running of sports activities and ordinary maintenance works. In fact, it is possible to suggest that, with the insolvency of local authorities, all the activities are stopped but for the very essential ones. Therefore, but for activities such as the collection of the rubbish, and the maintenance of major roads, it is possible to say that the Council of Birmingham would shut down all their activities, including the running of sports venues and the organisation of events.

In a similar way, in 2016 the City of Chicago was named as Junk City,[116] as a result of both severely underfunded public employee pension systems and a large amount of bonded debt. For this second aspect, indeed, the credit rating agency, Moody's downgraded the City of Chicago's general obligations bonds to "Bal" with a negative outlook because these bonds were junk.[117]

5.6.1 The aetiology of the insolvency of the councils

The reason that Birmingham Council has recently collapsed is not yet so clearly identifiable. The explanations are already multifarious. The first "suspect" seems to be the cost of the organisation of major events: the first of these seems to be the Commonwealth Games in 2022, where Birmingham was the host city. Although the event has been deemed very successful and with a huge number of viewers and spectators, the costs for the public (local) taxpayers were not negligible. The games were given to the city well before the dates on which they took place, but they got entrapped in the cost-of-living crisis of the post-pandemic. However, it can be also counterargued that for games of this kind sponsors offer generous "financial buffers," with the aim of providing the council enough oxygen to continue without major concern. In this case, the event may not have been properly funded by private operators. This seems confirmed by the fact that in Brisbane, Australia, where the Commonwealth Games were expected to take place in 2026, they have announced all of a sudden, two months ago, before the financial crisis at Birmingham's Council was disclosed, that they would no longer be prepared to host the games.

However, there might be a further reason that may explain the Birmingham crisis. We are referring, very simply, to a technical mistake in accountancy. This council, a few years before, was sued before an employment tribunal for a massive claim for violation of the principle of equal pay. Male employees were for decades paid more than women, albeit for the identical or similar jobs. The violation of the law (Equal Pay Act 1970) – more so because the actions were backdated – were so massive that the cost of the claim was in the region of 800 million pounds. In these circumstances, a good risk manager and a good management body would set

116 (Jones 2015).
117 (Chaudhury, Levitin and Schleic 2019; Myers 2022).

aside, in the balance sheet of the organisation they are in charge of, a yearly amount of money adequate to pay the potential claimants, were the latter to be victorious in court. This safe move would not burden, all of a sudden, the finances of the organisation. Unfortunately, in this case, the opposite has happened. The council estimated the cost of the claims at zero. This means that, when last year, the claims were upheld by the tribunal, the council needed to pay an unpredicted amount of money which has crashed not only the liquidity of the council but also its stability. The ensuing insolvency is the most logical outcome of this.

In summarising the reasons for this insolvency in Birmingham (but examples could multiply soon), it is possible to say that we are dealing with an insolvency caused, mainly, by accountancy incompetence. In the era of technology, where algorithms and programmes are able to engineer balance sheets of organisations, those in charge of the council failed to do what they should have done, in a sound and prudent way. And this is something that the techno-models of accountancy do not suggest, nor do they work on going beyond the technology and using good principles of accountancy, which human beings, with their own expertise and common sense too, should do. However, human beings did not identify the problem: to set aside a risk of loss in a controversy. They did not tick the relevant box, because they may have relied on the algorithm.

The issue that is unfolding more and more now is that the Birmingham Council does not appear to be an isolated episode of the soap opera. Other councils in the UK are said to be in financial difficulties and even on the verge of declaring bankruptcy. Councils cannot be declared insolvent; rather, they rely on the benefit from being under an obligation to honour their obligations. The difference is made up by government, either the central one or the regional one (Scotland, Northern Ireland, Wales, England) and the amount of money they are available to fill in, as far as the remaining obligations are concerned.

In summarising this aetiology, it is possible to say that a combination of gigantism and, even more, an increasing incompetence of the human being in the techno-era could be the likely reason for the failure. Technology, on the one hand, is simplifying the activity of businesses and its workers and, on the other hand, is affecting that level of attention that any professional should pay to its activities. Even the simplest assessment of a litigation cost, something learned and put in practice by chartered accountants for centuries, is neglected and forgotten, because it is becoming more and more common to rely on the machine. The self-pilot of the machine replaces the sound judgement of the individuals who, eventually, overlook the most basic principles governing their work.

5.6.2 The evolution of this insolvency: from the public bail-in to the private bail-in

While 15 years ago it was said that the financial crises were a deadly combination of moral hazard (*e.g.* to believe in an ever-growing market) and fraudulent business (*e.g.* opaque securitised products sold to retail customers, while the same bankers ignored the risk entailed in the transactions), in what could be the new public sector crises, the essence seems to lie with expertise and competence: the illiteracy of the managers, or better their incapability to apply their knowledge, either because they relied on references (*e.g.* the Commonwealth Games are major events, a bank cheque shall be signed by the public body) or for the reason that they relied on the technology and machinery of their of accountancy programs.

5.6.3 The consequences, also sociological, of a (global versus regional) insolvency of public entities

Whatever the cause of events is, it is still empirical rather than already enshrined in theory – because it lies in an unchartered territory – to ascertain the kind of reaction that needs to be taken by policymakers, as well as the interpretation that shall be given.

While 15 years ago the response to the financial collapse of banks was the bail-out (politicians using taxpayers' money to avoid the demise of banks), it is not unlikely that, for the more recent financial crises, banks and bankers are going to take revenge against their former enemies. Banks (now thriving because losses from the financial crises have been eventually absorbed, and interest rates are booming) may step up to the plate and buy, at a very cheap price, "bits and pieces" of councils or sections of them. The consequence of this may be dear in an era of a cost-of-living crisis. Services provided by councils may become unaffordable, because potentially offered by privatised entities, acting for purely economic interests.

Another option is the bail-out of councils by central government. In detail, this may be a potential public upstream bail-out because it comes from the first tier of the government. In fact, in a United Kingdom – but Italy may well be the case too – where between the government in London and the council, there is the medium of the "nations" (Scotland, Northern Ireland, Wales), each with its own devolution, we may end up staring, baffled, at rows and disputes between central and local government, as to who is in charge of what, as far as the public bail-out of councils is concerned. The British example could apply, *mutatis mutandis*, to different countries, depending on their constitutional structure.

As regards Italy and the European Union, the scenario may appear less problematic, but this analysis seems to be correct only in the short-term. After the pandemic, different countries of the European Union have started benefiting from a resilience plan, public money that, via tranches, is given by the EU to each country, in order to fund public investment by authorities, including local ones. The gist, though, is that this money, perceived as "public" and unrecoverable, constitutes debt that will appear in the finances of public central and local authorities. As result of this, two issues may play havoc: because the origin of this money is public, and from a "far" source: the distance between Brussels and Italy and other countries is not simply geographical. Additionally, because of the cost-of-living crisis, the huge loan granted to each member state can be perceived as inadequate, if compared to the various projects to the completed. Finally, should the repayment be pegged to variable – and during the current days increasing – rates, the cost of this plan could end up very dear. Therefore, in looking at the EU from the UK, the grass of the neighbour may not be necessarily as green as one might be inclined to believe.

Some questions, in a scenario of "insolvency" of public entities (better "forced inability to pay"), need some thoughtful reflections. First, it is dubious whether a crisis of public entities may be as global as the crisis of banks 15 years ago. Banks lend each other money, whereas councils offer services to the public. However, it is likely that other councils may have "contracted" the same virus as Birmingham: a loose approach to finances, coupled with accountancy illiteracy in the area of risk management. It is more likely that the crisis of councils may affect specific countries, certainly the UK, but also those having a similar *modus operandi* in their management. The real contagion, though, can be towards the public. In cities and villages where fundamental services are no longer offered, the public infrastructure, traditional value-for-money, offered by the councils may fade away. This may be replaced by either wealthy classes and wealthy areas (but just for their own interests), or they may simply fade way. Consequences to highlight, therefore, are also sociological, with potentially a model of life – a level playing field of services for everyone – which may become soon the legacy of the past.

5.6.4 The US experience

In the US legal system some scholars have already cogitated on the consequences of a collapse of a city council or, to put it in American English, a municipality.

First and foremost, the bankruptcy of a municipal corporation raises fundamental issues regarding the nature of the organisation. From a historical perspective, prior to 1933 there was no such thing as a federal legislation in the area of municipal bankruptcy. At the beginning it appeared that the American Constitution prevented from scratch any "tier" of government from dealing with the subject.

First and foremost, from the standpoint of the federal government, to do so would have meant to sneak into the governance of the state and their political ramification. Thus, this would violate state sovereignty. In a similar way, for the state government to do so would have driven a coach and horses through the obligations arising out of a contract, hence the reluctance of the federal government to wade into this area.[118]

This approach changed in 1938 with the landmark case *United States v Bekins*: the Court upheld Congress's second attempt to pass a municipal bankruptcy statute and, in 1942, *Faitoute Iron & Steel Co. v Asbury Park* issued the relevant rules to apply. In the latter, it was held that a state's authority may compel unwilling creditors to join in a plan of arrangement of debts owed by the municipality.

Based on the foregoing, it is not too arduous to affirm that the fundamental premises of current laws applicable to the US were shaped by pre-1938 constitutional

118 See *Hanover Nat'l Bank v Moyses*, 186 US 181, 188 (1902) ("[Congress's power under the Bankruptcy Clause] includes the power to discharge the debtor from his contracts and legal liabilities, as well as to distribute his property. The grant to Congress involves the power to impair the obligations of contracts, and this the States were forbidden to do"); (McConnell 1988).

consideration: the contract clause explains why we have a federal bankruptcy statute for municipalities while the principle of state autonomy explains its narrow scope. This was in contrast with private bankruptcy law. Therefore, the 1937 Act was originally adopted as a temporary emergency measure and was to expire in 1940;[119] however, it was extended several times and was made permanent in 1946.[120]

However, Congress substantially revised the act in 1976,[121] by making additional changes as part of the enactment of the 1978 Code and tinkered with the statute in 1984[122] and 1988.[123]

The first federal municipal bankruptcy statute, passed in 1933, was designed solely to deal with a pending issue: when individual creditors were threatened with facing a negotiated debt plan in the best interest of both the debtor and the creditors as a group.[124]

The bill was passed at the instance of municipal officials with the acquiescence of representatives of the creditor class: trust estates, insurance companies, endowment funds, pensions funds and other major holders of municipal bonds.

In *Ashton v Cameron County District*, the court struck down the first federal municipal bankruptcy statute on constitutional grounds. This decision was based on the theory that this piece of legislation "might materially restrict respondent's control over its fiscal affairs." The court elaborated that "[i]f obligations of States or their political subdivisions may be subjected to the interference here attempted, they are no longer free to manage their own affairs; the will of Congress prevails over them."[125]

One year after *Aston*, the Congress enacted a new municipal bankruptcy statute, albeit only marginally different from the one declared as non-valid. Although the statute was challenged, on this occasion the court decision was upheld since it was against the constitutional principles under *Ashton*.

119 See, for example, Act of June 28, 1940, 54 Stat 667, 670 c 438 (1940) (extending the act until 1942)

120 60 Stat 409, codified at 11 USC §§ 401 et seq (1946).

121 Pub L 94-260, 90 Stat 315, codified at 11 USC §§ 401 et seq (1976).

122 Bankruptcy Amendments and Federal Judgeship Act of 1984, PL 98-353, 98 Stat 333, 383-84, codified at 11 USC §§ 490-98 (1984

123 2 Municipal Bankruptcy Amendments, Pub L 100-597, 102 Stat 3028 (1988)

124 This feeling was explained by its principal sponsor in the follow terms: "The object and purpose of the bill is, of course, to enable counties, towns, and tax districts to adjust their debts effectively. In every instance where a governmental unit finds itself in financial difficulty and is able to make some satisfactory agreement of adjustment with the majority of its creditors, there is always a small minority who hold out and demand preferential treatment. These minority creditors are prompted in this action by the thought that someone will buy them out rather than have the whole plan collapse. The difficulty, of course, is that if one creditor by holding out can gain preferential treatment the others withdraw and nothing comes of the efforts at settlement or adjustment. It is to remove this difficulty that the bill has been drawn and introduced. If this bill is enacted, the minority creditors will be forced to accept the terms of adjustment which have been agreed upon by the officials of the political subdivision and the vast majority of creditors and approved by the court as being fair and equitable." Id at 22 (statement of Rep. J. Mark Wilcox). 109 Id at 40 (testimony of Charles Taylor).

125 298 US 513 (1936). m Id at 530. 1 Id at 531.

The case to be referred was *United States v Bekins*.[126] In this, the court held that, although it did not overrule *Ashton*, the new act did not identify any specific points of distinction from the earlier act. On this occasion, the court averred that the act was not a derogation from state and local sovereignty, rather, more precisely, "an aid" to those powers. In other words, it needed to be qualified as an expression of sovereignty representing an ability to make contracts. Furthermore, the act gave consent, bearing upon the exertion of government power; thus, the bankruptcy would remove an obstacle to do so. In the court's view, the only possible obstacle, from a constitutional perspective, was the right of the state to prevent a municipality from seeking bankruptcy protection. However, the latter objection did not represent a relevant argument in the specific case due to the fact that the state gave its consent.

The only changes of constitutional interest between the 1933 Act and the 1937 Act were the omission of the express provision of the requirement about the approval of bankruptcy petitions by states. The latter was replaced with the requirement that a petitioning municipality show that it "is authorized by law to take all action necessary to be taken by it to carry out the plan."[127] Moreover, it excluded counties from the act.

After this change, a *decisum*, *Faitoute Iron & Steel Co. v Asbury Park*,[128] was issued. Before *Faitoute Iron*, it was assumed that states were incompetent to relieve municipalities from their debts and debtors. The reason was that any plan of involuntary settlement of debts would impair the obligation of the creditor's contract in violation of the contractual clauses. By contrast, the court stressed that a federal statute was necessary. This was due to the fact that the preclusion for states from passing laws for the composition of municipal debts.

Despite this, in *Faitoute*, the court upheld a 1933 New Jersey law that permitted a plan of adjustment of municipal debt over the objection of minority creditors if the city and 85% of the creditors agreed. According to this line of reasoning, the strong argument was that such plans do not impair the obligations of a contract, but rather they are "the only proven way for assuring payment of unsecured municipal obligation." The verdict of this case law was overturned by Congress, because federal law now prohibited US states from exercising any power whereby they would be compelled to arrange for a settlement of municipal debt.[129]

Federal bankruptcy law is divided into three chapters, and the most important is Chapter 9, which covers municipalities. This legal provision provides a mechanism for the "Adjustment of Debts of a Municipality": a municipality may make a simple-form bankruptcy petition. The latter may be accepted only if (1) the municipality is insolvent, (2) the filing is authorised by state law and (3) the petition has

126 304 US 27 (1938).

127 Act of 16 August 1937, 50 Stat 654, 655 c 10 § 83(e)(6).

128 316 US 502 (1942).

129 (McConnell and Picker, When Cities Go Broke: A Conceptual Introduction to Municipal Bankruptcy 1993).

been negotiated in good faith with any class of creditors whose claims it intends to impair by Chapter 9.[130]

As far as insolvency is concerned, it is defined, if referred to a municipality, as unavailability of funds "to pay its debts as they come due" or "generally not paying its debts as they become due."[131]

The good faith principle gives discretion to the court in order to determine whether a municipality has filed for bankruptcy in good faith.[132] More precisely, it is required that debtors must show one of the following elements: (1) the majority of the creditors in each class gave their consent, (2) it has negotiated with creditors in good faith and failed to come to an agreement, and (3) it is unable to negotiate with creditors, or a creditor is trying to obtain a preferential transfer of some kind. For instance, in *Re Sullivan County Regional Refuse Disposal District*,[133] the court dismissed a petition on the basis that there was a lack of good faith. To elaborate, in this specific case, although the municipality was insolvent, it refused to exercise its authority to assess its taxation.[134]

When a municipality files for Chapter 9, most collection efforts against the municipality, outside the bankruptcy court, continue being dealt with via a federal injunction. During the bankruptcy, the municipality continues to manage its assets and affairs. It is possible that the municipality will propose a plan for adjustment of its debts. This plan shall classify creditor's claims into separate classes that specify the treatment of the claims and provide for means its implementation. A municipal debt adjustment plan can propose a broad range of things, including paying little or nothing on particular classes of claims, with the collection of any unpaid amounts the permanently enjoined.

After the court-approved disclosure of plan terms, creditor's vote may be solicited on the plan of adjustment. This plan may be confirmed if it is approved by the requisite majorities of creditors and comports with other various statutory requirements, including the well-known concept of "in the best interest of creditors."[135] In the case in which the plan is confirmed, any debts owed by the municipality are discharged to the extent they are not provided for by the plan.

It is crucial to be note that in America Chapter 9 derives from Chapter 11, the chapter in the Bankruptcy Code that is used for corporate reorganisation and liquidations, but it is not designed to deal with debtor conglomerates. The main problem, in other words, is that the Bankruptcy Code was shaped on small firm. To elaborate, the pragmatic debtor was more similar to a small shop and not to a firm, such as Coca-Cola. Additionally, the Code lacks attention to multi-entity firms because multi-entity firms, per se, do not have legal personhood, only their component entities. Thus, creditors and shareholders are specific to a particular entity

130 From a critical perspective, see Lawton (2020).
131 11 U.S.C. § 109(cX3); 11 U.S.C. § 101(32)(BXi) and (ii).
132 11 U.S.C. § 921(c) (2012).
133 *In re Sullivan County Regional Refuse Disposal Dist.*, 165 B.R. 60, 82-83 (Bankr. DN.H. 1994).
134 (Chaudhury, Levitin and Schleic 2019).
135 11 U.S.C. § 943(b) (2012).

and not a conglomerate as a whole. It is clear that bankruptcy petitions are filed on a per-entity basis rather than by firm.

Bearing this in mind, the more problematic aspect concerns the difficulty of transferring corporate bankruptcy doctrines, *i.e.* Chapter 11, to a Chapter 9 context. Chapter 11 encompasses, at least, two main procedures: joint administration and substantive consolidation.

The first one states that jointly administered debtors would, in the absence of anything further, each be required to have their own plans be confirmed. Accordingly, a joint plan would have to be separately confirmed for each entity. Separate confirmation would mean that the creditors and holders of interest in each affiliated debtor would have to be classified separately and vote separately for each plan. Further, the requirement that there must be one impaired class accepting the plan, not counting insiders, would have to be satisfied for each individual debtors' entity.

The second one, the substantive consolidation, means that corporate separateness is disregarded and the assets of liabilities of separate, substantively consolidated entities are treated as the common assets and liabilities of a single entity. Therefore, the claims of creditors of separate entities would all become one claim against a single consolidated entity that would hold the assets of all the separate entities.

Another element to highlight is that the Federal Rule of Bankruptcy Procedure 1015 does not apply to overlapping municipal governments. By contrast, it applies only to "a debtor and an affiliate" whose cases are in the same Court. The definition of "affiliate" is to entities with common equity ownership or control. Overlapping municipalities are not "affiliate"; hence, they are not under common equity ownership.[136]

Another element concerns the difference between the concept of the best interest under Chapter 9 and under Chapter 11. In Chapter 11, "best interest" does not appear in the statute, while it is used to refer to a requirement that a plan to pay all impaired, non-accepting creditors at least as much value as they would receive in a hypothetical liquidation of the debtor. By contrast, under Chapter 9, the "best interest" test compares how creditors fare under the proposed plan to how they would fare without any plan at all.[137]

References

Alexander, K. "Principles v Rules in Financial Regulation: Re-Assessing the Balance in the Credit Crisis: Symposium at Cambridge University." *European Business Organization Law Review* 10, no. 2 (2009): 169–173.

Anderson, J. "Struggling Lehman Plans to Lay Off 1,500." *NY Times*, 2008.

Baker, L. "Procurement, Finance and the Energy Transition: Between Global Processes and Territorial Realities." *EPE: Nature and Space* 5, no. 4 (2023): 1738–1764.

Barr, M.S., H.E. Jackson, and M.E. Tahyar. "The Financial Response to the COVID-19 Pandemic." *U of Michigan Law & Econ Research Paper*, no. 20-040 (2020).

136 (Chaudhury, Levitin and Schleic 2019).

137 See, also, *In re City of Detroit*, 524 B.R. 147,213 (Bankr. E.D. Mich. 2014).

Blakeley, G. "Financialization, Real Estate and COVID-19 in the UK." *Community Development Journal* 56, no. 1 (2021): 79–99.
Bokhorst, D., and F. Corti. "Governing Europe's Recovery and Resilience Facility: Between Discipline and Discretion." *Government and Opposition* (2023): 1–17.
Bolton, P., W. Jiang, and A. Kartasheva. "The Credit Suisse CoCo Wipeout: Facts, Misperceptions, and Lessons for Financial." *Journal of Applied Corporate Finance* 32, no. 23 (2023): 66–74.
Boot, A.W., and M. Marinč. "The Evolving Landscape of Banking." *Industrial and Corporate Change* 17, no. 6 (2008): 1173–1203.
Brunnermeier, M., A. Crockett, C. Goodhart, A. Persaud, and H. Shin. "The Fundamental Principles of Financial Regulation." *Geneva Report on the World Economy* 11, 2009.
Bush, D. "Is the European Union Going to Help Us Overcome the COVID-19 Crisis?" *Capital Markets Law Journal* 15, no. 3 (2022): 347–367.
Changlun, J., and T. Xiujuan. "Enhanced Safe-Haven Status of Bitcoin: Evidence from the Silicon Valley Bank Collapse." https://ssrn.com/abstract=4560087 (2023).
Chaudhury, A., A.J. Levitin, and D. Schleic. "Junk Cities: Resolving Insolvency Crises in Overlapping Municipalities." *California Law Review* 107, no. 2 (2019): 459–526.
Chiu, I. H.-Y., A. Kokkinis, and A. Miglionico. "Relief and Rescue: Suspensions and Elasticity in Financial Regulation, and Lessons from the UK's Management of the COVID-19 Pandemic Crisis." *Washington University Journal of Law & Policy*, no. 64 (2021): 63–112.
Ciuriak, D. "The Silicon Valley Bank Failure: Historical Perspectives and Knock-on Risks." *Ciuriak Consulting – Policy Commentary*, 2023.
Congleton, D.R. "The Political Economy of the Financial Crisis of 2008." In *Lessons from the Financial Crisis*, edited by W.R. Kolb. John Wiley & Sons, 2010.
Cooper, J. *The Integration of Financial Regulatory Authorities – The Australian Experience. Australian Securities & Investments Commission, Australia.* Rio de Janeiro: Ecurities and Exchange Commission of Brazil 30th Anniversary Conference, Assessing the Present, Conceiving the Future, 2006.
Cranston, R., E. Avgouleas, K.V. Zwieten, C. Hare, and T.V. Sante. *Principles of Banking Law*. Oxford: Oxford University Press, 2017.
D'Arcy, C. "Why Lehman Brothers Collapsed?" *The Economy*, 2009.
de Gioia Carabellese, P., and C. Della Giustina. *The Law of Securitisations. From Crisis to Techno-Sustanability*. London and New York: Routledge, 2023.
Di Mascio, F., A. Natalini, and S. Profeti. "The Draghi Government Put to the Test by the National Recovery and Resilience Plan." *Contemporary Italian Politics* 14, no. 4 (2022): 402–408.
Franklin, A., and E. Carletti. "An Overview of the Crisis: Causes, Consequences and Solutions." *Willey Online Library* (2010).
German, H. "From Lehaman to Silicon Valley Bank and Beyond: Why Are Mistakes Repeated in the US Banking System?" *Policy Center for the New South*, 2023.
Giese, J., and A. Haldane. "COVID-19 and the Financial System: A Tale of Two Crises." *Oxford Review of Economic Policy* 36, no. S1 (2020): S200–S214.
Greenwood, R., S.G. Hanson, J. Stein, and A. Sunderam. "The Financial Regulatory Reform Agenda in 2017." *Project on Behavioral Finance and Financial Stability Working Paper*, no. 9. Harvard Business School, 2017.
Gros, D. "The West's COVID-19 Learning Curve." *Project Syndicate* (2020), online.
Guan, Y., J. Yan, Y. Shan, Y. Zhou, Y. Hang, R. Li, Y. Liu, B. Liu, Q. Nie, B. Bruckner, and K. Feng. "Burden of the Global Energy Price Crisis on Households." *Nature Energy* 8, no. 8 (2023): 304–316.

Hafiz, H., S.-H. Oei, D. Ring, and N. Shnitser. "Regulating in Pandemic: Evaluating Economic and Financial Policy Responses to the Coronavirus." *Boston College Law School* (2020): 14–15.

Hosp, P. "Problematic Practices of Credit Rating Agencies: The Neglected Risks of Mortgage-Backed Securities." In *Lessons from the Financial Crisis*, edited by R.W. Kolb. Hoboken: John Wiley & Sons, 2010.

Jackson, H.E., and P. Rothesian. "The Analysis of Benefits in Consumer Protection Regulations." *Harvard Business Law Review* 197, no. 9 (2019): 207–209.

Jackson, H.E., and S.L. Schwarz. "Protecting Financial Stability: Lessons from the COVID-19 Pandemic." *Harvard Business Law Review* 11, no. 2 (2021): 192–232.

Jones, T. *Five Reasons Chicago Is in Worse Shape Than Detroit*. Bloomberg, 2015.

Khoo, G.-S. "Commentary: Lessons from SVB's Collapse on Sustainability Finance: Ensuring Resilience from "Unsustainability." *The Journal of Risk Finance* 24, no. 3 (2023): 386–389.

Kolb, R.B. *Lessons from the Financial Crisis*. Hoboken: John Wiley & Sons, Inc, 2010.

Lawton, A. "What Problem? A Response to How Cities Fail: Service Delivery Insolvency and Municipal Bankruptcy." *Michigan State Law Review*, no. 1 (2020): 233–252.

Leino, P. *Next Generation EU: Breaking a Taboo or Breaking the Law? CEPS in Brief*. Centre for European Policy Studies, 2020.

Leledarkis, G.L., and E.G. Pyrgiotakis. "US Bank M&As in the Post-Dodd – Frank Act Era: Do They Create Value?" *Journal of Banking & Finance* 135, no. 1 (2022): 105576.

Liu, K. "The Impact of the Dodd-Frank Act on Small US Banks." 2023.

Lui, A. "Single or Twin? The UK Financial Regulatory Landscape After the Financial Crisis of 2007–2009." *Journal of Banking Regulation* 1, no. 13 (2012): 24–35.

Luo, C.-M. "The Covid-19 Crisis: The EU Recovery Fund and Its Implications for European Integration – a Paradigm Shift." *European Review* 30, no. 3 (2021): 374–392.

MacNeil, I. "The Trajectory of Regulatory Reform in the UK in the Wake of the Financial Crisis." *European Business Organization Law Review* 11, no. 4 (2010): 438–526.

Marique, Y., and E. Vaccari. "Birmingham's Bankruptcy Is Only the Tip of the Iceberg – Local Authorities Across England Are at Risk." *The Conversation*, 2023.

McConnell, M.W. "Contract Rights and Property Rights: A Case Study in the Relationship between Individual Liberties and Constitutional Structure." *California Law Review* 76, no. 2 (1988): 267–296.

McConnell, M.W., and R.C. Picker. "When Cities Go Broke: A Conceptual Introduction to Municipal Bankruptcy." *University of Chicago Law Review* 60, no. 2 (1993): 425–496.

Mensah, K.M.J. "Appraisal and Improvement of Organizations' Performance: A Case Study of Accra." http://ssrn.com/author=1761405, 2012.

Milzen, P. "The Credit Crunch of 2007–2008: A Discussion of the Background, Market Reactions, and Policy Responses." *The Credit Crunch of 2007–2008: A Discussion of the Background, Market Reactions, and Policy Responses* 90, no. 3 (2008): 531–568.

Murphy, A. "An Analysis of the Financial Crisis of 2008: Causes and Solution." https://ssrn.com/abstract=1295344, 2008.

Myers, S. "Public Employee Pensions and Municipal Insolvency." *Online*, 2022.

Nguyen, A.T., L. Parker, L. Brennan, and S. Lockrey. "A Consumer Definition of Eco-Friendly Packaging." *Journal of Cleaner Production*, no. 252 (2020): 119792.

Ozili, P.K. "Global Economic Consequence of Russian Invasion of Ukraine." ssrn.com/abstract=4064770, 2022.

Ozili, P.K. "Causes and Consequences of the 2023 Banking Criss." *SSRN Electronic Journal*, 2023.

Peek, J., and E. Rosengren. "The Capital Crunch: Neither a Borrower Nor a Lender Be." *Journal of Money, Credit and Banking* 27, no. 3 (1995): 625–638.
Pichardo, C., and F. Bacon. "The Lehman Brothers Bankruptcy: A Test of Market Efficiency." *Allied Academies International Conference* 14, no. 1 (2009): 43–48.
Pilati, M. "National Recovery and Resilience Plan: Impowering the Green and Digital Transitions?" Discussion Paper. *European Policy Centre*, 2021.
Purnanandam, A. "Originate-to-Distribute Model and the Subprime Mortgage Crisis." *The Review of Financial Studies* 24, no. 6 (2011): 1881–1915.
Ramskogler, P. "Tracing the Origins of the Financial Crisis." *OECD Journal: Financial, Market Trends* 17, no. 2 (2015).
Rizk, A. "Banking Regulation After the Financial Crisis Has Made Banks Safer." *International Journal of Management Research and Economics* 2, no. 2 (2022): 47–59.
Schramm, L., U. Krotz, and B. De Witte. "Building 'Next Generation' After the Pandemic: The Implementation and Implications of the EU Covid Recovery Plan." *JCMS: Journal of Common Market Studies*, no. 60 (2022): 114–124.
Sher, V., and G.G. Iyanatul. *The Great Recession of 2008–2009: Causes, Consequences and Policy Responses*. The Institute for the Study of Labor, 2010.
Song Shin, H. "Reflections on the Northern Rock: The Bank Run That Heralded the Global Financial Crisis." *Journal of Economic Perspective* 23, no. 1 (2009): 101–119.
Sykes, B.J. *Regulatory Reform 10 Years After the Financial Crisis: Congressional Research*. https://fas.org/sgp/crs/misc/R45162.pdf, 2018.
Taylor, J.B. "The Financial Crisis and the Policy Responses: An Empirical Analysis of What Went Wrong." Working Paper, no. 14631. *National Bureau of Economic Research*, 2009.
Verick, S., and I. Islam. *The Great Recession of 2008–2009: Causes, Consequences and Policy Responses*. The Institute for the Study of Labor, 2010.
Vlukas, A.R. "Lehman Brothers' Examiners Repor." *SMC Blackboard* 1, no. 2 (2010).
Weaver, A.K., J.R. Gould, E.J. Carlton, and J.V. Remais. "Environmental Factors Influencing COVID-19 Incidence and Severity." *Annual Review of Public Health* 43, no. 2 (2023): 271–291.
Wojcik, D., and S. Ioannou. "Covid 19 and Finance: Market Developments So Far and Potential Impacts on the Financial Sector and Centres." *Tijdschrift voor economische en sociale geografie* 111, no. 3 (2020): 387–400.

Index

Note: Page numbers with n indicate footnotes.

acquisition finance 200
active interest 43
actual events of default 207
additional duty of investment firm 117–118
Admission Directive 146
Agricultural Credits (Scotland) Act, 1929 27
Agricultural Marketing Act, 1958 27
agriculture-based derivatives 172
agri-food market 169–174; elements affecting 169–170; financialisation of 170; index-based agricultural insurance and 173–174; speculation and 171
akhlaq 265
al-bay 266
Alcor Care Trust Supporting Organization (ACT) 344–345
Alcor Life Extension Foundation 344
all moneys guarantee 204
alternative dispute resolution 129–134; Financial Ombudsman 133–134; Online Dispute Resolution 132–133; overview of 129; restorative justice 129–132
alternative funding means 78–79n118
Alternative Investment Fund Managers (AIFM) 188, 192–194
alternative investment funds 192–194
Amsterdam Stock Exchange 140
aqidah (faith) 265
arranger 145–146, 196
Ashton v Cameron County District 383
asset finance transaction 200
asset separation 78
Association of German Public Banks 134
authorisation of banking business 60–63; European passport 61–62; non-compliance and 62–63; TFEU and 60
authorisation process, investment firm(s) 180–182
availability/commitment period of loan 199
avatars 309
Ayr Bank growth case study 25

bad bank 78
bail-in 2
bail-in tool 78, 89; moral hazard and 100
bail-out 78n115; as form of moral hazard 100
balance sheet lending 200
balloon payment 202
banco, defined 351n2
bank account 7, 43, 45, 47–48n11, 312, 328
bank authorisation 9, 13, 60–63
bank branch 47–48
bank industry holding 31, 37, 52–53
Banking Act, 1933 36–37
banking and financial crises, 2007–08 5, 16–17, 46, 98, 353–363; agri-food market following 170; beginning of crisis 355–358; Dodd-Frank Wall Street Reform and Consumer Protection Act 358–359; EU regulation 360–361; post-crisis regulation 358–363; pre-existing scenario 353–355; UK approach to 361–363
banking groups 49–50
Banking Holding Company Act, 1956 31, 37
banking law: alternative dispute resolution 129–134; consumer protection 108–129; human rights in 3; insolvency/resolution 71–108; introduction to 2–3; medical law and 4; organizations of banks 43–56; supervision of banks 56–71; *see also individual headings*

Banking Reform Act of 2013 362
banking system, Islamic finance 269–271
Bank Insurance Fund 34
Bank of America 33
Bank of England 5, 21–22, 301, 302; approach to green transition 306–307; Financial Policy Committee 60; from financial services authority to 22; financial stability 18–20; "ideal post-EU regulatory framework" 19
Bank of Scotland 24; coins and 25; origin of paper money 25–26
Bank Recovery and Resolution (BRRD) 2, 56, 74–76; early intervention measures 77; *mutatis mutandis* and 89; no creditor worse off principle 84–85, 90–94; recovery planning 76–77; resolution 77–78, 80; resolution conditions 81; resolution of bank under 80–83; structure 76–80
bankrupt 351
bankruptcy remote 248
bank(s): banking groups 49–50; branches 47–48; categories of 31, 45–51; commercial 45; defined 31; domestic 50–51; financial stability and prudential supervision 63–64; industry and 51–54; international 50–51; investment 45; subsidiaries 48–49; transformation function of 44; universal, *versus* multifunctional groups 45–47
Bank Secrecy Act, 2018 39–40
bank subsidiary 48–49
bank supervision, United States 40–41
Banque de France 302
Barnier, Michel 18
Barroso, José 13
Basel Accords 64, 353, 360
Basel Committee on Banking Supervision (BCBS) 64
Benchmarks Regulation 297–298
best efforts underwriting 145
Big Nature Impact Fund (BNIF) 301
bilateral loan 195
Birmingham Council case 377–386; aetiology of council insolvency 379–380; consequences of insolvency 381–382; introduction to 377–379; from public to private bail-in 380–381; US experience 382–386
bitcoin 311
blockchain 309–311; definitions of 309–310; elements of 310
blue economy, EU 291
BlueInvest 291
BNP Paribas 356
boilerplate clause 210–213; agent 211; changes to parties of agreement 210–211; conditions precedent 212–213; described 210; governing law 212; waivers 211–212
bonds, securities as 150
bonds markets, Islamic finance 275
Bounce-Back Loans Scheme (BBLS) 365
branches 47–48; CRR definition of 48
break costs 202
Brexit: Financial Services and Markets Act 2023 239; introduction to 1–2; UK consumer protection legislation 125–126; UK regulation and 17–18
bridge finance 200–201
bridge institution 78
British Financial Conduct Authority 338
British Linen Bank 26
brokerage houses 177
BRRD *see* Bank Recovery and Resolution (BRRD)
Brussels financial law legislation 8–16; De Larosière Report 13–15; European passport 10–11; First Banking Directive 9; Lamfalussy Report 11–13; overview of 8–9; Second Banking Directive 9–11; Single Supervisory Mechanism 15–16
bullet loan 199
bullet payment 202

calculation agent 219
Cameron, David 17
capital: adequacy, increasing 67; defined 65; going concern 66; gone concern 66; types of 66
capital buffers 64–67; categories of 66–67; characteristics of 65
capital markets, Islamic finance 271–272
Capital Markets Union Action Plan 185
Capital Requirements Directive IV (CRD IV) 12–13, 44, 49, 56, 64; Article 23 54; banking activities and 54–55; BRRD and 75–76
Capital Requirements Regulation (CRR) 48, 56, 64; BRRD and 75–76
cash-credit accounts, Scotland 24
central bank role in green transition 301–307; Bank of England approach to 306–307; climate change and

301–302; European Central Bank role 304–306; green bank concept 303–304; introduction to 301–303; Network for Greening the Financial System and 302
chacun pour soi solution 13
change of control 210
Charter of Nice 88–90
Charter of the Fundamental Rights of the European Union 7, 7n10
circular economy, transition to 292
circumvention 30
Citigroup 33
City Councils crises *see* Birmingham Council case
clauses 201–203
Clean Growth Fund 300–301
Climate Bonds Initiative (CBI) 296
climate change 292; mitigation/adaptation 292
Climate Delegated Act 292
Clinton, Bill 38
closed-end funds 189n227
club loan 195
COCOs *see* conversion or cancellation operation (COCOs)
collateral 213; *see also* security
commercial bank(s) 32, 45
Commercial Paper Funding Facility 368
Commission Regulation on Resolution Financing Arrangements 95
Committee on Payment and Settlement Systems 317
Commodity Exchange Act, 1936 171, 172
Commodity Futures Modernization Act of 2000 172
Commodity Futures Trading Commission 172
Companies (Floating Charges) (Scotland) Act, 1961, 1972 27, 29–30
competent authority 156
conditions precedent 212–213
conflicts of interest, identification of 118–119
consumer, defined 108, 119
consumer credit 119, 120
Consumer Credit Directive 119–122; consumer defined in 119; credit agreements and 119; digitalisation/technological advancements and 120; right to be forgotten in oncology element 120; structure of 121–122
Consumer Duty 186–187
Consumer Financial Protection Bureau (CFPB) 38
consumer protection 108–129; challenges 128–129; Consumer Duty and 187; described 108; domestic abuse, financial training and 126–127; financial/banking legislation 114–124; overview of 108–109; in UK 124–126; Unfair Terms Directive 108, 109–114
Consumer Protection Act 124
Consumer Rights Act 125
contingent liability facility 200
conversion or cancellation operation (COCO) 97–99
Coronavirus Aid, Relief, and Economic Security Act 367
Coronavirus Business Interruption Loans Scheme (CBILS) 365, 366
Coronavirus Corporate Financing Facility (CCFF) 365
corporate governance 69–70
Corporate Sustainability Reporting Directive 294
cost-of-living crisis 373
costs 203
Covid-19 pandemic 363–372; consumer protection and 128–129; EU approach to 369–372; financial instruments and 363–365; securitisations and 259–260; UK approach to 365–367; US management of 367–369
CRD IV *see* Capital Requirements Directive IV (CRD IV)
credit crunch 372–373
credit default swap (CDS) 216
credit derivatives 219–220
credit event 219
credit institution 43, 54
creditors' protection 84–99; *ex post* resolution funds 94–99; no creditor worse off principle 84–85, 90–94; property right under international legislation 85–90
credit risk 250–251
credit squeeze 372
Credit Suisse 376–377
crisis 351–386; banking and financial crises, 2007–08 353–363; Birmingham Council case 377–386; Covid-19 pandemic 363–372; from credit-crunch to cost-of-living 372–373; financial crisis 2023 374–377; introduction to 351–353; *see also individual headings*
cross-acceleration 209
cross-default 208–209
crowdfunding 340–342
CRR *see* Capital Requirements Regulation (CRR)

cryo-finance 343–345; described 4
cryptocurrencies 311–315
cultural heritage market 174–175
custody agreements 227–242; introduction to 227–229; of money and securities 229–232; security custody 232–236; transfer of money and securities 236–239; UK financial regulation 239–242

data protection 3
dealer 178n184
debt capital 195–196
debt securities 149
decarbonisation 298
decentralised autonomous organisation (DAO) 315–316
decentralised finance (DeFi) 264, 316
defaults, loan contract 207–210; change of control 210; cross-default 208–209; described 207–208; material adverse change 209; types of 207–208
De Larosière, Jacques 13
De Larosière Report 12, 13–15, 57, 360
demand loan 199
depositors' protection 243
depositors' protection schemes 243
depositum irregulare 227, 228, 229, 232
depositum regulare 227, 235
de-risking 340
derivatives 215–226; credit 219–220; described 215; EMIR and 225–226; forwards as 218; ISDA master agreement for 220–224; legal structure of 215–217; legislation and regulation 225–226; MiFIR and 226; options as 217–218; swaps as 219
digital banking 3, 316–335; described 316; digital euro 325–332; facial recognition technology 334–335; mobile payment 316–318; payment service directives 319–324; personal data as money 324–325; privacy and 332–334; smart-banking contracts 318–319
digital euro 325–332; advantages to 326–327; cross-currency payments and 330; described 325–326; European Central Bank and 326; legal tender status of 329–330; money laundering prevention and 330–331; online *vs.* offline models 328–329; privacy and data protection 329; sustainability issues 331–332
digitalisation 2, 3
digital market 175–176
Digital Operational Resilience Act (DORA) 337
Digital Service Act 175; applications of 175, 175n176; issues 175
Directive on Bank Recovery and Resolution (BRRD) 56
Directive on Deposit Guarantee Scheme 57
directives 7–8
directors, investment firm 182–183
Disclosure Delegated Act 292
distance contracts: defined 113; Unfair Terms Directive and 112–113
Distance Financial Services Directive 113–114
Distributed Ledger Technologies (DLT) 338
Dodd-Frank Wall Street Reform and Consumer Protection Act, 2010 38–39, 46–47, 358–359
domestic abuse, financial training and 126–127
domestic banks 50–51
dual banking system 40
Dubai Multi Commodities Centre (DMCC) Commodity Murabahah Trading Platform 277
Dutch East India Company 140

East India Company 23
EBA *see* European Banking Authority (EBA)
economic justice, components of Islamic 267
economic system, Islamic finance 265–267
elective client 116
eligible counterparties 116–117
Emissions Trading Schemes 307
Enforcement Regulation 125, 126
enhanced equivalence model 18
Environmental Delegated Act 292–293
equity capital 195
equity crowdfunding 341
equity kicker 201
equity markets, Islamic finance 275–277
equity securities 148–149
ESG (environmental, social and governance) 2; in Islamic finance 283
ESG factors as business model 289–346; central bank role in green transition 301–307; European Union approach to 290–298; fintech and 307–345; green

finance in UK regulation 298–301; introduction to 289; techno-digital economy, green and 345–346; *see also individual headings*
EU *see* European Union (EU)
Euro 56–57; digital 325–332; European Central Bank and 58
European Banking Authority (EBA) 14, 56, 57–58
European banking supervision 56–58; EBA 57–58; European Central Bank 58; Single Supervisory Mechanism 56–57
European Central Bank 15–16n40, 58, 301; blockchain definition 309; green transition role 304–306; Single Supervisory Mechanism 15–16
European Coal and Steel Treaty 6n5
European Economic Area (EEA) 11, 62, 76
European Green Bond Standard 295
European Green Deal 290, 296
European Insurance and Occupational Pensions Authority (EIOPA) 14
European market infrastructure regulation (EMIR) 225–226
European passport 10–11, 61–62
European Securities and Markets Authority (ESMA) 14, 109, 337
European Stability Mechanism (ESM) programme for Greece 105
European Systemic Risk Board (ESRB) 14–15
European System of Central Banks 58
European System of Financial Supervision (ESFS) 14, 56, 57, 360–361
European Union (EU) 6; banking activities 54–56; Climate Transition Benchmarks 298; Paris-aligned Benchmarks 298; regulation of securitisations 256–257
European Union approach to ESG 290–298; financial policy 293–295; financial product 295–297; green finance 291–293; overview of 290–291; regulatory instruments 297–298
European Union regulation 5–16; Brussels financial law legislation 8–16; directives 7–8; overview of 5; regulations 7–8; statutes 5–8; *see also* Brussels financial law legislation
European Union Securitisation Regulation 256
European Union statutes 5–8; overview of 5–6; treaties 6–7
European Union Withdrawal Act, 2018 20
eurozone 13, 16, 57–58, 79; digital euro and 326; ECB and 58; SRM and 75–76
eurozone debt crisis 13, 56, 76n94
EU-US Data Privacy Framework 333–334
ex ante solution 93, 96–99
ex post resolution funds 93, 94–96

FaceNet 334
facial recognition technology 334–335
factoring 10, 45, 50n20, 53, 247
Faitoute Iron & Steel Co. v Asbury Park 382, 384
Farmer and Finance project 307
Federal Deposit Insurance Act 36–37
Federal Deposit Insurance Corporation (FDIC) 31, 34, 37
Federal Farm Loan Act of 1916 171
Federal Open Market 367
Federal Reserve Act, 1914 35
Federal Reserve Bank 302, 367
Federal Reserve System 31, 34, 35
Federated Hermes and Finance Earth 301
fees 203
finance loans 194–213; *see also* loan contract
financial/banking legislation for consumer protection 114–124; Consumer Credit Directive 119–122; MiFID legislation 115–119; Mortgage Credit Directive 122–124; overview of 114–115
Financial Conduct Authority (FCA) 5n3, 19, 22, 60; Consumer Duty 186–187
financial contracts 194–213; loan contract 194–213; Unfair Terms Directive and 111–112; *see also individual headings*
financial crisis 2007–2008 *see* banking and financial crises, 2007–08
financial crisis 2023 374–377; consequences of 374; Credit Suisse and 376–377; First Republic Bank and 377; introduction to 374; Signature Bank and 376; Silicon Valley Bank collapse 375–376
financial instruments 140, 140n1; bonds 150; investment fund and 188; investment services/activities and 179; MA Directive and 161–162; shares 150
financial law: custody agreements 227–242; financial contracts 194–213; human rights in 3; introduction to 2–3; investments and funds 176–194; Islamic finance 264–283; legislation, Brussels 8–16; market organisation 139–176;

medical law and 4; security 213–226; spare banking and conduits 242–264; themes, post pandemic crisis 2; *see also* Brussels financial law legislation; *individual headings*
financial market infrastructure (FMI) 240–241
financial materiality 295
Financial Ombudsman 133–134
financial policy, European Union, ESG and 293–295
Financial Policy Committee 5n2, 362
Financial Regulation Authority 22
financial salesman, investment firm 183–185
financial services, IT and 335–345; crowdfunding 340–342; cryo-finance 343–345; described 335; lending technologies 342–343; roboadvice 335–337; sandbox regulation 338–340
Financial Services Act, 2012 5
Financial Services and Markets Act 2000 134, 313
Financial Services and Markets Bill, 2022 20
Financial Services Authority (FSA) 22, 60
financial stability 63–64
Financial Stability Board (FSB) 16
Financial Stability Oversight Council (FSOC) 38, 358
financial system principles, Islamic finance 267–277
financial transactions as green and blue 3
fintech 3, 307–345; blockchain and 309–311; cryptocurrencies and 311–315; decentralised autonomous organisation and 315; decentralised finance and 316; digital banking and 316–335; elements of 307–308; financial services, IT and 335–345; introduction to, in green transition 307–309; in Islamic finance 277–279; IT transactions 309–316; *see also* digital banking; financial services, IT and
firm commitment underwriting 145
First Banking Directive, 1977 9, 9n16
First Republic Bank 377
fixed rate term loan 199
flash crash 337
floating charges 23, 27, 29–30; requiring registration 30; security and 213n288
floating rate term loan 199
floor figures 148n36
flows, securitisations and 250–251
forwards 218
Framework for Financial Data Access (FFDA) 334
freely negotiable shares 148–149
FSA Regulatory Response 361
Future Regulatory Framework (FRF) Review 239

Gasus Dosier-Und Fordertechnik GmbH v Netherlands 86
ghabun concept 276
giro deposits 235
Glass-Steagall Act, 1933 36–37
going concern capital 66
gone concern capital 66
Gram-Leach-Billey Act, 1999 38
Great Depression 5, 32, 36
Greece case for state aid 104–105
green bank concept 303–304
green finance 244, 257; defined 299; European Union 291–293; techno-digital economy and 345–346; UK regulation of 298–301
green securitisations 257–259
greenwashing 297
grey market 174
guarantees 204–207

harmonisation: between General Data Protection and Payment Services Directive 320; of legislation 10–11, 15; securities markets and 147; stock market/exchange and 141, 146; UCITS and 189
Hellenic Deposit and Investment Guarantee Fund 105
Hellenic Financial Stability Fund 104–105
herding risk 337
Holland, John 24
home country control principle 11
human rights 2; in banking and financial law 3
hypotheca 28

ibadat 265
impact materiality 295
index-based agricultural insurance 173–174
industry, banks and 51–54; bank owning industry 52–53; commercial businesses/industries owning bank 53–54
initial coin offerings (ICOs) 341
inside information: defined 163–164; disclosure of 164–165, 167–169

insider, MA Regulation definition of 163
insider dealing 162–164
insider information: MA Regulation definition of 163–164; unlawful disclosure of 164–165
insider lists 168
insolvency, defined 351n1
Insolvency Directive 74n87
insolvency/resolution 71–108; creditors' protection 84–99; introduction to 71–72; moral hazard 100–103; resolution mechanism 82–84; state aid and 103–108; Winding-up Directive 72–82
insurtech 335
inter alia 132
interdisciplinary challenges 4
interest 43
interest rates 203
Interim Reports Directive 146
intermediation/disintermediation activities in Islamic finance 272–273
International Banking Act, 1978 37–38
international banks 50–51
International Capital Market Association (ICMA) 296
International Swaps and Derivatives Association (ISDA) 220–224; master agreement 220–221; netting arrangement 223–224; principal terms and conditions 221–223
Investment Account Platform (IAP) 277
investment activities 178n183
investment adviser 178n184
investment bank(s) 45, 177
investment-based (IB) crowdfunding 341
investment contracts 178n184
investment firm(s) 176–187; authorisation process 180–182; defined 176, 178; directors and shareholders 182–183; financial salesman 183–185; initial capital and 180; investment protection 185–187; under MiFID regulation 177–187; overview of 176–177
investment fund(s) 188–194; alternative 192–194; overview of 188; rules of transparency and 191–192; UCITS V Directive and 189–191
investment grade borrowers 196
investment protection 185–187
investment services 178n183
Investment Services Directive 1993/22/EC (ISD) 115
investment under MiFID regulation 177–187
ISDA *see* International Swaps and Derivatives Association (ISDA)
Islamic finance 264–283; banking system 269–271; bonds markets 275; capital markets 271–272; economic system principles 265–267; equity markets 275–277; ESG factors in 283; financial system principles 267–277; Fintech in 277–279; intermediation/disintermediation activities 272–273; introduction to 264–265; metaverse and 280–282; securitisation 273–275; two-tier *mudarabah* model 268; *wikala*-based model 269
issuer, defined 158n86
IT transactions 309–316; blockchain 309–311; cryptocurrencies 311–315; decentralised autonomous organisation 315; decentralised finance 316

Johnson, Boris 18
JPMorgan Chase 33
judicial resolution, alternative approach to 3

Lamfalussy, Alexandre 11
Lamfalussy Report 11–13; levels of regulation 12
landmark status 174
large exposure 68–69
leasing 45, 50n20, 53; financial 55; green 4; Islamic banks and 270, 272, 280
legal issues with securitisations 252–256
legal safety 220n308
Lehman Brothers collapse 357–358
Lehman Brothers International 230–231
lender of last resort (LOLR) 21
lending technologies 342–343
leverage 67–68
liens 28
Liikanen, Erkki 47
liquidity 67
Listing Directive 147–148
Listing Particulars Directive 146
loan-based (LB) crowdfunding 341
loan contract 194–213; boilerplate 210–213; clauses 201–203; costs and 203; defaults, events of 207–210; documentation structure/facilities 198–200; fees and 203; guarantees, representations, and undertakings

204–207; interest rates and 203; Loan Market Association and 197; loan purpose and 200–201; margins and 203; overview of 194–195; purposes of 195–196; syndication and 196–197
Loan Market Association 195, 197
loan purpose, loan contract and 200–201
Local Government Act 1974 378
London Stock Exchange 140
Love v Marshall and Others 30

Maastricht Treaty 6, 11, 58
MA (Market Abuse) Directive 159, 160, 161–164; market manipulation subcategories under 165–166; overview of 161–162
management body, stock market 143–144, 143n16, 144n19
managers' transactions 169
Marckx v Belgium 86
MA (Market Abuse) Regulation 159–161; inside information, defined 163–164; inside information, disclosure of 167–169; insider, defined 163; insider dealing and 162–164; market manipulation subcategories 165–167; market sounding reference 165; unlawful disclosure of inside information 164–165
margins 203
market abuse: directive on (MA Directive) 161–164; regulation on (MA Regulation) 159–161; *see also* MA (Market Abuse) Directive; MA (Market Abuse) Regulation
Market in Financial Instruments Directive II, EU 20–21
market manipulation 165–167
market organisation 139–176; inside information, disclosure of 167–169; market manipulation 165–167; parallel markets 169–176; primary market 139–158; secondary market 158–165
Markets in Crypto-assets (MiCA) Regulation 313–314
Markets in Financial Instruments Directive (MiFID) 115, 337; additional duty of investment firm 117–118; best execution clause 118; categorisation of clients 116; components of 115; conflicts of interest, identification of 118–119; eligible counterparties 116–117; legislation 115–119
Markets in Financial Instruments Directive II (MiFID II) 109
Markets in Financial Instruments Directive (MiFID) regulation, investments and funds under 177–187
Markets in Financial Instruments Regulation (MiFIR) 109, 226
market sounding 165
material adverse change 209
May, Theresa 17, 18
McCulloch v Maryland 33n93
McFadden Act, 1927 36
McKellar v McKellar 30
means of distance communication 113–114
medical law 4
megabanks 33
member bank(s) 34
Merchandise Marks Act 124
mergers and acquisitions (M&A transactions) 45
meta-banks 308
meta-*ijara* lease agreement 281
meta-*istisna/ijara* lease 281–282
meta-*murabaha* 280, 281
meta-*sukuk* 282
metaverse: described 308; Islamic finance and 280–282
mezzanine finance 201
MiFID *see* Markets in Financial Instruments Directive (MiFID)
MiFID Implementing Directive 115
mining 311
mismatch facilities 201
mobile payment 316–318
Mobilising Green Investment 299
money and securities, transfer of 236–239; settlement/clearing of 236–237; Settlement Finality Directive and 237–239
money and securities custody agreements 229–232
money-market instruments 179
Money Market Mutual Fund Liquidity Facility 368
moral hazard 100–103; in banking law 101; described 100; Northern Rock example 101–102; and risk taking 102–103
Morgan Grenfell v Welwyn Garden and Hartfield DC 217
Mortgage Credit Directive 122–124
MREL (minimum requirement for own funds and eligible liabilities) 91–92
muamalat 265

multifunctional groups *versus* universal banks 45–47
multilateral trading facility (MTF) 142n4
murabaha financing 280
musharakah aqd 275
musharakah mulk 275
mutatis mutandis 89, 181
mutual exchange, Islam definition of 266
mutual fund 188n222; *see also* investment fund
mutual recognition *see* passported activities

National Banking Act, 1863, 1864 33, 35
national bank(s) 32–33
National Monetary Commission 35
national supervision of banks 58–60
natural resource protection 292
negative pledge clause 206
netting agreements 74n88
netting arrangement, ISDA 223–224
Network for Greening the Financial System 302
Next Generation EU 370–371
no creditor worse off principle 84–85, 90–94
non-compliance 62–63
Non-Financial Reporting Directive 294
non-member state bank(s) 34
Northern Rock failure 356–357

offerer, defined 158n86
offer of securities 150–152
Office of the Comptroller of the Currency (OCC) 32
Olczak v Poland 87
Ombudsman 133–134
Online Dispute Resolution 132–133
Online Safety Bill 176
Open Banking Implementation Entity 333, 333n173
Open Banking Standard 333
Open Banking Working Group 333
open-end funds 189n227
options 217–218
Orderly Liquidation Authority (OLA) 359
organised trading facility 142n4
organizations of banks 43–56; categories of banks 45–51; EU banking activities 54–56; industry, bank and 51–54; introduction to 43–45
originate-to-distribute model 355
originate-to-hold model 354–355
originator 248
other parallel markets 3
overdraft facility 199–200
overdrafts, described 195
own funds requirement 65–66

parallel banking *see* parallel markets
parallel debt 214–215, 254–255
parallel markets 3, 169–176, 264; agri-food market 169–174; cultural heritage market 174–175; digital market 175–176; in Islamic finance 280, 281
pari passu 97, 196, 205, 205n266, 227, 230
Paris Agreement 290
passive interest 43
passported activities 10, 10n19, 13
passporting 10, 181
Patient Care Trust (PCT) 344
Payment Services Directive (PSD1/PSD2) 229, 319–324
Peel Bank Act, 1844 25
peer-to-peer (P2P) lending 342–343
peer-to-peer securitisations 3, 263–264
personal data, securitisations and 263–264
personal data as money 324–325
personal revival trust (PRT) 345
persons closely associated, defined 169
pignus 28
pledge/pledgers 28–29
Positive Money Europe 326
Possfund Custodian Trustee Ltd v Diamond 158n84
precise information 163–164n110
premium 218
prepayments 202
Primary Dealer Credit Facility 368
primary market 139–158; history of 139–140; securities law/regulation 147–158; stock market/exchange regulation 140–147; *see also individual headings*
Primary Market Corporate Credit Facility (PMCCF) 368
privacy 3; digital banking and 332–334; securitisations and 3, 262–263
private placement 155n69
professional clients 116
prohibition of *riba* 265
project finance transaction 200
ProMediate 3, 132
property, Islamic definition of 266
property right under international legislation 85–90
Proposal for a Regulation on European Green Bonds (European Commission) 296

pro rata parte 227
prospective events of default 208
prospectus concept 151
Prospectus Directive 146, 151, 151n50, 152–158; application requirements of 152; competent authority identification 156; elements of 153; exemptions from obligation of 154–155, 155n71–74; investor protection and 152; obligation to publish circumstances 154; product driven definition of 151n50
Protection Regulation 125–126
Prudential Regulation Authority (PRA) 5n3, 20, 60
prudential supervision 63–71; bank financial stability and 63–64; capital buffers, solvency ratio and 64–67; corporate governance 69–70; large exposure and 68–69; leverage and 67–68; liquidity and 67; remuneration and 70–71
Public Offer Prospectus Directive 146

qualified investors 155n68

rating agency 250
ratio essendi 151
Recovery and Resilience Task Force 371
recovery planning 76–77, 77n104
reference entity 219
refinancing 201
regulated market 154, 154n65; of transferable securities 159
regulations 7–8
remuneration 70–71
representations 204–207
reserved activities 10
residential mortgage 101, 251, 257, 353
resolution authority 77
resolution financial arrangements 78–79
resolution tools 2, 77–78; conditions for adoption of 78; *see also* state aid and resolution mechanism
restorative justice 129–132; described 129–130; elements of 130; legal documents pertaining to 130–131
Re Sullivan County Regional Refuse Disposal District 385
retail clients 116
Retail Investment Package (European Commission) 185–186
revolving loan 199
riba 266, 276
Riegle-Neal Interstate Banking and Branching Efficiency Act, 1994 36, 37
Right to Financial Privacy Act of 1978 333, 334
risk sharing 266
risk-taming 340
risk-washing fintech 339, 340
Risk Weighted Assets (RWA) 66
RisolviOnline 3, 132
roboadvice 335–337; systemic risks 337
roll over term loan 199
Royal Bank of Scotland 22, 23–24, 26; coins and 25

sandbox regulation 338–340
Saporta, Victoria 19
Savings Association Insurance Fund 34
Scotland banking law 22–30; circumvention in 30; floating charges 23, 29–30; history 23–26; overview of 22–23; securities 26–29
secondary market 158–165; directive on market abuse 161–164; insider information unlawful disclosure 164–165; *vs.* primary market 158–159; regulation on market abuse 159–161
Secondary Market Corporate Credit Facility (SMCCF) 368
Second Banking Directive, 1989 9–11, 9n17, 12
sectorial supervision 59; *see also* national supervision of banks
securities, offer of 150–152
securities, Scotland 26–29; definition of 27; forms of 26–27; hypothec 28; liens and 28; over corporeal movables 28; over incorporeal movables 29; pledge and 28–29; qualifications of 28; trustee in bankruptcy of 27
Securities Exchange Act of 1934 151
securities law and regulation 147–158; debt securities 149; equity securities 148–149; listing and legal liabilities 149–150; Listing Directive 147–148; offer of securities 150–152; Prospectus Directive 152–158
securitisations 244–264; Covid-19 259–260; EU regulation of 256–257; flows 250–251; green 257–259; Islamic finance and 273–275; legal issues with 252–256; overview of 244–247; peer-to-peer 3, 263–264; personal data 263–264; privacy and 3, 262–263;

shadow banking and 264; structure 247–250; UK regulation of 260–262
security 213–226; derivatives 215–226; many secured creditors and 213–214; purposes of 213; trustees 213–215
security custody 232–236; MiFID and 232–234; private or commercial law rules for 234–236
security rights 254
servicer 249
set-off 202–203
settled assets 236
Settlement Finality Directive 237–239
shadow banking 3, 242–244; definitions of 242–243; securitisations and 264
shareholders, investment firm 182–183
shares, securities as 150
shari'ah 265, 269, 272
short selling, Islamic finance and 276–277
Signature Bank 376
Silicon Valley Bank collapse 375–376
Single Euro Area Payment (SEAP) Regulation 312
Single European Payments Area 228–229; Payment Services Directive 229
Single Resolution Board (SRB) 74–76, 79, 83
Single Resolution Fund 79
Single Resolution Mechanism Regulation 79
Single Supervisory Mechanism (SSM) 15–16, 56–57, 76, 79
smart-banking contracts 318–319
smart city 345
smart finance, described 4
Snow Crash (Stevenson) 309
spare banking 3
spare banking and conduits 242–264; introduction to 242; securitisations 244–264; shadow banking 242–244
speculation 171
spread 44
SRB *see* Single Resolution Board (SRB)
stand-by loan 199
standby underwriting 145
state aid and resolution mechanism 103–108; Greece case 104–105; overview of 103–104; requirements for 104; *Tercas* case 106–108
state bank(s) 33
state chartering authority 31
Stevenson, Neal 309
stock market/exchange 140; arranger and 145–146; described 141; financial instruments 144–146; harmonisation at EU level 141, 146; history of 139–140; management body 143–144, 143n16, 144n19; MiFID I/II regulation 141–143; regulation 140–147; underwriting and 145, 145n25
Stran Greek Refineries v Greece 86–87
STS Regulation 257
subsidiaries 48–49; CRD IV definition of 49
sukuk 274–275, 274n439
supervision of banks 56–71; authorisation of banking business 60–63; European 56–58; national 58–60; prudential 63–71
sustainability 3; consumer protection and 128; factors 258
sustainable 290
sustainable finance 244, 257
Sustainable Finance Disclosure Regulation 293–294
swaps 219, 219n306
syndicated loan 195, 196–197

takāful technology 277
taktech 277
techno-digital economy, green and 345–346
Tercas case for state aid 106–108
Term Asset-Backed Securities Loan Facility 368
term loans 195, 198–199
term sheet 196
TFEU *see* Treaty on the Functioning of the European Union (TFEU)
Threadneedle Street 22
tied agent 185
Tiffany v National Bank of Missouri 33n95
token 311
tranching 248
transformation function 44
transparency, investment funds and rules of 191–192
Transparency Obligations Directive 146
Travelers Group 38
treaties 6–7
Treaty of Amsterdam 58
Treaty of Lisbon 6–7
Treaty of Rome 6, 7
Treaty of the European Economic Community 6, 6n5
Treaty on European Union (TEU) 7, 58; Article 50 of 17
Treaty on the Functioning of the European Union (TFEU) 7, 60

trigger event 98
Trotter, Archibald 24
true sale 252
trust, defined 214n290
trustees, security and 213–215
Turner Review 361
twin peaks model of supervision 59, 60, 362
two-tier *mudarabah* model, Islamic finance 268

UCITS Directive 188
UCITS V Directive 189–191
UK Financial Conduct Authority and Competition & Markets Authority 333
UK financial regulation, custody agreements and 239–242
UK regulation of securitisations 260–262
uncommitted facility 199
undertakings 204–207; UCITS as 189
undertakings for collective investment in transferable securities (UCITS) 188
underwriting 145, 145n25; and placement 178n186
Unfair Terms Directive 108, 109–114; conditions of 110–111; consumer category under 109–110; distance contracts and 112–113; Distance Financial Services Directive 113–114; financial contracts and 111–112; legal protection afforded by 110; means of distance communication 113–114; pillars of concerns under 114; terms presumed unfair 111
United Kingdom regulation 16–30; Bank of England role 21–22; Brexit and 17–18; consumer protection 124–126; custody agreements and 239–242; financial stability and 18–20; introduction to 16–17; proposal 20–21; Scotland banking law and 22–30; of securitisations 260–262
United States banking system 31–34; banks, defined 31; categories of banks 31; commercial banks 32; member banks 34; national banks 32–33; non-member state banks 34; overview of 31–32; state banks 33
United States legal system framework 34–40; Banking Act, 1933 36–37; Banking Holding Company Act, 1956 37; Bank Secrecy Act, 2018 39–40; Dodd-Frank Act, 2010 38–39; Federal Reserve Act, 1914 35; Gram-Leach-Billey Act, 1999 38; International Banking Act, 1978 37–38; McFadden Act, 1927 36; National Banking Act, 1863 35; overview of 34–35
United States regulation 31–41; banking system described 31–34; bank supervision 40–41; legal framework 34–40
United States v Bekins 382, 384
universal banks: defined 46; *versus* multifunctional groups 45–47
Universal Stock Exchange v Strachan 217n304
US Grain Futures Act, 1922 171
US National Banking System 35

Veazia Bank v Fenno 33n93
venture capital 201
Volcker Rule 46–47

wikala-based model, Islamic finance 269
Winding-up Directive 71, 72–82, 352; BRRD and 74–76; BRRD structure 76–80; insolvency procedures 72–73; overview of 72–74; resolution under BRRD 80–82; SRM and 74–76

For Product Safety Concerns and Information please contact our EU representative GPSR@taylorandfrancis.com
Taylor & Francis Verlag GmbH, Kaufingerstraße 24, 80331 München, Germany

www.ingramcontent.com/pod-product-compliance
Ingram Content Group UK Ltd.
Pitfield, Milton Keynes, MK11 3LW, UK
UKHW020156200926
475702UK00016B/2730
9781032628578